M*acroeconomics*

Macroeconomics

SIXTH EDITION

Stephen L. Slavin

Union County College
Cranford, New Jersey

The New School University
New York City

Boston   Burr Ridge, IL   Dubuque, IA   Madison, WI   New York   San Francisco   St. Louis
Bangkok   Bogotá   Caracas   Lisbon   London   Madrid
Mexico City   Milan   New Delhi   Seoul   Singapore   Sydney   Taipei   Toronto

McGraw-Hill Higher Education

*A Division of The **McGraw-Hill** Companies*

MACROECONOMICS

Published by McGraw-Hill, an imprint of The Mcgraw-Hill Companies, Inc., 1221 Avenue of the Americas, New York, NY, 10020. Copyright © 2002, 1999, 1996, 1994, 1991, 1989 by The McGraw-Hill Companies, Inc. All rights reserved. No part of this publication may be reproduced or distributed in any form or by any means, or stored in a database or retrieval system, without the prior written consent of The McGraw-Hill Companies, Inc., including, but not limited to, in any network or other electronic storage or transmission, or broadcast for distance learning.

Some ancillaries, including electronic and print components, may not be available to customers outside the United States.

This book is printed on acid-free paper.

1 2 3 4 5 6 7 8 9 0 QPD/QPD 0 9 8 7 6 5 4 3 2 1

ISBN 0-07-237409-8

Publisher: *Gary Burke*
Executive sponsoring editor: *Paul Shensa*
Senior developmental editor: *Tom Thompson*
Marketing manager: *Martin D. Quinn*
Project manager: *Christina Thornton-Villagomez*
Senior production supervisor: *Lori Koetters*
Media producer: *Craig Atkins*
Director of design BR: *Keith J. McPherson*
Lead supplement producer: *Szura*
Supplement associate: *Kate Boylan*
Photo research coordinator: *Judy Kausal*
Cover/Interior design: *Jamie O'Neal*
Cover illustrator: *Maria Rendon*
Typeface: *10/12 Times Roman*
Composition and project management: *The GTS Companies, Inc.*
Printer: *Quebecor World Dubuque Inc.*

Library of Congress Cataloging-in-Publication Data

Slavin, Stephen L.
    Macroeconomics / Stephen L. Slavin.—6th ed.
        p.   cm.
    Includes bibliographical references and index.
    ISBN 0-07-237412-8 (pbk.)
    1. Macroeconomics.   I. Title.
  HB172.5.S554   2001
    339—dc21   2001034549

http://www.mhhe.com

Preface to the Instructor

More than 25 years ago, while still a graduate student, I got a part-time job helping to ghostwrite an introductory text for a major publisher. I asked my editor why so many economics texts were ghostwritten. She smiled and said, "Economists can't write."

Economics can be a rather intimidating subject, with its extensive vocabulary, complicated graphs, and quantitative tendencies. Is it possible to write a principles text that lowers the student's anxiety level without watering down the subject matter? To do this, one would need to be an extremely good writer, have extensive teaching experience, and have solid academic training in economics. In this case, two out of three is just not good enough.

Why did I write this book? Probably my moment of decision arrived about 15 years ago when I mentioned to my macro class that Kemp-Roth cut the top personal income tax bracket from 70 percent to 50 percent. Then I asked, "If you were rich, by what percentage were your taxes cut?"

The class sat there in complete silence. Most of the students stared at the blackboard, waiting for me to work out the answer. I told them to work it out themselves. I waited. And I waited. Finally, someone said, "Twenty percent?"

"Close," I replied, "but no cigar."

"Fourteen percent?" someone else ventured.

"No, you're getting colder."

After waiting another two or three minutes, I saw one student with her hand up. One student knew that the answer was almost 29 percent—*one* student in a class of 30.

When do they teach students how to do percentage changes? In high school? In junior high or middle school? Surely not in a college economics course.

How much of *your* time do you spend going over simple arithmetic and algebra? How much time do you spend going over simple graphs? Wouldn't you rather be spending that time discussing economics?

Now you'll be able to do just that, because all the arithmetic and simple algebra that you normally spend time explaining are covered methodically in this book. All you'll need to do is tell your students which pages to look at.

The micro chapters offer scores of tables and graphs for the students to plot on their own; the solutions are shown in the book. This will cut down on the amount of time you'll need to spend putting these problems on the board.

As an economics instructor for more than 30 years at such fabled institutions as Brooklyn College, New York Institute of Technology, St. Francis College (Brooklyn), and Union County College, I have used a variety of texts. But each of their authors assumed a mathematical background that the majority of my students did not have. Each also assumed that his graphs and tables were comprehensible to the average student.

The biggest problem we have with just about any book we assign is that many of our students don't bother to read it before coming to class. Until now, no one has written a principles text in plain English. I can't promise that every one of your students will do the readings you assign, but at least they won't be able to complain anymore about not understanding the book.

Distinctive Qualities

My book has six qualities that no other principles text has.

1. **It reviews math that students haven't covered since middle school and high school.** (See, for example, the box "A Word About Numbers," Chapter 5, page 112, or "Calculating Percentage Changes," Chapter 9, page 223.)

2. **It's an interactive text, encouraging active rather than passive reading.**

3. **It's a combined textbook and workbook.** Each chapter is followed by workbook pages that include multiple-choice and fill-in questions, as well as numerical problems.

4. **It costs less than virtually every other text on the market.** The sixth edition has the lowest list price on the market for this combined textbook-workbook.

5. **It's written in plain English without jargon.** See for yourself. Open any page and compare my writing style with that of any other principles author. This book is written to communicate clearly and concisely with the students' needs in mind.

6. **It is written with empathy for students.** My goal is to get students past their math phobias and fear of graphs by having them do hundreds of problems, step-by-step, literally working their way through the book. Students learn economics best by actively "doing."

Special Features

Three special features of my book are its integrated coverage of the global economy, its extra help boxes, and its advanced work boxes.

The Global Economy

Until the early 1970s our economy was largely insulated from the rest of the world economy. All of this changed with the oil price shock of 1973, our subsequent growing appetite for fuel-efficient Japanese compact cars, as well as for TVs, VCRs, camcorders, and other consumer electronics made in Asia. As our trade deficits grew, and as foreigners bought up more and more American assets, every American became quite aware of how integrated we had become within the global economy.

The sixth edition has three chapters devoted entirely to the global economy—Chapter 18 (International Trade), Chapter 19 (International Finance), and Chapter 8 (The Export-Import Sector). This new chapter is part of the sequence (C, I, G, and X_n) leading up to the chapter on GDP. In addition, we have integrated a great deal of material dealing specifically with the global economy throughout the text.

Here are some of the things we look at:

- The "Isms": Capitalism, Communism, Fascism, and Socialism (Ch. 4, p. 98)
- China: The Premier Communist Power (Ch. 4, p. 104)
- Foreign Investment in the United States (Ch. 6, p. 148)
- The World's Leading Trading Nations (Ch. 8, p. 200)
- World Trade Agreements and Free Trade Zones (Ch. 8, pp. 202)
- Global Comparison: Breakdown of GDP Expenditures for Selected Countries (Ch. 9, p. 215)
- Trillion-Dollar Economies, 2000 (Ch. 9, p. 228)
- Comparative Unemployment Rates (Ch. 10, p. 255)
- How Independent Is Our Central Bank in Comparison to Other Leading Central Banks? (Ch. 14, pp. 370–371)
- The Effectiveness of Monetary Policy in an Open Economy (Ch. 14, p. 390)
- The Productivity of Labor: An International Comparison (Ch. 16, p. 468)
- Economic Growth in Less-Developed Countries (Ch. 16, p. 469)
- U.S. Merchandise Trade Deficit with Japan and China (Ch. 18, p. 538)
- How the Japanese Drove American TV Manufacturers Out of Business (Ch. 18, p. 541)
- Exchange Rates: Foreign Currency per American Dollar (Ch. 19, p. 561)

Extra Help Boxes

Students taking the principles course have widely varying backgrounds. Some have no problem doing the math or understanding basic economic concepts. But many others are lost from day one.

I have provided dozens of Extra Help boxes for the students who need them. They are especially useful to instructors who don't want to spend hours of class time going over material that they assume should be understood after one reading.

Of course these boxes can be skipped by the better prepared students.

Here are some of the topics covered in the extra help boxes:

- Read Only if You Still Don't Understand Why C is 1,000 (Ch. 5, p. 120)
- More on Finding Autonomous and Induced Consumption (Ch. 5, p. 124)
- Calculating Percentage Changes (Ch. 9, p. 223)
- Read Only if You're Not Sure How to Calculate the Unemployment Rate (Ch. 10, p. 253)
- Finding Percentage Changes in the Price Level (Ch. 10, p. 262)
- Differentiating Between the Deficit and the Debt (Ch. 12, p. 326)
- Finding the Percentage of Income Share of the Quintiles in Figure 1 (Ch. 17, p. 481)

Advanced Work Boxes

There are some concepts in the principles course that many instructors will want to skip. (Of course, if they're not included in principles texts, this will make other instructors quite unhappy.) These boxes are intended for the better prepared students who are willing to tackle these relatively difficult concepts.

Here is a sampling of my Advanced Work boxes:

- Post-World War II Recessions (Ch. 1, p. 15)
- APCs Greater Than One (Ch. 5, p. 116)
- Nominally Progressive, Proportional, and Regressive Taxes (Ch. 7, p. 148)
- Why NNP Is Better Than GDP (Ch. 9, p. 218)
- The Accelerator Principle (Ch. 10, p. 247)
- The Paradox of Thrift (Ch. 12, p. 320)
- Three Modifications of the Deposit Expansion Mul-

tiplier (Ch. 14, p. 381)

- Rational Expectations vs. Adaptive Expectations (Ch. 15, p. 419)
- The Negative Income Tax (Ch. 17, p. 504)

Changes in the Sixth Edition

We made a few major organizational changes in the sixth edition. There's now a much stronger emphasis on supply and demand toward the beginning of the text, and we've added a new chapter on the export-import sector of GDP. We've detailed the chapter-by-chapter changes near the beginning of the Instructor's Manual.

Two basic ways this book is different from all other principles texts is that it is a smoother read and it is interactive. The sixth edition improves on these features.

Most of the really hard stuff is in Advanced Work boxes and appendices. This relatively difficult material can be skipped, or perhaps assigned for extra credit. The really easy stuff—for example, math that should have been learned in high school—is covered in Extra Help boxes. These boxes save professors hours of valuable class time. For example, students who can't figure out percentage changes can get help from the boxes on pages 223 and 262. In the sixth edition I've added a dozen new boxes.

Unlike all other principles texts, which encourage passive reading, my book encourages active reading. Students work their way through each chapter, tackling numerical problems, filling in tables, and drawing graphs. Then, at the end of each chapter is a workbook section with multiple-choice and fill-in questions, and problems. In the sixth edition we now have about 100 problem sheets in the Instructor's Manual, which can be torn out, photocopied, and handed out to the students. Let's say a professor assigned the first 10 pages of Chapter 12 (Fiscal Policy and the National Debt). A problem sheet would have a graph and three questions: (1) Is this an inflationary gap or a deflationary gap? (2) How big is it? (3) What two fiscal policy measures would you use to remove it? There's a problem like this in the workbook section of Chapter 12, but this problem comes up at the beginning of a very long chapter. Having these problem sheets saves the professor from having to put this graph on the board and having students spend class time figuring out the answers.

The Supplement Package

In addition to the workbook, which is built in, *Macroeconomics* has a supplemental package to help students and instructors as they use the text.

Instructor's Manual

I prepared the instructor's manual to give instructors ideas on how to use the text. The manual includes a description of the textbook's special features, a chapter-by-chapter discussion of material new to the sixth edition, and a rundown of chapter coverage to help instructors decide what they can skip.

In the sixth edition, the IM has undergone the most radical change. Until now it had consisted of answers to the workbook questions at the end of each chapter in the text, worksheets, and worksheet solutions. We've now added answers to the Questions for Thought and Discussion at the end of each chapter. And, Mark Maier, who has used the text for several editions, has added three new IM sections for each chapter—learning objectives, ideas for use in class, and homework questions and projects (including scores of very useful Web sites). The IM now provides a rich source of interesting ideas of classroom activities and discussion involving concepts and issues included in the text.

Test Bank (Micro and Macro Versions)

The test bank, which I had updated and revised for each edition, had some 7,000 multiple-choice questions, fill-ins, and problems. Jim Watson has looked carefully at each of these, updating some, revising some, and dropping some. He then made up more than 1,000 new questions. To be quite frank, parts of my test bank had been getting somewhat stale, and Jim has greatly improved it.

Teaching Transparencies

The most important graphs and tables from the text are reproduced as two-color transparencies. Use of these acetates will aid the instructor's classroom presentations and the students' understanding.

Computerized Testing

The Micro and Macro test banks are available in computerized versions for PCs. Developed by the Brownstone Research Group, this state of the art software has the capability to create multiple tests, "scramble," and produce high-quality graphs.

Videos

A selection of videos is available to adopters, including both tutorial lessons and programs that combine historical footage, documentary sequences, interviews, and analysis to illustrate economic theory. There is also a 15-minute video that explains how to get the most out of the book. This may be played during the first day of class.

A series of instructional videos, whose content was reviewed by Nobel Laureate Robert Solow, is being created for McGraw-Hill's Principles of Economics texts. These brief but compelling pieces explain the core ideas of economics (for example, opportunity costs), dimishing returns, mutual gains from trade, marginal analysis, and comparative advantage.

Web Site

Some of the text's unique qualities are incorporated in a dynamic new Web site. Its remedial nature, with attention toward helping students further overcome math anxiety and graphing difficulties, will take on a self-help orientation for needy students. The quizzing practice offers questions not found in the Workbook or the Test Bank and serves to reinforce the material covered in every chapter. Instructors will find material from the IM and PowerPoints. Several sections, of interest to both instructors and students, provide useful and thought-provoking material and broaden understanding of the scope of economics.

One-Semester Courses from Economics, 6e

Here are some syllabi for one-semester courses with varying orientations:

Macro oriented:

Chapters 1–9; 12–14; 17; 29–33.
Chapters 1–3; 10; 12–14; 16–17; 26; 29–33.
Chapters 1–10; 16–17; 26; 31–33.

Micro oriented:

Chapters 2–4; 10; 16–26.
Chapters 1–4; 16–25; 32–33.
Chapters 2–3; 17–21; 27–33.

Balanced approach:

Chapters 1–9; 17–21; 32–33.
Chapters 1–4; 16–21; 26–31.

Here's another possibility—a one-semester course that focuses on contemporary problems:

Chapters 2–4; 10; 12–14; 16; 26; 29–33.

Acknowledgments

It is one thing to write an unconventional, even controversial, principles text, and it is quite another to get it published. Gary Nelson, the sponsoring editor at the time my book was signed, saw the project through from its inception to its completion, and I want to thank him for making this book possible. Gary oversaw the development from a bare bones text to a full-fledged principles package.

Paul Shensa, who succeeded Gary Nelson as sponsoring editor, has been a great advocate of my book, both inside and outside the company. Paul, who may well be the most experienced economics textbook editor in the industry, was especially helpful in getting the reviewers' suggestions incorporated into the text and the supplements. I also wish to thank Gary Burke, my publisher, who put together the group that edited and produced the book.

Chantal Guillemin, the developmental editor, saw this project through from the first reviews, the chapter-by-chapter revisions, the Test Bank revisions, and the dozens of deadlines that we met, to the time the book finally went to press. Chantal was great at keeping all the plates spinning, dealing with a diverse group of personalities, making sure that all the pieces fit, and seeing to it that the text and the supplements were ready to go to the printer.

Project manager Christina Thornton-Villagomez, with whom I worked day to day, managed the copyediting, artwork, and page proofs, and saw to it that we stayed not just on schedule, but ahead of schedule. Stacey Sawyer, the copyeditor with the light touch, suggested hundreds of improvements, large and small, while smoothing out the rough edges of the manuscript. Keith McPherson oversaw the design of the book from cover to cover. Supplements producer Becky Szura made sure the supplement production process went smoothly.

Every economist knows that no product sells itself. Without major sales and marketing efforts, my text could not sell very well. Marty Quinn, the marketing manager for economics, has done a great job publicizing my book, and he deserves a good deal of the credit for its expanding sales, as does Meg McCormick, the associate marketing manager. But most of the credit goes to all the Irwin/McGraw-Hill and Glencoe/McGraw-Hill sales reps for all their efforts to sell my book. And I would like to especially thank the reps in Dubuque, Iowa, who have personally accounted for about a quarter of our sales.

I'd also like to thank the many reviewers who helped improve this text over the last five editions:

Carlos Aguilar, *El Paso Community College*
James Q. Aylsworth, *Lakeland Community College*
Kevin Baird, *Montgomery Community College*
Robert G. Bise, *Orange Coast College*
Michael Cohik, *Collin Community College*
Steve Cole, *Bethel College*
Ana-María Conley, *DeVry Institute of Technology–Decatur*
Daniel Fischer, *University of Arizona*
Russell L. Flora, *Pikes Peak Community College*
Arthur Friedberg, *Mohawk Valley Community College*
Harold Friesen, *Friends University*
Eugene Gendel, *Woodbury University*
Cindy Goodyear, *Webster University*
Sanford B. Helman, *Middlesex County College*
Mark G. Johnson, *Lakeland Community College*
James Kelly, *Rio Hondo College*
Kenneth E. Kimble, *Sinclair Community College*
Jack Klauser, *Chaminade University of Honolulu*

Wayne Klutarits, *Jefferson College*
Harry Kolendrianos, *Danville Community College*
Stephen E. Lile, *Western Kentucky University*
Paul Lockard, *Black Hawk College*
Steven B. McCormick, *Southeastern Illinois College*
John E. Michaels, *University of Phoenix*
Green Miller, *Morehead State University*
Joan O'Brien, *Quincy College*
Alannah Orrison, *Saddleback College*
Louis A. Patille, *University of Phoenix*
Eric Rahimian, *Alabama A&M University*
W. H. Segur, *University of Redlands*
Don M. Soule, *University of Kentucky*
Bruno Stein, *New York University*
Stephen Steller, *University of Phoenix*
Edward Stevens, *Nebraska College of Business*
James Watson, *Jefferson College*
Marc Weglarski, *Macomb Community College*
Elaine Gale Wrong, *Montclair State College*

Many reviewers helped me to improve the text as it developed into the sixth edition. I thank the following reviewers for their suggestions:

Jim Angus, *Dyersburg State Community College (Tennessee)*
Lyndell L. Avery, *Penn Valley Community College (Missouri)*
Gerard A. Cahill, *Florida Institute of Technology*
Perry A. Cash, *Chadwick University (Alabama)*
Dave Cook, *Western Nevada Community College*
Thomas O. Depperschmidt, *University of Memphis*
Stacey Edgington, *San Diego State University*
Deborah M. Figart, *Richard Stockton College (New Jersey)*
Marilyn Fuller, *Paris Junior College (Texas)*
Charles W. Harrington Jr., *Nova Southeastern University (Florida)*
M. Moosa Khan, *Prairie View A&M University (Texas)*
Michael J. Kuryla, *SUNY-Broome Community College (New York)*
Alan Levinsohn, *SUNY-Morrisville (New York)*
Mark H. Maier, *Glendale Community College (California)*
Eddi Marlow, *Dyersburg State Community College (Tennessee)*
Ronan O'Beirne, *American Institute of Computer Sciences (Alabama)*
Michael L. Palmer, *Maple Woods Community College (Missouri)*
Thomas R. Parsons, *Massachusetts Bay Path Community College*
Ronald Picker, *St. Mary of the Woods College (Indiana)*
George Radakovic, *Indiana University of Pennsylvania*
Judith K. Robinson, *Massachusetts Bay Path Community College*
Michael Rosen, *Milwaukee Area Technical College*
Rose M. Rubin, *University of Memphis (Tennessee)*
Mourad Sebti, *Central Texas College*
Karen Spellacy, *SUNY-Canton (New York)*
John Somers, *Portland Community College (Oregon)*
Denver O. Swaby, *Columbia Union College (Maryland)*
Max Tarpley, *Dyersburg State Community College (Tennessee)*
Bette Lewis Tokar, *Holy Family College (Pennsylvania)*
Jim Watson, *Jefferson College (Missouri)*
Marc Weglarski, *Macomb Community College (Michigan)*
Steven White, *Glendale Community College (California)*
Sandy Zingo, *Rogers State University (Oklahoma)*

Finally, to all adopters of the past five editions, thank you. Your comments and concerns have helped me to write the 2002 edition of *Economics*.

—*Stephen L. Slavin*

Preface to the Student

What have you heard about economics? That it's dull, it's hard, it's full of undecipherable equations and incomprehensible graphs? If you were to read virtually any of the introductory economics textbooks, that's exactly what you would find.

How is this book different from all other books? For starters, this is the first economics book that is reader friendly. While you're reading, I'll be right there with you, illustrating various points with anecdotes and asking you to work out numerical problems as we go along.

Are you a little shaky about the math? Your worries are over. If you can add, subtract, multiply, and divide (I'll even let you use a calculator), you can do the math in this book.

How do you feel about graphs? Do you think they look like those ultramodernistic paintings that even the artists can't explain? You can relax. No graph in this book has more than four lines, and by the time you're through, you'll be drawing your *own* graphs.

In nearly every chapter you'll find one or two boxes labeled "Extra Help." Sometimes you can master a concept when additional examples are given. Don't be too proud to seek extra help when you need it. And when you don't need it, you may skip the boxes.

Unlike virtually every other economics text, this one includes a built-in workbook. Even if your professor does not assign the questions at the end of each chapter, I urge you to answer them because they provide an excellent review.

I can't guarantee an *A* in this course, but whether you are taking it to fulfill a college requirement or planning to be an economics major, you will find that economics is neither dull nor all that hard.

—Stephen L. Slavin

Contents

10 Economic Fluctuations, Unemployment, and Inflation 243

11 Classical and Keynesian Economics 279

12 Fiscal Policy and the National Debt 303

13 Money and Banking 339

14 The Federal Reserve and Monetary Policy 373

15 Twentieth-Century Economic Theory 403

About the Author

Stephen L. Slavin received his B.A. in economics from Brooklyn College and his M.A. and Ph.D. in economics from New York University. He has taught at New York Institute of Technology, Brooklyn College, St. Francis College (Brooklyn), and in the M.B.A. program at Fairleigh Dickinson University, and he now teaches at the New School University in New York City and at Union County College in Cranford, New Jersey.

He has written eight other books: *The Einstein Syndrome: Corporate Anti-Semitism in America Today* (University Press of America); *Jelly Bean Economics: Reaganomics in the Early 1980s* (Philosophical Library); *Economics: A Self-Teaching Guide, All the Math You'll Ever Need, Math for Your First- and Second-Grader, Quick Business Math: A Self-Teaching Guide* (all four published by John Wiley & Sons); *Chances Are: The Only Statistics Book You'll Ever Need* (University Press of America); and *Everyday Math in 20 Minutes a Day* (LearningExpress). He is the co-author of three other Wiley books, *Practical Algebra, Quick Algebra Review,* and *Precalculus.*

Dr. Slavin's articles have appeared in *Studies in Family Planning, Economic Planning, Journal of BioSocial Science, Business and Society Review, Bankers Magazine, Education for Business, Public Management, Better Investing, Northwest Investment Review, U.S.A. Today Magazine, Patterns in Prejudice, Culturefront,* and *Conservative Review.* In addition, he has written more than 500 newspaper commentaries on public policy, demographic economics, politics, urban economics, international trade, investments, and economic fluctuations.

Introduction

What Is Economics All About, How Do We Use This Book, and Why Is This Book Different from All Other Introductory Economics Textbooks?

You've just started reading what may be the shortest introduction with the longest title ever to appear in an introductory economics textbook. Why is this introduction so short? Mainly because I believe in economizing. What is economizing? Funny you should ask.

Economics deals with efficiency—getting rid of waste. That's why this introduction is so short. In fact, that's why this entire book—a textbook and a workbook combined—is so short. We've eliminated most of the extraneous material, the stuff that almost no one reads and virtually no one can understand. What you'll be getting here is 99.44 percent pure introductory economics. If this book were sold in supermarkets, you'd find it with the rest of the no-frills products.

What is economics? Basically, economics is a set of tools that enables us to use our resources efficiently. The end result is the highest possible standard of living.

Economics operates on two levels, the macro level and the micro level. *Macroeconomics* deals with huge aggregates like national output, employment, the money supply, bank deposits, and government spending—and how we can deal with inflation and recession. The first half of the book *Economics* (through Chapter 16) is devoted to macroeconomics.

Microeconomics operates on the level of the individual business firm, as well as that of the individual consumer. How does a firm maximize its profits, and how do consumers maximize their satisfaction? These are the types of questions answered by microeconomic analysis, which begins with Chapter 17 of *Economics* (or Chapter 5 of *Microeconomics*).

This book differs from every other introductory text in several ways. Not only is it shorter, but it is much more readable. To modify an old computer term, it is reader-friendly. There are plenty of jokes and anecdotes to illustrate points. And you will be able to do the math even if you are mathphobic.

The format of the book encourages you to read actively rather than passively. You will be asked to answer questions and do calculations. Then you'll check your work against my answers.

> An economist is a man who states the obvious in terms of the incomprehensible.
> —Alfred A. Knopf

Before you are asked to do any calculations (and we rarely go beyond eighth-grade arithmetic), there will be a section that reviews the math. For example, just before we explore the subject of consumption (Chapter 5 of *Economics* and *Macroeconomics*), which is expressed in trillions of dollars, there is a section showing you how to deal with large numbers. If you happen to be one of those people who doesn't know billions from trillions, then this section is for you. But if you do know your billions and trillions, you can pass this section, go directly into the chapter, collect $200, and roll the dice again.

Actually, I won't claim that reading this book will be quite as much fun as playing Monopoly, or that you will get to collect $200 whenever you skip a section. But you do get to save some money.

This text gives you two books in one: the conventional textbook and the workbook. Go into any college bookstore and check out the prices. Almost every standard textbook/workbook package will cost you more than $90, so you're already economizing. And yet, in the words of the Carpenters' golden oldie, "We've only just begun."

Chapter 1

A Brief Economic History of the United States

More than two centuries ago, some Americans believed it was "manifest destiny" that the 13 states on the eastern seaboard would one day be part of a nation that stretched from the Atlantic to the Pacific. Was it also our manifest destiny to become the world's economic superpower?

CHAPTER OBJECTIVES

In this chapter you'll learn:

- How we grew from a primarily agricultural nation of 4 million people to an industrial power of over 280 million.

- How the Civil War, World War I, and World War II affected our economy.

- How our nation was shaped by suburbanization after World War II.

- What major factors affected our economic growth decade by decade from the 1920s into the new millennium.

- What the "new economy" is and how it differs from the "old economy."

Introduction

Our economy is a study in contrasts. We have poverty in the midst of plenty; we have rapidly expanding industries like computer software and medical technology, and we have dying industries like shipbuilding and consumer electronics; we have won the cold war against communism, but we may be losing the trade war against Japan and China.

Which country has the largest economy in the world, the United States or Japan? Believe it or not, our national output is more than double that of Japan.

America is the sole superpower and has one of the highest standards of living in the world. Communism, to borrow a phrase from Karl Marx, has been "swept into the dustbin of history"—at least the version that dominated the former Soviet Union after the 1920s and Eastern Europe after World War II is no more.

The baby-boom generation has earned higher incomes than any other generation in history. Indeed, Americans once considered it their birthright to do better than their parents. But that ended some 30 years ago, and a lot of young people are worrying about their futures.

In the decade following the 1990–91 recession, our economy generated more than 22 million new jobs. That's the good news. The bad news is that half of them pay less than $15,000 per year. These so-called McJobs are often low-level, minimum wage, dead-end positions with no health benefits.

The children of the first baby boomers have already entered the job market. And their parents, after paying $25,000 or more a year to educate them, are wondering about their children's job prospects.

Between 1997 and early 2001, the job market was the strongest in memory, partly because large corporations, in their aggressive downsizing drives, may have laid off too many workers of their parents' generation. Jim Morin, a cartoonist, put it this way: "Hi dad. The good news is I found a job. The bad news is it's the same job you were downsized out of last year."

In these first few chapters, we'll be looking at how our economy uses its basic resources, at the workings of the law of supply and demand, and at how capitalism and other economic systems work. But first we need to ask how we got here. After all, the American economic system evolved over a period of more than 300 years.

Those who cannot remember the past are condemned to repeat it.
–George Santayana–

What did the great philosopher mean by this? Perhaps he meant that those who do not learn enough history the first time around will be required to repeat History 101. But whatever he meant, it is clear that to understand our economy today, we need to know how it developed over the years.

Did you see *Back to the Future*? You may have seen parts 1, 2, and 3, but let's stick with just part 1. Imagine being sent back to the 1950s. The way people lived then was very different from the way we live today—and the 1950s represented life on the fast track compared to daily existence during the first decade of the 20th century. So before we worry about today's economy, we'll take a few steps back and look at life in this country about 200 years ago.

Part 1: The American Economy in the 19th Century

Agricultural Development

America has always had a large and productive agricultural sector. At the time of the American Revolution, 9 out of every 10 Americans lived on a farm; 100 years later, however, fewer than 1 out of every 2 people worked in agriculture. Today, it's fewer than 2 in 100, but those 2 not only feed America but also produce a huge surplus that is sold abroad.

America had an almost limitless supply of land.

Unlike Europe, 200 years ago America had an almost limitless supply of unoccupied fertile land. The federal government gave away farmland—usually 160-acre plots (one-quarter of a square mile)—to anyone willing to clear the land and farm on it. Although sometimes the government charged a token amount, it often gave away the land for free.

Mass Production and Mass Consumption

Mass production is possible only if there is also mass consumption. In the late 19th century, once the national railway network enabled manufacturers to sell their products all over the country, and even beyond our shores, it became feasible to invest in heavy machinery and to turn out volume production, which, in turn, meant lower prices. Lower prices, of course, pushed up sales, which encouraged further investment and created more jobs. At the same time, productivity, or output per hour, was rising, which justified companies in paying higher wages. and a high-wage workforce could easily afford all the new low-priced products.

Henry Ford personified the symbiotic relationship between mass production and mass consumption. Selling millions of cars at a small unit of profit allowed Ford to keep prices low and wages high—the perfect formula for mass consumption.

So we had a mutually reinforcing relationship. Mass consumption enabled mass production, while mass production enabled mass consumption. As this process unfolded, our industrial output literally multiplied, and our standard of living soared. And nearly all of this process took place from within our own borders with only minimal help from foreign investors, suppliers, and consumers.

After World War II, the Japanese were in no position to use this method of reindustrialization. Not only had most of their plants and equipment been destroyed by American bombing, but also Japanese consumers did not have the purchasing power to buy enough manufactured goods to justify mass production of a wide range of consumer goods. And so the Japanese industrialists took the one course open to them: As they rebuilt their industrial base, they sold low-priced goods to the low end of the American market. In many cases they sold these items—textiles, black-and-white TVs, cameras, and other consumer goods—at half the prices charged in Japan.

Japanese consumers were willing to pay much higher prices for what was often relatively shoddy merchandise, simply because that was considered the socially correct thing to do. Imagine American consumers acting this way! Within a couple of decades, Japanese manufacturers, with a virtual monopoly in their home market and an expanding overseas market, were able to turn out high-volume, low-priced, high-quality products. We will look much more closely at Japanese manufacturing and trade practices in the chapter on international trade.

The great abundance of land was the most influential factor in our economic development during the 19th century. Not only did the availability of very cheap or free land attract millions of immigrants to our shores, but it also encouraged early marriage and large families, since every child was an additional worker to till the fields and handle the animals. Even more important, this plenitude of land, compared to amount of labor, encouraged rapid technological development.

At the time of George Washington's inauguration in 1789, there were about 4 million people living in the United States. By the time of the War of 1812, our population had doubled. It doubled again to 16 million in 1835 and had doubled still again by 1858. Our numbers continued to grow, but at a somewhat slower pace, reaching the 100 million mark in 1915, the 200 million mark in 1968, and reached 281 million in 2000.

America's large and growing population has been extremely important as a market for our farmers and manufacturers. After World War II, Japanese manufacturers targeted the American market, while the much smaller Japanese market remained largely closed to American manufactured goods. Japan—with less than half our population and, until very recently, much less purchasing power than the United States—has largely financed its industrial development with American dollars. (See box titled "Mass Production and Mass Consumption.")

Although all regions of the United States remained primarily agricultural in the years following the Civil War, New England, the Middle Atlantic states, and the Midwest—with their already well-established iron, steel, textile, and apparel industries—were poised for a major industrial expansion that would last until the Great Depression. In contrast, the South, whose economy was based on the cash crops of cotton, tobacco, rice, and sugar, as well as on subsistence farming, remained primarily an agricultural

Southern economic development remained agricultural.

Two Economic Conflicts Leading to the Civil War

In the decades before the Civil War, the economic interests of the North and South came into sharp conflict. Northern manufacturers benefited from high protective tariffs, which kept out competing British manufacturers. The Southern states, which had only a small manufacturing sector, were forced to buy most of their manufactured goods from the North and to pay higher prices than they would have paid for British goods had there been no tariff.*

As the nation expanded westward, another conflict reached the boiling point: the expansion of slavery into the new territories. In 1860, when Abraham Lincoln had been elected president, most of the land between the Mississippi River and the Pacific Ocean had not yet been organized into states. As newly formed states applied for membership in the Union, the big question was whether they would come in as "free states" or "slave states." Lincoln—and virtually all the other leaders of the new Republican Party—strenuously opposed the extension of slavery into the new territories of the West.

The Southern economy, especially cotton agriculture, was based on slave labor. The political leaders of the South realized that if slavery were prohibited in the new territories, it would be only a matter of time before these territories entered the Union as free states and the South was badly outvoted in Congress. And so, as Abraham Lincoln was preparing to take office in 1861, 11 Southern states seceded from the Union, touching off the Civil War, which lasted four years, cost hundreds of thousands of lives, and largely destroyed the Southern economy.

The two major consequences of the war were the freeing of 4 million black people who had been slaves and the preservation of the Union with those 11 rebel states. It would take the nation a full century to overcome the legacies of this conflict.

---

*Tariffs are fully discussed in the chapter on international trade.

region well into the 20th century. Its railroads had been largely destroyed by invading Northern armies during the war. Indeed, to this day there are places in Georgia where you can see evidence of the destruction caused by General William Tecumseh Sherman's army. Do you know what the twisted rails were called? Sherman's bow ties.

The South continued to be the poorest section of the country, a relative disadvantage that was not erased until the growth of the Sun Belt took off in the 1960s. The post–Civil War rallying cry "The South will rise again" did not even *begin* to ring true until 100 or so years later. (See box titled "Two Economic Conflicts Leading to the Civil War.")

Southern agriculture developed very differently from agriculture in the other regions of the nation. We know, of course, that most of the labor was provided by slaves whose ancestors had been brought here in chains from Africa. On the average, Southern farms were large. By 1860, four-fifths of the farms with more than 500 acres were in the South. The plantation owners raised commercial crops such as cotton, rice, sugar, and tobacco, while the smaller farms, which were much less dependent on slave labor, produced a wider variety of crops.

In the North and the West, self-sufficient, 160-acre family farms were most common. Eventually, corn, wheat, and soybeans became important commercial crops. But in the years following the Civil War, increasing numbers of people left the farms of the North to take jobs in manufacturing.

Bad times for agriculture

Times were bad for agriculture from the end of the Civil War until the close of the century. The government's liberal land policy, combined with increased mechanization, vastly expanded farm output. The production of the nation's three basic cash crops—corn, wheat, and cotton—rose faster than did its population through most of that period. Why did production rise so rapidly? Mainly because of the rapid technological progress made during that period (see box titled "American Agricultural Technology"). This brings us to

Supply and demand

supply and demand, which is covered in Chapter 3 and which explains why times were bad for agriculture despite expanded output. If the supply of corn increases faster than the demand for corn, what happens to the price of corn? It goes down. And this happened to wheat and cotton as well. Although other countries bought up much of the surpluses, the prices of corn, wheat, and cotton declined substantially from the end of the Civil War until the turn of the century.

American Agricultural Technology

In the 19th century, a series of inventions vastly improved farm productivity. In the late 1840s, John Deere began to manufacture steel plows in Moline, Illinois. These were a tremendous improvement over the crude wooden plows that had previously been used.

Cyrus McCormick patented a mechanical reaper in 1834. By the time of the Civil War, McCormick's reaper had at least quadrupled the output of each farm laborer. The development of the Appleby twine binder, the Marsh brothers' harvesting machine, and the Pitts thresher, as well as Eli Whitney's cotton gin, all worked to make American agriculture the most productive in the world.

The mechanization of American agriculture, which continued into the 20th century with the introduction of the gasoline powered tractor in the 1920s, would not have been possible without a highly skilled farm work force. Tom Brokaw described the challenge that farmers faced using this technology:

> Farm boys were inventive and good with their hands. They were accustomed to finding solutions to mechanical and design problems on their own. There was no one else to ask when the tractor broke down or the threshing machine fouled, no 1-800-CALLHELP operators standing by in those days.[*]

[*]Tom Brokaw, *The Greatest Generation,* New York: Random House, 1999, p. 92. The "greatest generation" was the one that came of age during the Great Depression and won World War II.

The National Railroad Network

The completion of a national railroad network in the second half of the 19th century made possible mass production, mass marketing, and mass consumption. In 1850, the United States had just 10,000 miles of track, but within 40 years the total reached 164,000 miles. The transcontinental railroads had been completed, and it was possible to get virtually anywhere in the country by train. Interestingly, however, the transcontinental lines all bypassed the South, which severely retarded its economic development well into the 20th century.

In 1836, it took a traveler an entire month to get from New York to Chicago. Just 15 years later, he could make the trip by rail in less than two days. What the railroads did, in effect, was to weave the country together into a huge social and economic unit, and eventually into the world's first mass market (see again box titled "Mass Production and Mass Consumption").

John Steele Gordon describes the economic impact of the railroads:

> most East Coast rivers were navigable for only short distances inland. As a result, there really was no "American economy." Instead there was a myriad of local ones. Most food was consumed locally, and most goods were locally produced by artisans such as blacksmiths. The railroads changed all that in less than 30 years.[1]

Before railroads, shipping a ton of goods 400 miles could easily quadruple the price. But by rail, the same ton of goods could be shipped in a fraction of the time and at one-twentieth of the cost.

The Age of the Industrial Capitalist

The last quarter of the 19th century was the age of the industrial capitalist. The great empire builders—Carnegie (steel), Du Pont (chemicals), McCormick (farm equipment), Rockefeller (oil), and Swift (meat packing), among others—dominated this era. John D. Rockefeller, whose exploits will be discussed in the chapter on corporate mergers and antitrust, built the Standard Oil Trust, which controlled 90 percent of the oil business. In 1872, just before Andrew Carnegie opened the Edgar Thomson works, the

The completion of the transcontinental railroads

Andrew Carnegie, American industrial capitalist (National Portrait Gallery/Art Resource)

[1]John Steele Gordon, "The Golden Spike," *Forbes ASAP,* February 21, 2000, p. 118.

The Development of the Automobile Industry

*Nothing is particularly hard
if you divide it into small jobs.*

—Henry Ford—

Who was the first automobile manufacturer to use a division of labor, to use a moving assembly line, and to bring the materials to the worker instead of the worker to the materials? Was it Henry Ford? Close, but no cigar. The man was Henry Olds, who turned the trick in 1901 when he started turning out Oldsmobiles on a mass basis. Still another Henry, Henry Leland, believed it was possible and practical to manufacture a standardized engine with interchangeable parts. By 1908, he did just that with his Cadillac.

Henry Ford was able to carry mass production to its logical conclusion. His great contribution was the emphasis he placed on an expert combination of accuracy, continuity, the moving assembly line, and speed, through the careful timing of manufacturing, materials handling, and assembly. In a sense, then, Henry Ford was the precursor to today's Japanese automaker.

Back in 1908, just 200,000 cars were registered in the United States. In 1915, Ford produced more than one-third of the 880,000 motor vehicles built that year. In 1923, Ford built 57 percent of the 4 million cars and trucks produced. But soon General Motors supplanted Ford as the country's number one automobile firm, a position it continues to hold. In 1929, motor vehicle production peaked at 5.3 million units, a number that was not reached again until 1949.

United States produced less than 100,000 tons of steel. Only 25 years later, Carnegie alone was turning out 4 million tons, almost half of the total American production. Again, as supply outran demand, the price of steel dropped from $65 to $20 a ton.

Part 2: The American Economy from 1900 through World War I

Until the last quarter of the 19th century, American economic history was largely agricultural history. Thereafter, the emphasis shifted to manufacturing. By the end of World War I, agriculture played a relatively minor role in our economic development.

Industrial Development

On the world's technological cutting edge

By the turn of the century, America had become an industrial economy. Fewer than 4 in 10 people still lived on farms. We were among the world's leaders in the production of steel, coal, steamships, textiles, apparel, chemicals, and agricultural machinery. Our trade balance with the rest of the world was positive every year. And although we continued to export most of our huge agricultural surpluses to Europe, increasingly we began to send the countries of that continent our manufactured goods as well.

We were also well on our way to becoming the world's first mass-consumption society. The stage had been set by the late-19th-century industrialists. At the turn of the 20th century, we were on the threshold of the automobile age (see box titled "The Development of the Automobile Industry"). The Wright brothers would soon be flying their plane at Kitty Hawk, but commercial aviation was still a few decades away.

American technological progress—or, if the South can forgive me, Yankee ingenuity—runs the gamut from the agricultural implements previously mentioned to the telegraph, the telephone, the radio, the TV, and the computer. It includes the mass-production system perfected by Henry Ford, which made possible the era of mass consumption and the high living standards that the people of all industrialized nations enjoy today. America has long been on the world's technological cutting edge, as well as being the world's leader in manufacturing.

Henry Ford, American automobile manufacturer (The Granger Collection, New York)

This technological talent, a large agricultural surplus, the world's first universal public education system, and the entrepreneurial abilities of our great industrialists combined to enable the United States to emerge as the world's leading industrial power by the time of World War I. Then, too, fortune smiled on this continent by keeping it out of harm's way during the war. This same good fortune recurred during World War II; so, once again, unlike the rest of the industrial world, we emerged from the war with our industrial plant intact.

Agricultural Development

Agricultural conditions really turned around in the first two decades of the 20th century. Production stabilized, and agriculture enjoyed mild prosperity from 1900 to 1913. Then came world War I, which brought the farmer unprecedented prosperity despite a huge increase in output. Wheat production, for example, which exceeded 1 billion bushels in 1915, passed the 3-billion-bushel mark in 1920.

But in the years immediately after the war, agriculture went into a terrible slump. The price of corn, which had been $1.50 a bushel in 1919, fell to just 30 cents. Wheat fell from $2.15 to 40 cents. And cotton went from 36 cents a pound all the way down to a nickel. It was not until the New Deal, World War II, and the massive federal farm-subsidy program that followed the war that farmers finally were able to get on their feet again.

Part 3: The American Economy between the Wars

When did the United States emerge as a mature industrial economy? We'll take as our starting point the decade of the 1920s, when America truly became a mass-consumption economy. But that economy did not have any distinct time of departure. It evolved from a set of powerful forces that were described in the first part of this chapter.

Let's proceed with a brief decade-by-decade account of the country's economic performance since the end of the first World War. Actually, not all these decades are *exactly* 10 years long, but nothing's perfect. Like the rest of life, economic history does not unfold into uniform periods of ups and downs.

The Roaring Twenties

World War I ended on November 11, 1918. After a mild and very brief recession, during which our economy reverted to peacetime production, we enjoyed a short economic boom from the spring of 1919 through January 1920. This boom was set off mainly by pent-up consumer demand for housing, clothing, and automobiles; the existence of a large amount of cash, bank deposits, and savings bonds just waiting to be spent; a high foreign demand for American products; and continuing high spending by the federal government. (These same forces, albeit on a much larger scale, were to fuel the prosperity enjoyed in the years immediately following World War II.)

The postwar boom

The Roaring Twenties actually began and ended with depressions. In early 1920, consumers, upset with high prices, began cutting back on their purchases. The Federal Reserve,[2] which controls our money supply, had already begun to tighten credit. Meanwhile, the federal government quickly managed to cut its large wartime budget deficit to zero, which also depressed the economy.[3]

The postwar depression

---

[2] I'll discuss how the Federal Reserve controls the growth of our money supply in the chapter on the monetary policy of the Federal Reserve in *Economics* and *Macroeconomics*.

[3] Federal budget deficits and their effect on our economy are discussed in a later chapter of *Economics* and *Macroeconomics*.

Our Financial House of Cards

Buying stocks on margin was one of the more visible financial excesses of the Roaring Twenties. The Florida real estate boom, which included thousands of spectacular underwater properties, was another. But the major abuse was the erection of a financial superstructure of holding companies and investment trusts that came crashing down in the early 1930s.

When the crash came, the banks that had financed these ventures began to fail, since the speculators were in no position to repay their loans. And as these banks failed, other banks around the country began to fail as well, either because they had large deposits at the failing banks or because depositors, nervous about the safety of their deposits, began withdrawing their savings. So even the banks that had little or nothing to do with the financial excesses of the 1920s were forced to close. And when they did, millions of depositors found that they had lost their entire life savings.

Retailers, stuck with heavy inventories, curtailed their purchases from manufacturers. Wholesale prices dropped 45 percent. Within months, a worldwide depression was in the works. But recovery began very quickly in the United States as excess inventory was worked off. The most important factor in the recovery was that the long-term investment opportunities that existed in 1919–20 were still present in 1921.

Like the pent-up demand for residential housing, there was a tremendous demand for commercial buildings. The automobile industry was growing rapidly and required a further expansion of auxiliary industries such as steel, glass, and rubber, as well as service stations and new roads.

The spreading use of electricity

Another important development in the 1920s was the spreading use of electricity. During this decade, electric power production doubled. Not only was industrial use growing, but by 1929 about two out of every three homes in America had been wired and were now using electrical appliances. The telephone, the radio, the toaster, the refrigerator, and other conveniences became commonplace during the 1920s.

Between 1921 and 1929, national output rose by 50 percent. Despite two minor recessions in 1924 and 1927, most Americans thought the prosperity would last forever. The stock market was soaring, and instant millionaires were created every day, at least on paper.

How to become a millionaire in the stock market

It was possible, in the late 1920s, to put down just 10 percent of a stock purchase and borrow the rest on margin from a stockbroker, who, in turn, borrowed that money from a bank. If you put down $1,000, you could buy $10,000 worth of stock. If that stock doubled (that is, if it was now worth $20,000), you just made $10,000 on a $1,000 investment. Better yet, your $10,000 stake entitled you to borrow $90,000 from your broker, so you could now own $100,000 worth of stock.

This was not a bad deal—as long as the market kept going up. But, as you've heard so many times, what goes up must come down. And, as you well know, the stock market came crashing down in October 1929 (see box titled "Our Financial House of Cards"). Although no one knew it at the time, the economy had already begun its descent into a recession a couple of months before the crash. And as the economy continued to sink, that recession became the Great Depression.

Curiously, within days after the crash, several leading government and business officials—including President Hoover and John D. Rockefeller—each described economic conditions as "fundamentally sound." The next time you hear our economy described in those terms, you'll know we're in big trouble.

The Great Depression

The August 1929 recession

By the summer of 1929, the country had clearly built itself up for an economic letdown. The boom in sales of cars and electrical appliances was over. The automobile market was saturated. Nearly three out of four cars on the road were less than six years old, and model changes were not nearly as important then as they are today. The tire industry had been overbuilt, and textiles were suffering from overcapacity. Residential construction was already in decline, and the general business investment outlook was not that rosy.

Had the stock market not crashed and had the rest of the world not gone into a depression, we might have gotten away with a moderate business downturn. Also, had the federal government acted more expeditiously, it is quite possible that the prosperity of the 1920s, after a fairly short recession, could have continued well into the 1930s. But that's not what happened. What did happen completely changed the lives of the people who lived through it, as well as the course of human history itself.

Even through 1930 there was no clear indication that we were in anything worse than a bad recession. A recession is a decline in national output for at least six months. There was a slight, abortive recovery in the early months of 1930, with rises in both automobile production and residential construction. Wage rates were well maintained throughout the year. But prices began to decline, investment in plant and equipment collapsed, and a drought wiped out millions of farmers. In fact, conditions grew so bad in what became known as the Dust Bowl that millions of people from the Midwest just packed their cars and drove in caravans to seek a better life in California. Their flight was immortalized in John Steinbeck's great novel *The Grapes of Wrath,* which was later made into a movie. Although most of these migrants came from other states, they were collectively called Okies, because it seemed at the time as if the entire state of Oklahoma had picked up and moved west.

The Dust Bowl and the "Okies"

By the end of 1930, thousands of banks had failed and the generally optimistic economic outlook had given way to one of extreme pessimism. Yet in the early months of 1931, the economy seemed to be attempting to stage another recovery. But whatever chance it had was crushed that spring by the collapse of the entire international financial structure. From here on, it was all downhill. By the beginning of 1933, banks were closing all over the country; by the first week in March, every single bank in the United States had shut its doors.

The bank failures

When the economy hit bottom, in March 1933, national output was about one-third lower than it had been in August 1929. The official unemployment rate was 25 percent, which meant that some 16 million Americans were out of work at a time when our country's population was less than half its present size. To lend some perspective, at the low point of the 1990–91 recession, nearly 10 million Americans were officially unemployed.

Hitting bottom

But official figures tell only part of the story. Millions of additional workers had simply given up looking for work during the depths of the Great Depression, as there was no work to be had. Yet according to the way the government compiles the unemployment rate, these people were not even counted since they were not actually looking for work.[4]

The Depression was a time of soup kitchens, people selling apples on the street, large-scale homelessness, so-called hobo jungles where poor men huddled around garbage-pail fires to keep warm, and even fairly widespread starvation. "Are you working?" and "Brother, can you spare a dime?"[5] were common greetings. People who lived in collections of shacks made of cardboard, wood, and corrugated sheet metal scornfully referred to them as Hoovervilles. Although Herbert Hoover did eventually make a few halfhearted attempts to get the economy moving again, his greatest contribution to the economy was apparently his slogans. When he ran for the presidency in 1928, he promised "two cars in every garage" and "a chicken in every pot." As the Depression grew worse, he kept telling Americans that "prosperity is just around the corner." It's too bad he didn't have Frank Perdue in those days to stick a chicken in every pot.

Herbert Hoover, thirty-first president of the United States (National Portrait Gallery/Art Resource)

Herbert Hoover and the Depression

---

[4]How the Department of Labor computes the unemployment rate is discussed in the chapter on economic fluctuations in *Economics* and *Macroeconomics.* In Chapter 2, we'll be looking at the concept of full employment, but you can grasp intuitively that when our economy enters even a minor downturn, we are operating at less than full employment.

[5]"Brother, Can You Spare a Dime?" was a depression era song written by Yip Harburg and Jay Gorney.

The New Deal

When Franklin D. Roosevelt ran for president in 1932, he promised "a new deal for the American people." Action was needed, and it was needed fast. In the first 100 days Roosevelt was in office, his administration sent a flurry of bills to Congress that were promptly passed.

The New Deal is best summarized by the three Rs: relief, recovery, and reform. Relief was aimed at alleviating the suffering of a nation that was, in President Roosevelt's words, one-third "ill-fed, ill-clothed, and ill-housed." These people needed work relief, a system similar to today's workfare (work for your welfare check) programs. About 6 million people, on average, were put to work at various jobs ranging from raking leaves and repairing public buildings to maintaining national parks and building power dams. Robert R. Russell made this observation:

> The principal objects of work-relief were to help people preserve their self-respect by enabling them to stay off the dole and to maintain their work habits against the day when they could again find employment in private enterprises. It was also hoped that the programs, by putting some purchasing power into the hands of workers and

suppliers of materials, would help prime the economic pump.*

The government hoped that all this spending would bring about economic recovery, but the most lasting effect of the New Deal was reform. The Securities and Exchange Commission (SEC) was set up to regulate the stock market and avoid a repetition of the speculative excesses of the late 1920s, which had led to the great crash of 1929. After the reform, bank deposits were insured by the Federal Deposit Insurance Corporation (FDIC) to prevent future runs on the banks by depositors, like those experienced in the early 1930s. Also, an unemployment insurance benefit program was set up to provide temporarily unemployed people with some money to tide them over. The most important reform of all was the creation of Social Security. Although even today retired people need more than their Social Security benefits to get by, there is no question that this program has provided tens of millions of retired people with a substantial income and has largely removed workers' fears of being destitute and dependent in their old age.

*Robert R. Russell, *A History of the American Economic System* (New York: Appleton-Century-Crofts, 1964), p. 547.

Why did the downturn reverse itself?

Why did the downturn of August 1929 to March 1933 finally reverse itself? Well, for one thing, we were just about due. Business inventories had been reduced to rock-bottom levels, prices had finally stopped falling, and there was a need to replace some plant and equipment. The federal budget deficits of 1931 and 1932, even if unwillingly incurred, did provide a mild stimulus to the economy.

Clearly a lot of the credit must go to the new administration of Franklin D. Roosevelt, which reopened the banks, ran large budget deficits, and eventually created government job programs that put millions of Americans back to work (see box titled "The New Deal"). Recognizing a crisis in confidence, Roosevelt said, "The only thing we have to fear is fear itself." Putting millions of people back to work was a tremendous confidence builder. A 50-month expansion began in March 1933 and lasted until May 1937. Although output did finally reach the levels of August 1929, more than 7 million people were still unemployed.

Franklin D. Roosevelt, thirty-second president of the United States (Franklin D. Roosevelt Library)

By far, the most important reason for the success of the New Deal's first four years was the massive federal government spending that returned millions of Americans to work. This huge infusion of dollars into our economy was just what the doctor ordered. In this case, the doctor was John Maynard Keynes, the great English economist, who maintained that it didn't matter *what* the money was spent on—even paying people to dig holes in the ground and then to fill them up again—as long as enough money was spent. But in May 1937, just when it had begun to look as though the Depression was finally over, we plunged right back into it again.

What went wrong? Two things: First, the Federal Reserve Board of Governors, inexplicably more concerned about inflation than about the lingering economic depression, greatly tightened credit, making it much harder to borrow money. Second, the Roosevelt administration suddenly got that old balance-the-budget-at-all-costs religion. The cost of that economic orthodoxy—which would have made sense during an economic boom—was the very sharp and deep recession of 1937–38. Tight money and a balanced budget are now considered the right policies to follow when the economy is heating up and

The recession of 1937–38

prices are rising too quickly, but they are prescriptions for disaster when the unemployment rate is 12 percent.[6]

The ensuing downturn pushed up the official unemployment count by another 5 million, industrial production fell by 30 percent, and people began to wonder when this depression would ever end. But there really *was* some light at the end of the tunnel.

In April 1938, both the Roosevelt administration and the Federal Reserve Board reversed course and began to stimulate the economy. By June, the economy had turned around again, and this time the expansion would continue for seven years. The outbreak of war in Europe, the American mobilization in 1940 and 1941, and our eventual entry into the war on December 7, 1941, all propelled us toward full recovery.

When we ask what finally brought the United States out of the Great Depression, there is one clear answer: the massive federal government spending that was needed to prepare for and to fight World War II.

Part 4: From World War II to the Vietnam War

For most Americans the end of the Depression did not bring much relief, because the nation was now fighting an all-out war. For those who didn't get the message in those days, there was the popular reminder, "Hey, bub, don't yuh know there's a *war* goin' on?"

The country that emerged from the war was very different from the one that had entered it less than four years earlier. Prosperity had replaced depression. Now inflation had become the number one economic worry.

Globally, we were certainly at the top of our game. With just 7 percent of the world's population, we accounted for half the world's manufacturing output, as well as 80 percent of its cars and 62 percent of its oil. Our potential rivals, Japan, Germany, France, and the United Kingdom would need at least 15 years to repair their war-damaged industrial plant and begin competing again in world markets.

The United States and the Soviet Union were the only superpowers left standing in 1945. When the cold war quickly developed, we spent tens of billions of dollars to prop up the sagging economies of the nations of Western Europe and Japan, and we spent hundreds of billions more to provide for their defense. In the four decades since the close of World War II we expended 6 percent of our national output on defense, while the Soviet Union probably expended at least triple that percentage. This great burden certainly contributed to the collapse of the Soviet Union in 1990–91, and our own heavy defense spending continues to divert substantial resources that might otherwise be used to spur our economic growth.

The 1940s: World War II and Peacetime Prosperity

Just as the Great Depression dominated the 1930s, World War II was the main event of the 1940s, especially from the day the Japanese bombed Pearl Harbor until they surrendered in August 1945. For the first time in our history, we fought a war that required a total national effort. Although the Civil War had caused tremendous casualties and had set the South back economically for generations, we had never before fought a war that consumed half of our nation's total output.

At the peak of the war, more than 12 million men and women were mobilized and, not coincidentally, the unemployment rate was below 2 percent. Women, whose place was supposedly in the home, flocked to the workplace to replace the men who had gone off to war. Blacks, too, who had experienced great difficulty finding factory jobs, were hired to work in the steel mills and the defense plants in the East, the Midwest, and the West.

Between 1939 and 1944, national output of goods and services nearly doubled, while federal government spending—mainly for defense—rose by more than 400 percent. By

---

[6]These policies will be discussed in later chapters of *Economics* and *Macroeconomics.*

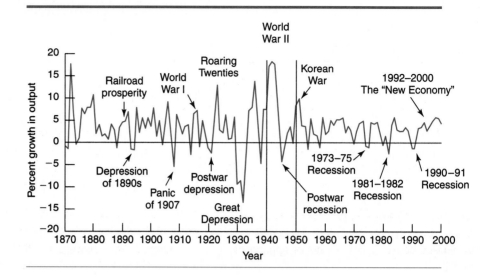

Figure 1

Annual Percentage Growth of U.S. Output of Goods and Services, 1870–2000

Although there were plenty of ups and downs, in most years output grew at a rate of between 2 and 5 percent. What stands out are the booms during World War I, the Roaring Twenties, the abortive recovery from the Great Depression (in the mid-1930s), World War II, and the late 1990s. The two sharpest declines in output occurred during the Great Depression and after World War II. The drop after World War II was entirely due to a huge cut in defense spending, but our economy quickly reconverted to producing civilian goods and services, so the 1945 recession was actually very mild.

Sources: U.S. Department of Commerce, AmeriTrust Company, Cleveland.

the middle of 1942, our economy reached full employment for the first time since 1929. To hold inflation in check, the government not only instituted price and wage controls but also issued ration coupons for meat, butter, gasoline, and other staples.

During the war, 17 million new jobs were created, while the economy grew 10 or 11 percent a year. Doris Kearns Goodwin attributed "a remarkable entrepreneurial spirit" not only to the opportunity to make huge wartime profits but to a competitiveness "developed within each business enterprise to produce better than its competitors to serve the country." A sign hanging in many defense plants read: "PLEDGE TO VICTORY: The war may be won or lost in this plant."[7]

The United States entered a very slight recession for a few months in 1945, as the economy underwent reconversion to put it on a peacetime footing. A somewhat longer, but still mild, downturn occurred from late 1948 through late 1949, but the decade was basically one of rapid economic expansion. (See box, "Post–World War II Recessions," for a description of each economic downturn since World War II.)

Figure 1 provides a snapshot of U.S. economic growth since 1870.

Within a year after the war ended, some 12 million men and several hundred thousand women returned home to their civilian lives. Very little housing had been built during the war and the preceding depressed period, so most veterans lived in overcrowded houses and apartments, often with three generations under one roof. The first thing they wanted was new housing.

The suburbanization of America

The federal government obligingly facilitated this by providing Veterans Administration (VA) mortgages at about 1 percent interest and often nothing down to returning veterans. The Federal Housing Administration (FHA) supplemented this program with FHA mortgages to millions of other Americans. Where were these houses built? In the suburbs. By 1945, little land was available in the cities, so suburbanization was inevitable.

---

[7]Doris Kearns Goodwin, "The Way We Won: America's Economic Breakthrough during World War II," *The American Prospect,* Fall 1992, p. 68.

Post–World War II Recessions

Since World War II, the United States has had 10 recessions of varying length and severity. The longest was from 1973–75, but the most severe was the 1981–82 recession.

February 1945–October 1945 Even though the war had not yet ended, we began to reconvert into peacetime production. This process was relatively painless, and the recession was perhaps the mildest in the last six decades.

December 1948–October 1949 This was another very mild downturn, really a pause after consumers had satisfied their pent-up demand for cars, major appliances, and new homes.

August 1953–May 1954 A decline in defense spending after the end of the Korean War and a reduction in business inventories built during the last months of the war were the main culprits. This was the third mild recession in a row.

August 1957–April 1958 Business, which had been flat from early 1956 through the summer of 1957, finally sank into a recession. Although brief, the decline was rapid. Investment in plant and equipment fell sharply, but spending by consumers fell only slightly. This was the worst recession since the Great Depression, but it ended in just nine months.

April 1960–February 1961 A long steel strike in 1959 and a swing to a balanced federal budget set off this very mild recession. National output fell almost imperceptibly.

December 1969–November 1970 This was another very mild downturn with another almost imperceptible decline in national output. The downturn coincided with an automobile strike and a strike at General Electric.

November 1973–March 1975 This was the worst downturn since the end of the Great Depression. It was set off by a fourfold increase in the price of oil engineered by the OPEC nations (which we'll talk a lot more about in the chapter on economic fluctuations in *Economics* and *Macroeconomics*). Simultaneously, there was a worldwide shortage of foodstuffs, which drove up food prices. To make matters worse in this country, we struck a deal to export about one-quarter of our wheat and other grains to the Soviet Union. Output fell about 5 percent, and, to make matters still worse, the rate of inflation remained unacceptably high.

January 1980–July 1980 A doubling of oil prices by OPEC and a credit crunch set off by the Federal Reserve Board of Governors, which had been alarmed by an inflation rate that had reached double-digit levels, pushed us into a very brief, but fairly sharp, recession. When interest rates rose above 20 percent, the Federal Reserve allowed credit to expand and the recession ended.

August 1981–November 1982 This downturn was also set off by the Federal Reserve, which was now determined to wring inflation out of our economy. By the end of the recession—which now held the dubious distinction of being the worst downturn since the Great Depression—the unemployment rate had reached almost 11 percent. But the inflation rate had been brought down, and in late summer 1982, the Federal Reserve once again eased credit, setting the stage for the subsequent recovery. At the same time, the federal government had been cutting income tax rates, further helping along the business upturn.

July 1990–March 1991 After the longest uninterrupted peacetime expansion in our history, a fairly mild downturn was caused by a combination of sharply rising oil prices (due to Iraq's invasion of Kuwait on August 2 and the ensuing Persian Gulf War), tight money, and a deficit-cutting budget agreement between President George Bush and Congress in October. The agreement, which called for a package of tax increases and federal government spending reductions totaling nearly $500 billion over five years, was supposed to bring down the deficit. What it *did* was make the recession somewhat worse than it might otherwise have been and also retard the ensuing recovery. President Bush himself termed the recovery "anemic," and its slow pace was largely responsible for his loss of the 1992 election to Bill Clinton. Unemployment continued to rise—to a peak of 7.8 percent—well into the recovery, which took an unusually long 18 months. Indeed, it was not until the very last week of 1992 that economists were certain that the recession was over and that we had fully recovered.

And how would these new suburbanites get to work? By car. Thus more highways were needed. Once again, the federal government stepped in. Before long a federally subsidized interstate highway network was being built, along with thousands of state and local highways, parkways, and freeways, as well as local streets and roads.

Hence the late 1940s and the 1950s were one big construction boom. Highway building and home construction provided millions of jobs. The automobile industry, too, was prospering after a total shutdown during the war. In the postwar era, we not only supplied all the new suburbanites with cars, but we also became the world's leading auto exporter. The industrial plants of West Germany and Japan had been destroyed or damaged during the war; it wasn't until the mid-1960s that those nations reentered the world market, and it took them another decade to capture more than 10 percent of the American car market.

The returning veterans, like the nation, had a lot of catching up to do. Couples had been forced to put off having children, but after the war the birthrate shot up and stayed high until the mid-1960s. This baby boom and low gasoline prices added impetus to the nation's suburbanization. Why continue to live in cramped urban quarters when a house in the suburbs was easily affordable?—as it was to most middle-class and working-class Americans (see box titled "Levittown, U.S.A.").

In 1944 Congress passed the GI Bill of Rights, which not only offered veterans mortgage loans, as well as loans to start businesses, but also provided monthly stipends for veterans who wanted help with educational costs. By 1956, when the programs ended, 7.8 million veterans, about half of all who had served, had participated. A total of 2.2 million went to college, 3.5 million to technical schools below the college level, and 700,000 to agricultural instruction of farms. The GI bill made college affordable to men from working-class and lower-middle-class backgrounds and was almost entirely responsible for enrollments more than doubling between 1940 and 1949.

The only jarring economic notes were very minor recessions in 1945 and 1948–49 (see again the box titled "Post–World War II Recessions") and a serious bout of inflation

Levittown, U.S.A.

Levittown, Long Island, a tract development of 17,000 nearly identical homes, was built right after World War II, largely for returning veterans and their families. These 800-square-foot, prefabricated homes sold for $8,000 each, with no down payment for veterans. William Levitt described the production process as the reverse of the Detroit assembly line:

> There, the car moved while the workers stayed at their stations. In the case of our houses, it was the workers who moved, doing the same jobs at different locations. To the best of my knowledge, no one had ever done that before.[*]

Levittown became the prototype of suburban tract development, and the Levitts themselves built similar developments in New Jersey, Pennsylvania, and Maryland. And so, while tens of millions of Americans were able to move into new suburban homes in the decades after World War II, a popular cartoon of the 1950s depicted this scene: Ten men with briefcases are getting out of their cars. Ten identical dogs rush out of 10 identical homes to greet them while 10 wives, each with two children, wait at the front doors.

In 1963, civil rights demonstrations targeted William Levitt's housing development in Bowie, Maryland. Levitt admitted he had refused to sell houses to black families, because, he said, integrating his developments would put him at a competitive disadvantage. Levitt's discriminatory sales policy was no different from most other developers, who did not relent until well into the 1960s, when government pressure forced them to do so. To this day, most of the communities built by the Levitts remain overwhelmingly white.

Of course racism was hardly confined to developers like Levitt. James T. Patterson, a historian, wrote that the Federal Housing Administration "openly screened out applicants according to its assessment of people who were 'risks.'"[†] These were mainly blacks, Jews, and other "unharmonious racial or nationality groups." In so doing it enshrined residential segregation as a public policy of the United States government.

---

[*]Eric Pace, "William J. Levitt, 86, Pioneer of Suburbs, Dies," *New York Times,* January 29, 1994, p. A1.

[†]James T. Patterson, *Grand Expectations* (New York: Oxford University Press, 1997), p. 27.

immediately after the war when consumer prices rose 35 percent in three years. Then, just when inflation had been brought under control, the Korean War, which the country entered in June 1950, brought on another wave of price increases.

The 1950s: The Eisenhower Years

The economy was further stimulated by the advent of television in the early 1950s, as well as by the Korean War. It didn't really matter what individual consumers or the government spent their money on, as long as they spent it on something.

General Dwight D. Eisenhower, one of the great heroes of World War II, made two key promises in his 1952 campaign for the presidency: He would end the war in Korea, and he would end the inflation. Eisenhower made good on both promises. Although three recessions occurred during his eight years in office, the country continued to suburbanize, and economic growth, although not as fast as it had been in the 1940s, was deemed satisfactory by most Americans (see the box "The Consequences of Suburbanization").

Eisenhower would end the war and end the inflation.

What may be most significant about the Eisenhower years is what *didn't* happen rather than what did. Eisenhower made no attempt to undo the legacies of the New Deal such as Social Security, unemployment insurance, or the regulatory reforms that had been instituted. The role of the federal government as a major economic player had become a permanent one. Twenty-eight years later, when President Ronald Reagan left office after having paid great lip service to "getting the government off the backs of the American people," that role had grown even greater.

The Soaring Sixties: The Years of Kennedy and Johnson

When John F. Kennedy ran for president in 1960, the country was mired in the third Eisenhower recession. Kennedy pledged to "get the country moving again." The economy *did* quickly rebound from the recession and embarked on an uninterrupted eight-year expansion. An assassin shot Kennedy before he could complete his first term; he was succeeded by Lyndon Johnson, who in his first speech as president stated simply, "Let us continue." A major tax cut, which Kennedy had been planning, was enacted in 1964 to stimulate the economy. That and our growing involvement in the Vietnam War helped bring the unemployment rate down below 4 percent by 1966. But three major

---

The Consequences of Suburbanization

Suburbanization was the migration of tens of millions of middle-class Americans—nearly all of them white—from our nation's large central cities to newly developed suburban towns and villages. Instead of getting to work by public transportation, these commuters now went by car. Truck transport replaced railroads as the primary way to haul freight. Millions of poor people—the large majority of whom were black or Hispanic—moved into the apartments vacated by the whites who had fled to the suburbs.

Suburbanization left our cities high and dry. As middle-class taxpayers and millions of factory jobs left the cities, their tax bases shrank. There were fewer and fewer entry-level jobs for the millions of new arrivals, largely from the rural South. Throughout the 1950s, 1960s, and 1970s, a huge concentration of poor people was left in the cities as the middle-class workers—both black and white—continued to flee to the suburbs. By the mid-1970s, the inner cities were rife with poverty, drugs, and crime, and had become socially isolated from the rest of the country.

Still other consequences of suburbanization were our dependence on oil as our main source of energy and eventually, our dependence on foreign sources for more than half our oil. Indeed, America's love affair with the automobile has not only depleted our resources, polluted our air, destroyed our landscape, and clogged our highways but also has been a major factor in our imbalance of trade.[*]

---

[*]The damage we are doing to our nation's environment and to that of our planet is alarming, but discussing it goes beyond the scope of this book. However, in the chapter on international trade, we do have a lengthy discussion of our trade imbalance and how our growing oil imports have contributed to it.

spending programs, all initiated by Johnson in 1965, have had the most profound long-term effect on the economy: Medicare, Medicaid, and food stamps.

However, as the federal deficit mounted and as the money supply grew too quickly, another round of inflation began; it was not brought under control until the mid-1980s.

Part 5: From the Vietnam War to the Breakup of the Soviet Empire

Our country has been at relative peace—with the exceptions of the very brief wars against Iraq in 1990–91 and Serbia in 1999—since our withdrawal from Vietnam in the early 1970s. Nevertheless, we have continued to spend over 3 percent of our national output on defense. With the breakup of the Soviet Union and its Eastern European military alliance came great hopes of a "peace dividend," but the government has made only minimal cuts in defense spending since 1990, and these hopes have been receding.

The Sagging Seventies: The Stagflation Decade

In 1968, Richard Nixon said he had a plan to end the Vietnam War and to bring inflation under control. Soon after taking office, he was greeted by a relatively minor recession (see again the box titled "Post–World War II Recessions"), but his main problem was with inflation. On August 15, 1971, Nixon suddenly announced wage and price controls, but these were applied halfheartedly and did not seem to make much of an impact. Nevertheless, Nixon was reelected by a landslide in 1972, though by then he seemed unwilling or unable to get our economy back on course—perhaps because he had other things to worry about, such as getting impeached.

Stagnation + inflation = stagflation.

The 1970s brought Americans crashing back to economic reality. In 1973, we were hit by the worst recession since the 1930s. This came on the heels of an oil price shock: The Organization of Petroleum Exporting Countries (OPEC) had quadrupled oil prices in the fall of 1973, and by then, too, we were mired in double-digit inflation, an annual rate of increase in prices of at least 10 percent. About the only good thing during this period was that we were able to add a new word to our vocabularies—*stagflation*. The first part of this word is derived from stagnation. Our rate of economic growth, which had been fairly rapid for 25 years after World War II, had slowed to a crawl. Usually when this happened, prices would stop rising or would at least slow their rate of increase. But now the opposite had happened: We had a bad case of inflation, which gave us the second part of the word *stagflation*.

Nixon's successor, Gerald Ford, did have a little success with respect to inflation, although his main weapon seemed to be a button he liked to wear that said WIN, which stood for "Whip Inflation Now."

Jimmy Carter's economic problems

The president who seemed to have the worst economic luck of all was Jimmy Carter. He presided over mounting budget deficits that, coupled with a rapid growth of the money supply, pushed up the inflation rate to nearly double-digit levels. And then suddenly, in 1979, the Iranian revolution set off our second oil shock. Gasoline prices went through the ceiling, rising from about 70 cents a gallon to $1.25 in June and July of that year.

Alarmed at the inflation rate, which had nearly doubled in just three years, the Federal Reserve literally stopped the growth of the money supply in October 1979. By the following January we were in another recession, while the annual rate of inflation reached 18 percent. Talk about stagflation!

Still another disturbing development was a slowing of our nation's productivity growth, or output per hour worked. By the late 1970s, it had dropped to only 1 percent, just about one-third its postwar rate.[8] Until we found a way to boost our productivity, our economy would continue to stagnate.

The 1980s: The Age of Reagan

Ronald Reagan, who overwhelmingly defeated incumbent Jimmy Carter in the 1980 presidential election, offered the answers to our most pressing economic problems. For too long, he declared, we had allowed the federal government to "tax, tax, tax, spend, spend, spend." Big government was not the answer to our problems. Only private enterprise could provide meaningful jobs and spur economic growth. If we cut tax rates, said Reagan, people would have more incentive to work, output would rise, and inflation would subside. After all, if inflation meant that too many dollars were chasing too few goods, why not produce more goods?

This brand of economics, supply-side economics, was really the flip side of Keynesian economics. Both had the same objective: to stimulate output, or supply. The Keynesians thought the way to do this was to have the government spend more money, which, in turn, would give business firms the incentive to produce more. The supply-siders said that if tax rates were cut, people would have more of an incentive to work and would increase output.

Personal income taxes were cut by a whopping 23 percent in 1981 (stretched over a three-year period), and business taxes were also slashed. This was the heart of the supply-side program.

In January 1981, it was Ronald Reagan's ball game to win or lose. At first he seemed to be losing. He presided over still another recession, which, by the time it ended, was the new postwar record holder, at least in terms of length and depth. The second-worst recession since World War II had been that of 1973–75. But the 1981–82 recession was a little longer and somewhat worse.

By the end of 1982, the unemployment rate reached nearly 11 percent, a rate the country had not seen since the end of the Depression. But on the upside, inflation was finally brought under control. In fact, both the inflation and unemployment rates fell during the next four years, and stagflation became just a bad memory.

Still, some very troubling economic problems surfaced during the period. The unemployment rate, which had come down substantially since the end of the 1981–82 recession, seemed stuck at around 6 percent, a rate that most economists consider to be unacceptably high. A second cause for concern was the megadeficits being run by the federal government year after year. Finally, there were the foreign trade deficits, which were getting progressively larger throughout most of the 1980s.

In 1988, George Bush, who had served as Reagan's vice president for eight years and claimed to be a convert to supply-side economics, made this famous campaign promise: "Read my lips: no tax increase." Of course, the rest is history. Bush won the election, and a couple of years later, in an effort to reduce the federal budget deficit, he agreed to a major tax increase. Not only did his words come back to haunt him when he ran for reelection in 1992, but the deficit continued to rise. And to completely ruin his party, we suffered a lingering recession that began in the summer of 1990 and from which we did not completely recover until the end of 1992, with the unemployment rate still hovering above 7 percent.

The budget deficit had become a concern. When Ronald Reagan took office in 1981, the deficit was $79 billion, but just 11 years later it had climbed to $290 billion. We'll return to the deficit and the humongous national debt in the chapter on fiscal policy in *Economics* and *Macroeconomics*.

Supply-side economics

The recession of 1981–82

"Read my lips."

---

[8]Productivity is output per hour worked, a concept we'll examine further in a chapter on economic growth and productivity in *Economics* and *Macroeconomics* and a chapter on unions, labor markets, and wage rates in *Economics* and *Microeconomics*.

Part 6: To the Millennium and Beyond

How would you grade our economic performance since the end of the 1990–91 recession (see box, "Post–World War II Recessions" on page 15)? I'd give it an A-minus, with several areas that need improvement. Let's look at those first, and then we'll move on to what has been termed the "new economy."

The Military

All our major wars have had very strong influences on our economy, generally setting off bouts of inflation and often speeding up our economic growth and reducing our unemployment as well. But our country has been more or less at peace since the early 1970s, when we withdrew from Vietnam.

Although defense spending continues at more than $300 billion, for the first time in at least six decades, our nation has virtually no military rivals. So the question is: What do we need to spend for a modern, high-tech, and more mobile military that can respond to an emergency?

The debate today is why, since the fall of the Berlin Wall and the demise of the Soviet Union, we need to divert so much of our resources to defense. These resources might otherwise be used to ameliorate our many social and economic problems—areas that clearly need improvement.

Real Wages

Economists use the term "real wages" to let us know how much we can buy with our wages after allowing for inflation. For example, if you earned 20 percent more than you did last year, but prices also went up by 20 percent, then your wages just kept up with inflation, and you could buy about the same amount of goods and services as you did last year. Despite all our economic growth, real wages for most workers today are actually slightly lower than they were back in 1973. In that year, urban wage earners and clerical workers earned $8.55 an hour (in real wages paid in dollars of the year 1982 purchasing power). By November of 2000 these workers averaged only $7.91.[9]

Why have real wages fallen since 1973? There are numerous explanations. Plant closings and corporate downsizing have done away with millions of well-paid jobs. (See box, "The New Vocabulary of Corporate Downsizing.") The weakening of labor unions and the alternative of cheaper workers abroad have exerted downward pressure on wages. Still another factor has been the increasing tendency of business to replace full-time workers with temporary and part-time employees. Apparently almost one-third the new jobs our economy has generated since 1991 have been part-time or temporary.

The State of American Agriculture

The story of American agriculture is the story of vastly expanding productivity. The output of farm labor doubled between 1850 and 1900, doubled again between 1900 and 1947, and doubled a third time between 1947 and 1960. In 1800 it took 370 hours to produce 100 bushels of wheat. By 1960 it took just 15 hours. In 1820 one farmer could feed 4.5 people. Today that farmer could feed about 100 people.

While agriculture is one of the most productive sectors of our economy, only about 4.5 million people live on farms today, and less than half of them farm full time. Despite hundreds of billions of dollars in price-support payments to farmers for crops in the years

---

[9]Economic Report of the President, 2001, p. 330.

The New Vocabulary of Corporate Downsizing

It may be no consolation to the millions of Americans who have been "downsized" during the 1990s, but this phenomenon has certainly enriched our vocabulary. Here is some of the euphemistic new corporate lingo that tries to put a positive spin on these massive lay-offs.

AT&T—"Force management program"

Bank of America—"Release of resources"

Bell Labs—"Involuntary separation from payroll"

Clifford of Vermont—"Career-change opportunity"

Digital Equipment Corp.—"Involuntary severance"

GM—"Career-transition program"

Harris Bank of Chicago—"Rightsizing the bank"

National Semiconductor—"Reshaping"

Newsweek—"Reduction in force (RIF)"

Pacific Bell—"Elimination of employment security policy"

Procter & Gamble—"Strengthening global effectiveness"

Stanford University—"Repositioning"

Stouffer Foods Corp.—"Schedule adjustments"

Tandem Computers—"Reducing duplication or focused reduction"

Wal-Mart—"Normal payroll adjustment"

Source: Compiled by William Lutz, appearing in *Newsweek,* August 12, 1996, p. 57.

---

since World War II, the family farm is rapidly vanishing. This is certainly ironic, since the primary purpose of these payments has been to save the family farm. During the more than six decades that this program has been in operation, 7 out of every 10 family farms have disappeared, while three-quarters of the payments go to large corporate farms. One by one, the dairy farmers, the poultry farmers, the grain growers, and the feedlot operators are being squeezed out by the huge agricultural combines.

If you were to ask, the overwhelming majority of farmers would tell you that the state of American agriculture is not good. Mainly because of overproduction, prices are way down, and we have been in a farm recession—some would say depression—since 1997. For example, a farmer in early 2001 was getting just $1 for a 100-pound sack of potatoes, down from $8 a few years earlier, and well below the $5 needed to cover the cost of production. Wheat farmers would lose about $2 on every bushel of wheat they grow if they brought it to market. Even though the Freedom to Farm Act of 1996 stipulated drastically reduced payments to farmers, as crop prices sank to 10- and 20- year lows in 2000, payments to farmers were a record $28 billion, about half of all farm income.

While we have lingering images of family farms, large farms—those with more than $250,000 in sales—now account for more than three-quarters of all agricultural sales. In the mid-1980s, their share was actually less than half. To keep costs down, especially when growing corn, wheat, and soybeans, a farmer needs a lot of expensive equipment and, consequently, must plant on a huge acreage.[10] In other words, you've got to become big just to survive.

American farms are so productive that we often export more than one-third of our corn, wheat, and other crops. And yet millions of Americans go to bed hungry every night. Back in the depths of the Great Depression, hungry Americans resorted to soup kitchens for their only meals. Today some 35 million Americans make use of food pantries, soup kitchens, and other food distribution programs.

---

[10]The average farm has gone from 139 acres in 1910 to 435 acres today.

Other Social and Economic Problems

Even in extremely good economic times, ours is a society beset with monumental problems. Crime, drugs, the disposal of nuclear waste, the permanent underclass, and our decaying central cities are largely neglected issues. After years of neglect, our interstate highway network remains, at best, a work-in-progress, highlighted by those orange signs, plastic barrels, flashing arrows, and one-lane stretches that seem to have become a permanent part of our landscape. And we have become a nation of consumption junkies who have run up a public and private debt exceeding $20 trillion—more than twice the value of our annual national output.

On a personal level, you might be asking: Will I be able to find a decent job when I graduate? Will I be able to live as well as my parents did? Or will I have to live with them because I won't be able to afford a place of my own? Will I be able to collect Social Security benefits when I retire, or will the whole system go bankrupt before then?

Which company is the largest employer in the U.S.A.? General Motors? Exxon? Wal-Mart? Do you give up? Our largest employer is Manpower, Inc., a temporary employment agency. And temp agencies like Manpower are our future. Bank of America, now NationsBank, which has been cutting the number of its full-time employees for years, hopes to soon reach its goal of having 80 percent of its staff made up of part-time employees working less than 20 hours a week—and ineligible for benefits like medical insurance. Indeed, some 45 million Americans have no medical insurance coverage.

Less than 20 years ago we were the world's largest creditor nation, but now we're the largest debtor. We are steadily losing our manufacturing base (although still the world's largest manufacturer), while hemorrhaging millions of well-paid blue-collar jobs. Our educational system turns out 1 million functional illiterates every year, but we still have the best college and university system in the world (more than half a million foreign students are enrolled). More than one in 10 Americans is officially classified as poor, and there is a growing permanent underclass of hundreds of thousands of fourth- and fifth-generation welfare families. All this exists despite the passage of the Welfare Reform Act of 1996, which we'll discuss in the chapter on income distribution and poverty near the end of the book. And even though we hold 2 million people in prison, many of our streets remain unsafe, and drug dealers operate with impunity.

The "New Economy" of the Nineties

"We've never been better off, but can America keep the party going?"

　—Jonathan Alter, *Newsweek,*
February 7, 2000.

What exactly *is* the "new economy"? And is it really all that new? It is a period marked by major technological change, low inflation, low unemployment, and rapidly growing productivity. Certainly that is a fair description of the 1990s, but one may ask if other decades—the 1920s and most of the 1960s—might be similarly described. Perhaps judging the appropriateness of the term "new economy" might best be left to the economic historians of the future. But new or not new, the 1990s will surely go down in history as one of the most prosperous decades since the founding of the republic.

The new economy could trace its beginning back to the late 1970s when the federal government began an era of deregulation, giving the market forces of supply and demand much freer reign. In the 1980s federal income tax rates were slashed, allowing Americans to keep much more of their earnings, thereby providing greater work incentives. But the 1980s and early 1990s also saw a huge increase in federal budget deficits; economic growth was lagging, and inflation, while no longer of double-digit proportions, was still a major concern.

As the decade of the 1990s wore on, the economic picture grew steadily brighter. The deficit was reduced each year from 1993 through the end of the decade, by which time we were actually running budget surpluses. Inflation was completely under control, and an economic expansion that began in the spring of 1991 reached boom proportions by the last years of the decade. Optimism spread as the stock market soared, and by February, 2000, the length of our economic expansion reached 107 consecutive months—an all-time record.

The 1990s was the decade of computerization. In 1990 only a handful of households were on the Internet; by the end of 2000, about 40 percent were connected. Much more significant was the spread of computerization in the business world. Indeed, there is a terminal on almost every desk. Planes, cars, factories, and stores are completely computerized. All this has clearly made the American labor force a lot more efficient. Economists, as well as ordinary civilians, believe that our rapid economic growth has been largely the result of computerization of the workplace.

Economists also agree that competition spurs economic performance, and the flood of imports—ranging from cars and camcorders to computer chips and calculators—has pushed American firms into operating more efficiently, producing better products, and holding down their prices. Today American automobiles are considered, on the whole, virtually the equal of Japanese automobiles. That clearly was not the case just 10 or 15 years ago. And who benefits the most from all this competition? You guessed it: the American consumer.

Through most of the 1990s and well into the new millennium, consumers were spending money as if there were no tomorrow. This consumption binge has led to a growing trade deficit, which is now about $370 billion. As long as foreigners gladly accept our dollars, using most of them to buy up American stocks, bonds, real estate, and occasionally whole corporations, we should not have too much to worry about. But this cannot go on indefinitely, if only because, at some point, we won't have anything left to sell. We'll have a lot more to say about this problem in the last two chapters of the book.

The 1990s are often compared to the 1920s. In both decades the stock market soared, and many great fortunes were made. But in the 1920s only one in 10 Americans owned corporate stock. Today more than half our population owns stock, either through individual portfolios or mutual funds or pension funds. And there is strong political support to shift at least a fraction of the Social Security trust fund into corporate stocks. Such widespread stock ownership shows great public confidence that the market will continue to rise and that our economic boom will continue indefinitely.

Like the 1920s, the 1990s was a decade of great prosperity, some of which was fueled, as mentioned, by a spectacularly rising stock market. As we approached the new millennium, many people wondered if history would repeat itself. Would a stock market crash usher in another Great Depression?

Obviously it didn't happen—at least so far. Although the stock market had its share of ups and downs in 1999 and after, there was no crash, and certainly there was no depression. What kind of economy can we look forward to as the 21st century unfolds? As you continue reading, you'll make your own informed guess as to what lies ahead. And, quite frankly, your guess may be as good as mine.

Back in 1941 Henry Luce, the founder of *Life Magazine,* wrote an editorial, "The American Century." History has certainly proven Luce right. Not only had American soldiers and economic power won World Wars I and II, but we also contained communism from the 1940s through the 1980s. With the collapse of the Soviet Union, we were the only military and economic superpower left standing.

As we move farther into the 21st century, we continue to dominate the global economy. Someday our dominance may be challenged, perhaps by the European Union, Japan, or even by China. But if Henry Luce were alive today, he might well predict that we are now entering the second American century.

By the spring of 2001 there were some clouds on our economic horizon. The stock market had given up its huge gains of the previous two or three years, and Americans were growing increasingly pessimistic about the immediate future. Economic growth had slowed markedly during the second half of 2000, and there was still uncertainty among economic forecasters if this slowdown would degenerate into a full blown recession.

President Reagan used to say that, rather than fight over how the economic pie gets divided, let's just bake a bigger pie. Economics deals with how large a pie we bake (we call this production) and how that pie gets sliced up (which is distribution).

To bake a pie, you start with ingredients. The ingredients of our economic pie are our resources—land, labor, capital, and entrepreneurial ability—which we'll cover in the next chapter.

Questions for Further Thought and Discussion

1. Describe, in as much detail as possible, the impact of the Great Depression on the lives of those who lived through it. If you know anyone who remembers the 1930s, ask him or her to describe those times.

2. What were the main agricultural developments over the last two centuries?

3. How have wars affected our economy? Use specific examples.

4. Inflation has been a persistent problem for most of the 20th century. What were some of its consequences?

5. In what ways were the 1990s like the 1920s, and in what ways were the two decades different?

6. Although our economy has performed well during the last 10 years, there have been some major problems. Identify and discuss a few of these problems.

7. When our country was being settled, there was an acute shortage of agricultural labor. Over the last hundred years millions of Americans have left the farms. How have we managed to feed our growing population with fewer and fewer farmers?

8. Today America has the world's largest economy as well as a very high standard of living. What factors in our economic history helped make this possible?

9. List the main ways the "new economy" (since the early 1990s) differs from the "old economy."

Workbook for Chapter 1

Name _____ Date _____

Multiple-Choice Questions

Circle the letter that corresponds to the best answer.

1. Which statement is true?
   a) Twenty-five million Americans were officially unemployed in 1933.
   b) Our economy expanded steadily from 1933 to 1945.
   c) Once the Great Depression began in 1929, our economy moved almost steadily downhill until the beginning of 1940.
   d) None of the above.

2. In the early 19th century, the United States suffered from a scarcity of
   a) land and labor
   b) land—relative to labor
   c) labor—relative to land
   d) neither land nor labor

3. Which statement is false?
   a) President Eisenhower presided over three recessions.
   b) Our economy has not had an unemployment rate below 5 percent since the early 1940s.
   c) There were six straight years of economic expansion under President Reagan.
   d) None of the above. (All of the above are true.)

4. Which statement is true?
   a) There was a great deal of stagflation in the 1970s.
   b) We had full employment for most of the 1980s.
   c) We have had seven recessions since World War II.
   d) None of the above.

5. Each of the following were elements of the New Deal except _____.
   a) relief, recovery, reform
   b) a massive employment program
   c) unemployment insurance and bank deposit insurance
   d) a balanced budget

6. Which of these best describes the post-World War II recessions in the United States?
   a) They were all very mild, except for the 1981–82 recession.
   b) They were all caused by rising interest rates.
   c) None lasted more than one year.
   d) Each was accompanied by a decline in output of goods and services and an increase in unemployment.

7. At the time of the American Revolution, about _____ of every 10 Americans lived on a farm.
   a) one   c) five   e) nine
   b) three   d) seven

8. Between 1939 and 1944, federal government spending rose by _____.
   a) 100%   c) 300%   e) 500%
   b) 200%   d) 400%

9. Each of the following was a year of high unemployment except _____.
   a) 1933   c) 1944   e) 1982
   b) 1938   d) 1975

10. The year 2000 could be described as having had a relatively _____ unemployment rate and a relatively _____ rate of inflation.
    a) low, low   c) high, low
    b) high, high   d) low, high

11. Between 1929 and 1933, output fell _____.
    a) by about one-tenth   c) by about one-half
    b) by about one-third   d) by about two-thirds

12. The inflation rate declined during the presidency of _____.
    a) both Eisenhower and Reagan
    b) neither Eisenhower nor Reagan
    c) Reagan
    d) Eisenhower

13. Our national output is _____ that of Japan.
    a) one-half
    b) a little smaller than
    c) a little larger than
    d) almost twice

14. The transcontinental railroads completed in the 1860s, 1870s, and 1880s all bypassed the _____.
    a) Northeast
    b) Midwest
    c) South
    d) mountain states
    e) Far West

15. Which best describes the American economy at the end of the 20th century?
    a) high growth, low inflation, and low unemployment
    b) low growth, high inflation, and high unemployment
    c) except for a few million poor people, almost all Americans were prospering
    d) large federal budget deficit and a recession

16. The longest economic expansion in our history began in _____.
    a) the spring of 1961
    b) the winter of 1982
    c) the spring of 1991
    d) the fall of 1993

17. The age of the great industrial capitalists like Carnegie, Rockefeller, and Swift was in the _____.
    a) second quarter of the 19th century
    b) third quarter of the 19th century
    c) fourth quarter of the 19th century
    d) first quarter of the 20th century
    e) second quarter of the 20th century

18. We had a business downturn at the end of, or soon _____.
    a) after World War I and World War II
    b) after neither World War I nor World War II
    c) after World War II but not World War I
    d) after World War I but not World War II

19. Medicare and Medicaid were inaugurated under the administration of _____.
    a) Franklin Roosevelt
    b) Harry Truman
    c) Dwight D. Eisenhower
    d) John F. Kennedy
    e) Lyndon B. Johnson

20. Most of the recessions since World War II lasted _____.
    a) less than 6 months
    b) 6 to 12 months
    c) 12 to 18 months
    d) 18 to 24 months
    e) 24 to 36 months

21. Which statement is true?
    a) President Eisenhower attempted to undo most of the New Deal.
    b) There was a major tax cut in 1964.
    c) The federal budget deficit was reduced during President Lyndon Johnson's administration.
    d) None of the above.

22. There was a major tax cut in _____.
    a) both 1964 and 1981
    b) neither 1964 nor 1981
    c) in 1964, but not in 1981
    d) in 1981, but not 1964

23. Our economic growth began to slow markedly _____.
    a) in the early 1940s
    b) in the early 1960s
    c) in the early 1970s
    d) between 1982 and 1985

24. Wage and price controls were introduced by President _____.
    a) Eisenhower
    b) Kennedy
    c) Johnson
    d) Nixon
    e) Ford

25. In the 1970s, our economy suffered from _____.
    a) inflation but not stagnation
    b) stagnation but not inflation
    c) inflation and stagnation
    d) neither inflation nor stagnation

26. The recession of 1990–91 was _____, and the ensuing recovery was _____.
    a) deep, slow
    b) deep, fast
    c) shallow, slow
    d) shallow, fast

27. Our longest uninterrupted economic expansion took place mainly in the decade of the _____.
    a) 1940s
    b) 1950s
    c) 1960s
    d) 1970s
    e) 1980s
    f) 1990s

28. Since the end of the 1990–91 recession, our economy has generated more than _____ million additional jobs.
   a) 5   b) 10   c) 15   d) 20

29. Compared to today, in 1945, _____.
   a) our economy was plagued by high unemployment and slow economic growth
   b) we faced much greater competition from our economic rivals in Europe and Asia
   c) we were a much more dominant global economic power
   d) we accounted for almost one-quarter of the world's manufacturing output and slightly more than one-third of its output of automobiles

Fill-In Questions

1. The low point of the Great Depression was reached in the year _____.

2. In 1790, about _____ of every 10 Americans lived on farms.

3. The worst recession we had since World War II occurred in _____.

4. The country with the world's largest output is _____.

5. In 1933, our official unemployment rate was _____%.

6. Bills providing for Medicare and Medicaid were passed during the administration of President _____.

7. Today one American farmer feeds about _____ _____ people.

8. During President Dwight D. Eisenhower's two terms, there were _____ recessions.

9. Rapid technological change in agriculture during the first half of the 19th century was brought on mainly by _____.

10. The main factor in finally bringing us out of the Great Depression was _____.

11. Since World War II there have been _____ recessions.

12. The quarter century that was completely dominated by the great industrialists like Andrew Carnegie and John D. Rockefeller began in the year _____.

13. Passage of the _____ in 1944 enabled nearly 8 million veterans to go to school.

14. The _____ century was termed the "American Century."

Chapter 2

Resource Utilization

Economics is defined in various ways, but scarcity is always part of the definition. We bake an economic pie each year, which is composed of all the goods and services we have produced. No matter how we slice it, there never seems to be enough. Some people feel the main problem is how we slice the pie, while others say we should concentrate on baking a larger pie.

CHAPTER OBJECTIVES

In this chapter you'll learn:

- The definition of economics.
- The central fact of economics.
- The four economic resources.
- The concepts of opportunity cost, full employment, and full production.

- Productive and allocative efficiency.
- What enables an economy to grow.
- The law of increasing costs.

Economics Defined

Economics is the efficient allocation of the scarce means of production toward the satisfaction of human wants. You're probably thinking, What did he say? Let's break it down into two parts. The scarce means of production are our resources, which we use to produce all the goods and services we buy. And why do we buy these goods and services? Because they provide us with satisfaction.

The only problem is that we don't have enough resources to produce all the goods and services we desire. Our resources are limited while our wants are relatively

Economics is the efficient allocation of the scarce means of production toward the satisfaction of human wants.

Economics is the science of
greed.

—F. V. Meyer

unlimited. In the next few pages, we'll take a closer look at the concepts of resources, scarcity, and the satisfaction of human wants. Keep in mind that we can't produce everything we'd like to purchase—there's scarcity. This is where economics comes in. We're attempting to make the best of a less-than-ideal situation. We're trying to use our resources so efficiently that we can maximize our satisfaction. Or, as François Quesnay put it back in the 18th century, "To secure the greatest amount of pleasure with the least possible outlay should be the aim of all economic effort."[1]

The Central Fact of Economics: Scarcity

Scarcity and the Need to Economize

Most of us are used to economizing; we save up our scarce dollars and deny ourselves various tempting treasures so we will have enough money for that one big-ticket item— a new car, a stereo system, a trip to Europe. Since our dollars are scarce and we can't buy everything we want, we economize by making do with some lower-priced items— a Cadillac instead of a Rolls Royce, chicken instead of steak, a videotape rental instead of a neighborhood movie.

If there were no scarcity, we would not need to economize, and economists would need to find other work. Let's go back to our economic pie to see how scarcity works. Most people tend to see scarcity as not enough dollars, but as John Maynard Keynes[2] pointed out more than 60 years ago, this is an illusion. We could print all the money we want and still have scarcity. As Adam Smith noted in 1776, the wealth of nations consists of the goods and services they produce, or, on another level, the resources—the *land, labor, capital,* and *entrepreneurial ability*—that actually produce these goods and services.

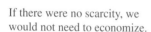

If there were no scarcity, we would not need to economize.

The Economic Problem

In the 1950s, John Kenneth Galbraith coined the term *the affluent society,* which implied that we had the scarcity problem licked. Americans were the richest people in the world (we've since slipped to fourth or fifth). Presumably, we had conquered poverty. But within a few years, Michael Harrington's *The Other America*[3] challenged that contention.

The economic problem, however, goes far beyond ending poverty. Even then, nearly all Americans would be relatively poor when they compared what they have with what they would like to have—or with what the Rockefellers, Gateses, Buffetts, Allens, and Ellisons have.

Human wants are relatively limitless (see box titled "E.T. and the Satisfaction of Human Wants"). Make a list of all the things you'd like to have. Now add up their entire cost. Chances are you couldn't earn enough in a lifetime to even begin to pay for all the things on your list.

John Kenneth Galbraith, American economist and social critic (UPI/Bettmann)

The Four Economic Resources

We need four resources, often referred to as "the means of production," to produce an output of goods and services. Every society, from a tiny island nation in the Pacific to the most complex industrial giant, needs these resources: *land, labor, capital,* and *entrepreneurial ability.* Let's consider each in turn.

---

[1]François Quesnay, *Dialogues sur les Artisans,* quoted in Gide and Rist, *A History of Economic Doctrines,* 1913, pp. 10–11.

[2]Keynes, whose work we'll discuss in later chapters of *Economics* and *Macroeconomics,* was perhaps the greatest economist of the 20th century.

[3]Michael Harrington, *The Other America* (New York: Macmillan, 1962).

E.T. and the Satisfaction of Human Wants

Remember the movie *E.T.*? Well, suppose E.T. were to return to Earth and hand each person $50 million. What would happen when everyone rushed out to spend this money? There simply would not be enough goods and services available. Still, assuming E.T.'s money was good, storekeepers would accept it. But since there would not be enough goods and services to go around, they would have to raise their prices. After all, what would you do if a line eight miles long formed outside *your* store?

Now an extraterrestrial like E.T. would never want to cause inflation, so you can be sure he would have made some provision for more goods and services to be made available. Imagine that he and his friends set up an E.T. shopping mall in every city and town in the world and continued to charge the old prices rather than

the new inflated prices. Everyone would be able to buy as much as he or she desired without having to worry about inflation.

Now we come to the greatest benefit of all. No one would ever have to take a course in economics. Why not? Because E.T. has eliminated the two conflicting forces that made economics necessary in the first place. Since we now have all the goods and services we desire, human wants are finally satisfied. Or, alternatively, the means of production are sufficient to produce everything people desire. We can no longer call them the "scarce means of production."

Of course, there may well be some people who would want even more than $50 million worth of goods and services. These people would still need to economize. And they'd still need to take courses in economics.

Land

As a resource, land has a much more general meaning than our normal understanding of the word. It includes natural resources (such as timber, oil, coal, iron ore, soil, and water) as well as the ground in which these resources are found. Land is used not only for the extraction of minerals but for farming as well. And, of course, we build factories, office buildings, shopping centers, and homes on land. The basic payment made to the owners of land is rent.

Labor

Labor is the work and time for which employees are paid. The police officer, the computer programmer, the store manager, and the assembly-line worker all supply labor. About two-thirds of the total resource costs are paid to labor in the form of wages and salaries.

Capital

Capital is "man"-made goods used to produce other goods or services. It consists mainly of plant and equipment. The United States has more capital than any other country in the world. This capital consists of factories, office buildings, and stores. Our shopping malls, the Empire State Building, and automobile plants and steel mills (and all the equipment in them) are examples of capital. The return paid to the owners of capital is interest.

Entrepreneurial ability

Entrepreneurial ability is the least familiar of our four basic resources. The entrepreneur sets up a business, assembles the needed resources, risks his or her own money, and reaps the profits or absorbs the losses of this enterprise (see the box titled "The Young Entrepreneur"). Often the entrepreneur is an innovator, such as Andrew Carnegie (U.S. Steel), John D. Rockefeller (Standard Oil), Henry Ford (Ford Motor Company), Steven Jobs (Apple Computer), William Gates (Microsoft), and Sam Walton (Wal-Mart).

We may consider land, labor, and capital passive resources, which are combined by the entrepreneur to produce goods and services. A successful undertaking is rewarded by profit; an unsuccessful one is penalized by loss.

In the American economy, the entrepreneur is the central figure, and our long record of economic success is an eloquent testimonial to the abundance of our entrepreneurial talents. The owners of the 23 million businesses in this country are virtually all entrepreneurs. The vast majority either work for themselves or have just one or two employees. But they have two things in common: Each runs a business, and each risks his or her own money.

Sometimes entrepreneurs cash in on inventions—their own or someone else's. Alexander Graham Bell and Thomas Edison were two of the more famous inventors who *did* parlay their inventions into great commercial enterprises. As you know, tens of billions of dollars were earned by the founders of America Online, Amazon, eBay,

The Young Entrepreneur

An entrepreneur is a person who sees an opportunity to make a profit and is willing and able to risk his or her funds. I went to school with such a person.

When he was 14, he was standing in line with several hundred other boys waiting for an application for a summer job. He got hungry, so he asked the guy in back of him to hold his place in line while he got a hot dog. On his way back, several boys along the line asked him where he had gotten that hot dog. Dollar signs immediately danced before his eyes.

"I went back to the store and bought as many as I could carry. They gave me a carton of them. I went up and down the line, and I charged 10 cents more than I paid." He quickly ran out. Then, using the money he had collected, he went back to that store again and again.

He made more money working that line than he made for the first two weeks on that summer job. Before he was 30, he became a vice president of Helmsley-Spear, the giant real estate company. I don't know if he's still peddling hot dogs.

Bill Gates: The Ultimate Entrepreneur

An entrepreneur is someone who sees a profit opportunity and is willing and able to risk his or her money—or someone else's—to achieve it. Bill Gates, who cofounded and ran Microsoft for most of the 1980s and 1990s, was arguably America's greatest entrepreneur. But was he an *innovator*?

The biggest innovations developed and marketed by Microsoft were Microsoft Word, the premier word processing program; Excel, the spreadsheet program; and Windows, the graphic user interface coupled with an operating system that has become the virtual standard in the personal computer industry. Did these three innovations originate within Microsoft? No! Each had been developed elsewhere before there were patents for software.*

The great contribution by Microsoft was to successfully position itself between the innovators and the users, taking from one and selling to the others. Was Bill Gates an innovator? Hardly. But he was the ultimate entrepreneur.

---

*Microsoft, which has spent tens of billions of dollars on product development, has been at the forefront of software development. But none of its three major products originated at Microsoft.

Yahoo!, and the thousands of other so-called dot.coms when they went public. These folks were all entrepreneurs (see box, "Bill Gates: The Ultimate Entrepreneur.") And have you heard of Tim Berners-Lee, the creator of the World Wide Web? Berners-Lee worked long and hard to ensure that the Web remained a public mass medium in cyberspace, an information thoroughfare open to all. He came up with the software standards for addressing, linking, and transferring multimedia documents over the Internet. And most amazing, Tim Berners-Lee did not try to cash in on his years of work.

Is this man an entrepreneur? Clearly he is not. He is an inventor of the first rank—like Bell and Edison—but the act of invention is not synonymous with being an entrepreneur.

Perhaps nothing more typifies American entrepreneurial talent than the Internet, which *The New York Times* termed the "Net Americana." Steve Lohr observed that "all ingredients that contribute to the entrepreneurial climate in the United States—venture capital financing, close ties between business and universities, flexible labor markets, a deregulated business environment, and a culture that celebrates risk-taking, ambition and getting very, very rich"—fostered the formation of the Internet. Lohr goes on to say that "United States corporations collect 85 percent of the revenues from the Internet business and represent 95 percent of the stock market value of Internet companies."[4]

---

[4]Steve Lohr, "Welcome to the Internet, the First Global Colony," *The New York Times,* January 9, 2000, Section 4, p. 1.

Resources are scarce because they are limited in quantity. There's a finite amount of land on this planet, and at any given time a limited amount of labor, capital, and entrepreneurial ability is available. Over time, of course, the last three resources can be increased.

Our economic problem, then, is that we have limited resources available to satisfy relatively unlimited wants. The reason why you, and everyone else, can't have three cars, a town house and a country estate with servants, designer clothing, jewels, big screen TVs in each room, and a $50,000 sound system is that we just don't have enough resources to produce everything that everyone wants. Therefore, we have to make choices, an option we call opportunity cost.

Opportunity Cost

Because we can't have everything we want, we must make choices. The thing we give up (that is, our second choice) is called the opportunity cost of our choice. Therefore, *the opportunity cost of any choice is the forgone value of the next best alternative.*

> The opportunity cost of any choice is the forgone value of the next best alternative.

Suppose a little boy goes into a toy store with $15. Many different toys tempt him, but he finally narrows his choice to a Monopoly game and a magic set, each costing $15. If he decides to buy the Monopoly game, the opportunity cost is the magic set. And if he buys the magic set, the opportunity cost is the Monopoly game.

If a town hires an extra police officer instead of repaving several streets, the opportunity cost of hiring the officer is not repaving the streets. Opportunity cost is the cost of giving up the next best alternative.

In some cases the next best alternative—the Monopoly game or the magic set—is virtually equal no matter what choice is made. In other cases, there's no contest. If someone were to offer you, at the same price, your favorite eight-course meal or a Big Mac, you'd have no trouble deciding (unless, of course, your favorite meal *is* a Big Mac).

> Even children learn in growing up that "both" is not an admissible answer to a choice of "which one?"
> —President Warren G. Harding

The state of California has a limited number of tax dollars to spend. Two of its biggest expenditures are college education and prisons. The opportunity cost of building more prisons is building fewer colleges. Between 1967 and 1997 California built 21 prisons and only one new state university. Between 1990 and 1997, California's universities laid off 10,000 employees, while in the same period the number of state prison guards rose by 10,000. What then, is the opportunity cost of 10,000 more prison guards? It's 10,000 fewer university employees. Even more alarming, some of those laid off were economics professors.

Today, as we all know, people are living longer. This has set the stage for an ongoing generational conflict over how much of our resources should be devoted to Medicare, Social Security, nursing homes, and old age homes, and how much to child care, Head Start, and, in general, education. If we are to be a humane society, we must take care of our aging population. But if our economy is to be competitive, we need to devote more dollars to education.

What are some of the opportunity costs *you* have incurred? What is the opportunity cost of attending college? Owning a car? Or even buying this economics text? There's even an opportunity cost of studying for an exam. How would you have otherwise spent those precious hours?

In the next section we will be dealing with the production possibilities frontier, and once again, we will have to make choices. As we shall see, the more we produce of one product, the less we can produce of another product.

Full Employment and Full Production

Everyone agrees that full employment is a good thing, even if we don't all agree on exactly what full employment means. Does it mean that every single person in the United States who is ready, willing, and able to work has a job? Is *that* full employment?

If economists were laid end to end, they would not reach a conclusion.

—George Bernard Shaw

The answer is no. There will always be some people between jobs. On any given day thousands of Americans quit, get fired, or decide that they will enter the labor force by finding a job. Since it may take several weeks, or even several months, until they find the "right" job, there will always be some people unemployed.

If an unemployment rate of zero does not represent full employment, then what rate does? Economists cannot agree on what constitutes full employment. Some liberals insist that an unemployment rate of 4 percent constitutes full employment, while there are conservatives who feel that an unemployment rate of 6 percent would be more realistic.[5]

Similarly, we cannot expect to fully use all our plant and equipment. A capacity utilization rate of 85 or 90 percent would surely employ virtually all of our usable plant and equipment.[6] At any given moment there is always some factory being renovated or some machinery under repair. During wartime we might be able to use our capacity more fully, but in normal times 85 to 90 percent is the peak.

In a global economy, not only has it become increasingly difficult to define which goods and services are made in America and which originate abroad, but one may even question the relevance of a plant's location. If our steel industry were operating at full capacity, we could get still more steel from Germany, Japan, Korea, Brazil, and other steel-producing nations. In the context of the global economy, our capacity utilization ratio is clearly much less important than it was just a few decades ago.

As long as all available resources are fully used—given the constraints we have just cited—we are at our production possibilities frontier. A few additional constraints should also be considered because they too restrict the quantity of resources available. These are institutional constraints, the laws and customs under which we live.

The so-called blue laws restrict the economic activities that may be carried out in various cities and states, mainly on Sundays. Bars and liquor stores must be closed certain hours. In some places, even retail stores must be closed on Sundays.

State and federal law carefully restrict child labor. Very young children may not be employed at all, and those below a certain age may work only a limited number of hours.

Traditionally, Americans dislike working at night or on weekends, particularly on Sundays. Consequently, we must leave most of our expensive plant and equipment idle except during daylight weekday hours. We don't consider that plant and equipment unemployed, nor do we consider those whose labor is restricted by law or custom unemployed. All of this is already allowed for in our placement of the location of the production possibilities frontier (shown in Figure 1 in the next section).

By full production, we mean that our nation's resources are being allocated in the most efficient manner possible. Not only are we using our most up-to-date technology, but we are using our land, labor, capital, and entrepreneurial ability in the most productive way.

We would not want to use the intersection of Fifth Avenue and 57th Street in Manhattan for dairy farming, nor would we want our M.D.s doing clerical work. But sometimes we do just that.

Until very recently in our history blacks, Hispanics, and women were virtually excluded from nearly all high-paying professions. Of course, this fact entails personal hurt and lost income; this discrimination also cost our nation in lost output. Until 1947, when Brooklyn Dodger owner Branch Rickey defied baseball's "color line" and signed Jackie Robinson for the team, major league baseball was played by whites only (see box, "The Jackie Robinson Story"). At that time, only a tiny handful of Hispanic players were tolerated. Today there are several black and Hispanic players on every team.

Whatever else one might say about professional basketball today, I don't think it would exactly be described as a "white man's sport." Nor, for that matter would the National Football League. But until the late 1940s, blacks were almost entirely banned

---

[5]Since the unemployment rate has recently hovered around 4 percent, why not call *that* rate full employment? Because from 1971 through 1996 our unemployment rate was above 5 percent. However, if it stays this low much longer, I'll relent and call an unemployment rate of 4 percent full employment.

[6]Technically, this is the rate at which the nation's factories, mines, and utilities are operating.

The Jackie Robinson Story

Blacks had been banned from almost all professional sports since the turn of the century, but most notoriously by major league baseball. For decades there was a parallel association for blacks called the Negro leagues. Finally, the color barrier was broken in 1947 when Jackie Robinson began playing for the Brooklyn Dodgers.

Looking back, then, to all those years when black ball players were not permitted to play major league baseball, basketball, and football, hundreds of athletes were underemployed. Not only did they suffer economically and psychologically, but the American public was deprived of watching innumerable talented athletes perform.

In 1991 I met a few of the men who played in the Negro leagues when I was visiting Kansas City, where the Negro League Baseball Museum is located. They all knew Satchel Paige, a legendary pitcher whose fastball was so fast, the batters often couldn't even see it, let alone hit it. Sometimes Paige would wind up and pretend to throw a pitch. The catcher pounded his glove and the umpire called a strike. Then the catcher, who had the ball all along, threw it back to Paige. As great as he was, Satchel Paige didn't play in the major leagues until the twilight of his career, when he was in his late 40s.

by those professional sports. And as late as the 1950s, only a few stereotypical roles were available to blacks in the movies and TV. And, except for Desi Arnaz (Ricky Ricardo of "I Love Lucy"), there were virtually no Hispanic-Americans in these entertainment media. That was America not all that long ago, when employment discrimination was the rule, not the exception.

And until recently only a tiny minority of women employed in the offices of American business were not typists or secretaries. In the 1950s and even into the 1960s, virtually every article in *Fortune* was written by a man and researched by a woman. What a waste of labor potential!

I can still picture one ad that appeared in several business magazines back in the 1950s. Four or five young women were on their knees on an office carpet sorting through piles of papers. This was an advertisement for a collator. The caption read, "When your office collator breaks down, do the girls have to stay late for a collating party?"

This ad said a great deal about those times. Forget about political correctness! Every woman (but almost no men) applying for office jobs was asked, "How fast can you type?" because those were virtually the only jobs open to women in corporate America—even to college graduates. Typing, filing, and other clerical positions were considered "women's work." The high-paying and high-status executive positions were reserved for men. So when the collator broke down, it seemed perfectly logical to ask the "girls" to stay late for a "collating party."

These are just a few of the most blatant examples of employment discrimination, a phenomenon that has diminished but has not yet been wiped out. Employment discrimination automatically means that we will have less than full production because we are not efficiently allocating our labor. In other words, there are millions of Americans who really should be doctors, engineers, corporate executives, or whatever but have been condemned to less exalted occupations solely because they happen not to be white Protestant males (see boxes titled "The Glass Ceiling: Employment Discrimination at the Top" and "Cracks in Canada's Glass Ceiling.")

To date only three Fortune 500 companies have black CEOs. Franklin Raines is the head of the mortgage-financing giant, Fannie Mae, A. Barry Rand runs Avis, and Kenneth Chenault was appointed to head American Express in 2001.

Finally, there is the question of using the best available technology. Historically, the American economy has been on the cutting edge of technological development for almost 200 years; the sewing machine, mechanical reaper, telephone, airplane, automobile, assembly line, and computer are all American inventions.

Using the best technology

Now it's the computer software industry. Not only are we on the cutting edge in this rapidly expanding industry, but we produce and export more software than the rest of

The Glass Ceiling: Employment Discrimination at the Top

You probably never heard of Linda Wachner or Jill Elikann Barad. Through the late 1990s they were the only female chief executive officers (CEOs) of Fortune 500 industrial companies. For the record, Ms. Barad headed Mattel, and Ms. Wachner ran Warnaco, which, among other things, manufactures Calvin Klein underwear.

In 1999 they finally got some company. Carleton (nicknamed Carley) Fiorina was named president and chief executive officer of Hewlett-Packard, the world's second largest computer maker. So now there were three women among the CEOs of the Fortune 500. However, in February of 2000, Jill Barad, who had made Barbie into a megabrand, stepped down from the top post at Mattel. So now we were back again to just two female CEOs at the Fortune 500. But Anne Mulcahy, the president and chief operating officer of Xerox may soon bring that total back up to three.

These women are the exceptions that prove the rule: In today's wonderful world of equal opportunity, you need to be a white male to get ahead in large corporations. There is a glass ceiling beyond which female executives do not rise. Although the barriers are coming down—at once exclusively male dining clubs; at country clubs; in executive recruitment programs; and in law school, business school, and medical school admission—there's an invisible "Men Only" sign posted on the entrances to most corporate executive suites.

Surveys by Catalyst, a nonprofit women's research and advocacy group, found that women constituted only 3.3 percent of the top earners at the nation's largest 500 companies. And it can evidently get quite lonely at the top. Only three companies—Sallie Mae, Avon Products, and H. F. Abmanson—had more than one woman in their roster of the five top officers.*

Elite business schools began admitting large numbers of women in the mid-1970s. Because senior executives of major corporations usually have an MBA and at least 25 years of experience, we should see further increases in the number of women in senior corporate posts by the beginning of the new millennium. But according to the Federal Glass Ceiling Commission report released in 1995, "At the highest levels of business there is indeed a barrier only rarely penetrated by women or persons of color."

One area where women *have* been reaching the highest levels is in the federal government. Frances Perkins, the Labor Secretary in President Franklin Roosevelt's cabinet, and Ovetta Culp Hobby (who has an airport named after her in Houston), Secretary of Health, Education, and Welfare in President Dwight Eisenhower's cabinet, were the first women to serve in presidential cabinets. Today, of course, women cabinet officers have plenty of company, and, in 1997 President Bill Clinton named Madeleine Albright the first female Secretary of State. And yet, even during this period of widely expanding opportunity, *The Voice of America* and the U.S. Information Agency agreed to pay 1,100 women a record sum of $508 million for having routinely discriminated against them in hiring and promotion. But as one litigant said at the time, "I wish I could be compensated for the desperation and sense of worthlessness I had then." Teri Schaefer, today an education reporter for Fox News in Kansas City, had passed tests to join *Voice of America* in 1983 but could never land a job, while men were hired routinely. "The money doesn't make up for that," she said.†

---

*See *Business Week*, November 22, 1999, p. 86.

†Peter T. Kilborn, "For Women in Bias Case, the Wounds Remain," *The New York Times*, March 24, 2000, p. A14.

---

the world combined. Microsoft, Cisco, Netscape, Oracle, and a host of other American companies are household names not just in the United States but all across the globe.

Full employment and underemployment

We need to tie up one more loose end before moving on to the main focus of this chapter, the production possibilities frontier. We need to be clear about distinguishing between less than full employment and underemployment of resources.

If we are using only 70 percent of our capacity of plant and equipment, as we do during some recessions, this would be a case of our economy operating at less than full employment of its resources. Anything less than, say, an 85 percent utilization rate would be considered below full employment.

More familiarly, when the unemployment rate is, say, 10 percent, there is clearly a substantial amount of labor unemployed. But how much *is* full employment? We never really answered that one.

As a working definition, we'll say that an unemployment rate of 5 percent represents full employment. Why not use 4 percent, as the liberal economists suggest, or the

Cracks in Canada's Glass Ceiling*

Two of the three largest companies on Canada's Financial Post 500 list are run by women. These are the CEOs of General Motors of Canada and the Ford Motor Company of Canada. Overall, women now run 10 of the largest companies in Canada.

That's the good news. The bad news is that of the 13 largest Canadian companies with women as chief executives, 9 are subsidiaries of American companies. There are some who say that Canada's "branch plant economy" is responsible for the relatively high number of women running major companies. After all, the last time we looked, there weren't any women running General Motors, Ford, or any other traditional giants of American industry.

*James Brooke, "Cracks in Canada's Glass Ceiling," *The New York Times,* October 30, 1999, page C1.

---

6 percent figure favored by the conservatives? Because 5 percent represents a reasonable compromise. So we'll be working with that figure from here on, but keep in mind that not everyone agrees that a 5 percent unemployment rate represents full employment.

Unemployment means that not all our resources are being used. Less than 95 percent of our labor force is working, and less than 85 percent of our plant and equipment is being used. It also means that our land and entrepreneurial ability are not all being used.

What is underemployment of resources? To be at full production, not only would we be fully employing our resources, we would also be using them in the most efficient way possible. To make all women become schoolteachers, social workers, or secretaries would grossly underuse their talents. Equally absurd—and inefficient—would be to make all white males become doctors or lawyers and all black and Hispanic males become accountants or computer programmers.

Now let's talk about a large group of the underemployed that *you* may soon be joining—college graduates. Your degree should be a credential that helps you get a relatively high paying job. But millions of college graduates have not been helped by that credential (see box, "Underemployment of College Graduates.")

Similarly, we would not want to use that good Iowa farmland for office parks, and we would not want to locate dairy farms in the middle of our cities' central business districts. And finally, we would certainly not want to use our multimillion-dollar computer mainframes to do simple word processing.

These are all examples of underemployment of resources. Unfortunately, a certain amount of underemployment is built into our economy, but we need to reduce it if we are going to succeed in baking a larger economic pie.

This brings us, at long last, to the production possibilities frontier. As we've already casually mentioned, the production possibilities frontier represents our economy at full employment and full production. However, a certain amount of underemployment of resources is also built into our model. How much? Although the exact amount is not quantifiable, it is fairly large. But to the degree that employment discrimination has declined since the early 1960s, underemployment of resources may be holding our output to 10 or 15 percent below what it would be if there were a truly efficient allocation of resources.

> The production possibilities frontier represents our economy at full employment and full production.

The Production Possibilities Frontier

Since scarcity is a fact of economic life, we need to use our resources as efficiently as possible. If we succeed, we are operating at full economic capacity. Usually there's some economic slack, but every so often we *do* manage to operate at peak efficiency. When this happens, we are on our production possibilities frontier (or production possibilities curve).

Underemployment of College Graduates

According to the Bureau of Labor Statistics, one in five college graduates has a job that does not require a college degree. And many of the jobs they hold that do require a bachelor's degree are dead-end, low-wage positions.

There are about 1 million college graduates working as salesclerks; 1.5 million as typists, file clerks, and receptionists; and another 1.3 million as construction or assembly-line workers.

That's the *good* news. The bad news is that by 2005, according to Labor Department economists, 3 out of every 10 college graduates will have jobs like these.

Thomas Geoghegan, a labor lawyer, tried to learn exactly what was the difference between a college job and a noncollege job:

> What does the Bureau of Labor Statistics define as a college job?
> Manager of a Blockbuster video store? Yes.
> Assistant manager of Blockbuster? Maybe.
> Legal secretary? Can be.

Police officer? Perhaps.
Claims adjuster? Maybe.*

When I graduated from college, I met a recruiter from the Continental Baking Company who wanted to hire economics majors to be truck drivers. "How will I use my economics?" I asked. He had a great answer: "You can economize on the gasoline." I told him that I didn't go to college for four years so that I could drive a truck. He might have answered by asking if I would rather be *under*employed or *un*employed.†

You are spending a great deal of time and money on your education. Unless our economic prospects improve substantially, you and your friends may spend a large part of your working lives underemployed. Who knows, that truck driving job may still be open.

---

*Thomas Geoghegan, "Overeducated and Underpaid," *New York Times*, June 3, 1997, p. A23.

†Less than 2 percent of college graduates were unemployed in early 2001.

Often economics texts cast the production possibilities frontier in terms of guns and butter. A country is confronted with two choices: It can produce only military goods or only civilian goods. The more guns it produces, the less butter and, of course, vice versa.

If we were to use all our resources—our land, labor, capital, and entrepreneurial ability—to make guns, we would obviously not be able to make butter at all. Similarly, if we made only butter, there would be no resources to make any guns. Virtually every country makes *some* guns and *some* butter. Japan makes relatively few military goods, while the United States devotes a much higher proportion of its resources to making guns.

You are about to encounter the first graph in this book. This graph, and each one that follows, will have a vertical axis and a horizontal axis. Both axes start at the origin of the graph, which is located in the lower left-hand corner and usually marked with the number 0.

In Figure 1 we measure units of butter on the vertical axis. Each line or box stands for one unit. On the horizontal axis we measure units of guns. As we move to the right, the number of guns increases—1, 2, 3, 4, 5.

The curve shown in the graph is drawn by connecting points A, B, C, D, E, and F. Where do these points come from? They come from Table 1. Where did we get the numbers in Table 1? They're hypothetical. In other words, I made them up.

Guns and butter

Table 1 shows six production possibilities ranging from point A, where we produce 15 units of butter and no guns, to point F, where we produce 5 units of guns but no butter. This same information is presented in Figure 1, a graph of the production possibilities curve of frontier. We'll begin at point A, where a country's entire resources are devoted to producing butter. If the country were to produce at full capacity (using all its resources) but wanted to make some guns, they could do it by shifting some resources away from butter. This would move them from point A to point B. Instead of producing 15 units of butter, they're making only 14.

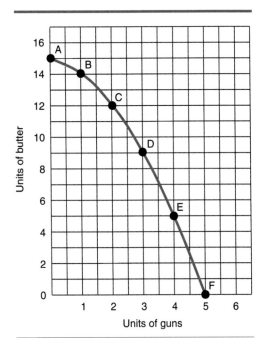

Figure 1

Production Possibilities Curve

This curve shows the range of possible combinations of outputs of guns and butter extending from 15 units of butter and no guns at point A to 5 units of guns and no butter at point F.

TABLE 1	Hypothetical Production Schedule for Two-Product Economy	
Point	Units of Butter	Units of Guns
A	15	0
B	14	1
C	12	2
D	9	3
E	5	4
F	0	5

Before we go any further on the curve, let's go over the numbers at points A and B. We're figuring out how many guns and how much butter is produced at each of these points. Starting at the origin, or zero, let's check out point A. It's directly above the origin, so no guns are produced. Point A is at 15 on the vertical scale, so 15 units of butter are produced.

Now we'll move on to point B, which is directly above 1 unit on the guns axis. At B we produce 1 unit of guns and 14 units of butter (shown vertically). Incidentally, to locate any point on a graph, first go across, or horizontally, then up, or vertically. Point B is 1 unit to the right, then 14 units up.

Now locate point C: 2 units across and 12 up. At C we have 2 guns and 12 butters. Next is D: 3 across and 9 up (3 guns and 9 butters). At E: 4 across and 5 up (4 guns and 5 butters). And finally F: 5 across and 0 up (5 guns and no butter).

The production possibilities curve is a hypothetical model of an economy that produces only two products—in this case, guns and butter (or military goods and civilian goods). The curve represents the various possible combinations of guns and butter that could be produced if the economy were operating at capacity, or full employment.

Since we usually do not operate at full employment, we are seldom on the production possibilities frontier. So let's move on to Figure 2, which shows, at point X, where

The production possibilities curve represents a two-product economy at full employment.

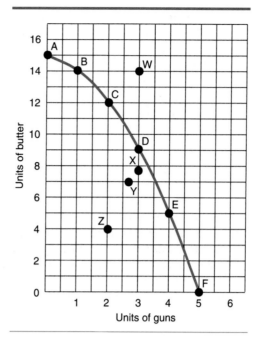

Figure 2

Points Inside and Outside the
Production Possibilities Curve

Since the curve represents output of
guns and butter at full employment,
points X, Y, and Z, which lie inside,
or below, the curve represent output
at less than full employment.
Similarly, point W represents output
at more than full employment and
is currently unattainable.

we generally are. Sometimes we are in a recession, with unemployment rising beyond 8
or 9 percent, represented on the graph by point Y. A depression would be closer to the
origin, perhaps shown by point Z. (Remember that the origin is located in the lower left-
hand corner of the graph.)

What if we were at the origin? What would that represent? Think about it. What
would be the production of guns? How about the production of butter? They would both
be zero. Is that possible? During the Great Depression in the 1930s, the U.S. economy
sank to point Z, but no economy has ever sunk to the origin.

Move back to the production possibilities curve, say, at point C, where we are producing 2 units of guns and 12 units of butter. Is it possible to produce more guns? Certainly. Just move down the curve to point D. Notice, however, that we now produce
fewer units of butter.

At D we have 3 units of guns and 9 units of butter. When we go from C, where we
have 2 guns, to D, where we have 3, gun production goes up by 1. But at the same time,
butter production declines from 12 at C to only 9 at D (a decline of 3).

If we're at point C, then, we can produce more guns, but only by sacrificing some
butter production. The opportunity cost of moving from C to D (that is, of producing 1
more gun) is giving up 3 units of butter.

Let's try another one, this time moving from C to B. Butter goes up from 12 to
14—a gain of 2. Meanwhile, guns go down from 2 to 1, a loss of 1. Going from C to
B, a gain of 2 butters is obtained by sacrificing 1 gun. The opportunity cost of producing 2 more butters is 1 gun.

Except at point A, we can go somewhere else on the production possibilities curve
and increase our output of butter. Similarly, anywhere but at point F, we can go somewhere else on the curve and raise our output of guns. It is possible to increase our output of *either* guns *or* butter by moving somewhere else on the curve, but there is an
opportunity cost involved. The more we produce of one (by moving along the curve),
the less we produce of the other. It is not possible, then, if we are anywhere on the curve,
to raise our production of both guns *and* butter. Of course, over time it is possible to
produce beyond our current production possibilities curve as our economy grows. We'll
get to economic growth in a few minutes.

What if we're somewhere inside the production possibilities frontier? Would it be
possible to produce more guns *and* more butter? The answer is yes. At point Z we have

an output of 2 guns and 4 butters. By moving to point D we would have 3 guns and 9 butters. Or, by going to point E, output would rise to 4 guns and 5 butters.

We are able to increase our output of both guns and butter when we move from Z to D or E because we are now making use of previously unused resources. We are moving from depression conditions to those of full employment. But when we go from C to D, we stay at full employment. The only way we can produce more guns is to produce less butter, because resources will have to be diverted from butter to gun production.

Productive Efficiency and Allocative Efficiency

So far we've seen that our economy generally falls short of full production. Now we'll tie that failure in to our definition of economics.

At the beginning of this chapter, we defined economics as *the efficient allocation of the scarce means of production toward the satisfaction of human wants.* The scarce means of production are our resources, land, labor, capital, and entrepreneurial ability. So how efficiently do we use our resources?

An economy is efficient whenever it is producing the maximum output allowed by a given level of technology and resources. *Productive efficiency is attained when the maximum possible output of any one good is produced, given the output of other goods.* This state of grace occurs only when we are operating on our production possibilities curve. Attainment of productive efficiency means that we can't increase the output of one good without reducing the output of some other good.

> Productive efficiency is attained when the maximum possible output of one good is produced, given the output of other goods.

As we've seen, our economy rarely attains productive efficiency, or full production. We have managed this state of grace since the summer of 1997 when the unemployment rate dipped below 5 percent. The previous time our economy actually operated on its production possibilities frontier was during the Vietnam War, in 1968 and 1969.

Now we come to allocative efficiency, which occurs when no resources are wasted. *When an efficient allocation of resources is attained, it is not possible to make any person better off without making someone else worse off.* No society has ever come anywhere close to allocative efficiency.

> When an efficient allocation of resources is attained, it is not possible to make any person better off without making someone else worse off.

In our hypothetical examples of production possibilities curves, we assumed that our economy produced just two goods or services. If our economy limited its production to two goods or services—or even 10—would this be an *efficient* allocation of our resources? Remember that the goal of economics is to satisfy human wants. Could *your* wants be satisfied with just 10 goods and services? Most people could easily make up lists totaling dozens of different goods and services which they consider basic necessities, and perhaps hundreds of additional goods and services which they would *like* to have.

Economists have long puzzled over the question of allocative efficiency, but we have more pressing things to consider—such as economic growth, the subject of the next section.

Economic Growth

If the production possibilities curve represents the economy operating at full employment, then it would be impossible to produce at point W (of Figure 2). To go from C to W would mean producing more guns and more butter, something that would be beyond our economic capabilities, given the current state of technology and the amount of resources available.

Every economy will use the best available technology. At times, because a country cannot afford the most up-to-date equipment, it will use older machinery and tools. That country really has a capital problem rather than a technological one.

> The best available technology

As the level of available technology improves, the production possibilities curve moves outward, as it does in Figure 3. A faster paper copier, a more smoothly operat-

Figure 3

Production Possibilities Curves

A move from PPC$_1$ to PPC$_2$ and
from PPC$_2$ to PPC$_3$ represents
economic growth.

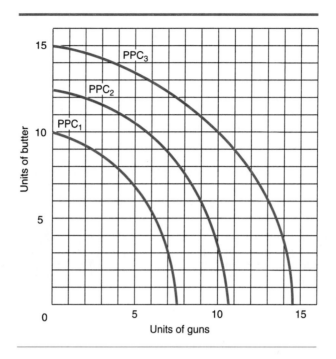

ing assembly line, or a new-generation computer system are examples of technological advances. And increasingly, industrial robots and bank money machines are replacing human beings at relatively routine jobs.

Our economic capacity is also expanded when there is an expansion of labor or capital. More (or better trained) labor and more (or improved) plant and equipment would also push the production possibilities curve outward. This is illustrated in Figure 3, as we go from PPC$_1$ to PPC$_2$, and from PPC$_2$ to PPC$_3$.

In the 1950s, when Nikita Khrushchev, then the head honcho of the Politburo, said, "We will bury you," he wasn't trying to drum up business for his funeral parlor. He meant that the Soviet Union would overtake the United States in output of goods and services. At that time the U.S.S.R. was growing much faster than we were. But in the 1960s, our rate of economic growth sped up, while the Soviet rate slowed down. Since then, of course, it was all downhill for the U.S.S.R., while the American economy continued to grow. However, since the early 1970s, our rate of growth, which had averaged more than 3 percent a year during the last two centuries, slowed to only a little more than 2 percent. Americans were consuming too much and producing too little.

Another way of putting this is that Americans were not saving enough, and business firms were not investing enough. This is shown by the two alternate graphs of Figure 4.

Why can't we operate at point B of Figure 4 rather than at point A? That's a very good question. Probably the best answer is that Americans, for whatever reason, have come to believe in the adage "Buy today, pay tomorrow."

Let's go back again to the days of World War II when our economy began to expand at an extremely rapid rate. The question I raise in the box titled "The Production Possibilities Frontier during World War II" is this: Can we have more guns *and* more butter?

Buying "on time" became popular after World War II, along with relatively easy-to-obtain home mortgages, federal income tax preferential treatment for home ownership and personal borrowing,[7] and, over the last three decades, the tremendous expansion in

---

[7]Until 1987, interest paid on all consumer loans—for example, car loans, credit card loans, bank personal loans, and installment loans—was deductible from federal personal income taxes.

People who own their homes can deduct mortgage interest and property taxes from their federal personal income tax.

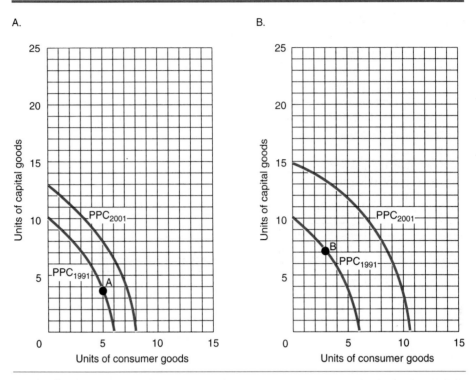

Figure 4

Production Possibilities Curves
Over Time

The panel on the right represents
much faster economic growth than
the panel on the left.

the use of credit cards. In addition, Americans are bombarded by more than $225 billion worth of advertising a year. The products may vary, but the message remains the same: Buy! Buy! Buy!

The more we buy, the less we save. In fact, by 1986, Americans were saving only about 2 percent of their incomes after taxes, which was just one-third the rate of the 1960s. Also contributing to our shortfall of savings has been the federal government, which ran budget deficits approaching $300 billion by the early 1990s. (Today, of course, we are running surpluses.)

It all came down to this: The funds needed by business firms for investment in plant and equipment were no longer being provided in sufficient quantity by private savers, and the federal government was sopping up much of the savings that were available. Foreign investors, who had been accumulating surplus dollars from our trade deficits, were lending us back some of our own money. But this was insufficient to provide all the investment funds needed to spur our rate of economic growth.

Although our savings rate continued to lag, our economic growth rate shot up in the latter half of the 1990s. Much of this advance was supported by a huge influx of foreign capital. and then, too, our tremendous investment in computerization had finally begun to pay off in faster economic growth.

The main factors spurring growth are an improving technology, more and better capital, and more and better labor. Using our resources more efficiently and reducing the unemployment of labor and capital can also raise our rate of growth. This topic is discussed more extensively in Chapter 16 of *Economics* and *Macroeconomics*.

The Production Possibilities Frontier During World War II

World War II was a classic case of guns and butter, or, more accurately, guns *or* butter. Almost two years before we became actively involved in the war, we began increasing our arms production and drafting millions of young men into the armed services. Did this increase in military goods production mean a decrease in the production of consumer goods?

Gee, that's a very good question. And the answer is found when you go from point A to point B on the first figure shown here.

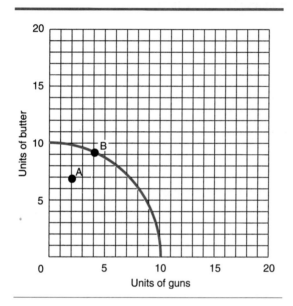

How were we able to increase the production of both guns and butter in 1940 and 1941? Because there was still a great deal of economic slack in those years. It was the tail end of the Great Depression described in Chapter 1, and there were still millions of people out of work and a great deal of idle plant and equipment that could be pressed into use.

Now we're in the war, and we're at point B in the first figure. Is it possible to further expand our output of both guns and butter? Think about it.

Is there any way we could do it? How about if there's economic growth? In the second figure shown here, we went from point B to point C by moving to a higher production possibilities curve. Is this *possible*? Over a considerable period of time, yes. But in just a couple of years? Well, remember what they used to say: There's a *war* going on. So a move from point B to point C in just a couple of years is possible during a war.

Now we're really going to push it. How about a move from point C to point D in the second figure? Is *this* move possible? Can we raise our production of both guns *and* butter to a point beyond our production possibilities frontier without jumping to a still higher production possibilities curve?

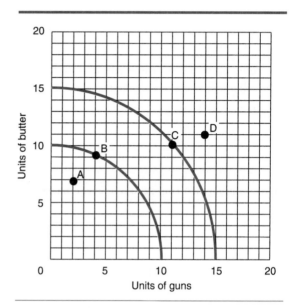

Well, what do you think? Remember, there's a war going on. The answer is yes. In 1942, 1943, and 1944 we did push our official unemployment rate under 3 percent, well below the 5 percent rate we would consider full employment today. Employers were so desperate for workers that they would hire practically anybody, and people who wouldn't ordinarily be in the labor market—housewives, retired people, and teenagers—were flocking to the workplace.

Meanwhile, business firms were pressing older machinery and equipment into use, because it was almost impossible to get new machinery and equipment built during the war. And so we were operating not only at full capacity but well beyond that point.

How long were we able to stay at point D? Only as long as there was a war going on. Point D represents an output of guns and butter that our economy can produce temporarily if it operates beyond its production possibilities frontier. It's almost like bowling 300. You can't expect to go out and do it every night.*

---

*One can argue that we were temporarily operating on a higher production possibilities frontier, and, at the end of the war, we returned to the lower production possibilities frontier.

Questions for Further Thought and Discussion

1. If you were in a position to run our economy, what steps would you take to raise our rate of economic growth?

2. Under what circumstances can we operate outside our production possibilities curve?

3. Give an example of an opportunity cost for an individual and a nation.

4. Would it be harder for a nation to attain full employment or full production? Explain.

5. Could a nation's production possibilities frontier ever shift inward? What might cause such a shift to occur?

6. What is the opportunity cost you incurred by going to college?

7. Although the U.S. is one of the world's wealthiest nations, some of the federal government's budget decisions are severely constrained by scarcity. Can you think of one such decision that was in the recent economic news?

8. Why is scarcity central to economics?

9. Can you think of any decisions you have recently made that incurred opportunity costs?

10. Do you know any entrepreneurs? What do they do?

11. Why is entrepreneurship central to every business firm?

Workbook for Chapter 2

Name _____ Date _____

Multiple-Choice Questions

Circle the letter that corresponds to the best answer.

1. The word that is central to the definition of economics is _____.
   a) resource   c) scarcity
   b) wants   d) capital

2. We would not need to economize if _____.
   a) the government printed more money
   b) there was no scarcity
   c) there was less output of goods and services
   d) everyone received a big pay increase

3. Human wants are _____.
   a) relatively limited
   b) relatively unlimited
   c) easily satisfied
   d) about equal to our productive capacity

4. Which of the following is an economic resource?
   a) gold   c) labor
   b) scarcity   d) rent

5. Each of the following is an example of capital except _____.
   a) land   c) a computer system
   b) an office building   d) a factory

6. The opportunity cost of spending four hours studying a review book the night before a final exam would be _____.
   a) the cost of the review book
   b) missing four hours of TV
   c) a higher grade on the exam
   d) the knowledge gained from studying

7. An economy operating its plant and equipment at full capacity implies a capacity utilization rate of _____.
   a) 40 percent   c) 85 percent
   b) 70 percent   d) 100 percent

8. The full-production level of our economy implies _____.
   a) an efficient allocation of our resources
   b) zero unemployment
   c) our plant and equipment being operated at 100 percent capacity
   d) a high unemployment rate

9. Underemployment means _____.
   a) the same thing as unemployment
   b) underutilization of resources
   c) a recession
   d) slow economic growth

10. The production possibilities frontier represents _____.
    a) our economy at full employment but not full production
    b) our economy at full production but not full employment
    c) our economy at full production and full employment

11. If we are operating inside our production possibilities frontier _____.
    a) there is definitely recession going on
    b) there is definitely not a recession going on
    c) there is definitely less than full employment
    d) there is definitely inflation

12. The closer we are to the origin and the farther away we are from the production possibilities frontier _____.
    a) the more unemployment there is
    b) the less unemployment there is
    c) the more guns we are producing
    d) the more butter we are producing

13. Economic growth will occur if any of the following occur except _____.
    a) a better technology becomes available
    b) the level of consumption rises and the savings rate falls
    c) more capital becomes available
    d) more labor becomes available

14. To attain a higher rate of economic growth, we need to devote _____.
    a) a higher proportion of our production to capital goods and a lower proportion to consumer goods
    b) a higher proportion of our production to consumer goods and a lower proportion to capital goods
    c) a higher proportion of our production to both consumer goods and capital goods
    d) a lower proportion of our production to both consumer goods and capital goods

15. Each of the following has contributed to our low rate of economic growth except _____.
    a) our high rate of savings
    b) our high rate of consumption
    c) our federal budget deficits
    d) our low rate of investment

16. Statement 1: As we move toward a more global economy, our capacity utilization rate becomes more relevant.
    Statement 2: A capacity utilization rate of 100 percent means that our economy is operating at full capacity.
    a) Statement 1 is true and statement 2 is false.
    b) Statement 2 is true and statement 1 is false.
    c) Both statements are true.
    d) Both statements are false.

17. Statement 1: The old Negro leagues provide an example of underemployment.
    Statement 2: Underemployment means basically the same thing as unemployment.
    a) Statement 1 is true and statement 2 is false.
    b) Statement 2 is true and statement 1 is false.
    c) Both statements are true.
    d) Both statements are false.

18. Employment discrimination is most closely related to _____.
    a) specialization   c) unemployment
    b) technology   d) underemployment

19. A woman who has a Harvard MBA who is working as a secretary would almost definitely be _____.
    a) unemployed
    b) underemployed
    c) both unemployed and underemployed
    d) neither unemployed nor underemployed

20. Which of the following is the most accurate statement?
    a) Women now hold about one-third of the senior management positions in Fortune 500 companies.
    b) The glass ceiling no longer exists.
    c) Underemployment of women, blacks, and other Americans has declined substantially since the 1950s.
    d) Although there was substantial employment discrimination in the past, there is virtually none today.

21. Which statement is true?
    a) America has always had a shortage of entrepreneurs.
    b) Our economic problem is that we have limited resources available to satisfy relatively unlimited wants.
    c) America has less economic resources today than we had 40 years ago.
    d) Aside from a few million poor people, we have very little scarcity in the United States.

22. Suppose you had $1,000 to spend. If you spent it on a vacation trip rather than on new clothes, your second choice, or 1,000 lottery tickets, your third choice, what was your opportunity cost of going on a vacation trip?
    a) $1,000
    b) the vacation trip itself
    c) not buying the new clothes
    d) not buying the lottery tickets
    e) missing out on the $10 million lottery prize

23. Which of the following best describes the role of an entrepreneur?
   a) the inventor of something with great commercial possibilities
   b) anyone who made a fortune by purchasing stock in a dot-com before its price shot up
   c) inventors who parlay inventions into commercial enterprises
   d) any employee earning at least $200,000 at a Fortune 500 company

24. Which is the most accurate statement?
   a) Employment discrimination against women was extremely prevalent before the 1960s.
   b) Although there was some employment discrimination against women in the 1950s, you would never know it by viewing period ads for office equipment.
   c) While a glass ceiling clearly exists in the United States, it has virtually disappeared in Canada.
   d) More than 10 percent of the CEOs of Fortune 500 companies are women.

Fill-In Questions

1. The main reason for our lagging rate of economic growth has been not enough _____.

2. The central fact of economics is (in one word) _____.

3. Human wants are relatively _____, while economic resources are relatively _____.

4. List the four economic resources (1) _____; (2) _____; (3) _____; and (4) _____.

5. Opportunity cost is defined as _____ _____.

6. If you went into a store with $25 and couldn't decide whether to buy a pair of jeans or a jacket, and you finally decided to buy the jeans, what would be the opportunity cost of this purchase? _____.

7. Full employment implies an unemployment rate of about _____ percent.

8. List some constraints on our labor force that prevent our fully using our plant and equipment 24 hours a day, seven days a week.

   (1) _____;

   (2) _____;

   and (3) _____.

9. Employment discrimination results in the _____ of our labor force.

10. When we are efficiently allocating our resources and using the best available technology, we are operating on our _____.

11. Most of the time our economy is operating _____ _____ its production possibilities frontier.

12. Economic growth can be attained by:

   (1) _____ and

   (2) _____.

13. Economics is defined as the allocation of the _____ toward the _____.

Problems

1. If we were at point C of Figure 1, could we quickly produce substantially more houses *and* more cars?

Figure 1

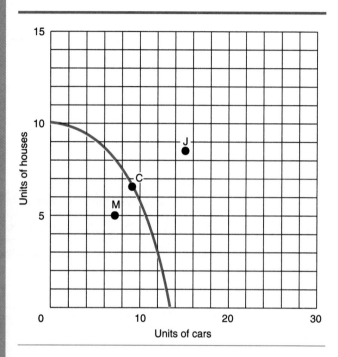

2. If we were at point M of Figure 1, could we quickly produce substantially more houses *and* more cars?

3. If we were at point C on Figure 1, could we quickly go to point J?

4. Fill in the following points on Figure 2.

   Point X: where our economy generally operates

   Point Y: a serious recession

   Point Z: a catastrophic depression

   Point W: economic growth

Figure 2

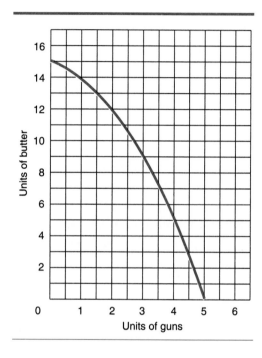

5. In Figure 3, fill in a new production possibilities frontier representing substantial economic growth.

6. In Figure 3, place point M where there is 100 percent unemployment.

Figure 3

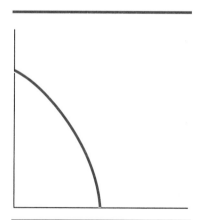

7. Fill in the following points on Figure 4.

   Point A: an unemployment rate of 100 percent

   Point B: an unemployment rate of 20 percent

   Point C: an unemployment rate of 2 percent

Figure 4

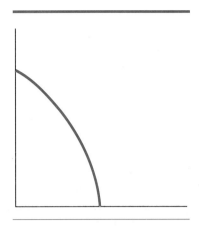

Appendix

The Law of Increasing Costs[1]

You may notice that Figure A-1 is an exact duplication of Figure 1. You may also notice that, as we shift production from guns to butter, we have to give up increasing units of guns for each additional unit of butter. Or, shifting the other way, we would have to give up increasing units of butter for each additional unit of guns we produce.

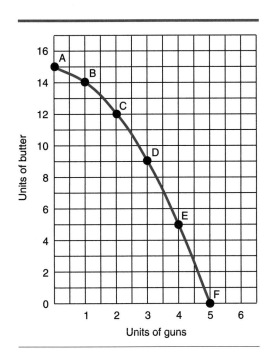

Figure A-1

Production Possibilities Curve

Diminishing Returns in the New York Region

The New York region, which includes the 15 counties in and around New York City, is extremely overcrowded, particularly with respect to getting around. In a sense, then, diminishing returns have set in when it takes 90 minutes to make a 20-mile trip to work, when daytime traffic moves at less than five miles per hour in midtown Manhattan, and when rush-hour gridlock threatens to prevent any movement whatsoever. The Houston area provides another example of overdevelopment resulting in near immobility.

The law of increasing costs

We will be calling this "the law of increasing costs." Stated formally, this law says that *as the output of one good expands, the opportunity cost of producing additional units of this good increases.* In other words, as more and more of a good is produced, the production of additional units of this good will entail larger and larger opportunity costs.

The law of increasing costs is based on three concepts: (1) the law of diminishing returns, (2) diseconomies of scale, and (3) factor suitability. We've already alluded to factor suitability when we talked about using our resources in the most efficient way possible. One example was to use our computer mainframe for sophisticated data analysis rather than for simple word processing.

The law of diminishing returns, which we'll take up more formally in a later chapter, is defined this way: *If units of a resource are added to a fixed proportion of other resources, eventually marginal output will decline.* Suppose one farmer working with one tractor can produce 100 bushels of wheat on one acre of land. Two farmers, working together, can produce 220 bushels. And three, working together, can produce 350.

The marginal output of the first farmer is 100. (In other words, the first farmer added 100 bushels to output.) The marginal output of the second farmer is 120. And the marginal output of the third farmer is 130. So far, so good. We call this increasing returns.

If we keep adding farmers, do you think we'll continue to enjoy increasing returns? Won't that single acre of land start getting a little crowded? Will that one tractor be sufficient for four, five, and six farmers? Suppose we did add a fourth farmer and suppose output rose from 350 to 450. By how much did marginal output rise?

It rose by only 100. So marginal output, which had been rising by 120 and 130, has now fallen to 100. We call this diminishing returns. (See box, "Diminishing Returns in the New York Region.") And it is one of the bases for the law of increasing costs.

Diseconomies of scale is a new term. As a business firm grows larger, it can usually cut its costs by taking advantage of quantity discounts, the use of expensive but highly productive equipment, and the development of a highly specialized and highly skilled workforce. We call these *economies of scale.* But as the firm continues to grow, these economies of scale are eventually outweighed by the inefficiencies of managing a bloated bureaucracy, which might sometimes work at cross-purposes. Most of the day could be spent writing memos, answering memos, and attending meetings.[2] Labor and other resources become increasingly expensive, and not only are quantity discounts no longer available, but now suppliers charge premium prices for such huge orders. As costs begin to rise, diseconomies of scale have now overcome economies of scale.[3]

Let's look at some increasing costs. We have already seen how we have had to give up the production of some guns to produce more butter and vice versa. We'll now take this a step further. To produce additional units of guns—one gun, two guns, three guns—we will have to give up increasing amounts of butter. Similarly, to produce additional units of butter, we will have to give up increasing numbers of guns.

---

[2]The time wasted performing these "managerial functions" is aptly described by Maryann Keller in *Rude Awakening* (New York: William Morrow, 1989), a book about General Motors Corporation.

[3]Economies and diseconomies of scale are more fully discussed in a later chapter.

TABLE A-1	Production Shifts from Butter to Guns	
Shift from Point to Point	Change in Gun Production	Change in Butter Production
A to B	+1	−1
B to C	+1	−2
C to D	+1	−3
D to E	+1	−4
E to F	+1	−5

How many units of butter would we have to give up to produce each additional gun? This is shown in Table A-1, which is derived from Figure A-1, or, if you prefer, from Table 1 of Chapter 2.

In Table A-1, as we begin to switch from butter to guns, we move from point A to point B. We give up just one unit of butter in exchange for one unit of guns. But the move from B to C isn't as good. Here we give up two butters for one gun. C to D is still worse: We give up three butters for one gun. D to E is even worse: We give up four units of butter for one gun. And the worst trade-off of all is from E to F: We lose five butters for just one gun.

This is why we call it the law of increasing relative costs. To produce more and more of one good, we have to give up increasing amounts of another good. To produce each additional gun, we have to give up increasing amounts of butter.

There are three explanations for the law of increasing relative costs. First, there's diminishing returns. If we're increasing gun production, we will need more and more resources—more land, more labor, more capital, and more entrepreneurial ability. But one or more of these resources may be relatively limited. Perhaps we will begin to run out of capital—plant and equipment—or perhaps entrepreneurial ability will run out first.

Three explanations for the law of increasing relative costs

Go back to our definition of the law of diminishing returns. *If units of a resource are added to a fixed proportion of other resources, eventually marginal output will decline.* Had we been talking about farming rather than producing guns, the law of diminishing returns might have set in as increasing amounts of capital were applied to the limited supply of rich farmland.

A second explanation for the law of increasing costs is diseconomies of scale. By shifting from butter to guns, the firm or firms making guns will grow so large that diseconomies of scale will eventually set in.

The third explanation, factor suitability, requires more extensive treatment here. We'll start at point A of Table A-1, where we produce 15 units of butter and no guns. As we move to point B, gun production goes up by one, while butter production goes down by only one. In other words, the opportunity cost of producing one unit of guns is the loss of only one unit of butter.

Why is the opportunity cost so low? The answer lies mainly with factor suitability. We'll digress for a moment with the analogy of a pickup game of basketball (see Figure A-2). The best players are picked first, then the not-so-good ones, and finally the worst. If a couple of players from one side have to go home, the game goes on. The other side gives them their worst player.

If we're shifting from butter to guns, the butter makers will give the gun makers their worst workers. But people who are bad at producing butter are not necessarily bad at making—or shooting—guns.

When all we did was make butter, people worked at that no matter what their other skills. Even if a person were a skilled gun maker, or a gun user, what choice did he have? Presumably, then, when given the choice to make guns, those best suited for that occupation (and also poorly suited for butter making) would switch to guns.

Figure A-2

Choosing Players for a Basketball
Team

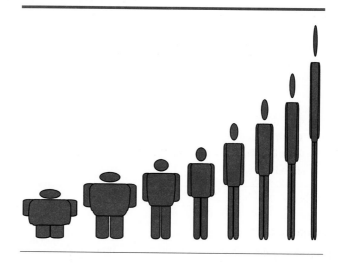

As resources are shifted from butter to guns, the labor, land, capital, and entrepreneurial ability best suited to guns and least suited to butter will be the first to switch. But as more resources are shifted, we will be taking resources that were more and more suited to butter making and less and less suited to gun making.

Take land, for example. The first land given over to gun making might be terrible for raising cows (and hence milk and butter) but great for making guns. Eventually, however, as nearly all land was devoted to gun making, we'd be giving over fertile farmland that might not be well suited to gun production.

Each of these three reasons—diminishing returns, diseconomies of scale, and factor suitability—helps explain the law of increasing costs. But now that the law is explained, we won't have to worry too much about it, because we would never devote all of our production to just one, or even a few, goods and services. Nevertheless, the law does have an applicability in certain localities and regions, or in particular economic sectors that may grow too large relative to the rest of the economy.

The law of increasing costs explains why we don't expand certain industries or sectors too far and what would happen if we did. That there are few examples of such overexpansion is eloquent testimony to the potency of the law.

Questions for Further Thought and Discussion

1. Explain the law of increasing costs, using a numerical example.
2. Discuss the three concepts on which the law of increasing costs is based.

Workbook for Appendix to Chapter 2

Name _____ Date _____

Multiple-Choice Questions

Circle the letter that corresponds to the best answer.

1. As we produce increasing amounts of a particular good, the resources used in its production _____.

    a) become more suitable

    b) become less suitable

    c) continue to have the same suitability

2. The law of increasing costs is explained by each of the following except _____.

    a) the law of diminishing returns

    b) diseconomies of scale

    c) factor suitability

    d) overspecialization

3. As a firm grows larger, _____.

    a) economies of scale set in, then diseconomies of scale

    b) diseconomies of scale set in, then economies of scale

    c) economies of scale and diseconomies of scale set in at the same time

    d) neither economies of scale nor diseconomies of scale set in

4. The law of increasing costs states that, as _____.

    a) output rises, cost per unit rises as well

    b) the output of one good expands, the opportunity cost of producing additional units of this good increases

    c) economies of scale set in, costs increase

    d) output rises, diminishing returns set in

Fill-In Questions

1. Large firms are able to lower their costs by taking advantage of _____.

2. When firms get too big, _____ set in.

3. The law of increasing costs states that, as the output of one good expands, _____.

4. The law of diminishing returns, diseconomies of scale, and factor suitability each provide an explanation for the law of

    _____.

Problems

1. Given the information in Table A-2, below, what is the opportunity cost of going from point B to point C? And of going from point D to point C?

TABLE A-2	Hypothetical Production Schedule for Two-Product Economy	
Point	Units of Butter	Units of Guns
A	15	0
B	14	1
C	12	2
D	9	3
E	5	4
F	0	5

2. Use Figure A-3 to answer these questions:

   a) What is the opportunity cost of going from point B to point C?

   b) What is the opportunity cost of going from point D to point C?

   c) What is the opportunity cost of going from point B to point A?

   d) What is the opportunity cost of going from point C to point D?

3. Use the data in Figure A-3 to illustrate the law of increasing costs numerically. (Hint: Start at point E and move toward point A.)

Figure A-3

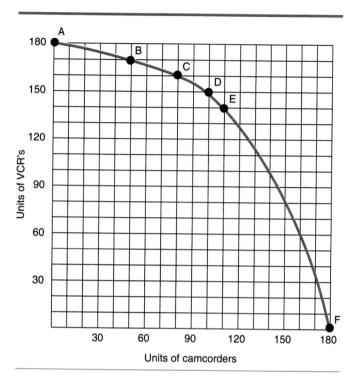

Chapter 3

Supply and Demand

Should your college charge you for parking, or should parking be free? Should the federal government put a ceiling of, say, $2 a gallon on gas prices? And should drug companies be forced to make prescription drug prices affordable to senior citizens?

Our price system is constantly sending buyers and sellers thousands of signals. Running an economy without that system would be like flying a jumbo jet plane without an instrument panel.

Our economy has a built-in guidance system that allocates resources efficiently. This guidance system, which includes the interaction of the forces of supply and demand in the marketplace, is known as the price system. How does it work? You're about to find out.

How are you at reading graphs? Economists love to draw them, so if you're going to get through this course, you'll need to be able to read them. The main graph we like to draw has just two curves: the demand curve and the supply curve. By observing where they cross, we can easily find not only the price of a good or service, but the quantity sold.

CHAPTER OBJECTIVES

In this chapter you will learn how to:

- Define and explain *demand* in a product or service market.
- Define and explain *supply.*
- Determine the equilibrium point in the market for a specific good, given data on supply and demand at different price levels.

- Understand what causes shifts in demand and supply.
- Understand how price ceilings cause shortages.
- Understand how price floors cause surpluses.

Demand

We define *demand* as *the schedule of quantities of a good or service that people are willing to buy at different prices.* And as you would suspect, the lower the price, the more people will buy.

How much would people living in Denver or in Chicago be willing to pay for a round-trip plane ticket for weekday travel between the two cities? Suppose we conducted a survey and were able to draw up a demand schedule like the one shown in Table 1.

Note that, as the price declines, increasing quantities of tickets are demanded. Now look at Figure 1 to see how a graph of this demand schedule looks.

The demand curve slopes downward and to the right. That's because of the way we've set up our graph. Prices are on the vertical axis, with the highest price, $500, at the top. From here on, the vertical axis of every graph in this book will be measured in terms of money. The horizontal axis of Figure 1 measures the quantity sold, beginning with zero, at the origin of the graph, and getting to progressively higher quantities as we move to the right. In all the demand and supply graphs that follow, price will be on the vertical axis, and quantity on the horizontal.

TABLE 1	Hypothetical Daily Demand for Coach Seats on Round-Trip Weekday Flights between Denver and Chicago	
Price	Quantity Demanded
$500	1,000
450	3,000
400	7,000
350	12,000
300	19,000
250	30,000
200	45,000
150	57,000
100	67,000

Figure 1

Hypothetical Daily Demand for Coach Seats on Round-Trip Weekday Flights between Denver and Chicago

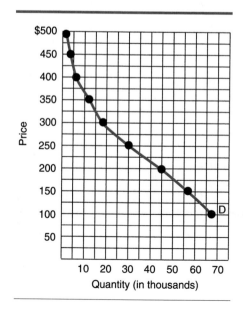

Supply

Supply is defined as *the schedule of quantities of a good or service that people are willing to sell at different prices.* If you compare the definition of supply with that of demand, you'll find that only one word is changed. Can you find that word?

If you are a supplier, then you are willing to *sell* a schedule of quantities at different prices; if you are a buyer, then you are willing to *buy* a schedule of quantities at different prices. What's the difference, then, between supply and demand? At higher prices the suppliers are willing to sell larger and larger quantities, while the buyers are willing to buy smaller and smaller quantities. Similarly, as price declines, buyers are willing to buy more and sellers are willing to sell less. But we're getting a little ahead of ourselves, since you haven't yet been formally introduced to a supply schedule. So first check out Table 2, and then Figure 2, which is a graph drawn from the numbers in the table.

What happens, then, to quantity supplied as the price is lowered? It declines. It's as simple as that.

Definition of supply: the schedule of quantities of a good or service that people are willing to sell at different prices.

TABLE 2	Hypothetical Daily Supply for Coach Seats on Round-Trip Weekday Flights between Denver and Chicago
Price	Quantity Supplied
$500	62,000
450	59,000
400	54,000
350	48,000
300	40,000
250	30,000
200	16,000
150	7,000
100	2,000

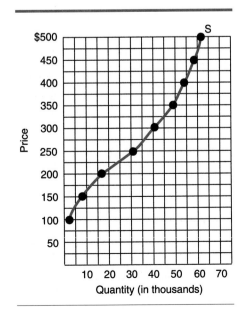

Figure 2

Hypothetical Daily Supply for Coach Seats on Round-Trip Weekday Flights between Denver and Chicago

But on the other hand, as economists like to say, we have skipped over a couple of very important considerations. In our definitions of demand and supply, we talked about a schedule of quantities of a good or service that people are willing to buy or sell at different prices. But what if they just don't have the money? Then those buyers are simply not counted. We say that they are not in the market. Similarly, we would exclude from the market any sellers who just don't have the goods or services to sell. I'd *love* to sell my services as a $500-an-hour corporate lawyer, but quite frankly, I just don't have those services to sell.

That brings us to a second consideration not included in our definitions of supply and demand. The supply and demand for any good or service operates within a specific market. That market may be very local, as it is for food shopping; regional, as it is for used cars; national, as it is for news magazines; or even international, as it is for petroleum.

Equilibrium

You've heard a lot about supply and demand—or is it demand and supply? It doesn't matter whether you put demand or supply first. What *does* matter is placing them together on the same graph. Look at Figure 3.

Can you find the equilibrium price? Did you say $250? Good! And how much is equilibrium quantity? Right again! It is 30,000.

Let's step back for a minute and analyze what we've just done. We've figured out the equilibrium price and quantity by looking at the demand and supply curves in Figure 3. So we can find equilibrium price and quantity by seeing where the supply and demand curves cross.

What is equilibrium price? It's the price at which quantity demanded equals quantity supplied. What is equilibrium quantity? It's the quantity sold when the quantity demanded is equal to the quantity supplied.

Equilibrium price is the price at which quantity demanded equals quantity supplied.

Surpluses and Shortages

Is the actual price, or market price, always equal to the equilibrium price? The answer is no. It could be higher and it could be lower. Suppose the airlines were selling tickets for $400. How many tickets would be demanded? Look back at Table 1 or, if you prefer, Figure 1 or Figure 3.

Figure 3
Demand and Supply Curves

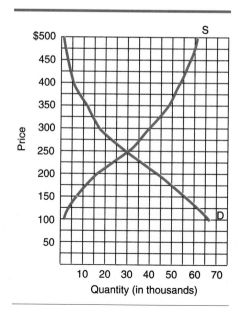

A total of 7,000 tickets would be demanded. And at a price of $400, how many tickets would be supplied?

The quantity supplied would be 54,000. What we've got here is a surplus. This occurs when the actual price, or the market price, is greater than the equilibrium price. How much is that surplus? You can measure it by finding the horizontal distance between quantity demanded and quantity supplied in Figure 3. Or, you can subtract the quantity demanded that you found in Table 1 (at a price of $400) from the quantity supplied in Table 2 (also at a price of $400). Either way, the surplus comes to 47,000.

A surplus occurs when the market price is above the equilibrium price.

The quantity that sellers are willing to sell (54,000) is much greater than the quantity buyers are willing to buy (7,000). This difference (54,000 − 7,000) is the surplus (47,000). The amount that sellers can sell is restricted by how much buyers are willing to buy.

What happens when there's a surplus? The forces of demand and supply automatically work to eliminate it. In this case, some of the airlines, which would be very unhappy about all those empty seats, would cut their prices. If the market price fell to $300, would there still be a surplus?

A glance at Figure 3 tells us that there would be. And how much would that surplus be?

It would be 21,000 seats. So *then* what would happen?

Some of the airlines would cut their prices to $250, and the buyers would flock to them. The other airlines would have no choice but to cut their price—or stop flying the Denver-Chicago route altogether. At $250, these flights would be at the equilibrium point. There would be no tendency for the price to change.

What if the market price were below equilibrium price? Then we'd have a shortage. How much would that shortage be if the market price in Figure 3 price were $200?

A shortage occurs when the market price is below the equilibrium price.

At a price of $200, quantity demanded would be 45,000, while quantity supplied would be just 16,000. So the shortage would be 29,000.

This time the buyers would be unhappy, because they would be quite willing to pay $200 for a round-trip ticket, but most would be unable to get one without waiting for months. Many of the buyers would be willing to pay more. So what do you think would happen?

You guessed it! The market price would rise to $250. At that price—the equilibrium price—quantity demanded would equal quantity supplied, and the shortage would be eliminated.

Thus we can see that the forces of demand and supply work together to establish an equilibrium price at which there are no shortages or surpluses. At the equilibrium price, all the sellers can sell as much as they want and all the buyers can buy as much as they want. So if we were to shout, "Is everybody happy?" the buyers and sellers would all shout back yes!

Shifts in Demand and Supply

So far we've seen how the forces of demand and supply, or the price mechanism, send signals to buyers and sellers. For example, the surplus that resulted from a price of $400 sent a clear signal to sellers to cut their prices. Similarly, a price of $200 was accompanied by a shortage, which made many buyers unhappy. And sellers quickly realized that they could raise their price to $250 and *still* sell all the tickets they wanted to sell.

Now we'll see how shifts in supply curves and shifts in demand curves change equilibrium price and quantity, thereby sending new sets of signals to buyers and sellers. Figure 4 has a new demand curve, D_2. This represents an increase in demand because it lies entirely to the right of D_1, the original demand curve. There has been an increase in demand if the quantity demanded is larger at every price that can be compared.

Why did the demand for airline tickets increase? Let's say that newer planes were introduced that cut travel time by 30 percent.

I'd like you to find the new equilibrium price and the new equilibrium quantity. When you do, please write down your answers.

How Changes in Demand Affect Equilibrium

If demand falls and supply stays the same, what happens to equilibrium price and equilibrium quantity? To answer those questions, sketch a graph of a supply curve, S, and a demand curve, D_1. Then draw a second demand curve, D_2, representing a decrease in demand. I've done that in this figure.

The original equilibrium price was $50, and the original equilibrium quantity was 10. Equilibrium price fell to $35, and equilibrium quantity fell to 8. So a decrease in demand leads to a decrease in equilibrium price and quantity.

What would happen to equilibrium price and equilibrium quantity if demand rose and supply stayed the same? Equilibrium price and quantity would rise.

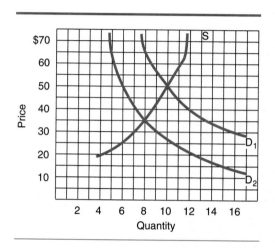

Figure 4
Increase in Demand

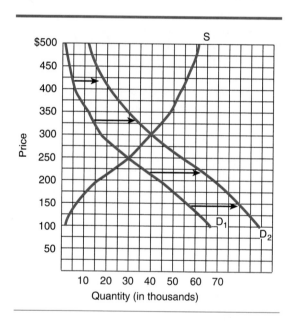

The new equilibrium price is $300, and the new equilibrium quantity is 40,000. So an increase in demand leads to an increase in both equilibrium price and quantity.

Next question: What would happen to equilibrium price and quantity if there were a decrease in demand?

There would be a decrease in both equilibrium price and quantity. Need a little extra help? Then see the box "How Changes in Demand Affect Equilibrium."

OK, one more set of shifts and we're out of here.

Figure 5 shows an increase in supply. You'll notice that the new supply curve, S_2, is entirely to the right of S_1. There has been an increase in supply if the quantity supplied is larger at every price that can be compared.

64

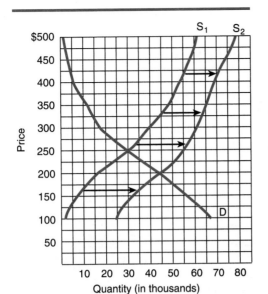

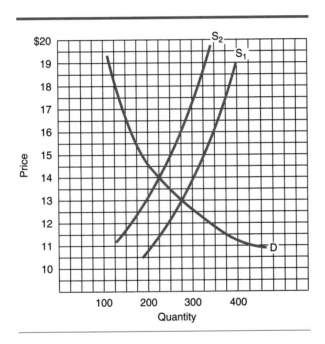

F*igure* 6

Why did supply increase? Let's assume that the cost of jet fuel fell by 50 percent. In response, the airlines scheduled more flights.

Please find the new equilibrium price and quantity, and write down your answers.

The new equilibrium price is $200, and the new equilibrium quantity is 45,000. So an increase in supply lowers equilibrium price and raises equilibrium quantity. One last question: If supply declines, what happens to equilibrium price and equilibrium quantity?

When supply declines, equilibrium price rises and equilibrium quantity declines. As you make your way through this text, supply and demand graphs will pop up from time to time. In every case you'll be able to find equilibrium price and quantity by locating the point of intersection of the demand and supply curves. If you need extra help, see the box "How Changes in Supply Affect Equilibrium."

Now let's work out a couple of problems. First, look at Figure 6 and write down your answers to this set of questions: (*a*) If the supply curve is S₁, how much are the equilibrium price and quantity? (*b*) If supply changes from S₁ to S₂, does that represent an increase or decrease in supply? (*c*) How much are the new equilibrium price and quantity?

An increase in supply lowers equilibrium price and raises equilibrium quantity.

How Changes in Supply Affect Equilibrium

If supply rises and demand stays the same, what happens to equilibrium price and equilibrium quantity? Again, to answer those questions, sketch a graph of a demand curve, D_1, and a supply curve, S_1. Then draw a second supply curve, S_2, representing an increase in supply. I've done that in this figure.

The original equilibrium price was $12, and the original equilibrium quantity was 20. Equilibrium price fell to $9, and equilibrium quantity rose to 26. So an increase in supply leads to a decrease in equilibrium price and an increase in equilibrium quantity.

What happens to equilibrium price and equilibrium quantity if supply falls and demand stays the same? Equilibrium price rises and equilibrium quantity falls.

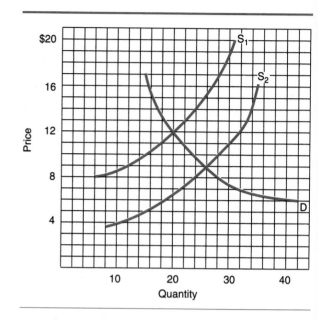

Figure 7

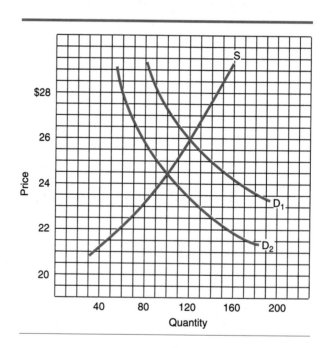

Here are the answers: (*a*) $13; 275; (*b*) decrease; and (*c*) $14; 225.

Next problem: Use Figure 7 to answer these questions: (*a*) If the demand curve is D_1, how much are the equilibrium price and quantity? (*b*) If demand changes from D_1 to D_2, does that represent an increase or decrease in demand? (*c*) How much are the new equilibrium price and quantity?

Here are the answers: (*a*) $26; 120; (*b*) decrease; and (*c*) $24.50; 100.

OK, you're taking an exam, and here's the first question: Demand rises and supply stays the same. What happens to equilibrium price and quantity? Just sketch a graph (like the one in Figure 4). Then you'll see that an increase in demand raises equilibrium price and quantity.

What happens to equilibrium price and quantity when there's a decrease in demand? Again, just sketch a graph, and you'll see that a decrease in demand lowers equilibrium price and quantity.

Next question: What happens to equilibrium price and quantity when there's an increase in supply? If your sketch looks like the one in Figure 5, you'll see that an increase in supply leads to a lower equilibrium price and a higher equilibrium quantity.

And finally, how does a decrease in supply affect equilibrium price and quantity? A decrease in supply leads to a higher equilibrium price and a lower equilibrium quantity.

Now let's return to that exam. When you're asked: How does an increase or decrease in demand affect equilibrium price and quantity, what do you do?

You just sketch a graph of a demand and supply curves and then another demand curve representing an increase or decrease in demand. Similarly, if you're asked how an increase or decrease in supply affects equilibrium price and quantity, just draw a sketch. It leads you to the right answers.

Price Ceilings and Price Floors

One of the most popular sayings of all time is "You can't repeal the law of supply and demand." Maybe not, but our government sure has a lot of fun trying. Price floors and price ceilings, which Washington has imposed from time to time, have played havoc with our price system. And taxes on selected goods and services have also altered supply and demand.

What's the difference between a floor and a ceiling? If you're standing in a room, where's the floor and where's the ceiling? As you might expect, economists turn this logic upside down. To find floors, we need to look up. How high? Somewhere above equilibrium price. And where are ceilings? Just where you'd expect economists to place them. We need to look down, somewhere below equilibrium price. A *price floor* is so named because that is the lowest the price is allowed to go in that market. Similarly, a *price ceiling* is the highest price that is allowed in that market.

Figure 8 illustrates a price floor. Equilibrium price would normally be $10, but a price floor of $15 has been established. At $15 businesses are not normally able to sell everything they offer for sale. Quantity supplied is much larger than quantity demanded. Why? At the equilibrium price of $10, sellers are willing to sell less while buyers are willing to buy more.

At a price of $15, there is a surplus of 30 units (quantity demanded is 20 and quantity supplied is 50). The government has created this price floor and surplus to keep the price at a predetermined level. This has been the case for certain agricultural commodities,

> You can't repeal the law of supply and demand.

> Floors and surpluses

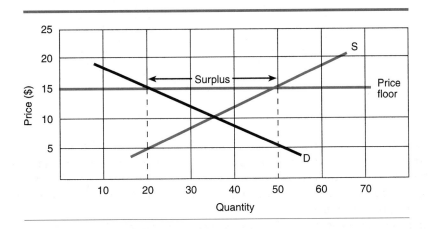

Figure 8

Price Floor and Surplus

The price can go no lower than the floor. The surplus is the amount by which the quantity supplied is greater than the quantity demanded.

Figure 9

Price Ceiling and Shortage

The price can go no higher than the price ceiling. The shortage is the amount by which quantity supplied is greater than quantity demanded.

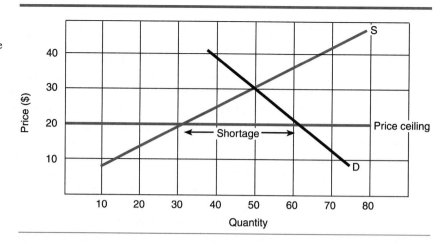

Figure 9

Price Ceiling and Shortage

The price can go no higher than the price ceiling. The shortage is the amount by which quantity supplied is greater than quantity demanded.

most notably wheat and corn. It was hoped that these relatively high prices would encourage family farms to stay in business. That the bulk of farm price support payments has gone to huge corporate farms has not discouraged Congress from allocating billions of dollars a year toward this end.

The way the government keeps price floors in effect is by buying up the surpluses. In the case of Figure 8, the Department of Agriculture would have to buy 30 units.

Another important price floor is the minimum wage. Today the vast majority of Americans are guaranteed a minimum of $5.15 an hour. Thus the wage rate, which is the price of an hour's labor, is, in effect, at least $5.15.

Price ceilings are the mirror image of price floors. An example appears in Figure 9.

Price ceilings are set by the government as a form of price control. "No matter what," the government tells business firms, "don't charge more than this amount."

Ceilings and shortages

A ceiling prevents prices from rising. The last time we had widespread price ceilings was during World War II. Because ceilings cause shortages, a rations system was worked out to enable everyone to obtain their "fair share" of such commodities as butter, meat, and sugar.

I remember World War II. I remember the ration books and the coupons you'd tear out when you went to the store. But chances are, even your parents don't remember the war, with its attendant shortages and rationing.

Ceilings and gas lines

Those over 30 may remember the gas lines we had in 1979, and real old-timers even recall the ones we had back in 1973. If not, imagine waiting a couple of hours in a line of cars six blocks long just to fill up your tank. What was the problem? In 1973 it was the Arab oil embargo, while the crisis in 1979 was set off by the Iranian Revolution.

How shortages are eliminated

In both cases, there was ostensibly an oil shortage. But according to the law of supply and demand, there can't really *be* any shortages. Why not? Because prices will rise. For example, in Figure 9, at a price of $25, there's a shortage. But we know the price will rise to $30 and eliminate that shortage. Why? Who drives it up? The dissatisfied buyers (the people who would rather pay more now than wait) drive it up because they are willing to pay more than $25. Note that as the price rises, the quantity demanded declines, while the quantity supplied rises. When we reach equilibrium price, quantity demanded equals quantity supplied, and the shortage is eliminated.

Now, I left you back in that gas line, and I know you don't want to wait two hours until it's your turn at the pump. Wouldn't you be willing to pay a few cents more if that meant you didn't have to wait? Let's suppose the gas station owner posted a higher price. What would happen? Some people would get out of line. What if he posted a still higher price? Still more people would leave the line. And as gas prices rose, more stations would miraculously open, and the others would stay open longer hours. What would happen to the gas lines? They'd disappear.

Who actually caused the shortage?

So now, let's ask the obvious question: What *really* caused the gasoline shortage? Who was the *real* villain of the piece? You guessed it! It was the federal government, which had set a ceiling on gasoline prices.

Rent Control: The Institution People Love to Hate

I grew up in a rent-controlled apartment and still believe that rent control worked very well at the time it was instituted. Very little new housing had been built during the 1930s because of the Great Depression and during the first half of the 1940s because of World War II. If rents had been allowed to rise to their market value in the late 1940s, my family, and hundreds of thousands— if not millions—of other families would have been forced out of their apartments.

Rent control is an institution that landlords, economists, libertarians, and nearly all good conservatives just love to hate. In fact, about the only folks who still seem to support rent control are the tenants whose rents are below what the market would have set and the politicians who voted for these laws in the first place.

Rent controls establish ceilings for how much rent may be charged for particular apartments and how much, if at all, these rents may be raised each year. The case for rent control is that it keeps down housing costs for the poor and the elderly. Actually, it keeps down housing costs for a lot of middle-class and rich people as well. Because the rent ceiling is established for each apartment regardless of who is living there, an awfully large number of people are paying a lot less than they could afford.

One of the perverse effects of rent control is to reduce vacancy rates. First, those paying low rents are reluctant to move. Second, real estate developers are reluctant to build apartment houses if their rents will be subject to controls. Still another perverse effect has been the large-scale abandonment of apartment buildings, especially in the inner cities, when landlords find that it makes more sense to walk away from their buildings than to continue losing money. These landlords had been squeezed for years by rising maintenance costs and stagnant rent rolls.

Richard Arnott has noted that "Economists have been virtually unanimous in their opposition to rent control." Why? Arnott provides a full list of reasons:

There has been widespread agreement that rent controls discourage new construction, cause abandonment, retard maintenance, reduce mobility, generate mismatch between housing units and tenants, exacerbate discrimination in rental housing, create black markets, encourage the conversion of rental to owner-occupied housing, and generally short-circuit the market mechanism for housing.*

After rent control was imposed in New York City in 1943, many landlords stopped taking care of their buildings and eventually walked away from 500,000 apartments.

Today nearly 200 cities, mostly in New York, New Jersey, and California, have some form of rent control. It is clear that this price ceiling has kept rents well below their equilibrium levels and consequently has resulted in housing shortages.

From a policy standpoint, do we want to eliminate rent controls? Would skyrocketing rents drive even more families into the ranks of the homeless? Perhaps a gradual easing of rent controls and their eventual elimination in, say, 10 or 15 years would send the right message to builders. But because these are local laws, only local governments can repeal them. And because the name of the political game is getting reelected, it is unlikely that many local politicians will find it expedient to repeal these popular laws.

*Richard Arnott, "Time for Revisionism on Rent Control?" *Journal of Economic Perspectives,* Winter 1995, p. 99.

Let's return once more to Figure 9, the scene of the crime. What crime? How could you forget? Our government was caught red-handed, trying to violate the laws of supply and demand.

In Figure 9, when a ceiling of $20 is established, there is a shortage of about 30 units. Had price been allowed to stay at the equilibrium level of $30, there would have been no shortage. However, at this lower price, business firms will sell about 18 units fewer than they'll sell at equilibrium, and consumers will demand about 12 units more. This explains the shortage.

One way the market deals with a shortage is to create what is known as a black market. Products subject to the price ceiling are sold illegally to those willing to pay considerably more. During World War II there was an extensive black market.

Two important price ceilings are rent control laws (see box "Rent Control: The Institution People Love to Hate") and usury laws, which put a ceiling on interest rates. Usury laws go back to biblical times when the prophets debated what, if anything, was a "fair" rate of interest. This same debate was carried on more than two millennia later by Christian scholars. And to this day we ask whether it is "moral" to charge high interest rates.

Usury laws put a ceiling on interest rates.

Price Ceilings, Price Floors, Shortages, and Surpluses

Let's look at Figure 1. See if you can answer these three questions: (1) Is $10 a price ceiling or a price floor? (2) Is there a shortage or a surplus? (3) How much is it?

Figure 1

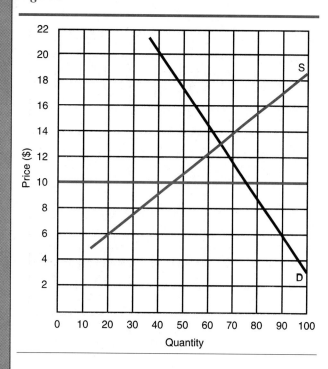

Let's look at Figure 2. We see that the quantity demanded is 75 and the quantity supplied is 45. The shortage is equal to quantity demanded less quantity supplied (75 − 45 = 30).

Figure 2

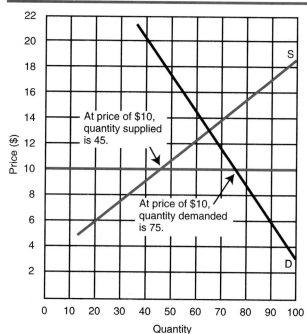

Solution: (1) $10 is a price ceiling because it is below equilibrium price: The ceiling is holding the market price *below* equilibrium price. (2) There is a shortage because quantity demanded is greater than quantity supplied. (3) The shortage is 30.

One dictionary definition of usury is "an unconscionable or exorbitant rate or amount of interest."[1] Many states have usury laws that prohibit banks, savings and loan associations, and certain other financial institutions from charging above specified rates of interest. What effect, if any, do these laws have?

Until the late 1970s interest rates were well below their legal ceilings. But then came double-digit inflation rates; sharply rising interest rates; and, as these interest rates reached their legal ceilings, a full-fledged credit crunch. In other words, these interest rate ceilings created a shortage of loanable funds—which is exactly what one would expect to

[1]*Webster's Collegiate Dictionary,* 10th ed., p. 1302.

Moving right along, answer these three questions with respect to Figure 1. (1) Is $40 a price ceiling or a price floor? (2) Is there a shortage or a surplus? (3) How much is it?

Figure 1

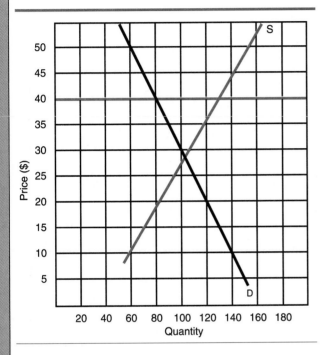

Let's look at Figure 2. We see the quantity supplied is 130 and quantity demanded is 80. The surplus is equal to quantity supplied less quantity demanded (130 − 80 = 50).

Figure 2

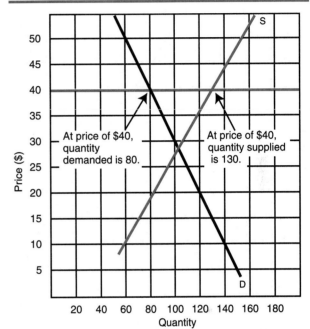

Solution: (1) $40 is a price floor because it is above equilibrium price: The floor is holding market price *above* equilibrium price. (2) There is a surplus because quantity supplied is greater than quantity demanded. (3) The surplus is 50.

happen when a price ceiling is set below the market's equilibrium price. In this case we're talking about the market for loanable funds and their price, the interest rate.

The confusion over the location of price floors and ceilings on the graph may be overcome by considering what the government is doing by establishing them. Normally, price would fall to the equilibrium level, but a price floor keeps price artificially high. Think of a floor holding price above equilibrium; therefore, a price floor would be located above equilibrium price.

By the same logic, a price ceiling is intended to keep price *below* equilibrium. If not for that ceiling, price would rise. Therefore, an effective price ceiling must be located below equilibrium to keep price from rising to that level.

Keep in mind, then, that the normal tendency of prices is to move toward their equilibrium levels. A price ceiling will prevent prices from rising to equilibrium, while a price floor will prevent prices from falling to equilibrium. If you need more information about ceilings, floors, shortages, and surpluses, see the box, "Price Ceilings, Price Floors, Shortages, and Surpluses."

Applications of Supply and Demand

Throughout this book we encounter many applications of supply and demand—so many, in fact, that I'm going to give you a quiz. But it will be an extremely easy quiz. There's just one answer to all these questions. Are you ready?

1. Interest rates are set by_____ .
   Did you answer "supply and demand"? Good.
2. Wage rates are set by _____ .
3. Rents are determined by _____ .
4. The prices of nearly all goods are determined by _____ .
5. The prices of nearly all services are determined by _____ .

Occasionally, however, government intervention interferes with the price mechanism and imposes price floors (or minimums) or price ceilings (or maximums). This gets economists very upset because it not only prevents the most efficient allocation of resources. It also happens to make it much harder to read our supply and demand graphs.

Interest Rate Determination

Let's take a closer look at the determination of the interest rate. I want to state right up front that there is no "interest rate" but rather scores of interest rates, such as mortgage rates, commercial loan rates, and short-term and long-term federal borrowing rates, as well as the interest rates paid by banks, credit unions, and other financial intermediaries. Figure 10 shows a hypothetical demand schedule for loanable funds and a corresponding hypothetical supply schedule.

We can see that $600 billion is lent (or borrowed) at an interest rate of 6 percent. In other words, the market sets the price of borrowed money at an interest rate of 6 percent.

Figure 10
Hypothetical Demand for and Supply of Loanable Funds

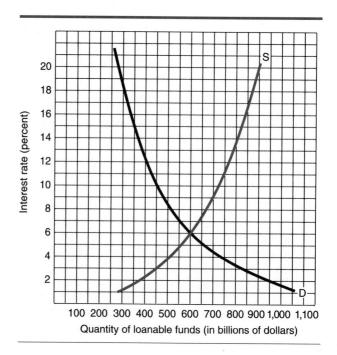

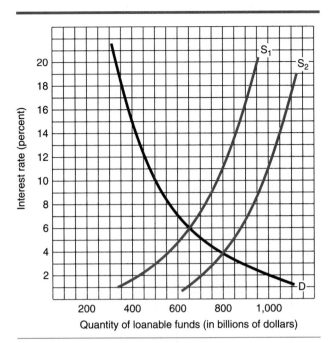

Figure 11
Hypothetical Demand for and
Supply of Loanable Funds

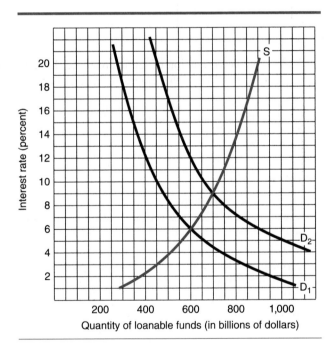

Figure 12
Hypothetical Demand for and
Supply of Loanable Funds

What would happen to the interest rate and to the amount of money borrowed if the supply of loanable funds increased?

Did you figure it out? If you did, then you can confirm your answers by glancing at Figure 11. A rise in the supply of loanable funds leads to a decrease in the interest rate to 4 percent and an increase in the amount of money borrowed to $800 billion.

One more question: What happens to the interest rate and to the amount of money borrowed if the demand for loanable funds rises?

Did you say that the interest rate would rise and the amount of money borrowed would also rise? Good. Then what you must have done was to sketch a graph like the one shown in Figure 12. The interest rate rose to 9 percent, and the amount of money borrowed rose to $700 billion.

College Parking

One of the big complaints on college campuses is the lack of parking spots for students. Which means that, if you get to school after 9 o'clock, you may have to walk a half mile or even more to get to class.

Should parking be free at your school?

Is parking free at your school? Although you may well believe it should be, let's look at the consequences of free parking. The school has set the price of parking at zero. That's a price ceiling of zero. We may conclude that this price ceiling has caused a shortage of available parking spots.

Suppose that the college administration decided to charge $25 a semester to students, faculty members, administrators, and other employees (and eliminated reserved parking as well). Would this fee eliminate the parking shortage? Surely it would cut down on the quantity of parking spots demanded. But if the shortage were not completely eliminated, perhaps a fee of $50 might do the trick. Or even $100. In short, if the price of parking were set high enough, the parking shortage would disappear.

Price-Setting in the Soviet Union

For decades, before the collapse of the Soviet Union in 1989–1991, the prices of nearly all goods and services were set by the government. In fact, they were often set so low that people would wait in long lines for hours for such basic goods as meat, tooth paste, and toilet paper.

The rulers of the Soviet Union may have believed that, as long as the people had bread, they would not rebel. They may have been thinking of the insensitive remark made by Marie Antoinette, the wife of the King of France some two centuries earlier. When told that the people had no bread, Marie Antoinette helped set off the French Revolution by replying, "Let them eat cake." Back in the 1980s the Soviets had the opposite problem. There was so much bread that even the cows were eating it.

The government had decided to keep the price of bread very low so that everyone could afford it, even cows. That's right! Soviet farmers found that it was cheaper to feed their cows bread than hay.

They did this by very heavily subsidizing bread production by devoting a huge amount of resources to it. The price of bread was much lower than the cost of producing it. No private business firm could afford to take this huge loss year after year, but the Soviet rulers were willing to do this to keep the price of bread affordable to all its citizens. Could we say, then, that the price of bread was kept low by a price ceiling? No, it was kept low by a huge subsidy. The government was selling bread at a price that was far below cost.

Here's how the system worked. Farmers shipped their wheat to mills to be ground into flour. From there it went to huge government bakeries where workers baked the flour into bread. A lot of that bread was then sent back to the farms, where it was fed to the cows. But after the breakup of the Soviet Union, the price of bread skyrocketed and the cows had to make do with hay and other less elegant fare.[2] The point is that the Soviet government attempted to dictate the prices of basic goods and services, but this prevented the price system from performing its most important function: rationing.

Low Wages in a High-Tech Economy

Many people earn very high salaries while millions of others earn just the minimum wage of $5.15 an hour.[3] Steven Rattner, a former deputy chairman at the investment banking firm, Lazard Frères, had *this* explanation:

---

[2]See Peter Passell, "Where Communist Economics Fell Short," *New York Times,* December 17, 1989, p. E–3.

[3]The legal minimum hourly wage was $ 5.15 as of March, 2001. When you read this it may have been raised.

First you understand the problem, which is a shift in the demand for labor. There have been huge increases in the demand for skilled labor, so wages have gone up, and falling demand for unskilled labor, so wages have gone down. Once you agree that that's the main problem, then the solution becomes fairly obvious: You have to train people to compete for better jobs, which will also reduce the supply of unskilled workers and force up wages at McDonald's.[4]

In a sense, the price mechanism has failed poor people. Many are working as hard as they can—sometimes working 50 or 60 hours a week—but they are still poor. Rattner's suggestion of training unskilled workers would help *some* of them, but such training programs can be very expensive.

Another possible solution would be to raise the minimum wage rate, but doing so would intervene with the price system by setting a price floor for wages (think of wages as the price of labor). Again, we'll take up *that* issue in the chapter on "Labor Markets and Wage Rates" in *Economics* and *Microeconomics*.

The Rationing Function of the Price System

If gasoline went up to $3 a gallon, would you cut back on your driving? Maybe you would try to do all your shopping in one trip instead of in two or three. And if gasoline went still higher, maybe you would even agree to join a car pool.

The price system is constantly sending buyers and sellers thousands of signals. The price of *this* service has gone through the roof. *That* product is on sale. *This* good is over-priced and *that* one is a bargain. When something becomes very expensive, we generally cut back. We do this not because the government ordered us to do so or because it issued ration coupons entitling everyone to only three gallons a week, but because the price system itself performed this rationing function.

At the beginning of Chapter 2, I defined economics as *the efficient allocation of the scarce means of production toward the satisfaction of human wants.* In a free-market, private-enterprise economy such as ours, we depend on the price mechanism, or the forces of supply and demand, to perform that job.

In the next chapter, we'll see how the price mechanism plays the central role in allocating resources under capitalism. The forces of demand and supply operate as an automatic guidance system that enables our economy, and others like it, to provide consumers with an endless stream of goods and services.

---

[4]See James Fallows, "The Invisible Poor," *The New York Times Magazine,* March 19, 2000, p. 112.

Questions for Further Thought and Discussion

1. **a.** If market price is above equilibrium price, explain what happens and why.
   b. If market price is below equilibrium price, explain what happens and why.

2. **a.** As the price of theater tickets rises, what happens to the quantity of tickets that people are willing to buy? Explain your answer.
   b. As the price of theater tickets rises, explain what happens to the quantity of tickets that people are willing to sell. Explain your answer.

3. Where is a price ceiling with respect to equilibrium price? What will be the relative size of quantity demanded and quantity supplied?

4. How is equilibrium price affected by changes in (*a*) demand and (*b*) supply?

5. What are the two ways to depict a demand schedule? Make up a demand schedule for some good or service you often buy.

6. What is equilibrium? Why is it advantageous for the market price to be at equilibrium?

7. If you were a landlord, why would you be against rent control?

8. Explain the difference between (*a*) demand and quantity demanded and (*b*) supply and quantity supplied.

Workbook for Chapter 3

Name _____ Date _____

Multiple-Choice Questions

Circle the letter that corresponds to the best answer.

1. When demand rises and supply stays the same, _____.

   a) equilibrium quantity rises

   b) equilibrium quantity declines

   c) equilibrium quantity stays the same

2. When supply rises and demand stays the same, _____.

   a) equilibrium quantity rises

   b) equilibrium quantity falls

   c) equilibrium quantity stays the same

3. At equilibrium price, quantity demanded is _____.

   a) greater than quantity supplied

   b) equal to quantity supplied

   c) smaller than quantity supplied

4. When quantity demanded is greater than quantity supplied, _____.

   a) market price will rise

   b) market price will fall

   c) market price will stay the same

5. What happens to quantity supplied when price is lowered?

   a) It rises

   b) It falls

   c) It stays the same

   d) It cannot be determined if it rises, falls, or stays the same

6. What happens to quantity demanded when price is raised?

   a) It rises

   b) It falls

   c) It stays the same

   d) It cannot be determined if it rises, falls, or stays the same

7. When market price is above equilibrium price, _____.

   a) market price will rise

   b) equilibrium price will rise

   c) market price will fall

   d) equilibrium price will fall

8. At equilibrium, quantity demanded is _____ equal to quantity supplied.

   a) sometimes

   b) always

   c) never

9. Market price _____ equilibrium price.

   a) must always be equal to

   b) must always be above

   c) must always be below

   d) may be equal to

10. A demand schedule is determined by the wishes of _____.

   a) sellers

   b) buyers

   c) buyers and sellers

   d) neither sellers nor buyers

11. In Figure 1, if market price were $110, there would be _____.

    a) a shortage

    b) a surplus

    c) neither a shortage nor a surplus

12. In Figure 1, if market price were $140, there would be _____.

    a) a shortage

    b) a surplus

    c) neither a shortage nor a surplus

Figure 1

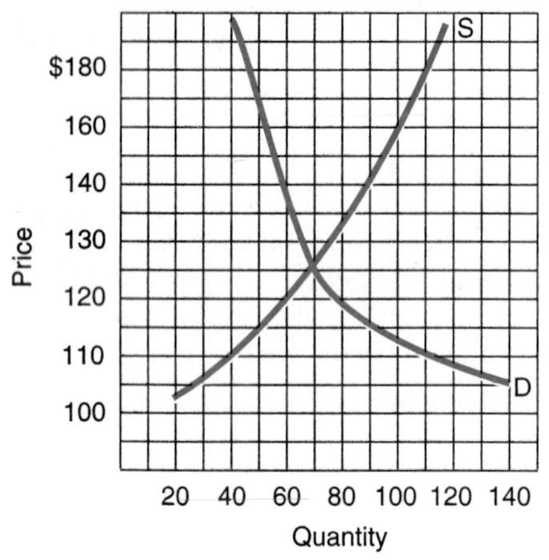

13. Market price may not reach equilibrium if there are _____.

    a) both price ceilings and price floors

    b) neither price ceilings nor price floors

    c) only price ceilings

    d) only price floors

14. Gas lines in the 1970s were caused by _____.

    a) price floors

    b) price ceilings

    c) both price floors and price ceilings

    d) neither price floors nor price ceilings

15. Statement 1: Price ceilings cause shortages.

    Statement 2: Interest rates are set by supply and demand, but wage rates are not.

    a) Statement 1 is true and statement 2 is false.

    b) Statement 2 is true and statement 1 is false.

    c) Both statements are true.

    d) Both statements are false.

16. If the equilibrium price of corn is 30 cents an ear, and the government imposes a floor of 40 cents an ear, the price of corn will _____.

    a) increase to 40 cents

    b) remain at 30 cents

    c) rise to about 35 cents

    d) be impossible to determine

17. Usury laws tend to _____.

    a) create a shortage of loanable funds

    b) create a surplus of loanable funds

    c) make it easier to obtain credit

    d) have no effect on the amount of loanable funds available

18. If the price system is allowed to function without interference and a shortage occurs, quantity demanded will _____ and quantity supplied will _____ as the price rises to its equilibrium level.

    a) rise, rise   b) fall, fall

    c) rise, fall   d) fall, rise

19. Which statement is true?

    a) A price floor is above equilibrium price and causes surpluses.

    b) A price floor is above equilibrium price and causes shortages.

    c) A price floor is below equilibrium price and causes surpluses.

    d) A price floor is below equilibrium price and causes shortages.

20. An increase in supply while demand remains unchanged will lead to _____.
   a) an increase in equilibrium price and a decrease in equilibrium quantity
   b) a decrease in equilibrium price and a decrease in equilibrium quantity
   c) an increase in equilibrium price and an increase in equilibrium quantity
   d) a decrease in equilibrium price and an increase in equilibrium quantity

21. A decrease in demand while supply remains unchanged will lead to _____.
   a) an increase in equilibrium price and quantity
   b) a decrease in equilibrium price and quantity
   c) an increase in equilibrium price and a decrease in equilibrium quantity
   d) a decrease in equilibrium price and an increase in equilibrium quantity

22. As price rises, _____.
   a) quantity demanded and quantity supplied both rise
   b) quantity demanded and quantity supplied both fall
   c) quantity demanded rises and quantity supplied falls
   d) quantity demanded falls and quantity supplied rises

23. When quantity demanded is greater than quantity supplied, there _____.
   a) is a shortage
   b) is a surplus
   c) may be either a shortage or a surplus
   d) may be neither a shortage nor a surplus

24. When quantity supplied is greater than quantity demanded _____.
   a) price will fall to its equilibrium level
   b) price will rise to its equilibrium level
   c) price may rise, fall, or stay the same, depending on a variety of factors

Use Figure 2 to answer questions 25 and 26.

Figure 2

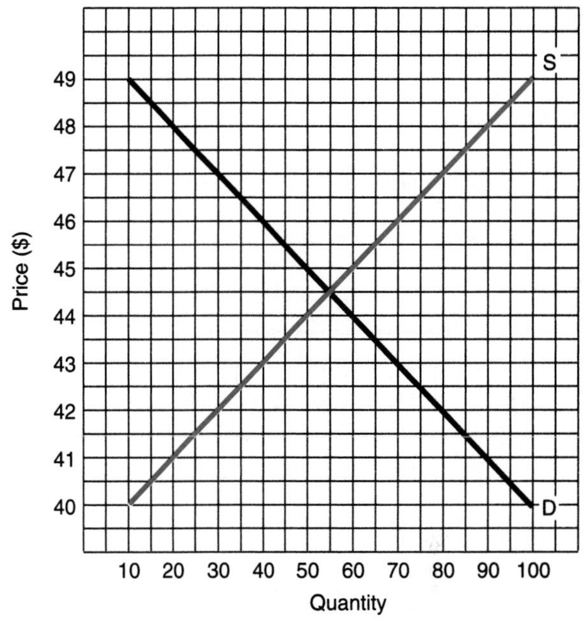

25. At a market price of $47, there is _____.
   a) a shortage
   b) a surplus
   c) both a shortage and a surplus
   d) neither a shortage nor a surplus

26. At a market price of $42, there is _____.
   a) a shortage
   b) a surplus
   c) both a shortage and a surplus
   d) neither a shortage nor a surplus

Fill-In Questions

1. If demand falls and supply stays the same, equilibrium price will _____, and equilibrium quantity will

   _____.

2. If supply rises and demand stays the same, equilibrium price will _____, and equilibrium quantity will

   _____ .

3. If quantity supplied were greater than quantity demanded, market price would _____ .

4. Equilibrium price is always determined

   by _____ and _____ .

5. As price is lowered, quantity supplied_____ .

6. Shortages are associated with price _____;

   surpluses are associated with price _____ .

7. If supply falls and demand remains the same, equilibrium price will _____, and equilibrium quantity will _____ .

8. Price floors and price ceilings are set by _____ .

9. Interest rates are set by _____

   _____ and _____ .

10. What happens to interest rates when the demand for money rises?_____

11. When the supply of money falls, interest rates

   _____ .

Use Figure 3 to answer questions 12 through 15.

Figure 3

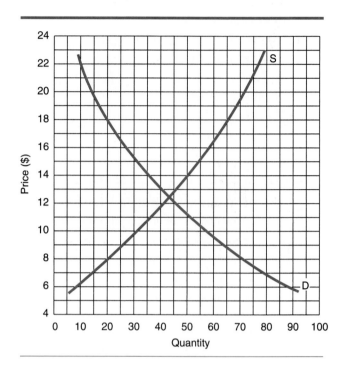

12. Equilibrium price is about $_____ .

13. Equilibrium quantity is about _____ .

14. If price were $20, there would be a (shortage or surplus) _____ of _____ units of quantity.

15. If price were $8, there would be a (shortage or surplus) _____ of _____ units of quantity.

16. Price floors keep prices _____ equilibrium price; price ceilings keep prices _____ equilibrium price.

Problems

1. In Figure 4, find equilibrium price and quantity.
2. Draw in a new demand curve, D_1, on Figure 4, showing an increase in demand. What happens to equilibrium price and quantity?

Figure 4

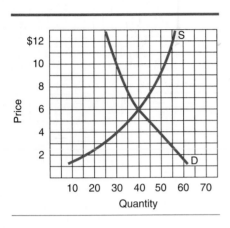

3. In Figure 5, find equilibrium price and quantity.
4. Draw in a new supply curve, S_1, on Figure 5, showing a decrease in supply. What happens to equilibrium price and quantity?

Figure 5

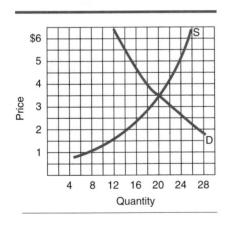

5. a) In Figure 6, if the demand curve is D_1, how much are equilibrium price and quantity? b) If demand changes from D_1 to D_2, does that represent an increase or decrease in demand? c) How much are the new equilibrium price and quantity?

Figure 6

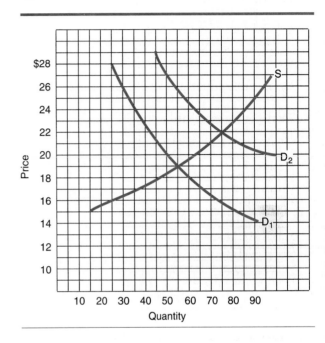

6. a) In Figure 7, if the supply curve is S_1, how much are equilibrium price and quantity? b) If the supply changes from S_1 to S_2, does that represent an increase or decrease in supply? c) How much are the new equilibrium price and quantity?

7. Given the information in Figure 8: a) Is $12 a price ceiling or a price floor? b) Is there a shortage or a surplus? c) How much is it (in units of quantity)?

Figure 7

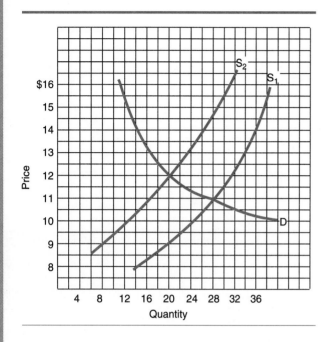

Figure 8

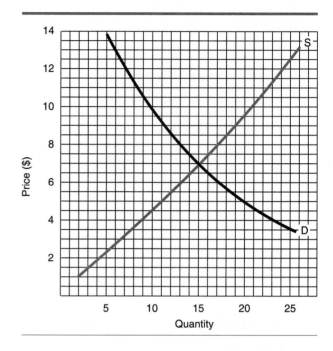

8. Given the information in Figure 9: a) Is $16 a price ceiling or a price floor? b) Is there a shortage or a surplus? c) How much is it (in units of quantity)?

Figure 9

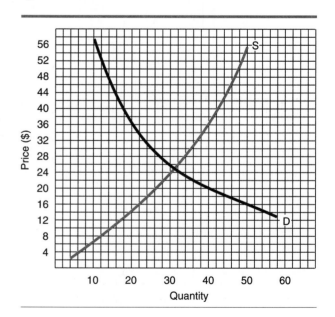

Chapter 4

The Mixed Economy

Ours is a mixed economy because there is a private sector and a public sector. Close to 90 percent of our goods and services originate in the private sector, although the government co-opts some of this production for its own use. China also has a mixed economy, although the public sector produces the large majority of goods and services. As we shall see, the Chinese are, to some degree, lackeys of the capitalists while Americans are, to some degree, running dogs of the communists.

CHAPTER OBJECTIVES

In this chapter we'll cover:

- The three questions of economics.
- The concepts of the profit motive, the price mechanism, competition, and capital.
- The circular flow model.
- Market failure and externalities.

- The economic role of capital.
- Specialization and its consequences.
- The "isms": capitalism, fascism, communism, and socialism.
- The decline and fall of the communist system.

The Three Questions of Economics

Because every country in the world is faced with scarce (limited) resources, every country must answer three questions: (1) What shall we produce? (2) How shall these goods be produced? (3) For whom shall the goods be produced? We'll take up each in turn.

What Shall We Produce?

What shall we produce?

In the United States, most of our production is geared toward consumer goods. More than 3 percent goes toward military goods. In the former Soviet Union, a much higher proportion was devoted to armaments, with a proportionately smaller percentage devoted to consumer goods. Japan has concentrated on building up its plant and equipment but devotes just 1 percent of its production to military goods.

Who makes these decisions? In the United States and Japan, there is no central planning authority but rather a hodgepodge of corporate and government officials, as well as individual consumers and taxpayers. The Soviets, as you probably guessed, *did* have a central planning authority. In fact, every five years the Soviet government used to come up with a new plan that set goals for its economy in numbers of cars, TVs, factories, and bushels of wheat and corn to be produced.

The resulting shortage of consumer goods was a perennial source of jokes in the former Soviet Union. One that was making the rounds a few years ago went like this:

A man walks into a store and asks the manager, "Is this the store that has no meat?"

"No," the manager replies. "This is *not* the store that has no meat."

"What store *is* this, then?"

"This is the store that has no fish. The store that has no meat is around the corner."

Shortages of consumer goods generally mean long lines, even when there is only a rumor that a shipment has arrived. In a *New York Times* article about his experiences while living in the Soviet Union, Marc Greenfield told this anecdote:

On a bus one summer day, I overheard this conversation between two women, one of them with a pair of Austrian boots:

"Did you have to stand long?"

"Not very. Only overnight."

"Overnight! You call that not long?"

"It's worse in winter, when you have to sleep in the doorways. This time it was fine. It was warm."

"Do they fit?"

"No; two sizes too big. But I wasn't going to stand in line for nothing."[1]

Here's another one:

A man goes into a Leningrad car dealership and orders a new car. The salesman tells him that the car will be delivered to him on June 15, 2009.

"Morning or afternoon?"

"What difference could it possibly make?" asks the salesman.

"Well, on the morning of June 15, 2009, the plumber is coming to fix the toilet."

How Shall These Goods Be Produced?

How shall these goods be produced?

In our country—and in most others as well—nearly everything is produced by private businesses. Not only are all the goods and services that consumers purchase produced by businesses, but so are most of what the government purchases. For example, when our astronauts landed on the moon, a long list of contractors and subcontractors was released. It read like a who's who in American corporations.

In socialist countries, of course, the government is the main producer of goods and services. But even in the most strictly communist country, China, there is still a substantial role for private enterprise.

---

[1] Marc Greenfield, "Life among the Russians," *New York Times,* sect. 6, October 24, 1982, p. 96.

For Whom Shall the Goods Be Produced?

For whom shall the goods be produced?

Economics may be divided into two parts: production, which we dealt with in the first two questions, and distribution. In the first question, we asked what the economic pie should be made of; in the second, we talked about how the pie would be made. Now we are ready to divide up the pie.

Our distribution system is a modified version of one dollar, one vote. In general, the more money you have, the more you can buy. But the government also has a claim to part of the pie. Theoretically, the government takes from those who can afford to give up part of their share (taxes), spends some of those tax dollars to produce various government goods and services, and gives the rest to the old, the sick, and the poor. (Nevertheless, the rich reap a major share of the subsidies to airlines, shipping companies, defense contractors, and agriculture.)

In theory, the Soviets' distributive system was diametrically opposed to ours. The communist credo "From each according to his ability, to each according to his needs" was something the Soviet leaders claimed to follow, and it does have a nice ring to it. But in actuality, their income distribution system, with its jerry-built structure of wage incentives, bonus payments, and special privileges, was probably no more equitable than our own.

Henry Fairlie has come up with a capitalist credo: From each according to his gullibility. To each according to his greed.

This point is illustrated by a story about Leonid Brezhnev. His mother visited him at the Kremlin just after he took power in the mid-1960s. He wanted to show off, so he told her how well he was living, but she didn't say anything. He showed her his magnificent quarters, but she didn't seem very impressed. He took her for a ride out to his country estate. Still, nothing. No reaction. He couldn't understand how his aged mother, a woman of humble peasant origin, could fail to be impressed with how well her son was doing. So finally he blurted out, "Babushka![2] Tell me! What do you think?" "Leonid," the old lady replied, "what if the communists come back?"

The Invisible Hand, the Price Mechanism, and Perfect Competition

We have just set the stage for a comparison between our economic system and those of several other countries. We'll start with the competitive economic model, which is based on the law of supply and demand, then talk about the economic roles of government and of capital, and then discuss specialization. These concepts, common to all economies, need to be understood before we can make comparisons among the economies of different nations.

Back in the 1950s, there was a popular song that went:

Love and marriage
Love and marriage
Go together like a horse and carriage
Dad was told by mother
You can't have one without the other.

Just as love and marriage go together, so do the invisible hand, the price mechanism, and perfect competition.[3] Maybe a little less catchy than the words to a popular song, it admittedly has a beat; most economists kind of like to dance to it.

---

[2]*Babushka* is an affectionate term that is roughly translated as "little grandmother." It really sounds much better in Russian, and it's OK to address an old peasant woman, not necessarily your grandmother, in this manner.

[3]Perfect competition is the topic of Chapter 22 in *Economics* and Chapter 10 in *Microeconomics.* It exists only in industries in which there are many firms selling an identical product, where there are no legal, technical, or economic barriers keeping new firms from entering the industry.

And like love and marriage, the invisible hand, the price mechanism, and perfect competition really do go together like a horse and carriage. In fact, you never can have one without the others.

The Invisible Hand

Some students go through their entire principles of economics course believing that the invisible hand is something that once grabbed them in a dark movie theater. But when Adam Smith coined the term, he was actually thinking about some kind of economic guidance system that always made everything come out all right.

In fact, he believed that if people set out to promote the public interest, they will not do nearly as much good as they would if they pursued their own selfish interests. That's right! If all people are out for themselves, everyone will work harder, produce more, and we'll all be the richer for it. And that premise underlies the free-enterprise system.

Smith said that the entrepreneur is motivated by self-interest:

> He generally, indeed, neither intends to promote the public interest, nor knows how much he is promoting it. By preferring the support of domestic to that of foreign industry, he intends only his own gain, and he is in this, as in many other cases, led by an invisible hand to promote an end which was no part of his intention. . . . By pursuing his own interest he frequently promotes that of the society more effectually than when he really intends to promote it.[4]

Whenever a businessperson runs for public office, he or she invariably brings up the fact that his or her opponent never met a payroll. This businessperson, motivated solely by a quest for profits, provided jobs for perhaps hundreds, or even thousands, of people. His or her firm produced some good or service so desirable that buyers were willing to pay for it. And so, this aspiring politician, who went into business solely to make money, now claims credit for creating jobs and promoting the public interest. And not a word of thanks to the invisible hand.

President Ronald Reagan was long a believer in supply-side economics, which placed great faith in the workings of the free-enterprise system. Supply-side economics is aimed at providing people with tax-cut incentives to work, save, and invest. Instead of appealing to their sense of patriotism, supply-side economics appeals to their self-interest by letting them keep more of their earnings. One might add, parenthetically, that if all people wanted to do good, we might not have needed such strong incentives.

Perhaps the central axiom of supply-side economics is that the government's economic role has been too big. Ideally, if we reduce that role, individuals will take up the slack by performing charitable or public-spirited acts on a voluntary basis. Unfortunately, however, the response of our economy during the Reagan years was somewhat underwhelming.[5]

Less than 15 years ago, about one-third of the food in the Soviet Union was produced on just 2 percent of the land under cultivation. That 2 percent was made up of small, privately owned plots; the other 98 percent was in the form of large collective farms. Obviously, the same farmers worked much harder on their own land than on the land whose produce was owned by the entire society. As Adam Smith said, a person pursuing his own interest "frequently promotes that of society more effectively than when he really intends to promote it."

The invisible hand, then, is really the profit motive or, more broadly, economic self-interest, that guides us. It motivates us to do good by helping us do well.

Adam Smith, Scottish professor of philosophy (Historical Pictures/Stock Montage)

The invisible hand is really the profit motive.

---

[4]Adam Smith, *The Wealth of Nations,* Book IV (London: Methuen, 1950), chap. II, pp. 477–78.

[5]Supply-side economics and four other economic policy schools are covered in Chapter 14 of *Economics* and *Macroeconomics.* Three major accomplishments of the Reagan years were sharply reduced rates of inflation and interest and the longest peacetime economic expansion on record.

The Price Mechanism[6]

It is often said that everyone has a price, which means that nearly all of us, for a certain sum of money, would do some pretty nasty things. The key variable here is *price*. Some of us would do these nasty things for $100, others for $1,000, others perhaps only for $1 million.

Not only does everyone have a price, but everything has a price as well. The price of a slice of pizza or a gallon of gasoline is known to all consumers. Although they vary somewhat, gas prices rarely fall below a dollar, and hardly anyone would pay $5 for a slice of pizza.

Just as prices send signals to consumers, they also signal producers or sellers. If pizza goes up to $5 a slice, I'll put an oven in my living room and open for business the next day.

Prices send signals to producers and consumers.

The price system, which we examined in Chapter 3, is based on the law of supply and demand. When the sugar supply was curtailed about a dozen years ago, prices soared. And when people began driving less and the economy was in a recession, gasoline prices dropped in early 1982.[7]

When consumers want more of a certain good or service, they drive the price up, which, in turn, signals producers to produce more. If the price rise is substantial and appears permanent, new firms will be attracted to the industry, thereby raising output still further.

During the 1970s, when we experienced some of the worst inflation in our history, many people called for price controls. These were very briefly and halfheartedly instituted by President Nixon, and their results in controlling inflation were decidedly mixed. Critics of controls believe they interfere with our price mechanism and the signals that mechanism sends to producers and consumers. Others, most notably John Kenneth Galbraith, have argued that the prices of our major products are administered or set by the nation's largest corporations rather than in the marketplace. What this disagreement boils down to is whether our economic system is basically competitive, with millions of buyers and sellers interacting in the marketplace, or whether our economy is dominated by a handful of corporate giants who have subverted the price system by setting prices themselves.

Competition[8]

What is competition? Is it the rivalry between Chase and Citibank? GM and Ford? Most economists will tell you that to have real competition, you need many firms in an industry. How many? So many that no firm is large enough to have any influence over price. Thus, by definition, an industry with many firms is competitive.

Competition makes the price system work.

When GM or Ford announces its new prices, *those* are the prices for American cars. When Bank of America, Chase, Citibank, or any of the other six or eight leading banks announces the new prime lending rate, *that* is the benchmark interest rate on which nearly every loan will be based.[9] No ifs, ands, or buts. No give-and-take in the marketplace. And the price mechanism? It just doesn't apply here.

To allow the price mechanism to work, we need many competing firms in each industry. Would seven or eight U.S. auto firms be considered many? Or the dozen oil firms that refine over half the oil sold in the American market? Surely some among a

---

[6]By the way, economists sometimes refer to the price system as the price mechanism. What's the difference between these two terms? There is none. To avoid confusion, I'll try to use just the price system from now on.

[7]Not only did demand for gasoline fall in the early 1980s, but a glut of oil developed in the world market. Price declines may result, then, from declines in demand, increases in supply, or some combination of the two.

[8]I use the terms *competition* and *perfect competition* interchangeably. We won't define perfect competition until later, but, for now, let's go with the definition given in the first paragraph of this section.

[9]This is not to say that the nation's leading banks are free to set the prime at 50 percent or, for that matter, at 5 percent. However, within parameters set by credit market conditions—monetary policy, credit demand, availability of funds, and inflation—the banks are free to set the prime rate.

handful of companies can influence price. Although there's no clear dividing line, probably most economists would consider the automobile industry at least somewhat competitive if there were 15 or 20 firms. And if there were about double the number of oil companies, that industry would also have a considerable degree of competition.

If large sectors of American industry are not very competitive, then the price system doesn't work all that well, and the invisible hand becomes even more invisible. However, even without a perfectly competitive economic system, we can't just toss the price mechanism out the window. The forces of supply and demand, however distorted, are still operating. With all their price manipulation, even the largest corporations must guide themselves by the wishes of their consumers. In conclusion, then, let's just say that we have an imperfectly functioning price system in a less than competitive economy that is guided by a not too vigorous invisible hand.

Equity and Efficiency

Under our economic system, most of the important decisions are made in the marketplace. The forces of supply and demand (that is, the price system) determine the answers to the three basic questions we raised at the beginning of the chapter: What? How? And for whom? Most economists would agree that this system leads to a very efficient allocation of resources, which, incidentally, happens to conform to our definition of economics: *Economics is the efficient allocation of the scarce means of production toward the satisfaction of human wants.*

Is our income distributed fairly?

So far, so good. But does our system lead to a fair, or equitable, distribution of income? Just look around you. You don't have to look far to see homeless people, street beggars, shopping-bag ladies, and derelicts. Indeed, there are about 33 million Americans whom the federal government has officially classified as "poor." Later in this chapter, we'll see that one of the basic functions of our government is to transfer some income from the rich and the middle class to the poor. Under the capitalist system, there are huge differences in income, with some people living in mansions and others in the streets. One of the most controversial political issues of our time is how far the government should go in redistributing some of society's income to the poor.

Very briefly, the case for efficiency is to have the government stand back and allow everyone to work hard, earn a lot of money, and keep nearly all of it. But what about the people who don't or can't work hard, and what about their children? Do we let them starve to death? The case for equity is to tax away some of the money earned by the rich and the middle class and redistribute it to the poor. But doing so raises two questions: (1) How much money should we redistribute? and (2) Won't this "handout" just discourage the poor from working? We'll discuss this further in the chapter on Income Distribution and Poverty toward the end of the book.

The Circular Flow Model

In Chapter 2 we talked about the four basic resources—land, labor, capital, and entrepreneurial ability. Who owns these resources? We all do. Nearly all of us sell our labor, for which we earn wages or salaries. In addition, many people own land or buildings for which they receive rent. A landlord may have just one tenant paying a few hundred dollars a month, or he or she may own an office building whose rent is reckoned by the square foot.

We also may receive interest payments for the use of our funds. Since most of the money we put into the bank is borrowed by businesses to invest in plant and equipment, we say that interest is a return on capital.

Finally, there are profits. Those who perform an entrepreneurial function (that is, own a business) receive profits for income.

The question we are asking here is, What do people do with their incomes? What

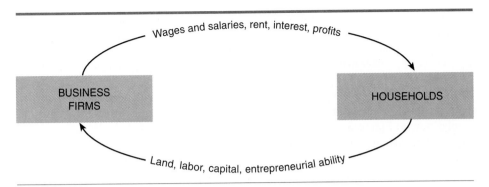

F*igure* 1

The Flow of Resources and Payments for Them

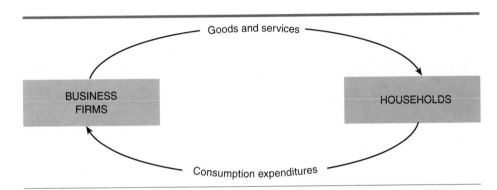

F*igure* 2

The Flow of Goods and Services, and Payments for Them

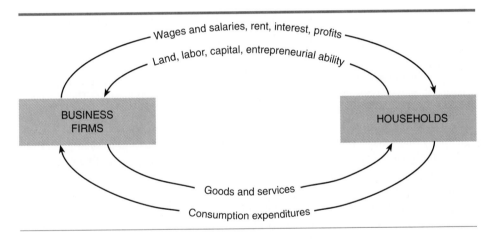

F*igure* 3

The Circular Flow

happens to the tremendous accumulation of rent, wages and salaries, interest, and profit? Mostly, it is spent on consumer goods and services, which are produced by private businesses.

This is the essence of what economists call the *circular flow model*. A model is usually a smaller, simplified version of the real thing. (Think of a model plane or a model ship.) An economic model shows us how our economy functions, tracing the flow of money, resources, and goods and services. Let's take the circular flow model step by step.

First we have some 104 million households receiving their incomes mainly from the business sector. A household may be a conventional family—a father, mother, and a couple of children—it may be a person living alone, or it may be two cohabiting adults. Any combination of people under one roof—you name it—is defined as a household.

We diagram the household's income stream in Figure 1. Businesses send money income (rent, wages and salaries, interest, and profits) to households. We've ignored the government sector (that is, Social Security checks, welfare benefits, food stamps).

Who owns our resources? It is not the employer who pays wages—he only handles the money. It is the product that pays wages.

—Henry Ford

In Figure 2 we show where this money goes. It goes right back to the businesses as payment for all the goods and services that households buy. In sum, the households provide business with resources—land, labor, capital, and entrepreneurial ability—and use the income these resources earn to buy the goods and services produced by these same resources.

In effect, then, we have a circular flow of resources, income, goods and services, and payments for these goods and services. By combining Figures 1 and 2, we show this circular flow in Figure 3.

There are two circular flows.

We can distinguish two circular flows in Figure 3. In the inner circle, we have resources (land, labor, capital, and entrepreneurial ability) flowing from households to business firms. The business firms transform these resources into goods and services, which then flow to the households.

The outer circular flow is composed of money. Households receive wages and salaries, rent, interest, and profits from business firms. This money is spent on goods and services, so it is sent back to business firms in the form of consumer expenditures.

Thus we have two circular flows: (1) money and (2) resources, and goods and services. These two flows represent the economic activities of the private sector. Whenever any transaction takes place, someone pays for it, which is exactly what *does* happen whenever we do business.[10]

Although the ciruclar flow model may appear fairly complex, it actually oversimplifies the exchanges in our economy by excluding imports, exports, and the government sector. I leave it to your imagination to picture the additional flow of taxes, government purchases, and transfer payments such as unemployment and Social Security benefits. We shall now look at the government's economic role, but our analysis will be separate from our analysis of the private sector.

The Economic Role of Government

The government under our federal system has three distinct tiers. At the top is the federal, or national, government, which we generally refer to as "the government." There are also 50 state governments and tens of thousands of local governments.

Each of these units of government collects taxes, provides services, and issues regulations that have a profound effect on our economy. By taxing, spending, and regulating, the government is able somewhat to alter the outcome of the three questions: What? How? and For whom?

The government provides the legal system under which our free enterprise economy can operate. It provides for the enforcement of business contracts and defines the rights of private ownership. Our legal system works so well that bribery is the very rare exception, rather than the rule, as it is in so many other countries, especially many in Asia and Africa.

Everyone wants to live at the expense of the state. They forget that the state lives at the expense of everyone.
—Frederic Bastiat

The government also maintains our competitive system and ensures the relatively unfettered operation of the law of supply and demand. Barriers to competition are sometimes broken down by the government, particularly when a few large firms attempt to squeeze their smaller competitors out of a market. We'll discuss those efforts more fully in the chapter on corporate mergers and antitrust in *Economics* and in *Microeconomics*.

Some of what we produce is done in response to government demand for roads, schools, courthouses, stamp pads, and missile systems. Government regulations have prevented business firms from producing heroin, cyclamates (from the mid-1960s to the late 1970s), and alcoholic beverages (from 1920 to 1933), as well as prostitutes' services (except in part of the state of Nevada, where they are legal).

How things are produced is also influenced by child labor laws, health and safety regulations, and pollution control. And finally, the government, by taking over $1.5 trillion

---

[10]Resource markets and the determination of rent, interest, wages, and profits are fully discussed in later chapters of *Economics* and *Microeconomics*.

away from wage earners in taxes, redistributes some of these funds to the old and the poor, thus strongly altering the outcome of the question "For whom?"

The size of our government depends largely on how well private enterprise does the job of efficiently allocating our resources. In the next section, we'll see that our price system does not always work perfectly, so the government is called on to fix problems.

Market Failure

If our price system worked perfectly, there would be no such thing as market failure, and you wouldn't need to read these next couple of pages. *When our resources are not allocated efficiently, we have market failure.*

We'll examine two basic classes of market failure: externalities and public goods. Both provide the government with the opportunity to improve on the work of Adam Smith's invisible hand. Another cause of market failure, monopoly, is the subject of a later chapter in *Economics* and *Microeconomics*.

Externalities

When you drive to school, how much does your ride cost you? Once you figure in the cost of gas, oil, and the depreciation on your car, you might come up with a figure of, say, 25 cents a mile. We call that 25 cents the *private cost* of driving to school.

But there's also an *external cost.* You cause a certain amount of pollution and congestion, and we could even factor in the cost of highway construction and maintenance. It would be hard to actually come up with a monetary figure, but there is no question that your drive to school imposes a definite social, or external, cost on society.

You probably never thought that driving to school was such a terrible thing, especially if there is no convenient public transportation. But you will be happy to know that you are capable of doing many socially beneficial things as well. If you paint your house and plant a beautiful garden in your front yard, you will not only add to the beauty of your neighborhood, but you will also enhance its property values. So now you will provide an *external benefit.*

Let's define *external cost* and *external benefit. An external cost occurs when the production or consumption of some good or service inflicts costs on a third party without compensation. An external benefit occurs when some of the benefits derived from the production or consumption of some good or service are enjoyed by a third party.*

The private market, governed solely by the forces of supply and demand, does not take into account external costs and external benefits. This is market failure. When the market failure imposes a high cost on society, we demand that the government do something about it.

Basically, the government can take three types of action. If you are doing something that provides an external benefit, such as running a family farm, the government may provide you with a subsidy to encourage you to continue farming. As we saw back in Chapter 1, although the federal government has paid out hundreds of billions of dollars in farm subsidies since World War II, not only have most family farms disappeared, but huge corporate farms have gotten most of the subsidies.

If you are incurring external costs, the government can discourage these activities in two ways. It can tax you, or it can impose stringent regulations.

Let's consider what the government can do about air and water pollution. It could tax these activities highly enough to discourage them. A hefty tax on air pollution will force the biggest offenders to install pollution-abatement equipment. What about the disposal of nuclear waste? Do we let nuclear power plants dump it into nearby rivers but make them pay high taxes for the privilege? Hardly. The federal government heavily regulates nuclear plants.

Basically, we want to encourage activities that provide external benefits and discourage those that incur external costs. One method now used in many states is the

External cost

External benefit
Definition of external cost and benefit

Shipbreaking

When ships grow too old and expensive to run—usually after about 25 or 30 years—their owners sell them on the international scrap market, where the typical freighter may bring a million dollars for the weight of its steel. Are the ship owners behaving in an environmentally correct manner, like those of us who return our soda cans to the grocery or deposit them in recycling bins? It turns out that they are not.

About 90 percent of the world's annual crop of 700 condemned ships are sailed right up on the beaches of Pakistan, India, and Bangladesh, where they are dismantled. Predictably, these once pristine beaches have become an environmental wasteland. In an *Atlantic Monthly* article, William Langewiesche described the risks to which the workers were exposed: "falls, fires, explosions, and exposure to a variety of poisons from fuel oil, lubricants, paints, wiring, insulation, and cargo slop. Many workers are killed every year."[*]

What the United States and other industrial nations have done is exported our environmental problems to the less developed countries of the world. Langewiesche explained how this came about:

> Shipbreaking was performed with cranes and heavy equipment at salvage docks by the big shipyards of the United States and Europe until the 1970s, when labor costs and environmental regulations drove most of the business to the docksides of Korea and Taiwan. Eventually, however, even these entrepreneurial countries started losing interest in the business and gradually decided they had better uses for their shipyards. This meant that the world's shipbreaking business was again up for grabs. In the 1980s enterprising businessmen in India, Bangladesh, and Pakistan seized the initiative with a simple, transforming idea: to break a ship they did not need expensive docks and tools; they could just wreck the thing— drive the ship up onto a beach as they might a fishing boat, and tear it apart by hand.[†]

*William Langewiesche, "The Shipbreakers," *The Atlantic Monthly,* August 2000, p. 34.

†*Ibid.*, p. 33.

five-cent deposit on cans and bottles. Millions of people have a monetary incentive to do the right thing by returning these bottles and cans for recycling.

A major part of the external costs of manufacturing and commerce affect our environment. Obvious examples include strips of tires along the highways, abandoned cars, acid rain, and toxic waste. The accompanying box discusses an international example of external costs—shipbreaking.

An activity that depletes a commonly held resource—for example, mining, cutting lumber, or fishing—involves significant negative externalities. With respect to fishing, if it is excessive, the fish will be unable to reproduce sufficiently to maintain their population, and the fishery will be depleted. In "A Tale of Two Fisheries," we see how this negative externality was dealt with very differently in Rhode Island and in Australia.

Lack of Public Goods and Services

A wide range of goods and services is supplied by our federal, state, and local governments. These include national defense; a court system; police protection; the construction and maintenance of streets, highways, bridges, plus water and sewer mains; environmental protection; public parks; and public schools. Few of these would be supplied by private enterprise because entrepreneurs would not be able to make a profit.

Interestingly, many of these goods and services *were* once supplied by private enterprise. The nation's first toll road, Pennsylvania's Lancaster Turnpike, was built two centuries ago. Private toll bridges were constructed all over the country. Even today, there are more than twice as many people who work in private security ("rent-a-cops," store and hotel detectives, building security, campus security, and private investigators, for example) than there are city and state police. Our national rail lines were once privately owned, with such fabled names as the Pennsylvania (or Pennsy) Railroad; the Baltimore

A Tale of Two Fisheries*

Lobstermen use 4-foot-long steel cages that they lower to the ocean floor to catch lobster. Let's consider the work of lobster catchers based in Point Judith, Rhode Island, and catchers in Port Lincoln in southern Australia.

Over the last few decades, as they depleted the fishing grounds, the Rhode Island lobster catchers gradually doubled the number of cages and the life expectancy of the lobsters plummeted. They had gotten caught up in a vicious circle: The more they depleted the lobster population, the less they caught; the less they caught, the more cages they used; the more cages they used, the more they depleted the lobster population.

> Their life expectancy plummeted. "Lobsters used to live for 50 or 75 years," recalled Robert Smith, who has been lobstering at Point Judith since 1948. "When I started, it was not unusual to get a 30-pound lobster. It's been 20 years since I got one that was even 20 pounds." Last year, the biggest one he caught was 4 pounds, and that was an anomaly. Most lobsters don't even make it to 2 pounds.

Why doesn't the government do something? Because politicians think ahead only to the next election. In the long run it would certainly be better for fishermen if the government limited each year's catch, but that would incur the political wrath of many fishermen who would be unwilling to sacrifice their current livelihoods for the prospect of future benefits. And so, instead of limiting lobstering, the state and federal governments continue offering tax breaks and other incentives to the lobstermen at Point Judith.

Back in the 1960s, the government in Australia set a limit on the total number of traps (or cages) used by the fleet in Port Lincoln.

> The government started it in the 1960s by setting a limit on the total number of traps used by the fleet in Port Lincoln. Licenses for those traps were assigned to the working fishermen, and from then on, any newcomer who wanted to set a trap in those waters had to buy a license from someone

already in the business. It's like New York's taxicab system, which has a fixed number of taxi licenses or "medallions": a newcomer who wants to own a cab must buy a medallion from someone who is retiring.

Daryl Spencer bought his first trap licenses for $2,000 apiece in Australian dollars. Today he owns 60 traps.

> Nowadays, they would sell for $35,000, which means that Spencer's are worth a total of $2.1 million, or about $1.2 million in American dollars. He has done well by doing good: His licenses have become more valuable because the lobstermen are conservationists. They pay for scientists to monitor the fishery, and they have imposed strict harvesting limits that allow the lobsters to grow into sizable adults.

In the old days, like the Rhode Islanders, the Australians used to protest when anyone suggested reducing their catch.

> But they began taking the long view as soon as they saw the rising price of their licenses for their lobster pots, as they call the traps. Like any property owner, they began thinking about resale value. "Why hurt the fishery?" Spencer said. "It's my retirement fund. No one's going to pay me $35,000 a pot if there are no lobsters left. If I rape and pillage the fishery now, in 10 years my licenses won't be worth anything."

By fishing less, the Australian fishermen leave more lobsters out there to produce more eggs, which will make it easier for them to catch lobsters in the future. In Rhode Island and in Australia the government intervened to deal with the effects of a negative externality—overfishing. In Australia, that intervention produced a win-win situation for the lobsters and for the lobstermen. In Rhode Island, the lobstermen are still looking for answers.

---

*This is the title of an article written by John Tierney in *The New York Times Magazine,* August 27, 2000, pp. 38–43. The quotes herein are from this article.

and Ohio (you'll still find the B&O on the Monopoly board); the Seaboard; the Southern; the Great Northern; the New York Central; the New York, New Haven, and Hartford; the Boston and Maine; the Southern Pacific; and the storied Atchison, Topeka, and the Santa Fe.

Difference between public and private goods

Let's talk about the difference between *public* goods and *private* goods. Private goods are easy. You buy a car. It's your car. But a public good is something whose consumption by one person does not prevent its consumption by other people. Take our national defense. If you want to pay to have your home defended from nuclear attack, then everyone on your block is defended as well, even though they don't chip in a cent.

Or, if your block association hires a private security firm to patrol your neighborhood, even your neighbors who were too cheap to pay their dues are protected.

Not everything produced by the public sector is a public good. We mentioned defense as a public good—something whose consumption by one person does not prevent its consumption by other people. What about a ride on a public bus? Or driving on the Jersey Turnpike? These are not public goods because only those who pay get to ride.

Public goods tend to be indivisible; they usually come in large units that cannot be broken into pieces for purchase or sale in private markets. Often there is no way they can be produced by private enterprise because there is no way to exclude anyone from consuming the goods even if she or he did not pay for them. National defense is a classic example. Could you imagine putting *that* service on a pay-as-you-go basis? "I think this year I'll just skip being defended." We can't exactly move the nuclear umbrella away from my house while continuing to shield those of all my neighbors.

Karl Marx, German economist, historian, and philosopher (Historical Pictures/Stock Montage)

Capital consists of plant and equipment.

The central economic role of capital

Capital

Capital is the crucial element in every economic system. Karl Marx's classic *Das Kapital*[11] examined the role of capital in the mid-19th-century industralizing economy of England. According to Marx, the central figure of capitalism is the capitalist, or business owner, who makes huge profits by exploiting his workers. Capitalism is denigrated by communist societies whose own economic system has been labeled *state capitalism.*

Capital consists of plant and equipment. Marx said that whoever controlled a society's capital controlled that society. In today's economy, it takes a great deal of wealth to control much capital, so whether or not you agree with Marx's conclusions, you'd have to agree that the people who own large chunks of America's leading corporations are not exactly without influence.

Furthermore, Marx observed that one's social consciousness was determined by one's relationship to the means of production. Inevitably, he believed, there would be a clash between the capitalists and the workers, leading to an overthrow of capitalism and the establishment of a communist society. Then the workers would own the means of production. In the Soviet Union, incidentally, the means of production *were* owned by the workers, but the ruling elite, the top Communist Party officials, had real economic and political control.

The role of capital in the production process is central to why our country is rich and most of the rest of the world is poor. The reason an American farmer can produce 10 or 20 times as much as a Chinese farmer is that the American has much more capital with which to work—combines, tractors, harvesters, and reapers. And the reason the American factory worker is more productive than the Brazilian factory worker is that our factories are much better equipped. We have a tremendous stock of computers, assembly lines, warehouses, machine tools, and so on.

Take the example of the word processor. In the past, a lot of business letters had to be personally or individually typed, although they were really only form letters. Today we have a word processor that can be programmed to type out identical texts with different addressees at better than a letter a minute.

Our stock of capital enables us to turn out many more goods per hour of labor than we could produce without it. Much backbreaking as well as tedious labor has been eliminated by machines. Without our capital, we would have the same living standard as that of people throughout Asia, Africa, and Latin America.

---

[11] Karl Marx, *Das Kapital* (New York: International Publishers, 1967).

Where Capital Comes From

The following hypothetical situation will illustrate the value of capital. Suppose it takes a man 10 hours to make an optical lens, while someone working with a machine can make one in just 5 hours. Let's assume that it would take 1,000 hours to build such a machine.

Assume, however, that a person working 10 hours a day is barely able to support himself and his family. (Karl Marx observed that, in most working-class families, not only did wives work, but they didn't have to worry about day care centers or baby-sitters for the children because factories employed six- and seven-year-olds.) If he could not afford to spend 100 days (1,000 hours) building the machine, he still had two choices. He could cut back on his consumption—that is, lower his family's standard of living—by working nine hours a day on the lenses and one hour a day on building the machine. Or he could work, say, an extra hour a day on the machine.

In either case, it would take 1,000 days to build the machine. If he cut back on his consumption *and* worked an extra hour a day, it would take him 500 days to build the machine.

Once he had the machine, he'd really be in business. He could double his daily output from one lens a day to two a day (remember that a person working with a machine can turn out a lens in just 5 hours).

Each day, if he held his consumption to the same level, he would produce two lenses and sell one for food, rent, and other necessities. The other lens he'd save. At the end of just 100 days, he'd have saved 100 lenses. Those 100 lenses represent 1,000 hours of labor, which is exactly the same amount of labor that went into building a machine. He would probably be able to buy another machine with those 100 lenses.

Now he's really a capitalist! He'll hire someone to run the second machine and pay him a lens a day. And in another 100 days, he'll have a surplus of 200 lenses, and he'll be able to buy two more machines, hire a foreman to run his shop, retire to a condominium in Miami Beach at the age of 36, and be the richest kid on the block.

Where did capital come from? Essentially from savings. Some people would set aside part of their savings, go into business, and purchase plant and equipment (see box, "Where Capital Comes From"). But we're really skipping a step.

Initially there was no capital, except for some crude plows and other farm tools. People worked from sunrise to sunset just to produce enough food to put on the table. But a few farmers, a little more prosperous than their neighbors, were able to spare some time to build better farm tools. Or they might have had enough food stored away to employ someone to build these tools. Either way, some productive resources were diverted from producing consumer goods to producing capital goods.

The factory conditions of the 19th-century England that Marx described in *Das Kapital* were barbaric, but the end result was that a surplus of consumer goods was produced. The factory owner, by paying his workers meager wages, was able to use this surplus to buy more capital goods. These enabled his factory to be more productive, creating still greater surpluses that were used to purchase still more plant and equipment.

Under Joseph Stalin, the Russians devoted a large part of their production to capital goods, literally starving the Russian population of consumer goods. To this day there is a great shortage of consumer goods in the former Soviet Union. But this shortage is no longer due to diversion of resources from production of consumer goods to the production of capital goods. It is due to the inefficiencies of the economic system itself—something we'll be looking at more closely in the closing pages of this chapter.

In the years following World War II, Japan and the countries of Western Europe, struggling to rebuild their shattered economies, held down their consumption as they concentrated on building new plant and equipment. The South Koreans and Taiwanese have followed this model of building capital by holding down consumption.

Capital, then, is the key to every society's standard of living. In the late 1980s, as our productivity and economic growth continued to lag, economists pointed to our slow rate of capital growth as the basic problem. Americans, they told us, were consuming too much and saving too little. There is no question that U.S. society cannot continue on this spending binge indefinitely, but Americans should also keep in mind that we

Where did capital come from?

Capital is past savings accumulated for future production.

—Jackson Martindell

Capital is the key to our standard of living.

have the largest stock of capital of any country in the world. Whether we are sufficiently modernizing that stock of plant and equipment and adding to it is an entirely different question.[12]

The world's developing nations face nearly insurmountable obstacles—rapidly growing populations and very little plant and equipment. The experience of the industrializing nations in the 19th century was that, as people moved into cities from the countryside and as living standards rose, the birthrate invariably declined. But for industrialization to take place, capital must be built up. There are two ways to do this: Cut consumption or raise production. Unfortunately, most developing nations are already at subsistence levels, so no further cuts in consumption are possible without causing even greater misery. And production cannot easily be raised without at least some plant and equipment.

With the exception of the OPEC nations, which have been able to sell their oil in exchange for plant and equipment, the poorer nations of Africa, Asia, and Latin America have little hope of rising from extreme poverty.[13] An exchange of letters that legend has it took place between Mao Tse-tung and Nikita Khrushchev when China and the Soviet Union were allies in the early 1960s illustrates the futility of a third way out—foreign aid.

Mao: Send us machinery and equipment.
Khrushchev: Tighten your belts.
Mao: Send us some belts.

Specialization and Its Consequences

We could not have a modern, highly productive economy without specialization and exchange. Imagine if we all had to be self-sufficient. Each of us would live on a farm where we would grow our own food, weave our own cloth, build our own homes, make our own tools and clothes—even our pins and needles and nails.

In modern economies, virtually everyone specializes. We can sell whatever good or service we produce. By specializing, we get good at producing something, and we are able to sell it for a relatively low price. So instead of spending hours trying to make your own nails, you can buy all the nails you need at the hardware store for less than a dollar.

But specialization may lead to boredom and alienation, especially if our job requires us to do repetitive tasks. A certain degree of work alienation is inevitable in a modern economy, but some employers have been more successful at minimizing it than others.

Specialization and Exchange

When people specialize, they are usually far more productive than if they attempt to be jacks-of-all-trades. Doctors, lawyers, accountants, engineers, and, of course, college professors, all specialize (see box, "Specialization in Economics").

If all of us become really good at something and concentrate on that one specialty, we will produce much more than if we try to do everything. A family that tries to be self-sufficient will have a relatively low standard of living because it takes a lot of time to do the hundreds of things that need to be done—all on an individual basis. Imagine not just making your own nails and pins, but weaving your own cloth, growing all your food, and building your own means of transportation. Think how many hours it would take you to weave a yard of cloth when you could buy it in the store for a couple of dollars.

---

[12]We'll have a lot more to say about our lagging rates of saving in Chapter 16 of *Economics* and *Macroeconomics*.

[13]Many of these less developed countries have only one or two primary exports, usually agricultural products, with which to obtain foreign exchange. Furthermore, most are deeply in debt to banks in developed countries as well as to foreign governments and international lending organizations.

Specialization in Economics

People specialize in every field of learning. Your economics professor, for example, may have specialized in banking, and not only can tell you all the dirt on the 1980s savings and loan scandal, but can explain exactly how banks operate, how they determine the creditworthiness of borrowers, and even how you can wire money to other countries.

Of course, you can overspecialize. A colleague of mine was the nation's leading expert on the Bland-Allison Act of 1878, which authorized the secretary of the treasury to purchase 2 to 4 million ounces of silver every month. Now that's a great thing to know, but the man tried to teach economics by relating most things to the Bland-Allison Act.

Specialization is fine only if there is a demand for your specialty. One way there would be a demand for what you make or do is if someone wants what you have. If this person has what you want, you can trade. This is called *barter*. Today we use money to facilitate exchange. Thus, instead of having to find someone who has what you want and wants what you have, all you need to do is buy what you want and find someone to buy what you have.

Barter, unlike buying something for money, can get pretty complicated. When we use money, we can pay for something and be out of the store in a minute. But when we need to barter, we may be there all day trying to think of something that we have that the storekeeper will accept as payment.

The lack of money obviously inhibits trade, or exchange, and without exchange, people can't specialize. Imagine calling someone to fix your air conditioner and trying to pay this person with piano lessons, a psychotherapy session, or by correcting their overbite or fixing their transmission. It's much easier to specialize when you don't have to buy from the same person who buys from you.

> Without money, very little exchange; without exchange, no specialization.

Specialization and Alienation

Many factory workers have become little better than cogs in some huge industrial wheel. People whose sole function is to tighten a couple of bolts or place front right fenders on auto bodies eight hours a day for most of their lives understandably get a little bored. Some express their unhappiness by frequent absences, while some, like the workers in a Chevy Vega plant in Lordstown, Ohio, many years ago, actually sabotage some of the cars they are assembling.

> Working the line at G.M. was like being paid to flunk high school for the rest of your life.
> —Ben Hamper, *Rivethead: Tales from the Assembly Line*

One of the most boring jobs in the world has got to be that of a telemarketer. "Hello, may I speak with Mr. Smith?" (which he manages to mispronounce). . . "How are *you* this evening?" (Fine, until you interrupted my dinner.) And then he goes into his canned talk, which, I can tell you from painful memories of selling cemetery plots on the phone, is tacked to the wall in front of him. Imagine calling dozens of people a night and delivering, *verbatim,* the same talk again and again and again.

In a book simply titled *Working,* Studs Terkel recounted tape-recorded interviews with hundreds of American workers. Here's what a spot welder in a Chicago Ford auto assembly plant said about his work:

> I stand in one spot, about a two- or three-foot area, all night. The only time a person stops is when the line stops. We do about thirty-two jobs per car, per unit. Forty-eight units an hour, eight hours a day. Thirty-two times forty-eight times eight. Figure it out. That's how many times I push that button.[14]

---

[14]Studs Terkel, *Working* (New York: Avon Books, 1972), pp. 221–22.

One of the problems here is that the workers never see the product of their labor. Attempts have been made in Western Europe, particularly in Sweden, as well as in Japan, to involve the workers in making a larger segment of the product. Some degree of specialization is sacrificed in an effort to bolster employee morale. Although these new production modes have been successful, American factories have made only a few tentative efforts in this area.

No one seems to be asking what we can do to make jobs more interesting. Why must clerical workers do repetitive tasks instead of switching off with one another? Perhaps the classic boring job is that of elevator operator. Let's face it: being enclosed in a box riding up and down all day long is enough to drive anyone up a wall. Maybe my observations are not completely accurate, but most of these people seem ready to jump out of their skins. Couldn't they be given desk jobs for half the day and let the deskbound people ride the elevators—or be given the shaft, as they say in the trade when they're not saying the job has its ups and downs—thereby keeping everybody at least half happy and half sane?

Seymour Melman, a longtime observer of the corporate scene, had this to say about how the factory floor bred worker alienation:

> Managements that have long viewed the industrial worker as a replaceable, animated, special-purpose machine have given little, if any, thought to the impact of the physical conditions of the workplace on the men and women employed there. As a result, the environment is often dangerous, or noisy, or dirty, or poorly ventilated, too hot or too cold, or some combination of these.[15]

In some respects, office workers glued to a video display terminal or a word processor are no better off than assembly-line operators. They are often isolated, completely out of contact with other workers, and very likely to become bored, apathetic, and alienated. Each worker must discipline herself or himself to the system imposed by the machine, most often working with computer terminals that have been strictly programmed to perform only one task.

A developed or industrial economy must necessarily have most of the features we have discussed in this chapter. Obviously, a huge capital stock is required, and a fairly large government sector is inevitable. Specialization is also inevitable, but worker alienation could probably be avoided, at least to a greater degree than it has been in this country.

The "Isms": Capitalism, Communism, Fascism, and Socialism

Q: What is the difference between capitalism and socialism?
A: Under capitalism, man exploits man. Under socialism, it's just the opposite.

—Overheard in Warsaw[16]

Property is the exploitation of the weak by the strong.
Communism is the exploitation of the strong by the weak.

—Pierre-Joseph Proudhon[17]

During the 20th century, perhaps no three opprobriums have been hurled more often at political opponents than those of Communist! Capitalist! and Fascist! Depending on where and when you lived, you might have been called any of these three. In the United

---

[15]Seymour Melman, *Profits without Production* (Philadelphia: University of Pennsylvania Press, 1987), p. 123.

[16]Lloyd G. Reynolds, *Microeconomic Analysis and Policy,* 6th ed. (Burr Ridge, IL: Richard D. Irwin, 1988), p. 435.

[17]Pierre-Joseph Proudhon, *What Is Property?* chap. V, Part II.

Specialization and International Trade

We've seen that, when you specialize in a certain type of work, you can get very good at it and have a much higher standard of living than you would as a jack-of-all trades. In this case, what makes sense for individuals also makes sense for nations. Nations generally export the goods and services they can produce efficiently (that is, cheaply), and they import the goods and services that other nations produce more efficiently.

Because of our abundant fertile farmland and eventually our tremendous stock of farm equipment, we have been a major exporter of wheat, corn, and soybeans since colonial times. In recent years we have been the world's leading exporter of computer software and entertainment goods and services. In contrast, we used to be a major exporter of steel and textiles, but now that other nations can produce these more cheaply, we have now become a major importer of these products. Similarly, immediately after World War II we produced more than 60 percent of the world's oil, much of which we exported. Now that we have exhausted most of our easily extractable reserves, we import more than half our oil. If we didn't import any oil, we might well be paying more than $10 a gallon for gasoline.

So we may conclude that specialization and exchange make a great deal of economic sense to both individual and to nations. We'll return to this issue in Chapter 8 of *Macroeconomics* and *Economics,* as well as in the next-to-last chapter of this book.

States in the 1920s, it was bad to be a communist. In the 1930s and the first half of the 1940s, being a communist was acceptable in many quarters, but being a fascist was not. Although being a fascist had gone completely out of style in Germany and the rest of Europe by 1945, communism was "in" only in Eastern Europe. In Western Europe in the late 1940s and the 1950s, it was tolerated; but in the United States, many politicians made careers by claiming to hunt down "card-carrying" communists in all walks of life. "Excuse me, ma'am, may I see your card?" And heaven help you if your card was red.

All of this time, in the Soviet Union, if you were a bad guy in the 1930s and early 1940s, you were probably a fascist (except between 1939 and 1941, when the Soviet Union and Germany were nominal allies). That alliance vanished when Hitler's armies invaded the Soviet Union in mid-1941, and suddenly a new alliance was born as we American capitalists shipped the Soviets billions of dollars in war material. But after 1945, the capitalists in that country became the oppressed minority, card or no card. Then in the 1990s, of course, communism was out and capitalism was in throughout the length and breadth of Russia and the rest of what was once the Soviet empire.

Enough about political freedom. Let's compare the four great economic systems. Capitalism, as we've already seen, is characterized by private ownership of most of the means of production—that is, land, labor, capital, and entrepreneurial ability. Individuals are moved to produce by the profit motive. Production is also guided by the price system. Thus, we have millions of people competing for the consumer's dollar. The government's role in all of this is kept to a minimum; basically, it ensures that everyone sticks to the rules.

Capitalism

"The theory of the Communists may be summed up in the single sentence: Abolition of private property," declared Karl Marx and Friedrich Engels in *The Communist Manifesto.* Who would own everything? The state. And eventually the state would wither away and we would be left with a workers' paradise.

Communism

In the Soviet version of communism, under which the state had evidently not yet withered away, most of the capitalist roles were reversed. Instead of a guidance system of prices to direct production, a government planning committee dictated exactly *what* was produced, *how* it was produced, and *for whom* the goods and services were produced. After all, the state owned and operated nearly all of the means of production and distribution.

All of the resources used had to conform to the current five-year plan. If the goal was 2 million tractors, 100 million tons of steel, 15 million bushels of wheat, and so on, Soviet workers might have expected to be putting in a lot of overtime.

The big difference between the old Soviet economy and our own is what consumer goods and services are produced. In our economy, the market forces of supply and demand dictate what gets produced and how much of it gets produced. But a government planning agency in the Soviet Union dictated what and how much was made. In effect, central planning attempted to direct a production and distribution process that works automatically in a market economy.

How well did the Soviet communist system work? Remember the chronic shortages of consumer goods we mentioned earlier in the chapter? Although Soviet president Mikhail Gorbachev went to great lengths to shake up the bureaucracy and get the economy moving again, his efforts were futile. To raise output, he found he needed to somehow remove the heavy hand of bureaucracy from the economic controls. But as he stripped away more and more of the Communist Party's power, he found that his own power had been stripped away as well.

If the Soviet Union did not exemplify pure communism, then what country did? In the box "Real Communism," you'll read that we have had pure communism right under our noses for many years.

One of the fundamental economic problems with *any* economy that attempts to substitute government planning for the price system (or to replace the law of demand and supply with government decrees) is that changes in price no longer help producers decide what and how much to produce. In a capitalist country, higher microwave oven prices would signal producers to produce more microwave ovens. But in the Soviet Union, there was very little inflation even though there were widespread shortages of consumer goods. In fact, the Soviets came up with a great cure for inflation. Just let everyone wait in line.

The entire Soviet economy was a Rube Goldberg contraption[18] of subsidies, fixed prices, bureaucratic rules and regulations, special privileges, and outright corruption. Had Gorbachev not acted, the entire Soviet system may well have come apart by itself over another couple of generations.

A joke that circulated in the late 1980s went like this: Under communism your pockets are full of money, but there isn't anything in the stores you can buy with it. Under capitalism, the stores are full, but you have no money in your pockets.

Fascism

Fascism hasn't been in vogue since Hitler's defeat in 1945, but it does provide another model of an extreme. In Nazi Germany the ownership of resources was in private hands, while the government dictated what was to be produced.

The problem with describing the fascist economic model is that there really *is* no model. The means of production are left in private hands, with varying degrees of governmental interference. Generally those in power are highly nationalistic, so a high proportion of output is directed toward military goods and services.

They pretend to pay us, and we pretend to work.
—Polish folk definition of communism

Real Communism

Several years ago, I knew a history professor at St. Francis College in Brooklyn who loved to shock his students by telling them that he had been a communist. As a young man, he had joined a Catholic religious order, lived in a commune, and shared all his possessions with his fellow seminarians. "What could be more communist than living in a commune with no private property?" he asked his students.

And so we may ask whether what they had in the Soviet Union and in Eastern Europe was really communism. How would Karl Marx have reacted to those huge bureaucratic dictatorships? Marx had foreseen "the withering away of the state," until all that was left was a society of workers who followed his credo "From each according to his ability; to each according to his needs." This sounds a lot more like that history professor's seminary than what was passing for communism in the old Soviet empire.

The Soviet regime collapsed not just because of its bureaucratic inefficiencies but also because it supported a huge military establishment that claimed between one-fifth and one-quarter of its resources and national output.

---

[18]Such a device is designed to accomplish by complex means what seemingly could be done simply.

Fascists have been virulently anticommunist but have also been completely intolerant of any political opposition. The one-party state, suppression of economic freedom, and a militaristic orientation have been hallmarks of fascism.

The early 1940s were evidently the high-water mark of fascism. Although from time to time a fascist state does pop up, it appears to be a temporary phenomenon. With the possible exception of Hitler's Germany, which did put most Germans back to work after the Great Depression, albeit largely at military production, most fascist states have been economic failures that apparently collapsed of their own weight.

No countries today are admittedly fascist, although Salazar's Portugal and Franco's Spain, both holdouts from the 1930s, functioned as fascist regimes until the 1960s. The military dictatorships of Africa, South America, and Saddam Hussein's Iraq have also been likened to the fascist model, but there is nothing today to compare with Hitler's Germany or Mussolini's Italy.

Socialism has not gotten the bad press that capitalism, fascism, and communism have received, perhaps because those who dislike the socialists prefer to call them communists. In fact, even Soviet government officials used to refer to themselves as socialists and their country, the U.S.S.R., was formally called the Union of Soviet Socialist Republics, although President Ronald Reagan referred to the Soviet Union as the evil empire. And the countries with socialist economies were our military allies.

Socialism

The economies of such countries as Sweden, Canada, Great Britain, and, recently, France and Greece have been described as socialist, not only by government officials in those countries but by outside observers as well. In general, these economies have three characteristics: (1) government ownership of some of the means of production; (2) a substantial degree of government planning; and (3) a large-scale redistribution of income from the wealthy and the well-to-do to the middle class, working class, and the poor.

One of the most familiar characteristics of socialist countries is cradle-to-grave security. Medical care, education, retirement benefits, and other essential needs are guaranteed to every citizen. All you need to do is be born.

Where does the money to pay for all of this come from? It comes from taxes. Very high income taxes and inheritance taxes fall disproportionately on the upper middle class and the rich. In Israel several years ago, a joke went around about a man who received an unusually large paycheck one week. He couldn't figure out what had happened until his wife looked at his check stub and discovered that he had been sent his deductions by mistake. Although only the very wealthy must give the government more than half their pay in socialist countries, the story *did* have a ring of truth to it.

> The vice of capitalism is that it stands for the unequal sharing of blessings; whereas the virtue of socialism is that it stands for the equal sharing of misery.
> —Winston Churchill

Rather than allow the market forces to function freely, socialist governments sometimes resort to very elaborate planning schemes. And since the government usually owns the basic industries and provides the basic services, this planning merely has one hand directing the other.

Sweden is often considered the archetypal socialist country, although perhaps 90 percent of the country's industry is privately owned. It is the government's massive intervention in the private economy that gives Swedish society its socialist tone. Not only has the Swedish government kept the unemployment rate generally below 3 percent for several decades by offering industry and workers a series of subsidies and incentives, but it provides one of the most elaborate cradle-to-grave programs in the world. The government doles out $100 monthly allowances for each child and provides day care centers, free education from nursery school through college, free medical care, and very generous unemployment and retirement benefits. Women may take a year off work after the birth of a child while receiving 80 percent of their pay.

Of course, taxes are very high in Sweden. In 1999 about 63 percent of the nation's output was paid out in taxes, compared to just 32 percent in the United States. Critics of the Swedish system have questioned whether the high tax rates haven't hurt work incentives. Even if they have, Sweden not only has one of the most equal income distributions in the world but also has one of the highest living standards. So the Swedes must be doing something right.

But Sweden's brand of socialism pales in comparison to that of Norway, its Scandinavian neighbor. In addition to free day care, subsidized housing and vacations, and free medical care, Norwegians receive annual stipends of more than $1,600 for every child under 17, retirement pay for homemakers, and 42 weeks of fully paid maternity leave. How do they pay for all of this? Not only does Norway have the world's highest income tax rates, but it has a 23 percent sales tax and a gasoline tax of about $5 a gallon. Hallmarks of Norwegian society are a great disdain for the trappings of wealth and power and a profound sense of equality, which militate against a wide disparity in pay.

In much of Western Europe the unemployment rate was more than 10 percent in 1996 and 1997. Critics of the socialist welfare states have noted that extremely high jobless benefits provide a disincentive to work. Why bother working when you can collect benefits equal to, say, 90 percent of what you could have earned? In addition, employers must pay very high taxes for each worker they hire. In France there are taxes for family allowances, for a fund offering low-cost housing loans, for unemployment insurance for pensions, for the improvement of security on building sites, for professional training, and even for reducing the social security deficit.

Perhaps this joke, which has made its rounds on the Internet, may best sum up the four isms:

Socialism: You have two cows. State takes one and gives it to someone else.
Communism: You have two cows. State takes both of them and gives you milk.
Fascism: You have two cows. State takes both of them and sells you milk.
Capitalism: You have two cows. You sell one and buy a bull.

The Decline and Fall of the Communist System

Under Joseph Stalin and his successors, from the late 1920s through the 1960s, Soviet economic growth was very rapid, as government planners concentrated on building the stock of capital goods, largely neglecting consumer goods. The government purposely set prices on consumer goods very low, often not changing them for decades. They wanted even the poorest people to be able to afford the basic necessities.

Whether intended or not, what they ended up with were constant shortages. We've illustrated such a shortage in the graph shown in Figure 4. When the quantity demanded is much greater than the quantity supplied, and when price is inflexible, then a shortage is inevitable. And so are the lines of people waiting to buy the underpriced goods. As a colleague who taught Russian literature remarked to me as he got off the line for a sumptuous buffet, I've already waited on enough lines in the Soviet Union.

Way back in the 1950s, America and its allies believed that we were faced by an implacable foe—monolithic world communism, with its headquarters in Moscow. The Chinese, the North Koreans, the revolutionaries in Vietnam, and the "captive" nations of Eastern Europe, were all part of what President Reagan later called "the evil empire." Sounds a lot like "Star Wars," but, in those days, we called it the cold war. Although there were occasional hot wars, most notably in Korea, Vietnam, and Afghanistan, the communists and the "free world" confronted each other with trillions of dollars worth of nuclear and conventional weapons, engaging in a 45-year-long war of nerves.

By the early 1970s, when Richard Nixon became the first American president to visit China, we had come to realize that there were vast political and economic differences between the Soviet Union and China. Indeed, much of our foreign policy was aimed at playing off these great powers against each other. But what we failed to see was that the economies of both nations had been faltering and that the heavy weight of bureaucratic planning was stifling economic growth.

By the late 1970s, China began reforms, very gradually evolving into a market economy. However the Soviet Union, through the 1980s, continued to stagnate, devoting most of its talent and capital to its military establishment. Most of its armed forces served, basically, as an army of occupation in Eastern Europe. By the time that army was withdrawn, in 1989, and defense expenditures slashed, the Soviet Union was in political

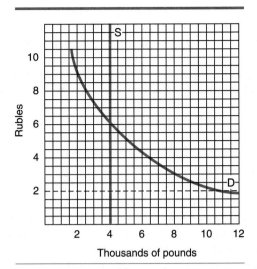

Figure 4

Hypothetical Demand for and
Supply of Butter

The price of butter is set by the
government at 2 rubles. This is a
price ceiling. How much would the
market price be if there were no
price ceiling? The market price
would be 6 rubles. How much is
the shortage of butter at a price of
2 rubles? The shortage is about
7,500 pounds (at a price of $2,
quantity supplied is 4,000 and
quantity demanded is 11,500).

turmoil. Within two years the communists, along with the huge central planning apparatus were gone, the Soviet Union was dismembered into 15 separate nations, the largest of which was Russia, and President Boris Yeltsin and his revolving door of economic and political lieutenants had found that their economic problems had only just begun.

In the closing months of 1989, the communist governments of Eastern Europe came tumbling down like falling dominoes. As democratically elected governments replaced Soviet-backed dictatorships, there was a strong movement away from government-owned and operated economies to market economies. These transitions are still evolving, and the final mix of private enterprise and government ownership is far from certain in any of these countries.

Two basic problems they have encountered are inflation and rising unemployment. The lifting of government price controls, as well as the removal of government subsidies for such basic necessities as meat, bread, eggs, milk, and butter, made price increases inevitable. And as some of the less efficient government enterprises have been shut down, hundreds of thousands of workers have been thrown out of work.

In the Soviet Union, the economic power of the government had been based largely in Article 10 of the Soviet constitution:

> The foundation of the economic system of the USSR is socialist ownership of the
> means of production in the form of state property (belonging to all the people), and
> collective farm and cooperative property.

In March 1990, the Soviet parliament passed a property law giving private citizens the right to own small factories, stores, and other businesses. It also permitted the creation of worker-owned cooperatives. But it remains to be seen whether these plans will create a truly mixed economy. A lot depends on whether the bureaucrats who control the huge state-run enterprises will cooperate with or sabotage these new competitors by refusing to sell them needed machinery, equipment, and supplies.

The communists ran the Soviet Union for more than 70 years, so even if their entire bureaucratic structure of state-owned farms, factories, offices, and stores were to be privatized, the process would take years, even decades. The whole system of economic planning and the millions of bureaucrats whose jobs depend on the state will not just disappear in a puff of smoke. The process of privatization so far has been relatively limited in comparison to what has already taken place in Poland, the former East Germany, Hungary, and a few of the other Eastern European countries.

Russia has made tremendous strides toward ridding itself of the old, inefficient Soviet bureaucracy, but it is also greatly burdened by the problems of transforming into a market economy. Rampant inflation, high unemployment, and a huge budget deficit

Two basic problems—inflation
and rising unemployment

have threatened to derail economic reform. The income of the average Russian is barely half what it was before the collapse of the communist system in 1990–91.

And yet a great deal of progress has been made. In early 1993 the government employed about 97 or 98 percent of the Russian industrial workforce, but by 2000 more than 75 percent worked for private enterprises. More than 100,000 state companies—from small shops to huge, enormously inefficient factories—have been transferred to private ownership. The question remains whether these largely inefficient enterprises can be transformed into lean and mean competing business firms.

The economic situation is bad, but improving. Average wages are just $65 a month, but, under president Vladimir Putin, more taxes are being collected, the ruble is stable, and inflation is under control.

Will the Soviet economy evolve into a clone of American capitalism? Probably not. For one thing, seven decades of egalitarian ideology have left their mark on every facet of Russian life. A new class of rich and superrich would cut against the grain of that deep-seated belief.

Perhaps a word of caution is in order about the political and economic changes that have swept across Eastern Europe and the Soviet Union over the last few years. The situation in each country will be fluid, if not volatile, for years to come. It is very possible that most or all of these nations will peacefully evolve into socialist or capitalist democracies. But then again, the pendulum may swing back toward communist autocracy. Either way, the next few years will be very interesting.

Will the Soviet Union go capitalist?

Collapse of communism is not a vote of confidence in American capitalism.

China: The Premier Communist Power

The communists came to power in 1949, taking over one of the world's poorest nations. For the first three decades, largely under Mao Tse-tung (his friends called him Chairman Mao, and he liked the rest of the Chinese to refer to him as "the Great Helms-man"), the Chinese economy was dominated by Soviet-style central planning. Even though the economy absorbed two extremely disruptive setbacks—the Great Leap Forward (1958–60), during which perhaps 30 million people starved to death, and the Cultural Revolution (1966–75), both of which Mao used to consolidate power—economic growth may have averaged 9 percent a year. China was pulled up from a backward country plagued by periodic famine to one in which everyone had enough to eat and many could afford to buy TVs, refrigerators, cameras, and some of the other amenities we in the United States take for granted. In 1978 there were 1 million TV sets in China; by 1998 there were nearly 300 million.

In China, as in the former Soviet Union, the big boss of a province, or of the entire country, has held the modest title of First Secretary of the Communist Party. Back in 1978 a man named Zhao Ziyang was the First Secretary in Szechuan province, which was becoming world famous for its wonderful cuisine. Until 1978, the highly centralized Chinese planning system had slowed economic growth. Zhao issued an order that year freeing six state-owned enterprises from the control of the central planners, allowing the firms to determine their own prices and output, and even to keep any profits they earned. In just two years some 6,600 firms had been cut loose, Zhao had become the Chinese head of state, and China was well on its way to becoming a market, or capitalist, economy.

Beginning in 1979 many provincial leaders across China, independent of the central authorities in Beijing, shifted the responsibility of operating huge collective farms to the families that lived on the farms. Although each family was given a production quota to meet, any additional output could be sold at a profit. By 1984 more than 90 percent of China's agricultural land was farmed by individual households.

Finally free to farm their own land, and able to actually earn a profit from their labor, most farmers put forth a much greater effort. Farm output, which had been growing at an annual rate of about 2½ percent between 1953 and 1978, grew at a rate of almost 7 percent over the next five years. In 1978 farmers sold just 8 percent of their crops privately, but, by 1990, that share had increased to 80 percent.

Rather than being given the chance to own the farms outright, farmers were generally given 15-year leases, which could be extended for additional 15-year periods when they expired. Why not allow the farmers to actually own this land? Communist party officials were afraid that private ownership of farmland could give rise to a new class of very wealthy absentee landlords, who would then exploit the farmers who rented their land. Immediately after the end of the Chinese civil war in 1949, hundreds of thousands of wealthy absentee landlords were "liquidated" (executed). Over the next three decades, hundreds of millions of farm workers labored on government-run huge collective farms. By the late 1970s, the Communist party leadership had reached the conclusion that neither extreme—private ownership or collective farming—was acceptable. Since then, however, their compromise solution of providing 15-year leases has definitely stimulated agricultural production.

In the late 1970s and early 1980s, reform began to take hold in the industrial sector as well. State firms were free to sell any surplus output, after having met their quotas. Simultaneously millions of tiny family-run enterprises were springing up all across the land, ranging from street peddlers, owners of tiny restaurants, and bicycle repair shops, to large factories and international trading companies. By the late 1980s, many of these large private factories were at least partially owned by Chinese businessmen from Hong Kong and Taiwan, as well as by investors from Japan, other Asian countries, and even some from Western Europe and the United States. China's southern provinces, and especially her coastal cities, have become veritable "export platforms," sending out a stream of toys, consumer electronics, textiles, clothing, and other low-tech products mainly to consumers in Japan, Europe, and North America. Between 1978 and 2000, Chinese exports rose from $5 billion to more than $200 billion.

The agricultural and industrial reforms diluted the ideological purity that had marked the first 30 years of communist rule. Indeed, by 1984 the Communist Party's Central Committee went so far as to depart from the traditional communist credo "From each according to his ability, to each according to his needs." The new slogan was "More pay for more work; less pay for less work." What this did, implicitly, was to say to budding entrepreneurs, "It's OK if you get rich—you worked hard for your money." Apparently the reformers, led by Deng Xiaoping, the nonagenarian revolutionary who had survived Mao's purges, believed that a large degree of economic freedom should be tolerated but that free political expression was an entirely different matter, as the student demonstrators in Beijing's Tienanmen Square were to learn in 1989.[19]

> To get rich is glorious.
> —Deng Xiaoping

More than 70 percent of all investment in China goes into state-owned factories run by managers appointed by the Communist Party, up from about 60 percent in 1990. Although they soak up a growing percentage of investment funds, these factories produce a shrinking share of China's economic output. Indeed, privately owned factories now produce about 60 percent of all output and may reach 75 percent in 2002.

During the 1980s and 1990s the Chinese economy grew by about 9 percent every year, but by 1999 and 2000, that growth had slowed considerably. In 2000 there were still 400 million peasant farmers in China. Another 180 million people worked for private, or partly private companies, and 125 million were employed by state-owned industries. As the economy slowed, unemployment grew to 10 percent in the cities and about 30 percent in rural areas. Factories were turning out goods that could not be sold, and consumer prices fell for the twenty-second consecutive year. Millions of workers, laid off state-owned companies, were left without work. Unless government efforts to revive consumer demand are successful, the Chinese economic miracle of the 1980s and 1990s may give way to much slower growth, or even economic stagnation.

Although average family income has at least quintupled since 1978, China remains a relatively poor agricultural nation with three-quarters of its population living in rural areas. But it has 1.3 billion people (one out of every five people on this planet lives in China), and it has become a middle-rank industrial power. Should its economy continue

---

[19]Deng died in 1997, at the age of 92.

to grow at 6 or 8 percent a year, within another few decades China may well replace Japan as our most formidable economic rival.

Will China eventually overtake the United States as the world's leading economic power? China is already the world's largest producer of coal, cement, grain, fish, and cotton; it ranks third in steel production and fifth in crude oil output. But the Chinese economy is just one-tenth the size of ours. China may yet surpass the United States, but probably not in the 21st century.

Last Word: The Mixed Economy

The first words of this chapter were these: Ours is a mixed economy because there is a private sector and a public sector. The next time you're in the supermarket, pick up a jar of mixed nuts and see if the label proclaims, "No more than 70 percent peanuts." Think of our economy as a jar of mixed nuts. If the privately held sector were peanuts, what would the label say? Probably, "No more than 90 percent peanuts."

No economy is wholly government owned and operated. In the old Soviet Union, there were privately held plots of farmland and hundreds of thousands of tiny business firms. And in China today, there is a huge and rapidly growing private sector that includes millions of manufacturing firms, retailers, and service providers. Indeed, the largest chunk of private property is held by officers of the Peoples' Liberation Army. The Chinese government has had great difficulty preventing these enterprises from producing and selling pirated American computer software, CDs, jeans, and videos. Although most Chinese still work for government-owned and -operated factories, stores, and farms, perhaps one-third of the Chinese economy is in private hands.

So where does all of this leave us? It leaves us with one conclusion: Every nation in the world has a mixed economy.

Questions for Further Thought and Discussion

1. The circular flow model is a simplified version of our economy. Describe how this model works.

2. What are the three basic economic questions that all economies must answer? Describe the differences in the ways capitalism and socialism answer these questions.

3. What was Adam Smith's invisible hand, and what economic function did it serve?

4. What are the two basic classes of market failure? What would be an example of each?

5. What are the consequences of overspecialization? Give an example of a job that is overspecialized.

6. What factors contributed to the collapse of the Soviet economy?

7. How far has China evolved into a market economy? To what degree has this evolution contributed to China's economic growth?

8. For many years Americans referred to the People's Republic of China as "Communist China." Why would that label be misleading today?

9. Explain why you would prefer to live in a socialist or a capitalist country.

W*orkbook* for Chapter 4

Name _____ Date _____

Multiple-Choice Questions

Circle the letter that corresponds to the best answer.

1. We have a mixed economy because _____.
   a) we produce guns and butter
   b) we consume domestically produced goods as well as imports
   c) we consume both goods and services
   d) there is a private sector and a public sector

2. Which does not fit with the others?
   a) competition
   b) government planning and regulation
   c) the invisible hand
   d) the price mechanism

3. Adam Smith believed the best way to promote the public interest was to _____.
   a) have the government produce most goods and services
   b) let people pursue their own selfish interests
   c) wait for individuals to set out to promote the public interest
   d) get rid of the price mechanism

4. Supply-side economists believe cutting taxes will _____.
   a) hurt the economy
   b) give people an incentive to work, save, and invest
   c) have little or no economic effect
   d) help during recessions, but be less effective than government spending increases

5. In the Soviet Union, _____.
   a) the most productive plots of land were privately owned
   b) there was no private ownership of agricultural land
   c) private plots produced more food than collective farms
   d) there was more privately owned land than government-owned land

6. Adam Smith believed people are guided by all of the following except _____.
   a) the profit motive   c) the public good
   b) self-interest   d) the invisible hand

7. The price system is based on _____.
   a) government regulation (i.e., the government sets most prices)
   b) the individual whim of the businessperson who sets it
   c) the feelings of the individual buyer
   d) supply and demand

8. Which statement is true?
   a) American industry is very competitive.
   b) There is no competition in American industry.
   c) To have competition, you need to have many firms in an industry.
   d) The American automobile industry is very competitive.

9. In the United States, nearly all resources are owned by _____.
   a) the government   c) individuals
   b) business firms   d) foreigners

10. The Australian lobster catchers were able to prevent the depletion of their lobster population _____.
    a) through government subsidies
    b) through voluntary restraint
    c) through a system of government licensing of lobster traps
    d) fishing far from Australian shores

11. Wages, rent, interest, and profits flow from _____.
    a) business firms to households
    b) households to business firms
    c) business firms to the government
    d) the government to business firms

12. The government performs each of the following economic functions except _____.

a) collecting taxes

b) spending

c) issuing regulations

d) operating the price mechanism

13. Private ownership of most of the means of production is common to _____.

a) capitalism and communism

b) capitalism and fascism

c) capitalism and socialism

d) fascism and communism

14. The price mechanism is least important under _____.

a) capitalism   c) fascism

b) socialism   d) communism

15. The five-year plan had been the main economic plan of _____.

a) the United States   c) Nazi Germany

b) Sweden   d) the U.S.S.R.

16. Fascism peaked in the _____.

a) 1920s   c) 1940s

b) 1930s   d) 1950s

17. The strongest criticism of Sweden's economic system has been that _____.

a) it provides too many benefits

b) its taxes are too high

c) its taxes are too low

d) it doesn't provide enough benefits

18. The strongest indictment of the capitalist system was written by _____.

a) Adam Smith   c) Rose D. Cohen

b) John Maynard Keynes   d) Karl Marx

19. Karl Marx said that _____.

a) whoever controlled a society's capital controlled that society

b) in the long run, capitalism would survive

c) the U.S.S.R.'s communist system was "state capitalism"

d) capitalists and workers generally had the same economic interests

20. The main reason the American farmer can produce more than the farmer in China is that he _____.

a) has more land   c) has more labor

b) has more capital   d) is better trained

21. Capital comes from _____.

a) gold   c) high consumption

b) savings   d) the government

22. All modern economies depend on _____.

a) alienation

b) government ownership of the means of production

c) free enterprise

d) specialization

23. Alienation is one result of _____.

a) exchange   c) underspecialization

b) overspecialization   d) self-sufficiency

24. An individual can build up his/her capital by _____.

a) working longer hours only

b) cutting back on consumption only

c) both cutting back on consumption and working longer hours

d) only by borrowing

25. Which is the most accurate statement about the Chinese economy?

a) It will probably be bigger than ours before the year 2040.

b) Most of its workers are now employed by industry rather than agriculture.

c) Its growth rate slowed considerably in 1999 and 2000.

d) Its private sector is very small.

26. Which is the most accurate statement about shipbreaking?

a) It is generally done in a manner that is environmentally sound and that minimizes dangers to workers.

b) It is an extremely profitable activity that is sought after by the world's largest shipbuilders.

c) Ship owners whose boats have grown too old and expensive to run usually abandon them at sea or sink them.

d) The United States and other industrial nations have exported their environmental problems like shipbreaking to less developed countries such as India, Bangladesh, and Pakistan.

Fill-In Questions

1. The invisible hand is generally associated with (1) the _____ and (2) _____.

2. Adam Smith believed that if people set out to promote the public interest, they will not do nearly as much good as they will if they _____.

3. Supply-side economists believe the way to provide people with incentives to work, save, and invest is to _____.

4. Supply-side economists feel that the government's economic role is _____.

5. In the Soviet Union most of the farmland was in the form of _____.

6. Under private enterprise, production is guided by _____.

7. The price system is based on the law of _____ _____.

8. Critics feel that price controls interfere with the _____.

9. Under competition, there are so many firms that no firm is large enough to _____.

Chapter 5

The Household-Consumption Sector

In this chapter we begin our examination of the four sectors of gross domestic product (GDP): C (consumption), I (investment), G (government spending), and Xn (net exports). We look at consumption: why people spend money, what they buy, and why they save so little of their incomes. We will also introduce graphing techniques as a tool for macroeconomic analysis, which will be covered in Chapters 11 and 12.

CHAPTER OBJECTIVES

In this chapter we will introduce eight economic concepts:

- The average propensity to consume.
- The average propensity to save.
- The marginal propensity to consume.
- The marginal propensity to save.
- The consumption function.
- The saving function.
- The determinants of consumption.
- The permanent income hypothesis.

GDP and Big Numbers

Consumption, investment, and government spending are the three main sectors of GDP. But what, exactly, is GDP? Gross domestic product is a term that you'll find quite frequently in the financial section of your newspaper, as well as in the *Wall Street Journal, BusinessWeek, Fortune,* and other financial publications. Gross domestic product, which is the subject of Chapter 9, is the *nation's expenditure on all the final goods and services produced during the year at market prices.*

    I'm going to be throwing very large numbers at you—millions, billions, and trillions. The box titled "A Word about Numbers" provides a lucid explanation of how to deal with these numbers; so if you don't know your billions from your trillions, you definitely need to read it.

What's the difference between mathematics and economics? Mathematics is incomprehensible, economics just doesn't make sense.

111

A Word about Numbers

The time has come to talk about numbers—big numbers. We need to keep our thousands, millions, billions, and trillions straight, so I've devised a little test. This will help you gauge what you know and don't know. And by the time you finish this section, believe me, you will know.

I'd like you to express some numbers in words. I'll do the first one.

(a) 1,591 <u>One thousand, five-hundred, and ninety-one</u>

(b) 4,338,500,000 _____

(c) 468,374 _____

(d) 2,847,600,000,000 _____

(e) 216,129,000 _____

You'll find the answers at the end of the box. But don't look yet—I have a few more problems for you. OK, I'll do the first one—then you do the rest. This time we translate words into numbers.

(f) Seventy-six billion, three-hundred million
76,300,000,000 _____

(g) Two-hundred nineteen thousand, four hundred

_____

(h) Six trillion _____

(i) Forty-five million, three-hundred eighty-eight
thousand _____

Summary

1. Thousands come after the first comma: for example, 17,000 (seventeen thousand); 391,000 (three-hundred ninety-one thousand).

2. Millions come after the second comma: for example, 6,000,000 (six million); 410,000,000 (four-hundred ten million).

3. Billions come after the third comma: for example, 924,500,000,000 (nine-hundred twenty-four billion, five-hundred million); 86,000,000,000 (eighty-six billion).

4. Trillions come after the fourth comma: for example, 31,000,000,000,000 (thirty-one trillion); 570,000,000,000,000, (five-hundred seventy trillion).

Answers

(b) four billion, three-hundred thirty-eight million, five-hundred thousand
(c) four-hundred sixty-eight thousand, three-hundred and seventy-four
(d) two trillion, eight-hundred forty-seven billion, six-hundred million
(e) two-hundred sixteen million, one-hundred twenty-nine thousand
(g) 219,400
(h) 6,000,000,000,000
(i) 45,388,000

Speaking of numbers, so they don't have to write out 12 zeros, economists write one trillion dollars like this: 1,000, or sometimes, 1000. It's a lot faster than writing, $1,000,000,000,000.

How would they write $100 billion? See if you can do it. The answer is 100. Now maybe you *do* need to read "A Word about Numbers."

Consumption

The average American spends virtually all of her income after taxes. The total of everyone's expenditures is consumption, designated by the letter C. The largest sector of GDP, C, is now just over two-thirds of GDP.

Consumers spend more than half their money on services such as medical care, eating out, video rentals, life insurance, and legal fees. The rest is spent on durable goods, such as television sets and furniture, or on nondurable goods, such as food and gasoline. All consumption falls into one of the two categories of goods or services.

The consumption function states that as income rises, consumption rises, but not as quickly.

Although consumption is not a steady percentage of disposable income, until the late 1990s, it was usually between 90 and 95 percent. John Maynard Keynes (pronounced "canes") noted that consumption is a stable component of income. His theory, called the

TABLE 1	Consumption and Disposable Income

Disposable Income	Consumption
1,000	1,400
2,000	2,200
3,000	3,000
4,000	3,800
5,000	4,600

consumption function, states that *as income rises, consumption rises, but not as quickly.*[1] For example, if a country's disposable income rises by 300 (from 2,000 to 2,300), its C will rise, but by less than 300. If C were 1,800, it might rise by 250 to 2,050.[2]

The consumption function is illustrated by the hypothetical figures in Table 1. Let's start with a disposable income of 1,000 (read as $1,000 billion, or $1 trillion) and consumption of 1,400 ($1,400 billion, or $1.4 trillion). Now let's move up to a disposable income of 2,000. You'll notice that C rose to 2,200. So an increase of 1,000 (from 1,000 to 2,000) in disposable income pushes up C by 800 (from 1,400 to 2,200). This relationship remains the same as we raise disposable income to 3,000, 4,000, and 5,000. Each 1,000 increase in disposable income gives us an 800 increase in C.

So, as disposable income rises in increments of 1,000, C rises in increments of 800, which conforms to the consumption function: *As income rises, consumption rises, but not as quickly.*

When we say, then, that consumption is a function of disposable income, we mean that it *varies* with disposable income. When disposable income goes up, so does consumption, though by a smaller amount. And when disposable income declines, so does consumption, but again, by a smaller amount.

Saving

Saving is simply not spending. Since the average family spends 90 to 95 percent of its disposable income, it saves just 5 to 10 percent, one of the lowest savings rates among industrialized nations. In recent years Japan has had a savings rate of about 20 percent; Italy and Korea have averaged more than 20 percent; and Taiwan has averaged more than 30 percent. But the prize for savings may go to China, which has a rate of 35 to 40 percent.

Since the early 1990s our savings rate seems to be performing its own version of the limbo. In answer to the question, "How low can you go?" you'll see in Figure 1 that in 2000 we managed to get our savings rate all the way down to 0 percent. In other words, in the year 2000, the average American family saved no money at all. And if you really want to be accurate, our savings rate in 2000 was actually −0.1 percent, which means that saving was negative.

Figure 1 shows our savings record over the last four decades. During nearly all of that period the savings rate was less than 10 percent of disposable personal income, and there has been a marked downward trend since the mid-1980s. A low savings rate and a high consumption rate are just flip sides of the same coin. The more we spend, the less we save.

When one has had to work so hard to get money, why should he impose on himself the further hardship of trying to save it?
—Don Herold

[1]His exact words were, "Men are disposed, as a rule and on the average, to increase their consumption as their income increases, but not by as much as the increase in their income."

[2]No more Mr. Nice Guy. From here on I'll refer to billions of dollars in this shorthand way. The number 2,050 represents $2,050 billion (or $2.05 trillion). Remember that 2,000 represents $2,000 billion, or $2 trillion. This is a convention all economists use when writing about billions and trillions of dollars.

Figure 1

Savings as a Percentage of
Disposable Personal Income,
1960–2000

There has been a marked decline in
our savings rate since the early
1980s.

Source: Economic Report of the
President, 2001; Business Cycle
Indicators, March 2001

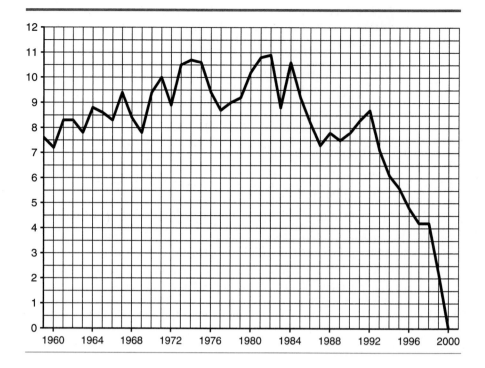

And a low savings rate leads to a low rate of productivity growth. Why? Because without savings to invest in new and better capital, we can't raise our productivity very quickly.

Why has the savings rate sunk so low, or, alternatively, why are Americans spending virtually all of their take-home pay? These are good questions. But never mind the why and wherefore—at least for now. We'll get into the mechanics of saving and consuming, run a few graphs by you, and then, near the end of the chapter, get around to answering why we save so little and spend so much. Let's let the suspense build for a while.

Average Propensity to Consume (APC)

The average propensity to consume is the percentage of disposable income spent. Using the data in Table 2, let's calculate the APC.

TABLE 2	
Disposable Income	Consumption
$40,000	$30,000

$$APC = \frac{Consumption}{Disposable\ income}$$

To find the percentage of disposable income spent, we need to divide consumption by disposable income.

$$APC = \frac{Consumption}{Disposable\ income} = \frac{\$30,000}{\$40,000} = \frac{3}{4} = .75$$

Let's review how this is done. We use the three-step method of solving this problem. First, write the formula. Then, substitute the numbers into the formula. Finally, solve the formula.

You know that \$30,000/\$40,000 can easily be reduced to 3/4. To change the fraction (3/4) into decimal form, divide 3 by 4. (Remember always to divide the bottom number into the top number.)

$$4\overline{)3.00}^{\,.75}$$

Average Propensity to Save (APS)

The APS is the mirror image of the APC. It is the percentage of disposable income saved. Using the data in Table 2, calculate the APS.

Use the same three-step method we used to calculate the APC: (1) Write the formula, (2) plug in your numbers, and (3) solve. Do it right here.

Now we'll check your work. The formula is:

$$APS = \frac{Saving}{Disposable\ income}$$

Next we'll substitute into the formula. You already know from Table 2 that disposable income is \$40,000. How much is saving? It's not in Table 2, but since consumption is \$30,000, we can find saving by subtracting consumption from disposable income: \$40,000 − \$30,000 = \$10,000. Now we can complete the problem.

$$APS = \frac{Saving}{Disposable\ income} = \frac{\$10,000}{\$40,000} = \frac{1}{4} = .25^3$$

Note that the APC and the APS add up to 1. Let's work out another one, using the data in Table 3.

TABLE 3	
Disposable Income	Saving
\$20,000	\$1,500

Use the space below to calculate the APC and the APS.

---

[3]To convert ¼ into a decimal, we must divide the bottom number, 4, into the top number, 1.

APCs Greater than One

Is it possible to have an APC greater than one? You bet it is! How much would your APC be if you had a disposable income of $10,000 and your consumption was $12,000? Figure it out:

$$\text{APC} = \frac{\text{Consumption}}{\text{Disposable income}} = \frac{\$12,000}{\$10,000} = \frac{12}{10} = 1.2$$

Where would this extra $2,000 come from? Let's round up the usual suspects. You might take money out of the bank, borrow on your credit cards, take out a car loan, or buy on the installment plan. The bottom line is that many people find it quite easy to spend more than they earn year after year, whether by drawing down their savings, borrowing money, or some combination thereof.

Incidentally, if your APC *were* 1.2, how much would your APS be? Work it out right here:

$$\text{APS} = \frac{\text{Saving}}{\text{Disposable income}} = \frac{-\$2,000}{\$10,000} = \frac{-2}{10} = -0.2$$

Is it possible to have a negative APS? If your savings happens to be negative (that is, you spend more than your income), then your APS will definitely be negative. And you'll notice that your APC (1.2) plus your APS (-0.2) add up to 1.0.

Solutions:

$$\text{APC} = \frac{\text{Consumption}}{\text{Disposable income}} = \frac{\$18,500}{\$20,000} = \frac{185}{200} = \frac{37}{40}$$

$$40\overline{)37.000} = 4\overline{)3.7^10^20} \quad .925$$

$$\text{APS} = \frac{\text{Saving}}{\text{Disposable income}} = \frac{\$1,500}{\$20,000} = \frac{15}{200} = \frac{3}{40}$$

$$4\overline{)3.00} = 4\overline{).30^20} \quad .075$$

APC + APS = 1

Note that once again APC (.925) and APS (.075) add up to 1. This is your check to ensure that you haven't made a mistake in your calculations. (But can the APC ever be greater than 1? See the box, "APCs Greater than One.")

Now that we've done all this work, what does it mean to say that a person has an APC of .925 and an APS of .075? Think about it for a moment. Go back to the formulas for the APC and the APS. Think of the APC and the APS as percentages. Obviously, then, the APC is the percentage of a person's income that he or she spends. And the APS? It is the percentage of the person's income that is saved. In other words, 92.5 percent is spent and 7.5 percent is saved.

Just two more questions: How much is the APC for the United States? How much is the country's APS? From 1998 to 2000 the APC has averaged .98 and the APS .02. In other words, Americans spend about 98 percent of their disposable incomes and save the remaining 2 percent.

Marginal Propensity to Consume (MPC)

When income changes, so does consumption. When income rises, consumption also rises, but by less than does income. This is the consumption function, introduced at the beginning of the chapter.

The formula for calculating the MPC is:

$$\frac{\text{Change in C}}{\text{Change in income}}$$

$$MPC = \frac{\text{Change in C}}{\text{Change in income}}$$

TABLE 4

Year	Disposable Income	C
2000	$30,000	$23,000
2001	40,000	31,000

Using the data in Table 4, calculate the MPC in the space below.

Solution:

$$MPC = \frac{\text{Change in C}}{\text{Change in income}} = \frac{\$8,000}{\$10,000} = \frac{8}{10} = .8$$

Marginal Propensity to Save (MPS)

When income changes, not only does consumption change, but so does saving. When income rises, both consumption and saving will rise. Similarly, when income falls, both consumption and saving fall.

The formula for calculating the MPS is:

$$MPS = \frac{\text{Change in saving}}{\text{Change in income}}$$

$$MPS = \frac{\text{Change in saving}}{\text{Change in income}}$$

Using Table 4 again, calculate the MPS. (Note: Remember how to find saving when you have disposable income and consumption.)[4]

---

[4]From Table 4: Disposable income − Consumption = Savings
(2000) $30,000 − $23,000 = $7,000
(2001) $40,000 − $31,000 = $9,000

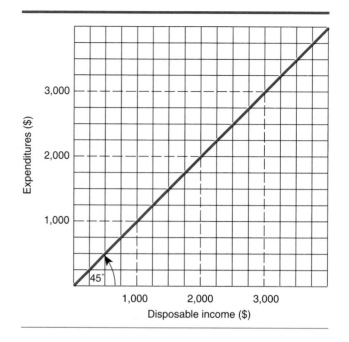

Solution:

$$\text{MPC} = \frac{\text{Change in saving}}{\text{Change in income}} = \frac{\$2,000}{\$10,000} = \frac{2}{10} = .2$$

We'll be using the APC, APS, MPC, and MPS later in this chapter, and occasionally in later chapters.

Graphing the Consumption Function

Through the ages, generations of economics students have been traumatized by graphs. The consumption function, savings, and, later, investment, aggregate demand, and equilibrium GDP have been undecipherable quantities. Estimating these variables on a graph is like being called on to read an exotic foreign language—without being permitted to use a dictionary.

Our first step will be to learn how to read a graph. The key to reading economic variables from a graph is knowing where to look for them; so before we even look at graphs, let's just talk about them for a moment. There is a vertical line on the left side of every graph called the *vertical scale,* and there is a horizontal line on the bottom side of every graph called the *horizontal scale.* Take a peek at Figure 2 to see what I'm talking about.

Every graph you will ever see in an economics text will have these two dimensions: the horizontal and the vertical. The vertical scale is almost always measured in dollars. In Figure 2 we have an expenditures scale with the numbers 1,000, 2,000, and 3,000, which represent expenditures of $1 trillion, $2 trillion, and $3 trillion, respectively. Note that the distances between each of the successive numbers are equal. If you used a ruler to measure the distances between 0 and 1,000; 1,000 and 2,000; and 2,000 and 3,000, they would be exactly the same. This is a very important point, because in a few pages you'll need to estimate distances between these numbers.

The horizontal axis in Figure 2 measures disposable income, also in units of 1,000, 2,000, and 3,000. In the graphs you'll encounter in future chapters, the horizontal scale will sometimes be based on units of time or units of output, but here we are measuring disposable income, which is measured in terms of dollars.

Nearly every variable is read from the vertical scale. The only exception we will encounter is disposable income, which is read from the horizontal scale.

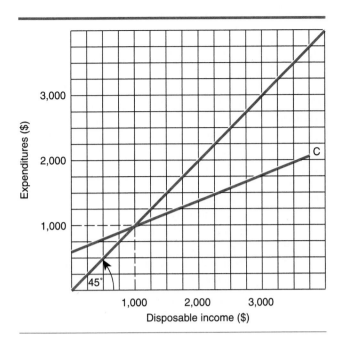

Figure 3
Consumption and Disposable Income

At a disposable income of 1,000, the C line crosses the 45-degree line. So consumption expenditures are equal to disposable income at 1,000.

The graph in Figure 2 shows expenditures along the vertical scale and disposable income along the horizontal scale. Figure 2 has only one line: a 45-degree line. This line has one purpose: to equate the horizontal scale with the vertical scale, that is, expenditures with disposable income.

Note the dotted line rising from a disposable income of 1,000. It meets the 45-degree line and then moves horizontally to the vertical scale. For a disposable income of 2,000, there is another dotted line rising to the 45-degree line and then moving straight across to the vertical scale. The same pattern occurs at a disposable income of 3,000.

Let's take that first point on the 45-degree line, just above 1,000 on the disposable income scale and directly across from 1,000 on the expenditures (vertical) scale. That point is exactly 1,000 units from both the vertical and horizontal scales. Point 2 is 2,000 units from each scale. Thus, we see that points on the vertical scale are equal to their corresponding points on the horizontal scale.

Now we're ready to graph the consumption function. First we'll review it: *As income rises, consumption rises, but not as quickly.* How should it look on a graph? Suppose disposable income rises by 1,000. By how much should C rise? According to our definition of the consumption function, it should rise by less than 1,000.

If the consumption function stated that C rises as quickly as income, can you guess what a graph of the consumption function would look like? That's a hard one. It would look like the 45-degree line. Each point would be the same number of units from the two scales.

Figure 3 illustrates that consumption does not rise as quickly as the 45-degree line. Since C does not rise as quickly as disposable income, the consumption line is flatter than the 45-degree line in Figure 2.

OK, now we're ready to read the graph in Figure 3. How much is consumption when disposable income is 1,000? Don't wait for me to tell you. Find a disposable income of 1,000 on the horizontal axis and work your way vertically (that means straight up) to the consumption line (C line). Then move across to the vertical axis. Now how much is C? You're not sure? OK, get a ruler or some other straightedge. Don't worry. I'll wait for you right here. Now let's go back to that disposable income of 1,000. Using the ruler, draw a line straight up to the C line. Now draw another line, this one perfectly horizontal (that means straight across), to the vertical axis. Now read the number. It is 1,000. Voilà! (If you need extra help, see the Extra Help box.)

Expenditures are measured on the vertical scale and disposable income along the horizontal scale.

Read Only If You Still Don't Understand Why C Is 1,000

If you're still trying to figure out why C is 1,000, we'll use the analogy of football. Suppose your team is about to receive a kickoff. One of your players catches the ball on the goal line and runs it out to your own 10-yard line. How far was his return yardage? Obviously 10 yards. How do you know it was exactly 10 yards? Because you saw him start at the goal line and get tackled at the 10. In fact, there are even markers on the sideline.

If we were to ask how much C is when disposable income is 1,000, we go vertically (or downfield) from the horizontal axis to the 1,000 mark, which we find on the vertical axis. How far did we go? We went 1,000. We

have a scale on the vertical axis that enables us to measure how far we've gone—just like in football.

Now suppose a team has a first down, say, on the 25-yard line. On the next play it moves the ball to about the 35. Is this another first down? What will the referees do? They'll measure. How? That's right, they'll bring out the chains.

You may do the same thing to measure C or any other variable measured against the vertical axis. Not only is there a scale on the vertical axis (or yard markers), but you may use a ruler (chains) to make your measurements.

We both know that I really did that one. Those lines were already on the graph. There are no guidelines for the next one. Find the level of C when disposable income is 2,000. Are you ready? Go ahead then. Just remember: up from a disposable income of 2,000 to the C line and then straight across. Oops! I'm giving it away. Go ahead: You do it, and I'll let you know if you're right or not.

What did you get? To me it looks like about 1,400. Anything close to 1,400 is fine. But if you got 1,300, then you probably thought that each box is worth 200. Check Figure 3 again. Each box is worth 250, because there are four boxes between 1,000 and 2,000. Incidentally, how much is the marginal propensity to consume? Figure it out in the space below using the three-step method: formula, substitute, and solve.

Solution:

$$\text{MPC} = \frac{\text{Change in C}}{\text{Change in disposable income}} = \frac{400}{1,000} = \frac{4}{10} = .4$$

Let's try another problem. How much is C when disposable income is 3,000?

What did you come up with? Your answer should be around 1,800. While we're at it, how much is the average propensity to consume? Again, use the three-step method.

Solution:

$$\text{APC} = \frac{\text{Consumption}}{\text{Disposable income}} = \frac{1,800}{3,000} = \frac{18}{30} = \frac{3}{5} = .6$$

Remember that C is measured vertically. Note that, as disposable income (which is measured horizontally) increases, C moves higher and higher. But it doesn't rise as quickly as disposable income.

At very low levels of disposable income, note that the C line is higher than the 45-degree line. When that happens, consumption is greater than disposable income. How is that possible? Believe me, it happens—especially during depressions. Besides, didn't your consumption ever exceed your income? What's that? Your consumption always exceeds your income? Well, then, you might not have any money in the bank, but you should intuitively grasp the notion that a nation can spend more than its disposable income.

Some nations have gone into debt for tens of billions of dollars. A few years ago, Mexico, Brazil, and Argentina headed the list of big debtors. However, the new champion is the United States, with an external net debt that is approaching \$2 trillion.[5]

At low income levels, C is greater than disposable income.

The Saving Function

The saving function is virtually the same as the consumption function: *As income rises, saving rises, but not as quickly.*

Now we're ready to find saving on the graph in Figure 4. First, how much is saving when disposable income is 1,000? Go ahead and figure it out. Even with no listing of saving on the graph, you can figure out how much saving is from the information you already have—you already figured the level of C when disposable income is 1,000.

Your answer should be zero. If disposable income is 1,000 and C is 1,000, saving must be zero. Note that saving is the vertical distance between the C line and the 45-degree line.

Next problem. How much is saving when disposable income is 2,000? After you do that, find saving when disposable income is 3,000.

The answers to both questions are worked out in the graph in Figure 4. All you need to do is take the vertical distance between the C line and the 45-degree line. (To figure out what C is when disposable income is zero, see box "Autonomous Consumption versus Induced Consumption.")

The saving function: As income rises, saving rises, but not as quickly.

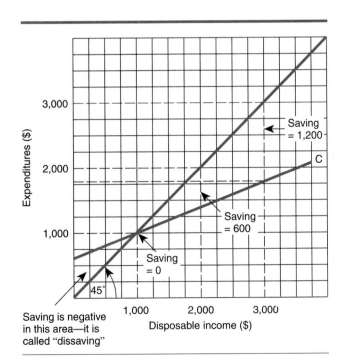

Figure 4

Consumption, Saving, and Disposable Income

Saving is the vertical distance between the C line and the 45-degree line. When the C line lies above the 45-degree line, saving is negative.

---

[5]In the last chapter of this book, we'll examine this problem in detail.

Autonomous Consumption versus Induced Consumption

You may have noticed in Figure 4 that, when disposable income is zero, C is about 600. We call this *autonomous consumption* because people will spend a certain minimum amount on the necessities of life—food, clothing, and shelter. Whether one has to dig into one's savings, go on welfare, or else beg, borrow, or steal, one will spend that minimum amount. And on a national level, we will all spend a minimum amount—what we are calling autonomous consumption—even if national disposable income is zero.*

If the autonomous level of consumption were 600, then it would continue to be 600 no matter what the level of disposable income was. We know from the consumption function that consumption rises as disposable income rises; therefore an increase in consumption is induced. At any given level of disposable income there is a corresponding level of consumption. Part of that consumption is autonomous and part is induced. Because autonomous consumption stays the same—no matter how much disposable income varies—we can easily figure out how much consumption is induced. Just subtract autonomous consumption from total consumption.

Let's start with a disposable income of zero in Figure 4. Autonomous consumption *is* total consumption because a disposable income of zero cannot induce any consumption.

Let's go to a disposable income of 1,000. How much are autonomous consumption and induced consumption? Autonomous consumption would continue to be 600. Because total consumption is 1,000, induced consumption is 400.

We'll try one more. How much is autonomous consumption and how much is induced consumption when disposable income is 3,000? Autonomous consumption continues to be 600. If total consumption is estimated at 1,800, then induced consumption is 1,200 (1,800 − 600).

---

*Of course, national disposable income would never actually fall to zero because people are always spending that minimum amount, so other people are receiving most of that amount in income. For example, if people spent $20 each on food, clothing, and shelter each week, this money would end up in the pockets of those who supplied these goods and services. They, in turn, would spend most of this money on their own necessities. This analysis anticipates our discussion of the multiplier, which we will get to in Chapter 11.

Figure 5

Consumption, Saving, and Disposable Income

Note that each box in this graph is 250. There are six boxes between 1,500 and 3,000.

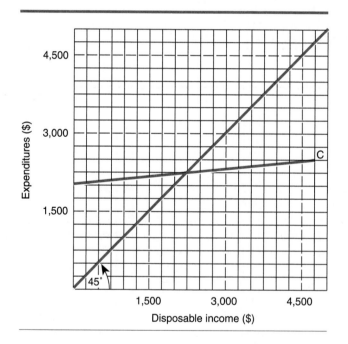

Let's stop for a minute to define two terms—autonomous consumption and induced consumption. *Autonomous consumption is our level of consumption when disposable income is 0.* It's called *autonomous consumption* because it's autonomous, or independent, of changes in the level of disposable income. *Induced consumption is that part of consumption which varies with the level of disposable income.* As disposable income rises, induced consumption also rises, and when disposable income falls, induced con-

autonomous consumption

induced consumption

On Reading Graphs

So far, we've had graphs with just two lines—the C line and the 45-degree line. In Chapter 6 we'll be adding the C + I line and in Chapter 7 the C + I + G line.

Not everyone can read a graph the first time out, but usually, with a little practice reading graphs becomes easier. So if you're not yet comfortable with graphs, I'd like you to go back a few pages to the section headed Graphing the Consumption Function. After you've reread it and reworked each of the problems, you should be considerably more comfortable with graphs.

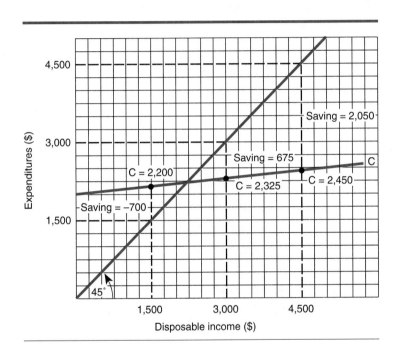

F*igure* 6

Consumption, Saving, and Disposable Income

Please note that C is the vertical distance between the horizontal axis and the C line. Saving is the vertical distance between the C line and the 45-degree line. C and saving always add up to disposable income.

When disposable income is 1,500, C is 2,200, so saving must be −700.

When disposable income is 3,000, C is 2,325 and saving is 675.

When disposable income is 4,500, C is 2,450 and saving is 2,050.

These are only approximations. Your answers may vary slightly as long as your saving and consumption add up to disposable income.

sumption also falls. We say that changes in the level of disposable income **induce** changes in the level of consumption.

If you are having any trouble measuring these vertical distances, remember that all vertical distances are measured on the vertical axis. Horizontal dotted lines have been drawn in Figure 4 to locate points on the vertical axis.

Let's try another graph to make sure we're clear on how to measure consumption and saving at various levels of disposable income. In Figure 5, find the levels of consumption and saving when disposable income is (*a*) 1,500, (*b*) 3,000, and (*c*) 4,500. To check your work, see Figure 6. (For extra help on reading graphs, see the boxes "On Reading Graphs" and "More on Finding Autonomous and Induced Consumption.")

Each box is 250. From 1,500 to 3,000 is a distance of 1,500. Divide 1,500 by 6 and you get 250. The C line begins two lines or boxes above 1,500, which means that autonomous C is 2,000—that is, 1,500 + (2 × 250).

Once you know autonomous consumption, you can figure out induced consumption for any level of disposable income. Start with a disposable income of zero. How much is induced consumption? Figure it out.

extra | HELP | extra

More on Finding Autonomous and Induced Consumption

We are going to find autonomous and induced consumption in Figure 6. That is, you're going to find them, and then I'll tell you whether you're right. Ready? Good. How much is autonomous consumption? Did you get 2,000? That's correct.

How much is induced consumption when disposable income is (1) 0; (2) 1,500; (3) 3,000; and (4) 4,500? Write your answers here: (1)_____; (2)_____; (3) _____; and (4) _____.

Your answers should be: (1) 0; (2) 200; (3) 325; and (4) 450. (If you got everything right, then you know how to find autonomous and induced consumption, so you may skip the rest of this box.)

First we'll go over the autonomous consumption, which is the level of consumption when disposable income is zero. In Figure 6, when disposable income is zero, which is at the lower left-hand corner of the graph, you can see that consumption is between 1,500 and 3,000, but somewhat closer to 1,500. The distance between 1,500 and 3,000 is six boxes or lines. How much is each box (the distance between two consecutive lines)? Figure it out.

Each box is 250. From 1,500 to 3,000 is a distance of 1,500. Divide 1,500 by 6 and you get 250. The C line begins two lines or boxes above 1,500, which means that autonomous C is 2,000—that is, 1,500 + (2 × 250).

Once you know autonomous consumption, you can figure out induced consumption for any level of disposable income. Start with a disposable income of zero. How much is induced consumption? Figure it out.

The answer is zero. At a disposable income of zero, total consumption is 2,000. Because autonomous consumption is also 2,000, induced consumption must be zero. Remember: Total consumption, or C, is the sum of autonomous consumption and induced consumption.

Next question: How much is induced consumption when disposable income is 1,500?

The answer is 200. Total consumption is 2,200. Total consumption (2,200) − autonomous consumption (2,000) = induced consumption (200). Remember: Autonomous consumption stays the same for all levels of disposable income. So once you find autonomous consumption, you can find induced consumption for any amount of disposable income by subtracting autonomous consumption from total consumption.

How much is induced consumption when disposable income is 3,000?

It's 325. Total consumption (2,325) − autonomous consumption (2,000) = induced consumption (325).

One more. How much is induced consumption when disposable income is 4,500?

The answer is 450. Total consumption (2,450) − autonomous consumption (2,000) = induced consumption (450).

The answer is zero. At a disposable income of zero, total consumption is 2,000. Because autonomous consumption is also 2,000, induced consumption must be zero. Remember: Total consumption, or C, is the sum of autonomous consumption and induced consumption.

Next question: How much is induced consumption when disposable income is 1,500?

The answer is 200. Total consumption is 2,200. Total consumption (2,200) − autonomous consumption (2,000) = induced consumption (200). Remember: Autonomous consumption stays the same for all levels of disposable income. So once you find autonomous consumption, you can find induced consumption for any amount of disposable income by subtracting autonomous consumption from total consumption.

How much is induced consumption when disposable income is 3,000?

It's 325. Total consumption (2,325) − autonomous consumption (2,000) = induced consumption (325).

One more. How much is induced consumption when disposable income is 4,500?

The answer is 450. Total consumption (2,450) − autonomous consumption (2,000) = induced consumption (450).

What the Consumer Buys

Consumption is traditionally divided into three categories: durables, nondurables, and services. Durables are things that last a while—say, at least a year or two. Nondurables, such as food, gasoline, and children's clothing, don't last long. (In fact, a case could be made that the clothing worn by fashion-conscious adults doesn't last either, although the reason it doesn't last is that fashions change rather than that it wears out.)

Durable goods include appliances, cars, and furniture. They last—or, at least, they're supposed to last. The big change in our economy since World War II has been in the service sector, which now produces over half of what consumers buy. Medical care, education, legal and financial services, and entertainment are some of the fields that have grown rapidly in the last five decades.

Figure 7 summarizes where the consumer's dollar went in 1955 and where it went in 2000. There has been a huge shift from expenditures on durables and nondurables to expenditures on services.

In 1955 Americans spent only 36 cents out of every consumer dollar on services; but today, 58 cents goes toward services. Why this massive shift? For one thing, Americans are spending a much larger part of their incomes on medical care than they did in the 1950s. This trend has been reinforced as our population grows older. More Americans are going to college, eating out, and suing one another than ever before. Computer services, financial services, and personal services have expanded rapidly. Basically, we're paying people to do things for us that we either did for ourselves in the 1950s or didn't do at all.

Do you bring your lunch to school every day? Do you know anyone who does? Had you gone to college 45 years ago, the chances are you would have brown-bagged it. How does a homemade lunch go into GDP? It goes into the category of nondurable goods. But the lunch you buy in the cafeteria or at Burger King is classified as a service. Similarly, if you buy lettuce, tomatoes, carrots, and other raw vegetables, cut them up at home, and eat a salad, the components of that salad classify as nondurables. But if you stop at a salad bar and buy the identical components, which have been cut up for you—and pay about 10 times as much per pound—then this expenditure would count as a service.

Americans spent nearly $7 trillion on consumer goods and services in 2000. This came to more than two-thirds of GDP. What did we buy? See Table 5.

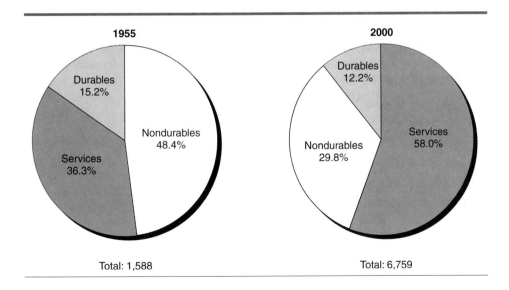

Figure 7

Consumer Spending, 1955 and 2000 ($ billions)

The major change in consumer spending has been a massive shift from nondurables to services.
Source: Economic Report of the President, 2001.

Thorstein Veblen, American sociologist and economist (Historical Pictures/Stock Montage)

In mid-March, 2001, American stocks were worth about $11 trillion. Economists estimate that consumers cut back spending by about 4 cents for every dollar's worth of wealth they lose in the market, so a $1 trillion stock market plunge would cause about a $40 billion drop in annual consumption, or less than one-half of one percent of total spending. Of course, if the market were to continue to rise, we would see a corresponding *increase* in consumption.

In addition to *feeling* rich, if your liquid assets rise, you do indeed have more money to spend. That is, you can quickly convert some of these assets into money, then go out and spend it. Economists have found that there is some correlation between consumption and the amount of liquid assets held. The reasoning here is that if you don't have it, you can't spend it, and if you do have it, you will spend some of it.

Stock of Durable Goods in the Hands of Consumers

In 1929, radios, toasters, vacuum cleaners, waffle irons, and other appliances were relatively new because most of the country had been electrified only over the last decade and a half. More than 95 percent of the cars on the road were less than 10 years old. By 1930, the market for consumer durables was temporarily saturated.

When few people own items such as personal computers, VCRs, or video games, sales will rise. But when the market is saturated (and people own relatively late models), it will be some time before sales pick up again.

Consumer durables are now a relatively small part of total consumption—only about 12 percent of all goods and services sold to consumers in 1997. However, their sales are somewhat erratic, largely because they vary inversely with the stock of consumer durables in the hands of consumers. When people hold a large stock of consumer durables, consumer durable sales tend to be low; when that stock is low, sales tend to be high.

Keeping Up with the Joneses

Wealth has never been a sufficient source of honor in itself. It must be advertised, and the normal medium is obtrusively expensive goods.
　　—John Kenneth Galbraith,
　　　　The Affluent Society

Conspicuous consumption

Our necessities are few but our wants are endless.
　　　　—Inscription found
　　　　　in a fortune cookie

Most of us, at least a few times in our lives, have been guilty of showing off our expensive clothes, our jewelry, our cars, or even our Florida tans. And most of us have been tempted to keep up with our neighbors, relatives, and friends. When the Joneses buy something, we have to go out and buy one, too—even if we can't afford it—because if we don't buy it, we won't be keeping up.

Why do some people spend $2,000 on a wristwatch, $150 for a pair of sneakers, or $5,000 for an evening gown? To a large degree, they're showing off. I have so much money, they seem to be saying, that I can afford these indulgences.

About 90 years ago Thorstein Veblen coined the term *conspicuous consumption.* In a marvelous book titled *The Theory of the Leisure Class,* Veblen stated, "Conspicuous consumption of valuable goods is a means of reputability to the gentleman of leisure." He went on to say, "With the exception of the instinct of self-preservation, the propensity for emulation is probably the strongest and most alert and persistent of the economic motives proper."[7]

Consumer Expectations

When people expect inflation, they often buy consumer durables before prices go up. On the other hand, when they expect recession, they tend to reduce their purchases of such big-ticket items as cars, furniture, and major appliances. Many people fear being laid off or having their income reduced because of recessions, so they tend to postpone major purchases until times get better.

---

[7]Thorstein Veblen, *The Theory of the Leisure Class,* Chapters 4 and 5.

The Permanent Income Hypothesis

According to Milton Friedman, a prominent conservative economist, the strongest influence on consumption is one's estimated average lifetime income. No one knows what his or her average lifetime income will actually be, but people can generally figure out if they are earning more or less than that average.

If a factory worker earning $25,000 a year expects to remain a factory worker, she can estimate her future earnings until she retires. According to Friedman, people gear their consumption to their expected earnings more than to their current income.

Suppose someone's income temporarily contracts, say, because of a factory layoff. Would the person cut back very sharply on her consumption? No, she would not, says this theory, since she knows she will be back on the job within a few months. She has to continue paying her rent, meeting her car payments, and eating three times a day.

Earnings tend to rise until late middle age (about 55 or so) and then decline. Therefore the permanent income hypothesis would predict that most people's consumption is greater than their income until their mid or late 20s. From the late 20s to the early 60s, current disposable income is usually greater than consumption. In old age, the relationship between consumption and current disposable income is again reversed, so consumption is greater than income.

Thus, our consumption is determined by our average expected income, or permanent income. That income is a constant; consumption is a constant percentage of that income. For most Americans, consumption would be more than 95 percent of permanent income.

According to Friedman's hypothesis, if you suddenly win the lottery, make a huge sum of money on a quiz show, or experience some other windfall, you will not spend much of it. You will spend *some* of it because it will raise your permanent income, but you will spend only a small part of it.

For example, suppose you receive a windfall of $100,000. If the permanent income hypothesis applies, you might spend an extra $6,000 or $8,000 a year over the next 15 years or so. Is this how most lottery winners have handled their windfalls? Apparently there are quite a few deviations from the behavior predicted by the permanent income hypothesis.

Milton Friedman, winner of Nobel prize, 1976, for work on monetary theory (© The Nobel Foundation)

Determinants of the Level of Saving

Savings may be viewed as a residual of disposable income, what is left after most or nearly all of it has been used on consumption. Some people spend virtually all of their income, while others manage to spend more than they earn year after year.

Still, most Americans manage to save at least a small part of their income. Some people are saving for a big-ticket item like a couch, a new bedroom set, a car, or a VCR. Others are saving for a vacation or perhaps the down payment on a house. Many Americans try to put away some money each year for their children's education. Some people save money every year for a rainy day or their old age, while still others are simply penny-pinchers.

There are many reasons why people save.

On the average, Americans save about 2 percent of their disposable income. Can you figure out from this one fact how much our APS and APC are?

APS =   APC =

If you remembered what we covered near the beginning of the chapter, you said that the APS is .02 and APC is .98. In other words, we spend, on the average, 98 percent of our disposable income and save 5 percent.

For most of the 20th century, Americans saved between 7 and 10 percent of their disposable incomes. A decline to 5 percent (and even less in recent years) may not seem like much, but it amounts to an enormous amount of money when we consider that our disposable personal income is about $7 trillion. Now figure out by how many dollars our savings would decline if the savings rate fell by 2 percent. Work it out here and then check the solution in the space below.

Solution: $7,000,000,000,000 × .02 = $140,000,000,000 (or $140 billion).

Incidentally, this problem can be reduced to a very simple problem in arithmetic. How much is $7 trillion × 2? It's $14 trillion. Write it out: $14,000,000,000,000. OK. Now when you multiply a number by .02, how many zeros do you take from it? I hope you said two. Thus we have $14,000,000,000,000. When we move the commas over, we get $140,000,000,000.

A much easier way to do this calculation is to write $7 trillion as 7000 (which stands for 7 thousand billion). Then 7000 × .02 = 140.

A $140 billion shortfall is particularly important at a time when we need all the savings we can lay our hands on to finance the hundreds of billions of investment funds that large corporations need to build new plant and equipment.

Why Do We Spend So Much and Save So Little?

Murray Weidenbaum, President Reagan's first chief economic advisor (© 1993 Susan Muniak)

It seems a lot of trouble if, instead of having to earn money and save it, you can just go and borrow it.
—Winston Churchill

Americans have been on a spending binge these last 20 years. In fact, the national motto might well be "Buy now, pay later," "Shop till you drop," or "We want it all, and we want it now!" The "me generation" has had a fascination for every conceivable type of electronic gadget, has had to buy new wardrobes every six months as the fashions change, and has had to drive the latest-model, fully-loaded luxury foreign car. In fact, much of what we buy is made by foreigners. Murray Weidenbaum, who served as President Ronald Reagan's first chief economic advisor, summed up our profligacy this way:

> As citizens of the United States, we are consuming more than we are producing, borrowing more than we are saving, and spending more than we are earning. We are rapidly approaching the time when we will have to pay the piper.[8]

The federal government has actually underwritten our spending binge. Until 1987, interest paid on consumer loans was fully deductible from our federal income taxes. Mortgage interest and property taxes remain fully deductible. So buy a home and charge part of your costs to Uncle Sam.[9] And if you need to borrow still more money, just take out a second mortgage and use this money to finance your ever-growing consumption expenditures.

The tremendous expansion of bank credit cards, installment credit, and consumer loans has further fueled the consumer binge of the last dozen years. Every day Americans are offered millions of credit cards, whether they asked for them or not. In fact, from 1990 to 2000 household debt doubled to $7 trillion. Some people call credit cards "mall money."

Young Americans getting married, buying their first homes, and starting families will not be able to begin saving until they are well into their 30s. Traditionally, it is the middle-aged who do the bulk of the nation's saving. But today's middle-aged, the baby boomers born in the late 1940s and in the 1950s, are spending as if there were no

---

[8]Murray Weidenbaum, *Rendezvous with Reality* (New York: Basic Books, 1988). p. 4.

[9]Tax deductions are a marvelous way to reduce your tax bill. In Chapter 7 we'll talk about how the tax system works and how you can beat it.

tomorrow. Much of this spree is financed by tax-deductible home equity loans (see box "Home Equity Loans: A Tax Subsidy for Consumption").

In America, we like to say that the consumer is king. See the box "Is the Consumer Really King?" for a view almost diametrically opposed to the one I've been expressing all this time. Does the consumer really have all that many choices, or does our suburban lifestyle make it almost impossible for most families to save?

Our saving rate might not have been so low were it not for two factors that have become increasingly important over the last five decades—Social Security and widespread home ownership. Most Americans do not feel the pressing need to save for their old age because they will receive Social Security benefits, not to mention private pensions. Similarly, home ownership is seen as a form of saving, especially during a period of rising real estate prices.

> Nobody goes to the mall anymore because they're too crowded.
> —Standard retail industry joke

Home Equity Loans: A Tax Subsidy for Consumption

Until the Tax Reform Act of 1986, consumer spending was subsidized by the federal government in two ways. Money spent on sales tax could be deducted from federal taxes. Also deductible was interest on consumer loans. These two subsidies were taken away, but a loophole the size of a house was left in place.

Homeowners are able to continue taking the interest paid on home equity loans off their taxes. So if you need money for a new car, a trip around the world, or a plain old-fashioned shopping spree, just take out a home equity loan. Since it's treated by the IRS as mortgage borrowing, it's tax deductible.

One of the consequences of this spending binge by the middle-aged is that they will leave much less to their children than *their* parents left to them. Alfred Malabre observes that "the coming generation of Americans won't be able to afford the standard of housing enjoyed by their parents, since their parents will have spent their inflated equity and left behind a mountain of debt."[*]

---

[*]Alfred L. Malabre, Jr., *Beyond Our Means* (New York: Random House, 1987), p. 46.

Is the Consumer Really King?

Before we even receive our paychecks today, nearly all those dollars already have someone else's name on them. *Think* about it. How much of *your* family's paychecks goes toward paying off your mortgage, credit card debt, your cars, school tuition, insurance, medical bills, and home repair? Of course you would have had a lot more to spend if the government hadn't already taken *its* share of your pay before you even saw your paycheck.

Let's start with what is, by far, our most important purchase—a home. Once that purchase is made, there aren't a whole lot of choices with respect to mortgage payments, real estate taxes, heating bills, homeowner's insurance, upkeep, and repairs. Back in 1949, the average 30-year-old head of household needed to spend just 14 percent of his paycheck to make the payments on his home. By 1970 it took more than 21 percent of his paycheck to pay for that home. And today the average 30-year-old has to shell out more than 40 percent of his take-home pay.

The American dream has gradually become a financial nightmare. I recently asked my students how many cars their families owned. The majority owned three or four.

Suburban sprawl has almost completely obviated the use of mass transit. Indeed, it is economically unfeasible to have any kind of mass transit—even express bus service during peak travel times—unless there's a minimum population density of five families per acre. This means that the typical suburban family must be completely dependent on its cars. The trip to work, to school, to the store, to little league practice, and to virtually anywhere else must be made by car.

The cost of car payments, insurance, gas, maintenance, and repairs takes another large chunk—often more than 25 percent—out of the typical suburban family's income. So it's no wonder that most households depend on two full-time incomes, and often one or two additional part-time incomes as well.

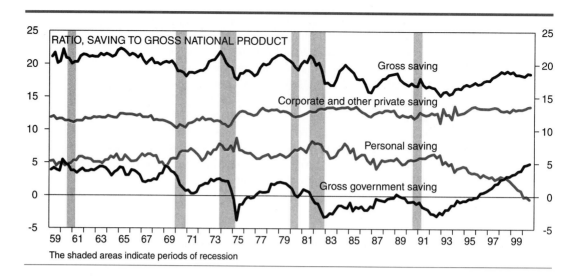

The shaded areas indicate periods of recession

F*igure* 8

The Three Components of National Saving, 1969–2000

Personal saving has been on the decline since the mid-1980s, while government saving (by the federal, state, and local governments) was negative for most of the 1980s and 1990s, and has become positive as the federal government swings from huge budget deficits to huge surpluses. By far, the most important component of national saving is business saving.

Source: Survey of Current Business, February 2001.

Bruce Steinberg, a Merrill Lynch economist, takes a contrarian view, by claiming that the savings rate is badly biased downward. His view was summarized by *BusinessWeek:*[10]

> In calculating the rate, he notes, the government inconsistently subtracts capital-gains taxes from income while failing to count as income the gains on which those taxes are paid.
>
>   If realized capital gains were counted as income (which is how most people see them), Steinberg figures the current savings rate would be 10%—close to its historic level. In other words, people have not been dipping into their unrealized capital gains, as some charge.

How *have* we been able to put off paying the piper for so long? By borrowing. As individual consumers, we borrow; as giant corporations, we borrow; and as the federal government, we borrow. And who lends us this money? Increasingly, the answer is foreigners.

Total Saving: Individual Saving + Business Saving + Government Saving

Every economy depends on saving for capital formation. That saving is the total of individual saving, business saving, and government saving.[11] We've seen that individual saving has dwindled in recent years. Businesses set aside savings in the form of depreciation allowances and retained earnings, while our local, state, and federal governments save by running surpluses and dissave by running deficits.

As you can see in Figure 8, the decline in household saving has been offset since 1993 by a sharp rise in government saving and business saving. It is appropriate, then, that the business investment sector and the government sector are covered in the next two chapters.

---

[10]*BusinessWeek,* "Are Americans Spendthrifts?" November 22, 2000, p. 18.

[11]Government saving = federal surplus (or deficit) + state and local surplus.

Questions for Further Thought and Discussion

1. Explain the relationship between consumption and saving.

2. Explain the difference between autonomous consumption and induced consumption.

3. Explain how the stock of consumer durables in the hands of consumers and credit availability each affect the level of consumption.

4. Since the 1950s a massive shift in consumption patterns with respect to nondurable goods and services has taken place. What is this shift and how can it be explained?

5. How little do Americans save? Why do they save so little?

6. How is it possible for a nation's consumption to sometimes exceed its disposable income?

7. The marginal propensity to consume (MPC) for a nation is .85. Explain what this means.

8. Why is the demand for consumer nondurable goods more stable than that for consumer durable goods?

Workbook for Chapter 5

Name _____ Date _____

Multiple-Choice Questions

Circle the letter that corresponds to the best answer.

1. Since 1955 Americans have been spending _____.
   a) a larger percentage of their incomes on services
   b) a smaller percentage of their incomes on services
   c) about the same percentage of their incomes on services

2. When the C line crosses the 45-degree line, saving is _____.
   a) positive
   b) negative
   c) zero
   d) impossible to calculate because there is not enough information to know.

3. When disposable income is zero, _____.
   a) autonomous consumption is equal to induced consumption
   b) autonomous consumption is equal to total consumption
   c) induced consumption is equal to total consumption

4. The minimum amount that people will spend even if disposable income is zero is called _____ consumption.
   a) autonomous
   b) induced
   c) total

5. According to the permanent income hypothesis, if a person received a windfall of $100,000, he would spend _____ that year.
   a) some of it
   c) nearly all of it
   b) most of it
   d) all of it

6. As disposable income rises, _____.
   a) autonomous C rises
   c) induced C rises
   b) autonomous C falls
   d) induced C falls

7. The largest component of GDP is _____.
   a) net exports
   c) consumption
   b) investment
   d) government purchases

8. The largest component of C is _____.
   a) durable goods
   b) services
   c) nondurable goods

9. The consumption function tells us that, as income rises, consumption _____.
   a) declines
   b) remains the same
   c) rises more slowly than income
   d) rises more quickly than income

10. When income levels are very low, C is _____.
    a) zero
    b) lower than income
    c) higher than income

11. When income is equal to consumption, saving is _____.
    a) negative
    b) zero
    c) positive
    d) impossible to calculate because there is insufficient information

12. Which of the following relations is *not* correct?
    a) MPC + MPS = 1
    d) 1 − APS = APC
    b) APC + APS = 1
    e) 1 − MPC = MPS
    c) MPS = MPC + 1

13. Induced consumption expenditures _____.
    a) fall as income rises
    b) are always equal to autonomous consumption expenditures
    c) plus saving equals total consumption expenditures
    d) represent consumption that is independent of income
    e) are influenced mainly by income

14. Autonomous consumption expenditures are _____.
    a) equal to induced consumption expenditures
    b) proportional to disposable income
    c) not influenced by income
    d) influenced primarily by the saving function

15. The average propensity to save _____.
    a) is disposable income divided by savings
    b) is a measure of the additional saving generated by additional income
    c) is negative at very high income levels
    d) varies directly with income; as income rises, the APS rises

Fill-In Questions

1. About _____ percent of what Americans spend on consumption is spent on services.

2. The average propensity to consume is found by dividing _____ by _____.

3. The APS + the APC = _____.

4. The consumption function states that _____.

5. Dissaving takes place when _____.

6. Induced consumption is induced by _____.

7. According to the saving function, as disposable income rises, _____.

8. The most important determinant of the level of consumption is _____.

9. The average propensity to consume in the United States today is about _____.

10. 1 − MPS = _____.

11. When the C line crosses the 45-degree line, saving is equal to _____.

Problems

1. Given the information shown in Table 1, calculate the APC and the APS.

TABLE 1

Disposable Income	Consumption
$10,000	$8,400

2. Given the information shown in Table 2, calculate the MPC and MPS. (Assume disposable income rises from $35,000 to $37,000.)

TABLE 2

Year	Disposable Income	Saving
2002	$35,000	$4,600
2003	37,000	5,300

3. Using the information in Figure 1, how much are consumption and saving when disposable income is:

	C	Saving
a) 1,000	_____	_____
b) 2,000	_____	_____
c) 3,000	_____	_____

4. Using your answers from question 3a, calculate the APC and the APS.

5. Using your answers from questions 3a and 3b, calculate the MPC and the MPS when disposable income rises from 1,000 to 2,000.

6. Using the data in Figure 1, how much is autonomous consumption?

7. Using the data in Figure 1, determine induced consumption when disposable income is:

   a) 1,000

   b) 2,000

   c) 3,000

8. If C is $4 trillion, disposable income is $5 trillion, and autonomous consumption is $3 trillion:

   a) How much is saving?

   b) How much is induced consumption?

   c) How much is the APS?

   d) If the APS falls by .01, how much does saving fall?

Figure 1

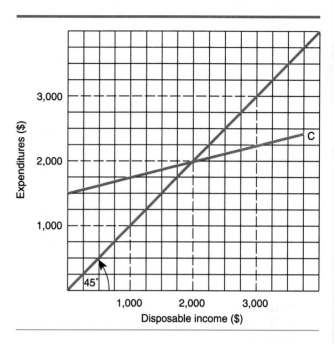

Chapter 6

The Business-Investment Sector

Unlike in Vietnam, Cuba, North Korea, and dozens of other communist and socialist nations, most investment in the United States is carried out by private business firms rather than by the government. That investment consists of the production of new plant and equipment, residential housing, and additions to our inventories.

CHAPTER OBJECTIVES

In this chapter you'll learn about:

- The three types of business firms.
- How investment is carried out.
- The difference between gross investment and net investment.

- How capital is accumulated.
- The determinants of the level of investment.
- The graphing of the C + I line.

Proprietorships, Partnerships, and Corporations

There are three types of business firms in the United States. Proprietorships are owned by individuals and are almost always small businesses. Partnerships, which are also usually small, are owned by two or more people. There are relatively few large businesses in our country, and virtually all of them are corporations. Most corporations, like most businesses, are small.

Most businesses are small.

The Proprietorship

A typical proprietorship would be a grocery, a barbershop, a candy store, a restaurant, a family farm, or a filling station. Chances are, nearly all of the places in the neighborhood where you shop are proprietorships.

To start a proprietorship, a person simply decides to go into business, either opening a new firm or taking over an existing one. With a proprietorship, there are fewer legal complications than with any other form of business organization. Another advantage is that you are your own boss. You don't have to consult with other owners, partners, or stockholders. Finally, there are tax advantages. A proprietor's income is taxed only once—when she or he pays personal income tax. But if the same firm were to incorporate, its income would be taxed twice—once as the income of the firm (the corporate income tax) and again as the personal income of the owner.

The Partnership

Advantages of a partnership

Two or more people can form a partnership. Although the typical partnership has two people, some law and accounting firms have hundreds of partners. Two key advantages of forming a partnership are being able to raise more capital and to divide the work and responsibility of running the business.

A typical division of labor between partners would be production and sales, or, in the parlance of business, inside and outside. The advantages of forming a partnership must be weighed against two basic disadvantages. The first is that the partnership must be dissolved when one of its members dies or wants to leave the business. A second disadvantage is that of unlimited liability.

Disadvantages of a partnership

Both proprietors and partners are liable for all debts incurred by their businesses. For example, if the firm is sued for negligence, the owners are personally liable to pay the amount awarded if the firm cannot do so. If one partner absconds with funds, the other partners may lose their homes and cars even though they were innocent victims. The way to avoid ever having to face this dilemma is to incorporate.

The Corporation

The main advantage to incorporating is limited liability.

The key advantage of the corporation is limited liability. That is, each owner's liability is limited to the amount of money he has invested in the business. If there's a negligence suit or someone absconds with funds, the most you can lose is your investment. No one can touch your house, car, or any other personal property.

Corporation: An ingenious device for obtaining individual profit without individual responsibility.
—Ambrose Bierce,
The Devil's Dictionary

A corporation is a legal person. As such, it can sue and be sued. What is significant about this attribute is that the people who own the corporation—the stockholders—cannot be sued no matter how grievous the transgressions of the corporation. However, the courts have, on occasion, found stockholders liable (for example, when stockholders form a corporation for fraudulent purposes).

A second advantage of a corporation is its potentially perpetual life. While a partnership must be dissolved when one of the partners leaves the business, a corporation can continue indefinitely: The stock owned by the principal who wants to pull out is purchased by someone else. In the case of large, publicly held corporations, such transactions take place routinely at the major stock exchanges.

A third advantage is paying lower federal personal income tax. If you're a small business owner making at least $40,000, says Judith McQuown, author of *Incorporate Yourself,*[1] you can actually save on your taxes by incorporating. But won't you now have to pay corporate income tax *and* personal income tax? Yes, but the sum of these two taxes could be thousands of dollars less than you paid in personal income tax before incorporating. You can find all of this spelled out in McQuown's book,[2] and, if you decide to incorporate, you'll want to hire an accountant to calculate your tax savings.

Still another advantage of incorporating is that the company can sell stock to the public to raise more money. Because the owners have limited liability and the firm itself

---

[1]Judith McQuown, *Inc. Yourself: How to Profit by Setting Up Your Own Corporation,* 9th ed., (New York: Broadway Books, 1999).

[2]*Ibid.,* Chapter 1.

Small Corporations

The typical corporation is very small, like the old North American Uniform Cap Corporation. Although the company had a rather impressive name, its officers were Jonas Lewy, president; Nadja Lewy, vice president; and their son, Henry Lewy, secretary-treasurer. They ran their business out of a tiny loft in Manhattan's garment district, sewing up work caps, military caps, and what are now called "gimme caps." They had about a half-dozen sewing machines, and Henry's parents—the president and the vice president—operated two of them. During the "busy season," they hired another three or four operators.

The North American Uniform Cap Corporation never grew into a large enterprise, although the Lewys were always waiting for that one big order—like maybe a few million caps for the Chinese Peoples Liberation Army. But the big order never came, and, like 85 percent of all corporations, North American Uniform Caps never managed to do a million dollars worth of business in a single year.

TABLE 1	The Top Ten in U.S. Sales, 2000	
		2000 Sales in Billions
1	ExxonMobil	$211
2	Wal-Mart Stores	186
3	General Motors	185
4	Ford Motor	170
5	General Electric	130
6	Citigroup	112
7	Enron	101
8	IBM	88
9	AT&T	66
10	Verizon	65

Source: Business Week, February 26, 2001.

has ongoing life, the corporation is in a better position than the proprietorship or partnership to go to the public to raise funds.

Of course, only a tiny fraction of all corporations ever go public. Nearly all are relatively small businesses that are completely owned by a few individuals. (See box, "Small Corporations.")

Most corporations are small firms.

The largest 10 corporations are shown in Table 1. Who's number one? It's Exxon Mobil, with sales of $211 billion.

You'll notice that *Business Week* ranks corporations in terms of sales. They may also be ranked in size of assets, profits, number of employees, or some other attribute. If you're curious, in 2000, Exxon Mobil led the nation in profits with $17.7 billion, followed closely by Citigroup ($13.5 billion), and General Electric ($12.7 billion).

There are two disadvantages to incorporating. First, you have to have papers drawn up and pay a fee for a charter. The expense of doing this varies, but most states charge filing fees of less than $200. A second disadvantage is that you will have to pay federal, and possibly state, corporate income tax. Although the rates are very low for small corporations, those with profits of more than $10 million must pay 35 percent of anything above that amount to the Internal Revenue Service.[3] Still another disadvantage of incorporating is being subject to double taxation. After a corporation's profits are subject to the corporate income tax, much of what remains is paid out in dividends, on which one must pay personal income taxes.

Two disadvantages to incorporating

---

[3]Corporations earning smaller profits pay lower rates.

The New Hybrid Varieties

Some companies seem to fall into the cracks between partnerships and corporations. There are limited partnerships, which not only avoid paying corporate income taxes but, as their name implies, also minimize legal risk to their investors. There are S corporations—named after the subchapter of the Internal Revenue Code that authorizes them—which offer their shareholders limited liability and pay no corporate income tax. Since 1988, the Internal Revenue Service has also authorized limited liability companies, which have the legal insulation of a corporation and the preferred tax treatment of a limited partnership.

You can also form a limited liability company, or limited liability partnership, to protect your personal assets if your business is sued. A suit can place only the assets of your business at risk. Between 1992 and 1994 more than 40 states—with California a prominent exception—passed limited liability legislation. A limited liability company carries the same benefits as the S corporation, with taxes assessed solely at the individual level; the owners pay personal income tax on their profits but do not have to pay corporate income tax.

But all of this said, these are still the exceptions that prove the rule. The vast majority of businessowners incorporate to secure limited liability, and are then subject to paying corporate income taxes. The hybrid entities do provide loopholes, but so far only a small minority of businessowners have crawled through.

The box titled "The New Hybrid Varieties" describes companies that are a cross between partnerships and corporations.

Stocks and Bonds

Stockholders are owners of a corporation. Bondholders lend money to a company and are therefore creditors rather than owners. This distinction becomes important when we consider the order in which people are paid off when the corporation is doing well and when it goes bankrupt.

Two types of stock

There are two types of corporate stock: common and preferred. The advantage of owning preferred is that you will receive a stipulated dividend, say 6 percent of the face value of your stock, provided there are any profits out of which to pay dividends. After you are paid, if some profits remain, the common stockholders will be paid.

Why bother to own common stock? Mainly because only common stockholders may vote on issues of concern to the corporation as well as on who gets to run the corporation. Both preferred and common stockholders own the corporation, or hold equity in the company, but only common stockholders vote.

Bondholders are creditors—not owners.

Bondholders are creditors rather than owners of a corporation. Like the preferred stockholders, they must be paid a stipulated percentage of the face value of their bonds, say 8 percent, in the form of interest, but they must be paid whether or not the company makes a profit. In fact, the interest they receive is considered one of the costs of doing business. And should a company go bankrupt, the bondholders, as creditors, have to be paid off before the owners of preferred and common stock see any money.

Capitalization and Control

A corporation's total capital, or capitalization, consists of the total value of its stocks and bonds. For example, a $4 billion corporation may have $1 billion in bonds, $500 million in preferred stock, and $2.5 billion in common stock. Similarly, a corporation with $200 million in bonds, $100 million in preferred stock, and $300 million in common stock would be capitalized at $600 million.

One might ask how much money would be needed to gain control of a large corporation. Let's consider a corporation that's capitalized for $500 million—$300 million in bonds, $120 million in preferred stock, and $80 million in common stock. Theoretically, you would need slightly over $40 million, or 50 percent plus one share of the common stock.

But most large corporations are rather widely held; that is, there are many stockholders with only a few holding even 1 percent. Furthermore, many stockholders either don't bother to vote their shares or they give proxies to others who will. Usually, then, holding about 5 percent of the common stock of a company will be sufficient for control. So, in this case, by holding $4 million worth of common stock (5 percent of $80 million), you should be able to control this $500 million corporation.

Now let's work out a problem testing your knowledge of capitalization and control: If the XYZ corporation has $4 billion in preferred stock, $6 billion in common stock, and $3 billion in bonds: (*a*) How much is its capitalization? (*b*) Theoretically, how much would it take to control it? (*c*) Practically speaking, it may take only about how much to control it?

Work out your answers here:

Solutions: (*a*) $4 billion + $6 billion + $3 billion = $13 billion
(*b*) $6 billion × .50 = $3 billion, or, technically speaking, $3 billion + $1
(*c*) $6 billion × .05 = $300 million

Many economists believe that you really need to hold about 10 percent of the common stock to be assured of control. In *that* case, we have: $6 billion × .10 = $600 million. So to be fair, we would have to accept an answer of either 5 percent of the common stock or 10 percent of the common stock. Or, for that matter, any percentage between 5 and 10.

The Business Population

There are some 24 million business firms in the United States. As you can see in Table 2, the most numerous are proprietorships, followed by corporations, and then partnerships.

TABLE 2 The Business Population by Form of Legal Organization, 2000

Form	Number of firms
Proprietorships	17,176,000
Partnerships	1,759,000
Corporations	4,710,000
Total	23,645,000

Source: Statistical Abstract of the United States, 2001.

We show the comparative percentage shares of the business population in panel (a) of Figure 1. Then, in panel (b) of Figure 1, we have the percentage share of sales of each of proprietorships, partnerships, and corporations. Corporations account for nearly $9 out of every $10 of sales.

Investment

Investment is really the thing that makes our economy go. When we have prosperity, investment is high and rising. And when we're in a recession, it is low and falling. Let's define investment and then see how it varies.

Figure 1

The Business Population and
Shares of Total Sales, 1997

Source: Statistical Abstract of the United
States, 2001

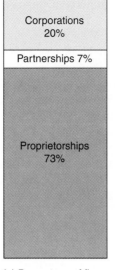

(a) Percentage of firms   (b) Percentage of sales

Investment is any new plant, equipment, additional inventory, or residential housing.[4] Plant includes factories, office buildings, department and other retail stores, and shopping malls. Examples of equipment are assembly lines, machine tools, display cases, cash registers, computer systems, and office furniture—as long as businesses purchase them. For example, if you buy a car for your personal use, it's a consumption expenditure. But if Shell Oil buys a car for its executives to ride around in (on company business), then it's an investment. The key question we must ask is whether the purchase adds to a company's plant, equipment, or inventory. If not, then it's not investment. What if your town buys a new police car or a new word processor, or puts up a new school? Is this investment? Close, but no cigar. When the government makes these purchases, it's government spending rather than investment. This may sound arbitrary, but it's part of the rules of national income accounting, which we discuss fully in Chapter 9.

What if you were to purchase 100 shares of Intel stock? Would that be investment? Does that add (directly) to Intel's plant, equipment, or inventory? It doesn't? Then it isn't investment. It's merely a financial transaction. When Intel uses those funds to buy plant, equipment, or inventory, *then* it's investment.

Inventory includes goods on store shelves waiting to be sold, cars in a showroom or car lot, finished goods in a factory waiting to be shipped, and even parts of a product ready to be assembled. Business firms do not want to hold more inventory than they need because that inventory ties up money and also incurs storage costs. Suppose you owned a toy store and had sales of $10,000 a week. Would you want to carry an inventory of $100,000 toys? Today, with inventory computerization, many firms use the just-in-time method of inventory control. Stores and factories, many tied to the Internet, have found they can cut costs by shrinking the warehouses where they store the materials they use in production or the goods they sell later to consumers.

Calculating inventory investment is a little tricky. We include only the net change from January 1 to December 31 of a given year. For example, how much was inventory investment for General Motors in 2003 (using the figures in Table 3)?

How much was GM's inventory investment in 2003? $25 million? Nope. $395 million? Nope. The answer is $10 million. All you have to do is look at the levels of inventory on January 1 and December 31 and calculate the difference.

You are investing if you are adding to your firm's plant, equipment, or inventory.

How to calculate inventory investment

[4]Residential construction does not properly belong in a chapter on business investment, but I am prepared, just this once, to dispense with propriety, because I don't know where else to put it.

TABLE 3	Hypothetical Inventory Levels of General Motors
Date	Level of Inventory
January 1, 2003	$120 million
July 1, 2003	145 million
December 31, 2003	130 million

TABLE 4	Hypothetical Inventory Levels of Shell Oil
Date	Level of Inventory
January 1, 2004	$230 million
May 15, 2004	215 million
September 1, 2004	240 million
December 31, 2004	220 million

Let's try another one. Using the data in Table 4, calculate the inventory investment for Shell Oil in 2004.

Your answer should be −$10 million. Between the first day of the year and the last day of the year, the level of Shell's inventory went down by $10 million. In other words, inventory investment was negative.

The fact that we can have negative inventory investment is significant. Because investment is one sector of GDP, declining inventories will be a drag on GDP. That's what happens during recessions.

A glance at Figure 2 shows just how unstable inventory investment has been over the last 40 years. In fact, you've probably never been on a roller coaster that had as many steep ups and downs as inventory investment. Most of the steep drops are associated with

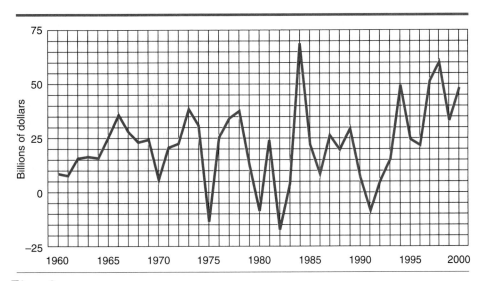

F*igure* 2

Inventory investment, 1960–2000 (in billions of 1987 dollars)

This is the most volatile sector of investment. Note that inventory investment was actually negative during three recessions.

Source: Economic Report of the President, 2001; Business Cycle Indicators, March 2001.

I hope your answer is $120. If it isn't, here's how to calculate the interest:

$$\text{Interest rate} = \frac{\text{Interest paid}}{\text{Amount borrowed}}$$

$$.12 = \frac{x}{\$1,000}$$

Now, multiply both sides by $1,000:

$$\$120 = x$$

You won't invest if interest rates are too high.

In general, the lower the interest rate, the more business firms will borrow. But to know how much they will borrow—or whether they will borrow at all in any particular instance—we need to compare the interest rate with the expected rate of profit on the investment.

(4) The Expected Rate of Profit

Economists are not happy unless they give virtually the same concept at least three different names. Therefore, the expected rate of profit is sometimes called the marginal efficiency of capital or the marginal efficiency of investment. We'll define it this way:

$$\text{Expected rate of profit} = \frac{\text{Expected profits}}{\text{Money invested}}$$

Now, of course, we have to work out a problem. Here's an easy one: How much is the expected profit rate on a $10,000 investment if you expect to make a profit of $1,650? You know how things work around here. Do it yourself, then check your result against mine. I'm always right. But you can't be unless you try.

$$\text{Expected rate of profit} = \frac{\text{Expected profits}}{\text{Money invested}}$$

$$= \frac{\$1,650}{\$10,000}$$

$$= 16.5 \text{ percent}$$

You won't invest unless the expected profit rate is high enough.

The relationship between the interest rate and the expected profit rate was underscored by John Maynard Keynes in his landmark *The General Theory of Employment, Interest, and Money.* Keynes said that every profit opportunity would be exploited as long as the expected profit rate (which he called the "marginal efficiency of capital") exceeded the interest rate: "The rate of investment will be pushed to . . . where the marginal efficiency of capital in general is equal to the market rate of interest."[10]

Suppose your business firm is interested in borrowing $100,000 at the going interest rate of 15 percent to buy inventory. If your expected profit rate is 18 percent, would it pay to borrow? In other words, after you paid off the interest, how much money would you have left? ($18,000−$15,000 in interest = $3,000.) You would stand to make $3,000 profit. Of course you would borrow the money.

Now we're ready for an easy three-part problem. Suppose you could borrow money at 20 percent interest and someone offered to buy 100 pounds of a certain substance from you at $1,300 a pound. It costs you only $1,000 a pound to grow this substance. The only problem is that the money you borrow will be tied up for a year until you are able to pay it back.

---

[10]John Maynard Keynes, *The General Theory of Employment, Interest, and Money* (New York: Harcourt Brace Jovanovich, 1958), pp. 136–37.

Investing Your Own Money

Business firms do not always borrow the money that they use for investment projects. Actually, American businesses invest hundreds of billions of dollars a year that they have accumulated in depreciation allowances and retained earings. If this money is not borrowed and no interest needs to be paid on it—it would be kind of silly to pay interest to yourself—then why even *think* about the interest rate?

If a firm didn't invest this money internally, what would it *do* with this money? Suppose that it lent the money to another firm at the going rate of interest. Back in Chapter 2 we talked about the concept of opportunity cost. Do you remember its definition? *The opportunity cost of any choice is the forgone value of the next best alternative.* The firm has two choices: It can use the money itself, or it can lend it to another firm and collect interest. If it uses the money itself, it forgoes the interest it would have otherwise been able to collect. That's why a firm must take the interest rate into account even if it is using its own funds.

Let's use a concrete example. The political consulting firm of Nixon, Ford, Reagan, and Bush is thinking of opening a branch office. It already has the $1 million it would need. It has an expected profit rate of 14 percent on its in-vestment. Its other choice is to lend the money to its competitor, McGovern, Carter, Mondale, and Dukakis.

Question: What does it do? You need to ask *me* a question before you can answer. And what question is that? You need to ask me how much the going interest rate happens to be. Suppose that the going interest rate is 5 percent. What should Nixon, Ford, Reagan, and Bush do? Lend the money to their competitor or use it themselves? Your answer? They should use it themselves. Why? Because their expected profit rate is substantially higher than the interest rate. In terms of opportunity cost, they can get a much higher rate of return by investing the money in their own firm than by lending it to someone else.

What should Nixon, Ford, Reagan, and Bush do if the going rate of interest is 18 percent? Lend the money to their competitor or use it themselves? What do you think? I think they should lend the money to their competitor, because they would collect a sure 18 percent interest, which is 4 percentage points higher than their *expected* (but not guaranteed) profit rate. Again in terms of opportunity cost, by lending the money out, they would be getting a return 4 points higher than if they invested it in their own firm.

Answer yes or no to each of these three questions:

1. Would you accept the deal as it stands?
2. Would the deal be acceptable if the interest rate were 10 percent?
3. Would the deal be acceptable if the interest rate were 30 percent?

You stand to make a profit of 30 percent using borrowed money. From those profits, you need to pay interest on your loan. If you borrowed the money at (*a*) 20 percent interest, you would still have money left over (net profit) after you paid the interest, so it would pay to accept the deal. If you borrowed money at (*b*) 10 percent interest, it would be even more profitable than at 20 percent interest. But if you accepted the deal at (*c*) 30 percent interest, after you paid the interest from your 30 percent profit, there would be no money left over from your sales. (See the box, "Investing Your Own Money.")

Why Do Firms Invest?

We've talked about *when* firms tend to invest—(1) when their sales outlook is good; (2) when their capacity utilization rate is high; (3) when interest rates are low; and (4) when their expected profit rate is high. But *why* do they invest?

Some firms invest merely to replace worn-out equipment. A related purpose is to replace this equipment with equipment that is more technologically advanced. For example, an old photocopy machine that did 10 copies a minute may be replaced with a high-speed machine that can do more tricks than Houdini. In effect, then, we are replacing machinery and equipment that may not only be dilapidated but obsolete as well. A firm may have to do this just to keep up with the competition. So, in a large sense, just keeping up with current technology requires a substantial amount of investment.

153

Figure 5
The Consumption Function

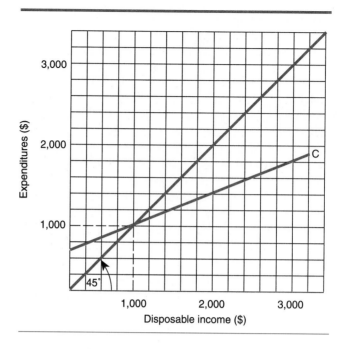

A business may also invest to become larger. Of course, the incentive to invest is based on the sales outlook. No one will want to grow if it means operating at only 50 percent of capacity. In that case, you might be the biggest kid on the block, but you would certainly not be the richest—*or* the smartest.

Graphing the C + I Line

Do you remember the consumption function from Chapter 5? As income rises, consumption rises, but not as quickly. Do you remember induced consumption? As income rises, more consumption is induced.

Figure 5 reproduces the consumption function graphed in Figure 3, p. 119. You'll note that, as income rises, the C line slopes upward. Higher income levels induce higher levels of consumption.

Would it be reasonable to assume that there is a parallel concept of induced investment? That as income rises, the level of investment rises as well? What do *you* think?

At very low levels of income, the country is in a depression. Nobody invests. At somewhat higher levels of income, more and more investment takes place, because people are able to save *some* money and those funds are invested. So it would be reasonable to say that as income rises, higher levels of investment are induced.

That would be a reasonable assumption, but we need to keep things simple here, because we want to be able to read our graphs. So we're going to assume the level of investment stays the same for all levels of income. We know that in the real world, as income rises, I rises, but we're going to trade off some reality for some simplicity.

So far we've had a graph with just two lines—the 45-degree line and the C line, or consumption function. From this two-line graph, C and savings could be calculated. To calculate I (actually the C + I line), a third line is necessary. Figure 6 graphs a C + I line, which is drawn parallel to the C line. This is the same graph as in Figure 5, with the C + I line added.

The question for you to solve has three parts: How much is I when disposable income is (*a*) 1,000, (*b*) 2,000, and (*c*) 3,000? Look at the graph and figure out the answers. Keep in mind that the C line and the C + I line are parallel.

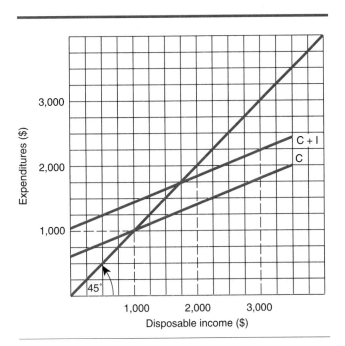

The answer to the question "How much is I when disposable income is (*a*) 1,000, (*b*) 2,000, and (*c*) 3,000?" is "around 425" (400, 410, 420, 430, 440, or 450 are acceptable). More important, since the C line and the C + I line are parallel, the vertical distance between them remains the same. If you estimated I at 410 with a disposable income of 1,000, it remains 410 when disposable income is 2,000 or 3,000.

We're about halfway through our graphs. Before you go any further, you need to ask yourself this question: Self, do I really know how to measure I, or investment, in Figure 6? If the answer is a definite yes, then go directly to the last section of this chapter, The Summing Up of Investment. But if you'd like a little extra help, you'll find it in the box "Reading the C + I Graph."

The Summing Up of Investment

We're finally ready to include the last part of investment: residential construction spending. The data shown in Table 5 indicate the relative size of the components of investment.

TABLE 5	Gross Investment, 2000
Plant and equipment	1,203
Residential construction	403
Inventory change	43
Total	1,650*

*Numbers don't add up due to rounding.
Source: Economic Report of the President, 2001.

Reading the C + I Graph

Do you remember how, in the last chapter, we found C, or consumption, at various levels of disposable income? All we did was take the vertical distance

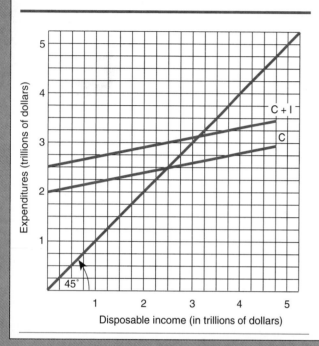

between the horizontal axis and the C line. For example, in the figure shown here, how much is C at a disposable income of $4 trillion? It's just a tad over $2.75 trillion—say $2.8 trillion.

How do we find I? Well, you tell *me*. How much is I, or investment, at a disposable income of $4 trillion? If you're not sure, just guess. Did you come up with about $500 billion, or $.5 trillion? The way we measure I is to take the vertical distance between the C line and the C + I line. At a disposable income of $4 trillion, that vertical distance is about two boxes. Since each box counts for one-quarter of a trillion dollars (because there are four boxes between each trillion dollars), then two boxes equal half a trillion dollars, or $500 billion. Incidentally, if you're still having trouble distinguishing between millions and billions, and between billions and trillions, then you definitely need to reread the box "A Word about Numbers," which appears near the beginning of Chapter 5.

Now we'll do one more. How much is I when disposable income is $2.5 trillion? Did you get $500 billion, or $.5 trillion? I certainly hope so. Just remember that we measure I by taking the vertical distance between the C line and the C + I line. It's as easy as counting the boxes.

How does our level of investment stack up against those of other leading industrial nations? We're somewhere in the middle, quite a bit lower than South Korea and Japan (see Figure 7).

Figure 7

Gross Investment as a Percentage of GDP, Selected Nations, 1999

Source: National Acounts of OECD Countries, 2001.

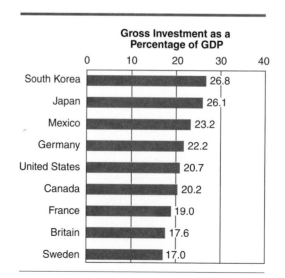

Questions for Further Thought and Discussion

1. What are the advantages and disadvantages of the corporation as a form of business organization?

2. Explain how the capacity utilization rate and the interest rate affect the level of investment.

3. Explain why building up capital takes a great deal of sacrifice.

4. The Carolina Textile Corporation is capitalized at $200 million. If you wanted to buy control of this company, how much money would you have to invest? Since you don't have nearly enough information to make this decision, just make some reasonable assumption about its bonds, preferred stock, and common stock.

5. What has happened to our personal savings rate in recent years, and how has that affected our level of investment?

6. If you owned a business and were considering increasing your level of investment, what would be the most important factor you would consider in determining how much you planned to invest? Explain why you chose that factor.

7. Why are virtually all large business firms corporations?

Workbook for Chapter 6

Name _____ Date _____

Multiple-Choice Questions

Circle the letter that corresponds to the best answer.

1. In the United States, investment is done _____.
   a) entirely by the government
   b) mostly by the government
   c) about half by the government and half by private enterprise
   d) mainly by private enterprise

2. Which of these is not investment?
   a) additional inventory
   b) the building of a county courthouse
   c) the building of a shopping mall
   d) the building of an automobile assembly line

3. There are about _____ business firms in the United States.
   a) 2 million   c) 24 million
   b) 12 million   d) 36 million

4. A business firm with one owner is _____.
   a) a proprietorship   c) a corporation
   b) a partnership   d) none of these

5. A partnership _____.
   a) must have exactly two owners
   b) must have more than two owners
   c) must have more than one owner
   d) may have more than one owner

6. A key advantage of a partnership over a proprietorship is _____.
   a) limited liability
   b) division of responsibility
   c) perpetual life of the business firm
   d) none of these

7. A _____ is a legal person.
   a) proprietorship   c) corporation
   b) partnership   d) business firm

8. Most corporations are _____.
   a) publicly held   c) very small
   b) very large   d) none of these

9. Corporations collect about _____ percent of all business receipts.
   a) 10   c) 60
   b) 30   d) 90

10. A key disadvantage of incorporating is that _____.
    a) you will have to pay corporate income tax
    b) you will have to charge sales tax
    c) you will have to sell stock
    d) you will have to reorganize the corporation whenever an officer resigns or dies

11. Corporations are controlled by the _____.
    a) employees   c) common stockholders
    b) bondholders   d) preferred stockholders

12. The last to be paid off, whether the corporation does well or goes bankrupt, are the _____.
    a) employees   c) common stockholders
    b) bondholders   d) preferred stockholders

13. Ownership of a corporation is based on _____.
    a) whether you work for the company
    b) whether you buy from the company
    c) whether you hold the bonds of the company
    d) whether you hold stock in the company

14. A corporation's capitalization is based on all of the following except _____.
    a) preferred stock   c) bonds
    b) common stock   d) sales

15. Which is not investment?
    a) the purchase of 100 shares of IBM
    b) the construction of a new factory
    c) the purchase of a new delivery truck
    d) the purchase of inventory

16. Inventory investment is _____.
    a) always positive
    b) always negative
    c) can be either positive or negative
    d) can be neither positive nor negative

17. Inventory investment is _____.
    a) very stable
    b) fairly stable
    c) fairly unstable
    d) very unstable

18. During severe recessions, inventory investment is _____.
    a) negative
    b) stable
    c) fairly high
    d) very high

19. Gross investment _____.
    a) plus depreciation equals net investment
    b) minus depreciation equals net investment
    c) plus net investment equals depreciation
    d) equals net investment minus depreciation

20. Each of the following might be used to acquire capital except _____.
    a) working more
    b) consuming less
    c) borrowing
    d) consuming more

21. Karl Marx said that capital is produced by _____.
    a) the worker
    b) the capitalist
    c) the government
    d) money

22. Which is the least stable?
    a) investment in plant and equipment
    b) investment in residential housing
    c) investment in inventory
    d) overall investment

23. Business firms invest in plant and equipment during recession years for each of these reasons except _____.
    a) interest rates are lower
    b) it has been planned years ahead
    c) it replaces worn-out plant and equipment
    d) it is needed because capacity may be fully utilized

24. During bad recessions, investment in plant and equipment will _____.
    a) be negative
    b) fall by around 15–20 percent
    c) fall somewhat
    d) rise

25. Each of the following is business investment except _____.
    a) inventory investment
    b) investment in new plant
    c) investment in new equipment
    d) investment in new residential housing

26. Investment will be high when the capacity utilization rate is _____ and the interest rate is _____.
    a) high, high
    b) low, low
    c) high, low
    d) low, high

27. Our capacity utilization rate is usually between _____.
    a) 10 and 30
    b) 30 and 50
    c) 50 and 70
    d) 70 and 90

28. Firms will most likely borrow money for investment when _____.
    a) interest rates are low
    b) interest rates are high
    c) the interest rate is higher than the expected profit rate
    d) the expected profit rate is higher than the interest rate

29. Which statement is the most accurate?
    a) Almost all corporations are very large.
    b) If you want to be your own boss and don't want to share any of the decision making, the business form that would best suit you is a proprietorship.
    c) It is very expensive to form a corporation.
    d) Most business firms are partnerships.

30. Statement I. Inventory computerization has tended to reduce inventory levels.

    Statement II. Inventory investment tends to rise during recessions.
    a) Statement I is true and statement II is false.
    b) Statement II is true and statement I is false.
    c) Both statements are true.
    d) Both statements are false.

Fill-In Questions

1. Of the big three spending sectors of GDP, the least stable is _____ .

2. There are about _____ million business firms in the United States.

3. A partnership is owned by _____ people.

4. The key advantage of incorporating is _____ .

5. The two main disadvantages of incorporating are (1) _____ and (2) _____ .

6. A corporation is owned by its _____ and its _____ .

7. A corporation is controlled by its _____ _____ .

8. The creditors of a corporation are mainly its _____ .

9. Theoretically, you would need an investment of about $ _____ to control a corporation that had $100 million in preferred stock, $50 million in common stock, and $350 million in bonds.

10. The least stable form of investment is _____ investment.

11. Gross investment − _____ = Net investment.

12. According to Karl Marx, capital was created by the _____ and expropriated by the _____ .

13. In Marx's terms, the people who wait outside the factory gates for work are the _____ .

14. During severe recessions, our capacity utilization rate falls to around _____ percent.

15. The expected profit rate is found by dividing _____ by _____ .

16. An investment will be undertaken if the expected profit rate is higher than the_____ _____ .

17. Total investment is found by adding (1)_____ ; (2)_____ ; and (3)_____ .

Problems

1. If a corporation has $100 million in preferred stock, $150 million in common stock, and $250 million in bonds: a) How much is its capitalization? b) Theoretically, how much would it take to control it? c) Practically speaking, it may take only about how much to control it?

2. If a corporation has gross investment of $150 million and depreciation of $40 million, how much is its net investment?

3. Given the information in Table 1, find inventory investment in 2005.

TABLE 1

Date	Level of Inventory
January 1, 2005	$500 million
July 1, 2005	530 million
December 31, 2005	485 million

4. Use the information in Figure 1 to fill in Table 2:

Figure 1

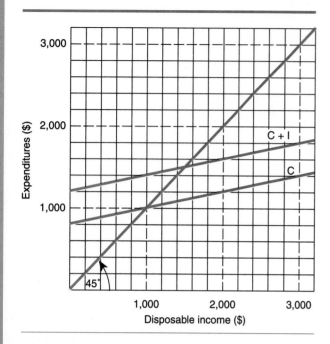

TABLE 2

Disposable Income	Consumption*	Savings*	Investment
(a) 1,000	———	———	———
(b) 2,000	———	———	———
(c) 3,000	———	———	———

*If you don't remember how to find consumption and savings, you'll need to review parts of Chapter 5.

5. If a corporation has $2 billion in common stock, $1 billion in preferred stock, and $4 billion in bonds: a) How much is its capitalization? b) Theoretically, how much would it take to control it? c) Practically speaking, it may take only about how much to control it?

6. If net investment is 400 and depreciation is 175, how much is gross investment?

7. Given the information in Table 3, find inventory investment in 2006.

8.

TABLE 3

Date	Level of Inventory
January 1, 2006	$2.0 billion
May 1, 2006	2.1 billion
Sept. 1, 2006	1.8 billion
Dec. 31, 2006	2.3 billion

Suppose you could borrow $200,000 for one year at an interest rate of 10 percent. You are virtually certain that you can invest this money in inventory that you could sell over a year for $300,000. If your selling costs were $50,000 and you were to pay your interest out of your profits, how much would your expected profit rate be on your investment?

9. Derek Jeter, George Steinbrenner, and Tino Martinez would like to gain control of the Sports Trading Card Corporation of America. If that corporation has $200 million in common stock, $300 million in preferred stock, and $500 million in bonds: a) Theoretically, how much would they need to invest to control it? b) Practically speaking, how much would they need to invest to control it?

Chapter 7

The Government Sector

The last two chapters covered consumption and investment. In this chapter we'll look at the last of the three main sectors of GDP: government spending. While we're at it, we'll see how the government affects our economy through spending, taxation, regulation, and income redistribution.

CHAPTER OBJECTIVES

We'll be looking at these topics:

- Government spending.
- The graphing of the C + I + G line.
- Types of taxes.
- The average and marginal tax rates.

- Sources of government revenue.
- Principles of taxation.
- The economic role of the government.

Introduction: The Growing Economic Role of Government

The role of government has grown tremendously over the past seven decades. Actually, most of that growth took place between 1933 and 1945, during the administration of Franklin Delano Roosevelt. The two major crises of that period—the Great Depression and World War II—dwarfed anything our nation has faced since. In fact, we would have to go back to the Civil War to find an event as cataclysmic as either the Depression or what people over 60 still refer to as "the war."

Most of the growth was due to the Depression and World War II.

163

Figure 1

The Federal Government
Dollar—Fiscal Year 2001
Estimate

Eighty-two cents of each dollar of
federal revenue comes from
individual income taxes and social
insurance receipts, while slightly
more than half of all federal
expenditures goes for direct benefit
payments for individuals. Note also
that, because federal tax revenue
($2,019 billion) is greater than
federal government spending
($1,835 billion), we have a budget
surplus of $184 billion.

*Source: Budget of the United States
Government,* Fiscal Year 2001.

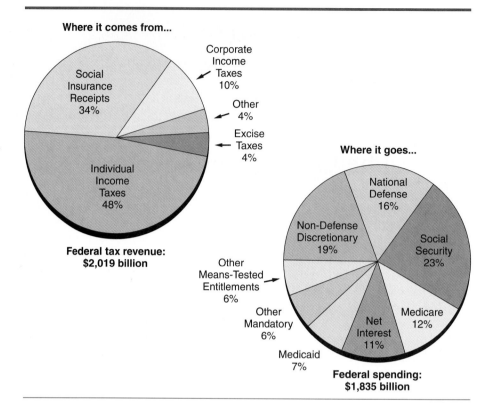

Where it comes from...

Corporate
Income
Taxes
10%

Social
Insurance
Receipts
34%

Other
4%

Excise
Taxes
4%

Individual
Income
Taxes
48%

**Federal tax revenue:
$2,019 billion**

Where it goes...

National
Defense
16%

Non-Defense
Discretionary
19%

Social
Security
23%

Other
Means-Tested
Entitlements
6%

Other
Mandatory
6%

Net
Interest
11%

Medicare
12%

Medicaid
7%

**Federal spending:
$1,835 billion**

Government is not the solution
to our problem. Government is
the problem.

—Ronald Reagan

    Since 1945, the roles of government at the federal, state, and local levels have
expanded, but the seeds of that expansion were sown during the Roosevelt administration. Americans seem determined never to experience again the traumatic events that
overtook us during the 30s and 40s. *Never again* will we leave ourselves vulnerable to
a depression or a military attack by another nation.

    The government exerts four basic economic influences: It spends more than
$3 trillion, levies even more in taxes, redistributes hundreds of billions of dollars, and
regulates our economy. For the last three and a half decades, the state and local governments have managed to raise enough money in taxes to pay for their expenditures
and still run a surplus each year. In other words, total tax revenue of all state and local
government has exceeded total spending. And over this same period, the federal government has spent much more than it has raised in taxes. It has made up the difference
each year by borrowing. But since 1998 the federal government has been running large
and growing budget surpluses.

    What does the government *do* with all our money? Some of it is spent on goods
and services (that is, highways, police protection, defense), and some of it is redistributed to the poor, to retirees, and to the holders of government bonds.

What does the government do
with all our money?

    The government also has an important regulatory role in our economy. We are sub-
ject to myriad local, state, and federal laws governing how business may be conducted.
These will be examined toward the end of this chapter.

Government Spending

Federal Government Spending

Thank God we don't get all the
government we pay for.

—Will Rogers

In fiscal year 2001 the federal government spent over $1.8 trillion. Who got the biggest
bite of the pie? As you can see from Figure 1, it went to Social Security recipients. (For
an explanation of budget preparation and the fiscal year, see the boxes "The Chronology
of Federal Budget Preparation" and "Why the Fiscal Year Starts on October 1.")

The Chronology of Federal Budget Preparation

Preparation of the budget begins about two years before the beginning of the fiscal year. We'll be looking at the timetable for the preparation of the budget for fiscal year 2001, which began on October 1, 2000.

During early 1999, after months of internal studies, each department presented its budget for fiscal year 1999 to the Office of Management and Budget (OMB). That agency has the job of coordinating all budget requests to ensure that they are consistent with the president's economic program. The OMB then put together a tentative budget for the president.

President Bill Clinton was concerned not just with individual spending programs—foreign aid, defense, food stamps, Social Security—but with the bottom line, or total spending. The president and the director of the OMB then established spending ceilings for each department and the federal agencies, which were then asked to prepare a second round of expenditure plans over the summer.

During the fall of 1999 the OMB reviewed these revised programs, and in the late fall the budget was presented to President Clinton for final approval. The final budget message was then drafted for submission to Congress in January 2000.

Over the next eight months the ball was in Congress's court. Both houses of Congress have budget committees that prepare "concurrent resolutions" to be reported to their respective houses by April 15. These resolutions contain two key figures: overall expenditures and overall revenue. By May 15 Congress must pass a single concurrent resolution.

Between May 15 and October 1, Congress passed various appropriations bills—agricultural subsidies, veterans' benefits, aid to mass transit, public assistance—while trying to stay within the limits set by the concurrent resolution. Finally, a second budget resolution had to be passed by October 1, the first day of the fiscal year.

Why the Fiscal Year Starts on October 1

The federal government, as you might expect, often has to do things a little differently. While nearly all business firms issue annual reports based on the normal calendar year—January 1 to December 31—the federal government's financial, or fiscal, year begins on October 1 and runs through September 30 of the following year.

Do they start on October 1 just to be different, or is there a reason for this unorthodox starting time? There actually *is* a reason. A new Congress is elected every second November and takes office the following January. This gives congresspeople eight months to work on the next year's federal budget. Of course, if the new budget did not go into effect until January 1, they'd have 11 months. Since Congress tends to leave its most important business for last, it would be trying to wrap

up business while worrying about getting home for Christmas. So members *do* have a reason for starting on October 1—maybe not a great reason, but a reason nevertheless.

By the way, what has probably been lost in my cogent explanation of why the fiscal year starts on October 1 is what a fiscal year actually is. It is a 12-month period over which the government projects a certain amount of spending and a certain level of tax receipts. The government might budget expenditures of $2.2 trillion and tax receipts of $2.3 trillion, leaving a surplus of how much?

The surplus would come to $100 billion (or $.1 trillion). If this math still bothers you, you would do well to reread the box "A Word about Numbers" on the second page of Chapter 5.

During the last 30 years, federal transfer payments have gone through the roof. How come? There are several explanations for this huge increase in social spending. Much of it reflects continued expenditures on the Great Society programs of the 1960s, particularly Medicare, Medicaid, and food stamps. A second reason for the increase is that the prosperity our nation has enjoyed in recent years has not spread to tens of millions of poor Americans. Consequently, spending on public assistance, unemployment insurance benefits, and food stamps has shot up since the early 1970s. Finally, in 1955 relatively few people were collecting full Social Security benefits, because that program was then only 20 years old. Today, however, the number of retired people on the rolls is more than twice that of 1955, and benefits have gone up substantially because they are indexed

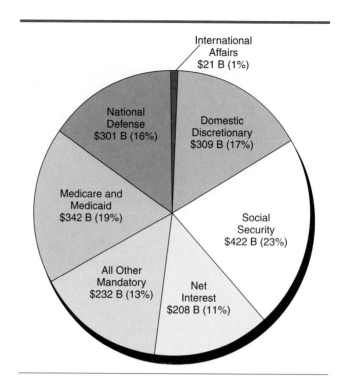

for inflation. For example, if the consumer price index were to go up by 1.2 percent in the third quarter of 2002, then Social Security benefits would rise by 1.2 percent in the fourth quarter of that year.

The next big-ticket item is defense expenditures, budgeted in fiscal 2001 at $292 billion. This comes to $1,000 for each person in the United States. President Ronald Reagan had long been an advocate of a strong national defense; he managed to get Congress to nearly double military spending between 1981 and 1986. Ironically, Mr. Reagan was critical of Democratic social programs "for throwing money at problems."

One of the fastest-growing federal expenditures in the 1980s and early 1990s was interest on the national debt. The national debt is six times its 1980 size. When you owe six times as much, you have to pay a lot more interest.

So far we've covered the big three of federal spending. If you'd like to see more, I've summarized President Bill Clinton's spending proposals for fiscal year 2002 in Figure 2. But none of these figures is written in stone. After all, the president proposes and Congress disposes. In fact, much of the data presented in these last few chapters will be out of date before the book even gets to the printer. I'd even be willing to place a little side bet that defense spending, which is budgeted at $301 billion, will come in at more than $310 billion, once the Republican majorities in the House and the Senate have a chance to vote on the defense appropriations bill. Keep in mind, too, that George W. Bush, who moved into the White House in January 2001, has somewhat different spending priorities from those of President Clinton. So it would be extremely helpful for you to consult newspapers, news magazines, and government periodicals (the Commerce Department's *Survey of Current Business* is *my* favorite) for more up-to-date figures.

If you're like most taxpayers, you'd like to see the government trim some of the fat from its budget. So I'd like you to pick up your heaviest ax and start hacking away at Figure 2. But be careful—as soon as you lift your ax, a lot of people will start howling.

Begin with defense. You'll not only make the president unhappy, but you'll incur the wrath of the secretary of defense, the armed forces' top brass, and thousands of defense contractors—not to mention the millions of your fellow citizens who think any cut in the defense budget is the same as just handing the country over to our enemies,

Government is the great fiction, through which everybody endeavors to live at the expense of everybody else.

—Frédéric Bastiat, *Essays on Political Economy,* 1872

Are We Giving Away the Store?

Many taxpayers are asking whether it makes sense to be spending so much money to help foreigners when we have so many poor people in the United States. During fiscal year 2001, we provided our friends, our allies, and many of the poorer nations of the world with about $15 billion in economic and military aid. About half went to Israel, Egypt, Russia, and the other states of the former Soviet Union.

How does foreign aid spending stack up against what the federal, state, and local governments spend on public assistance, food stamps, Medicaid, and public housing? It turns out that we spend more than 10 times as much on our own poor as we do on foreigners. Recent polls found that two out of five Americans believe foreign aid is the largest single item in the federal budget.

In the chapter on income distribution and poverty I'll argue that the government could do a lot more about poverty in the United States, but just now I'm trying to put the federal government's spending programs in perspective. Our foreign aid bill comes to less than 1 percent of the federal budget, or less than 0.2 percent of our GDP. Fifteen billion dollars is a lot of money, and much of it, especially the military aid, is being questioned in light of the receding Russian military threat. But in relative terms, it's just a drop in the federal budgetary bucket.

whoever they are. And besides, even if everyone agreed to major cuts, we are legally obligated to pay defense contractors hundreds of billions of dollars for the next few years for weapons systems already in the pipeline. And just one other thing—can you actually "fire" the Army? That elusive "peace dividend" we heard so much about when the Soviet Union disappeared along with the communist menace has yet to materialize. Although defense spending is down substantially from its $380–$390 billion levels of 1985 and 1986 (in 2001 dollars), it has bottomed out, and may be rising substantially as long as the Republicans continue to control Congress and the White House.

OK, let's cut Social Security and Medicare. Just try it! There are more than 45 million recipients of these benefits, and nearly all of them vote. What about federal pensions? It's too late—we're legally obligated for the next 50 years or so.

Want to cut the other mandatory spending? First, we're legally obligated to pay pensions and other benefits to retired federal employees and veterans. Second, there's a political problem. Veterans' benefits have a powerful constituency. Just drop by your local American Legion hall and ask the people there how *they* would feel about the government cutting these benefits.

Can we cut the interest we pay on the national debt? Yes! As long as we continue running federal budget surpluses—and barring a major rise in interest rates—we should be able to keep reducing the national debt and the interest payments that we owe each year.

State and Local Government Spending

State and local government spending has been rising rapidly since World War II, but it is still just a little more than half the level of federal spending. Well over half of all state and local government expenditures goes toward education, health, and welfare. One of the problems faced by these governments is that they are expected to provide more and more services with limited tax bases. For example, more than 20 million teenagers are currently attending high school or college. Sixty years ago most people were working by the time they were 14, but now they are still in school. Supporting public education has traditionally been the role of the state and local governments, although in recent years Washington has provided supplementary funds covering about 6 percent of the costs of educating children through high school.

Big state and local expenditures are education, health, and welfare.

Another expenditure that has increased enormously is police protection. Although this is another traditional function of local government, rising crime and perhaps the deterioration of neighborhoods have made it necessary to hire many more police officers. Until the 1950s, neighborhoods largely policed themselves informally, mainly because people spent a great deal of time on the street, most urban areas were more densely populated, and people tended to know one another. All this has changed, and now the police are being called on to perform functions that neighborhoods used to handle.

Government Purchases versus Transfer Payments

The federal, state, and local governments spend more than $3 trillion a year. Nearly half goes to individuals as transfer payments, and the rest is government purchases. We represent these purchases by the letter G, and they go into our GDP equation: GDP = C + I + G + X_n.

$$GDP = C + I + G + X_n$$

What do you think the biggest government purchase is? It's defense, which accounts for 16 cents out of every dollar that goes into G. Other biggies are education, police, health, and highway construction. A government purchase is the spending of government funds to purchase or provide the public with some good or service.

Transfer payments cannot be counted because they do not represent that kind of spending. What is the largest government transfer payment? I'm sure you know that it's Social Security. Of the trillion dollars that the federal, state, and local governments pay out in transfer payments, $422 billion goes to Social Security recipients.

You may want to ask why we bother to distinguish between government purchases and transfer payments. OK, go ahead and ask. The reason is that we need to come up with a figure for GDP—the nation's expenditures on all final goods and services produced during the year at market prices. So we want to add in only what we produced and purchased that year. Don't people receiving transfer payments spend that money on consumer goods and services, or C in our GDP equation? Yes, they do. And so as soon as they spend those Social Security, public assistance, or government employees' retirement and veterans' benefits, that money will go into GDP.

Federal purchases were as high as they were from the mid-1960s through the early 1970s partially because of defense spending on the Vietnam War. Defense spending, which had been as much as 7 percent of GDP, has fallen to just 3 percent. Overall total government purchases have been declining since the late 1960s, and now are just 17 percent of GDP.

Federal and state and local transfer payments have grown from just 6 percent of GDP in 1960 to more than 10 percent today. Most of the impetus has come from two of President Lyndon Johnson's Great Society programs of the 1960s—Medicare and Medicaid—and from the rising proportion of retirees who are now collecting Social Security. It is conceivable that, in 30 years, when all the baby boomers have retired, total government transfer payments will be more than one-quarter of GDP.

Graphing the C + I + G Line

In Chapter 5 we graphed the C line. In the last chapter we graphed the C + I line. Now we add another line to our graph: the C + I + G line. By now this should be old hat to you, so I'm going to ask you to figure out how much G is in Figure 3 (assuming the C + I + G line is parallel to the C + I line).

What did you get? You should have gotten 400 or thereabouts (each box is 200). You'll notice that the level of G remains at 400 no matter what the level of disposable income. Is this realistic? It can be argued that, at low levels of income, the government might spend more money than at higher income levels. Why? Because low income levels represent periods of recession and depression, when the government might well be spending a lot of money to get the economy moving again. We'll see just how the government would do this in Chapter 13, when we look at fiscal policy.

It could also be argued that, at higher levels of disposable income, the government would be taking in more tax dollars and thus have more money to spend. So, rather than take sides here, I'll just say that the government spends a constant amount of money, no

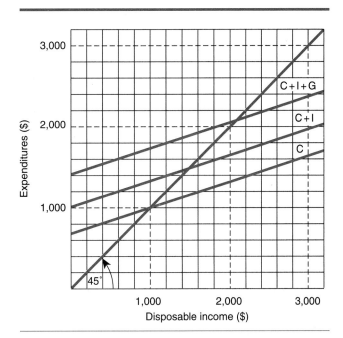

Figure 3
Measuring Government
Spending

matter what the level of disposable income. The main reason for doing this is to keep our graph as simple as possible.

We're not quite finished with our graphs. We still need to draw the C + I + G + X_n line, but that won't happen until the beginning of the next chapter.

Taxes

Taxes are so pervasive that more than half the chapter will be devoted to them. Before we even begin to consider how much taxes are, we'll need to understand something about tax rates and the types of taxes that exist. Once that's done, we'll see just how onerous the American tax system really is.

The Average Tax Rate and the Marginal Tax Rate

If someone asked you what your tax rate was, would you have a ready answer? Generations of attorneys have taught us that the best answer to any question (and especially those to which you don't know the answer) is another question. So the answer to the question "What's your tax rate?" is "Which tax rate are you referring to? My average tax rate or my marginal tax rate?"

But what if your questioner replies, "What is your average tax rate?" What do you do then? You tell her. And if she then happens to ask you your marginal tax rate, you tell her that as well.

We all pay tax at two different rates: the average rate and the marginal rate. The average rate is the overall rate you pay on your entire income, while the marginal rate is the rate you pay on your last few hundreds (or thousands) of dollars earned. Your marginal rate is often referred to as your tax bracket. In nearly all cases, I'm talking about the average and marginal rates that you're paying in personal income tax, but I'll apply the average tax rate to the Social Security tax as well.

The Average Tax Rate   I kind of left you hanging there, didn't I? How do you answer the question "What is your average tax rate?"

The art of taxation consists in so plucking the goose as to obtain the largest possible amount of feathers with the smallest amount of hissing.
—Jean-Baptiste Colbert

Types of Taxes

There are two basic divisions of taxes. First we'll be looking at the difference between direct and indirect taxes. Then we'll take up progressive, proportional, and regressive taxes.

In this world nothing can be said to be certain, except death and taxes.
    —Benjamin Franklin

Direct Taxes   A direct tax is a tax with your name written on it. The personal income and Social Security taxes are examples. They are taxes on particular persons. If you earn a certain amount of money, you must pay these taxes.

The corporate income tax is also a direct tax. You might not think so, but a corporation is considered a legal person. For example, in court, you would sue a corporation rather than its owners or officers. Thus, if a corporation makes a profit, it must pay a corporate income tax, and this is a direct tax.

Indirect Taxes   These are not taxes on people but on things. Some of us may have trouble making this distinction, especially given our problematic relationships with some of our family, friends, and co-workers, but in economics we *do* make a sharp distinction between people and things. Taxes on things include sales and excise taxes. Examples are a state sales tax on most retail purchases and the excise taxes on tires, gasoline, movie tickets, cigarettes, and liquor.

The distinction between direct and indirect taxes was made by John Stuart Mill more than a century ago:

> A direct tax is one which is demanded from the very persons who, it is intended or desired, should pay it. Indirect taxes are those which are demanded from one person in the expectation and intention that he shall indemnify himself at the expense of another.[1]

Now we shall take up, in turn, progressive, proportional, and regressive taxes. The key variable we use to differentiate them is where the tax burden falls.

John Stuart Mill, English philosopher and economist (Brown Brothers)

Progressive Taxes   A progressive tax places a greater burden on those best able to pay and little or no burden on the poor. The best example is, of course, the federal personal income tax. For the vast majority of American taxpayers today, the more they earn, the higher percentage they pay. In terms of the average tax rate, then, people in higher income brackets pay a substantially higher average tax rate than those in lower brackets.

But the federal income tax was much more progressive before the passage of the Economic Recovery Tax Act of 1981 and the Tax Reform Act of 1986. At the upper end of the income scale, the maximum marginal tax rate of 70 percent before 1981 went to just 50 percent that year, and to just 28 percent in 1988.[2] Also, the number of tax brackets was reduced from 14 in 1986 to just 2 in 1988 and then nudged up to 3 in 1990. By lumping all taxpayers into only three brackets, the government further cut down on the progressiveness of the personal income tax.[3]

Proportional Taxes   Proportional taxes place an equal burden on the rich, the middle class, and the poor. Sometimes a flat tax rate is advanced as a "fair" or proportional tax, but it is neither. For example, a flat income tax rate of, say, 15 percent with no deductions, would place a much greater burden on the poor and the working class than

---

[1] John Stuart Mill, *Principles of Political Economy,* Book IV, ed. William J. Ashley (Philadelphia: Porcupine Press, 1979), p. 823.

[2] In 1990 the maximum marginal tax rate was raised to 31 percent, and in 1993 to 39.6 percent.

[3] This loss of progressivity can best be illustrated by looking at the marginal tax brackets of upper-middleclass families and of millionaires. A family earning, say, $75,000 of taxable income is in the 28 percent tax bracket, while the family with a taxable income of $75 million is in the 39.6 percent bracket. Back in 1980 the $75,000 family had a marginal tax rate of about 40 percent and the millionaire family had a marginal tax rate of 70 percent.

Nominally Progressive, Proportional, and Regressive Taxes

We have already defined these taxes in accordance with their effect, or burden, on taxpayers in different income groups. The burden of a progressive tax falls most heavily on the rich; the burden of a proportional tax falls equally on all income groups; and the burden of a regressive tax falls most heavily on the poor.

This three-part graph presents an alternative view of these types of taxes. I'll tell you up front that I strongly disagree with the implications of this view. Let's look at each part of this graph and see how *you* feel.

The graph in part (*a*) is nominally progressive because higher-income people pay a higher tax rate than lower-income people. For example, those earning $10,000 pay only 4 percent of their incomes, while those earning $100,000 pay 8 percent. But is this, in effect, a progressive tax? Is it as easy for a poor family to pay $400 as it is for a rich family to pay $8,000? We could argue it either way. And, unfortunately, economic analysis cannot supply an answer. Now, I personally feel that a $400 tax bill imposes a greater burden on a family earning $10,000 than an

$8,000 tax bill imposes on a family earning $100,000. What do *you* think?

Let's move on to the next part of the graph, (*b*), which shows a nominally proportional tax rate of 10 percent. Here's the question: Is it as easy for a poor family to hand over 10 percent of its income to the IRS as it is for a middle-class family, or a rich family? What do *you* think? My own view is that it isn't and that this nominally proportional tax is, in effect, a regressive tax.

The last part, (*c*), is easy. This is a nominally regressive tax because the tax rate declines as income rises. Obviously, by any measure, the burden falls most heavily on the poor.

Economists should avoid making value judgments, so perhaps I have gone a bit too far in claiming that nominally progressive taxes *could* be regressive in effect. And that nominally proportional taxes *are* regressive in effect (although this is somewhat less controversial). So if you disagree with my conclusions it doesn't make one of us wrong and the other right. It means only that our values are different.

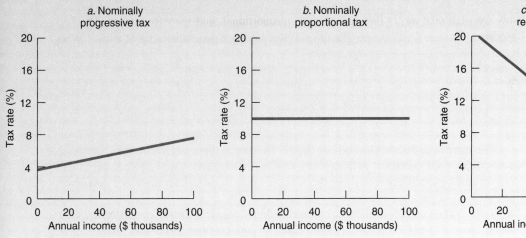

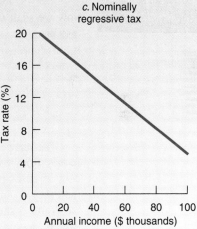

on the rich[4] (See box, "Nominally Progressive, Proportional, and Regressive Taxes.") It would be much harder for a family with an income of $10,000 to pay $1,500 in income tax (15 percent of $10,000) than it would be for a family with an income of $100,000 to pay $15,000 (15 percent of $100,000).

---

[4]Steve Forbes, whose net worth is estimated to be about $400 million, made his flat tax proposal his major issue in his campaigns for the Republican presidential nomination in 1996 and 2000. He advocated a flat tax on wages and salaries, exempting profits, interest, and dividends. And for good measure, Forbes, who inherited his wealth, would abolish the federal tax on inheritances.

Regressive Taxes   A regressive tax falls more heavily on the poor than on the rich. The examples I have already given illustrate this (a tax may be set forth as progressive or proportional when it may be regressive in actuality). Another example is the Social Security tax. In 2001 the rate was 6.2 percent on all wages and salaries up to $80,400. The maximum you had to pay was $4,984.80. Where did this figure come from? I'll give you some space to come up with the answer:

That's right: multiply $61,200 by 6.2 percent, or .062.

$$
\begin{array}{r}
\$80{,}400 \\
\times\ .062 \\
\hline
160800 \\
482400 \\
\hline
\$4{,}984.80\cancel{0}
\end{array}
$$

Now that I've had you do all these calculations, I have some bad news for you. The 6.2 percent of your wages deducted from your paycheck is not *all* the government takes. The Medicare tax of 1.45 percent is also taken out, but, unlike the Social Security tax, there's no wage-base limitation. If you earned $1 million, you'd pay a Medicare tax of $14,500.

So let's go back to the drawing board. The deduction from your pay is 7.65 percent (6.2 percent for Social Security and 1.45 percent for Medicare). How much, then, is deducted per year for these programs from the pay of a person earning $10,000? Work it out right here:

The answer is $765 ($10,000 × .0765). Of course, your employer also withholds money from your check for personal income taxes. But guess what! More than 70 percent of all taxpayers pay more in payroll taxes (that is, Social Security and Medicare) than they do in personal income tax.

Table 1 shows the Social Security taxes paid by people with various incomes. Only earned income (wages and salaries) is subject to this tax; rental income, interest, dividends, and profits are not. It might appear at first glance that the Social Security tax is proportional; but as you examine Table 1, you should observe that it is not only regressive in effect, but nominally as well.

Take a yearly income of $100,000, for example. This person pays the maximum of $4,984.80 (that is, 6.2 percent of the first $80,400). Now, what percentage of a $100,000 income is taxed? It comes to just 5 percent. Not bad. Everyone with an income below $80,400 paid 6.2 percent. What happens, then, is that as income rises above $80,400, people pay the same tax—$4,984.80—while the proportion of their income that goes to the Social Security tax falls steadily. In fact, the person making $1 million a year also pays $4,984.80, which comes to just 0.5 percent of his or her income.

What would be an ideal tax—one that would not fall disproportionately on the poor, the middle class, *or* the rich? In principle, an ideal tax would be a tax that is proportional *in effect*. It would therefore be a tax that is nominally progressive, looking something like the one in graph (*a*) in the box "Nominally Progressive, Proportional, and Regressive Taxes" on page 173.

TABLE 1	The Incidence of the Social Security Tax at Various Income Levels in 2001[*]		
Level of Earned Income	Taxes Paid		Average Tax Rate
$ 10,000	$ 620.00		6.2%
80,400	4,984.80		6.2%
100,000	4,984.80		5.0%
1,000,000	4,984.80		0.5%

[*]The Social Security tax rate is set by law at 6.2 percent. Each year, however, the inflation rate of the previous year raises the wage base.

So far, so good. The only problem is that, when we try to come up with actual tax rates for different income groups, there is a great deal of screaming and carrying on by those who feel they are being forced to pay too much. Remember that in 1980 Ronald Reagan was elected president largely because he promised—and delivered—a massive personal income tax cut. In 1984, when he ran for reelection, he declared that taxes would be increased only "over my dead body." In 1988 George Bush made his fateful "Read my lips: No new taxes" pledge, which he broke less than two years later. Finally, in the 1992 election, Bush tried to make up for his indiscretion by pledging new tax cuts, while Bill Clinton, not to be outdone, also said he would cut the taxes of the middle class. But only a few weeks after taking office, Clinton announced that no one would be getting a tax cut after all. And in 1993 we had a substantial tax increase that fell almost entirely on the rich.

Sources of Federal Revenue

The Personal Income Tax   As we saw in Figure 1, the federal government has three main sources of tax revenue, the largest of which is the personal income tax. This tax was only a minor source of federal revenue until World War II. It now accounts for 46 cents out of every tax dollar collected by the Internal Revenue Service. (To find out how to save on your income tax, see box with this title.)

The largest source of federal revenue is the personal income tax.

The personal income tax would be an even greater source of revenue were it not for two landmark tax laws passed in the 1980s. First, the Economic Recovery Tax Act of 1981, better known as the Kemp-Roth tax cut,[5] lowered the average citizen's tax bill by 23 percent over a three-year period. The maximum rate was cut from 70 percent to 50 percent, and, most analysts agreed, the wealthiest third of the population got most of the benefits.

The Economic Recovery Tax Act of 1981

Then came the Tax Reform Act of 1986, which cut personal income taxes still further. The maximum rate was lowered to 28 percent, and most taxpayers ended up in the lower bracket—15 percent. This meant the nation's wealthiest people had marginal tax rates of 28 percent, the upper middle class was taxed at 28 percent, and the working class and lower middle class were taxed at 15 percent. At the same time, millions of poorer families were taken off the income tax rolls entirely. In 1990, however, the top marginal rate was raised to 31 percent, and in 1993 the top bracket was raised to 36 percent, with a 10 percent surtax on incomes over $271,000. That makes the top bracket 39.6 percent (36 + 10 percent of 36 or 3.6). Figure 4 shows changes in the maximum marginal tax rate since 1979. In 1981 the top marginal tax rate was lowered in stages to 50 percent, a rate that was

The Tax Reform Act of 1986

Where there is an income tax, the just man will pay more and the unjust less on the same income.

—Plato

---

[5]Kemp was Representative Jack Kemp from upstate New York. He had been a star quarterback for the Buffalo Bills and was a 1988 Republican presidential contender. In 1989, he joined President Bush's cabinet as secretary of housing and urban development, and in 1996 he was Bob Dole's vice presidential running mate. William Roth was a Republican senator from Delaware. He lost his bid for reelection to a sixth term.

How to Save on Your Income Tax

The personal income tax would be even more progressive in effect were it not for two methods of beating the Internal Revenue Service out of some of its tax proceeds. One method is tax evasions, which are illegal. The other, tax avoidance, is not only legal but has been purposely put into the Internal Revenue Code by Congress. These provisions are commonly known as "loopholes."

The most popular way of evading taxes is to not report income. We may think first of cabdrivers, waiters and waitresses, barbers and beauticians, and domestics, who often don't report all their income from tips. People who work "off the books" and those engaged in illegal activities are also frequently cited. But we usually miss the big boys—the businesspeople, doctors, dentists, and others who work for themselves.

According to the IRS, the worst tax cheats are auto dealers, restaurateurs, and clothing store operators, who underreport 40 percent of their taxable income. The IRS estimates that small businesses that deal mostly in cash are reporting only 20 cents of each dollar they receive.

Often you can tell when a businessperson isn't reporting income. He will tell you that there's no sales tax if you pay cash. Now isn't that nice of him?

Another way of evading income tax is to take phony deductions. Even President Richard Nixon was not above cheating on his taxes. He had made a gift of his vice presidential papers to the National Archives and valued them at $576,000. So far, so good. The only trouble was that, a year before he made this gift, Congress had passed a law that made such gifts nondeductible. No problem. Nixon simply backdated his signature on a deed of his gift to reflect the time before the law's passage. The president could have pleaded ignorance of the law. The only problem was that Nixon himself had signed the bill into law.

Tax avoidance, unlike evasion, is quite legal, In fact, the Internal Revenue Code is set up to help rich people avoid a large chunk of their tax liability. Perhaps the most blatant example is the treatment of interest on state and municipal bonds. Unlike interest you might earn on savings accounts or corporate bonds, you pay no federal income tax on the interest earned from state and municipal bonds. The reason for this is to make it easier for state and local governments to borrow by making their securities more attractive to investors.

Now, guess who the *big* investors are in state and municipal bonds? The rich. They hold most of these bonds. Why? Because they're tax exempt.

Imagine you have $100 million lying around the house. If you were to buy some of these bonds, you might earn 7 percent interest, or $7 million a year. With other bonds you would have to pay 39.6 percent of this income to the federal government, but, because the interest on these bonds isn't taxed, you don't have to pay one penny. When the rich invest in these securities, we call that tax avoidance. And what's so nice about it is that it's perfectly legal.

People want just taxes more than they want lower taxes. They want to know that every man is paying his proportionate share according to his wealth.
—Will Rogers

maintained from 1983 to 1987. Under the Tax Reform Act of 1986, it was lowered in stages to 28 percent in 1988. In 1990 the top marginal tax rate was raised to 31 percent, a rate that was in effect from 1991 through 1993. In 1993 the top tax bracket was raised to 36 percent, with a 10 percent surtax for those making more than $250,000. In effect, then, since 1994, the top marginal tax rate has been 39.6 percent (36 percent + 3.6 percent).

You don't have to pay tax on your entire income. In fact, a married couple with children earning less than $20,000 pays no federal income tax at all, because of a combination of deductions, exemptions, and child care tax credits. If you were single, earned $10,000, and were entitled to $9,000 in deductions and exemptions, how much federal personal income tax would you pay? Work it out right here:

Solution:
$10,000 − $9,000 = $1,000 taxable income. Since you would be in the lowest income tax bracket, 15 percent, you would pay $150 in federal personal income tax ($1,000 × .15).

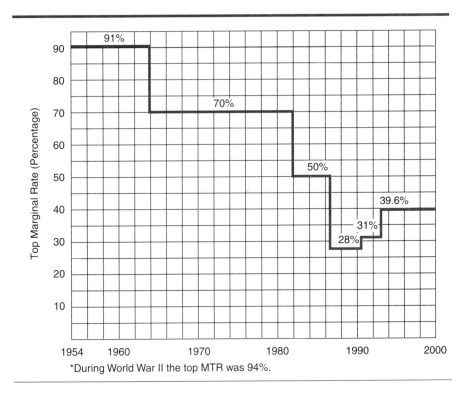

F*igure* 4

Federal Personal Income Tax:
The Top Marginal Tax Rate,
1954–2000

The top rate today is less than half
the top rate in 1962, but it is
substantially higher than the top
rate in the late 1980s.

One of the major issues of the presidential election of 2000 was how much of a personal income tax cut would go to the rich. Al Gore said that most of George Bush's proposed tax cut would go to the rich. He was right. George Bush said that the rich paid most of the taxes. And he was right. How much of our taxes are paid by the rich? The wealthiest one percent of all income tax filers—with incomes higher then $275,000 a year—pay one-third of all income taxes. And the wealthiest five percent pay more than half.

How does our top marginal tax rate compare with those of other wealthy countries? Would you believe it's the lowest in the group shown in Figure 5?

The Payroll Tax   What's the payroll tax? Remember the Social Security and Medicare taxes that you pay? What you pay is matched by your employer. When you pay 7.65 percent of your wages (6.2 percent for Social Security and 1.45 percent for Medicare), your employer also pays 7.65 percent of your wages.

The payroll tax is the federal government's fastest-growing source of revenue and now stands second in importance to the personal income tax. But the Social Security trust fund may be running out of money, because in the coming years medical and retirement payments may rise even faster than tax collections. (See the box titled "The Arithmetic of Social Security.")

We have seen that the Social Security tax is extremely regressive. This regressiveness lessened somewhat over the years as the earnings ceiling was raised. Recently, however, the ceiling has been raised each year at the same rate at which the consumer price index rose the previous year. In effect, then, the regressive structure of the Social Security tax is written in stone, at least until such time as the president and Congress change the law.

As we hear from time to time (see again the box about the arithmetic of Social Security), when the baby boomers begin to retire starting in the year 2011, the Social Security trust fund will be in big trouble. Around 2015 the Social Security trust fund will begin taking in less in payroll taxes than it is paying out in benefits.

So what should we do? Raise the age at which you can collect full benefits? We already did that. Right now people who are retiring can collect full benefits at the age of 65, but this will be raised gradually to 67 by 2022. Should we raise the wage base?

> Giving money and power to the government is like giving whiskey and car keys to teenage boys.
>
> —P. J. O'Rourke

Figure 5

Top Marginal Income Tax Rates
in 15 Leading Wealthy Nations,
2000

The U.S. has the lowest top
personal income tax rate among
these 15 nations.

Source: OECD, *The Economist,* August
5, 2000, p. 49.

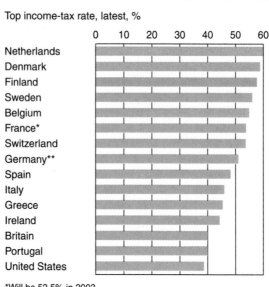

Top income-tax rate, *latest*, %

*Will be 52.5% in 2003.
**Will be 42% by 2005.

This, too, is being done. Each year the wage base is raised to keep pace with inflation. Of course we could raise the wage base *faster* than the inflation rate and we could also raise the tax rate from 6.2 percent to, say, 7 or 8 percent.[6] But further increases in Social Security taxes would surely meet with tremendous political opposition, especially from workers in their 20s and 30s, who are wondering whether there will be any money left in the trust fund for *their* retirement benefits.

As we can't immediately resolve this dilemma, let's make sure we're clear on what the Social Security, Medicare, and payroll taxes are. Our employers deduct 6.2 percent of our pay (up to $80,400) in Social Security taxes and 1.45 percent of our pay in Medicare taxes. In other words, we pay 7.65 percent in payroll tax on wages of up to $80,400, and 1.45 percent on all wages. The employer matches the employee's payments dollar for dollar. So how much payroll tax would the government collect on wages of $20,000?

Solution: It would collect $3,060 ($20,000 × .153). The employee would pay $1,530 ($20,000 × .0765), and this would be matched by the employer.

The power to tax involves the
power to destroy.
—Chief Justice John Marshall

The Corporate Income Tax   Until the late 1970s the corporate income tax was the second-largest source of federal revenue, but it is now a distant third. Under the Tax Reform Act of 1986, the maximum rate was lowered from 46 percent to just 34 percent, but most large corporations have ended up paying more tax because several deductions were reduced. At the present time the maximum rate is 35 percent.[7]

---

[6]Because the Social Security tax is very regressive, the burden of an increase in its rate would fall disproportionately on the working poor and the working class. Furthermore, an increase in its rate would discourage employers from hiring more workers because employers also pay this tax.

[7]All corporations earning profits of at least $335,000 pay an average tax rate of 35 percent. Of course, using loopholes in the tax law, virtually all major corporations are legally able to report much lower profits, and consequently, pay much lower taxes.

The Arithmetic of Social Security

Will Social Security be there for you when you retire? If you were born after 1950, the answer is no. The way things stand right now, in the year 2015, the Social Security system, which is currently accumulating huge surpluses, will begin paying out more in benefits than it will receive in tax revenue. And by 2037, according to government estimates, the fund will be empty. Of course, the chances are very good that sometime in the next few years, Congress will get around to dealing with this impending disaster.

Today more than 45 million Americans—retired, survivors, and disabled—collect Social Security benefits. As the baby boomers—those born between 1946 and 1964—begin reaching retirement age, the number of Social Security beneficiaries will swell to more than 50 million in the year 2010, to 65 million in 2020, and to 75 million in 2030. Look at it this way: In 1945, there were 42 workers for every beneficiary. In 1965, this ratio fell to 4 to 1. It's 3 to 1 today. And in 2030, it will be less than 2 to 1.

What it all comes down to is that our population is aging, so more and more people will be receiving Social Security payments while fewer and fewer people will be paying into the system. So if you think we have problems now, just wait until 2030. You should only *live* so long!

The corporate income tax is a tax on a corporation's profits. Those who believe profits provide our economy with its main incentive to produce goods and services are uneasy that they are so heavily taxed. However, corporate income taxes are now just 10 percent of all federal tax revenue, down from 15 percent in the 1970s.

Excise Taxes　An excise tax is a sales tax, but it is aimed at specific goods and services. The federal government taxes such things as tires, cigarettes, liquor, gasoline, and phone calls. Most excise taxes are levied by the federal government, although state and local governments often levy taxes on the same items. Cigarettes and gasoline, for example, are subject to a federal excise tax as well as to excise taxes in many states. In fact, the differential in state excise taxes encourages many people to "smuggle" cigarettes from North Carolina into New York.

Excise taxes, which account for about 4 percent of federal revenue, have another purpose beside serving as a source of revenue. They tend to reduce consumption of certain products of which the federal government takes a dim view. The surgeon general not only warns us about cigarettes but looks on approvingly as the government taxes them.

Excise taxes are generally regressive because they tend to fall more heavily on the poor and working class. The tax on a pack of cigarettes is the same whether you're rich or poor, but it's easier for the rich person to handle 60 or 80 cents a day it than it is for a poor person. The same is true of liquor and gasoline. In fact, a tax on most consumer goods is regressive because the poor tend to spend a higher proportion of their incomes on consumption than the rich (who save 20 to 25 percent of their incomes). (See the boxes regarding cigarette and gasoline excise taxes.)

Excise taxes are usually regressive.

The Estate Tax　A tax on estates of people who die, this has been termed by its opponents as the "death tax." It is a graduated tax that rises to 55 percent but is levied only on estates valued at $675,000 or more, an amount scheduled to rise to $1,000,000 by 2006. It accounts for about one and a half percent of federal tax revenue and is triggered by only 2 percent of all deaths. Most important, it falls on the relatively rich. More than 90 percent of estate taxes are paid by the estates of people with incomes exceeding $200,000 a year at the time of death. In 2000 Congress voted to repeal the tax, but this measure was vetoed by President Clinton. In the spring of 2001, at the behest of President George W. Bush, Congress again considered repealing, or at least modifying, this tax.

Conclusion

Americans often complain about the high taxes they pay, so let me ask you a question about that. Do most people pay more in income tax or payroll tax? The correct answer:

Should Cigarettes Be Taxed?

Economists don't like to get into issues involving value judgments, but this one is too good to pass up. Should cigarettes be taxed to discourage their consumption? Do cigarettes cause lung cancer, heart disease, and other terrible things? No less an authority than the surgeon general of the United States says that they do. Indeed, this official provides us with a reminder on every pack of cigarettes.

Should cigarettes be taxed? Why not? If the tax is high enough, it will discourage smoking. Of course, we don't want to make it too high, or nobody will smoke, and the federal government will be out about $8 billion a year.

But there are two good reasons why a tax on cigarettes is unfair (a word economists never use). OK, there are two reasons why it's inequitable. Whatever. First, it's regressive. We can see that it's harder for a poor person to pay a dollar a pack (or $1,095 a year, if that person has a three-pack-a-day habit) than it is for a rich person to pay a dollar a pack. But if you're poor, you're much more likely to smoke than if you're rich.

According to the U.S. Centers for Disease Control in Atlanta (where I actually once worked as a management trainee), 16 percent of all college graduates smoke, while 36 percent of all high school dropouts continue to puff away. Your average college student is much more affluent than your average high school dropout, which means a cigarette tax is almost targeted at the poor.

Here's a second good reason why a tax on cigarettes is inequitable. John Shover, a Stanford University economics professor, has calculated that "premature death saves society about $20,000 in Social Security benefits for each smoker."* So you can see that these guys are really paying their dues, so to speak. We single out relatively poor people, we tax them on something they really like to do, we overcharge them on Social Security taxes, and then, to add insult to injury, we make them stand outside the building. So put *that* in your pipe and smoke it.

*See Peter Passell, "So Long, Marlboro Man," *New York Times*, February 28, 1990, p. D2.

---

75 percent of all taxpayers pay more in payroll taxes than income taxes. Near the end of the chapter we'll compare our tax burden with that of the citizens of other countries.

Sources of State and Local Revenue

The sales tax is regressive.

The Sales Tax   More than half the taxes collected by the states come from the sales tax. This is a highly regressive tax. Although most food items are exempt, the poor consume a higher proportion of their incomes than the rich, who are able to save. In other words, a higher proportion of poor people's income is subject to this tax.

Furthermore, the rich can avoid or evade a large proportion of the sales tax by buying their big-ticket items—stereos, TVs, cars, and so on—in states that have low or no sales tax. They can also evade the sales tax by buying expensive items for cash (an option not feasible for the poor) from merchants who don't declare their cash incomes.

Still another problem with the sales tax is that it can distort business decisions about where to locate. Why did Amazon.com buy warehouses in Nevada near the California border to serve its West Coast market, when warehouses in California's Central Valley would probably have been more cost-effective? Because a physical presence in California would make Amazon responsible for collecting sales taxes on items sold to Californians, something which Amazon wants to avoid. According to the U.S. Constitution, one state cannot require businesses in another state to collect taxes for it.

The Property Tax   More than 80 percent of all local tax revenue is derived from the property tax. There is some disagreement about whether this is a regressive tax, but it *is* a deduction that you may take on your federal income tax. For example, if you paid $3,000 in property tax, you are entitled to a $3,000 deduction on your federal income tax return.

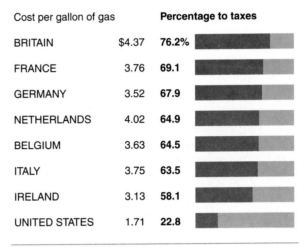

Should Our Gasoline Taxes Be Raised?

Are our gas taxes too high? They certainly are not too high relative to the taxes paid in other industrial countries. The table below shows gasoline prices per gallon before and after taxes in selected industrial countries for the week ending September 4, 2000.

	Cost per gallon of gas	Percentage to taxes	
BRITAIN	$4.37	76.2%	
FRANCE	3.76	69.1	
GERMANY	3.52	67.9	
NETHERLANDS	4.02	64.9	
BELGIUM	3.63	64.5	
ITALY	3.75	63.5	
IRELAND	3.13	58.1	
UNITED STATES	1.71	22.8	

Source: Energy Information Administration

The State and Local Fiscal Dilemma

Since World War II, state and local governments have been expected to provide an increasing number of services, most notably health, welfare, education, and police protection. According to the 1940 census, just one-third of all Americans who were 25 or older had gone beyond the eighth grade. Today more than 80 percent of those 25 or older are at least high school graduates. Education is perhaps the main job of local government, but it is paid for not just by local taxes, but by state and federal taxes as well. In 1945 state and local taxes were about 5 percent of GDP; now they are 10 percent (see Figure 6). During the 1960s and 1970s the federal government accommodated the fiscal needs of states and cities through increasing grants-in-aid and general revenue sharing. The Reagan administration not only stemmed this increase, but strongly reversed it.

Furthermore, under our federal system, neighboring states and local governments are in direct competition with one another for tax dollars. If one government's tax rates—particularly the sales and property taxes—rise too far above the levels of its neighbors, its citizens will vote with their feet. They will shop or even move to the areas that have lower tax rates. Were there a uniform national sales or property tax, it could be more easily raised when necessary. As long as neighboring government units are in direct competition, raising the necessary tax revenues will be difficult.

You probably never heard of the 1998 Internet Tax Freedom Act, which declared a three-year tax moratorium for online sales, exempting buyers from paying state and local sales taxes. As these sales multiply, the states stand to lose an increasing proportion of their most important source of revenue. However, there will apparently be no Internet sales tax in the foreseeable future.

Comparison of Taxes in the United States and Other Countries

Contrary to popular opinion, Americans are not heavily taxed in comparison with the citizens of other industrial countries. As we see in Figure 7, our taxes, which were 31.4 percent

Figure 6

Government Tax Receipts as
Percentage of GDP, 1929 and
2000

Taxes today are almost three times
as high as they were in 1929.

*Source: Economic Report of the
President,* 2001.

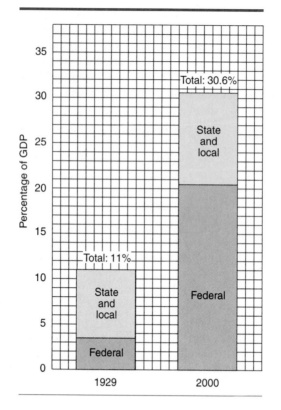

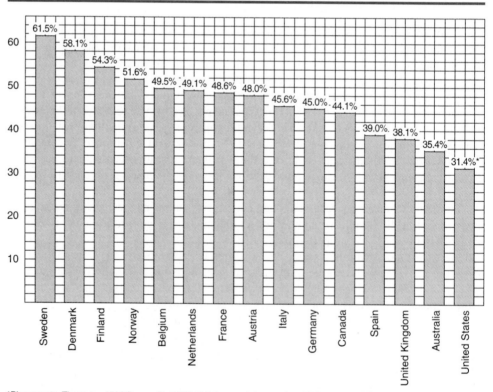

*Please note: These are 1999 figures. By 2000, U.S. tax receipts were just 30.6 percent of GDP, and, assuming a major tax cut in 2001 they may soon fall below 30 percent of GDP.

Figure 7

Tax Receipts as a Percentage of GDP in United States and Selected Countries, 1999

American taxpayers have a relatively low burden in comparison to taxpayers in other industrial nations.

Source: Organization for Economic Cooperation and Development.

of our GDP in 1999, are at the low end of the world's leading industrial countries. Keep in mind that these taxes include federal, state, and local taxes, and that about half of that total is redistributed in the form of transfer payments, such as Social Security, public assistance, food stamps, and unemployment insurance payments.

Who pays the highest taxes in North America? OK, I'll give you a hint: In which *province* do they pay the highest taxes? In case you didn't know, it's Quebec, which boasts a 51.7 percent tax bite, which includes a sales tax of about 15 percent. So the next time you hear someone complaining about high taxes, just tell them to move to Quebec.

So what's our problem? Why all this whining and carrying on about our high taxes when people in other countries pay so much more? Much of the dissatisfaction has to do with the tangible benefits we get in return for our taxes. In many European countries medical care is free, college is free, and day care is heavily subsidized. Indeed, parents of young children receive $1,000 or more every year in child care allowances from their governments. So the United States would definitely have many more happy campers if its citizens got to see more of what they've been paying for.

Do you remember the concept of *opportunity cost,* which we covered in Chapter 2? Because we're always having to make choices, *the opportunity cost of any choice is the foregone value of the next best alternative.* In the spring of 2001, at the urging of President George W. Bush, Congress began consideration of a massive tax cut, which may cost the U.S. Treasury up to $1.6 trillion over the subsequent decade. The tax cut debate is really over opportunity cost: What do we need to *give up* in exchange for lower taxes?

Because our federal budget surpluses will be smaller, the National Debt will be reduced more slowly. And then, too, the federal government will have less money available to pay for a drug prescription plan for senior citizens, to pay for more federal aid to education, or to pay for a missile defense system. The industrial nation with the lowest tax rates was about to drastically reduce those taxes. Consequently there would be fewer tax dollars available to provide government goods and services. Just as you can't have your cake and eat it too, the concept of opportunity cost shows us that we can't cut taxes *and* maintain the level of government spending that we would like.

> A tax is a compulsory payment for which no specific benefit is received in return.
> —U.S. Treasury

Two Principles of Taxation: Ability to Pay versus Benefits Received

Economists, politicians, moralists, and other people concerned with the fairness of taxation ponder and debate this issue endlessly: (1) Should the amount of taxes that people pay be based on their ability to pay? or (2) Should taxes be based on the benefits that people receive? Not surprisingly, the ability-to-pay and the benefits-received principles were quickly discovered.

If taxes were based solely on ability to pay, rich people would pay much higher proportions of their incomes to the Internal Revenue Service than middle-class people, who, in turn, would be paying a much higher proportion of their incomes than poor people. Is this fair? Yes—if we are concerned only with people's incomes.

But what if some people receive more benefits from the proceeds of these tax dollars than other people? If my house caught fire, I would receive the benefits of the fire department's services, whereas all my neighbors would not (unless, of course, the fire department, by putting out the fire in my house, prevented it from spreading to my neighbors' houses). Even more to the point, the family receiving food stamps or welfare payments is receiving greater benefits from the government than those who receive nothing.

Quite clearly, then, some people receive more benefits from the government than others. If we were to apply the benefits-received principle strictly, we would obtain some rather absurd results. We would take away in tax payments the food stamps or welfare payments that a poor family received. Would *this* make sense? And if you had the misfortune of a fire starting in your house, it might pay not to call the fire department; your insurance would probably cover most of your losses, while the fire department might

> That which angers men most is to be taxed above their neighbors.
> —Sir William Petty, *A Treatise of Taxes and Contributions,* 1662

> It is generally allowed by all, that men should contribute to the publick charge but according to the share and interest they have in the public peace; that is, according to their estates or riches.
> —Sir William Petty, *A Treatise of Taxes and Contributions,* 1662

Paying for Education with the Property Tax

Every so often a tax comes along that balances ability to pay with benefits received. Such a confluence occurred in the 1950s and 1960s when millions of 20- and 30-something couples with children moved into thousands of new suburban developments.

Few of these couples minded paying property taxes, which were used to pay for their children's schools. To paraphrase Marx and Engels's communist credo, "from each according to his ability, to each according to his needs," from each according to his property tax assess-ment, to each according to the number of his school-age children.

By the 1980s these children had all grown up and moved away, but their parents, now in retirement, were still paying high property taxes. And they began asking what they were getting in return for these taxes: "We're paying taxes to educate other people's children. Let them pay for it. We've already paid for ours. Now let somebody else pay for theirs."

---

charge you thousands of dollars for its services. And if your neighbors also opted to collect on *their* insurance policies as the fire spread, we'd end up with very few houses in your town—all because of the benefits-received principle.

Still another problem with the benefits-received principle is that we are not always clear about the value of the benefits we are receiving. Take, for instance, the so-called nuclear umbrella that the Department of Defense was kind enough to install several miles above our country. Even though our military leaders tell us that the Russians can easily get several thousand missiles through this umbrella, we are still paying more than $1,000 per capita every year for this protection. Talk about protection money!

Police protection is another case in point. How do we *know* when we are being protected? Does a masked man on a white horse perform some heroic act and then, just to make sure we get the message, leave behind a silver bullet? When a police patrol car drives by, this action may well avert a mugging, but does the potential muggee realize that he has just been saved?

So what we're left with are two undeniably noble principles that are not easily applied. The federal personal income tax is an attempt to apply the ability-to-pay principle, as it is fairly progressive. Local sewer taxes are based on water usage; they are, therefore, an application of the benefits-received principle. Another such application is the federal and state tax on gasoline, which is geared to the number of miles we drive on public roads. And, of course, all the highway and bridge tolls we pay are also based on the benefits-received principle. (See the box "Paying for Education with the Property Tax" for a discussion of education and taxes.)

We cannot, however, devise a tax based on both principles because they appear to be mutually exclusive. Unless we have a society in which everyone earns the same income and receives the same government benefits, we will have to compromise by basing some taxes on individuals' ability to pay and others on the benefits they receive.

The Economic Role of Government

This chapter has talked a lot about taxes and government spending. In short, the government giveth and the government taketh away.

One fact that should be readily apparent is that the federal government and, to a lesser degree, state and local governments have a tremendous impact on the economy. This analysis, however, will be confined to the federal government. Although there is a great deal of overlap, we are going to consider, sequentially, four specific economic functions of government: provision of public goods and services, redistribution of income, stabilization, and economic regulation. We covered some of these functions back in Chapter 4, but now we'll talk about them in greater detail.

(1) Provision of Public Goods and Services

Near the beginning of the chapter, I enumerated the range of goods and services provided by our federal, state, and local governments. Private enterprise would supply few of these because they are not profitable. Back in the 1950s, most of the country was served by private intercity bus lines. In New Jersey, when these companies began losing money, the state had to subsidize them just to keep the buses running. Finally, more than 20 years ago the state was forced to take over all the remaining private bus lines. Other states and regions were also forced to form public transportation authorities, while the federal government formed Amtrak to take over the national rail lines. Add to these all the other government operations and you're talking about some $1.8 trillion of public goods and services.

Some of the main services our government provides include defense of the country, maintenance of internal order and a nationwide highway network, and provision of a money supply to facilitate exchanges of goods and services. While certain services, such as public education and the running of the criminal justice system, are very obvious, others, such as bank inspections, environmental protection, and the carrying out of scientific research are less visible to most citizens.

(2) Redistribution of Income

The government is sometimes seen as a modern-day Robin Hood, redistributing money from rich taxpayers to poor welfare recipients, or from huge corporations to unemployment benefit recipients. Food stamps, Medicaid, and disability payments are all programs aimed mainly at the needy, while the relatively well-to-do taxpayer foots the bill.

Some would dissent from this view by arguing that there is also welfare for the rich, whether in the form of subsidies to corporate farmers and shipbuilders; tax breaks for defense contractors, oil companies, and other large corporations; or huge government contracts for missile systems.

Does the government take from the rich and give to the poor—or is it the other way around?

While one may well question whether the government takes from the rich and gives to the poor or vice versa, as former President Richard Nixon was fond of saying, "Let me make one thing perfectly clear": The government does redistribute hundreds of billions of dollars every year. The federal, state, and local governments combined provide Americans with over $1 trillion a year in the form of transfer payments such as Social Security and unemployment insurance benefits.

What is the economic impact of all this churning? The largest expenditure, Social Security, redistributes money from those currently working to those who have retired. The next largest expenditure, defense, provides contractors and subcontractors with hundreds of billions of dollars for building all those tanks, planes, guns, and missiles. But perhaps the most important economic impact of all this spending is the stabilization function, which we shall consider next.

(3) Stabilization

Two basic goals of the federal government are stable prices and low unemployment. Stated somewhat differently, the goals may be seen as a fairly high rate of economic growth (which would hold the rate of unemployment to a minimum) with no inflation.

It is the aim of good government to stimulate production, of bad government to encourage consumption.
—Jean-Baptiste Say

How the government might go about attaining these goals is the subject of Chapters 11 through 16. But at this time we can already gauge some of the economic impact of the federal budget and how that budget might affect the stability of our economy.

The $1,800 billion that the federal government now dispenses annually puts a floor under our economy's purchasing power. During the early stages of the Great Depression, the federal government was only a minor economic player. The total federal budget was less than 5 percent of GDP. Now it's more than 18 percent. Thus, no matter how bad things get, at least the government will provide a floor under total spending.

(4) Economic Regulation

Another important function of government is to provide the economic rules of the game and, somewhat more broadly, the social and political context in which the economy operates. Some of these rules are easily understood: the fostering of competition among business firms, environmental protection laws, child labor laws, the setting of a minimum hourly wage rate, consumer protection laws, and a court system to adjudicate disputes and punish offenders. Beyond these, the government helps provide the social and political framework within which individuals and business firms are able to function smoothly.

In Chapter 4 we talked about the role of competition and the price mechanism in our economic system. A competitive system will function only as long as there is competition. If there are only a handful of firms in several industries, there is no competition. The government's job is to make sure this doesn't happen.

Within our political and social framework, the government must also allow individuals and business firms to operate with the maximum degree of freedom. There are those who consider the current level of government regulation blatant interference with their economic freedom.

Does that freedom imply the right to pollute the environment or to monopolize an industry by driving competitors out of business? Perhaps Justice Oliver Wendell Holmes put it best when he noted that a person's freedom to swing his fist extended only as far as his neighbor's nose. Unfortunately, in the economic environment, there is little agreement as to how far economic freedom may be extended without interfering with society as a whole or the economic rights of specific individuals or business firms.[8]

Conclusion

Big government, like rock 'n' roll, is here to stay.

Until the early 1930s, just before the advent of President Roosevelt's New Deal, the federal government more or less followed the role prescribed by Adam Smith. Although Smith never would have approved of high protective tariffs, land subsidies to railroads, and possibly not even the antitrust legislation and trust-busting of the 1890–1915 period, until the 1930s the basic economic policy of the government could well have been described as laissez-faire.[9]

Adam Smith's dos and don'ts

In 1980 Ronald Reagan campaigned for the presidency by promising to "get the government off the backs of the American people." While he did attain a certain measure of success by cutting back some government spending programs, lowering income tax rates, and fostering a less rigorous approach to government regulation, it is obvious that big government is here to stay. An open question, though, is just how big big government will be.

Adam Smith, in his monumental *The Wealth of Nations,* published in 1776, summed up the dos and don'ts of economic endeavor: "Every man, as long as he does not violate the laws of justice, is left perfectly free to pursue his own interest his own way, and to bring both his industry and capital into competition with those of any other man, or order of men."[10]

Smith went on to define the economic role of government:

> According to the system of natural liberty, the sovereign has only three duties to attend to; three duties of great importance, indeed, but plain and intelligible to common understandings: first, the duty of protecting the society from the violence and invasion of other independent societies; secondly, the duty of protecting, as far as

---

[8]We discuss these issues in the chapters on monopoly and on corporate mergers and antitrust in *Economics* and in *Microeconomics.*

[9]This is a French expression that means "to leave alone" or "hands off." In this context, a laissez-faire policy means that the government keeps its hands off business, allowing it to operate without interference.

[10]Adam Smith, *The Wealth of Nations* (London: Methuen, 1950), p. 208.

possible, every member of the society from the injustice or oppression of every other member of it, or the duty of establishing an exact administration of justice; and, thirdly, the duty of erecting and maintaining certain public works and certain public institutions, which it can never be for the interest of any individual, or small number of individuals, to erect and maintain; because the profit could never repay the expense to any individual or small number of individuals, though it may frequently do much more than repay it to a great society.[11]

If we were to take Adam Smith's description of the government's economic role as our starting point, let's see how far it might be expanded. Should the government try to curb air and water pollution? What about prohibiting the dumping of toxic waste or regulating the disposal of nuclear waste?

In the 1992 presidential election, President George Bush tried to frame the issue of environmental protection as the balancing of two opposing forces—protecting jobs or protecting the spotted owl. Vice presidential candidate Albert Gore (whom Bush nicknamed "ozone man") countered that environmental protection actually generated a net gain of jobs. But the underlying issue was how far we want the federal government to go in protecting our environment.

How much should the government be involved in helping the homeless and the 32 million Americans officially classified as poor?[12] Or the 45 million people without medical insurance? And what more should be done about crime and drugs? In the new millennium, our government will become increasingly involved in dealing with these problems. The government's economic role has grown tremendously these last seven decades, and it will continue to grow in coming years. Indeed, when your children take macroeconomics, the author of their textbook may look back at the first decade of the 21st century as a period when the economic role of government was still relatively small.

Questions for Further Thought and Discussion

1. If a political candidate said that if she were elected to Congress, she would work toward cutting federal government spending by one-third over the next four years, would she stand much chance of fulfilling her promise? Why not?

2. When you retire, will you be able to collect Social Security benefits? Give the reasons why you might not be able to collect.

3. Discuss the pros and cons of having a high cigarette excise tax.

4. Make up a numerical example to show why the Social Security tax is regressive.

5. If Adam Smith were alive today, to what degree would he approve of the present economic role of the American government?

6. What additional goods and services do we expect from government today as opposed to 60 years ago?

7. Some politicians say that Americans pay too much in taxes. Explain why you agree or disagree with them.

8. Describe the growth of the economic role of the federal government since the 1930s.

9. Explain the difference between government spending and government purchases of goods and services.

10. Give two examples of public goods or services that you use.

---

[11]Ibid., pp. 208–9.

[12]Poverty is the subject of a later chapter.

Workbook for Chapter 7

Name _____ Date _____

Multiple-Choice Questions

Circle the letter that corresponds to the best answer.

1. The role of government grew most rapidly during the period _____.
   a) 1920–1933
   b) 1933–1945
   c) 1945–1960
   d) 1960–1975

2. The seeds of the expansion of the federal government's economic role were sown during the administration of _____.
   a) Franklin Roosevelt
   b) Dwight Eisenhower
   c) Richard Nixon
   d) Ronald Reagan

3. The federal government spends about $_____ a year.
   a) $1,800 million
   b) $1,800 billion
   c) $1,800 trillion
   d) $1,800 quadrillion

4. The key agency in the preparation of the president's budget is _____.
   a) the Treasury
   b) the OMB
   c) the Comptroller of the Currency
   d) the Department of Defense

5. The federal government's fiscal year begins on _____.
   a) January 1
   b) July 1
   c) October 1
   d) November 1

6. Transfer payments to individuals are _____ percent of the federal budget.
   a) 25
   b) 50
   c) 65
   d) 85

7. Which federal spending program grew the fastest in the 1980s?
   a) defense
   b) interest on the national debt
   c) aid to mass transit
   d) aid to education

8. Compared to federal spending, state and local spending is _____.
   a) twice as large
   b) about the same
   c) half as large
   d) one-quarter as large

9. The largest federal government purchase of final goods and services is _____.
   a) Social Security
   b) defense
   c) interest on the national debt
   d) foreign aid

10. If one person earns $10,000 and another person earns $100,000 a year, they both will pay Social Security tax _____.
    a) at the same average tax rate
    b) but the poorer person will pay at a higher average tax rate
    c) but the richer person will pay at a higher average tax rate
    d) but it is impossible to tell what their average tax rates are

11. The most progressive tax listed here is the _____.
    a) Social Security tax
    b) federal personal income tax
    c) federal excise tax
    d) state sales tax

12. Each of the following is a direct tax except the _____ tax.
    a) Social Security
    b) federal personal income
    c) corporate income
    d) federal excise

13. Which is true?
    a) The rich are hurt more than the poor by regressive taxes.
    b) The poor are hurt more than the rich by progressive taxes.
    c) The federal personal income tax is a regressive tax.
    d) None of these statements is true.

14. A tax with an average tax rate of 20 percent for the rich and 2 percent for the middle class is _____.
   a) progressive
   b) regressive
   c) proportional
   d) none of these

15. In 2001 a person earning $200,000 paid Social Security tax on _____.
   a) none of her income
   b) all of her income
   c) nearly all of her income
   d) less than half of her income

16. You can legally cut down on how much income tax you pay by means of _____.
   a) tax avoidance
   b) tax evasion
   c) both tax evasion and tax avoidance
   d) neither tax evasion nor tax avoidance

17. In 2001 a person making $5 million in interest on municipal bonds was taxed on this income at an average tax rate of _____.
   a) 39.6 percent
   b) 31 percent
   c) 28 percent
   d) 0 percent

18. The most important source of federal tax revenue is the _____.
   a) personal income tax
   b) corporate income tax
   c) federal excise tax
   d) payroll tax

19. Until 1981 the maximum marginal tax rate on the federal income tax was _____.
   a) 70 percent
   b) 50 percent
   c) 40 percent
   d) 33 percent

20. Today for every retired person there is (are) _____ person(s) in the labor force.
   a) one
   b) two
   c) three
   d) four

21. In 2001 the maximum corporate income tax rate was _____ percent.
   a) 50
   b) 46
   c) 40
   d) 35

22. Each of the following is subject to a federal excise tax except _____.
   a) phone calls
   b) gasoline
   c) cigarettes
   d) paper products

23. Taxes (including federal, state, and local) are about _____ of our GDP.
   a) 10 percent
   b) 20 percent
   c) 30 percent
   d) 40 percent

24. The most important source of state tax revenue is the _____ tax.
   a) property
   b) income
   c) excise
   d) sales

25. The most important source of local tax revenue is the _____ tax.
   a) property
   b) income
   c) excise
   d) sales

26. Compared with the citizens of other industrial countries, Americans are _____.
   a) much more heavily taxed
   b) somewhat more heavily taxed
   c) taxed at about the same rate
   d) not as heavily taxed

27. As a redistributor of income, the federal government plays _____.
   a) no role
   b) a very minor role
   c) a major role
   d) a completely dominating role

28. Adam Smith endorsed each of the following roles of government except _____.
   a) providing for defense
   b) establishing a system of justice
   c) erecting a limited number of public works
   d) guaranteeing a job to every person ready, willing, and able to work

29. An example of a public good is _____.
   a) a Honda Accord
   b) a movie theater
   c) a Boeing 747
   d) a lighthouse

30. Public goods are usually _____.
   a) very low-priced
   b) efficiently produced
   c) indivisible
   d) sold by private firms

31. Which statement is true?

    a) Americans pay the highest taxes in the world.

    b) Public goods are provided by private enterprise.

    c) The economic role of the federal government has shrunk over the last 30 years.

    d) In 1990 and in 1993 taxes for the rich were increased substantially.

32. A person in which one of these occupations is least likely to cheat on his taxes?

    a) auto dealer   c) clothing store operator

    b) restaurateur   d) postal clerk

33. Statement 1: Americans pay a higher percentage of their income in taxes than most Western Europeans but also receive much greater benefits from the government. Statement 2: Public education is traditionally funded largely by local property taxes.

    a) Statement 1 is true and statement 2 is false.

    b) Statement 2 is true and statement 1 is false.

    c) Both statements are true.

    d) Both statements are false.

34. Gasoline taxes in the United States are _____ than they are in other leading industrial nations.

    a) much higher   c) a little lower

    b) a little higher   d) much lower

35. Statement 1: Payroll taxes and Social Security taxes are identical. Statement 2: The Social Security tax was 6.2 percent of your earnings on a wage base of $80,400 in 2001.

    a) Statement 1 is true and statement 2 is false.

    b) Statement 2 is true and statement 1 is false.

    c) Both statements are true.

    d. Both statements are false.

36. Statement 1: The Medicare tax is 1.45 percent on a wage base of $80,400. Statement 2: The Medicare tax is slightly less regressive than the Social Security tax.

    a) Statement 1 is true and statement 2 is false.

    b) Statement 2 is true and statement 1 is false.

    c) Both statements are true.

    d) Both statements are false.

37. Statement 1: The wage base for the Social Security tax is raised each year to keep pace with inflation. Statement 2: About one out of every three taxpayers pays more in payroll taxes than in personal income taxes.

    a) Statement 1 is true and statement 2 is false.

    b) Statement 2 is true and statement 1 is false.

    c) Both statements are true.

    d) Both statements are false.

Fill-In Questions

1. The economic role of the federal government began to get very large in the year _____.

2. Name basic economic influences of the federal government: (1) _____; (2) _____; and (3) _____.

3. Fiscal year 2000 began on _____ _____ (fill in month, day, and year).

4. The federal government agency that plays the central role in the preparation of the president's budget is _____.

5. In 2001 we spent about $ _____ on defense.

6. Interest on the federal debt in 2001 was about _____ _____.

7. In 2001 the federal government spent about $ _____ _____.

8. Total government spending in 2001 (including federal, state, and local) came to $ _____.

9. The largest federal government transfer payment is _____.

10. The average tax rate is found by dividing _____ by _____.

11. Progressive taxes place the greatest burden on the _____.

12. Examples of regressive taxes include _____ and _____.

13. In 2001 the Social Security tax rate was _____ percent.

14. The most important source of federal tax revenue is the _____ tax.

15. The Economic Recovery Act of 1981 was better known as the _____.

16. The maximum marginal tax rate today is _____ percent.

17. Most Americans are taxed at marginal rates of _____ percent and _____ percent.

18. If you earned $10,000 in 2001, how much would the federal government collect in payroll tax? $ _____ _____.

19. The state and local governments have been faced with a dilemma since World War II. They have been expected to _____ but they have had difficulty _____.

20. The benefits-received principle of taxation states that _____.

21. If Adam Smith were alive today, he would say that our government is too _____.

Problems

1. If a person earned $80,000 in 2001, how much Social Security tax did he pay?

2. If a person earned $10,000 in 2001, how much Social Security tax did she pay?

3. If you earned $20,000 and paid $1,000 in federal income tax, how much was your average tax rate?

4. If you had a marginal tax rate of 28 percent and earned an extra $10,000, how much tax would you pay?

5. If you earned an extra $1,000 and paid $150 in taxes on that income, how much would your marginal tax rate be?

6. If you were in the lowest personal income tax bracket, how much personal income tax would you have to pay on $5,000 of taxable income?

7. Suppose that Bill Gates's income were to increase by $100 million. How much more personal income tax would he have to pay?

8. If your taxable income rose from $30,000 to $40,000 and your tax bill rose from $4,500 to $7,000, how much is your marginal tax rate?

9. If you pay $5,000 on a taxable income of $40,000, how much is your average tax rate?

10. The Speedy Delivery Service paid its 10 drivers $30,000 each. How much did the company owe in payroll tax?

11. If you earned $100,000, how much would you pay in Social Security tax and in Medicare tax?

12. Prove that a married person with three dependents (including himself) and an income of $12,000 pays more in Social Security tax than in federal income tax.

13. If you were the only working member of a family of two adults and two children and earned $15,000, (a) approximately how much federal personal income tax would you pay? (b) How much Social Security and Medicare tax would you pay?

14. If you paid $1,000 in federal income tax, how much is your marginal tax rate and your total tax rate? (There is enough information for you to figure out the answer.)

Chapter 8

The Export-Import Sector

The American economy is, by far, the largest and most productive in the world. Consequently, we are the world's largest importer and exporter of goods and services. Yet foreign trade is less important to the U.S. economy than it is to those of nearly all other industrial nations. But, in spite of the relatively small percentage of U.S. GDP accounted for through foreign trade, we have become thoroughly integrated into the global economy.

So far we've looked at the three main sectors of GDP—C (consumption), I (investment), and G (government spending). Now let's consider X_n (net exports). X_n = exports − imports.

CHAPTER OBJECTIVES

In this chapter we'll cover:

- The basis for international trade.
- U.S. imports and exports.
- A summing up: $C + I + G + X_n$.

- The world's leading trading nations.
- World trade agreements and free-trade zones.

The Basis for International Trade

If you follow baseball, then you're familiar with trades. Let's say that the Houston Astros have five right-handed hitting outfielders and trade one of them to the Philadelphia Phillies. In exchange the Phillies send the Astros one of their four left-handed relief pitchers. Baseball folk would say that that was a trade that helped both teams. Of course, why else would they trade?

We're going to look at trading, first between individuals, and then between nations. There are a lot of people who like to putter around the house, doing their own repairs.

193

Figure 5
Measuring GDP (solution)

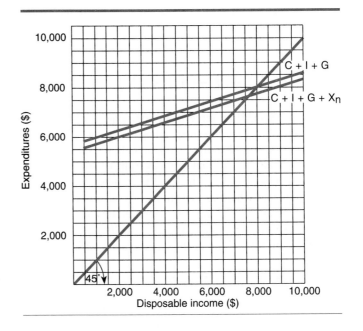

Why is the C + I + G + X$_n$ line drawn below the C + I + G line?

Why do we draw the C + I + G + X$_n$ line *below* the C + I + G line? Because X$_n$ is a negative number, so the sum of C + I + G + X$_n$ is *less* than the sum of C + I + G.

Let's suppose that we somehow eliminated our trade deficit. How much, then, would X$_n$ be? X$_n$ would be 0. Now, if X$_n$ were 0 instead of -370, then our GDP, or total output of goods and services, would be \$370 billion higher. That would mean we would be producing over \$1,300 worth more goods and services for each person living in the United States. So one may conclude that running a huge trade deficit represents producing a lot less output than would be produced if there were no deficit.[4]

This graph completes an odyssey we began back in Chapter 5 when we graphed the C line, and continued with the C + I line in Chapter 6, and the C + I + G line in Chapter 7. I'll give you a chance to catch your breath in this chapter and the next, but in Chapter 11 the graph of the C + I + G + X$_n$ line returns.

The World's Leading Trading Nations

Who is the world's leading trading nation? For most of the 18th and 19th centuries it was undoubtedly England, although for some of that time the Dutch certainly gave the English a run for their money. In Figure 6 it appears that the Netherlands (a.k.a. Holland) were now the world's leading trading nation, with Canada a distant second.

But now look at Figure 7. The United States exports more than any other nation. Indeed, the Netherlands didn't even make the top ten list. So, while trade is more important to the Dutch economy than to ours, we are the world's leading exporter. OK, given the data in Figure 7, who is the world's leading trading nation?

We are! In terms of world trade, we export more than any other nation. So, even though trade is less important to our economy than to those of the Netherlands, Canada, and many other nations, we are the world's leading trading nation because we export more than anyone else.

We also import more than anyone else. As you know, we have a very large negative balance of trade. In fact our negative balance of trade is much larger than that of any other nation.

---

[4]This is, of course, an oversimplification, mainly because it assumes we are operating below full employment.

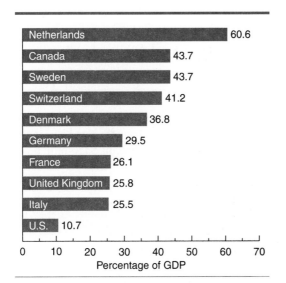

Figure 6

Exports of Goods and Services
as a Percentage of GDP,
Selected Countries, 1999
Source: OECD, *National Accounts of
OECD Countries,* 2001.

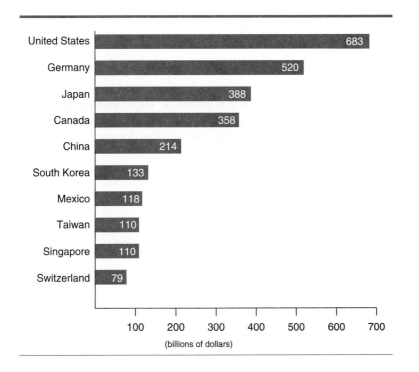

Figure 7

The World's Top Ten
Merchandise Exporting
Nations, 1999

The United States, Germany, and
Japan are the world's largest
exporters.
Source: World Trade Organization.

Which nation is the world's largest exporter? It's the United States. And which nation has the world's largest negative net exports? Also the United States. Can you explain how we can be the world's leading exporter and have the largest negative net exports? I'd like you to think about that and then read the box titled "How Can We Be the World's Leading Exporter and Have the Largest Negative Net Exports?".

World Trade Agreements and Free Trade Zones

Since the end of World War II in 1945 there has been an accelerating movement toward free trade. The formation of the European Common Market, renamed the European Union, and of NAFTA (the North American Free Trade Agreement), have placed most

How can we be the world's leading exporter and have the largest negative net exports?

You can see from the data in Figure 7 that we are the world's leading exporter. But we also lead the world in negative net exports. How can we be the world's leading exporter and have the largest negative net exports?

Answer: We also happen to be the world's largest im- porter. In fact our imports are so much larger than our exports that we have the largest negative net exports. In the year 2000 we bought $370 billion more goods and services from foreigners than they bought from us. We bought $1,469 billion, and they bought just $1,099 billion.

of the industrial world within two virtual free trade zones. In addition, the General Agreement on Trade and Tariffs (GATT), now the World Trade Organization, has reduced trade barriers worldwide.

Free Trade Zones

NAFTA   The North American Free Trade Agreement, which was ratified by Congress in 1993, created a free trade area including Canada, the United States, and Mexico, a market fast approaching 400 million consumers. Here is how the agreement is described in the 1994 *Economic Report of the President:*

> In addition to dismantling trade barriers in industrial goods, NAFTA includes agreements on services, investment, intellectual property rights, agriculture, and strengthening of trade rules. There are also side agreements on labor adjustment provisions, protection of the environment, and import surges.[5]

How well has the agreement worked so far? Has a flood of cheap Mexican goods resulted in "the sound of jobs being sucked out of the United States"? Hardly. Despite the precipitous fall of the peso against the dollar and other currencies in late 1994, our trade with Mexico was up about 20 percent, and we continued to run a very small trade surplus.

In early 1995, however, the full effects of the peso's fall turned our small trade surplus with Mexico into an annual deficit of more than $15 billion. The effect of NAFTA on jobs is more difficult to discern. Clearly the threat of moving operations to Mexico, where hourly wages and fringe benefits average about $1.50 an hour, has had a depressing effect on American factory wages. But there is little evidence that the agreement has cost more than 200,000 jobs, which is less than 2 one-thousandths of our total employment. Keep in mind, too, that since the advent of NAFTA in 1993 our unemployment rate fell from just under 7% to just over 4% in 2000.

Mexico is becoming a manufacturing export platform. Currently 62 percent of all U.S. exports to Mexico are eventually re-exported back to the United States—up from 40 percent before NAFTA. Mexican autoworkers performing sophisticated, highly productive manufacturing work that used to be done in America do it at one-eighth the U.S. wage.

Currently the United States absorbs 87 percent of Mexico's expots. This figure should fall substantially during the next decade, especially after the trade deal negotiated between Mexico and the European Union, which will abolish most tariffs between

[5]See page 225 of the *Report.*

Figure 8
Countries of the European Union

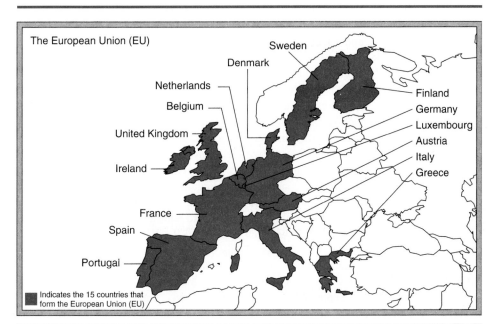

The European Union (EU)

Sweden
Denmark
Netherlands
Belgium
United Kingdom
Ireland
France
Spain
Portugal

Finland
Germany
Luxembourg
Austria
Italy
Greece

■ Indicates the 15 countries that form the European Union (EU)

them by 2007. Volkswagen, which makes the New Beetle solely in Mexico, currently pays a seven-percent duty when it ships to Europe, but under the new pact, these cars will be shipped to Europe duty-free.[6]

NAFTA was an extension of an earlier trade agreement with Canada, our most important trading partner, with whom we have been running a $10 billion to $15 billion trade deficit in recent years. Under the agreement, duties on most goods will be phased out within the next few years.

Canada remains our most important trading partner, and we, theirs. We import more from Canada than any other country, and we export more to Canada than any other country. Because of our mutual interdependence—and because of the integration of our economies—it would be unthinkable for either country to erect trade barriers to keep out imports from the other.

> Canada is our most important trading partner.

There has been talk of expanding NAFTA to include all 34 nations of the Western Hemisphere (except Cuba), a grouping tentatively called the "Free Trade Area of the Americas." The leaders of these nations met in Quebec in April 2001 at the third summit of the Americas, and agreed in principle to put the pack into operation no later than 2005. However, President George W. Bush must get authority from Congress to negotiate trade agreements that cannot be amended when ratified by Congress.

The European Union (EU)   Although this free trade association of 15 nations (see Figure 8) can trace its origins back to the 1950s, it wasn't until 1992 that a truly common market was formed. Freight was now able to move anywhere within the EU without checkpoint delays and paperwork. So-called "quality" codes such as German beer-purity regulations and Belgian chocolate-content restrictions were ended. Workers from any EU country could work in any other member country.

With a population and GDP comparable to those of the United States, the EU is already an economic powerhouse. In 1999, 11 EU countries formed the European Monetary Union, which established the euro as a common currency. The euro initially existed along with each country's own currency. In 2002 new euro coins and paper money will begin replacing the old national currencies. This common currency is

---

[6]See Geri Smith, "Mexico Pulls Off Another Trade Coup," *BusinessWeek,* February 7, 2000, p. 56.

expected to make trade among participating member nations much easier to conduct. A German tourist buying a meal in a Parisian restaurant will no longer have to convert her marks into francs, and a Dutch businessman buying Italian wine will no longer have to convert his guilders into lira.

How much will the euro increase trade among the 11 member nations? According to a study by Andrew K. Rose of the National Bureau of Economic Research (a private research company based in New York), nations with the same currency trade three times as much with one another as they would with different currencies.[7]

The introduction of the Euro went very smoothly, and it has eased trade and commerce among its 11 members. However, two major problems persist. First, Great Britain has so far refused to join, preferring to continue using its own currency for internal and international transactions.[8] And second, almost immediately after being introduced, the euro dropped steadily in value for a year. Initially it was set at $1.17; that is, you could exchange $1.17 for one euro. But within a year the euro had fallen below $ .90 and then traded for most of the year 2000 at between $.85 and $.95. We'll be covering the euro much more thoroughly in the last chapter of this book.

Exchange rate

A more general topic we'll be covering in that chapter is exchange rates. *An exchange rate is the price of one unit of a country's currency expressed in terms of another's.* We've already expressed exchange rates of euros and dollars. In a couple of pages we'll mention the exchange rate between U.S. dollars and Japanese yen. If you can get 90 yen for a dollar one day and 91 yen for a dollar the next, we would say that the dollar went up in value relative to the yen because you're getting more yen for your dollar. Similarly, we would say that the yen fell in value relative to the dollar because you would need to exchange more yen for one dollar.

Mercosur   Much less well known than NAFTA and the EU, this free trade zone includes Argentina, Brazil, Paraguay, and Uruguay and associate members Bolivia and Chile. It is the fourth largest integrated market after NAFTA, the EU, and Japan. Mercosur is an acronym for Mercado Común del Sur, or Common Market of the South. Formed in 1991, it has succeeded in eliminating all internal tariffs while imposing a common external tariff on goods imported from countries outside the union. However, some trade restrictions—especially between Brazil and Argentina— still persist.

World Trade Agreements

GATT   The General Agreement on Trade and Tariffs was drafted in 1947 and has since been signed by more than 135 nations. GATT is a uniform system of rules for the conduct of international trade. Its latest version, which was ratified by Congress in 1994, was the culmination of years of negotiations. It will reduce tariffs worldwide by an average of 40 percent, lower other barriers to trade such as quotas on certain products, and provide patent protection for American software, pharmaceuticals, and other industries.

Will GATT hurt our trade balance, unleash a flood of cheap foreign imports, and result in the loss of millions of American jobs? Although some industries will be affected adversely, the positive appears to outweigh the negative. First of all, on the average, foreign countries have more trade restrictions and tariffs on U.S. goods than we have on theirs, so GATT should help us much more than it hurts us. For the first time intellectual property rights like patents, trademarks, and copyrights will be protected. GATT will also open markets for service industries such as accounting, advertising, computer services, and engineering—fields in which Americans excel.

---

[7]See *BusinessWeek,* March 27, 2000, p. 30.

[8]In September of 2000, the people of Denmark voted against joining the European Monetary Union.

The WTO, the IMF, and the World Bank

What do the WTO and the IMF stand for, and what do they do? And what is the World Bank? You don't have a clue? Don't worry—you are not alone.

The WTO stands for the World Trade Organization, which was set up to encourage world trade by bringing down existing trade barriers. In the next section we'll see how it operates.

The International Monetary Fund (IMF), an organization of more than 150 nations, was set up in 1944 as a lender of last resort to discourage member nations from devaluating their currency. For example, the IMF would lend dollars to Japan if the Japanese yen were falling relative to the dollar. Let's say that 100 yen were trading for one dollar and the yen fell to 105 for one dollar, and then to 110 for one dollar. The IMF would lend reserves to Japan to stabilize the yen.

The World Bank, also created in 1944, makes long-term, low-interest loans to developing countries, mainly to build highways, bridges, dams, power generators, and water supply systems. In addition, it acts as a guarantor of repayment to encourage some private lending.

Finally, GATT brings agriculture under international trade rules for the first time. Many countries heavily subsidize their farmers (in 2000 the United States spent $28 billion in crop subsidies), but European subsidies dwarf those paid to American farmers. Clinton's Council of Economic Advisors noted that, "Since the United States has a strong underlying comparative advantage in agriculture, the mutual reduction in trade barriers and subsidization will be to the distinct advantage of U.S. producers."[9] Proportionately, the Europeans will have to reduce their subsidies a lot more than we'll have to, making American crop exports even more competitive.

WTO   The World Trade Organization was set up in 1995 as a successor to GATT. It is based on three major principles: (1) liberalization of trade; (2) nondiscrimination—the most-favored-nation principle; and (3) no unfair encouragement of exports. Let's consider each principle in detail.

Trade barriers, which were reduced under GATT, should continue to be reduced. Incidentally, barriers have been falling *within* free trade zones such as NAFTA and the European Union.

Under the most favored nation principle, members of the WTO must offer all other members the same trade concessions as any member country. Which is a lot like when the teacher says that if you bring candy to class, you must bring some for *everyone.*

Finally, no unfair encouragement of exports encompasses export subsidies, which are considered a form of unfair competition. American and European governments have long subsidized their farmers, who, in turn, have exported much of their crops. Boeing, and the European consortium, Airbus, have also received substantial export subsidies from the governments.

The WTO has a Dispute Settlement Body to handle trade disagreements among member nations. Many of the disputes involve the charge of the dumping of products below cost. Although many politicians in the United States have very reluctantly accepted the jurisdiction of the WTO, we have won almost all the more than two dozen cases in which we have been the complaining party.

At present, China is the largest economic power not yet a member of the WTO. Negotiations have begun over its conditions for entry. As a nation with some of the highest trade barriers in the world, China will have to agree to provide much greater access to its market before it will gain admission.

---

[9]*Economic Report of the President,* 1995, p. 208.

The Seattle Protest   When the WTO held a meeting in Seattle in late 1999 to formulate further trade agreements, tens of thousands of protesters descended on the city. Not only did they manage to disrupt the conference, but they wreaked so much havoc that the governor of Washington state was forced to call in the National Guard to restore order. Only a minority of the protesters were at all unruly, and prominent among them were labor union members, environmentalists, and human rights advocates.

BusinessWeek outlined the reasons for the protests:

> Environmentalists argue that elitist trade and economic bodies make undemocratic decisions that undermine national sovereignty on environmental regulation. Unions charge that unfettered trade allows unfair competition from countries that lack labor standards. Human rights and student groups say the IMF and the World Bank prop up regimes that condone sweatshops and pursue policies that bail out foreign lenders at the expense of local economies.[10]

In early 2000 there were protests in Washington and Prague targeting the WTO, the IMF, and the World Bank and in Quebec City in April 2001 against the summit of the Americas. Although there is little chance these institutions will be very much affected by the protests, they could well be an indication of spreading concern about the consequences of globalization.

Many Americans, as well as citizens of other leading industrial nations, have strong reservations about ceding their national sovereignty to international organizations, especially the WTO. Much of their concern centers on the possible loss of jobs and the reduction of wages in their countries if their workers were forced to compete with low-wage workers in the world's poorer countries, most of whom earn just one or two dollars a day. Is it fair to make American factories, which uphold relatively high environmental standards, compete with Third World factories that are not similarly burdened? If the United States and other industrial countries are subject to the rules and regulations of the WTO, their own governments would be unable to prevent a flood of cheap imports. In sum, the debate is not about "free trade," but about "fair trade."[11]

Questions for Further Thought and Discussion

1. Explain how and why trade barriers have come down in recent decades.
2. Do you think we should have joined NAFTA? Try to argue this question from both sides.
3. List the reasons why our trade deficit has grown so quickly since the mid-1990s. What we can do to help bring it down?
4. Identify the goods and services that you purchase that are imported. How would your lifestyle change if these imports were unavailable?
5. How would your life change if the United States were no longer the world's leading exporter?
6. Explain how international trade (exports and imports) affects a nation's output, employment, and income.

---

[10]*BusinessWeek,* April 24, 2000, p. 40.

[11]In a *BusinessWeek*/Harris poll conducted in April, 2000, 1,024 people were asked these questions:

Which of the following best describes your views about foreign trade? Do you consider yourself to be someone who believes in free trade or trade without any restrictions, someone who believes in fair trade or trade with some standards for labor and the environment, or someone who is protectionist, meaning that there should be rules to protect U.S. markets and workers from imports?

Here is how they answered:

Free trader . . . . . .10%   Fair trader . . . . .51%   Protectionist 37%
Don't know . . . . .3%   Refused 0%

(*BusinessWeek,* April 24, 2000, p. 44).

Workbook for Chapter 8

Name _____ Date _____

Multiple-Choice Questions

Circle the letter that corresponds to the best answer.

1. Today world trade is regulated by _____.
   a) NAFTA
   b) GATT
   c) WTO
   d) EU

2. During the last ten years our trade balance in merchandise was _____, and our trade balance in services was _____.
   a) positive, positive
   b) negative, negative
   c) negative, positive
   d) positive, negative

3. Which is the most accurate statement?
   a) Our trade deficit has narrowed since 1995.
   b) We export more merchandise than services (in terms of dollars).
   c) The largest service purchase that foreigners make from the United States is educational services.
   d) In recent years foreigners have generally refused to accept U.S. dollars in payment for their goods and services.

4. Since the early 1990s our trade deficit has _____.
   a) fallen substantially
   b) fallen slightly
   c) risen slightly
   d) risen substantially

5. In the 20th century our balance of trade was positive until the _____.
   a) 1950s
   b) 1960s
   c) 1970s
   d) 1980s
   e) 1990s

6. Statement I: The European Union was formed as a trading counterweight to NAFTA.
   Statement II: Since the formation of NAFTA, the United States has lost millions of jobs to Mexico.
   a) Statement I is true, and statement II is false.
   b) Statement II is true, and statement I is false.
   c) Both statements are true.
   d) Both statements are false.

7. The basis for international trade is that _____.
   a) a nation can import a particular good or service at a lower cost than if it were produced domestically.
   b) we stand to gain if we can sell more to other nations than they buy from us.
   c) there are winners and losers.
   d) it pays to trade, provided we remain independent by producing all our necessities.

8. Adam Smith believed that _____.
   a) people should never buy anything if they can make it themselves.
   b) what makes sense in the conduct of a private family's economic endeavors also makes sense in those of a nation.
   c) trading with other nations promotes full employment.
   d) A nation will gain if its citizens trade among themselves, but it will probably lose if it trades with other nations.

9. $GDP = C + I + G + X_n$. If X_n were not included, our GDP would be _____.
   a) higher
   b) about the same
   c) lower

10. The most-favored nation clause of the WTO agreement stipulates that _____.
    a) no member nation may impose a tariff on the goods of any other member nation.
    b) all member nations must offer all other member countries the same trade concessions as any member country.
    c) each member may designate another member as a favored nation, providing that nation with trade concessions.
    d) all member nations must sell their goods to other member nations at cost.

11. Statement I: The United States has a much larger population and GDP than the European Union.
Statement II: The European Union has attained a higher degree of economic integration than NAFTA.
    a) Statement I is true, and statement II is false.
    b) Statement II is true, and statement I is false.
    c) Both statements are true.
    d) Both statements are false.

12. Statement I: Our trade deficit, although still high, is lower than it was five years ago.
Statement II: We both export and import computers and semiconductors.
    a) Statement I is true, and statement II is false.
    b) Statement II is true, and statement I is false.
    c) Both statements are true.
    d) Both statements are false.

13. Most economists and people in the business community supported _____.
    a) both NAFTA and GATT.
    b) neither NAFTA nor GATT.
    c) NAFTA but not GATT.
    d) GATT but not NAFTA.

14. Which statement is true?
    a) X_n has always been positive.
    b) X_n has always been negative.
    c) X_n had been positive from the turn of the century until the 1970s.
    d) X_n had been negative from the turn of the century until the 1970s.
    e) None of these statements is true.

15. Statement I: Since the late 1990s, our negative balance of trade has become much larger.
Statement II: The United States has the world's largest negative balance of trade.
    a) Statement I is true, and statement II is false.
    b) Statement II is true, and statement I is false.
    c) Both statements are true.
    d) Both statements are false.

16. The world's largest exporter is _____.
    a) the United States
    b) Japan
    c) Germany
    d) the United Kingdom
    e) China

17. Since the passage of NAFTA our trade deficit with Mexico has gone _____ and our trade deficit with Canada has gone _____.
    a) up, up   c) up, down
    b) down, down   d) down, up

18. Statement I: The United States has a much less self-sufficient economy than those of countries in Western Europe.
Statement II: Mexico sends the United States more than 80 percent of its exports.
    a) Statement I is true, and statement II is false.
    b) Statement II is true, and statement I is false.
    c) Both statements are true.
    d) Both statements are false.

19. Mexico has recently signed a trade pact with _____.
    a) Japan   c) the European Union
    b) China   d) Brazil and Argentina

20. Each of the following is a characteristic of the European Union EXCEPT that _____.
    a) workers from any EU country could seek work in any other member country
    b) the euro replaced the domestic currencies (for example, francs, marks, lira) in 1999
    c) its population and GDP are comparable to those of the United States
    d) freight is able to move anywhere within the EU without checkpoint delays and paperwork

21. The trading bloc that has eliminated all internal tariffs is _____.
    a) the European Union
    b) NAFTA
    c) Mercosur
    d) the World Trade Organization

22. Which one of these statements best describes the complaints of the protesters at the 1999 WTO meeting in Seattle?
    a) They opposed military aid to Third World dictatorships.
    b) They opposed trade with poor countries because of the exploitative nature of that trade.
    c) They opposed free trade with nations whose people worked under sweatshop conditions and opposed ceding national sovereignty to an international group.
    d) They opposed strict environmental standards, which they felt would increase our cost of living.

23. Most Americans would describe themselves as being in favor of _____ .
    a) free trade   c) trade protection
    b) fair trade   d) no foreign trade

24. Which statement would best describe the situation of the American economy?
    a) We are more dependent on foreign trade than most other nations.
    b) We are much more dependent on foreign trade than we were 30 years ago.
    c) We are much less dependent on foreign trade than we were 30 years ago.
    d) We are virtually self-sufficient.

25. Which statement is false?
    a) During World War I and World War II, the sum of our imports and exports as a percent of GDP rose sharply.
    b) Foreign trade in goods is much more important to the American economy than foreign trade in services.
    c) Because the American economy is much larger than any other economy, we can continue running larger and larger trade deficits for as long as we like.
    d) We pay for a large chunk of our trade deficit with U.S. dollars.

Fill-In Questions

1. The world's leading exporting nation is _____ ; the nation with the largest trade deficit is _____ .

2. $X_n =$ _____ − _____ .

3. The three members of NAFTA are _____ , _____ , and _____ .

4. In the year 2000 we ran a trade deficit of $ _____ billion.

5. Our leading merchandise export is _____ , and our leading merchandise import is _____ .

6. Of all the goods produced in the United States, about _____ percent were imported.

7. The most prominent nation not yet a member of the World Trade organization is _____ .

8. Our exports of goods and services are about _____ percent of our GDP.

9. Our most important trading partner is _____ .

10. We run a trade deficit in _____ and a trade surplus in _____ .

11. As a percentage of GDP the sum of our imports and exports is more than _____ times as high today as it was 30 years ago.

12. The only trading bloc that has eliminated all its internal tariffs is _____ .

13. What was the main concern of the labor union members who were protesting against the WTO in Seattle in 1999?

14. Foreign trade was relatively unimportant to our economy until around the year _____ .

Chapter 9

Gross Domestic Product

When was the last time someone said to you, "Mine is bigger than yours?" My *what* is bigger than your *what*? My GDP is bigger than your GDP? Well, it just so happens that our country's GDP is bigger than everyone else's. Even Japan's. Gross domestic product, or GDP, measures a country's output over a year—which means the United States produces more goods and services every year than any other nation in the world.

CHAPTER OBJECTIVES

When you have finished this chapter, you will know the answers to these questions:

- What is GDP?
- How is GDP measured?
- What are the national income accounts?
- What is the difference between GDP and real GDP?

- How does our GDP compare to those of other nations?
- How is per capita GDP calculated?
- What are the shortcomings of GDP as a measure of national economic well-being?

What Is Gross Domestic Product?

What is GDP? *It is the nation's expenditure on all the final goods and services produced during the year at market prices.* For example, if we spent $18,000 per car on 10 million American cars, that $180 billion would go into GDP. We'd add in the 15 billion Big Macs at $3 for another $45 billion, and the 1.8 million new homes at $80,000 each for $144 billion. Then, for good measure, we'd add the 5 billion visits to doctors' offices at $75 apiece for $375 billion and the 20 billion nightclub admissions at $15 each for $300 billion. Add everything up and we'd get nearly $10 trillion in the year 2000.

Definition of GDP

Did you notice the word *final* in the definition of GDP? We include only those goods and services that consumers, businesses, and governments buy for their own use. So when you buy a telephone answering machine or you get your hair cut, or if the government repaves a highway, we count those goods and services in GDP. But if Liz Claiborne buys 10,000 yards of fabric to make dresses, that purchase is not recorded in GDP. When the dresses are sold, they are then counted in GDP.

An alternate definition of GDP is *GDP is the value of all goods and services produced within a nation's boundaries during the year.* This would include the wages, rent, interest, and profits earned by the few million foreigners who work in the United States. For example, there are a lot of Japanese in Tennessee and a lot of Germans in South Carolina who make cars. But our GDP would not include the wages, rent, interest, and profits earned by Americans living abroad.

$GDP = C + I + G + X_n$

Let's get back to our GDP equation:

$$GPD = C + I + G + X_n$$

Substituting the year 2000 data into this equation, we get:

$$GDP = 6,759 + 1,834 + 1,743 - 370$$

$$GDP = 9,966$$

In 2000 we produced almost $10 trillion worth of final goods and services (see Table 1). Over two-thirds were consumer goods and services, followed in size by government purchases, investment spending, and, finally, net exports, which were negative. Now we'll draw a few graphs and then move on to how GDP is measured.

Table 1 offers a detailed compilation of the components of GDP in 2000. As you can see, C was the largest, followed by I, G, and then X_n, which was negative.

TABLE 1	The Components of GDP, 2000 (in $ billions)*	
Consumption:		
Durable goods	820	
Nondurable goods	2,010	
Services	3,929	
C	6,759	6,759
Investment:		
Plant and equipment	1,361	
Residential housing	416	
Inventory change	57	
I	1,834	1,834
Government purchases:		
Federal	595	
State and local	1,148	
G	1,743	1,743
Net exports:		
Exports	1,099	
−Imports	−1,466	
X_n	−370	−370
GDP		9,966

*Figures may not add up due to rounding.
Source: Economic Report of the President, 2001.

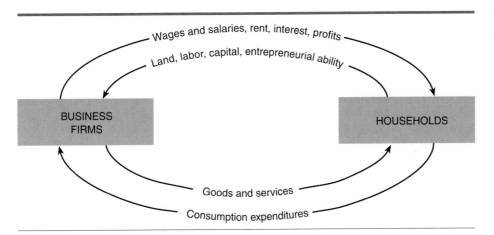

Figure 1
The Circular Flow

How GDP Is Measured

There are two basic ways of measuring GDP: the flow-of-income approach and the expenditures approach (which happens to be my favorite). Both are illustrated in Figure 1.

Both approaches are parts of the national income accounts, a series of numbers that only an economist could love. Figure 1 has the flow of income (resources and resource payments) on the top and the expenditures flow (consumer goods and services and consumer expenditures) on the bottom.

Unfortunately, Figure 1 is a gross simplification (no pun intended) of the way our economy works. We've left out business investment, savings, government purchases and transfer payments, and taxes, as well as imports and exports. Including each of these would have made our economic model more realistic, but Figure 1 would have looked like the intersection of two interstate highways with all those cloverleaves and entrance and exit ramps.

By the way, haven't you seen Figure 1 someplace before, or do you use that line on all the graphs you meet? Well, it turns out you did see virtually the same flowchart a few chapters ago. Check out Figure 3 of Chapter 4, and you'll see for yourself.

Two ways to measure GDP are the flow-of-income approach and the expenditures approach.

The Expenditures Approach

This approach will be used in the next few chapters. People buy consumer goods from business firms and pay for them. Note that we have a circular flow of expenditures and income by connecting the top and bottom loops of Figure 1. People receive incomes from business firms for their land, labor, and capital. This money flows right back to the firms in exchange for consumer goods and services. Hence the money keeps flowing around and around as more goods are produced and paid for.

We've excluded business investment expenditures (I), government expenditures (G), and net exports, X_n, until now.

The big three spenders of GDP

From time to time we will go back to the definition of GDP: *the nation's expenditure on all the final goods and services produced during the year at market prices.* Only "final" goods and services are counted. These include those goods and services purchased by their ultimate consumers. They are represented by the variables in our equation:

GDP is the nation's expenditure on all the final goods and services produced during the year at market prices.

$$GDP = C + I + G + X_n$$

Substituting the year 2000 data for these variables, we get:

$$9,966 = 6,759 + 1,834 + 1,743 - 370$$

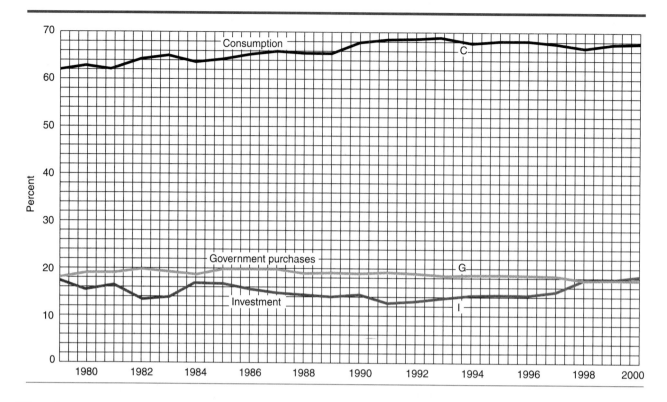

Figure 2

C, I, and G as Percentages of GDP, 1979–2000[*]

Consumption has consistently been between 60 and 70 percent of our GDP, with a slow upward trend over this period.

[*]C + I + G add up to more than 100% because X_n is negative.

Source: Economic Report of the President, 2000.

A careful perusal of Figure 2 will disclose three trends. Between the late 1970s and the late 1990s, the consumption percentage share of GDP rose from the low 60s to the high 60s. The government share stayed between 17 and 21 percent. And the investment share fluctuated within a range of 13 to 19 percent.

Even with our upwardly trending consumption line in Figure 2, the percentage of our GDP devoted to consumption is no higher than that of other leading industrial nations (see Figure 3).

The Flow-of-Income Approach

Business firms produce nearly all our goods and services. The firms pay people wages to get them to turn out these goods and services. Those who own the land and buildings used are paid rent, and those who supply the capital are paid interest. Add up all the goods and services produced and you have GDP. Or, alternatively, add up the incomes received by the factors of production (plus a couple of other things we'll be talking about) and you have GDP.

The flow-of-income approach to GDP is shown in the top part of Figure 1. Households provide business firms with resources (land, labor, capital, and entrepreneurial ability) and are paid by business firms in the form of rent, wages and salaries, interest, and profits.

We need to look at the flow of income in more detail than we looked at the expenditures flow because it has more components. Indeed, this approach is so complex, we'll divide it into three parts: national product (Table 2), national income (Figure 4), and personal income (Figure 4).

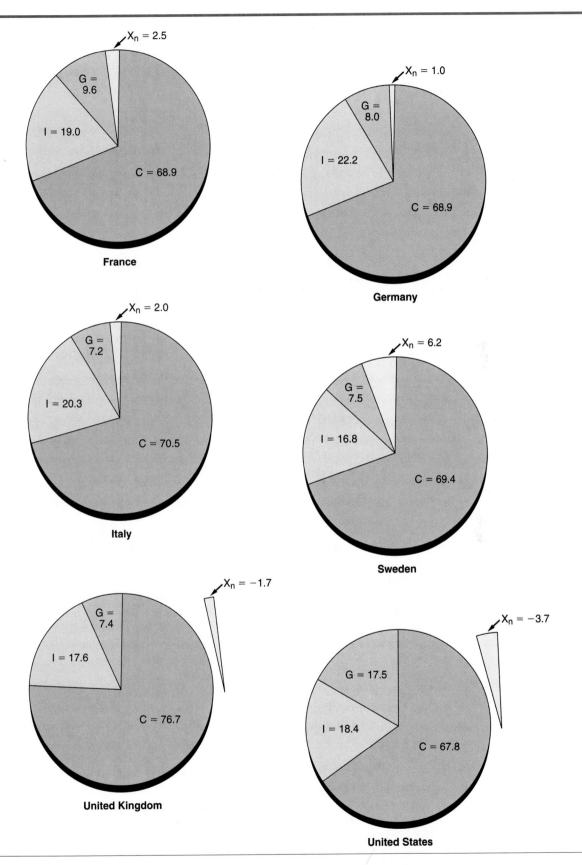

Figure 3

Global Comparison: Breakdown of GDP Expenditures for Select Countries, 2000

Compared to other countries, the United States has a relatively low percentage of its GDP expended on consumption.

Source: National Accounts of OECD Countries, 2001.

TABLE 2	Gross Domestic Product, 2000 (billions of dollars)*
Consumption	$6,759
Investment	1,834
Government spending	1,743
Net exports	−370
GDP	$9,966
(Plus) Receipts of factor income from rest of world	383
(Less) Payments of factor income to rest of world	−375
GNP	9,974
(Less) Depreciation	−1,257
Net domestic product	8,717
(Less) Indirect business taxes (plus) subsidies†	−715*
National income	$8,002†

*Indirect business taxes constitute nearly 90 percent of this figure. Subsidies are very small and positive. Also included are business transfer payments ($30 billion) and a statistical discrepancy (which, in 2000, was $84 billion which we somehow could not account for).

†The figures do not add up exactly because of rounding. Because subsidies are relatively small, we'll ignore them.

Source: Economic Report of the President, 2001.

GDP − Depreciation = NDP

1. National Product   Now we come to the fun part. Many economists are unhappy with the concept of gross domestic product. It's simply too gross. They much prefer net domestic product (NDP) (see box, "Why NDP Is Better Than GDP"). What's the difference? The main difference is depreciation.

Gross domestic product − Depreciation = Net domestic product

GDP includes, among other things, $1,361 billion worth of plant and equipment spending (see Table 1). This is money spent on new office buildings, shopping malls, factories, stores, assembly lines, office machines, computers, and a host of other machinery and equipment.

Why are we so anxious to get rid of depreciation? Depreciation represents the buildings and machinery (plant and equipment) that have worn out or become obsolete over the course of the year. Usually these are replaced with new plant and equipment, but this doesn't represent a net gain because the company ends up right where it started. For example, if a firm begins the year with eight machines and replaces three that wore out during the year, it still has eight machines at the end of the year.

Similarly, when we measure a nation's GDP, one of the things we are counting is the replacement of plant and equipment, which can lead to some dubious conclusions about a nation's economic well-being. For example, suppose Sweden and Canada each have a GDP of 200, but depreciation in Sweden is 50, while in Canada it is only 30. The NDP of Sweden would be 150 (GDP of 200 − Depreciation of 50); Canada's NDP would be 170 (GDP of 200 − Depreciation of 30). A more elaborate example appears in the box "Why NDP Is Better Than GDP."

Are you ready for a big question? All right then, here it comes. What's the difference between gross investment and net investment? *Gross* investment is the total amount we invest in new plant and equipment (as well as new residential housing and additional inventory). *Net* investment is the additional plant and equipment with which we end up by the end of the year. So we have this equation:

Gross investment − Depreciation = Net investment

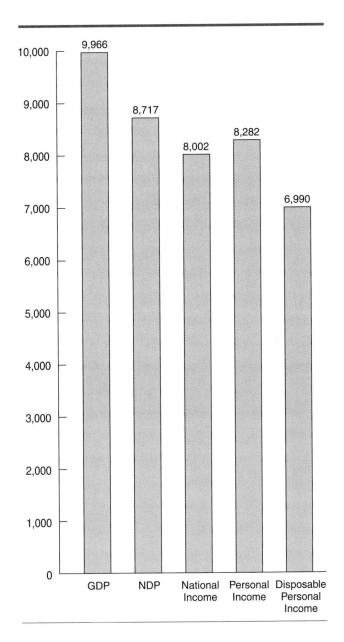

F*igure* 4

National Product and Income, 2000

Our GDP, which is nearly 10 trillion dollars, is the largest of these five variables, and disposable personal income is the smallest.

Source: Economic Report of the President, 2001.

The *I* in the equation GDP = C + I + G + X$_n$ is *gross* investment. We distinguished between *gross* investment and *net* investment back in Chapter 6.

Let's go over the arithmetic. In Table 2, we have a GDP of $9,966 billion (the sum of C + I + G + X$_n$). We add net receipts of factor income from the rest of the world (+$8 billion) and subtract depreciation ($1,257 billion) from GDP to get net domestic product ($8,717 billion). Are you ready to take up national income? All right then, here it comes.

2. National Income   Now we need to subtract indirect business taxes (mainly general sales taxes and taxes on specific items such as gasoline, liquor, and cigarettes) and subsidies (such as government payments to farmers).

We've talked about indirect taxes (sales taxes and taxes on cigarettes, gasoline, and liquor), and we've also talked about income taxes and Social Security taxes, which are direct taxes. Direct taxes are on *people* and indirect taxes are on *things*. (Direct and indirect taxes were discussed in Chapter 7.)

NDP − Indirect business taxes and subsidies = National Income

Why NDP Is Better Than GDP

Although people commonly use GDP when they talk about national output, most economists prefer NDP. Why? Because it allows for depreciation of plant and equipment. Let's illustrate this with two hypothetical countries in the table below:

North Atlantis		South Atlantis	
GDP	500	GDP	500
−Depreciation	50	−Depreciation	100
NDP	450	NDP	400

We see that North Atlantis and South Atlantis had identical GDPs, but that North Atlantis had depreciation of $50 billion while South Atlantis's depreciation was $100 billion.* Consequently, North Atlantis ended up with an NDP of $450 billion, while South Atlantis had an NDP of just $400 billion.

This distinction is important. North and South Atlantis had the same GDP, but North Atlantis's NDP was $50 billion greater than that of South Atlantis. Why? Because South Atlantis had to replace $100 billion of wornout or obsolete plant and equipment that year, while North Atlantis had to replace just $50 billion of plant and equipment.

In 1930 Babe Ruth held out for a salary of $80,000. A reporter asked him if it would be fair for a baseball player to earn more than Herbert Hoover, the president of the United States. "Why not? I had a better year than he did," the Babe replied. And so, we too may ask, who had a better year, North or South Atlantis? Based on GDP, they did equally well; based on NDP, North Atlantis did better.

South Atlantis had a lower NDP because it had to devote twice as much production to replacing worn-out and obsolete plant and equipment as did North Atlantis. When you are devoting such a large portion of your resources to replacing plant and equipment, these resources can't go toward adding to your stock of plant and equipment or, for that matter, to producing consumer goods and services.

Suppose North Atlantis devoted that extra $50 billion to production of more plant and equipment. It would now have $50 billion worth of additional plant and equipment. Or if it had produced $50 billion worth of consumer goods and services, its citizens would have enjoyed a much higher standard of living.

So who enjoyed a better year? Virtually every economist would tell you that North Atlantis did because it had a higher NDP. Stated differently, it's not as significant to know how much a country grossed as to know how much it netted.

---

*Economists use this shorthand way of writing billions (for example, 50 = $50 billion; 100 = $100 billion).

NDP − Indirect business taxes and subsidies = National Income

The big three of domestic product—GDP, NDP, and National Income—are lined up by size in Figure 4 for the year 2000. For other years, could they be in some other order? Could NDP, for example, be larger than GDP? The answer is no. Since GDP − Depreciation = NDP, the only way for NDP to be larger would be if depreciation were negative.[1]

Our National Income was $8,002 billion in the year 2000. The largest part, by far, was compensation of employees (see Figure 5). This compensation includes wages, salaries, and fringe benefits (such as medical insurance and sick, holiday, and vacation pay). Corporate profits are either paid out as dividends or plowed back into the corporation. Net interest is the total interest income of individuals minus interest paid by consumers to businesses and net interest paid by the government. (No one ever asks you to define net interest on an economics exam.) Rental income is the rent received by individuals (rent received by businesses is counted elsewhere). And finally, we have the fifth part of National Income: proprietors' income. This includes the total incomes of all unincorporated businesses (that is, rent, interest, profits, and compensation for labor).[2]

---

[1]Negative depreciation is a logical absurdity. It would mean that plant and equipment had somehow become *less* obsolete and *less* worn out during the year. Negative depreciation is actually appreciation.

[2]These are proprietorships and partnerships, which were discussed early in Chapter 6.

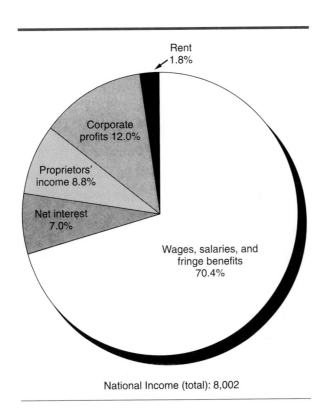

Rent
1.8%

Corporate
profits 12.0%

Proprietors'
income 8.8%

Net interest
7.0%

Wages, salaries, and
fringe benefits
70.4%

National Income (total): 8,002

Figure 5

Distribution of National
Income, 2000

Wages, salaries, and fringe benefits
account for more than 70 cents of
every dollar of our domestic
income.

*Source: Economic Report of the
President,* 2001.

National Income, then, is the sum of compensation to employees, corporate profits, net interest, rental income, and proprietors' income. These are all resource payments for the use of land, labor, capital, and entrepreneurial ability.

So far we've dealt with the domestic product and National Income. OK, two down, one to go.

3. Personal Income   Now we'll work our way down to personal income and disposable personal income. Starting with National Income, we subtract earnings not received (almost all Social Security taxes and corporate profits that were not paid out as dividends), add receipts not earned (mainly Social Security benefits and other government transfer payments, and interest income), and we get personal income, which was $8,282 billion in 2000.

You probably noticed in Figure 4 that personal income is larger than National Income. Why? Because receipts not earned were larger than earnings not received. But personal income is really just what we earn on paper, so to speak. The bottom line is disposable personal income, because it's the money that's ours to keep.

Starting with personal income, we need to subtract personal taxes (chiefly personal income taxes) and a few relatively minor items, such as traffic tickets and charges for government services. Disposable personal income gets its name because it is ours to dispose of, to spend and save as we see fit. In 2000 it came to $6,990 billion.

Do you need to know all of this stuff? Will you ever get to use it? The answer to both questions is a qualified no. GDP you definitely need to know (see the box "Reviewing the Two Approaches to GDP"). The other terms will crop up from time to time over the next eight chapters.

Reviewing the Two Approaches to GDP

First we'll go over the flow-of-income approach. If wages and salaries are $4.7 trillion, rent is $.1 trillion, interest is $.7 trillion, profits are $.5 trillion, indirect business taxes are $.8 trillion, and depreciation is $.6 trillion, find national income, NNP, and GDP:

Solution:

Wages and salaries	$4.7 trillion
Rent	.1
Interest	.7
Profits	.5
Domestic income	6.0
+ Indirect business tax	.8
NNP	6.8
+ Depreciation	.6
GDP	7.4

Now we'll do a problem that starts off with GDP and works its way down to domestic income. Given: GDP = 6,700, Indirect business taxes = 500, Depreciation = 700, and Direct taxes = 500. Find NDP and domestic income.

Solution:

GDP	6,700
Depreciation	−700
NDP	6,000
−Indirect taxes	−500
National income	5,500

I hope you didn't try to use direct taxes. Clearly, they don't belong in our calculations. Just because they're listed doesn't mean we should use them. Suppose you were baking a cake and you had placed your flour, sugar, butter, and other ingredients on a counter. If someone left out a can of turpentine there, would you pour it into your mixing bowl? I hope not, especially if you were planning to offer me a slice of that cake.

Well, then, why did I put direct taxes into the last problem? Because I wanted to see what you would do with it. Remember, just because something is there doesn't mean we have to use it.

Moving right along, let's work out a problem using the expenditures approach to GDP. Given: C = 4,100, I = 900, G = 1,200, Imports = 750, Exports = 650. Find GDP:

Solution: First we'll find net exports:

$$X_n = \text{Exports} - \text{Imports}$$

$$X_n = 650 - 750$$

$$X_n = -100$$

Next we'll write down our equation:

$$\text{GDP} = C + I + G + X_n$$

Then we substitute numbers for the letters:

$$\text{GDP} = 4,100 + 900 + 1,200 - 100$$

And finally, we solve:

$$\text{GDP} = 6,200 - 100$$

$$\text{GDP} = 6,100$$

We'll follow this general procedure for problem solving throughout the book: (1) Write down the equation, (2) substitute, and (3) solve.

Two Things to Avoid When Compiling GDP

Two mistakes are commonly made when GDP is compiled. First we'll talk about multiple counting, that is, counting a particular good at each stage of production. Then we'll look at the inclusion of transfer payments. To compile GDP correctly, we count each good or service only once, and we don't count transfer payments as part of GDP.

Multiple Counting

We need to avoid multiple counting when we compile GDP. Only expenditures on final products—what consumers, businesses, and government units buy for their own use—belong in GDP. This is clearly illustrated by the journey wheat makes from the farm to the supermarket.

The farmer gets about 2 cents for the wheat that goes into a loaf of bread. This wheat is ground into flour at a mill and is now worth, say, 4 cents. When it is placed in 100-pound packages, it is worth 5 cents, and when it is shipped to a bakery, it is worth 10 cents. Baked bread is worth 20 cents, packaged baked bread is worth 23 cents, and bread delivered to the supermarket is worth 35 cents. The supermarket sells it for 89 cents.

How much of this goes into GDP? Do we add up the 2 cents, 4 cents, 5 cents, 10 cents, 20 cents, 23 cents, 35 cents, and 89 cents? No! That would be multiple counting. We count only what is spent on a final good, 89 cents, which is paid by the consumer. Of this entire process, only 89 cents goes into GDP.

GDP, then, counts only what we spend on final goods and services—not those of an intermediate nature. We are not interested in the money spent on wheat or flour, but only that which the buyer of the final product, bread, spends at the supermarket. If we count intermediate goods, we will greatly inflate GDP by counting the same goods and services over and over again.

GDP counts only what we spend on final goods and services.

An alternate way of measuring GDP is the value-added approach.[3] The farmer grows 2 cents' worth of wheat, to which the flour mill adds 2 cents by grinding the wheat into flour and 1 cent by packaging it. The shipper adds 5 cents by getting that flour to the bakery. The baker adds 10 cents by baking the flour into bread and 3 cents more by packaging it. The person who delivers the bread to the supermarket adds another 12 cents to the value of the bread, and finally, the supermarket, by providing a convenient location for the sale of the bread, adds 54 cents. If you sum the value added by each stage—2 cents + 2 cents + 1 cent + 5 cents + 10 cents + 3 cents + 12 cents + 54 cents—you should get 89 cents. If you didn't, you better get a new battery for your calculator. Or if you got a different answer in your head, perhaps your own battery is beginning to run down.

Value-added approach to measuring GDP

Just as we don't include intermediate goods in GDP, we don't count used goods either. If you buy a used car, a 10-year-old house, or virtually anything from a flea market, your purchase does not go into GDP. Remember, we count only final goods and services that were purchased in the current year.

However, anything done this year to make a used product salable is counted (for example, paint job for a used car). What if you add a room to your house? If you do it yourself, then the cost of materials will be included in GDP. If you pay someone to build the addition, then we'll include the full cost of the job.

Treatment of Transfer Payments

At first glance, transfer payments appear to belong in GDP. When the government issues a Social Security or unemployment insurance check, isn't this a form of government

---

[3]The value-added approach to measuring GDP is rarely used. It amounts to summing the values added by all firms in the economy, plus any value added by the government.

spending? Shouldn't it be part of G, like defense spending or the salaries paid to government employees?

GDP includes only payments for goods and services produced this year. A person receiving a Social Security check is not being reimbursed for producing a good or service this year. But a government clerk or a defense contractor *is* providing a good or service this year and their pay would therefore be included under government purchases, designated by the letter G.

Because Social Security, public assistance, Medicare, Medicaid, and other government transfer payments—which now make up more than half of the federal budget—are not payments for currently produced goods and services, they are not included in GDP. However, those who receive these payments will spend nearly all of that money, so, ultimately, the payments will go toward GDP in the form of consumer spending. Note that consumer spending does involve the purchase of final goods and services produced in the current year.

Something else not counted in GDP is financial transactions. The purchase of corporate stocks and bonds does not add anything to GDP. Isn't it an investment? It certainly is from an individual's point of view; but in strictly economic terms, the purchase of corporate stocks and bonds, government securities, real estate, and other financial assets does not constitute investment because it does not represent the purchase of new plant and equipment. But aren't these funds used to buy new plant and equipment? Perhaps. If and when they are, those purchases qualify as investment and therefore as part of GDP.

Transfer payments don't go directly into GDP.

Financial transactions don't go into GDP.

GDP versus Real GDP

Suppose you have a birthday party every year and invite the same three guests, and every year you send out to the same pizzeria for a large pie with everything. Pretty wild, eh? In 1998 the pie cost you $8; in 1999, $9; in 2000, $10; and in 2001, $11. The pie was exactly the same size each year; the only thing that got bigger was its price. It's the same way with real GDP (the pie) and GDP (the price of the pie).

If we want to compare our domestic economic pie, or total production (real GDP), from one year to the next, we have to get rid of inflation. For example, the pizza pie that cost us $8 in 1998 and $11 in 2001. But we were getting exactly the same amount of pizza.

If our economy produced the same amount of output in 2001 as it did in 1998, then real GDP did not change. Prices may have gone up 37.5 percent (from $8 to $11), but we're still producing exactly the same amount of pizza.

To understand the concept of real GDP, you're going to need to calculate percentage changes. Here's one virtually all my students (and quite a few of my fellow economists) get wrong. If a number is tripled, by what percentage has it increased? Go ahead and try to figure it out.

Solution: Pick any number. An easy one is 100. Triple it. You have 300. Now find the percentage change.

Have you figured it out? Did you get 200 percent? If you did, then you might be able to skip the box that shows how to calculate percentage changes. If you're at all shaky on how to do this, this extremely helpful box will probably change your life.

GDP is the basic measure of how much the country produced in a given year. However, comparisons of GDP from one year to the next can be misleading. For example, say GDP went from $3 trillion in 1982 to $3.3 trillion in 1983. At first, it appears the United States has done extremely well, because GDP leapt by 10 percent. But before we get too excited, we should remember that GDP is a measure of all the final goods and services produced during a given year *at market prices*. For all we know, the entire 10 percent increase in GDP may be caused by inflation. This would obviously be the case if prices *did* rise by 10 percent in 1983.

To make year-to-year GDP comparisons, we have to get rid of inflation.

Calculating Percentage Changes

When we go from 100 to 120, that's an increase of 20 percent. From 150 to 200 is an increase of $33\frac{1}{3}$ percent. When we go from 50 to 25, that's a percentage decline of 50 percent. How do we know? We use this formula:

$$\% \text{ change} = \frac{\text{Change}}{\text{Original number}}$$

Using the first example, from 100 to 120 is a change of 20, and as our original number is 100, we have $^{20}\!/_{100}$. Any number divided by 100 may be read as a percentage —in this case, 20 percent.

Another way of figuring this out—and we'll need this method most of the time because 100 will rarely be the original number—is to divide the bottom number into the top number. Remember, whenever you have a fraction, you may divide the bottom number into the top:

$$\frac{\text{Change}}{\text{Original number}} = \frac{20}{100} \qquad 100\overline{)20.00} \quad .20 = 20\%$$

.20 is 20 percent. Any decimal may be read as a percent if you move the decimal point two places to the right and add the percent sign (%).

Now let's do the other two. First, the percentage change when we go from 150 to 200. Work it out yourself in the space provided here, and then go on to the last one—when we go from 50 to 25.

$$\frac{\text{Change}}{\text{Original number}} = \frac{50}{150} = \frac{5}{15} = \frac{1}{33} = 33\frac{1}{3}\%$$

And finally:

$$\frac{\text{Change}}{\text{Original number}} = -\frac{25}{50} = -\frac{1}{2} = -.50\% = -50\%$$

$$100\overline{)-25.00} \quad -.50$$

We need to be able to correct GDP for price increases so we can measure how much actual production rose. To do this we use the GDP deflator, which is calculated quarterly by the Department of Commerce. The GDP deflator is really a price index, like the consumer price index,[4] and it is used to measure price changes in the items that go into GDP (i.e., consumer goods and services, investment goods, and government goods and services).

The GDP deflator

Let's go back to the problem we posed earlier: GDP rose from $3 trillion in 1982 to $3.3 trillion in 1983. We need to deflate 1983's GDP to find out how much production rose. In other words, if GDP was $3 trillion in 1982, how much was GDP one year later in 1982 dollars? To find this we use the formula:

$$\text{Real GDP (current year)} = \text{GDP (current year)} = \frac{\text{GDP deflator (base year)}}{\text{GDP deflator (current year)}}$$

Deflating GDP to get real GDP

We'll adapt this general formula to our specific years. We're comparing 1983 (our current year) to 1982 (the base year). Therefore, our formula will now read:

$$\text{Real GDP}_{83} = \text{GDP}_{83} \times \frac{\text{GDP deflator}_{82}}{\text{GDP deflator}_{83}}$$

---

[4]The consumer price index is examined near the end of Chapter 9. The GDP deflator is a much broader concept, covering not just consumer goods and services but also investment goods and government goods and services.

To solve this equation, we need to substitute actual numbers for the three variables on the right side of the equation. We already know that GDP was $3.3 trillion in 1983. By convention, this number is written as 3,300. The GDP deflator for 1982, the base year, is 100, again by convention. The base year of virtually every index is 100.

We still need to know the GDP deflator for 1983. The Commerce Department publishes this figure, but let's assume it is 110. In other words, prices rose by 10 percent in 1983. Now we'll see if our formula works because our answer should be obvious. We're looking for the real GDP in 1983, and we see that GDP rose by 10 percent and prices also rose by 10 percent. Real GDP in 1983 should be equal to that of 1982. The formula is as follows:

$$\text{Real GDP}_{83} = \text{GDP}_{83} \times \frac{\text{GDP deflator}_{82}}{\text{GDP deflator}_{83}}$$

$$= \frac{3,300}{1} \times \frac{100}{110}$$

$$= \frac{\cancel{3,300}\,30}{1} \times \frac{100}{\cancel{110}\,1}$$

$$= 3,000$$

Let's go over a few of the mechanics of our solution. We put the 3,300 over 1 because this makes it easier to do cross division followed by multiplication. Incidentally, you are allowed to put any number over 1 because this means you are dividing that number by 1 (which doesn't change the number). For example, 5 is equal to 5/1. It means that 1 goes into 5 five times.

Another thing we did was reduce the fractions by division: 110 goes into 3,300 30 times. You don't have to reduce fractions, but usually you'll find that smaller numbers are easier to work with.

How do we know which is the base year and which is the current year? The base year is always the earlier year. In the last problem 1982 was the base year and 1983 was the current year.

Here's one more problem: GDP rises from $3 trillion in 1982 to $5 trillion in 1988. The GDP deflator in 1988 is 150. Find the real GDP in 1988. Find the percentage increase in real GDP between 1982 and 1988.

Solution:

$$\text{Real GDP}_{88} = \text{GDP}_{88} \times \frac{\text{GDP deflator}_{82}}{\text{GDP deflator}_{88}}$$

$$= \frac{5,000}{1} \times \frac{100}{150}$$

$$= \frac{33.33}{1} \times \frac{100}{1}$$

$$= 3,333$$

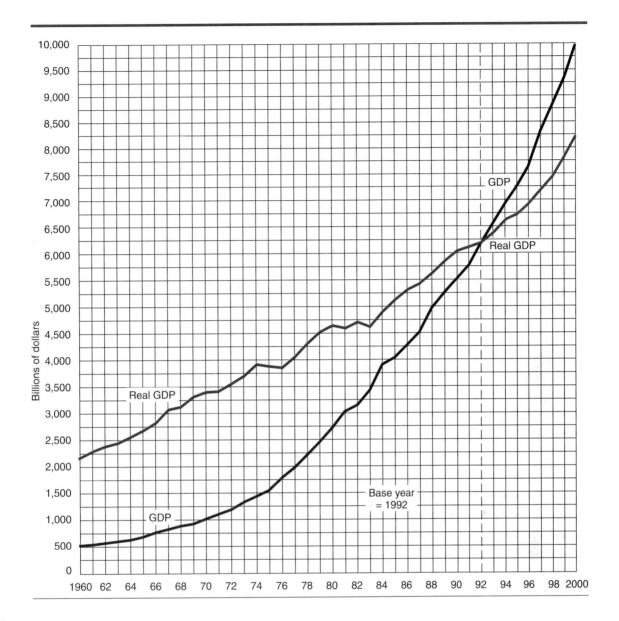

F*igure* 6

GDP and Real GDP (in 1992 Dollars), 1960–2000

GDP and real GDP are equal during the base year of 1992. To get an accurate picture of how much our output rose during this period, you would look at real GDP.

Source: Economic Report of the President, 2001.

Percentage change in real GDP from 1982 to 1988:

$$\frac{\text{Change}}{\text{Original number}} = \frac{333}{3,000} = 11.1 \text{ percent}$$

Real GDP in the current year enables us to compare the economy's output, or production, with that of the base year. This problem shows that output was 11.1 percent higher in 1988 than in 1982.

Now let's take a look at the record, which is shown in Figure 6. GDP rose steadily between 1960 and 2000. Not even during recession years (1970, 1973–75, 1980, 1981–82, and 1990–91) were there any declines. But real GDP *did* fall during those bad periods. How come? You tell *me*.

Read Only If You're Still Confused About the Difference Between a Change in GDP and Real GDP

From August 1981 through November 1982 we suffered our worst recession since the great depression of the 1930s. In 1981 our GDP was 3131, and in 1982 our GDP rose to 3259. Question: What must have happened to real GDP?

It went down from 4994 to 4900. (The base year is 1996, but you don't have to worry about that.) How can you explain a rise in GDP accompanied by a decline in real GDP, or actual output?

Prices, measured by the GDP deflator, must have gone up at a higher rate than output declined. OK, by what percentage did GDP go up, and by what percentage did real GDP go down?

GDP rose by 4.1 percent, and real GDP fell by 1.9 percent. See if you can figure out by what percentage prices (as measured by the GDP deflator) rose between 1981 and 1982. (Hint: You can figure out the answer by simple subtraction.)

Prices rose by 2.2 percent (4.1 percent − 1.9 percent). Let's look at this graphically:

There's a very simple relationship among percentage changes in GDP, real GDP, and the GDP deflator from one year to the next:

Percentage change in GDP = Percentage change in real GDP + Percentage change in GDP deflator

Question: If real GDP rose by 3 percent and the GDP deflator fell by 1.2 percent, what was the percentage change in GDP?

Solution: Percentage change in GDP = Percentage change in real GDP (3%) + percentage change in GDP deflator (−1.2%).

Percentage change in GDP = 3% + (−1.2%)
= 3% − 1.2% = 1.8%

One more question: If GDP rose by 3.8% and the GDP deflator rose by 2.5%, find the percentage change in real GDP.

Solution: Percentage change in GDP = Percentage change in real GDP + Percentage change in GDP deflator.

3.8% = Percentage change in real GDP + 2.5%

1.3% = Percentage change in real GDP

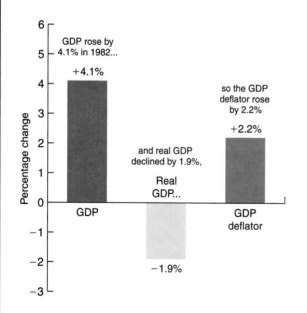

Real GDP reflects just our output, or production. Output falls during recessionary years; therefore real GDP, by definition, must also fall. But GDP, by definition, is *the nation's expenditure on all final goods and services produced during the year at market prices.* If prices rise by a larger percentage than output falls, then GDP will increase. For example, if output goes down by 4 percent and prices go up by 7 percent, by what percentage does GDP go up?

It goes up by 3 percent. Take another look at Figure 6. Real GDP starts out much higher than GDP in 1960. By 1992—the base year—they're equal. And after 1992, GDP soars far above real GDP. Why? Because prices are rising.

The GDP curve begins at a level of just over $500 billion in 1960 (much lower than the real GDP curve). But the GDP curve crosses the real GDP curve in 1992, and ends much higher than real GDP. What's going on here? What's going on is that GDP measures changes in output *and* prices. Real GDP measures just changes in output. GDP rose every year from 1960 to 2000. Even in recession years like 1974 and 1975 GDP rose. That's because price increases during those years were greater than output declines. How do we know that output went down in 1974 and 1975? Just look at the real GDP curve. It dipped in 1974 and 1975. In 1982 the same thing happened: GDP went up, but real GDP went down. What happened? It was another recession year. But it was also a year of inflation. In fact, so *much* inflation that the increase in prices was greater than the drop in output.

Now let's see if you can work out some verbal GDP problems. If GDP rises and real GDP falls, explain what happened.

Answer: The GDP deflator (or, rate of inflation) rose more than real GDP fell. For instance, if GDP rose by 3 percent, while real GDP fell by 2 percent, then the GDP deflator must have risen by 5 percent.

Next problem: Real GDP remains unchanged, while GDP falls. What happened?

Answer: What happened was deflation, or a decline in the price level (that is, the GDP deflator dropped below 100). Although those of us under 68 never experienced much deflation in our lifetimes, deflation *does* happen. We'll talk more about deflation toward the end of the next chapter.

One more problem: GDP doubles and the price level doubles. What happened to real GDP?

Answer: Real GDP stayed the same. Let's make up a problem with real numbers: GDP rises from 1000 to 2000, and the GDP deflator is 200 in the current year. What happened to real GDP?

$$\frac{\text{Real GDP}}{\text{(current year)}} = \frac{\text{GDP}}{\text{(current year)}} \times \frac{\text{GDP deflator (base year)}}{\text{GDP deflator (current year)}}$$

$$= \frac{\overset{10}{\cancel{2000}}}{1} \times \frac{100}{\underset{1}{\cancel{200}}} = 1,000$$

If you're still confused about the difference between a change in GDP and a change in real GDP, please see the Extra Help box.

International GDP Comparisons

Which country has the world's largest GDP? I hope you didn't forget that the United States does. Which country has the second largest? That's right; it's Japan. In Figure 7 we have the 2000 GDPs of the world's eight largest economies.

Different countries use different national income accounting systems, and international exchange rates fluctuate (we'll take up international exchange rates in the last chapter of this book). Hence GDP comparisons among countries cannot be made with great precision. Yet it's reasonable to say that such comparisons do give us fairly close approximations.

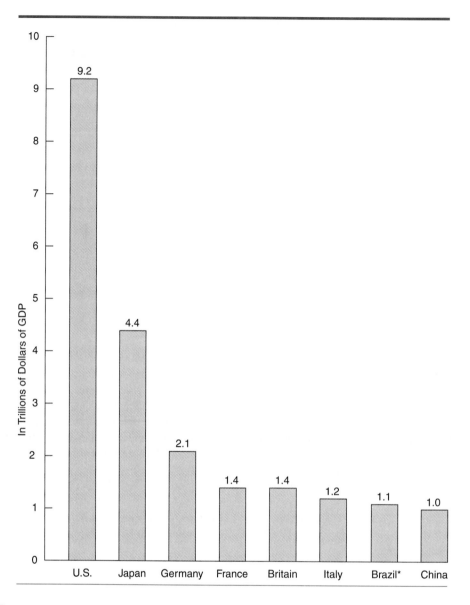

Figure 7

Trillion Dollar Economies, 2000

Our economy is by far the largest in the world. Japan's, which is the second largest, is less than half the size of ours.

*Estimates of Brazil's GDP range from $700 billion to $1.1 trillion.

Source: New York Times Almanac, 2001.

America has had the world's largest economy since the 1920s, but over the last 40 years we have spent a lot of time looking over our shoulders. In the 1950s and 1960s, we thought that the Soviet Union might overtake us. Then, in the 1970s and 1980s, it was the Japanese who were catching up. And now, as we approach the millennium, it appears that our biggest economic rival may soon be China.

Per Capita Real GDP

In spite of all this information, you may still be wondering, how *are* we doing? How are we doing in comparison to what? Or to whom? OK, how are we doing in comparison to other countries? We're doing just great—kind of.

TABLE 3	Per Capita Real GDP, Selected Years, 1929–2000 (in 2000 dollars)
Year	Per Capita Real GDP
1929	$ 9,087
1939	8,566
1949	11,566
1959	14,230
1969	18,813
1979	22,707
1989	25,231
2000	35,466

Sources: Economic Report of the President, 2001, Survey of Current Business, February 2001.

How can we tell? We can measure our GDP against that of any other nation. And ours is bigger. How much bigger? Well, our GDP is nearly $3 trillion larger than Japan's. Of course, Japan happens to have half as many people.

You'll notice a decline between 1929 and 1939 in Table 3. What happened? What happened was the Great Depression. In fact, per capita real GDP probably declined by 50 percent between 1929 and 1933. By 1939, per capita real GDP had made it most of the way back to its 1929 level. There were substantial increases in the 1940s, 1950s, and 1960s, but since then our economic growth has slowed. We'll keep coming back to this slowdown in subsequent chapters, and then, in Chapter 16, we'll finally get around to asking why our growth has slowed and what we can do to speed it up again.

GDP may be used to compare living standards among various countries or living standards during different time periods within one country. Such comparisons would usually be on a per capita basis. Per capita GDP = GDP/Population. In the United States, per capita GDP in 2000 was:

$$\frac{GDP}{Population} = \frac{\$9,966,000,000,000}{281,000,000} = \$35,466$$

This means that in 2000 we produced $35,466 worth of final goods and services for every man, woman, and child in this country.

To compare 2000 per capita GDP with that of another year, we would have to correct for inflation. In other words, we really need to revise our formula:

$$\text{Per capita real GDP} = \frac{\text{Real GDP}}{\text{Population}}$$

Per capita real GDP = Real GDP/Population

How does our per capita real GDP compare with earlier years? Just take a look at Table 3. Since 1939 per capita real GDP has quadrupled. The calculation of per capita real GDP is shown in the accompanying Advanced Work box.

Per capita real GDP comparisons over time

How valid are per capita real GDP comparisons over time? Over the short run, say, up to 10 years, they are quite valid. But comparisons over 20, 30, or 40 years become more and more like comparing apples and oranges, or, more to the point, like comparing video games and pocket calculators with nine-inch RCA TVs and those big old office adding machines whose lever you pulled every time you entered a number. Still more to the point, compare Ford T-birds with Model-T Fords. Over long periods of time, not only do different goods and services go into GDP, but the quality of those goods and services changes as well.

Calculating Per Capita Real GDP

Earlier in the chapter we worked out several problems in which we converted GDP into real GDP. And we've just done some per capita GDP problems. So what's left to do? Calculating per capita real GDP.

Suppose our GDP were to rise from $12 trillion in 2006 to $18 trillion in 2016, when the GDP deflator is 120. And suppose that our population rose from 280 million in 2006 to 300 million in 2016. What we want to find is (1) How much is per capita real GDP in 2016, and (2) By what percentage did per capita real GDP rise between 2006 and 2016?

See if you can work this out. I would suggest doing this problem in four steps: (1) Find real GDP in 2016; (2) find per capita real GDP in 2016; (3) find per capita real GDP for 2006; and (4) find the percentage rise in per capita real GDP between 2006 and 2016.

Solution:

$$(1)\ \text{Real GDP}_{2016} = \text{GDP}_{2016} \times \frac{\text{GDP deflator}_{2006}}{\text{GDP deflator}_{2016}}$$

$$= \frac{\overset{150}{\cancel{18,000}}}{1} \times \frac{100}{\underset{1}{\cancel{120}}}$$

$$= 15,000$$

$$(2)\ \begin{array}{l}\text{Per capita}\\ \text{Real GDP}_{2016}\end{array} = \frac{\text{Real GDP}_{2016}}{\text{Population}_{2016}} = \frac{15,000}{.3} = \$50,000$$

$$(3)\ \begin{array}{l}\text{Per capita}\\ \text{Real GDP}_{2006}\end{array} = \frac{\text{Real GDP}_{2006}}{\text{Population}_{2006}} = \frac{12,00\cancel{0}}{.28\cancel{0}}$$

$$= \frac{6000}{.14} = \frac{3000}{.07} = \$42,857$$

$$(4)\ \begin{array}{l}\text{Percentage}\\ \text{change}\end{array} = \frac{\text{Change}}{\text{Original Number}} = \frac{\$7,143}{42,857} = 16.7\%$$

International per capita real GDP comparisons

International comparisons of per capita real GDP must be made with even more caution. The per capita real GDP of America is perhaps 80 times the size of India's. Do we produce 80 times as much per capita? Probably not. The typical Indian, a farmer living in a rural village, is not subject to the psychological stresses, commuting problems, pollution, or crime that the average American is. Furthermore, the average Indian family produces most of its own food, clothing, and shelter—items that are not counted in GDP. Therefore, we are seriously underestimating India's real GDP.

Perhaps the American real GDP is not 80 times that of India, but just 25 times as high. Per capita real GDP is not an accurate measure of international differences in production levels, but it does provide a rough measure. Comparisons of countries at similar stages of economic development are much more accurate, however, than comparisons of countries at different stages.

How does our per capita GDP compare with those of other leading industrial nations? Twenty-five years ago, we were clearly number one. By the late 1980s, however, we had definitely lost our lead. As you can see in Figure 8. Luxembourg, Switzerland, Japan, Denmark, and Norway have passed us. But using an alternate measure, the World Bank placed the United States second in terms of actual living standard.

There are problems with translating the value of yen, marks, pounds, krona, and other currencies into dollars, and vice versa. Currency swings and different price levels make comparisons less than precise. So the best we can say is that our living standard is somewhere in the top eight.

From the close of World War II until 1990, the Soviet Union was our bitter rival. Since that nation's breakup, the standard of living of its main component, Russia, has progressively worsened. In the box "The Cost of Living in the United States and Russia: An Alternate Comparison," we've used another method to compare the living standards of the United States and Russia.

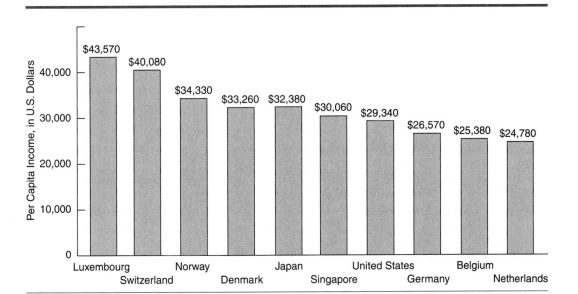

Figure 8

Per Capita GDP of the 10 Leading Nations, 1999

Although the United States is definitely not in the top five, international comparisons for per capita GDP are at least somewhat suspect because of varying national income accounting systems as well as fluctuations of foreign exchange rates.
Source: The World Bank, *World Development Indicators,* 2000.

The Cost of Living in the United States and Russia: An Alternate Comparison

One way around the problems of dealing with currency exchange rates and different national income accounting systems is to measure living standards in terms of the number of minutes of work needed to buy certain goods. The table below shows the minutes of work that were required in 1994 to pay for selected goods in the United States and Russia.* Clearly, our standard of living is perhaps six to eight times the Russian standard.

Good	U.S.	Russia
Sugar, per pound	3 minutes	29 minutes
Bread, per pound	5 minutes	14 minutes
Milk, half-gallon	9 minutes	1 hour, 10 minutes
Sausage, per pound	12 minutes	2 hours, 27 minutes
Gasoline, per gallon	8 minutes	1 hour, 16 minutes
Television, average	6 days	71 days

Sources: Russian State Statistics Committee, U.S. Bureau of Labor Statistics, U.S. Department of Agriculture, Electronic Industries Association.

    Does our eighth-place per capita GDP ranking mean our standard of living is falling? No. Our standard of living has been rising, although at a much slower rate these last 25 years than it was in the 1950s and 1960s. It means several nations have caught up with us, and if present trends continue, by the turn of the century our standard of living will be slightly higher than today's, but it will be only the 10th or 12th highest in the world.

In the immortal words of baseball great Satchel Paige, "Don't look back, because somebody may be gaining on you."

    We've used the terms *per capita GDP* and *standard of living* interchangeably, but what if half of our GDP were spent on defense—as it was during the Second World War? During those years our per capita GDP was about double our standard of living. Similarly, a nation like Japan, which devotes significantly more of its resources to capital production, has a much higher per capita GDP than living standard. Still another qualification is a nation's housing stock. Although the Japanese have a comparable per capita GDP, Americans live better. The average American family has three times the living space of its Japanese counterpart. So when we use per capita GDP and standard of living interchangeably, we need to take each of these additional factors into account.

    We've also used *per capita GDP* and *per capita real GDP* interchangeably. Technically, we use per capita real GDP comparisons over time. But if we're talking about just one year's per capita GDP, we drop the "real" because we're not making a year-to-year comparison.

*How much have things changed since 1994? Actually very little, except that today it might take just 4 days' work for the average American worker to buy a TV.

Shortcomings of GDP as a Measure of National Economic Well-Being

Production That Is Excluded

If a man marries his housekeeper or his cook, the national dividend is diminished.

—A. C. Pigou,
Economics of Welfare

Household Production   Household production consists mainly of the work done by homemakers—care of children, cleaning, shopping, and cooking. Were a housekeeper hired to do these tasks, this would be counted in GDP. Were two homemakers to work for each other as housekeepers (why, I don't know), their work would be counted in GDP. So why not count homemakers' work in their own homes? Because no money changes hands. No payments are recorded.

Food grown in backyard plots, home repairs, clothes made at home, and any other do-it-yourself goods and services that people make or do for themselves, their families, or their friends are not counted in GDP. (The National Gardening Association reports that about 35 million households have garden plots that produce over $1 billion worth of food. The most popular crop is tomatoes, which are grown on 85 percent of the plots.) When you buy these goods and services from other people, the goods and services are counted (assuming they are reported by the sellers as income).

Illegal Production   Illegal goods and services are not counted in GDP. The big three—dope, prostitution, and gambling—are ignored even though people spend hundreds of billions on these goods and services. Of course, if you place a bet at a racetrack or an offtrack betting parlor, it is legal and counts in GDP. But a bet placed with a bookie is illegal. If you play the state lottery, your bet is counted toward GDP, but not if you play the numbers.

Prostitution was legal in France before World War II. Although the same services continued to be provided after the war on an illegal basis, anyone scanning France's GDP figures right after the war might think that the country had been hit by a depression.

California is our leading agricultural state. Do you know its number one crop? Lettuce? Grapes? Citrus fruit? Sorry, it's none of the above. California's number one crop is grass—that's right, grass, as in marijuana. It is also the number one cash crop in Kentucky, Tennessee, and West Virginia. How much do Americans spend on illegal drugs? Estimates vary widely, but it is likely that more than $100 billion a year is spent on heroin and cocaine alone.

The Underground Economy   In every large city, on country roads, in flea markets, and even in suburban malls, there are people selling everything from watches to watermelons, and from corn to collectibles. Chances are, the proceeds of these sales are not reported to the government. Not only are no taxes paid, but the sales are not reflected in GDP.

Some of the items sold were stolen, but most are simply goods produced without the government's knowledge. Together with illegal goods and services, these markets form a vast underground economy. How vast? Maybe 10 or 15 percent of GDP.[5] Who knows? How much of *your* income is spent in the underground economy? Or perhaps I should be asking, how much of your income *comes* from the underground economy? (See box, "Pirated CDs and Videos.")

Our underground economy is not composed of only the street peddlers, cabdrivers, and low-life entrepreneurs who underreport their incomes. Oh no. The underground economy gets a very nice class of people—doctors, dentists, lawyers, and even, heaven forbid, accountants. In fact, there is a whole branch of accounting dedicated to the underground economy. It's called creative accounting. Often it involves keeping three separate sets of books—one for your creditors (showing an inflated profit), one for the government, and

---

[5]*Fortune* magazine (September 5, 1994, p. 104) reports that in India "the underground economy adds anywhere from 20% to 50% to the official GDP."

Pirated CDs and Videos

Not everything sold on the street "fell off the truck."*A lot of those "designer" clothing items are illegal "knockoffs" of the real thing. What about those $5 CDs and $10 videos? Where do *they* come from?

Hollywood producers were amazed to find videos of their films being sold in the street just days after they opened and months before their own videos were released. The mystery was easily solved. When the films opened, people with camcorders would seat themselves just off the center aisles of the theaters and tape the films. These tapes would then be reproduced in quantity, put in authentic-looking boxes, and sold on the street.

Pirating CDs is even easier. For an investment of about $3,000, anyone can buy a "CD burner" and copy CDs onto blank disks called CD-recordables, or CD-Rs, through a digital process that maintains the quality of the recording. Since CD-Rs cost just a dollar, there's a nice $4 markup when the CDs are sold by street peddlers. Meanwhile the customer gets a $15 CD of Britney Spears, TLC, the Backstreet Boys, or Puff Daddy for just five bucks. The only ones who lose are the record companies, the recording artists, and the government (assuming that no income is declared and no sales taxes are paid).

*A euphemism for goods that are stolen.

---

one for yourself, so you know how you're doing. The next time you're having your teeth realigned, just ask your dentist, "Would you prefer a check or cash?" Then, to make absolutely certain, ask if there's a discount for paying cash.

The underground economy adds hundreds of billions of dollars of goods and services to our national output. In addition, it is a safety valve, a generator of jobs and business opportunities that provide a great deal of economic support to the poor and near-poor. Go into any low-income housing project and you'll discover that many people are engaged in some underground economic activity—whether doing hairstyling, fixing cars, or providing childcare.

Illegal immigrants are heavily employed in activities that can easily be conducted off the books. Tens of thousands of women work in garment sweatshops, often for substantially less than the legal minimum wage of $5.15 an hour. In New York you'll often find illegal immigrants peddling T-shirts and mood rings on the sidewalk in front of the Immigration and Naturalization Service office.

Let's step back for a minute and look once again at our definition of GDP: *the nation's expenditure on all the final goods and services produced during the year at market prices.*

What exactly is production? What we produce? For once economists are in agreement and quite clear as well about what something means. *Production is any good or service that people are willing to pay for.* And that means anything!

> Production is any good or service that people are willing to pay for.

You go to a concert and fall asleep. How much was your ticket? $10? That was $10 worth of production.

You went to a brilliant lecture on the future of the universe. It was free. The speaker wasn't paid. No production.

You grow tomatoes in your backyard for your family's consumption. No production.

You take a course in philosophy. The professor walks into the room and lies down on the floor in the front of the class. This happens all term. How much tuition did you pay to take this course? That's how much production took place.

The problem we have, then, is an inconsistency between the definition of GDP and the way it is compiled by the U.S. Department of Commerce. There's a lot of stuff going on out there that the department misses. Why? Is it understaffed (one of the all-time favorite words of bureaucrats)? Perhaps. The government not only refuses to count the underground economy—legal *or* illegal—but it will not even admit its existence. The bottom line is that it does not go into GDP, even as an estimate. As a result, we are grossly (no pun intended) undercounting GDP.

perfect form, with his legs exactly perpendicular to his body. The physical benefits of being a gym teacher, farmer, or a health club employee are obvious.[8]

Today's GDP is produced by an entirely different type of labor force doing different work from that of 50 or 100 years ago. And our labor force works very differently from those of developing countries. This makes GDP comparisons that much less valid.

What Goes Into GDP?

Other problems with GDP as a measure of national economic well-being have to do with what goes into GDP (see again the box titled "Measure of Economic Welfare"). When a large part of our production goes toward national defense, police protection, pollution control devices, repair and replacement of poorly made cars and appliances, and cleanups of oil spills, a large GDP is not a good indicator of how we're doing. And if a large part of our labor force staffs the myriad bureaucracies of state, local, and federal governments, as well as those of the corporate world, we're not all that well off. GDP tells us how much we produce. We need to ask: how much of what?

We also need to ask about the production of new goods and services and about the improvement of product quality. Let's use television sets as an example. Very few American families had TV sets before the late 1940s, and those who did had 9″, 13″, or the "big screen" 17″ black-and-white sets. We counted the $600 17″ black and white Philco, RCA, or Dumont (American TV-makers back in prehistoric times) at its selling price in the 1948 GDP. But the $600 Samsung 28″ ultra-flat-screen stereo color TV also counts for just $600 in the 2001 GDP, even though television sets today are vastly superior to those of the late 1940s.

In general, the problem with using GDP as a measure of national economic well-being is that GDP is just one number, and no single number can possibly provide us with all the information we need. Try these examples.

My daughter is doing very well on her diet. She's down to 120 pounds. Of course she's only 3 feet 6 inches.

How's the weather? It's great; the temperature is 50. Oh yes, there's a hurricane.

My son got all As in his college courses this semester. Unfortunately, he's taking them in jail where he is serving 10 consecutive life sentences for mass murder. Oh well, as I always say, nobody's perfect.

James Tobin, winner of Nobel Prize, 1981, for work on the interrelationship between money and the real economy (© The Nobel Foundation)

The Last Word on GDP

I've said some nasty things about GDP that I hope you won't be repeating to your friends. I said it includes some things that really shouldn't be counted. And GDP has excluded some things that should be included. We've even attempted to refine GDP by correcting it for inflation (real GDP) and by subtracting depreciation (NNP). As pointed out in the box "Measure of Economic Welfare," James Tobin and William Nordhaus have actually come up with an alternative measure of national output. Nevertheless, if we can accept GDP while acknowledging all of its limitations, it serves us well, not only for the analysis of the next eight chapters, but in any discussion of macroeconomics beyond the pages of this book.

I'd like to close this chapter with some words that Robert Kennedy wrote more than a third of a century ago:

William Nordhaus, economist who served on President Jimmy Carter's Council of Economic Advisors (J. D. Levine/Yale University)

---

[8]Mr. Spalter must have been doing *something* right. Two Madison graduates have won the Nobel Prize in economics. Robert Solow, who graduated in 1940, won it in 1987, and Gary Becker, class of 1948, won it in 1992. Thus the high school I attended has had more economics Nobel Prize winners than any other high school in the country. And who knows, maybe lightning will strike a third time. If you're curious, I graduated in 1957.

We will find neither national purpose nor personal satisfaction in a mere continuation of economic progress, in an endless amassing of worldly goods. We cannot measure national spirit by the Dow Jones average, nor national achievement by the gross national product. For the gross national product includes air pollution and advertising for cigarettes, and ambulances to clear our highways of carnage. It counts special locks for our doors, and jails for the people who break them. The gross national product includes the destruction of the redwoods, and the death of Lake Superior.[9]

Questions for Further Thought and Discussion

1. Suppose we want to compare this year's GDP with those of previous years. As we go back in time—to 1980, to 1970, to 1960, and to still earlier years—what happens to the validity of these comparisons? Why does this happen?

2. If our GDP rose from 11,000 to 11,500, there could be a few different explanations. List each of these possibilities.

3. Which has been increasing faster, GDP or real GDP? Explain your answer.

4. GDP is not an ideal measure of national economic well-being. Make a list of all the things you would do to improve this concept. Include in your list the goods and services that GDP does not count.

5. "Americans enjoy the highest standard of living in the world." Discuss why this statement is not perfectly accurate.

6. Under what circumstances could real GDP for a given year be greater than GDP for that same year? For example, if 2015 were the base year and 2016 were the current year, how could real GDP in 2016 exceed GDP for 2016?

7. Explain how GDP is affected by the sale of
   a. a new house;
   b. an hour session with a physical trainer;
   c. 1,000 shares of U.S. West;
   d. an antique rolltop desk.

8. If you were comparing the economic well-being of two countries and had a choice of using one of the following four measures, which one would you choose and why would you choose it?
   a. GDP
   b. real GDP
   c. per capita GDP
   d. per capita real GDP

---

[9]Robert Kennedy, *To Seek a Newer World* (Garden City, NY: Doubleday, 1967), p. 264. If Robert Kennedy's name is not familiar, he was the brother of President John Kennedy, served as Attorney General from 1961–64, was a U.S. Senator from New York from 1965–68, and, like his brother John, he was assassinated.

Workbook for Chapter 9

Name _____ Date _____

Multiple-Choice Questions

Circle the letter that corresponds to the best answer.

1. Nearly all of our output is produced by _____.
   a) the government
   b) private business firms
   c) individual consumers

2. GDP may be found by _____.
   a) adding together money spent on goods and services and incomes received by the factors of production
   b) subtracting incomes received by the factors of production from the money spent on goods and services
   c) subtracting the money spent on goods and services from the incomes received by the factors of production
   d) adding the money spent on final goods and services

3. Which equation is correct?
   a) GDP − Depreciation = NDP
   b) NDP − Depreciation = GDP
   c) GDP + NDP = Depreciation

4. Each of the following is an indirect business tax except _____.
   a) sales tax
   b) excise tax
   c) business property tax
   d) corporate income tax

5. If Mexico had a GDP of 700 and depreciation of 100, while Italy had a GDP of 710 and a depreciation of 180, most economists would say that _____.
   a) Italy had a better year
   b) Mexico had a better year
   c) there is no way of determining which country had a better year

6. Pirated CDs and videos are _____.
   a) part of the underground economy
   b) sold only in other countries
   c) sold by recording studios and Hollywood movie producers
   d) encouraged by the federal government because their manufacture and sale provides tens of thousands of jobs to marginal workers

7. In declining order of size, which of these is the proper ranking?
   a) GDP, NDP national income
   b) NDP, GDP, national income
   c) National income, GDP, NDP
   d) National income, NDP, GDP
   e) GDP, national income, NDP
   f) NDP, national income, GDP

8. Wages, salaries, and fringe benefits constitute about _____ of domestic income.
   a) 25 percent   c) 70 percent
   b) 50 percent   d) 95 percent

9. The largest sector of GDP is _____.
   a) investment   c) net exports
   b) government spending d) consumer spending

10. Which is not counted in GDP?
    a) a Social Security check sent to a retiree
    b) government spending on highway building
    c) money spent on an airline ticket
    d) money spent by a company to build a new office park

11. Which one of these goes into the investment sector of GDP?
    a) the purchase of a new factory
    b) the purchase of 100 shares of Texaco stock
    c) the purchase of a 10-year-old office building
    d) the purchase of a U.S. savings bond

12. When there is inflation _____.

    a) real GDP increases faster than GDP

    b) GDP increases faster than real GDP

    c) GDP and real GDP increase at the same rate

    d) there is no way of telling whether GDP or real GDP increases faster

13. If GDP rose from $6 trillion to $9 trillion and prices rose by 50 percent over this period, _____.

    a) real GDP fell by 100 percent

    b) real GDP fell by 50 percent

    c) real GDP stayed the same

    d) real GDP rose by 50 percent

    e) real GDP rose by 100 percent

14. Which of the following is counted in GDP?

    a) household production   c) leisure time

    b) illegal production   d) government spending

15. Which statement is true?

    a) There is an inconsistency between the definition of GDP and the way it is compiled by the U.S. Department of Commerce.

    b) GDP is an accurate measure of production in the United States.

    c) U.S. GDP figures include estimates for production in the underground economy.

    d) Our GDP would grow faster if we had less inflation.

16. Suppose the GDP of Argentina were 10 times that of Uruguay. Which statement would be most accurate?

    a) There is no way of comparing the output of Argentina and Uruguay.

    b) Argentina's output is greater than that of Uruguay.

    c) Argentina's output is probably around 10 times that of Uruguay.

    d) Argentina's output is 10 times that of Uruguay.

17. Which statement is true?

    a) GDP tells us how much we produce as well as what we produce.

    b) GDP tells us neither how much we produce nor what we produce.

    c) GDP tells us what we produce.

    d) GDP tells us how much we produce.

18. The measure of economic welfare formulated by Tobin and Nordhaus starts with GDP and then _____.

    a) subtracts the economic bads and the regrettable necessities and adds household, unreported, and illegal production

    b) subtracts the economic bads, the regrettable necessities, and household, unreported, and illegal production

    c) adds the economic bads and the regrettable necessities and subtracts the household, unreported, and illegal production

    d) adds the economic bads and subtracts the regrettable necessities and household, unreported, and illegal production

19. Per capita real GDP is found by _____.

    a) dividing population by real GDP

    b) dividing real GDP by population

    c) adding population to real GDP

    d) multiplying real GDP by population

20. Which statement is true?

    a) Over longer and longer periods of time, comparisons of real per capita GDP become increasingly valid.

    b) Over the short run, say, up to 10 years, comparisons of per capita real GDP are quite valid.

    c) International comparisons of per capita real GDP may be made with less caution than comparisons over time within a given country.

    d) None of these statements is true.

21. Since 1929 our per capita real GDP has _____.

    a) declined   c) doubled

    b) stayed about the same   d) almost quadrupled

22. Which statement is true?

    a) The Japanese have a higher standard of living than we do.

    b) The Japanese have a larger GDP than we do.

    c) The typical Japanese family has more living space than the typical American family.

    d) None of these statements is true.

23. $C + I + G + X_n$ is _____ approach(es) to GDP.
    a) the flow-of-income
    b) the expenditures
    c) both the expenditures and the flow-of-income
    d) neither the expenditures nor the flow-of-income

24. Which statement is true about the period since 1984?
    a) Both the consumption and investment percentage shares of GDP rose.
    b) Both the consumption and investment percentage shares of GDP fell.
    c) The consumption percentage share of GDP rose, while the investment percentage share of GDP fell.
    d) The investment percentage share of GDP rose, while the consumption percentage share of GDP fell.

25. Which is the most accurate statement about the underground economy?
    a) It adds hundreds of billions of dollars to our GDP.
    b) It provides employment to hundreds of thousands of illegal immigrants.
    c) It is run almost entirely by organized crime.
    d) It makes the rich richer and the poor poorer.

26. Which would be the most valid statement?
    a) Because each nation uses its own system to compile its national accounts, international comparisons of per capita GDP are virtually useless.
    b) The standard of living of the average American is about twice that of the average Russian.
    c) The standard of living of the average American is comparable to that of the average person in Switzerland, Germany, and Japan.
    d) If the underground economy, illegal production, and household production were accurately measured and added to GDP, our GDP would probably rise by less than 1 percent.

Fill-In Questions

1. The nation's expenditure on all the final goods and services produced during the year at market prices is

   _____.

2. Nearly all our goods and services are produced by

   _____.

3. GDP − _____ = NDP.

4. NDP − _____ = national income.

5. A tax with your name on it is a(n) _____ tax.

6. A sales tax is a(n) _____ tax.

7. GDP includes only payments for _____

   _____ _____.

8. _____ measures total production in one year.

9. Goods and services produced without the government's knowledge are part of the

   _____ economy.

10. Economists call any good or service that people are willing to pay for _____.

11. Economists call the psychological strain associated with work _____.

12. The measure of economic welfare developed by Tobin and Nordhaus begins with GDP and subtracts

    _____ and _____ and adds _____ and _____ and_____.

13. Per capita real GDP is found by dividing_____

    _____ by _____.

14. Over time, per capita real GDP comparisons become

    _____ valid.

241

Problems

1. Given the following information, calculate NDP and national income: GDP = $5 trillion, Indirect business taxes = $300 billion, and Depreciation = $500 billion.

2. If national income is $3 trillion, depreciation is $400 billion, and indirect business taxes are $300 billion, how much are NDP and GDP?

3. If wages, salaries, and fringe benefits are $4 trillion, profit is $500 billion, interest is $300 billion, rent is $100 billion, and depreciation is $600 billion, how much is national income?

4. If wages, salaries, and fringe benefits are $3 trillion, profit is $400 billion, interest is $200 billion, rent is $100 billion, depreciation is $400 billion, and indirect business taxes are $300 billion, how much is national income, NDP and GDP?

5. If consumption spending is $3 trillion, investment is $800 billion, government spending is $1 trillion, imports are $1.2 trillion, and exports are $900 billion, how much is GDP?

6. If consumption is $3.8 trillion, investment is $1.1 trillion, government spending is $1.1 trillion, imports are $1.6 trillion, and exports are $1.4 trillion, how much is GDP?

7. GDP rises from $4 trillion in 1986, the base year, to $5 trillion in 1989. The GDP deflator in 1989 is 120. Find real GDP in 1989. Find the percentage increase in real GDP between 1986 and 1989.

8. GDP rises from $5 trillion in 1990, the base year, to $7 trillion in 1994. The GDP deflator in 1994 is 140. Find real GDP in 1994. Find the percentage increase in real GDP between 1990 and 1994.

9. Find the Tobin and Nordhaus measure of economic welfare if GDP is $5 trillion, the economic bads are $500 billion, the regrettable necessities are $400 billion, and the sum of household, unreported, and illegal production is $1 trillion.

10. Find per capita GDP when population is 100 million and GDP is $2 trillion.

11. Find per capita GDP when GDP is $1.5 trillion and population is 300 million.

12. Suppose our GDP were to rise from $10 trillion in 2007 to $20 trillion in 2027, when the GDP deflator is 125. And suppose that our population rose from 300 million in 2007 to 330 million in 2027. a) How much is per capita real GDP in 2027? b) By what percentage did per capita real GDP rise between 2007 and 2027? [Hint: Do the problem in four steps: (1) Find real GDP in 2027; (2) find per capita real GDP in 2027; (3) find per capita real GDP for 2007; and (4) find the percentage rise in per capita real GDP between 2007 and 2027.

13. Suppose the GDP of South Korea were to rise from $600 billion in 2005 to $1.5 trillion in 2015, when the GDP deflator is 150. And suppose that Korea's population rose from 40 million in 2005 to 50 million in 2015. a) How much is per capita real GDP in 2015? b) By what percentage did per capita real GDP rise between 2005 and 2015?

14. If GDP rises from $10 trillion to $10.4 trillion and real GDP rises from $10 trillion to $10.3 trillion, find the percentage change in the GDP deflator.

15. If real GDP goes up by 3.7% and the GDP deflator goes up by 1.6%, find t he percentage change in GDP.

Chapter 10

Economic Fluctuations, Unemployment, and Inflation

As the chapter title indicates, we'll be covering the major problems the U.S. economy has encountered, especially in the years since World War II. In later chapters we'll consider how the government can deal with these problems.

CHAPTER OBJECTIVES

In this chapter we will:

- Examine the business cycle.
- Consider various business cycle theories.
- Show how economic forecasting is done.
- Measure the GDP gap.

- Learn how the unemployment rate is computed.
- Look at the types of unemployment.
- Construct a consumer price index.
- Consider the theories of inflation.

Economic Fluctuations

Figure 1 shows the country's economic record since 1964, but before we are in a position to analyze that record, we need a little background information on the business cycle.

Let's look at the record.
—Alfred E. Smith
1928 Democratic
Presidential Candidate

Is There a Business Cycle?

Economists and noneconomists have long debated whether there is a business cycle. It all depends on what is meant by the term. If *business cycle* is defined as increases and decreases in business activity of fixed amplitude that occur regularly at fixed intervals, then there is no business cycle. In other words, business activity does have its ups and downs, but some ups are higher than other ups and some downs are lower than others.

243

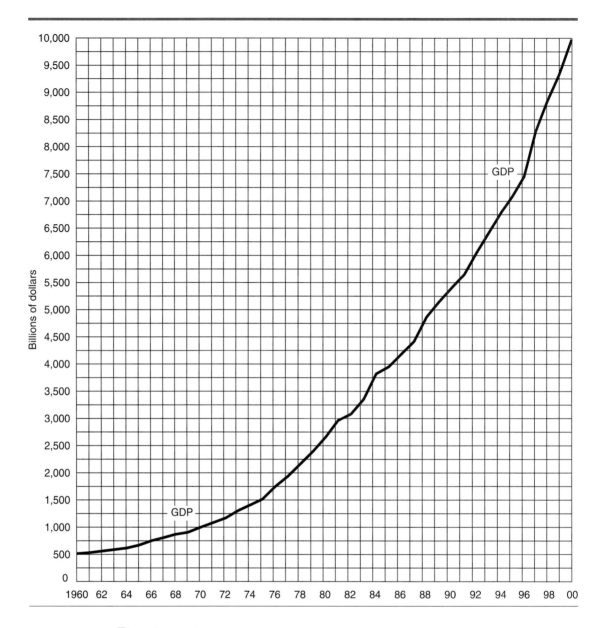

F*igure* 1

GDP 1960–2000

Sources: U.S. Dept. of Commerce, *Business Conditions Digest,* April 1982; and *Economic Report of the President,* 2001.

Furthermore, there is no fixed length to the cycle. For example, as Figure 1 shows, the United States went for nearly the entire decade of the 1960s without a recession but had back-to-back recessions in 1980 and 1981.

Upswings don't die of old age.
—economic saying

Since November 1982 we have had only one recession (at least through the end of 2000). The economic expansion that began in March 1991 is the longest in history. Can we say that our economy is finally recession-proof and that the business cycle is obsolete? I'm going to really stick my neck out on *this* one and make a prediction. This expansion will end. The only question is when.

If we define the business cycle as alternating increases and decreases in the level of business activity, of varying amplitude and length, then there is definitely a business cycle. What goes up will eventually come down, and what goes down will rise again.

Cycle Turning Points: Peaks and Troughs

Peaks

At the end of economic expansion, business activity reaches a peak (see Figure 1). Usually there is a certain degree of prosperity, but the last time there was full employment (before the boom beginning in the mid-1990s) was at the 1969 peak. In the month following the peak, the economy went into a decline.

Not all economic declines turn out to be recessions. As a rule of thumb, *most economists agree that a recession has occurred if real GDP declines for at least two consecutive quarters.* However, in the decline that occurred in the second half of 1981, real GDP actually rose slightly in the third quarter, but it is generally accepted that the recession started in August, the second month of the third quarter.

A recession occurs when real GDP declines for two consecutive quarters.

When the economy bottoms out, a trough occurs. From this low point, economic recovery sets in, and eventually most sectors share in the expansion.

Troughs

Business cycles may be measured from peak to peak, or trough to trough. As we have noted, these cycles vary greatly in amplitude and length. Note the severity of the 1973–75 and 1981–82 recessions in Figure 1 and the varying lengths of the cycles shown in the same graph.

Since the end of World War II, the economy's expansions have been as brief as 12 months and longer than 10 years (and counting). The contractions fall into a much narrower range—from 6 to 16 months. And so we may conclude that, like snowflakes, no two business cycles are exactly alike. For a blow-by-blow account of the 10 recessions since World War II, see the box "Post–World War II Recessions" in Chapter 1.

The Conventional Three-Phase Business Cycle

We'll begin our analysis with the first peak in Figure 2. The decline that sets in after the peak is called a recession, which ends at the trough. Occasionally there is a false recovery when business activity turns upward for a few months but then turns down again. If the next low point is the lowest since the previous peak, then *that* is the trough.

Recovery begins at the trough, but the expansion must eventually reach the level of the previous peak. Occasionally business activity rises without reaching the previous peak; unless it does, it does not qualify as a recovery.

Once recovery definitely *has* set in, GDP moves upward until it passes the level of the previous peak, when it enters the third phase of the cycle: prosperity. This phase does not necessarily mean there is full employment, or even that we are approaching full

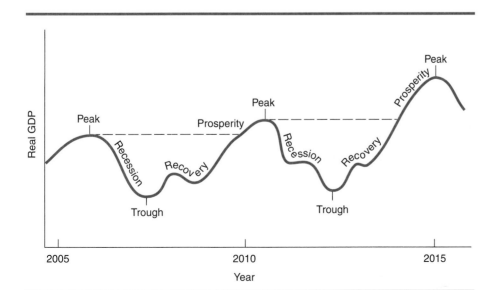

Figure 2

Hypothetical Business Cycles

The three-phase business cycle runs from peak to peak, beginning with a recession, which ends at a trough, followed by a recovery. When the level of the previous peak is attained, prosperity sets in, continuing until a new peak is reached.

employment. As long as production (real GDP) is higher than it was during the previous peak, we are in the prosperity phase.

Prosperity is the second part of the economic expansion and is accompanied by rising production, falling unemployment, and often accelerating inflation. Sooner or later we reach a peak and the process starts all over—recession, recovery, and prosperity.

This is the conventional three-phase cycle. Some people talk of a fourth phase: depression. Although depressions are relatively rare—we have not had one since the 1930s—there is always talk about the possibility that a recession could turn into a depression.

What is the dividing line between a recession and a depression? There is no agreed-on or official definition. Obviously, an unemployment rate of 20 percent would be a depression. But would 10 percent qualify?

Perhaps the best definition was proposed by, among others, the late George Meany, longtime president of the AFL-CIO. He said that if his neighbor were unemployed, it would be a recession. If *he* were unemployed, it would be a depression!

Some people say prosperity is when the prices of the things that you are selling are rising, and inflation is when the prices of things that you are buying are rising.

—Anonymous

What is the dividing line between recession and depression?

Business Cycle Theories

I have stated that business cycles are inevitable; what goes up must come down, and what goes down must come back up. Although economists generally agree that business cycles exist, they have many competing theories on their causes. We'll briefly consider two types of theories: endogenous (internal) and exogenous (external).

Endogenous Theories

Innovation theory

These theories place the cause of business cycles within rather than outside the economy. We'll consider first the theory of innovations, which was advanced primarily by Joseph Schumpeter.

When a businessman attempts to market a new product such as a car or a television set, at first he will encounter resistance ("Get that contraption off the road—it's frightening my horses!"). But when others perceive the profits being made by the innovator, they will imitate his new product with their own versions, and production will soar. Eventually the market will be saturated—as it was by cars in 1929 and televisions in 1953—and an economic downturn will occur. The downturn continues until a new innovation takes hold and the process begins anew.

Psychological theory

A second endogenous theory is the psychological theory of alternating optimism and pessimism, which is really an example of a more general theory of the self-fulfilling prophecy. If businessowners are optimistic, they will invest in plant, equipment, and inventory. This will provide more jobs and result in more consumer spending, justifying still more investment, more jobs, and more spending. But eventually businessowners will turn pessimistic, perhaps because they figure this prosperity can't continue. As pessimism sets in, investment, jobs, and consumer spending all decline, and a recession begins. The contraction continues until businessowners figure that things have gone down so far, there's no place to go but back up again.

Inventory cycle theory

Still another endogenous theory is that of the inventory cycle. During economic recovery, as sales begin to rise, businessowners are caught short of inventory, so they raise their orders to factories, thus raising factory employment. As factory workers are called back to work, they begin to spend more money, causing businessowners to order still more from factories. Eventually the owners are able to restock their inventories, so they cut back on factory orders. This causes layoffs, declining retail sales, further cutbacks in factory orders, and a general economic decline. The decline persists until inventory levels are depleted low enough for factory orders to increase once again. (See box, "The Accelerator Principle.")

The Accelerator Principle

The accelerator principle is a variant of the overinvestment theory of the business cycle. It is somewhat analogous to the predicament of the Red Queen in *Through the Looking-Glass* (the sequel to *Alice's Adventures in Wonderland*), who had to keep running just to stay where she was. The accelerator principle requires sales to keep increasing at the same rate to prevent investment from falling. The table below presents a hypothetical example of the accelerator principle.

Year	Sales	Machines	Net I (+)	Replacement I (=)	Gross I
1991	100	200	0	10	10
1992	110	220	20	10	30
1993	120	240	20	10	30
1994	130	260	20	10	30
1995	135	270	10	10	20
1996	130	260	−10	10	0

This particular example is based on three assumptions:

1. Two dollars' worth of machinery will produce $1 of output. This ratio of 2:1 is the capital-output ratio.

2. Each machine has a life of 20 years.

3. We'll assume sales have been 100 and we've had 200 machines for the past 20 years. Therefore, we need to replace 10 machines each year just to stay at 200 machines. In other words, each year we start out with 200 machines, 10 wear out, and we have to replace those 10 to still have 200.

Now we're ready to use the table. When sales are 100, we need 200 machines. In 1991 we start with 200 machines, which is the number we'll need that year since sales are 100 and the capital-output ratio is 2:1. We just need to replace the 10 machines that wore out. There's no Net I, but we replace 10 machines and have a Gross I total of 10 [Net I (0) + Replacement I (10) = Gross I (10)]. This, by the way, is the same as saying that Net I plus Depreciation equals Gross I.

In 1992 sales rise from 100 to 110. Because the capital-output ratio is 2:1, we need 220 machines. Net I is 20 machines and we replace 10 machines, so our Gross I is 30.

Machine makers, who had been making 10 machines a year for years, are suddenly deluged with orders. "Thirty machines! What should we do? Should we enlarge our plant and build more equipment to handle these orders? Will business continue to be so good?"

In 1993 sales go up to 120, which means we now need 240 machines. Again Net I is 20 and Replacement I is 10, which adds up to a Gross I of 30.

We've now arrived at what economists call "the Red Queen effect." We're running just to stay where we are. Sales went up by 10 and Gross I stayed at 30.

In 1994 sales again go up 10 to 130, 260 machines are needed, and Gross I stays at 30. Let's see what happens if sales go up by just 5, from 130 to 135. Now we need 270 machines, which leads to a Gross I of only 20.

An increase in sales has led to a decline in Gross I! Sales, which had been increasing by 10 in 1992, 1993, and 1994, rose by only 5 in 1995. So sales, which had been increasing at a constant rate during the previous three years, increased at a decreasing rate in 1995. This led to a decline in Gross I.

When orders for machines fall from 30 to 20, the machine maker must lay off one-third of his employees. And his plant is now being used at only two-thirds of capacity.

In Chapter 11 we will work out problems with the multiplier. Any change in C, I, or G has a multiplied effect on GDP. Now we have a decline of 10 in I. If the multiplier were 5, GDP would decline by 50. This means we are in a recession.

When machine makers lay off their workers, even though they'll collect unemployment insurance, they'll still cut back on their consumption. This, in turn, will depress sales in the following year, 1996. This decline of 5, from 135 to 130, means we need 10 fewer machines. Net I is actually negative, −10, canceling replacement demand of 10 so that Gross I is 0.

This is really a bad year. Gross I has fallen from 20 to 0. Sales are down by 5. The economy sinks still deeper into the recession.

What brings us out? Perhaps more machines wear out and have to be replaced. Maybe sales pick up. If, for some reason, sales eventually start to rise, then Gross I will rise and we'll be back on the ascending part of our roller coaster ride.

Let's recap. The accelerator principle states that, if sales or consumption is rising at a constant rate, Gross I will stay the same; if sales increase at a decreasing rate, both Gross I and GDP will fall.

Monetary theory

Yet another endogenous theory of the business cycle is the monetary theory. When inflation threatens, the monetary authorities slow or stop the growth of the money supply. This causes a recession. When they are satisfied that inflation is no longer a problem—or if the recession they have caused has become even more of a concern than inflation—the monetary authorities allow the money supply to grow at a faster rate, which brings about economic recovery. The monetary theory may well explain the 1980 and 1981–82 recessions, when the Federal Reserve stepped heavily on the monetary brakes, as well as our subsequent recoveries, when monetary growth was increased. We'll have a lot more to say about monetary policy in Chapter 14.

Underconsumption theory

One last theory and we're out of here. The underconsumption or overproduction theory stipulates that our economy periodically produces more goods and services than people want or can afford. A variant is the overinvestment theory, which says that business firms periodically overinvest in plant and equipment (again see box, "The Accelerator Principle").

Exogenous Theories

Just as endogenous theories place the causes of the business cycle within the economy, exogenous theories place the causes of the business cycle outside the economy.

The sunspot theory

I am perfectly convinced that these decennial crises do depend upon meteorological variations of like period, which again depend, in all probability, upon cosmic variations of which we have evidence in the frequency of sunspots, auroras, and magnetic perturbations.

—W. Stanley Jevons,
*Investigations in Currency
and Finance*

The very first exogenous business cycle theory, the sunspot theory, was formulated by William Stanley Jevons more than a century ago. Jevons believed that storms on the sun, which were observed through telescopes as sunspots, caused periodic crop failures. Because 19th-century economies were primarily agricultural, crop failures, by definition, caused declines in production, or recessions. Subsequent better harvests led to recovery, then prosperity, until the next sunspots occurred.

Is the sunspot theory valid today? Was it ever valid? Not really. Then why even mention it? Because it got people to thinking about what causes business cycles. If it isn't sunspots, it must be something else. Benjamin Franklin once said, "A question is halfway to wisdom." William Stanley Jevons asked the right question, so he deserves at least partial credit for his theory.

The war theory

Another external theory is the war theory. The production surge caused by preparation for war and war itself causes prosperity, and the letdown after war causes a recession. Our experiences before, during, and after World War II, the Korean War, and the Vietnam War seem to validate this theory.

Perhaps no single explanation, whether exogenous or endogenous, can explain each of the cycles we have experienced. The best we can do, then, is to treat each cycle separately, seeking causes that apply.

Business Cycle Forecasting

The most widely used forecasting device is the index of leading economic indicators, which is compiled monthly by the Conference Board, a private business group. This series, which is a weighted average of 10 variables, is a valuable forecasting tool, particularly when used with caution.

An economist is an expert who will know tomorrow why the things he predicted yesterday didn't happen today.

—Laurence J. Peter,
Peter's Quotations

To err is human; to get paid for it is divine.

—William Freund,
economic consultant

The 10 leading indicators consist of variables that "lead" general economic activity by several months (See box, "The Ten Leading Economic Indicators.") When the index turns downward, particularly for two or three months in a row, there is a good chance the economy may be heading into a recession. However, as some pundits have put it, the index has predicted 13 of the last 5 recessions. In other words, the index may have turned downward for two or three months a total of 13 times, but in only 5 instances did a recession follow.

If the index moves steadily upward, there is virtually no chance of a recession in the next few months. But when it begins to move downward, watch out! A downturn *may* be at hand.

Similarly, when the index of leading economic indicators moves down steadily for 11 months in a row, as it did from April 1981 through March 1982, we not only had a

The Ten Leading Economic Indicators

1. **Average workweek of production workers in manufacturing**   When workers get less overtime, output may be declining.

2. **Average initial weekly claims for state unemployment insurance**   When first-time claims for unemployment insurance benefits rise, employment may be falling.

3. **New orders for consumer goods and materials**   When manufacturers receive smaller orders, they may cut back on output.

4. **Vendor performance (companies receiving slower deliveries from suppliers)**   Better on-time delivery by suppliers means they have a smaller backlog of orders.

5. **New orders for capital goods**   If these orders drop, then businesses are planning less output.

6. **New building permits issued**   This provides a good indication of how much construction activity there will be three or four months from now.

7. **Index of stock prices**   Declining stock prices may reflect declining prospects for corporate sales and profits.

8. **Money supply**   If the Federal Reserve cuts the money supply, interest rates will rise, and it will be harder for businesses and individuals to borrow money.

9. **Spread between rates on 10-year Treasury bonds and Federal funds**   Long-term interest rates are usually substantially higher than short-term interest rates. Federal reserve policies designed to slow the economy raise short-term interest rates with little effect on long-term rates. So a smaller spread between short-term and long-term interest rates implies a restrictive monetary policy and a decline in output.

10. **Index of consumer expectations**   As consumers grow less confident about the future, they plan to make fewer major purchases.

---

recession, but there was virtually no chance of an upturn until later in the year, which is exactly what happened.

Figure 3 presents a record of the performance of the index of leading economic indicators. You may judge for yourself how well the index predicted recessions. (See box, "By How Many Months Do the Leading Indicators Lead?")

Where does all of this leave us? It leaves us with the observation that economics is an inexact science that attempts to forecast certain conditions in an uncertain world. For

Q: Why did God create economists?
A: To make weather forecasters look good.

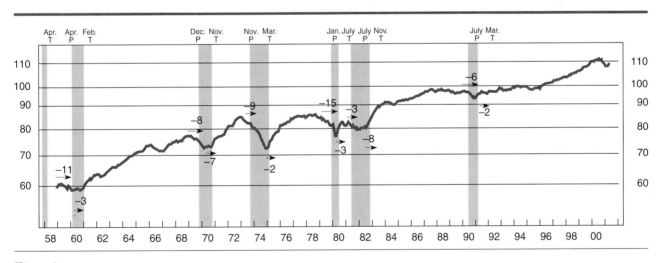

F*igure* 3

The Index of Leading Indicators, 1958–2001*

You'll note that the index has turned down well before recessions begin and turned upward before recoveries set in. For example, the index turned down 10 months before the 1960–61 recession and turned upward three months before the onset of the recovery.

Note: The numbers and arrows indicate length of leads (−) and lags (+) in months from business cycle turning dates.

*1996 = 100

Sources: Survey of Current Business, March 1995, *Business Cycle Indicators,* February 2001.

By How Many Months Do the Leading Indicators Lead?

Note those numbers with arrows in Figure 3. The note below the graph states numbers entered on the chart indicate lengths of leads (−) and lags (+) in months from reference turning dates. For example, a recession began in April 1959, but the Index of Leading Indicators turned down 10 months earlier. Similarly, a recovery that began in the second half of 1980 was "predicted" by an upturn in the index two months earlier.

There are two main problems in using the index to forecast business cycle turning points. First, it takes the

Department of Commerce a full month to tabulate all the necessary data. That means, for example, that the index for September is not announced until the end of October. A second problem is that we can't be sure for several months whether the index has had a turning point. Suppose the index actually turned downward in January. At the end of February, the Department of Commerce would report that the index had declined. And then again at the end of March. It would still be too early to predict a recession, and yet a recession might have already begun.

We have two kinds of forecasters: Those who don't know . . . and those who don't know they don't know.
—John Kenneth Galbraith

example, the index of leading indicators turned down eight months before the November 1973 peak, and it turned up one month before the March 1975 trough. Similarly, the index turned down two months before the July 1981 peak and turned up 10 months before the November 1972 trough.

The GDP Gap

The economic effects of unemployment are more quantifiable than the social effects. To measure them we will use the GDP gap, which is the difference between what we could potentially produce and what we actually produce.

We'll try an analogy first. Do you bowl? What's your high game? Suppose your high game were 180. If you went out tonight and bowled 178, how would you feel? Good? What if you bowled 185? Great?

Living up to our potential GDP

Our potential GDP is like our high game at bowling. We know we can do it—not often, but sometimes. And there's always the chance that we can do still better. Our potential GDP, then, is our output when our resources are fully employed and we are using the best available technology. Remember the production possibilities frontier in Chapter 2? If we are attaining our potential GDP, we are on our production possibilities frontier.

How often do we produce our potential GDP? About as often as we bowl our high game; it happens, but it's unusual. Usually our economy operates below our potential GDP.

Potential GDP and the production possibilities curve

What's the difference, then, between the production possibilities curve and potential GDP? They both represent output when the economy is at full employment (that is, with an unemployment rate of 5 percent), but the production possibilities curve (or frontier) represents the economy at a particular moment in time, while the graph of potential GDP shows how much the economy would produce over time if it were to operate at full employment. Thus, the production possibilities frontier is a snapshot of the economy at full employment at a particular time, while a graph of the potential GDP might show how much the economy would produce at full employment over a period of decades.

The GDP gap is the amount of production by which potential GDP exceeds actual GDP.

Figure 4 shows our country's economic record since World War II. In fact, you'll find that it's essentially a reproduction of Figure 1, except it has a smooth curve added to the record of our actual GDP. That's our potential GDP. Notice that potential GDP is greater than actual GDP for almost every year. There is a gap, which we call the GDP gap. It is the amount of production by which potential GDP exceeds actual GDP.

You'll also notice that in some years actual GDP exceeds potential GDP; there's no GDP gap at all. This is like having a high bowling game of 180 and going out and

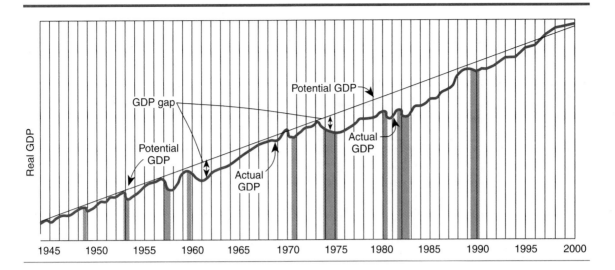

F*igure* 4

The GDP Gap, 1945–2000

Since potential GDP has exceeded actual GDP for most years since World War II, we have had a GDP gap. However in some periods, most recently from 1996 through 2000, actual GDP has been greater than potential GDP.

bowling a 185. These things *do* happen, but they happen so infrequently that we can safely say we don't often expect our actual GDP to exceed our potential GDP.

By looking at Figure 4, you can identify the years when there was no GDP gap. Jot them down and then I'll tell you which years *I've* identified.

I'd say we had no GDP gap in 1957, 1969, and 1997 through 2000. Our answers may differ slightly because everyone reads a graph a little differently. Incidentally, our unemployment rate has been below 5 percent since mid-1997. Since we consider a rate of 5 percent to represent full employment, we can say that in recent years our economy has exceeded its potential.

What, then, is the significance of the GDP gap? Obviously, it shows by how much we are leaving our potential unfulfilled. In 1992 the Congressional Budget Office made an estimate of the GDP gap. Had the unemployment rate been 5.5 percent that year, instead of 7.3 percent, then the United States would have produced an additional $271 billion in GDP.

What is the significance of the GDP gap?

Back in Chapter 2, I made the arbitrary decision that our economy is at full employment when the unemployment rate is 5 percent. But the unemployment rate has been below 5 percent since 1997, so a good case can be made to redefine full employment as an unemployment rate of 4 percent. Still, if we glance ahead at Figure 5, we'll see that our unemployment rate was above 5 percent for most of the 1970s, all of the 1980s, and most of the 1990s. So let's stick with the 5 percent unemployment rate—at least until the next edition of this book.

Unemployment

The Problem

One of the most devastating experiences a person can have is to be out of work for a prolonged period. Most of us have been unemployed once or twice, but only those who have been unable to find work after looking for six to eight months, or even longer, really know that feeling of hopelessness and self-doubt, not to mention a depressed standard of living.

How can you expect somebody who's warm to understand somebody who's cold?
—Aleksandr Solzhenitsyn, One Day in the Life of Ivan Denisovich

The Bureau of Labor Statistics (BLS) defines "discouraged workers" as those who have given up looking for work and have simply dropped out of the labor force. Where have all the discouraged workers gone?

Walk around the slums of our great cities. Walk through East St. Louis, Watts, Bedford-Stuyvesant, and the Hough district of Cleveland. Walk through Roxbury in Boston or central Newark, or through most of our nation's capital. Walk through any of these places in midafternoon and you'll see block after block of teenagers and adults hanging around with nothing to do.

Ask them what they want more than anything else. A bigger welfare check? More food stamps? A bigger TV? Most of them would tell you that all they want is a decent job. Not a dead-end, minimum-wage, low-status, menial job, but a *real* job.

Are these people unemployed? No, these people have given up, dropped out, and are, for all intents and purposes, no longer living in the United States. They may reside here physically, but they are not part of our society.

How the Unemployment Rate Is Computed

Where unemployment data comes from

The Bureau of Labor Statistics (BLS) is in charge of compiling statistics on the number of Americans who are employed and unemployed. Where does it get its data? Most people believe it gets statistics from unemployment insurance offices, but if you stop and think about it, only about one-third of all unemployed Americans are currently collecting unemployment insurance benefits. The BLS gets its unemployment statistics by conducting a random survey of more than 60,000 households.

Essentially, the bureau asks a series of questions: (1) Are you working? If the answer is no, (2) did you work at all this week—even one day? Anyone who has answered yes to questions 1 or 2 is counted as employed. For those who have not been working the BLS has one more question: (3) Did you look for work during the last month (that is, did you go to an employment agency or union hall, send out a résumé, or go on an interview)? If your answer is yes, you're counted as unemployed. If your answer is no, you're just not counted; you're not part of the labor force. If you want to work but have given up looking for a job, you're a "discouraged worker," but you are not in the labor force and you are not considered "unemployed."

The labor force consists of the employed and the unemployed. For example, in July 2000, 134,749,000 Americans were employed and 5,650,000 were unemployed. We can compute the unemployment rate by using this formula:

Unemployment rate = $\dfrac{\text{Number of unemployed}}{\text{Labor force}}$

$$\text{Unemployment rate} = \frac{\text{Number of unemployed}}{\text{Labor force}}$$

How much was the unemployment rate in July 2000? Work it out right here.

Did you get 4.0 percent? The key here is to figure out how many people are in the labor force. Add the employed (134,749,000) and the unemployed (5,650,000), and you'll get a labor force of 140,399,000. So in July 2000 the official unemployment rate was 4.0 percent. (If you need more help with this, see the Extra Help box.)

The liberals say the true unemployment rate is higher than the official rate.

The liberal economists (does anyone still call herself a "liberal"?) would say that the true rate of unemployment is somewhat higher, perhaps 6 or 7 percent, because we should count all the jobless people who are ready, willing, and able to work. Let's ask about the 2 or 3 million people who are not working but are not officially unemployed. If we asked the BLS, it would tell us that they are discouraged workers. Discouraged? Why discouraged? Because they're *so* discouraged they've given up looking for work. Therefore, they don't meet the BLS criteria for being officially unemployed. As I mentioned, if a person has not actively looked for a job during the last month—sent out a

Who are the discouraged workers?

Read Only If You're Not Sure How to Calculate the Unemployment Rate

In January 1995, 7,500,000 Americans were unemployed and 124,600,000 held jobs. Go ahead and calculate the unemployment rate:

$$\text{Unemployment rate} = \frac{\text{Number of unemployed}}{\text{Labor force}}$$

$$= \frac{7,500,000}{132,100,000}$$

OK, where did we get the 132,100,000? That's the labor force—the number of unemployed (7,500,000) plus the number of employed (124,600,000).

The next step is simple division: 132,100,000 into 7,500,000, which gives us an unemployment rate of 5.7 percent.

Incidentally, a common mistake in this type of problem is to divide 7,500,000 into 132,100,000. Some people insist on dividing the smaller number into the larger number. But the rule we must always follow is to divide the bottom number into the top number. (By the way, if you're interested, you may want to buy another book I wrote, *All the Math You'll Ever Need.**)

---

*It was published by John Wiley & Sons and is available in bookstores, or on amazon.com.

---

résumé, gone on a job interview, or visited an employment agency—that person is not counted as unemployed. He is not in the labor force. And as far as our unemployment rate statistics go, he is not there at all.

The liberals have a couple of additional bones to pick with the BLS definition. A person who worked one day in the last month is counted as employed. Also, someone who works part-time but wants to work full-time is counted as employed. The liberals ask, "Doesn't this sort of measurement overstate the number of employed?" When you put it all together, they maintain, the BLS is overstating employment and understating unemployment. The result is an unemployment rate that is perhaps a couple of points too low.

That's the liberal view. As you would expect, the conservatives say the official unemployment rate *over*estimates the true rate of unemployment. Using the BLS definition of an unemployed person—someone who has not worked this month and who has actively sought work—the conservative focuses on those who are required to report to state employment or other government employment offices to remain eligible for unemployment insurance, welfare, or food stamps. Is this, asks the conservative, really an effort to look for work, or are these guys just going through the motions?

> The conservatives say the true unemployment rate is lower than the official rate.

Some conservatives also cite the huge numbers of Americans—as well as illegal immigrants—working in the underground economy (see that section near the end of the previous chapter). There may be a couple of million people out there working as hair dressers, livery cab operators, unlicensed plumbers, carpenters, electricians, and auto mechanics, as well as street peddlers and sewing machine operators in illegal garment sweat shops. All these people are employed off the books, do not report their income, and are not counted as employed by the Bureau of Labor Statistics.

Another factor that conservatives cite as boosting the unemployment rate is the change in the composition of the labor force. The percentage of married women who work has risen from 25 percent in the late 1940s (when the birthrate was very high) to about 65 percent today. The advent of married women seeking work raises the unemployment rate in three different ways. First, married women who are reentering the labor force after having had children will have to find jobs (unless their employers held their old positions open for 5, 10, or 20 years). Second, because their husbands are employed,

> The effect of married women on the unemployment rate

253

When It's a Recession for Whites, It's a Depression for Blacks

In the first part of this chapter, I jokingly referred to the difference between recessions and depressions. For blacks, however, unemployment is no joking matter. Historically, the unemployment rate for blacks has been double that of whites. And black teenagers' "official" unemployment rate during the 1981–82 recession topped 50 percent. We can only guess at their true unemployment rate if all the "discouraged" black teenagers who dropped out of the labor force were counted.

A survey in the early 1980s by the Center for the Study of Social Policy turned up this interesting fact: Black college graduates earn about the same income as white high school graduates. So much for the notion of equal opportunity.

Of course, there have been major strides toward equality of economic opportunity since the mid-1960s, but they have left in their wake a huge black (and Hispanic) underclass. If you are black or Hispanic, your chances of being poor are three times as great, and your chances of being unemployed are twice as great.

It appears that two things can be done to ease the economic burden of minority groups. One is to make greater efforts to end employment discrimination. The other is to avoid recessions and keep the unemployment rate as low as possible.

The rate of unemployment is 100 percent if it's you who is unemployed.

—David L. Kurtz

they can shop around some for a job. And third, their husbands, if unemployed, can also shop around for a while if their wives are working.

It is interesting to note that in recent years there has been virtually no difference between the unemployment rates of women and men. It has also been pushed up as the baby-boom generation (those born from the late 1940s to the mid-1960s) came of age. Young adults tend to have a relatively high unemployment rate because, like the homemakers returning to the labor force, they need time to find that first job. Next, they tend to go from job to job until, like Goldilocks, they find a position that is "just right." Finally, because many young adults still live at home or receive help from their parents, they experience less pressure to take the first job that comes along. However, as the baby boomers have aged, the proportion of young people in the labor force has been lower than it was 25 years ago. (See box, "When It's a Recession for Whites, It's a Depression for Blacks," for a discussion of unemployment among blacks.)

The bottom line, according to the conservatives, is that perhaps a couple of million of the "officially" unemployed are not really looking for work. The liberal bottom line is that at least a couple of million people out there want to work but aren't being counted.

Are the conservatives or the liberals right? Guess what? I'm going to let *you* decide.

Figure 5 is a record of the official unemployment rate from 1948 through 2000. You'll notice a marked upward trend from the late 1960s through the mid-1980s, which apparently lends credence to the conservative interpretation—but all the results are not yet in. In fact, the trend seems to have reversed since the mid-1980s, by which time the baby boomers had all come of age.

The unemployment rate plays an important role in presidential elections. A high unemployment rate in 1992 was a very important factor in President George Bush's loss to Bill Clinton. And four years later, when Clinton defeated challenger Bob Dole, he made our low rate of unemployment a major campaign issue. Moreover, in every election since 1948, the party that occupied the White House held on to the presidency if the unemployment rate was falling in the second quarter of that year but lost the election if the unemployment rate was flat or rising.[1] This leading indicator has been right on the money in the last 13 elections; maybe we can dispense with the voting and just tote up the April, May, and June unemployment rates in every presidential year. (See box, "Comparative Unemployment Rates.")

---

[1]In March 2000 the unemployment rate was 4.1. It fell to 3.9 in April, rose to 4.1 in May, and fell to 4.0 in June. So was the unemployment rate going *up* or *down* in the second quarter of 2000? It's kind of hard to say, which seems to reflect the results of the Bush-Gore presidential election.

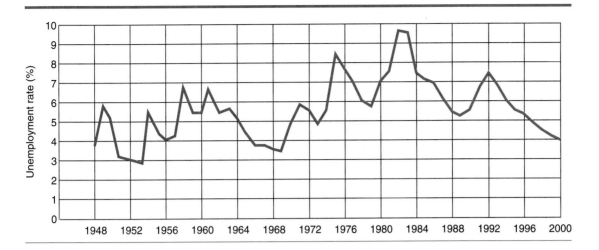

F*igure* 5

The Unemployment Rate, 1948–2000

Unemployment went up between 1969 and 1982 and went down after that.

Source: Economic Report of the President, 2001.

Comparative Unemployment Rates

Why is the American unemployment rate so low compared to those of other industrial nations? Part of the answer is our booming economy compared to the stagnating economies of Europe and Japan through most of the 1990s. Europe's cradle-to-grave safety net means not only that being out of work has become a viable way of making a living but that there is no longer much stigma attached to joblessness. In Sweden workers can collect nearly 80 percent as much as they could earn working, while in Spain it's 70 percent and in France, nearly 60 percent. But, in the United States and Japan, which also has a low unemployment rate despite an almost decade-long recession, unemployment benefits are less than 50 percent of what workers would earn on the job.

Only about one-third of workers who are out of work qualify for benefits in the United states and Japan, where newer members of the labor force and temporary workers are ineligible. Compare that with 89 percent of unemployed workers in Germany and 98 percent in France. While the limit for collecting unemployment benefits in the United States and Japan is 26 weeks, German unemployed workers can collect for at least five years, and in Britain, unemployed people can collect practically forever.

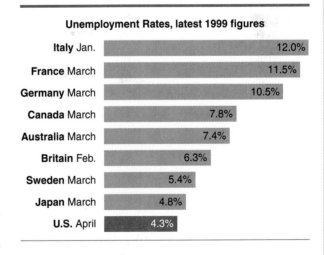

And then too, Western Europe is much more heavily unionized than the United States. Often, by law, their collective bargaining agreements (including job security) are extended to all firms in the industry, whether or not they are unionized. In addition, business firms are so tied up by government rules and regulations that they find it nearly impossible to dismiss employees.

Sources: Bureau of Labor Statistics; Organization of Economics Cooperation and Development; The Economist.

A Computer-Based Job Bank

Imagine a computer-based network that lists every job opening in the country and every person seeking employment. Every job opening and every job seeker will be matched instantly. What effect will this have on frictional unemployment? It will practically wipe it out in one fell swoop.

Why don't we set up such a system? Believe it or not, we have. Virtually every state employment office[*] has a computer data bank of job openings. There are just two problems.

First, only a small minority of employers list their jobs with their state employment services. One reason most employers don't is that they're reluctant to hire people who are collecting unemployment insurance because they are sometimes perceived as being lazy or having low motivation. Also, employers in general will look askance at anyone who is out of work. "*Why* are you unemployed?" You'll always stand a better chance of finding a job if you already have a job, or at least if people think you do.

A second reason why the state employment services can't perfectly match job openings to job seekers is that not everybody out of work registers at their state employment office. If they're collecting unemployment insurance benefits, they *have* to register. If they're not, they may. But in certain lines of work—executive posi-

tions, many professional jobs, and, in general, higher-paying positions—job applicants rarely register at their state employment service.

There's another computer-based job bank on the World Wide Web. The Internet can put you in touch with thousands of potential employers. Sounds too good to be true? Here are 10 job sites you can find on the Web:

monster.com	jobsonline.com	careerpath.com
headhunter.net	hotjobs.com	careerbuilder.com
jobs.com	dice.com	occ.com	careermosaic.com

Nearly all large corporations have their own E-recruitment Web sites. Unfortunately most are poorly designed. According to a *BusinessWeek* article by Stephen Wildstrom (September 20, 1999, p. 19), they employ "excessive use of graphics that add no real information and make pages pages very slow to load." Wildstrom concludes that "about three of every four online job seekers give up in frustration before submitting an application." On the bright side, these Web sites are improving virtually as you read these words.

---

[*]These are the employment agency counterparts to the state unemployment insurance offices where unemployed people sign up for their unemployment checks.

Types of Unemployment

Frictional Unemployment   Our economy is far from a well-tuned, efficient, smoothly functioning machine. When a job opening occurs somewhere, it is rarely filled instantaneously, even when there is someone ready, willing, and able to fill it. In a word, our economy has a certain degree of friction (see box, "A Computerized Job Bank").

The final solution for unemployment is work.
—Calvin Coolidge

About 2 to 3 percent of our labor force is always frictionally unemployed.

The frictionally unemployed are people who are between jobs or just entering or reentering the labor market. Because our system of filling jobs—newspaper classified ads, employment agencies, corporate recruiters, executive headhunters, help-wanted signs, and word of mouth—is imperfect, usually weeks or months pass before positions are filled.

At any given time, about 2 or 3 percent of the labor force is frictionally unemployed. Students who are looking for their first full-time jobs, homemakers reentering the labor market after 5, 10, or 20 years, and servicemen and -women who have recently been discharged by the armed forces are frictionally unemployed until they find jobs. In addition, there are those who leave their jobs voluntarily, perhaps so they can spend all their time looking for better jobs. Maybe they're looking in another part of the country. Add to these the people who get fired or quit. These people, too, are between jobs, or frictionally unemployed.

When people change jobs, they may have time between jobs, or they may leave one job on a Friday and start a new one on Monday. Officials at the Labor Department estimate that 40 percent of the labor force, or roughly 50 million workers, change jobs within a year.

The Effects of Structural Unemployment

In a book titled *Prosperity Lost,* Philip Mattera provides scores of stories of how structural unemployment has affected the lives of ordinary Americans. He talks about Ray Woolaghan, who was laid off his $12-an-hour job at U.S. Steel's Homestead, Pennsylvania, mill back in the mid-1980s, just 17 days short of qualifying for his pension. It took him two years to find steady work. What he found was a $5.23-an-hour custodial position at the University of Pittsburgh.

Then Mattera tells about another person who found himself structurally unemployed:

> After Bill Baudendistel of Goshen, Ohio, was laid off from his $13-an-hour factory job with General Electric in 1988, the best work he could find was a position as a night maintenance man at a shopping mall. The pay: $5 an hour. His wife had to take a part-time job as a secretary in a hospital, though she preferred to stay at home with their three children. Nonetheless, the Baudendistels, finding it hard to keep up, began buying their clothes at garage sales and stopped purchasing "luxuries" like fresh fruit.*

As both of these structurally unemployed workers eventually found much lower paying jobs, neither is counted among the unemployed. But both will spend the rest of their working lives at relatively low-paying jobs and adjust their living standards accordingly.

---

*Philip Mattera, *Prosperity Lost* (Reading, MA: Addison-Wesley, 1991), pp. 66–67.

Structural Unemployment Former U.S. Attorney General, Robert F. Kennedy,[2] once asked, "Have you ever told a coal miner in West Virginia or Kentucky that what he needs is individual initiative to go out and get a job where there isn't any?" A person who is out of work for a relatively long period of time, say, a couple of years, is structurally unemployed. The economy does not have any use for this person. The steelworker in Youngstown, Ohio, and the coal miner from Kentucky are no longer needed because the local steel mills and coal mines have closed. (See box, "The Effects of Structural Unemployment.") And the skills of clerical workers, typists, and inventory control clerks who once staffed a corporate office have been made obsolete by a computer system. Add to these the people whose companies have gone out of business or whose jobs have been exported to low-wage countries and you've got another 2 to 3 percent of the labor force structurally unemployed.

> About 2 to 3 percent of our labor force is always structurally unemployed.

One out of five adult Americans is functionally illiterate. These people cannot read, write, or do simple numerical computations. In a workplace that increasingly demands these minimal skills, more and more of these people are finding themselves virtually shut out of the labor force. Each year our educational system turns out 1 million more functional illiterates, most of whom will face long periods of structural unemployment. Many of these young adults come from very poor families where no one has held a job. They have no idea of how to dress for a job interview, what to say, or even the need to show up on time. Unless these people are given some kind of vocational training and provided with entry-level jobs, they will be out of work for most of their lives.

> The "unemployables"

Ours is a dynamic economy, and the opportunities for retraining and subsequent employment *do* exist. But the prospects for a 50- or 60-year-old worker embarking on a second career are not auspicious. To compound the problem, most of the structurally unemployed reside in the Rust Belt of the East and Midwest, while most of the new career opportunities are in the Sun Belt, and in several states on the East and West coasts.[3]

> When men are employed, they are best contented.
> —Benjamin Franklin

---

[2]Robert Kennedy also served as a U.S. senator from 1965 to 1968 and was the brother of President John F. Kennedy.

[3]Many large corporations, including IBM, AT&T, General Motors, Sears, Boeing, and GTE, have been downsizing by offering hundreds of thousands of employees early retirement, while other companies have been closing plants and putting millions of employees out of work.

What if someone were "between jobs" for six months, or a year, or even two years? When someone is out of work for a long period of time, he or she is classified as "structurally unemployed." But where do we draw the line between frictional and structural unemployment? The answer is that we don't. There *is* no clear dividing line.

Fluctuations in our unemployment rate are due to cyclical unemployment.

Cyclical Unemployment   As you know, our economy certainly has its ups and downs, a set of fluctuations known as business cycles. During a recession, the unemployment rate rises to 8, 9, or even 10 percent. During the Great Depression, the "official" unemployment rate hit 25 percent, which definitely understated the true unemployment picture.

If we allow for a certain amount of frictional and structural unemployment, anything above the sum of these two would be cyclical unemployment. Let's say that the sum of frictional and structural unemployment is 5 percent. If the actual rate of unemployment is 7.7 percent, then the cyclical rate is 2.7 percent.

If we take a 5 percent unemployment rate as our working definition of full employment, anything above 5 percent would be cyclical unemployment. You may wonder whether 5 percent is a reasonable level for full employment. Surely we can never expect our unemployment rate to reach zero, since we'll always have some frictionally and structurally unemployed people. Our unemployment rate did get down to 1.2 percent in 1944, but as they said then, "There's a war going on." With 12 million men in the armed forces and the economy going full-steam ahead, employers were desperate for help, and anyone who could walk and spell his or her name had no trouble finding a job.

There are liberal economists who insist that we could realistically get the unemployment rate down to 4 percent, while there are conservative economists who consider 6 percent the lowest attainable rate. As I've said before, we'll split the difference and call 5 percent full employment.

Read the box titled "Are You Eligible to Collect Unemployment Benefits?" You might be eligible, even if you're a full-time student. Hundreds of thousands of people are eligible right now but aren't collecting. Yet millions more are unemployed and

---

Are You Eligible to Collect Unemployment Benefits?

A large number of people who are eligible to collect don't know they're eligible. The eligibility requirements are a yes answer to these three questions:

1. Did you work for at least parts of 20 of the last 52 weeks (or 15 of the last 52 weeks and 40 of the last 104)?
2. Did you lose your last job through no fault of your own?
3. Are you ready, willing, and able to work?

The second question is open to interpretation. What if you were fired from your last job? Why were you fired? Did you provoke your own dismissal? Then you can't collect. What if you and your boss had an argument? Then you may be eligible.

What if you were fired because your boss didn't like you, or because you couldn't get the hang of the job, or because there was simply no work for you to do? Then you could collect. But what if you got fired because you were always late, often absent, or refused to do any work? You then provoked your own dismissal and are not eligible for unemployment benefits.

The answer to the second question is not always a clear-cut yes or no. As a onetime employee of the New York State Employment Service, I offer you this advice: If you lose your job and you think you *may* be eligible for unemployment benefits, it pays to apply. Numerous people collecting right now probably had even more dubious claims than you have. Just go down to your state unemployment insurance office and find out whether you're eligible.

ineligible to collect. Why? Many are new entrants or reentrants to the labor market; others are people who left their jobs voluntarily, those who provoked their dismissals, and finally, those whose unemployment insurance benefits ran out. Only one out of every three unemployed people is actually collecting benefits.

Seasonal Unemployment At any given time a couple of hundred thousand people may be out of work because this is their "slow season." The slack seasons in the ladies' garment industry are in the spring and fall after those seasons' new fashions have been shipped to the stores. The tourist season is slow all summer in Florida, and elsewhere some employees at Carvels and Dairy Queen are laid off in the winter. My aunt Betty, who worked in the garment industry for nearly 60 years, turned her seasonal unemployment to her advantage by arranging to get laid off each year in early November, registering for unemployment insurance benefits, and then taking off for Florida.

Seasonal unemployment is not nearly as large as frictional, structural, or cyclical unemployment, so it hasn't figured in our discussion of total unemployment. But if it weren't mentioned here, someone would be sure to ask why it wasn't included.

Natural Unemployment Rate

As the unemployment rate falls, and it becomes increasingly difficult to find employees, employers will bid up wage rates, pushing up the rate of inflation. Once the unemployment rate falls below its natural rate, which most economists estimate to be 5 or 6 percent, then inflationary wage pressure emerges.

Our unemployment rate fell below 6 percent in 1994, below 5 percent in 1997, and below 4.5 percent in 1998. Could it be that the natural rate of unemployment was falling? There are at least five reasons to support this view.

First, the natural unemployment rate tends to fall when the proportion of youths in the labor force is shrinking. The youth contingent has been shrinking since the late 1970s from a post-baby boom peak of nearly 25 percent to just 16 percent in recent years.

A second factor is the doubling of the adult population in prison since 1985—with 2.3 percent of the male labor force behind bars at last count. Assuming a fair number of these inmates would be counted as unemployed if they weren't locked up, this too has pushed down our natural unemployment rate.

Worker insecurity, based on massive corporate downsizing and plant closings, has also tended to reduce the natural unemployment rate. Even though unemployment rates are the lowest in 30 years, many workers are willing to accept small pay increases, rather than risk the ire of their employers.

Next, there is the rapid growth of the temporary-help industry, whose share of employment has jumped from 0.5 percent in the early 1980s, to more than 2.2 percent today. Not only do many people who would otherwise be unemployed now work as temps as they look for permanent jobs, but the availability of temp agencies allows employers to fill vacancies more easily and, in some cases, to minimize wage pressures by keeping the new hires on temp payrolls.

Finally, the labor force has been expanding rapidly. The Census Bureau estimates that as many as five million illegal immigrants are working here today. In addition, many new workers are unmarried mothers with at least one child younger than three years old. The percentage of these women now in the labor force rose to 66 percent in 1999 from only 54 percent in 1995.[4]

In the next part of this chapter, we'll see how rising wages, among other things, contribute to inflation. But first we'll need to answer the question "What is inflation?"

---

[4]This will be discussed further in the context of the Welfare Reform Act of 1996 in the chapter on income and poverty near the end of the book.

Inflation

Defining Inflation

What exactly *is* inflation? It is a rise in the price level. Generally, we consider inflation a sustained rise in the average price level over a period of years. In our own lifetimes, we have known little *but* inflation.

If the rate of inflation had been 4 percent, would that mean the price of every good and service went up by 4 percent? Of course not! The prices of some things went up by much more than 4 percent, and the prices of others rose by less than 4 percent. The prices of some things may not have changed. And when the overall price level is rising, the prices of some goods and services are actually going down. Can you think of any examples? In the 1970s and 1980s TV prices came way down. And then the price of VCRs declined. And more recently, prices of cellular phones, fax machines, CDs and CD players, camcorders, personal computers, beepers, laser printers, and graphing calculators have fallen.

U.S. inflation has been persistent since World War II, particularly in the 1970s when, for much of the decade, it was at double-digit proportions. And yet, when compared to an inflation rate of more than 100 percent in several Latin American countries during the 1980s and early 1990s,[5] ours has been relatively mild.

Ask the man on the street what inflation is and he'll tell you that everything costs more. To be more precise, the U.S. Department of Labor's Bureau of Labor Statistics compiles an average of all items that consumers buy—the prices of cars, appliances, haircuts, TVs, VCRs, steaks, medical services, Big Macs—and figures out how much it costs the average family to live. Every month several hundred BLS employees around the country check the cost of 90,000 items—ranging from airline tickets to cat food. Let's say that in January 1995 it cost the Jones family $20,000 to maintain a certain standard of living. If it cost the Joneses $22,000 to buy the same items in January 1999, we would say that the cost of living went up 10 percent.

The consumer price index (CPI), which measures changes in our cost of living, is reported near the middle of every month by the Bureau of Labor Statistics. For example, you'll hear on the radio, "There was some good news today on the inflation front. Consumer prices rose just two-tenths of 1 percent last month, and the consumer price index now stands at 136.4." Before you have a chance to digest this information, the announcer is doing sports and weather.

First let's consider that prices rose just two-tenths of 1 percent last month. Is that a lot of inflation? If we convert it to an annual rate, it comes to just under 2.7 percent.[6] An inflation rate of 2.7 percent a year certainly does not seem to be all that bad, especially when you compare it to the inflation we experienced from the early 1970s to the early 1980s (see Figure 6).

The radio announcer also said that our consumer price index now stands at 136.4. What does that tell us? Unless you're pretty familiar with the consumer price index, how it's constructed, and what it measures, you won't be able to fully appreciate the significance of that number. Well, your worries are over. In another few pages you'll know exactly what this index is all about.

The number 100 is a magic number. It lends itself well to calculating percentage changes. Suppose, for example, that we want to find out by what percentage prices rose since the base year for the consumer price index. The base year is set at 100. If the CPI

The consumer price index is based on what it costs an average family to live.

---

[5] In 1990 Brazil had an annual inflation rate of 2,360 percent, and Nicaragua had one of 33,600 percent. But Bolivia managed to attain an even more impressive rate of 50,000 percent in 1985.

[6] How did we get from 0.2 percent a month to just under 2.7 percent a year? There are three ways of doing this: (1) Use pencil and paper, if you happen to have about half an hour; (2) work it out with your pocket calculator; or (3) look it up in a book that has compound interest tables.

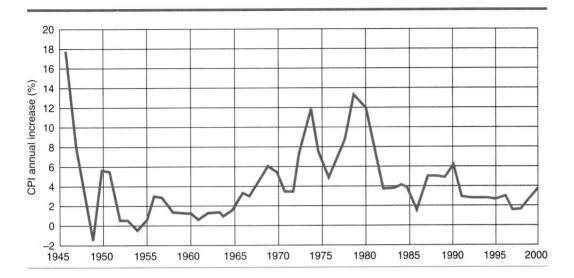

F*igure* 6

Annual Percentage Change in Consumer Price Index, 1946–2000

Since World War II we have had two periods of price stability—from 1952 through 1965, and from 1991 to the present.

Source: Economic Report of the President, 2001.

were 136.4 today, by what percentage did prices rise since the base year? They rose by 36.4 percent.

What I did was subtract 100 from 136.4. Try this one: If the CPI is now 201.6, by what percentages did prices rise since the base year? Work it out right here:

They rose by 101.6 percent (201.6–100). Now you're getting it—I hope. You'll notice that we take the CPI in the current year and subtract the CPI in the base year, which is always 100.

No one would complain if the cost of living rose 2 or 3 percent a year, but during the 10-year period from 1972 to 1982 the consumer price index rose from 125.3 to 289.1. By what percentage did the cost of living rise? Figure it out here:

It went up by 130.7 percent. In other words, it cost the typical American family more than twice as much to live in 1982 as it did 10 years earlier.

If you didn't get an increase of 130.7 percent, then it's a pretty good bet that you could use some extra help calculating percentage changes. You'll find that help in the box "Finding Percentage Changes in the Price Level."

Deflation and Disinflation

Deflation   *Deflation* is a decline in the price level, but once again, not for just a month or two but for a period of years. The last deflation the United States had was from 1929

Finding Percentage Changes in the Price Level*

First we'll work out the arithmetic of finding the percentage change in going from 125.3 to 289.1:

$$\text{Percentage change} = \frac{\text{Change}}{\text{Original number}} \times 100$$

$$= \frac{163.8}{125.3} \times 100$$

$$= 1.307 \times 100$$

$$= 130.7$$

Calculating percentage changes is an essential skill, not just in economics, but in everyday life. If you're *still* not comfortable with the arithmetic, please study the box "Calculating Percentage Changes," which is about halfway through Chapter 9.

If all this is beginning to sound like déjà vu all over again as baseball great Yogi Berra used to say, it should be. The reason we needed to compute percentage changes in Chapter 9 was to use them to gauge changes in real GDP. And to find real GDP itself, we employed the GDP deflator, which is a price index for GDP compiled by the Bureau of Labor Statistics. This organization also compiles the consumer price index (CPI), which measures price changes in consumer prices. So both the CPI and the GDP deflator are price indices, but the GDP deflator measures price changes in a much broader range of goods and services.

Here's a chance to work out a few more problems: Find the percentage change in prices since the base year if the CPI is now 94.7.

The answer is −5.3 percent. The price level declined (94.7−100 = −5.3). OK, one last problem and we're out of here. By what percentage did prices rise since the base year if the CPI is now 485.2?

They rose by 385.2 percent (485.2−100=385.2). So when you're figuring out the percentage change in prices since the base year, all you have to do is subtract 100 from the current CPI.

---

*This method varies slightly from that shown in the box "Calculating Percentage Changes" in Chapter 9.

---

to 1933, when prices fell 50 percent. Significantly, that deflation was accompanied by the Great Depression.

Until the inflationary recessions of the 1970s, business downturns were called deflations, for they were invariably accompanied by price declines. As much as business owners dislike inflation, particularly that of double-digit proportions, they hate deflation even more.

Suppose your store sells air conditioners, refrigerators, and other appliances. You place orders with manufacturers a couple of months before delivery and generally hold two months' worth of inventory in your warehouse. If there is a 2 or 3 percent rate of deflation, instead of the 2 or 3 percent rate of inflation you had been counting on, you'll probably have to charge about 5 percent less than you had been planning to charge. You paid your suppliers more than you should have, and you'll collect less from your customers than you had expected to. So just a little deflation can be very bad news to business firms, especially retailers.

But deflation is great news to consumers, because it means that they'll be paying lower prices. If you happen to have a lot of money—in the form of currency or bank deposits—you will be sitting pretty, because each dollar that you hold will be going up in value. And if you're living on a fixed income, you'll be able to buy more for your money.

Deflation has not been a concern in the United States since the 1930s, but it has become a problem of growing concern in Japan. Deflation is chipping away at asset values, increasing credit risks, pinching wages and salaries, and preventing the economy

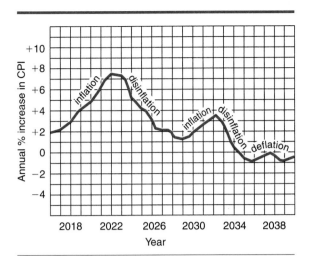

Figure 7
Hypothetical Annual Rate of
Increase of CPI, 2016–2040

from generating any sustained growth after a decade of stagnation. Stocks were trading at the same prices in early 2001 as they had been in the mid-1980s, and real estate prices had fallen for ten consecutive years. Consumer prices are dropping at an annual rate of about one percent, but the Japanese economy is running the risk of getting caught in a deflationary spiral similar to the Great Depression, when prices and wages fell sharply throughout the world.

Disinflation   You now know all about inflation and deflation. Get ready for a new one: *disinflation.* You may ask yourself, Do we really need another term, especially since *dis*inflation sounds a lot like *de*flation?

Until about 40 years ago, we would have had little use for the term *disinflation.* After all, if the price level was rising, that was inflation. If the price level was falling, that was deflation. And if prices were rising and output was going nowhere, we had stagflation. Immediately after World War II we had a great deal of inflation. But when recessions occurred, inflation would disappear and prices actually declined slightly.

By the late 1950s, even though the rate of inflation was quite moderate, recessions no longer eliminated rising prices. They continued to rise, albeit at a slower rate. This gave us our definition of disinflation: *Disinflation occurs when the rate of inflation declines.*

For example, during the recession of 1981–82, the rate of inflation fell from about 12 percent to about 4 percent. And again, since the recession of 1990–91, the rate of inflation fell from a little more than 4 percent to less than 2 percent (see Figure 6).

In Figure 7 we've constructed a hypothetical graph illustrating inflations, disinflation, and deflation.

The Post–World War II History of Inflation

During each war in U.S. history, prices rose sharply. Each war was accompanied by a combination of money supply increases and large budget deficits.

In 1945, as World War II ended, a tremendous pent-up demand for consumer goods was unleashed. Consumer prices rose sharply. Too many dollars were chasing too few goods. Just as the inflation was being brought under control, the Korean War broke out. This brought on another wave of consumer spending and price increases.

President Dwight David Eisenhower took office in 1953, pledging to end the war in Korea and the inflation at home. It took him only a couple of months to end the war, but it wasn't until 1960, three recessions later, that inflation was controlled.

Until 1965, consumer prices rose at an annual rate of only 1 percent (see Figure 6). Then the Vietnam War, accompanied by huge federal budget deficits, rekindled another inflationary fire.

At its present cost, life is worth about 30 cents on the dollar.
—Don Herold

By this time most Americans had become conditioned to rising prices; they seemed inevitable. When prices have been rising for some time, it is reasonable to assume they will keep rising. So what did we do? We ran out to buy still more goods and services before prices rose still further. And when businessowners saw that demand for their products was high, they were encouraged to raise *their* prices.

What was taking place was a self-fulfilling prophecy. We thought something would happen, and it did. In other words, so long as people *believe* inflation is inevitable, it is indeed inevitable!

Early in President Richard Nixon's first term, he recognized this self-fulfilling prophecy; he therefore reasoned that all he needed to do was convince people that prices would not be rising in the near future. Then they wouldn't stock up on goods, and prices wouldn't rise.

Nixon's premise was correct, as was his conclusion: If people believe prices will be stable, they won't buy too much and drive up those prices. However, no one believed Nixon when he told the country that prices would be leveling off.

Since then a lot has happened to affect the rate of inflation. Nixon's wage and price freeze didn't really take, perhaps because it was tried only halfheartedly. When OPEC quadrupled oil prices in the fall of 1973, inflation accelerated (see Figure 6). The deep recession that followed did damp down the inflation, but in the late 1970s it returned with renewed vigor. Not until the back-to-back recessions of 1980 and 1981–82 was the rate of inflation finally brought down to acceptable levels.

In the 1970s we did get to add a new word to our vocabulary—*stagflation*—which is a contraction of the words *stagnation* and *inflation.* The new word got a great deal of use during the recessions of 1973–75, 1980, and 1981–82, when we experienced the worst of both worlds: declining output *and* inflation.

Since 1992, the inflation rate has stayed below 3 percent in five of six years. What accounts for this? Four factors come to mind. First is the rising tide of imported goods. When these imports compete with goods made in America, the competition drives down prices. Imported goods reduce our inflation rate by 1 or 2 percent.

A second factor is the rise of huge discounters, like WalMart, Toys R Us, Staples, and Price-Costco. In 2000, discount stores sold almost 50 percent of all general merchandise, up from 37 percent just 10 years earlier. Discounters work closely with suppliers to minimize distribution costs, and these savings are largely passed on to consumers as lower prices.

A third cause of our low rate of inflation is the advent of E-commerce, which has added a new layer of competition. Nearly every item that can be purchased at a traditional retail store is available on the Web, and for cost-conscious consumers, this provides unparalleled leverage, because buyers can comparison-shop across dozens of stores at the click of a mouse. Books, for example, cost about 20 percent less online than in bookstores. For sellers, savings come via lower real estate and rental costs, as well as reduced outlays for advertising, inventory, and transportation—items that ordinarily account for some 40 percent of the consumer price of goods.

Finally, the efforts of business firms to become leaner and meaner have been paying off in rising efficiency and productivity. Wage increases have been held down, millions of workers have been discharged, and, again, savings have been passed on to consumers. Are the bad old inflationary days of the 1970s and early 1980s behind us, or will inflation come roaring back again?

How does our inflation rate compare to those of other industrial countries? In the decade of the 1990s it has been about average.

The Construction of the Consumer Price Index

The most important measure of inflation is the consumer price index. Now we'll see how the Bureau of Labor Statistics goes about constructing this index.

Construction of the Consumer Price Index

We're going to calculate how much it cost a family to live in March 1987 and in March 1995. In the table showing hypothetical costs of living for these months, part A has a month's expenditutes for 1987, the base year. To find these expenditures, we multiply quantity purchased by price. Then, adding up the money spent on each item, we find the total amount of money spent in March 1987.

Now we'll compare that amount with the amount spent in March 1995, which is shown in part B. What happened, then, was that the family spent $848 for these six items in 1987 and $994 for these same items in 1995. Obviously, their cost of living went up. But by how much?

To find out, we'll construct a consumer price index. To do this, divide the cost of living in the base year, 1987, into the cost of living in the current year, 1995. After you've done that multiply your answer by 100 to convert it into an index number.

Do your work in the space provided and then check it with the calculations shown.

$$994/848 = 1.172$$
$$1.172 \times 100 = 117.2$$

That's our consumer price index for 1995. You'll notice that we've carried it to one decimal place, which is exactly how the Bureau of Labor Statistics does it and how you'll find it listed in the newspaper.

One last question. By what percentage did prices rise between 1987 and 1995? The envelope please. Prices rose by 17.2 percent (117.2 − 100).

If you're still having trouble figuring out percentage changes, reread the box titled "Finding Percentage Changes in the Price Level," earlier in this chapter.

A. March 1987.

Item	Quantity	Price	Quantity × Price
Loaf of bread	10	.70	7.00
Quart of milk	15	.60	9.00
Pair of jeans	2	28.00	46.00
New car	0.02	7800.00	156.00
Mortgage payment	1	590.00	590.00
Movie admission	8	5.00	40.00
Total			848.00

B. March 1995.

Item	Quantity	Price	Quantity × Price
Loaf of bread	10	.90	9.00
Quart of milk	15	.80	12.00
Pair of jeans	2	31.00	62.00
New car	0.02	9000.00	180.00
Mortgage payment	1	675.00	675.00
Movie admission	8	7.00	56.00
Total			994.00

First a base year is picked. In early 1998 we used the period 1982–84 as our base, setting the average price level of those years equal to 100. By December 1997 the CPI stood at 161.3, which meant, of course, that the price level had risen 63.1 percent since 1982–84. So the CPI measured the rise in the cost of living from the base years to December 1997.[7]

If you're *really* curious about the mechanics of how the CPI is constructed, it's worked out in the Extra Help box "Construction of the Consumer Price Index." Of course, this is a very simplified version containing just six items. The Bureau of Labor Statistics compiles a market basket of hundreds of goods and services that the typical urban family buys in 1987. Assuming they buy that same market basket of goods and

---

[7]The Bureau of Labor Statistics usually overhauls the CPI every 10 years, doing a survey of some 10,000 families to find out what they're buying and how much they're paying.

The Declining Real Cost of Living

The CPI measures the cost of living in money terms. "The real cost of living," say W. Michael Cox and Richard Alm, "isn't measured in dollars and cents, but in the hours and minutes we must work to live."* For example, back in 1916, you would have needed to work 3,162 hours to buy a refrigerator, 333 hours in 1958, and just 68 hours in 1997. And the 1997 model could do a lot more tricks. In 1919 you would have worked 80 minutes to buy a dozen eggs, but by 1997 you would have worked just 5 minutes.

Of course not everything is cheaper, when measured in hours worked. Take private college tuition. Today it costs about 1500 hours of work; in the mid-1960s, it cost just 500 hours of work. If you happen to attend the University of Texas, the cost today of just over 200 hours' work is only a bit higher than it was in the mid-1930s.

*W. Michael Cox and Richard Alm, "Time Well Spent," *1997 Annual Report of the Federal Reserve Bank of Dallas.*

services in 1995, the BLS figures out how much that family would have had to spend. It then comes up with an index number for 1995. In fact, it does this every month.

In 1996 a commission headed by Michael Boskin (who had been the chief economic advisor to President George Bush) told Congress that the CPI overstated inflation by 1.1 percent. In response, statisticians at the Bureau of Labor Statistics did a major overhaul of the CPI, resulting in a lowering of the annual rate of inflation by about 0.5 percent.

The consumer price index tends to overstate the actual rate of inflation by failing to account completely for gains in the quality of the goods and services that people buy as well as improvements in technology. Back in 1987, when there were personal computers in just 18 percent of all American households, you would have paid a lot more for one than you would have paid 14 years later. By 2001, when there were personal computers in more than 60 percent of all households, you could have bought one with much greater capabilities for the same money. But the CPI utterly fails to take into account such improvements in product quality. In the accompanying box, we consider an alternate cost of living measure. (See "The Declining *Real* Cost of Living.")

Suppose that in 2002 the CPI is recalculated so that the rate of inflation is adjusted downward by 1 percent. Because Social Security benefits are raised by the same percent that the CPI rises, the average Social Security recipient would get about $100 less that year. In Chapter 11 we'll look at the effects of an adjustment in the CPI on government spending and tax receipts.

Anticipated and Unanticipated Inflation: Who Is Hurt by Inflation and Who Is Helped?

Why farmers like inflation

Creditors have better memories than debtors.
    —James Howell, 1659

Traditionally, inflation has hurt creditors and helped debtors. Throughout our history, the farmers have been debtors. During times of deflation or stable prices, the farmers' cries of anguish are heard loud and clear all the way to Washington; but during times of inflation, there is scarcely a peep out of them.

It is easy to see why. Suppose a farmer borrows $100, which he agrees to repay in one year along with 4 percent interest ($4). In one year he pays back $104. But what if, during the year, prices double? The money he pays back is worth much less than the money he borrowed.

Let's say that when the farmer borrowed the money, wheat was selling at $2 a bushel. He would have been able to buy 50 bushels of wheat ($100/$2). But farmers don't buy wheat; they sell it. So one year later, this farmer harvests his wheat and pays back the loan. If the price level doubles, assume the price of wheat doubles. How much wheat would the farmer need to sell at $4 a bushel to pay off the $104 he owes? He would need to sell only 26 bushels ($104/$4).

This farmer, who is a debtor, benefits magnificently from unanticipated inflation because he has borrowed money worth some 50 bushels of wheat and pays back his loan—with interest—in money worth only 26 bushels of wheat. Debtors, in general, gain from unanticipated inflation because they repay their loans in inflated dollars.

Just as obviously, those hurt by unanticipated inflation are people who lend out the money—the creditors. We generally think of creditors as banks, but banks are really financial middlemen. The ultimate creditors, or lenders, are the people who put their money in banks, life insurance, or any other financial instrument paying a fixed rate of interest. And the biggest debtor and gainer from unanticipated inflation has been the U.S. government. The national debt, which now totals $5.5 trillion, would be a lot easier to pay off if there were a great deal of inflation.

> The issuers may have, and in the case of government paper, always have, a direct interest in lowering the value of the currency, because it is the medium in which their own debts are computed.
> —John Stuart Mill

Another group helped by unanticipated inflation is businessowners. Just as businesses suffer losses on their inventory during periods of deflation, during inflations they obtain inventory price windfalls. Between the time inventory is ordered and the time it is sold, prices have crept upward, swelling profits.

Those who are hurt by unanticipated inflation are people who live on fixed incomes, particularly retired people who depend on pensions (except Social Security) and those who hold long-term bonds, whether corporate or U.S. government bonds. Finally, people whose wages are fixed under long-term contracts and landlords who have granted long-term leases at fixed rent are hurt by unanticipated inflation. In other words, under unanticipated inflation, some people gain and others lose. In fact, the gains and losses are exactly equal.

Who is hurt by inflation?

When inflation is fully anticipated, there are no winners or losers. The interest rate takes into account the expected rate of inflation. Normally, without anticipated inflation, the interest rate would be around 3 or 4 percent. In 1980, and again in 1981, when the rate of inflation ran at close to 15 percent, the prime rate of interest (paid by top credit-rated corporations) soared over 20 percent.

> If all prices and incomes rose equally, no harm would be done to anyone. But the rise is not equal. Many lose and some gain.
> —Irving Fisher, 1920

For inflation to be fully anticipated and built into interest rates, people need to live with it for several years. Although the country had relatively high inflation for most of the 1970s, it was only in 1979 that the prime interest rate (which top credit-rated corporate borrowers pay) finally broke the 12 percent barrier. Today, however, unanticipated inflation is largely a thing of the past.

Creditors have learned to charge enough interest to take into account, or anticipate, the rate of inflation over the course of the loan. This is tacked onto the regular interest rate that the lender would charge had no inflation been expected.

We'll work out a few examples. If the real rate of interest (the rate that would be charged without inflation) were 5 percent, and there was an expected rate of inflation of 3 percent, then obviously the creditors would charge 8 percent.

Real rate of interest

If the real rate of interest were 4 percent and the expected inflation rate were 6 percent, how much would the nominal rate (the rate actually charged) be? Good! I know you said 10 percent. Thus, the real rate of interest plus the expected rate of inflation equals the nominal rate of interest.

Are you ready for a tricky one? If the nominal interest rate is 6 percent and the expected rate of inflation is 8 percent, how much is the real rate of interest? Have you found it yet? The real rate of interest is −2 percent. How can a real rate of interest be negative? It can be negative if the rate of inflation is greater than the rate of interest that you pay or receive (that is, the nominal rate of interest).

If the nominal interest rate accurately reflects the inflation rate, then the inflation has been fully anticipated and no one wins or loses. This is a good thing for the economy because it means no one is hurt and no one is forced out of business because of inflation.

But if the rate of inflation keeps growing—even if it is correctly anticipated—our economy will be in big trouble. In a hyperinflation there are ultimately only losers.

In recent years Social Security benefits have been indexed for inflation; that is, they have gone up by the same percentage as the consumer price index, protecting those who collect Social Security from inflation. Many wage-earners, too, are protected against inflation by cost-of-living adjustment clauses (called COLA agreements) in

Is a Dollar Worth Only 50 Cents Today?

What this country needs is a good five-cent nickel.
                        —Franklin Pierce Adams

A dollar is worth only 50 cents today. Is that true? If it is, then would you be willing to give me a dollar for every 50 cents I give you? Think about it.

What you really mean when you say that a dollar is worth only 50 cents today is that a dollar today buys only half as much (or 50 percent of) what it bought, say, 10 years ago.

When you lament that a dollar is worth only 50 cents today—or 25 cents, or even 10 cents for that matter—you need to specify which year's dollar you are comparing with today's dollar. For example, in 1948 you could buy a hot dog for a dime or see a movie for 50 cents. So, in terms of what a dollar bought in 1948, a dollar today is worth only about 8 cents.

their contracts.[8] One way or another, then, many sectors of our society have learned to protect themselves from at least the short-term ravages of inflation. (But how much is a dollar worth? See box, "Is a Dollar Worth Only 50 Cents Today?")

Theories of the Causes of Inflation

Excessive demand causes demand-pull inflation

Demand-Pull Inflation   When there is excessive demand for goods and services, we have demand-pull inflation. What is excessive? When people are willing and able to buy more output than our economy can produce. Something's gotta give. And what gives are prices.

Demand-pull inflation is often summed up as "too many dollars chasing too few goods." The problem is that we can't produce any more goods because our economy is already operating at full capacity.

What happens next if demand keeps rising? What if people have money in their pockets and the desire to spend it? Again, something's gotta give. Output can't rise any more. There's only one thing that can go up: prices.

This usually happens during wars. The government spends a lot of money on uniforms, tanks, planes, rifles, bullets, bombs, and missile systems. Private citizens want more consumer goods and services. Business firms are also bidding for resources to build more plant and equipment, expand their inventories, buy more raw materials, and hire more employees. So everyone's out there spending a lot of money to buy what they want.

Inflation is a form of taxation that can be imposed without legislation.
                        —Milton Friedman

It would not be unreasonable to ask, Just *where* did all this money come from? Milton Friedman, a Nobel laureate in economics and the world's leading exponent of monetary economics, has long been rounding up the usual suspects: the seven governors of the Federal Reserve System, which controls the money supply's rate of growth. Chapter 14 provides a detailed account of how the Board of Governors exercises that control. Demand-pull inflation is shown graphically in the Advanced Work box, "Demand-Pull Inflation and the Aggregate Supply Curve."

The wage-price spiral

Cost-Push Inflation   There are three variants of cost-push inflation. Most prominent is the wage-price spiral. Because wages constitute nearly two-thirds of the cost of doing business, whenever workers receive a significant wage increase, this increase is passed along to consumers in the form of higher prices. Higher prices raise everyone's cost of living, engendering further wage increases.

Imagine a 3 percent rise in the cost of living. Labor unions will negotiate for a 3 percent catch-up increase and a 3 percent increase on top of that for an anticipated

---

[8]About one worker in four is covered by a COLA. See Chapter 30 of *Economics* or Chapter 18 of *Microeconomics*.

Demand-Pull Inflation and the Aggregate Supply Curve

To help explain what happens when there's excess demand, we'll select another term from the economist's tool kit—the *aggregate supply curve*. The figure here shows a hypothetical aggregate supply curve. It has a horizontal curve that begins to slope upward to the right and eventually becomes completely vertical. Note that it becomes vertical at full employment.

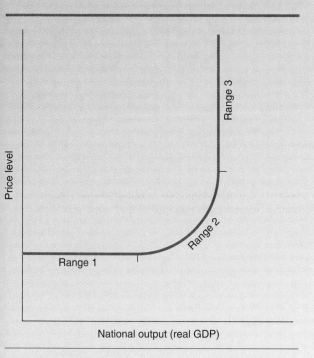

At very low levels of output—depression levels—it is easy to increase output without raising prices. After all, with high unemployment and idle plant and equipment those resources can be put back to work without raising costs much. For example, if a person who has been out of work for several months is offered a job at the going wage rate, she will jump at the chance to get back to work.

Look at the aggregate supply curve. In which range are we operating? Clearly we're in range 1.

As output expands, most of the idle resources will be back in production. Firms that need more plant and equipment will have to buy them. Employers will have to raise wages to induce new employees to work for them. In effect, then, businesses will have to bid for resources, and in doing so, they will bid up the prices of land labor, and capital. We are now in range 2 of the aggregate supply curve.

As their costs go up, business firms will be forced to raise their prices. We're moving closer and closer to full employment. It becomes increasingly difficult to get good help. New workers have to be lured away from other employers. There's only one way to do this—pay them more.

This pushes costs up still further until finally we've reached the full-employment level of output. Any further spending on goods and services will simply bid up prices without any corresponding increase in output. Welcome to range 3.

Our economy rarely operates in either range 1 or range 3. Both depressions and runaway inflations are relatively rare occurrences, though they *do* happen. The twin goals of macroeconomic policy are to avoid these extremes, or anything approaching them. But runaway inflations in particular are sometimes unavoidable. This happens when macroeconomic policy must subordinate itself to military necessity. During World War II, for example, the federal government bought up half the national output for military use. The only problem was that private citizens had plenty of money to spend and not enough output to spend it on. So civilians and the government had a bidding war for the country's limited resources. It was a classic case of too much money chasing too few goods.

We've actually gotten a bit ahead of ourselves. To fully understand the shape of the aggregate supply curve, we need to do some further analysis, which we'll put off until the next chapter.

cost-of-living increase *next* year. That's 6 percent. If every labor union gets a 6 percent increase, prices will undoubtedly rise not 3 percent but you guessed it—6 percent! In the next round of labor negotiations, the unions might want not just a 6 percent catch-up but 12 percent, to take care of next year as well.[9]

All of this can be described as the wage-price spiral. Regardless of who is to blame for its origin, once it gets started it spawns larger and larger wage and price increases. Round and round it goes, and where it stops nobody knows.

One man's wage rise is another man's price increase.
—Sir Harold Wilson, 1970

---

[9]Labor unions are covered in Chapter 30 of *Economics* and Chapter 18 of *Microeconomics*.

Graphing Demand-Pull and Cost-Push Inflation

Demand-pull inflation is set off by an increase in demand for goods and services without any increase in supply. The left graph shows how prices rise.

Cost-push inflation happens when production costs rise. Sellers can no longer supply the same output at current prices. This results in a decrease in supply. We see how prices go up in the right graph.

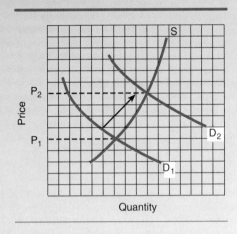

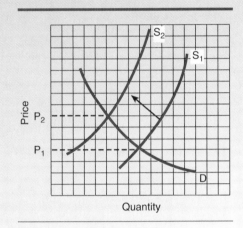

This variant of cost-push inflation may well explain a great deal of the inflation the country experienced through the early 1970s. However, in recent years the membership and power of U.S. labor unions have been sharply declining, so the wage-price spiral would serve today, at best, as a partial explanation for inflation.

Profit-push inflation

The second variant of cost-push inflation is profit-push inflation. Because just a handful of huge firms dominate many industries (for example, cigarettes, detergents, breakfast cereals, cars, and oil), these firms have the power to administer prices in those industries rather than accept the dictates of the market forces of supply and demand. To the degree that they are able to protect their profit margins by raising prices, these firms will respond to any rise in costs by passing them on to their customers.

Supply-side cost shocks

Finally, we have supply-side cost shocks, most prominently the oil price shocks of 1973–74 and 1979. When the OPEC nations quadrupled the price of oil in the fall of 1973, they touched off not just a major recession but also a severe inflation. When the price of oil rises, the cost of making many other things rises as well, for example, electricity, fertilizer, gasoline, heating oil, and long-distance freight carriage. And as we've seen again and again, cost increases are quickly translated into price increases. Cost-push inflation is shown graphically in the Advanced Work box "Graphing Demand-Pull and Cost-Push Inflation."

Inflation as a Psychological Process

Inflation takes on a life of its own.

Have you noticed that once inflation gets under way, the initial cause is of little consequence because the process takes on a life of its own? To come to grips with inflation, we must get at its roots. We have already discussed the psychology of inflation. If people believe prices will rise, they will act in a way that keeps them rising. The only way to curb inflation is to counter inflationary psychology.

Various things can set off an inflationary spiral—wars, huge federal budget deficits, large increases in the money supply, sudden increases in the price of oil—but once the spiral begins, inflationary psychology takes over.

When prices have been jolted upward, the original cause no longer matters; other forces are activated. Labor unions seek catch-up wage increases. Businesspeople raise their prices to keep up with costs—primarily wage increases. Consumers with money in their pockets spend it before prices rise further.

To stop inflation, then, we need to convince workers, businesspeople, and consumers that prices will stop rising. If we can do that, prices *will* stop rising.

Once we attain a period of price stability, the psychology of inflation will be destroyed. We will enjoy that stability as long as we can avoid triggering another round of inflation. In the early 1960s we attained such a period of stability, but then came the Vietnam War and its attendant federal budget deficits. Again in the mid-1980s we had a very low rate of inflation, but continuing deficits and rapid monetary growth may have rekindled the inflationary fires.

To break the back of the inflationary psychology is to bring down the rate of inflation for a sufficiently long period of time for people actually to expect price stability to continue. This has happened in the recent past only after successive recessions have wrung inflation out of the economy. To date, this has been the only cure we've come up with, and obviously it's a cure with some unpleasant side effects, particularly for those who lose their jobs during these recessions. After we examine creeping inflation and hyperinflation, we'll return to the problem of unemployment.

Breaking the back of the inflationary psychology

Creeping Inflation and Hyperinflation

Because *inflation* is a relative term, what may be considered creeping inflation in one country would be hyperinflation in another. Moreover, what might have been called creeping inflation in one particular country 10 years ago might now be considered hyperinflation in that same country.

Creeping inflation in one country would be hyperinflation in another.

For example, when the United States suffered from double-digit inflation in the mid-1970s and again in the late 70s and early 80s, a rate of 6 or 7 percent would have been welcomed as creeping inflation. But by the mid-1980s, some people would have considered anything above 4 percent to be hyperinflation.

Let's take an annual rate of increase in the consumer price index of 1 or 2 percent as something that virtually everyone would agree is creeping inflation. Very few people would be alarmed by this price-level increase. Businesspeople would generally like it because it would swell profits and basically be good for business. And as we have seen, many wage-earners and all Social Security recipients are protected from inflation by cost-of-living increases tied to the consumer price index.

But once we cross the line between creeping inflation and hyperinflation—which keeps shifting—we run into trouble. It becomes increasingly difficult to conduct normal economic affairs. Prices are raised constantly. It becomes impossible to enter into long-term contracts. No one is sure what the government might do.

Having a little inflation is like being a little pregnant.
—Leon Henderson

Prices serve as a signal system for business firms. If prices are rising, business firms will produce more goods and services. But what if costs are rising faster?

Suppose Nucor Steel agrees to supply General Motors with 50,000 tons of steel at $300 a ton. Suddenly Nucor's costs rise by 50 percent. Would GM go along with a $150 increase, raising the price from $300 to $450 a ton? Would you? Not if you had signed a contract calling for only $300 a ton.

Meanwhile, the government—meaning Congress, the president, and the Federal Reserve Board[10]—may decide to act precipitously. On August 15, 1971, President Nixon suddenly announced the imposition of wage and price controls—based on a law he had been saying he would never use. In October 1979 the Federal Reserve Board suddenly stopped monetary growth, sending interest rates through the roof and touching off a sharp recession.

---

[10]Technically, the Federal Reserve Board is not part of the government. We'll consider its role in regulating the rate of growth of our money supply in Chapter 14.

The German inflation

Hungary's pengö provides an
example of inflation

The classic hyperinflation took place in Germany after World War I. You may think that double-digit inflation (10 percent or more per year) is hyperinflation, but in Germany prices rose 10 percent an hour! The German government had to print larger and larger denominations—100-mark notes, then 1,000-mark notes, and, eventually, 1-million-mark notes. The smaller denominations became worthless; parents gave them to children as play money.

The German inflation eventually led to a complete economic breakdown, helped touch off a worldwide depression, and paved the way for a new chancellor named Adolf Hitler. No wonder the Germans get nervous whenever their inflation rate begins to inch up.

Another classic example is what happened in Hungary during and after World War II. Before the war, if you went into a store with a pengö, you had some money in your pocket. In those days a pengö was a pengö. But by August 1946, you needed 828 octillion pengös—that's 828 followed by 27 zeros—to buy what one pengö bought before the war.

When inflation really gets out of hand, people begin to refuse to accept money as a means of payment. Society is reduced to a state of barter, making it extremely difficult for the economy to function. If you don't have what I want or I don't have what you want, we can't do business.

When there is *any* inflation, even a creeping inflation of just 1 or 2 percent a year, people often worry that the rate will keep increasing until we have a runaway inflation. Does this always happen? The answer is a definite no. However, there's always the chance that things may get out of control. Like fire, a little inflation is not bad at all, but if it gets out of control, we'll be in big trouble.

Conclusion

One thing the economy has rarely been able to attain simultaneously is a low unemployment rate and stable prices. A British economist, A. W. Phillips, even had a curve named after him illustrating that there is a trade-off between price stability and low unemployment.

The misery index

As Phillips showed, in the 1950s and 1960s we attained price stability at the cost of higher unemployment and vice versa. In the 1970s, though, we had high unemployment *and* rapidly rising prices. During the presidential campaign of 1976, Jimmy Carter castigated President Gerald Ford with his "misery index," which was the inflation rate and the unemployment rate combined.[11] Anything over 10 was unacceptable, according to Carter.

In 1980 Ronald Reagan resurrected the misery index for the voters, reminding them that it had gone from 10, when President Carter took office, all the way to 20.

Although the misery index has obvious political uses, it also provides us with a snapshot view of our economic performance over the last four decades. From Figure 8 we can gauge just how stable our economy has been during this period. Which were the best two extended periods? I would say from the late 1950s through the late 1960s and since 1993. During both stretches our misery index stayed below 10.

Whatever else might be said about Bill Clinton's two terms as president (January 1993–January 2001), he enjoyed great popularity and was overwhelmingly reelected in 1996. Why was he all that popular? We need look no further than Figure 7. Both inflation and unemployment were not only quite low during his presidency, but the misery index declined almost steadily during both his terms. Evidently his political advisors got it right. Back in 1992 they posted a sign in their campaign headquarters. It said: "It's the economy, stupid." For eight years they stayed right on message.

It would certainly be hard to have a lower misery index then we have had in recent years. We'll begin to examine macroeconomic policy in Chapter 12 to learn how things

---

[11]During the 1960s Arthur Okun, while he was President Lyndon Johnson's Chairman of the Council of Economic Advisors, coined the term *economic discomfort index,* which Jimmy Carter renamed the *misery index.*

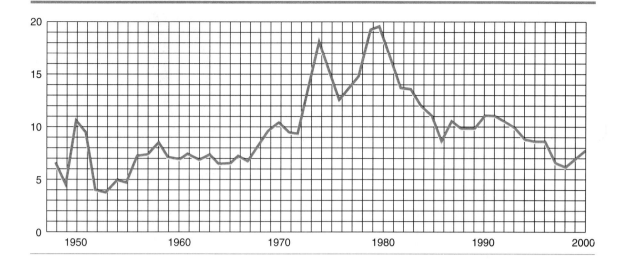

Figure 8

The Misery Index, 1948–2000

You'll note that this combined rate of unemployment and inflation rose to a peak in 1979 and has declined substantially since then.

Source: Economic Report of the President, 2001.

are supposed to work and why they sometimes don't. But first I'll try to tie things together a bit in the next chapter when we look at equilibrium GDP.

Questions for Further Thought and Discussion

1. Why is a high rate of inflation bad for the economy?

2. Right now, our economy is going through what phase of the business cycle? How do you know this?

3. Explain the difference between deflation and disinflation.

4. Being unemployed means different things to different people. Illustrate this by making up examples of three different unemployed people.

5. How would you improve upon the way the Bureau of Labor Statistics computes the unemployment rate?

6. How much is our misery index right now? How did you compute it?

7. Lev Trotski is laid off. How does he make ends meet until he finds another job?

8. If we succeeded in setting up a computer-based national job bank with listings of virtually every job opening, what type of unemployment would this nearly eliminate? Explain how this would happen.

9. Explain why cigarette excise taxes are regressive.

10. Explain how the GDP gap can be equated to an opportunity cost for the whole economy in terms of output.

W_orkbook_ for Chapter 10

Name _____ Date _____

Multiple-Choice Questions

Circle the letter that corresponds to the best answer.

1. If the CPI rose from 160.5 in 1998 to 168.7 in 1999 to 173.4 in 2000, this would be an example of _____.

   a) deflation

   b) disinflation

   c) inflation

2. Disinflation generally occurs during _____.

   a) recessions   c) periods of hyperinflation

   b) economic booms   d) times of deflation

3. In the three-phase business cycle, the prosperity phase is always followed immediately by _____.

   a) recovery   c) depression

   b) the trough   d) recession

4. If our economy is at full employment, the cyclical rate of unemployment would be _____.

   a) 0   c) 5 percent

   b) 2 percent   d) impossible to find

5. A business cycle forecasting method that tries to explain the entire economic process is _____.

   a) endogenous   c) barometric

   b) exogenous   d) analytic

6. If the CPI rose from 100 to 500, the price level rose by _____.

   a) 100 percent   d) 400 percent

   b) 200 percent   e) 500 percent

   c) 300 percent

7. *Prosperity Lost,* a book by _____, recounted scores of instances of structural unemployment.

   a) Joseph Schumpeter   d) Milton Friedman

   b) William Stanley Jevons e) Alfred Smith

   c) Philip Mattera

8. If there are 90 million people employed, 10 million unemployed, 5 million collecting unemployment insurance, and 5 million discouraged workers, there are _____ in the labor force.

   a) 90 million   d) 105 million

   b) 95 million   e) 110 million

   c) 100 million

9. During the 1970s, we experienced _____.

   a) high inflation and high unemployment

   b) low inflation and low unemployment

   c) high inflation and low unemployment

   d) low inflation and high unemployment

10. The misery index was highest in which of these years?

    a) 1989   d) 1977

    b) 1986   e) 1967

    c) 1980

11. The last time we had full employment was in _____.

    a) 1945   c) 1969

    b) 1957   d) the current year

12. We have business cycles of _____.

    a) the same length and amplitude

    b) the same length but different amplitudes

    c) the same amplitude but different lengths

    d) different lengths and amplitudes

13. During business cycles _____.

    a) troughs are followed by recessions

    b) troughs are followed by peaks

    c) peaks are followed by troughs

    d) peaks are followed by recessions

14. The second part of the expansion phase of the cycle is _____.

    a) recovery   c) recession

    b) prosperity   d) depression

15. An example of an exogenous business cycle theory would be _____.
    a) overinvestment   c) money
    b) inventory   d) war

16. The accelerator principle is a variant of the _____ theory.
    a) monetary   c) psychological
    b) innovations   d) overinvestment

17. The GDP gap is found by _____.
    a) subtracting actual GDP from potential GDP
    b) subtracting potential GDP from actual GDP
    c) adding potential GDP and actual GDP
    d) none of the above

18. When the unemployment rate rises, the GDP gap _____.
    a) will get wider
    b) will get narrower
    c) will remain the same
    d) none of the above is correct

19. The unemployment rate is computed by the _____.
    a) nation's unemployment insurance offices
    b) Bureau of Labor Statistics
    c) Department of Commerce
    d) Office of Management and Budget

20. If the number of unemployed stays the same and the number of people in the labor force rises, _____.
    a) the unemployment rate will rise
    b) the unemployment rate will fall
    c) the unemployment rate will stay the same
    d) there is not enough information to determine what will happen to the unemployment rate

21. Which statement is true?
    a) Both liberals and conservatives feel that the official unemployment rate is too high.
    b) Both liberals and conservatives feel that the official unemployment rate is too low.
    c) The liberals believe that the official unemployment rate is too high, and the conservatives feel that it is too low.
    d) The conservatives feel that the official unemployment rate is too high, and the liberals feel that it is too low.

22. Greater participation by young people in the labor force _____.
    a) tends to push the unemployment rate up
    b) tends to push the unemployment rate down
    c) has no effect on the unemployment rate
    d) has an unknown effect on the unemployment rate

23. Which statement is false?
    a) Over the last two decades there has been an upward drift in the unemployment rate.
    b) The unemployment rate for blacks is about twice that for whites.
    c) The official unemployment rate includes "discouraged" workers.
    d) None of the above is false.

Answer questions 24 through 29 by using one of these three choices:
    a) frictional unemployment
    b) structural unemployment
    c) cyclical unemployment

24. An autoworker who is still out of work two years after her plant closed is an example of _____.

25. A homemaker returning to the labor market after an absence of 10 years and looking for work is an example of _____.

26. A blue-collar worker who is laid off until business picks up again is an example of _____.

27. People who are "between jobs" are examples of _____.

28. A person in his mid-50s whose skills have become obsolete would be an example of _____.

29. When the unemployment rate goes above 5 percent, anything above that 5 percent level is _____.

30. An example of deflation since the base year would be a CPI in the current year of
    a) 90   b) 100   c) 110   d) 200

31. Inflation generally occurs _____.
    a) during wartime   c) during recessions
    b) before wars   d) during peacetime

32. The period of greatest price stability was _____.
    a) 1950–56   c) 1968–76
    b) 1958–64   d) 1976–82

33. Traditionally, those hurt by inflation have been _____
    _____.
    a) creditors and people on fixed incomes
    b) debtors and people on fixed incomes
    c) debtors and creditors

34. Farmers have generally been _____ by
    inflation.
    a) hurt
    b) helped
    c) neither helped nor hurt

35. Creditors generally do better when inflation is ____.
    a) anticipated
    b) unanticipated
    c) neither anticipated nor unanticipated

36. Businesspeople generally like a little _____
    but dislike a little _____.
    a) inflation, deflation
    b) deflation, inflation

37. Inflationary recessions first occurred in the _____.
    a) 1950s   c) 1970s
    b) 1960s   d) 1980s

Fill-In Questions

1. The worst recession since World War II began in
   _____.

2. Stagflation is a contraction of the words _____
   and _____.

3. To find the number of people in the labor force we
   need to add the _____ and the _____.

4. To find the unemployment rate we need to divide the
   _____ by the _____.

5. A person who is functionally illiterate faces long
   periods of _____ unemployment.

6. When the overall unemployment rate is 6.5 percent,
   the cyclical unemployment rate is _____.

7. The upper turning point of a business cycle is called
   the _____.

8. In the year _____ the OPEC nations
   quadrupled the price of oil.

9. The low point of a business cycle is the _____;
   _____ the high point is the _____.

10. Theories that place the cause of business cycles
    within the economy rather than outside are known as
    _____ theories.

11. According to the inventory theory of the business
    cycle, a recession is set off when retailers _____.

12. The monetary theory of the business cycle
    hypothesizes that recessions are set off when
    _____ and recoveries begin when the
    monetary authorities _____.

13. The acceleration principle requires sales to keep
    increasing at the _____ to prevent
    investment from _____.

14. Liberals say the unemployment rate is actually _____
    _____ than the BLS says it is;
    conservatives say it is really _____.

15. Between the mid-1970s and the mid-1980s, our
    unemployment rate never dipped below _____
    percent.

16. The unemployment rate for blacks is about _____
    times the white unemployment rate.

17. The misery index is found by adding the _____
    _____ and the _____.

18. When the unemployment rate declines, the GDP gap
    _____.

19. To be eligible for unemployment insurance, you need
    to have worked at least _____ or _____.

20. During a very severe recession when more than 11 percent of the labor force is out of work, most of the unemployment is _____ unemployment.

21. In 1973 the OPEC nations _____ the price of oil.

22. According to A. W. Phillips, there is a trade-off between _____ and _____.

23. If the consumer price index rises from 150 to 180, the cost of living rose by _____ percent.

24. Once inflation is under way, an _____ takes over.

25. To stop inflation, we need to convince people that _____.

Problems

1. If the unemployment rate is 7 percent, how much is cyclical unemployment?

2. Compute the unemployment rate given the following information: 8 million unemployed, 117 million employed.

3. Given the following information, how many people are in the labor force? 3 million people are collecting unemployment insurance; 7 million people are officially unemployed; 2 million people are discouraged workers; and 110 million people are employed.

4. How much would the nominal interest rate be if the real rate of interest were 6 percent and the expected rate of inflation were 7 percent?

5. How much would the real rate of interest be if the nominal interest rate were 12 percent and the expected rate of inflation were 4 percent?

6. If the CPI is currently 178.9, by what percentage did prices rise since the base year?

7. If the CPI rose from 200 in 1991 to 240 in 1997, by what percentage did prices increase?

8. If the rate of inflation is 5 percent, the prime rate of interest is 6 percent, and the unemployment rate is 7 percent, how much is the misery index?

9. If actual GDP is 4,400 and potential GDP is 4,600, state the GDP gap in dollars.

10. Label the graph in Figure 1 with respect to the three phases of the business cycle and the cycle turning points.

Figure 1

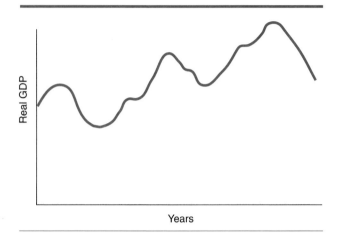

11. Answer these questions, given the following information: a) How many people are in the labor force? b) What is the unemployment rate? Employed: 90 million; discouraged workers: 4 million; unemployed: 10 million; people collecting unemployment insurance: 8 million.

12. a) If the CPI fell from 180 to 150, by what percentage did the price level fall? b) If the CPI rose from 150 to 180, by what percentage did the price level rise?

13. In which year was the misery index (a) the highest? (b) the lowest?

Year	Unemployment Rate (percent)	Inflation rate (percent)
1948	8.0	3.0
1949	5.9	−2.1
1950	5.3	5.9
1951	3.3	6.0
1952	3.0	0.8
1953	2.9	0.7
1954	5.5	−0.7
1955	4.4	0.4
1956	4.1	3.0
1957	4.3	2.9
1958	6.8	1.8
1959	5.5	1.7
1960	5.5	1.4
1961	6.7	0.7

Chapter 11

Classical and Keynesian Economics

This chapter is divided into three parts: (1) the classical economic system, (2) the Keynesian critique of the classical system, and (3) the Keynesian system. The basic difference between Keynes and the classicals is whether our economy tends toward full employment.

CHAPTER OBJECTIVES

In this chapter we shall take up:

- Say's law.
- Classical equilibrium
- Real balance, interest rate, and foreign purchases effects.
- Aggregate demand.
- Aggregate supply in the long run and short run.

- The Keynesian critique of the classical system.
- Equilibrium at varying price levels.
- Disequilibrium and equilibrium.
- Keynesian policy prescriptions.

Jean Baptiste Say, French economist and entrepreneur (Historical Pictures/Stock Montage)

Part I: The Classical Economic System

The centerpiece of classical economics is Say's law. Named for Jean Baptiste Say, a late-18th-century (that means the late 1700s) French economist, the law stated, "*Supply creates its own demand.*" Think about it. Somehow what we produce—supply—all gets sold.

A few years later the great English economist David Ricardo elaborated on Say's law:

> No man produces but with a view to consume or sell, and he never sells but with an intention to purchase some other commodity which may be immediately useful to him or which may contribute to future production. By producing, then, he necessarily

Say's Law

becomes either the consumer of his own goods, or the purchaser and consumer of the goods of some other person.[1]

People who produce things are paid. What do they do with this money? They spend it. On what? On what *other* people produce.

We can illustrate Say's law using the production figures in Table 1. Let's look at Table 1. Everyone eats tomatoes, bread, and butter, and wears Mao jackets and wooden shoes. Joe sells eight bushels of tomatoes, keeping two for his own use. Sally wears one of her Mao jackets and sells the other four. And so forth.

What do they do with the proceeds from their sales? They use them to buy what they need from each of the others. Joe, for example, buys a Mao jacket from Sally, four loaves of bread from Mike, two pounds of butter from Bill (they all like to put a lot of butter on their bread), and a pair of wooden shoes from Alice.

"Why does anybody work?" asked Say. Because a person wants money with which to buy things. Why do *you* work?

As long as everyone spends everything that he or she earns, we're OK. But we begin having problems when people start saving part of their incomes.

Basically, producers need to sell everything they produce. If some people save, then not everything produced will be sold. In a world with large companies instead of self-employed producers, some workers must be laid off when demand for production falls. In fact, as unemployment mounts, demand falls still further, necessitating further cutbacks in production and employment.

The villain of the piece is clearly saving. If only people would spend their entire incomes, we'd never have unemployment. But people do save, and saving is crucial to economic growth. Without saving we could not have investment—the production of plant, equipment, and inventory.[2]

Think of production as consisting of two products: consumer goods and investment goods (for now, we're ignoring government goods). People will buy consumer goods; the money spent on such goods is designated by the letter C. Money spent by businesses on investment goods is designated by the letter I.

If we think of GDP as total spending, then GDP would be C + I. Once this money is spent, other people receive it as income. And what do they do with their income? They spend some of it and save the rest.

If we think of GDP as income received, that money will either be spent on consumer goods, C, or saved, which we'll designate by the letter S. If we put all this together, we have two equations:

$$GDP = C + I$$

$$GDP = C + S$$

TABLE 1	Production in a Five-Person Economy
Joe	10 bushels of tomatoes
Sally	5 Mao jackets
Mike	20 loaves of bread
Bill	10 pounds of butter
Alice	5 pairs of wooden shoes

Sidebar quotes:

Everyone lives by selling something.
—Robert Louis Stevenson

One person's price is another person's income.
—President Calvin Coolidge

"Why does anybody work?"

Each of us puts in what he has at one point of the circle of exchange and takes out what he wants at another.
—P. H. Wicksteed, March 1914

$GDP = C + I$

$GDP = C + S$

---

[1]David Ricardo, *The Principles of Political Economy and Taxation* (Burr Ridge, IL: Richard D. Irwin, 1963), p. 166.

[2]In this chapter we're ignoring investment in residential housing and considering only business investment.

These two equations can be simplified to one short equation. First, because things equal to the same thing are equal to each other:

$$C + I = C + S$$

This step is justified because $C + I$ and $C + S$ are both equal to GDP. Therefore, they are equal to each other.

Next, we can subtract the same thing from both sides of an equation. In this case we are subtracting C:

$$C + I = C + S$$

$$I = S$$

Going back to Say's law, we can see that it holds up, at least in accordance with classical analysis. Supply does create its own demand. The economy produces a supply of consumer goods and investment goods. The people who produce these goods spend part of their incomes on consumer goods and save the rest. Their savings are borrowed by investors who spend this money on investment goods. The bottom line is that everything the economy produces is purchased.

This is a perfect economic system. Everything produced is sold. Everyone who wants to work can find a job. There will never be any serious economic downturns, so there is no need for the government to intervene to set things right.

Supply and Demand Revisited

We're going to be doing a considerable amount of supply and demand analysis, which you may remember dimly from Chapter 3. Rather than ask you to turn back to that chapter, I've drawn another supply and demand graph for you in Figure 1.

I'd like you to observe two things: equilibrium price and equilibrium quantity. How much is the equilibrium price? Good. And the equilibrium quantity? Good—you got that right, too. You followed the horizontal dotted line to a price of about $7.20 and the vertical dotted line to a quantity of 6.

Incidentally, we call the price that clears the market *equilibrium price* and the quantity purchased and sold *equilibrium quantity*. At the equilibrium price the quantity that buyers wish to purchase is equal to the quantity that sellers wish to sell.

Now let's see how the classical economists applied the law of supply and demand to help prove Say's law and, more specifically, to prove that $I = S$ (Investment = Saving). This is done in Figure 2, which graphs the demand for investment funds and the supply of savings.

(margin notes)

$C + I = C + S$
$I = S$

Equilibrium price and quantity

Figure 1

Demand and Supply Curves

The curves cross at a price of $7.20 and a quantity of 6.

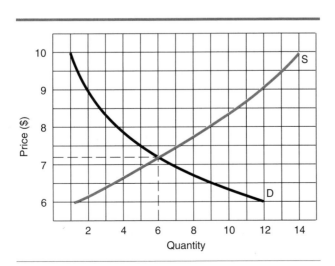

Figure 2

The Loanable Funds Market

The demand and supply curves cross at an interest rate of 15 percent.

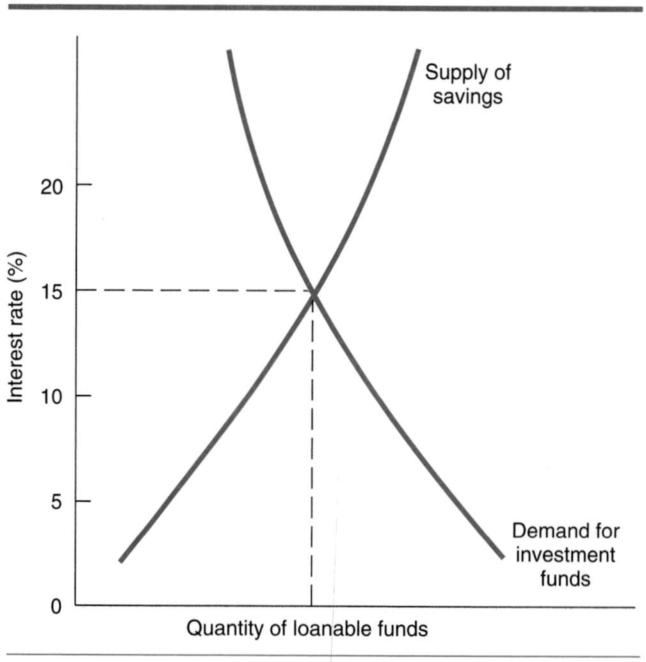

Figure 3

Market for Hypothetical Product

If the quantity supplied is greater than the quantity demanded at a certain price (in this case, $8), the price will fall to the equilibrium level ($6), at which quantity demanded is equal to quantity supplied.

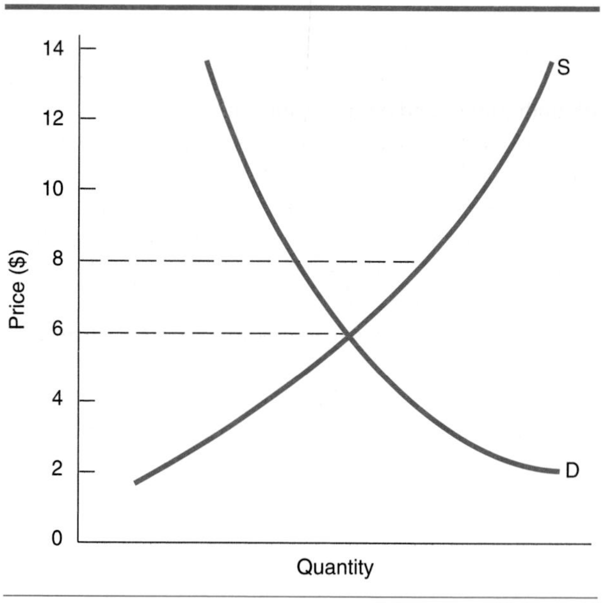

What if savings and investment were not equal? For instance, if savings were greater than investment, there would be unemployment. Not everything being produced would be purchased.

There's nothing to worry about, according to the classical economists. And they proved this by means of the two curves in Figure 2. If savings were greater than investment, the interest rate would fall. Why? Because some savers would be willing to lend at lower interest rates and some investors would be induced to borrow at lower interest rates.

Savings and investment will be equal.

The classical economists had a fallback position. Even if lower interest rates did not eliminate the surplus of savings relative to investment, price flexibility would bring about equilibrium between saving and investing. Business firms, unable to sell their entire output, would simply lower prices. And then people would buy everything produced.

Prices and wages will fall to bring about equilibrium between saving and investing.

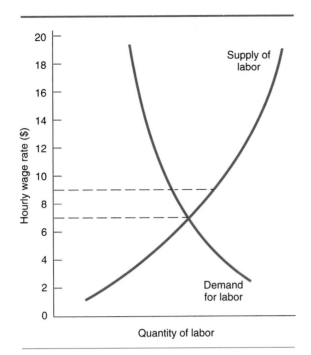

Figure 4

Hypothetical Labor Market

If the wage rate is set too high ($9 an hour), the quantity of labor supplied exceeds the quantity of labor demanded. The wage rate falls to the equilibrium level of $7; at that wage rate the quantity of labor demanded equals the quantity supplied.

One might ask whether business firms could make a profit if prices were reduced. Yes, answered the classical economists, if resource prices—particularly wages—were also reduced. Although output and employment might decline initially, they would move back up again once prices and wages fell. At lower prices people would buy more, and at lower wages employers would hire more.

Falling prices and falling wage rates can also be illustrated by a supply and demand graph. Look at Figure 3. If sellers of a particular good are not selling all they wish to sell *at the price,* some of them will lower their price. In Figure 3 the price falls from $8 to $6, which happens to be the equilibrium price.

Exactly the same thing happens in the labor market (see Figure 4). At a wage rate of $9 an hour, there are many unemployed workers. Some are willing to accept a lower wage rate. When the wage rate falls to $7 an hour, everyone who wants to work at that rate can find a job, and every employer willing to hire workers at that rate can find as many workers as she wants to hire.

The Classical Equilibrium: Aggregate Demand Equals Aggregate Supply

What exactly *is* equilibrium GDP? We've seen, on a micro level, that when quantity demanded equals quantity supplied, we're at equilibrium. Similarly, on a macro level, when aggregate demand equals aggregate supply, we're at equilibrium. At equilibrium there is a state of balance between opposing forces such that there is no tendency for change.

The classical economists believed our economy was either at, or tending toward, full employment. So at the classical equilibrium—the GDP at which aggregate demand was equal to aggregate supply—we were at full employment. And as long as aggregate demand and aggregate supply did not change, our economy would continue operating at full employment.

We've been weaving back and forth between macro and micro analysis. From here on it's going to be macro. We'll begin with the economy's aggregate demand curve, go on to the economy's aggregate long-run and short-run supply curves, and finally put these curves together to derive the economy's equilibrium GDP.

Our economy is either at or tending toward full employment.

The Aggregate Demand Curve

The aggregate demand curve shows that as the price level declines, the quantity of goods and services demanded rises.

The aggregate demand curve of Figure 5 depicts an inverse relationship between the price level and the quantity of goods and services demanded: as the price level declines, the quantity of goods and services demanded rises. Similarly, as the price level rises, the quantity of goods and services demanded declines. This relationship is illustrated by an aggregate demand curve that slopes downward to the right.

This is different from the aggregate demand curve in Figure 2 of Chapter 9. Why? Because in *that* graph, the price level was held constant. The C + I + G + Xn curve showed that as disposable income rose, there was a corresponding increase in the quantity demanded of goods and services, assuming no change in the price level.

Is it reasonable to assume constant prices? Instinctively, we would reject this assumption because in our lifetimes we have known almost nothing but inflation. Furthermore, as the economy approaches full employment, a certain amount of inflation is inevitable.

Definition of aggregate demand

What does this curve tell us? I'll begin by defining aggregate demand as *the total value of real GDP that all sectors of the economy are willing to purchase at various price levels.* You'll notice that as the price level declines, people are willing to purchase more and more output. Alternatively, as the price level rises, the quantity of output purchased goes down.

There are three reasons why the quantity of goods and services purchased declines as the price level increases.

There are three reasons why the quantity of goods and services purchased declines as the price level increases: (1) An increase in the price level reduces the wealth of people holding money, making them feel poorer and reducing their purchases; (2) the higher price level pushes up the interest rate, which leads to a reduction in the purchase of interest-sensitive goods, such as cars and houses; and (3) net exports decline as foreigners buy less from us and we buy more from them at the higher price level. The first of these reasons is called the real balance effect, the second is the interest rate effect, and the third is the foreign purchases effect. Let's consider each in turn.

(1) The Real Balance Effect   When the price level goes up, your purchasing power goes down. The money you have in the bank, your stocks and bonds, and all your other liquid assets shrink in terms of what they can buy. You *feel* poorer, so you'll tend to spend less.

The *real balance effect* is the influence of a change in your purchasing power on the quantity of real GDP that you are willing to buy. Here's how it works. Suppose you are holding $800 in money and your only other asset is $200 worth of shoes (you are a fan of Philippine former first lady Imelda Marcos, who managed to accumulate 3,000 pairs of shoes). Now, what if the prices of most goods and services fell, among them those of shoes. The $800 that you're holding now buys more goods than before. You've got a larger real balance.

Before prices fell, you were very happy holding 80 percent of your assets in the form of money ($800 of $1,000) and 20 percent in the form of shoes ($200 of $1,000). But now those shoes you're holding are worth less than $200 because their price has fallen, while your money is worth more. Let's say there was so much deflation that the purchasing power of your money doubled, to $1,600, while the value of your shoes fell to $100. Question: Wouldn't you like to take advantage of the price decrease to buy more shoes? Of course you would. And how many more dollars' worth of shoes would you buy if you wanted to keep 20 percent of your assets in the form of shoes (and 80 percent in the form of money)? Answer: Your total assets are now $1,700 ($1,600 in money and $100 in shoes), so you'd want to hold 20 percent of the $1,700, or $340, in shoes. In other words, you'd buy $240 worth of shoes.

Let's sum up. A decrease in the price level increases the quantity of real money. The larger the quantity of real money, the larger the quantity of goods and services demanded. Similarly, an increase in the price level decreases the quantity of real money. The smaller the quantity of real money, the smaller the quantity of goods and services demanded.

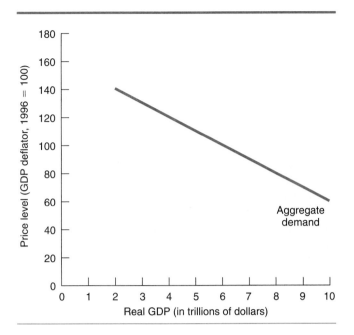

Figure 5

Aggregate Demand Curve (in trillions of dollars)

The level of aggregate demand varies inversely with the price level: As the price level declines, people are willing to purchase more and more output. Alternatively, as the price level rises, the quantity of output purchased goes down.

(2) The Interest Rate Effect   A rising price level pushes up interest rates, which in turn lower the consumption of certain goods and services and also lower investment in new plant and equipment. Let's look more closely at this two-step sequence.

First, during times of inflation, interest rates rise, because lenders need to protect themselves against the declining purchasing power of the dollar. If you lent someone $100 for one year and there was a 10 percent rate of inflation, you would need to be paid back $110 just to be able to buy what your original $100 would have purchased.

Second, certain goods and services are more sensitive to interest rate changes than others. Can you name some especially sensitive ones? Try auto purchases and home mortgages. Clearly, then, when interest rates rise, the consumption of certain goods and services falls, and when interest rates fall, their consumption rises.

Now let's see how a rising price level (which pushes up interest rates) affects investment spending. We saw in Chapter 6 that rising interest rates choke off investment projects that would have been carried out at lower rates. Some projects, especially in building construction, where interest is a major cost, are particularly sensitive to interest rate changes. So we know, then, that a rising price level pushes up interest rates and lowers both consumption and investment. Similarly, a declining price level, which pushed down interest rates, encourages consumption and investment. Clearly the interest rate effect can be very powerful.

(3) The Foreign Purchases Effect   When the price level in the United States rises relative to the price levels in other countries, what effect does this have on U.S. imports and exports? Because American goods become more expensive relative to foreign goods, our imports rise (foreign goods are cheaper) and our exports decline (American goods are more expensive).

In sum, when our price level increases, this tends to increase our imports and lower our exports. Thus, our net exports (exports minus imports) component of GDP declines. When the price level declines, the net exports component (and GDP) rises.

The Long-Run Aggregate Supply Curve

First I'll define aggregate supply as *the amount of real output, or real GDP, that will be made available by sellers at various price levels.* Next I'll show you what the long-run aggregate supply curve looks like. You'll note in Figure 6 that it's a vertical line.

Definition of aggregate supply

Figure 6

Long-Run Aggregate Supply
Curve (in trillions of dollars)

Why is this curve a vertical line?
The classical economists made two
assumptions: (1) In the long run,
the economy operates at full
employment; (2) in the long run,
output is independent of prices.

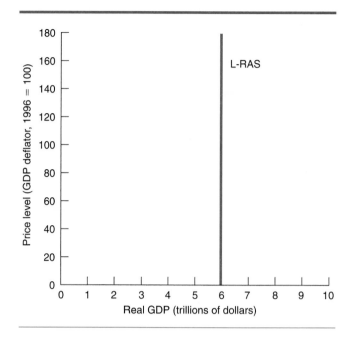

This curve is based on two assumptions of the classical economists. First, in the long run, the economy operates at full employment. (In Chapter 10 we decided that, because there would always be frictional and structural unemployment totaling about 5 percent of the labor force, a 5 percent unemployment rate meant the economy was operating at full employment.) Second, in the long run, output is independent of prices.

Ready for a little action? We're going to put the aggregate demand curve and the long-run aggregate supply curve together on one graph and see what happens. Figure 7 shows this.

The equilibrium full-employment level of real GDP

What happens is that we find two things: (1) the equilibrium full-employment level of real GDP and (2) the corresponding price level, which happens to be 100.

What does this *mean*? It means that in the long run our economy will produce the level of output that will provide jobs for everyone who wants to work (that is, the unemployment rate will be 5 percent). In other words, in the long run our economy will produce at full-employment GDP. And how much *is* full-employment GDP, according to Figure 7? It comes to exactly $6 trillion. One of the nice things about working with hypothetical numbers is that they come out so well rounded.

This is what the classical economists predicted and is completely consistent with Say's law: Supply creates its own demand. Our economy, then, will always be at full employment in the long run. But what about in the short run?

The Short-Run Aggregate Supply Curve

The economy may operate below full-employment GDP in the short run.

In the short run, according to the classical economists, some unemployment *is* possible. Some output *may* go unsold. And the economy *may* operate below full-employment GDP. Figure 8 shows all of this.

Why does the short-run aggregate supply curve sweep upward to the right? Because business firms will supply increasing amounts of output as prices rise. Why? Because wages, rent, and other production costs are set by contracts in the short run and don't increase immediately in response to rising prices. Your landlord can't come to you while your lease still has two years to go and tell you that he must raise your rent because *his* costs are going up. Your employees who are working under two- and three-year contracts can't ask you to renegotiate. (They can *ask* you to, but you probably won't.) And

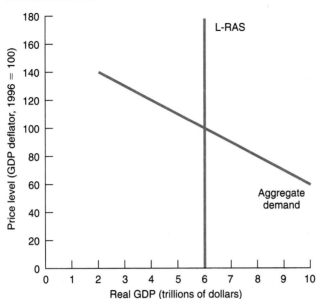

F*igure* 7

Aggregate Demand and Long-Run Aggregate Supply (in trillions of dollars)

The long-run equilibrium of real GDP is $6 trillion at a price level of 100.

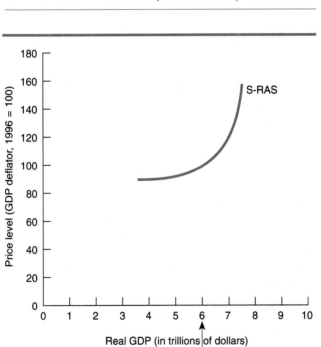

F*igure* 8

Short-Run Aggregate Supply Curve (in trillions of dollars)

Why does the short-run aggregate supply curve sweep upward to the right? Because business firms will supply increasing amounts of output as prices rise.

your suppliers may also have agreed contractually to send you their goods at set prices. So, in the short run, higher prices mean higher profit margins, which give business firms like yours an incentive to increase output.

As output continues to rise, land, labor, and capital become more expensive and less-efficient resources are pressed into service. To get homemakers to work, employers need to make wage rates attractive enough (and some even go to the expense of setting up child care facilities) to entice them back into the labor force. As output approaches full employment, antiquated machinery and less-productive facilities must be used. And so, as the full-employment level of GDP is approached, the short-run aggregate supply curve is becoming steeper and steeper. You'll notice that full-employment GDP is still $6 trillion, as in Figure 7.

As output rises, costs rise.

Beyond full employment

You'll also notice in Figure 8 that output continues to rise even after we've exceeded full-employment GDP. Is this *possible*? Can our real GDP ever exceed our full-employment GDP? Yes, it can. But only in the short run.

Do you remember the production possibilities curve back in Chapter 2? When the economy was operating on that curve, we were at full employment. Occasionally, however, we could exceed that output level and produce beyond the full-employment level. We also saw this near the beginning of the last chapter in Figure 4, when actual GDP exceeded potential GDP. How can we *do* this?

Let's extend the example of luring homemakers into the labor force with better pay. How about enticing full-time college students who are working part-time to give up their education (or perhaps switch to night school) and work full-time? Or how about persuading retired people, or those about to retire, to take full-time jobs? How would we do this? By paying attractive wage rates and providing whatever other incentives are necessary. We can also keep putting back into service aging or obsolete plant and equipment, and make use of marginal land as well.

Why, then, does the short-run aggregate supply curve eventually become vertical? Because there is a physical limit to the output capacity of the economy. There is just so much land, labor, and capital that can be put to work, and when that limit is reached, there is no way to increase production appreciably. During World War II, U.S. factories ran 24 hours a day, and millions of people worked 50 or 60 hours a week. But everyone simply could not have kept up this effort year after year. As Americans said at the time, "There's a war going on." Just in case someone hadn't noticed.

So, in the short run, we can push our output beyond the level of full-employment GDP and get our economy to operate beyond full employment. But this is only possible in the short run. In the long run, we're back at the long-run aggregate supply curve.

Figure 9 puts this all together for you. You see the point at which the short- and long-run aggregate supply curves intersect the aggregate demand curve? That's the long-run equilibrium level of GDP. At that point, the price level happens to be 100 and GDP is $6 trillion.

In the classical system, all the parts fit together neatly. The long-run aggregate supply curve, the short-run aggregate supply cost curve, and the aggregate demand curve come together at full employment. If there *is* some unemployment in the short run, it will automatically be eliminated as the economy returns to its long-run, full-employment equilibrium. And if there is more than full employment, this is again only a temporary phenomenon that will end as the level of economic activity returns to its full-employment level. In short, the economy can temporarily slide up and down its short-run aggregate supply curve, but it inevitably returns to its long-run equilibrium at full employment.

Do aggregate demand and aggregate supply remain constant? Of course not. Over time, as an economy grows, they grow, too. And during recessions, of course, they decline.

Part II: The Keynesian Critique of the Classical System

Our free enterprise system has rightly been compared to a gigantic computing machine capable of solving its own problems automatically. But anyone who has had some practical experience with large computers knows that they do break down and can't operate unattended.
—Wassily Leontief, March 1971

Until the Great Depression, classical economics was the dominant school of economic thought. Adam Smith, credited by many as the founder of classical economics, believed the government should intervene in economic affairs as little as possible. Indeed, laissez-faire economics was practiced down through the years until the time of Herbert Hoover, who kept predicting that prosperity was just around the corner. John Maynard Keynes finally proclaimed the end of the classical era when he advocated massive government intervention to bring an end to the Great Depression.

John Maynard Keynes, a prominent classically trained economist spent the first half of the 1930s writing a monumental critique of the classical system.[3] If supply creates its

---

[3] *The General Theory of Employment, Interest, and Money* is considered one of the most influential books of the 20th century.

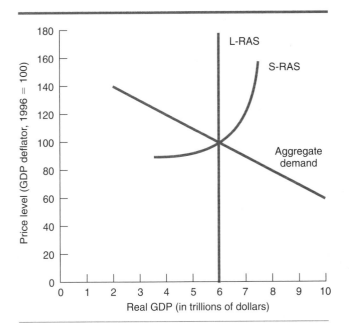

Figure 9
Aggregate Demand, Long-Run and Short-Run Aggregate Supply (in trillions of dollars)
The long-run aggregate supply curve, the short-run aggregate supply curve, and the aggregate demand come together at full employment.

own demand, he asked, why are we having a worldwide depression? Keynes set out to learn what went wrong and how to fix it.

Keynes posed this problem for the classical economists: What if saving and investment were not equal? For instance, if saving were greater than investment, there would be unemployment. Not everything being produced would be purchased.

Keynes asked, "What if saving and investment were not equal?"

You'll recall—at least I *hope* you will—that the classicals figured this was no problem. They just trotted out the graph in Figure 2, which showed that the interest rate would equilibrate savings and investment. If the quantity of savings exceeded the quantity of loanable funds demanded for investment purposes, the interest rate would simply fall. And it would keep falling until the quantity of savings and the demand for investment funds were equal.

Keynes disputed this view. Saving and investing are done by different people for different reasons. Most saving is done by individuals for big-ticket items, such as cars, stereo systems, and major appliances, as well as for houses or retirement. Investing is done by those who run business firms basically because they are trying to make a profit. They will borrow to invest only when there is a reasonably good profit outlook. Why sink a lot of money into plant and equipment when your factory and machines are half idle? Even when interest rates are low, business firms won't invest unless it is profitable for them to do so. This point was discussed at length toward the end of Chapter 6.

Keynes: Saving and investing are done by different people for different reasons.

Even *this* posed no major problem to the classical economists, because they assumed wages and prices were downwardly flexible. If there were unemployment, the unemployed would find jobs as wage rates fell. And, similarly, if sellers were stuck with unwanted inventory, they would simply lower their prices.

Keynes questioned whether wages and prices were downwardly flexible, even during a severe recession. In the worst recession since the Great Depression, the downturn of 1981–82, there were very few instances of price or wage declines even in the face of declining output and widespread unemployment. Studies of the behavior of highly concentrated industries indicate that prices are seldom lowered, while similar studies of large labor unions indicate that wage cuts (even as the only alternative to massive layoffs) are seldom accepted. Even if wages *were* lowered, added Keynes, this would lower workers' incomes, consequently lowering their spending on consumer goods.

All of this led Keynes to conclude that the economy was not always at, or tending toward, a full-employment equilibrium. Keynes believed three possible equilibriums existed—*below* full employment, *at* full employment, and *above* full employment. Using

We are not always at, or tending toward, full employment.

the same demand and supply analysis as the classicals, Keynes showed that full employment was hardly inevitable.

The Keynesian long-run aggregate supply curve was really a hybrid of the classical short-run and long-run aggregate supply curves. It is drawn in Figure 10.[4] At extremely low levels of real GDP, when output is at, say, $3 trillion, our economy is in a catastrophic depression. As the economy begins to recover, output can be raised to about $4.7 trillion without any increase in prices. Why? Because millions of unemployed workers would be happy to work for the prevailing wage, so wage rates would certainly not have to be raised to entice people back to work. Furthermore, businessowners would also be happy to sell additional output at existing prices. But as real GDP continues to rise above $4.7 trillion, costs begin to rise, and bottlenecks eventually develop in certain industries, making greater and greater price increases necessary. Eventually, of course, at a real GDP of $6 trillion, we are at full employment and cannot, in the long run, raise output above that level. (See the box, "The Ranges of the Aggregate Supply Curve.")

So, for all intents and purposes, the Keynesian and classical aggregate supply analyses are virtually identical. But they are completely at odds with respect to aggregate demand. Figure 11 shows three aggregate demand curves. AD_1 represents a very low level of aggregate demand, which, Keynes believed, was the basic problem during recessions and depressions. The AD_2 curve shows the same full-employment equilibrium shown in Figure 9. And finally, AD_3 represents excessive demand, which would cause inflation.

In the last chapter we talked about demand-pull inflation, which was described as "too much money chasing too few goods." Demand-pull inflation occurs in the intermediate range of the aggregate supply curve in the figure in the box "The Ranges of the Aggregate Supply Curve." Or, looking at Figure 11, start with an aggregate demand of AD_1 and imagine a series of higher and higher aggregate demand curves. At first we would have increases in real GDP without any price increases, but as aggregate demand moved closer to AD_2, we would eventually be able to keep pushing up real GDP only at the cost of some inflation. And as aggregate demand approached AD_2, we would be obtaining smaller and smaller increments of added output at the cost of larger and larger rises in the price level.

So we see that increases in aggregate demand will eventually lead to inflation. Applying this same analysis but moving in the opposite direction, we'll observe that decreasing aggregate demand leads to declining output and a decline in the rate of inflation. Starting at AD_2 and moving toward AD_1 in Figure 11, we see that real GDP is declining. As we noted toward the beginning of the last chapter, a decline in real GDP for two consecutive quarters is, by definition, a recession. And if continued decreases in aggregate demand pushed real GDP down still further, the recession would deepen and we might even sink into a depression.

Under this Keynesian analysis, we have three distinct possible equilibriums—below full employment, at full employment, and above full employment (with respect to prices, not output). Our economy, according to Keynes, does not necessarily tend toward full employment, as the classicals maintained.

Our economy, said Keynes, can get stuck at an equilibrium that is well below full employment:

> Indeed it seems capable of remaining in a chronic condition of subnormal activity for a considerable period without any marked tendency either toward recovery or toward complete collapse. Moreover, the evidence indicates that full, or even approximately full, employment is of rare and short-lived occurrence.[5]

The Keynesian and classical aggregate supply analyses are virtually identical.

John Maynard Keynes, British economist (The Bettmann Archives)

---

[4]The curve shown in Figure 10 is actually a slightly modified Keynesian aggregate supply curve. Keynes originally assumed prices would not rise at all until full employment was attained (when real GDP was $6 trillion), but we've allowed here for an accelerating rise in prices from a real GDP of about $4.7 trillion to one of $6 trillion.

[5]John Maynard Keynes, *The General Theory of Employment, Interest, and Money* (New York: Harcourt Brace Jovanovich, 1958), pp. 249–50.

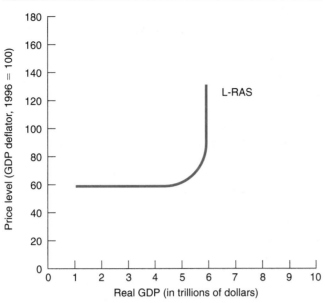

Figure 10

Modified Keynesian Aggregate
Supply Curve

As an economy works its way out
of a depression, output can be
raised without raising prices, so the
aggregate supply curve is flat.
However, as resources become
more fully employed and
bottlenecks develop, costs and
prices begin to rise. When this
happens the aggregate supply curve
begins to curve upward. When we
reach full employment (at a real
GDP of $6 trillion), output cannot
be raised any further.

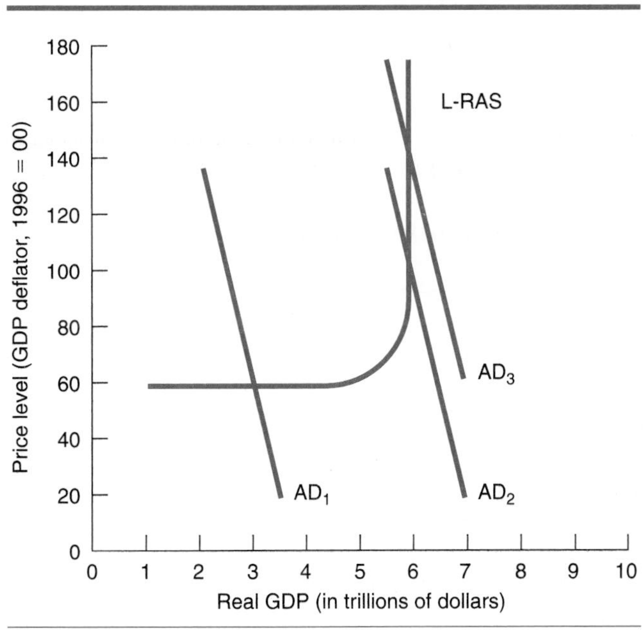

Figure 11

Three Aggregate Demand
Curves

AD₁ represents aggregate demand
during a recession or depression;
AD₂ crosses the long-run aggregate
supply curve at full employment;
and AD₃ represents excessive
demand.

What we need to do now is examine the Keynesian system in more detail, and then we'll be ready to consider what the government should (or should not) do to prevent or to moderate recessions and inflations.

Part III: The Keynesian System

The classical theory of equilibrium was great at explaining why we would be either at full employment or tending toward it. But it wasn't much good at explaining why, in the 1930s, the entire world was in a depression. We needed a new theory to explain what was happening, and we needed a policy prescription to bring us out of this depression. John Maynard Keynes provided both.

The classical equilibrium could not explain the Great Depression.

Keynes used the same aggregate demand and supply apparatus as the classicals had, but he came up with very different conclusions. The key to his analysis was the role of aggregate demand. According to Keynes, the equilibrium level of GDP was determined primarily by the volume of expenditures planned by consumers, business firms, governments, and foreigners. Keynes concentrated on aggregate demand because he viewed rapid declines in this variable as the villain in recessions and depressions. Changes in aggregate supply—changes brought about by new technology, more capital and labor, and greater productivity—came about slowly and could therefore be neglected in the short run.

What about Say's law that "Supply creates its own demand"? Keynes stood Say's law on its head. In fact, we can summarize Keynesian theory with the statement "Demand creates its own supply."

Keynes: Aggregate demand is our economy's prime mover.

Aggregate demand, said Keynes, is our economy's prime mover. Aggregate demand determines the level of output and employment. In other words, business firms produce only the quantity of goods and services they believe consumers, investors, governments, and foreigners will plan to buy.

The centerpiece of his model was the behavior of the consumer. If consumers decide to spend more of their incomes on goods and services—or less, for that matter—then the effect on output and employment can be substantial.

The Keynesian Aggregate Expenditure Model

Since the Keynesian model assumes a constant price level, we'll return to our original graphic presentation, which we began in Chapter 5. We'll be on familiar ground because we'll be using some of the concepts covered in Chapters 5 through 9. You already have quite a bit of Keynesian analysis under your belt without having known it.

The Ranges of the Aggregate Supply Curve

The curve shown in the figure to the right is just slightly more elaborate than that in Figure 10. Here we have the three ranges: Keynesian, intermediate, and classical. The Keynesian range is thus named because John Maynard Keynes was writing during the Great Depression. People were so anxious to find work that they were happy to take a job—virtually any job—at the going wage rate. Thus, business firms could easily expand output without encountering rising wages.

Would they raise prices? Not for quite a while. After suffering through a few years of extremely low sales, they would be grateful for more business, albeit at the same price.

As the economy expanded, bottlenecks would begin to develop, shortages of resources (especially labor) would occur here and there, and costs would begin to rise in some sectors and eventually spread throughout the economy. And then business firms would begin raising their prices as well.

Eventually the economy would reach the maximum output level, at which point the only give would be in the form of higher prices. This would be the classical range of the aggregate supply curve. Remember that the classical economists believed that full employment was our normal state of affairs.

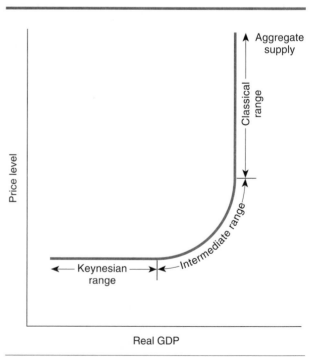

In a nutshell, here's what we're going to be working with: (1) the consumption function; (2) the saving function; and (3) investment, which will be held constant. To keep things as simple as possible, we are including only the private sector, so government purchases (and net exports, as well) are excluded from our model. This means changes in aggregate demand are brought about only by changes in C. And that's why I said the centerpiece of the Keynesian model was the behavior of the consumer.

The Consumption and Saving Functions   Here's the consumption function: *As income rises, consumption rises, but not as quickly.* It is a "fundamental psychological law," said Keynes "that men are disposed, as a rule and on the average, to increase their consumption as their income increases, but not by as much as the increase in their income."[6]

So what people do, then, as incomes rise, is spend some of this additional income and save the rest—which brings us to the saving function: *As income rises, saving rises, but not as quickly.* No surprises here.

Hypothetical consumption and savings functions appear in Figure 12. This should be old hat to you, since we covered the consumption and savings functions back in Chapter 5.

As disposable income rises, consumption and saving rise as well. Because disposable income rises as output, or real GDP, rises, we can say that as real GDP rises, consumption and saving rise. What about investment?

The Investment Sector   We learned in Chapter 6 that investment is the loose cannon on our economic deck. Keynes was well aware of this. What causes recessions in the Keynesian model? A decline in profit expectations, or, as Keynes puts it, in the marginal efficiency of capital, causes recessions. Although rising interest rates may play an important role in setting off recessions, Keynes stressed profit expectations:

Investment is unstable.

> But I suggest that a more typical, and often the predominant, explanation of the crisis is, not primarily a rise in the rate of interest, but a sudden collapse in the marginal efficiency of capital.[7]

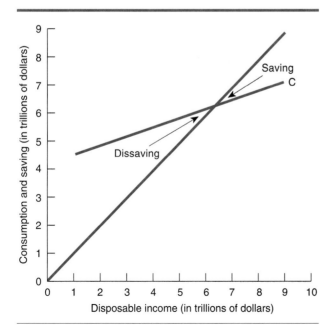

Figure 12

Disposable Income (in trillions of dollars)

When consumption is greater than disposable income, savings is negative; when disposable income is greater than consumption, savings is positive.

[6]*Ibid.*, p. 96.
[7]*Ibid.*, p. 315.

How do we allow for planned investment in the Keynesian model? We've seen that planned consumption rises with disposable income and real GDP. What about planned investment? It, too, probably varies directly with disposable income and real GDP. But we need to keep things simple. So we're going to come up with an arbitrary figure for planned investment—$500 billion—and keep it constant for all levels of real GDP.

We'll add just one line to our graph, the C + I line, and then we'll be able to wind up our analysis. We've done that in Figure 13. Assuming C + I constitutes aggregate demand, how much is equilibrium GDP? It comes out to $7 trillion.

And how much is investment? Also $500 billion.

So, at equilibrium GDP, all our ducks are in a line, so to speak. Aggregate demand, C + I (measured vertically), is equal to aggregate supply, or real GDP (measured on the horizontal scale). The level of output produced is exactly equal to the amount that buyers wish to purchase.

Also, saving and investment are equal. Saving is the vertical distance between the C line and the 45-degree line. The vertical distance between the C line and the C + I line is I. Therefore, the vertical distance between the C line and the 45-degree line must be equal to (actually, identical to) the vertical distance between the C line and the C + I line. (For extra help with finding equilibrium GDP, see box, "Finding Equilibrium GDP.")

Disequilibrium and Equilibrium

In both Keynesian and classical economic systems, the economy is always tending toward equilibrium, where aggregate demand and aggregate supply are equal. Let's look at this process from two perspectives: first, when aggregate demand is larger than aggregate supply and second, when aggregate supply is larger than aggregate demand.

(1) Aggregate Demand Exceeds Aggregate Supply

When aggregate demand
exceeds aggregate supply,
inventories decline.

When aggregate demand exceeds aggregate supply, a chain reaction is set off and continues until the economy is back in equilibrium. The first thing that happens is that inventories start declining. What do business firms do? They order more inventory.

Figure 13

Real GDP (in trillions of dollars)

When C + I represents aggregate demand, how much is equilibrium GDP? It's $7 trillion.

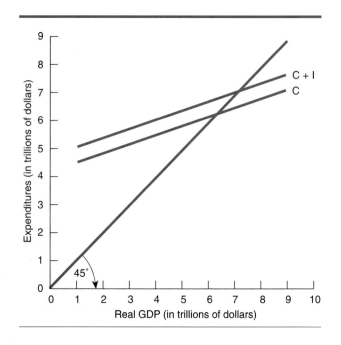

Finding Equilibrium GDP

Finding equilibrium GDP is as easy as finding the level of spending at which saving and investment are equal. Try to find that level of spending in the first figure here.

What did you get? Equilibrium real GDP is $5.5 trillion. Now, how much is saving? At equilibrium GDP, saving—the vertical distance between the C line and the 45-degree line—is about $1.7 trillion. And how much is I? It's the vertical distance between the C line and the C + I line—also about $1.7 trillion. And so, at an equilibrium GDP of $5.5 trillion, savings and investment are equal at $1.7 trillion.

After all the graphs we've gone through in this chapter, in the second figure here we come back to the C + I + G + X_n graph from Chapter 8. C + I + G + X_n is aggregate demand, or GDP. We've simply added the government and foreign sectors to the consumption and investment sectors.

How much is equilibrium GDP in the second figure? It's $5 trillion. We'll be making good use of this type of graph at the beginning of the next chapter.

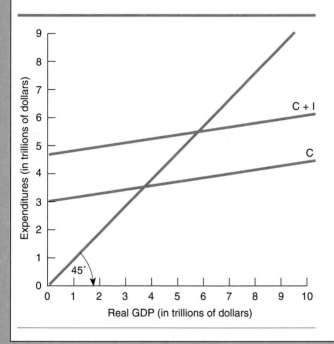

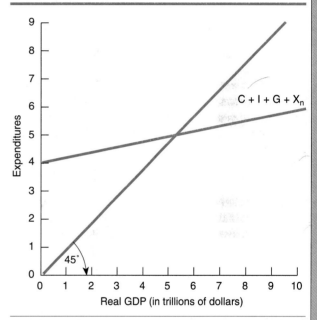

As I said, the first thing that happens when aggregate demand is greater than aggregate supply is that inventories are depleted. Consequently, orders to manufacturers rise, and, of course, production rises. Manufacturers will hire more labor, and eventually, as plant utilization approaches capacity, more plant and equipment is ordered.

Suppose you own an appliance store. You have been ordering 50 blenders a month because that's about how many you sell. But during the last month your blender sales doubled, so you decide to order 100 blenders instead of your usual 50. Think of what this does to the production of blenders, assuming the other appliance stores double their orders as well.

As more people find employment, they will consume more, raising aggregate demand. Business firms may also begin raising their prices. Retailers may perceive that their customers are willing to pay more. Eventually, the manufacturers may have trouble increasing output much farther because of shortages in labor, raw materials, plant and equipment, or the funds to finance expansion. These shortages will occur at some point—and consequently, prices will have to rise—because what is happening in the appliance industry is probably happening in the rest of the economy. As the economy approaches full capacity (and full employment), prices will have begun to rise.

We started with aggregate demand exceeding aggregate supply, but this disparity told manufacturers to increase aggregate supply. First, output was increased; eventually, so were prices. As final GDP (which is identical to aggregate supply) is defined as the nation's output of goods and services at market prices, it appears that there are two ways to raise aggregate supply—by increasing output and by increasing prices. By doing this, we raise aggregate supply relative to aggregate demand and quickly restore equilibrium.

(2) Aggregate Supply Exceeds Aggregate Demand

When aggregate supply is greater than aggregate demand, the economy is in disequilibrium. Aggregate supply must fall. Because aggregate supply is greater than aggregate demand, production exceeds sales, and inventories are rising. When retailers realize this, what do they do? They cut back on orders to manufacturers. After all, if you found you were accumulating more and more stock on your shelves, wouldn't you cut back on your orders? Remember, not only does it cost money to carry large inventories—shelf space as well as money is tied up—but also there is always the risk that you may not be able to sell your stock.

When manufacturers receive fewer orders, they reduce output and consequently lay off some workers, further depressing aggregate demand as these workers cut back on their consumption. Retail firms, facing declining sales as well as smaller inventories, may reduce prices, although during recent recessions price reductions have been relatively uncommon. Eventually, inventories are sufficiently depleted. In the meantime, aggregate supply has fallen back into equilibrium with aggregate demand.

When aggregate supply exceeds aggregate demand, inventories rise.

(3) Summary: How Equilibrium Is Attained

We can make an interesting observation about the entire process. When the economy is in disequilibrium, it automatically moves back into equilibrium. It is always aggregate supply that adjusts. When aggregate demand is greater than aggregate supply, the latter rises, and when aggregate supply exceeds aggregate demand, aggregate supply declines.

Please keep in mind that aggregate demand (C + I) must equal the level of production (aggregate supply) for the economy to be in equilibrium. When the two are not equal, aggregate supply must adjust to bring the economy back into equilibrium.

When the economy is in disequilibrium, it automatically moves back into equilibrium.

Keynesian Policy Prescriptions

Let's summarize the classical position. Recessions are temporary because the economy is self-correcting. Declining investment will be pushed up again by falling interest rates, while, if consumption falls, it will be raised by falling prices and wages. And because recessions are self-correcting, the role of government is to stand back and do nothing.

Keynes's position was that recessions were not necessarily temporary, because the self-correcting mechanisms of falling interest rates and falling prices and wages might be insufficient to push investment and consumption back up again. The private economy did not automatically move toward full employment. Therefore, it would be necessary for the government to intervene.

What should the government do? Spend money! How *much* money?[8] If the economy is in a bad recession, it will be necessary to spend a lot of money. And if it's in a depression, then it must spend even more. I'll be more specific in the next chapter.

The classicals believed recessions were temporary because the economy is self-correcting.

---

[8]We'll be much more specific in the next chapter. But let's be clear now that, when the government *spends* more money, that's not the same thing as *printing* more money. Generally it borrows more money and then spends it.

Aggregate demand is insufficient to provide jobs for everyone who wants to work; thus it is necessary for the government to provide the spending that will push the economy toward full employment. Just spend money; it doesn't matter on what. Keynes made this point quite vividly:

> If the Treasury were to fill old bottles with banknotes, bury them at suitable depths in disused coal mines which are then filled up to the surface with town rubbish, and leave it to private enterprise on well-tried principles of laissez-faire to dig the notes up again . . . , there need be no more unemployment. . . . It would, indeed, be more sensible to build houses and the like; but if there are political and practical difficulties in the way of this, the above would be better than nothing.[9]

If all it takes is government spending to get us out of a depression, then why didn't President Franklin Roosevelt's massive New Deal spending get us out of the Great Depression? First of all, it did succeed in bringing about rapid economic growth between 1933 and 1937. But then, just when the economy seemed to be coming out of its depression, Roosevelt suddenly decided to try to balance the federal budget; he raised taxes and cut government spending. On top of this, the Federal Reserve sharply cut the rate of growth of the money supply. So back down we went, with output plunging sharply and the unemployment rate soaring once again.

Why didn't New Deal spending get us out of the economic crisis of the 1930s?

Not until the huge federal government expenditures on World War II in the early 1940s did the United States finally emerge from the Depression. So what, then, did we learn from all of this? One possibility is that the only way to end a depression is to go to war (see the box, "A Dissertation upon Roast Pig"). But what I hope you learned is that massive government spending of *any* kind—whether on highways, school construction, AIDS research, crime prevention, space exploration, *or* military expansion—will pull us out of a depression.

In recent times, the most expensive application of Keynes' policy prescription for recessions has been carried out by Japan. For nearly the entire decade of the 1990s, the Japanese economy has been mired in recession. During this period Japan has spent more than $1 trillion, much of it on bridges, tunnels, airports, concert halls, and highways. Although none of these projects was as unproductive as burying bottles of banknotes, the new $10 billion Tokyo subway line, which was supposed to provide a direct route from the northern part of the city to the southwest, does not do so. It is just one of many Japanese public works projects that seem extravagant, wasteful, or even pointless. Construction contractors and the politicians who receive their contributions are the most obvious beneficiaries, and, indirectly, perhaps millions more derived some benefit. One might add, parenthetically, that Japanese politicians, even more than American politicians, must tailor their spending programs to local interest groups. While I don't know the Japanese term for that, in the American Congress the practice is known as pork barrel spending.

But the million-dollar question—or, in this case, the trillion-dollar question—is how this giant public works program benefited the Japanese economy. Clearly it has kept a lingering recession from slipping into a more severe one, or even into a depression. Maybe the Japanese government, like the American New Deal of the 1930s, just did not spend enough for long enough. Or just maybe, what really counts is not just how *much* you spend, but *how* you spend it.

Over the last seven decades, our economy has been racked by repeated bouts of inflation, recession, and, of course, the decade-long Great Depression. According to John Maynard Keynes, our problem during periods of recession and depression has been insufficient aggregate demand. And though he died in 1946, before we encountered periods of sustained inflation, he would have prescribed lowering aggregate demand to bring down the inflation rate.

[9]*Ibid.*, p. 129.

*A Dissertation upon Roast Pig**

This wonderful fable by Charles and Mary Lamb provides an analogy to going to war to end a depression. The story takes place in China many centuries ago.

> The swineherd, Ho-ti, having gone out into the woods . . . to collect mast for his hogs, left his cottage in the care of his eldest son, Bo-bo, a great lubberly boy, who being fond of playing with fire, as younkers of his age commonly are, let some sparks escape.

To make a long story short, the cottage burned down, and nine pigs, who were kept in the hut, were burned to death. Bo-bo touched one of the pigs, burned his fingers, and put them in his mouth to cool them off. And he discovered the joys of tasting roast pig. He proceeded to devour pig after pig. When his father, Ho-ti, returned home, he too burned his fingers on a pig, placed them in his mouth, and tasted roast pig.

Well, there was no question that they were onto something. Neighbors observed that Ho-ti's cottage was burnt down with great frequency. Pretty soon the secret was out, and all the neighbors were burning down *their* cottages to make roast pig.

> Thus this custom of firing houses continued until . . . a sage arose, who made a discovery, that the flesh of swine, or indeed of any other animal, might be cooked . . . without the necessity of consuming a whole house to dress it.

If the analogy isn't clear, let me clarify. To end a depression, or even a bad recession, we certainly don't need to go to war. All we need to do is spend as much money as we would have spent going to war. As Keynes said, it doesn't matter *what* the money is spent on, as long as enough of it is spent.

---

*Charles and Mary Lamb, "Dissertation upon Roast Pig," *The Works of Charles Lamb,* Vol. III (Boston: Crosby, Nichols, Lee, 1980), pp. 203–12.

In the next chapter we shall deal specifically with this Keynesian manipulation of the level of aggregate demand to deal with inflation and recession. Fiscal policy, which is the name that has been assigned to Keynesian taxation and government spending prescriptions, became the basic government policy tool to ensure price stability and high employment from the 1930s through the 1960s.

Questions for Further Thought and Discussion

1. The classical economists believed that our economy was always at full employment or tending toward full employment. If our economy were operating below full employment, what would happen, according to the classicals, to move the economy back toward full employment?

2. When the price level increases, the quantity of goods and services purchased declines. Why does this happen?

3. Explain the difference between the long-run aggregate supply curve and the short-run aggregate supply curve.

4. What were the major areas of disagreement between John Maynard Keynes and the classical economists?

5. Describe the chain reaction that is set off when (a) aggregate demand exceeds aggregate supply; (b) aggregate supply exceeds aggregate demand.

6. If you lived in a village cut off from the rest of the world, show how Say's law would apply to your village's economy.

Workbook for Chapter 11

Name _____ Date _____

Multiple-Choice Questions

Circle the letter that corresponds to the best answer.

1. Until the Great Depression, the dominant school of economic thought was _____.
   a) classical economics
   b) Keynesian economics
   c) supply-side economics
   d) monetarism

2. The classical economists believed in _____.
   a) strong government intervention
   b) laissez-faire
   c) a rapid growth in the money supply
   d) none of these

3. Say's law states that _____.
   a) we can have an inflation or a recession, but never both at the same time
   b) the normal state of economic affairs is recession
   c) demand creates its own supply
   d) supply creates its own demand

4. People work, according to Jean Baptiste Say, so that they can _____.
   a) spend   c) stay busy
   b) save   d) none of these

5. According to the classical economists, _____.
   a) people will always spend all their money
   b) any money that is saved will be invested
   c) saving will always be greater than investment
   d) saving will always be smaller than investment

6. Keynes believed _____.
   a) recessions were temporary
   b) once a recession began, it would always turn into a depression
   c) the real problem that modern economies faced was inflation
   d) none of these

7. "Our economy is always at full employment" was a claim made by _____.
   a) both Keynes and the classicals
   b) neither Keynes nor the classicals
   c) Keynes but not the classicals
   d) the classicals but not Keynes

8. According to the classical economists, if the amount of money people are planning to invest is greater than the amount that people want to save, _____.
   a) interest rates will rise and saving will rise
   b) interest rates will fall and saving will fall
   c) interest rates will fall and saving will rise
   d) interest rates will rise and saving will fall

9. Each of the following supports the classical theory of employment except _____.
   a) Say's law
   b) wage-price flexibility
   c) the interest mechanism
   d) government spending programs

10. Our economy is definitely at equilibrium in each case except when _____.
    a) saving equals investment
    b) aggregate demand equals aggregate supply
    c) the amount people are willing to spend equals the amount that producers are producing
    d) equilibrium GDP equals full-employment GDP

11. That we are always tending toward full employment is a belief of _____.
    a) Keynes   c) the supply-siders
    b) the classicals   d) the monetarists

12. Keynes said _____.
    a) the expected profit rate was more important than the interest rate
    b) the interest rate was more important than the expected profit rate
    c) the expected profit rate and the interest rate were equally important
    d) neither the expected profit rate nor the interest rate was important

13. John Maynard Keynes is most closely associated with the _____.
    a) American Revolution
    b) French Revolution
    c) the Great Depression
    d) inflation

14. The classical economists' aggregate supply curve is vertical _____.
    a) both in the short run and in the long run
    b) in neither the short run nor the long run
    c) in the short run, but not in the long run
    d) in the long run, but not in the short run

15. To end a bad recession, we need to _____.
    a) go to war
    b) spend a lot of money
    c) balance the federal budget

16. Which statement best describes the classical theory of employment?
    a) We will always have a great deal of unemployment.
    b) We will usually have a great deal of unemployment.
    c) We will occasionally have some unemployment, but our economy will automatically move back toward full employment.
    d) We never have any unemployment.

17. According to Keynes, our economy always tends toward _____.
    a) equilibrium GDP
    b) full-employment GDP
    c) recessions
    d) inflations

18. When saving is greater than investment, we are _____.
    a) at equilibrium GDP
    b) at full-employment GDP
    c) below equilibrium GDP
    d) above equilibrium GDP

19. Keynes considered full-employment GDP to be _____.
    a) the normal state of economic affairs
    b) a rare occurrence
    c) an impossibility
    d) none of these

20. Keynes was concerned mainly with _____.
    a) aggregate supply
    b) aggregate demand
    c) the interest rate
    d) inflation

21. When aggregate demand is greater than aggregate supply, _____.
    a) inventories get depleted and output rises
    b) inventories get depleted and output falls
    c) inventories rise and output rises
    d) inventories rise and output falls

22. When the economy is in disequilibrium, _____.
    a) production automatically rises
    b) production automatically falls
    c) it automatically moves back into equilibrium
    d) it stays in disequilibrium permanently

23. As the price level rises, _____.
    a) the quantity of goods and services demanded falls
    b) the quantity of goods and services demanded rises
    c) the quantity of goods and services demanded stays the same
    d) none of the above is correct

24. The slope of the aggregate demand curve is explained by each of the following except _____.
    a) the real balance effect
    b) the interest rate effect
    c) the foreign purchases effect
    d) the profit effect

25. Which of the following antirecession (or anti-depression) programs would not be one that John Maynard Keynes would have prescribed?

 a) the New Deal under President Franklin Roosevelt

 b) the one-trillion-dollar Japanese public works program of the 1990s

 c) letting the forces of supply and demand allow the economy to reattain full employment

 d) burying bottles containing banknotes

Fill In Questions

1. Laissez-faire was advocated by the _____ school of economics.

2. Say's law states that _____ _____.

3. According to Say's law, people work so that they can _____.

4. According to Say's law, people spend _____.

5. The classical economists believed savings would equal _____.

6. If supply creates its own demand, asked Keynes, why are we having a _____?

7. If saving were greater than investment, said the classical economists, they would be set equal by the _____.

8. The classical economists believed that wages and prices were _____ flexible.

9. The classical economists believed recessions were _____.

10. During recessions, said the classical economists, the government should _____.

11. Aggregate supply is _____ _____.

12. Aggregate demand is _____ _____.

13. At equilibrium GDP, _____ will be equal to _____ and _____ will be equal to _____.

14. Our economy always tends toward _____ _____ GDP.

15. When investment is greater than savings, we are _____ equilibrium GDP.

16. Full-employment GDP and equilibrium GDP are _____ equal.

17. Keynes was most concerned with one main variable, _____.

18. According to John Maynard Keynes, the level of aggregate supply is determined by the _____ _____.

19. When we are below the full-employment level of GDP, Keynes suggested that the _____ _____.

20. When aggregate supply is greater than aggregate demand, the economy is in _____.

21. When aggregate demand is greater than aggregate supply, inventories will _____ and output will _____.

22. When individuals, business firms, and the government are spending just enough money to provide jobs for everyone willing and able to work, we are at _____ GDP.

23. The real balance effect states that _____ _____ _____.

24. The two reasons why the aggregate supply curve moves upward to the right are: (1) _____ and (2) _____.

25. The interest rate effect states that _____ _____ _____.

26. The three reasons why the aggregate demand curve

    slopes downward are (1) _____;

    (2) _____;

    and (3) _____.

27. The foreign purchases effect states that _____ _____ _____.

Problems

1. If GDP = C + I and if GDP = C + S, then

    _____ = _____.

2. Given the information in Figure 1, and assuming an interest rate of 15 percent: a) Will the economy be at equilibrium? b) Will savings equal investment? c) What will happen, according to the classical economists?

Figure 1

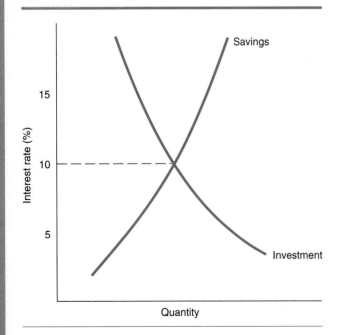

3. Given the information in Figure 2: a) If aggregate demand shifts from AD_1 to AD_2, what happens to the level of prices and to output? b) If aggregate demand shifts from AD_2 to AD_3, what happens to the level of prices and to output? c) If aggregate demand shifts from AD_3 to AD_4, what happens to the level of prices and to output?

Figure 2

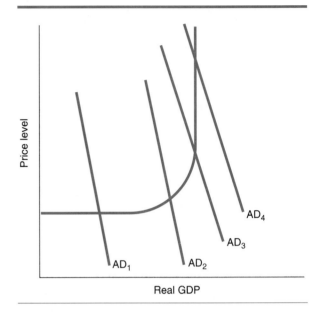

Chapter 12

Fiscal Policy and the National Debt

These are exciting times for economists. For nearly 30 years we worried about reducing the federal budget deficit. Now we are debating how to handle our soaring surpluses. The big question for you is whether you'll get a tax cut and how big it will be. You might also want to think about how much of the projected surpluses we should "spend" on a tax cut, added government spending, shoring up Social Security and Medicare, and paying down the national debt.

Fiscal policy is *the manipulation of the federal budget to attain price stability, relatively full employment, and a satisfactory rate of economic growth.* To attain these goals, the government must manipulate its spending and taxes. Later, in Chapter 14, we'll look at monetary policy, which uses very different means to promote the same ends.

CHAPTER OBJECTIVES

In this chapter you will learn about:

- The deflationary gap.
- The inflationary gap.
- The multiplier and its applications.
- Automatic stabilizers.

- Discretionary fiscal policy.
- Budget deficits and surpluses.
- The public debt.

Putting Fiscal Policy into Perspective

Until the time of the Great Depression, the only advice economists gave the government was to try to balance its budget every year and not to interfere with the workings of the private economy. Just balance the books and then stay out of the way. There was no such thing as fiscal policy until John Maynard Keynes invented it in the 1930s.

He pointed out that there was a depression going on and that the problem was anemic aggregate demand. Consumption was lagging because so many people were out of work. Investment was extremely low because businessowners had no reason to add to their inventories or build more plant and equipment. After all, sales were very low and much of their plant and equipment was sitting idle. So the only thing left to boost aggregate demand was government spending.

What about taxes? Well, certainly, we would not want to *raise* them. That would push aggregate demand even lower. We might even want to *cut* taxes to give consumers and businesses more money to spend. OK, now if we were to follow this advice, would the government be able to balance its budget? No way! But if we ran a big enough budget deficit, we could jump-start the economy and, in effect, spend our way out of this depression.

You don't have to be a great economist to see that we haven't been too successful at attaining our fiscal policy goals, particularly since the mid-1960s. It's important that the aggregate supply of goods and services equals the aggregate demand for goods and services at just the level of spending that will bring about full employment at stable prices.[1]

Equilibrium GDP tells us the level of spending in the economy. Full-employment GDP tells us the level of spending necessary to get the unemployment rate down to 5 percent (which we have been calling full employment). We'll see how fiscal policy is used to push equilibrium GDP toward full-employment GDP.

In terms of equilibrium GDP, sometimes we are spending too much, and at other times we are spending too little. When equilibrium GDP is too big, we have an inflationary gap, and when it's too small, a deflationary gap.[2] Remember Goldilocks and the Three Bears? Remember the porridge that was too hot and the porridge that was too cold? Like Goldilocks seeking the perfect porridge, our policy objective is to find a level of GDP that is just right. We will deal with deflationary and inflationary gaps and GDPs that are just right in the next few pages.

Economics is filled with dicta, some of which make perfect sense—you can't repeal the law of supply and demand—and some of which don't seem to make much sense at all. This chapter is based on two of the second type. First, we'll consider the following dictum: The federal budget must be balanced every year. In fact, during the 1980s, the required three-quarters of the state legislatures nearly approved a constitutional convention to consider an amendment that would have made an annually balanced budget the law of the land. Since then, in 1994, 1995, 1996, and in 1997 new efforts to pass a balanced budget amendment have been very narrowly defeated in Congress. You can read all about this in Part VI of this chapter.

The last part of this chapter will be devoted to a discussion of the public or national debt. The dictum in question is: The public debt is a burden on future generations. In fact, another dictum virtually contradicts this one: We owe it to ourselves. As we shall see, neither holds true. But as we shall also see, neither is completely wrong.

Part I: The Deflationary Gap and the Inflationary Gap

Equilibrium GDP is the level of output at which aggregate demand equals aggregate supply.

Before we go to the gaps, we need to go over some terms from Chapter 10. First: *equilibrium GDP*. Our economy is always at equilibrium GDP or tending toward it. *Equilibrium GDP is the level of output at which aggregate demand equals aggregate supply.* What is *aggregate demand*? It's *the sum of all expenditures for goods and services* (that is, $C + I + G + X_n$). And what is *aggregate supply*? Aggregate supply is *the nation's total output of final goods and services.* So at equilibrium GDP, everything produced is sold.

---

[1] That's a very long sentence whose meaning will become increasingly apparent as you read this chapter.

[2] Some economists call this a *recessionary* gap. If this term makes you happier, use it.

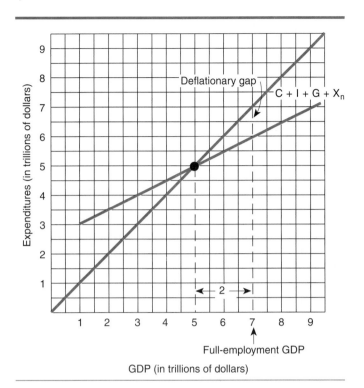

Figure 1

The Deflationary Gap

When full-employment GDP is greater than equilibrium GDP, there is a deflationary gap. How much is it in this graph? The deflationary gap is $1 trillion.

We need to review one more term: *full-employment GDP.* Full employment means nearly all our resources are being used. For example, if our plant and equipment is operating at between 85 and 90 percent of capacity, *that's* full employment. Or if only 5 percent of our labor force is unemployed, then *that's* full employment. So, what's full-employment GDP? Full-employment GDP is *the level of spending necessary to provide full employment of our resources.* Alternatively, it is the level of spending necessary to purchase the output, or aggregate supply, of a fully employed economy.

Full employment GDP is the level of spending necessary to provide full employment of our resources.

The Deflationary Gap

A *deflationary gap occurs when equilibrium GDP is less than full-employment GDP.* Equilibrium GDP is the level of spending that the economy is at or is tending toward. Full-employment GDP is the level of spending needed to provide enough jobs to reduce the unemployment rate to 5 percent. When too little is being spent to provide enough jobs, we have a deflationary gap, which is shown in Figure 1. Another way of expressing this state of economic affairs is to say that we are inside our production possibilities frontier (or curve), as we discussed in Chapter 2.

How much is equilibrium GDP in Figure 1? Write down the number. What did you get? Did you get $5 trillion? That's the GDP at which the C + I + G + X_n line crosses the 45-degree line.

How do we close this gap? We need to raise spending—consumption (C) or investment (I) or government expenditures (G)—or perhaps some combination of these.[3] John Maynard Keynes tells us to raise G. Or we may want to lower taxes. Lowering business taxes might raise I; lowering personal income taxes would increase C.

How can we close the deflationary gap?

How much would we have to raise spending to close the deflationary gap shown in Figure 1? Would you believe $1 trillion? That's right! This is *some* deflationary gap.

[3]We are leaving out net exports (X_n) for purposes of simplification. Increasing our exports and/or reducing our imports would reduce a deflationary gap, but these two variables are not very responsive to fiscal policy.

There would have to be a depression going on, so we would need to raise spending by $1 trillion. Anything less would reduce, but not eliminate, the gap.

Note that equilibrium GDP is $2 trillion less than the full-employment GDP of $7 trillion. In a few pages we'll do some multiplier analysis. This analysis will show us that raising G by $1 trillion will raise equilibrium GDP by $2 trillion and eliminate the deflationary gap. But let's not get ahead of ourselves.

Note how the points in Figure 1 line up. Equilibrium GDP is to the left of full-employment GDP. The deflationary gap is directly above the full-employment GDP. It is the vertical distance between the 45-degree line and the $C + I + G + X_n$ line.

The Inflationary Gap

Figure 2 shows the inflationary gap. The key difference between this graph and that of the deflationary gap is the position of equilibrium GDP. When there is an inflationary gap, equilibrium GDP is to the right of full-employment GDP. It is to the left when there's a deflationary gap. In other words, *equilibrium GDP is greater than full-employment GDP when there's an inflationary gap.* When there's a deflationary gap, full-employment GDP is greater than equilibrium GDP.

In both graphs the gap is the vertical distance between the $C + I + G + X_n$ line and the 45-degree line, and in both graphs the gap is directly above full-employment GDP.

In short, when there's a deflationary gap, equilibrium GDP is too small; when there's an inflationary gap, it's too big. To eliminate an inflationary gap, Keynes would suggest cutting G and raising taxes. Both actions are aimed at reducing spending and, therefore, equilibrium GDP.

In Figure 2 the inflationary gap is $200 billion ($1,200 billion–$1,000 billion). If we cut spending by $200 billion, it would have a multiplied effect on GDP. Equilibrium GDP would decline by $500 billion ($1,500 billion – $1,000 billion) to the full-employment level.

I'm tossing around billions and trillions as if they were pocket change. Remember that 1,000 billion equals 1 trillion. If you need a fast review, reread the box "A Word about Numbers," near the beginning of Chapter 5.

Deflationary gap: Equilibrium GDP is too small.

Inflationary gap: Equilibrium GDP is too large.

F igure 2

The Inflationary Gap

When equilirium GDP is greater than full-employment GDP, there is an inflationary gap. How large is the inflationary gap in this graph? The inflationary gap is $200 billion.

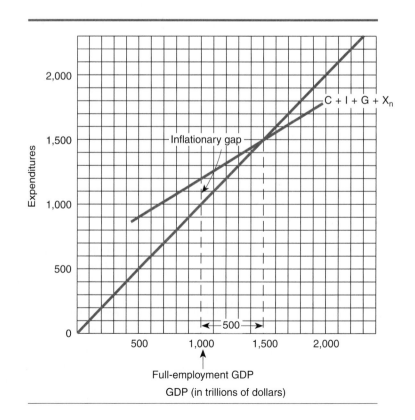

To summarize, if spending is too high, equilibrium GDP is above the full-employment level. To eliminate the inflationary gap, we cut G and/or raise taxes. If equilibrium GDP is less than full-employment GDP, we eliminate the deflationary gap by raising G and/or cutting taxes.

Over the last two decades Republicans have labeled every Democratic presidential candidate a "tax and spend liberal." And by inference these Republicans wanted to be called "low-tax and low-spend conservatives." To generalize, liberals seem to favor a high-spending, high-taxing, big government, and conservatives a low-spending, low-taxing, relatively small government. How would these philosophies lend themselves to fiscal policy?

If there were a recession, conventional fiscal policy calls for tax cuts and more government spending. If the liberal could choose just one of these measures, which would she favor? And which one would the conservative favor? The liberal would choose higher government spending (which would increase the role of government), while the conservative would cut taxes, thereby reducing the government's role.

Now figure out the liberal's and conservative's respective policy prescriptions for dealing with inflation. Write them down right here:

The liberal would raise taxes, and the conservative would cut government spending. To generalize—or perhaps overgeneralize—the liberal tends to favor bigger government, and the conservative, smaller government.

Part II: The Multiplier and Its Applications

We're going to put together some concepts introduced in earlier chapters: aggregate demand (Chapters 9 and 11), the marginal propensity to consume (Chapter 5), and equilibrium GDP (Chapter 11). We know that an increase in G will raise aggregate demand, but by how much? We also know that a tax increase will lower aggregate demand, but, again, by how much? The multiplier will tell us by just how much.

The Multiplier

The multiplier is based on two concepts covered in Chapter 9: (1) GDP is the nation's expenditure on all the final goods and services produced during the year at market prices. (2) GDP $= C + I + G + X_n$.

It is obvious that if C goes up, GDP will go up. Or if I goes down, so will GDP. Now we'll add a new wrinkle. When there is any change in spending, that is, in C, I, G, or X_n, it will have a multiplied effect on GDP.

When money is spent by one person, it becomes someone else's income. And what do we do with most of our income? We spend it. Once again, when this money is spent, someone else receives it as income and, in turn, spends most of it. And so, if a dollar were initially spent, perhaps someone who received that dollar would spend 80 cents, and of that 80 cents received by the next person, perhaps 64 cents would be spent. If we add up all the spending generated by that one dollar, it will add up to four or five or six times that dollar. Hence, we get the name *the multiplier.*

Any change in spending (C, I, or G) will set off a chain reaction, leading to a multiplied change in GDP. *How much* of a multiplied effect? A $10 billion increase in G might increase GDP by $50 billion. In that case, the multiplier is 5. If a decline of $5 billion in I causes GDP to fall by $40 billion, then the multiplier would be 8.

First we'll concentrate on calculating the multiplier, for which we'll use the formula:

$$\text{Multiplier} = \frac{1}{1-\text{MPC}}$$

$$\frac{1}{1-\text{MPC}}$$

Then we'll see how it is used to predict changes in GDP. (A reminder: MPC is marginal propensity to consume.)

The formula above is the same as 1/MPS. Remember, MPC + MPS = 1 (or 1 − MPC = MPS). Because the multiplier (like C) deals with spending, 1/(1 − MPC) is a more appropriate formula.

The MPC can thus be used to find the multiplier. If the MPC were .5, find the multiplier. Work this problem out in the space below. Write down the formula first, then substitute and solve.

Solution:

$$\text{Multiplier} = \frac{1}{1-\text{MPC}} = \frac{1}{1-.5} = \frac{1}{.5} = 2$$

Many students get lost at the third step. How do we get .5? How come 1−.5=.5? Look at it this way:

$$\begin{array}{r} 1.0 \\ -.5 \\ \hline .5 \end{array}$$

If it's still not clear, then think of 1 as a dollar and .5 (or .50) as 50 cents. How much is a dollar minus 50 cents?

Step four is just as easy. How many times does 50 cents go into a dollar? Or, you can just divide .5 into 1.0. Either way, it comes out to 2.

Let's try another problem. When the MPC is .75, how much is the multiplier?

Solution:

$$\text{Multiplier} = \frac{1}{1-\text{MPC}} = \frac{1}{1-.75} = \frac{1}{.25} = 4$$

After you've substituted into the formula, think of 1 as a dollar and .75 as 75 cents. From there (1/.25) we divide .25 into 1, or a quarter into a dollar.

The multiplier is really a shortcut for addition. In the case illustrated in Table 1, a consumer spends $1,000 of additional money. If the MPC is .5, that means the person who receives this $1,000 in additional income will spend $500. The $500 spent will add to others' incomes, and—still assuming an MPC of .5—they will spend $250. Ad infinitum (that's Latin for "without limit," or "forever").

TABLE 1	Step-by-Step Working of the Multiplier When MPC is .5

$1,000.00
500.00
250.00
125.00
62.50
31.25
15.625
7.8125
3.90625
1.953125
.9765625
.48828125
.244140625
.1220703125
.06103515625
.030517578125
.0152587890625
$1,999.9847402109375*

*In arithmetic, addition and multiplication are one and the same. Multiplication is just a shortcut. If we were to carry out even more steps in our addition, we would approach a sum of $2,000. It is surely much easier to use the multiplier of 2 (2 × $1,000 = $2,000) than to add up all these figures.

Applications of the Multiplier

Knowing the multiplier, we can calculate the effect of changes in C, I, and G on the level of GDP. If GDP is 2,500, the multiplier is 3, and C rises by 10, what is the new level of GDP?

The multiplier is used to calculate the effects of changes in C, I, and G on GDP.

A second formula is needed to determine the new level of GDP:

New GDP = Initial GDP + (Change in spending × Multiplier)

Note the parentheses. Their purpose is to ensure that we multiply before we add. In arithmetic you must always multiply (or divide) before you add (or subtract). Always. The parentheses are there to make sure we do this.

Copy down the formula, substitute, and solve.
Solution:

(1) New GDP = Initial GDP + (Change in spending × Multiplier)

(2)   = 2,500 + (10 × 3)

(3)   = 2,500 + (30)

             = 2,530

Here are a few variations of this type of problem. Suppose that consumer spending rises by $10 billion and the multiplier is 3. What happens to GDP?

Solution: It rises by $30 billion: $10 billion $\times$ 3.

Try this one: Government spending falls by $5 billion with a multiplier of 7.

Solution: $-$5 billion $\times$ 7 $=$ $-$35 billion. In other words, if government spending falls by $5 billion with a multiplier of 7, GDP falls by $35 billion.

Two more multiplier applications and we're through. First, how big is the multiplier in Figure 1? If you're not sure, guess. What's your answer? Is it 2? We can find the multiplier by using deductive logic. We know the deflationary gap is $1 trillion. We also know that equilibrium GDP is $2 trillion less than full-employment GDP. (Equilibrium GDP is $5 trillion and full-employment GDP is $7 trillion.) Suppose we were to raise G by $1 trillion. What would happen to the gap? It would vanish! And what would happen to equilibrium GDP? It would rise by $2 trillion and become equal to full-employment GDP.

Still not convinced? Let's redraw Figure 1 as Figure 3 and add $C_1 + I_1 + G_1 + X_{n1}$. You'll notice that $C_1 + I_1 + G_1 + X_{n1}$ is $1 trillion higher than $C + I + G + X_n$. You'll also notice that the deflationary gap is gone. And that equilibrium GDP equals full-employment GDP.

One more question: How big is the multiplier in Figure 2? Again, if you're not sure, guess. Is your answer 2.5? How do we get 2.5? OK, we know that the inflationary gap is 200, and we know equilibrium GDP is 500 greater than full-employment GDP. So if we lower G by 200, the inflationary gap disappears. And now equilibrium GDP falls by 500 and is equal to full-employment GDP.

Here's formula you can use to find the multiplier whether you have an inflationary gap or a deflationary gap:

$$\text{Multiplier} = \frac{\text{Distance between equilibrium GDP and full-employment GDP}}{\text{Gap}}$$

In Figure 4 the distance is 500 and the inflationary gap is 200. So 500/200 $=$ 2.5. You can also use this formula to find the multiplier if there is a deflationary gap. For example,

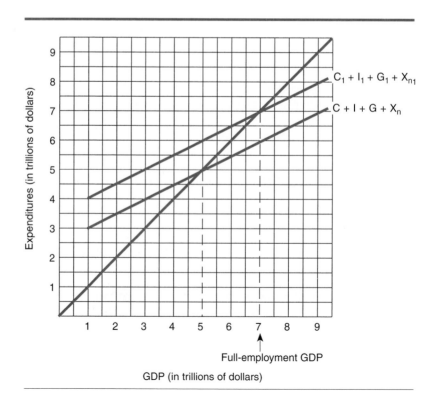

F*igure* 3

Removing the Deflationary Gap

Let's start with an aggregate demand of $C + I + G + X_n$ and an equilibrium GDP of $5 trillion. To remove the deflationary gap, we raise aggregate demand to $C_1 + I_1 + G_1 + X_{n1}$. This pushes equilibrium GDP to $7 trillion and removes the deflationary gap.

Finding the Multiplier

Let's assume that the full-employment GDP is $4 trillion in Figure 3 (use the $C + I + G + X_n$ line; ignore the $C_1 + I_1 + G_1 + X_{n1}$ line). See if you can answer these three questions:

1. Is there an inflationary gap or a deflationary gap?
2. How much is the gap?
3. How much is the multiplier?

Solution:

1. There is an inflationary gap because full-employment GDP is less than equilibrium GDP. If aggregate demand, or total spending, is greater than the spending necessary to attain full employment, that excess spending will cause inflation.
2. The inflationary gap is measured by the vertical distance between the 45-degree line and the

$C + I + G + X_n$ line at full-employment GDP. It appears to be half a trillion, or $500 billion, which we can write as 500.

$$\text{Multiplier} = \frac{\text{Distance between equilibrium GDP and full-employment GDP}}{\text{Gap}}$$

Now let's assume that full-employment GDP is $6 trillion.
Please answer the same three questions.

Solution:

1. There is a deflationary gap.
2. It is $500 billion, or 500.

3. $\text{Multiplier} = \dfrac{1,000}{500} = 2$

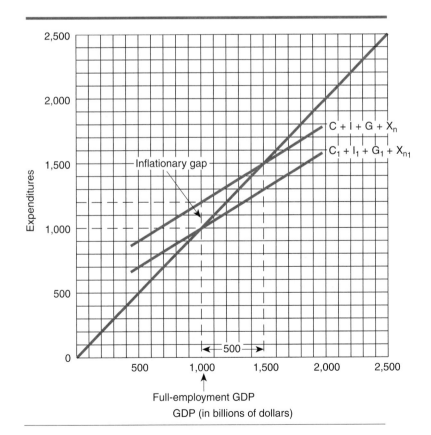

Figure 4

Removing the Inflationary Gap

We'll start with an aggregate demand of $C + I + G + X_n$ and an equilibrium GDP of 1,500. To remove the inflationary gap, we lower aggregate demand to $C_1 + I_1 + G_1 + X_{n_1}$. This pushes equilibrium GDP down to 1,000 and removes the deflationary gap.

311

advanced WORK

Tax Cuts and Tax Increases

A tax cut will have the same impact on the deflationary gap as an increase in G *only if people spend the entire tax cut.* If personal income taxes were cut by $100 billion, would people spend this entire amount? Maybe. They certainly would if their MPC were 1.0. But what if it were only .9? How much of it would they spend? Just $90 billion. And what would the multiplier be if the MPC were .9? It would be 10 (Multiplier = $1/(1 - \text{MPC}) = 1/(1-.9) = 1/.1 = 10$). So, if taxes were cut by $100 billion, by how much would equilibrium GDP rise? It would rise by $900 billion ($90 \times 10 = \$900$ billion).

The same logic applies to a tax increase. If personal-income taxes were raised by $100 billion and the MPC were .8, by how much would equilibrium GDP decline?

Solution:

$$\text{Change in GDP} = \text{Change in spending} \times \text{Multiplier}$$

$$= -80^* \qquad \times 5^\dagger$$

$$= -400$$

---

*We get -80 by multiplying the tax cut of $100 billion by the MPC of .8. We're assuming that if taxes had not been raised by $100 billion, people would have spent $80 billion of the income.

†Multiplier = $1/(1-\text{MPC}) = 1/(1-.8) = 1/.2 = 5$.

---

in Figure 3 the distance between equilibrium GDP and full-employment GDP is $2 trillion, which we can express as 2,000. And the deflationary gap is $1 trillion, or 1,000. Using the formula:

$$\text{Multiplier} = \frac{\text{Distance between equilibrium GDP and full-employment GDP}}{\text{Gap}} = \frac{2,000}{1,000} = 2$$

If you are still a bit uncertain and want a little more practice, then do the work in the Extra Help box, "Finding the Multiplier."

Because tax cuts and tax increases present a more complex problem, we'll put them in their own box. If you like more complex problems, read the Advanced Work box, "Tax Cuts and Tax Increases." And while you're at it, you may also find the box on the paradox of thrift (later in the chapter) of some interest. Otherwise, you may collect $200 and advance to Part III.

Part III: The Automatic Stabilizers

Have you ever been on an airborne plane when the pilot took a stroll through the cabin and you asked yourself, Who's flying the plane? Let's hope it's the copilot. Or maybe the plane is on automatic pilot, which is fine unless it hits some turbulence. If it does, then the pilot will rush back to the cockpit and take over the manual controls.

An analogy can be made with our economy. Our automatic stabilizers enable us to cruise along fairly smoothly, but when we hit severe economic turbulence, then we hope the president and Congress take the controls. Right now, we'll examine our automatic stabilizers, and in Part IV, we'll talk about discretionary fiscal policy, which is our manual control system.

In the 1930s the government built a few automatic stabilizers into the economy, mainly to prevent recessions from becoming depressions. Today, when the country hits routine economic turbulence, Congress does not need to pass any laws, and no new bureaucracies have to be created. All the machinery is in place and ready to go.

The automatic stabilizers protect us from the extremes of the business cycle.

Each of these stabilizers protects the economy from the extremes of the business cycle—from recession and inflation. They are not, by themselves, expected to prevent booms and busts, but only to moderate them. To do still more, we need discretionary economic policy, which we'll discuss in the next section.

Personal Income and Payroll Taxes

During recessions the government collects less personal income tax and Social Security tax than it otherwise would. Some workers who had been getting overtime before the recession are lucky to be hanging on to their jobs even without overtime. Some workers are less lucky and have been laid off. That's the bad news. The good news is that they don't have to pay any personal income tax or payroll tax because they have no income.

During recessions, tax receipts decline.

During prosperous times our incomes rise, and during times of inflation our incomes tend to rise still faster. As our incomes rise, we have to pay more taxes. These taxes tend to hold down our spending, relieving inflationary pressures.

During inflations, tax receipts rise.

During recessions, as incomes fall, federal personal income and Social Security tax receipts fall even faster. This moderates economic declines by leaving more money in taxpayers' pockets.

Personal Savings

As the economy moves into a recession, saving declines. Many Americans lose their jobs and others earn less overtime. As incomes fall, savings must fall as well. Looked at from another perspective, consumption rises as a percentage of income.

During recessions, saving declines.

Just as the loss of income is cushioned by a fall in saving, the reverse happens when the economy picks up again. Like higher taxes, during times of rapid economic expansion, increased saving tends to damp down inflationary pressures.

During prosperity, saving rises.

Credit Availability

Because most Americans now hold bank credit cards, mainly MasterCard and VISA, we may think of these as automatic stabilizers that work in the same way that personal savings does. During good times, we should be paying off the credit card debts that we run up during bad times.

Credit availability helps get us through recessions.

Although many of us are quite good at running up credit card debt during good times as well as bad, our credit cards, as well as other lines of credit, may be thought of as automatic stabilizers during recessions because they give us one more source of funds with which to keep buying things. You may have lost your job and have no money in the bank, but your credit cards are just as good as money.

Unemployment Compensation

Here's a great example of closing the barn door after the horses have run off. We came up with a great unemployment insurance program back in 1935, which happened to be the sixth year of the Great Depression.

Reason to study economics: When you are in the unemployment line, at least you will know why you are there.

During recessions, more people collect unemployment benefits.

When you lose your job, you can sign up for unemployment benefits if you qualify. To qualify you need to have worked at an insured job for 20 weeks during the last year or 40 weeks during the last two years. Also, you must have lost your job through no fault of your own. If you were laid off or your company moved out of town, you will be able to collect almost automatically.

During recessions, as the unemployment rate climbs, hundreds of thousands and then millions of people register for unemployment benefits. Benefit schedules and maximum payments vary from state to state. Most people who collect get almost 60 percent of their salaries, although those earning more than $40,000 a year get considerably less than half.

A man whose gross income is $200 a week and take-home pay is $160 receives between $110 and $120 in unemployment benefits. For this person, the loss of his job means an income decline of just $40. Without unemployment insurance it would have been a lot worse. Chances are, by dipping into his savings and borrowing a little here and there, he can more or less maintain his standard of living until he finds another job.

But *will* he find another job? There's a recession going on. Actually, the tens of billions of dollars of unemployment benefits being paid out establish a floor under purchasing power. People who are, they hope, only temporarily out of work will continue spending money. This helps keep retail sales from falling much, and even without further government help, the economy has bought some time to work its way out of the recession. As the economy recovers and moves into the prosperity phase of the cycle, people find jobs more easily and unemployment benefit claims drop substantially.

The maximum paid varies from state to state. In 1962, when the author collected for the full 26 weeks from New York, the maximum was just $50.

Sometimes during recessions, Congress will extend the benefit period beyond 26 weeks to 39 or even 52 weeks in certain cases. This action is part of discretionary policy, because it does not happen automatically. You cannot collect beyond 26 weeks unless Congress acts. During the recession of 1969–70, for example, a friend who had been "cut off" after 26 weeks unexpectedly heard from her local unemployment insurance office. "It was a miracle!" she told me. "They called me in and said I could collect for another 13 weeks!"

Clearly most people can protect themselves from relatively short-term losses of income. Because this is so, their continued spending helps provide a floor under consumer spending during recessions, which, in turn, helps keep recessions from turning into depressions. For a more personal example, see the box, "How the Automatic Stabilizers Help You Survive a Recession."

The Corporate Profits Tax

During recessions, corporations pay much less corporate income taxes.

Perhaps the most countercyclical of all the automatic stabilizers is the corporate profit (or income) tax. Corporations must pay 35 percent of their net income above $10 million to the federal government. During economic downturns, corporate profits fall much more quickly than wages, consumption, or real GDP; and, of course, during expansions, corporate profits rise much more rapidly. During the 1981–82 recession, corporate after-tax profits fell from an annual rate of $169 billion in the first quarter of 1981 to $119 billion just one year later. And during the much milder downturn almost a decade later, profits slid from an annual rate of $271 billion in the first quarter of 1989 to just $194 billion two years later.

Part of this decline is cushioned by the huge falloff of federal tax collections from the corporate sector. This leaves more money to be used for investment or distribution to shareholders in the form of dividends. And when corporate profits shoot up during economic booms, the federal government damps down economic expansion by taxing away 35 percent of the profits of the larger corporations.

Other Transfer Payments

Some people think that when a recession hits, the government automatically raises Social Security benefits. This might make sense, but it doesn't happen. Congress would have to pass special legislation to do so.

How the Automatic Stabilizers Help You Survive a Recession

Elizabeth Zimiles, who was earning $500 a week, lost her job during a recession. How was she able to make ends meet?

First of all, she no longer had to pay any federal or state income tax, and she didn't have to pay any payroll (Social Security and Medicare) tax. Let's see how this affected her aftertax income.

Before she lost her job, Ms. Zimiles earned $500, paid $100 in taxes, and took home $400. Now she earns nothing and takes home nothing. So her aftertax income fell from $400 to 0.

Suppose that when she was working, she saved $50 a week. Now that she has lost her job, she takes $100 a week out of her savings. Let's see how this affected her spending money.

Before Ms. Zimiles lost her job, she took home $400 a week, saved $50, and had $350 available for spending. But now she takes home no money, and draws $100 a week out of her savings to have available for spending. So her spending money has fallen from $350 to $100.

But you ain't seen nuthin' yet. She applies for unemployment insurance benefits, and receives $260 a week. Add that to her $100 of spending money and now she has $360.

	Earned Income	After tax Income	− Savings	Unemployment Insurance + Benefits	Spending Money
Before job loss	$500	$400	$ 50	0	$350
After job loss	0	0	−$100	$260	$360

Can you see where we're going with this? Before she lost her job, she had $350 to spend each week. But now she has $360. While I'm not suggesting that everyone can live better without a job than with one, I *am* suggesting that the automatic stabilizers can definitely help you survive a recession.

Three important payments do rise automatically because of laws on the books. Each is aimed at helping the poor. These are welfare (or public assistance) payments, Medicaid payments, and food stamps.

Whenever a recession hits, millions of people become eligible for welfare, or if they are already getting welfare payments, they become entitled to larger payments. Someone earning the minimum wage of $5.15 an hour brings home just $166.46 (based on a 35-hour week with payroll taxes—but not personal income taxes—deducted). This comes to just $8,656 a year, which most states deem inadequate support for a family of four, making this family eligible for public assistance and food stamps to supplement their income. During a recession, if this person loses her job and she collects unemployment benefits, these benefits will come to only a little more than half her pay, so her family will get larger welfare payments.

At the same time, this family will get more food stamps, as both public assistance and food stamps are based solely on family income. Furthermore, people who join the ranks of those on public assistance become eligible for Medicaid benefits.

These programs are important for two reasons. Not only do they alleviate human suffering during bad economic times, but they also help provide a floor under spending, which helps keep economic downturns from worsening.

The automatic stabilizers smooth out the business cycle, keeping the ups and downs within a moderate range. Since the Great Depression, we have had neither another depression nor a runaway inflation. But the stabilizers, by themselves, cannot altogether eliminate economic fluctuations.

Figure 5 shows the workings of the stabilizers. The solid line shows real GDP in an economy with no automatic stabilizers. The dotted line shows real GDP in an economy such as ours, which does have automatic stabilizers. The latter part of the expansions are held down in the hypothetical business cycle with stabilizers in place, and the contractions are less severe. Basically, then, the automatic stabilizers smooth out the business cycle but don't eliminate it.

A safety net for the poor

Figure 5

Hypothetical Business Cycles

Without the automatic stabilizers, real GDP would fluctuate much more widely. But you'll note that, while the stabilizers do smooth out the cycle, they do not eliminate it.

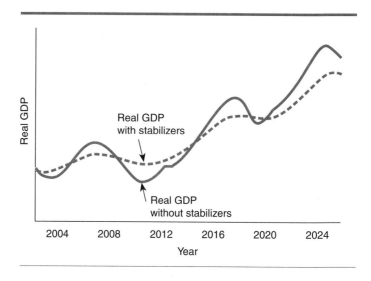

The automatic stabilizers may be likened to running our economy on automatic pilot—not well suited for takeoffs and landings, but fine for the smooth part of the flight. However, when the going gets rough, the economy must resort to manual controls. Discretionary policy is our manual control system.

Part IV: Discretionary Fiscal Policy

The first words of this chapter were *Fiscal policy is the manipulation of the federal budget to attain price stability, relatively full employment, and a satisfactory rate of economic growth.* The automatic stabilizers, which swing the federal budget into substantial deficits during recessions and tend to push down those deficits during periods of inflation, would appear to be part of fiscal policy. Because they are built into our economy, one might call them a passive fiscal policy. But our automatic stabilizers are now taken for granted; therefore we consider fiscal policy to be purely discretionary. Let's now consider the discretionary fiscal policy tools that are available to the federal government.

Making the Automatic Stabilizers More Effective

One problem with unemployment benefits is that they run out in six months while a recession can drag on for more than a year and its effects can last still longer. After the 1990–91 recession ended, the unemployment rate continued rising and did not begin to decline until a full year after the start of the recovery. Extending the benefit period is an example of discretionary fiscal policy because benefits are not extended automatically. An increase in the benefit ceiling or a widening of eligibility standards are other ways of making this stabilizer more effective.

One of the most devastating charges against President Bush during the 1992 election campaign was that he was insensitive to the suffering of the unemployed. The fact that he vetoed legislation extending unemployment benefits did not help his case, although he finally *did* relent and sign a bill that extended benefits in states with high unemployment for up to 20 more weeks.

Altering federal personal and corporate income tax schedules to make them more progressive is another example of discretionary fiscal policy. As the economy heats up and personal incomes and corporate profits rise, they would be taxed at progressively higher rates. Of course, the most recent adjustments in personal income taxes, the 1981 Kemp-Roth Act and the Tax Reform Act of 1986, have had the opposite effect, making the tax structure less progressive and therefore less countercyclical. Progressive taxes were more fully discussed in Chapter 7 if you'd like to review this material.

Public Works

During the Great Depression, the Roosevelt administration set up several so-called alphabet agencies to provide jobs for the long-term unemployed. Among them, the Works Progress Administration (WPA), the Civilian Conservation Corps (CCC), and the Public Works Administration (PWA) put millions of people to work doing everything from raking leaves to constructing government buildings.

> The main fiscal policy to end the Depression was public works.

One of the problems in getting these public works projects off the ground was a lack of plans. Not only did the government lack ready-to-go blueprints, but it did not even have a list of the needed projects. If the country is ever again to institute a public works program, it needs to be much better prepared than it was in the early 1930s. If not, by the time the program gets started, the recession will be over.

Although criticized as "make-work projects," the public works projects gave jobs to millions of the unemployed. These workers spent virtually their entire salaries, thereby creating demand for goods and services in the private sector, thus creating still more jobs. Unfortunately, in 1937, there was a complete turnaround in both fiscal and monetary policy, plunging the economy into a deep recession from which it did not fully recover until the massive arms buildup just before the country's involvement in World War II.

Public works is probably not the answer to recessions unless the downturns last so long that the projects can be carried out. Yet one might ask, if public works are so necessary, why wait for a recession to carry them out?

Transfer Payments

Just as the government could increase the amount of money given for unemployment compensation, it could add to the welfare, Social Security, and veterans' pensions during recessions. Like public works, this would channel money into the hands of consumers, who, by spending this money, would create jobs in the private sector.

> It seems ideally conceivable that the state . . . should undertake public works, that must be executed some time, in the slack periods when they can be executed at least expense, and will, at the same time, have a tendency to counteract a serious evil.
> —Philip H. Wicksteed
> *The Common Sense of Political Economy*

Increased transfer payments have the added advantage of working quickly. No plans or blueprints are needed. Just program the computer and put the checks in the mail.

Changes in Tax Rates

So far, the discretionary policy measures have dealt exclusively with recessions. What can we do to fight inflation? We can raise taxes.

This was done in 1968 when Congress, under President Lyndon Johnson, passed a 10 percent income tax surcharge. If your income was $15,000 and your federal income tax was listed in the tax table as $2,300, you had to pay a $230 surcharge, which raised your taxes to $2,530.

In the case of a recession, a tax cut would be the ticket. The recession of 1981–82 was somewhat mitigated by the Kemp-Roth tax cut, which called for a 5 percent cut in personal income taxes in 1981 and a 10 percent cut in July 1982. However salutary its effects, Kemp-Roth was seen by its framers as a long-run economic stimulant rather than an antirecessionary measure.

Corporate income taxes, too, may be raised during inflations and lowered when recessions occur. The investment tax credit, first adopted by the Kennedy administration, is another way of using taxes to manipulate spending.

A key advantage to using tax rate changes as a countercyclical policy tool is that they provide a quick fix. We have to make sure, however, that temporary tax cuts carried out during recessions do not become permanent cuts.

The Politics of Fiscal Policy

In a sense there really *is* no fiscal policy, but rather a series of political compromises within Congress and between the president and Congress. The reason for this lies within our political system, especially the way we pass laws.

To become a law, a bill introduced in either house of Congress must get through the appropriate committee (most bills never get that far) and then receive a majority vote from the members of that house. It must get through the other house of Congress in the same manner. Then a House–Senate conference committee, after compromising on the differences between the two versions of the bill, sends the compromise bill to both houses to be voted on once again. After receiving a majority vote in both houses, the bill goes to the president for his signature.

If the president does not like certain aspects of the bill, he can threaten to veto it, hoping Congress will bend to his wishes. If he gets what he wants, he now signs the bill and it becomes law. If not, he vetoes it. Overriding a veto takes a two-thirds vote in both houses—not an easy task.

Adding to the political difficulties, there were only six years between 1968 and 2000 when the president and the majority in both houses of Congress were in the same political party.[*] This necessitated still more compromise. For example, many Democrats in Congress wanted to scrap the third year of the Kemp-Roth tax cut scheduled to take effect July 1, 1983, while the president had considered asking Congress to make it effective January 1, 1983. Neither side got its way: The tax cut went into effect as scheduled, July 1, 1983. President Ronald Reagan wanted to cut social programs and raise military spending—priorities that many congressional Democrats wanted to reverse. Again, compromises had to be reached.

Although the president and the budget committees of the House and Senate come up with budgets for the coming fiscal year, the resulting fiscal policy is necessarily the product of political compromise. It's interesting that Republican and Democratic party leaders point the finger at each other when the economy doesn't improve. The suspicion here is that both sides are right.

---

[*]With substantial Democratic majorities in both houses of Congress, Bill Clinton enjoyed this political state of grace in 1993 and 1994, but since January 1995 the Republicans have held majorities in both houses of Congress. Technically, in 2001 the Senate was split 50-50 between the Democrats and the Republicans. But Vice President Richard Cheney, a Republican, was able to cast tie-breaking votes.

Changes in Government Spending

When we talked about increasing government transfer payments and embarking on public works projects to counter business downturns, we were calling for increased government spending. Looking back at the Depression, what finally pulled the United States out was the massive armament spending at the beginning of World War II. To generalize, then, we can beat any recession by having the government spend enough money.

But too much spending—whether C, or I, or G—will lead to inflation. To help solve that problem, we must cut government spending. Some critics of President Ronald Reagan had asked how he expected to end inflation by cutting social programs if, at the same time, he got Congress to raise defense spending even more. (See the box, "The Politics of Fiscal Policy.")

To summarize, discretionary fiscal policy dictates that we increase government spending and cut taxes to mitigate business downturns, and that we lower government spending and raise taxes to damp down inflation. In brief, we fight recessions with budget deficits and inflation with budget surpluses.

Who Makes Fiscal Policy?

Making fiscal policy is like driving a car. You steer, you keep your foot on the accelerator, and occasionally you use the brake. Basically, you should not go too fast or too slow, and you need to stay in your lane.

Would you mind letting someone else help you drive? Suppose you had a car with dual controls, like the ones driving schools have. Unless you and the other driver were in complete agreement, not only would driving not be much fun, but you'd be lucky to avoid having an accident.

So, if making fiscal policy is like driving a car, let's ask just who is doing the driving. Is it the president? Or is it Congress? The answer is yes to both questions. In other words, the conduct of our fiscal policy is a lot like driving a dually controlled car. Further complicating maneuvers, sometimes one political party controls Congress while the president belongs to the other party. In October 1990 the federal government all but shut down while President George Bush struggled with Congress in an effort to pass a budget. And in 1993, even though President Bill Clinton and a substantial majority of members of both houses were Democrats, each house passed a budget by just one vote. (See again the box, "The Politics of Fiscal Policy.")

Fiscal policy is indeed a powerful tool that may be used to promote full employment, stable prices, and a satisfactory rate of economic growth. But no one seems to be in charge of *making* fiscal policy. Nor is there widespread agreement among economists as to what effect any given fiscal policy measure has on our economy. Perhaps the words of Robert J. Gordon lend just the right perspective:

Unfortunately, policymakers cannot act as if the economy is an automobile that can quickly be steered back and forth. Rather, the procedure of changing aggregate demand is much closer to that of a captain navigating a giant super-tanker. Even if he gives a signal for a hard turn, it takes a mile before he can see a change, and 10 miles before the ship makes the turn.[4]

The huge budget deficits we've been running since the early 1980s have sharply limited the government's ability to use discretionary fiscal policy to create jobs and to stimulate the economy. Between legally mandated spending programs and legally mandated entitlement programs such as Social Security, Medicare, and Medicaid, there is little discretionary income to play with. Of course, the Treasury could borrow even more money, but only if Congress and the president were willing to allow the budget deficit to grow.

Part V: The Deficit Dilemma

Until the late 1990s, the federal budget deficit was considered a very serious problem. Now that problem has disappeared. Instead of running deficits, we are running surpluses, and those surpluses are expected to continue into the foreseeable future.

Deficits, Surpluses, and the Balanced Budget

To understand how fiscal policy works, we need to understand three basic concepts. First, the deficit. *When government spending is greater than tax revenue, we have a federal budget deficit.* The government is paying out more than it's taking in. How does it make up the difference? It borrows. Deficits have been much more common than surpluses. In fact, the federal government ran budget deficits every year from 1970 through 1997.

This is not to say that deficits are always bad. Indeed, during recessions, they are just what the economic doctor ordered. But as you are certainly aware, we have not had recessions every year between 1970 and 1997!

Second, budget surpluses are the exact opposite of deficits. They are prescribed to fight inflation. *When the budget is in a surplus position, tax revenue is greater than government spending.*

Finally, *we have a balanced budget when government expenditures are equal to tax revenue.* We've never had an exactly balanced budget; in many years of the 19th and early 20th

A deficit is created when the government is paying out more than it's taking in.

A billion here, a billion there, and pretty soon you're talking about *real* money.
—Everett Dirksen,
   U.S. Senator from Illinois in
   the 1960s and 1970s

---

[4]Robert J. Gordon, *Macroeconomics* (Boston: Little, Brown, 1978), p. 334.

The Paradox of Thrift[*]

Since childhood we have been taught that saving is good. Benjamin Franklin once said, "A penny saved is a penny earned." Franklin, it turns out, never followed his own advice. It also turns out that if we all try to save more, we'll probably end up with a really bad recession. This outcome is explained by the paradox of thrift.

You have probably heard that the sum of the parts does not necessarily add up to the whole. Consider, for example, what you would do if you were in a room full of people and that room suddenly burst into flames. Would you politely suggest to your companions that everyone file out of the room in an orderly fashion? Or would you bolt for the door?

What if the door opened inward (that is, into the room)? Whoever got there first would attempt to pull open the door. But if everyone made a dash for the door, they would all arrive at just about the same time. The person trying to pull open the door wouldn't have space to do this because everyone else would be pushing him against the door. Several people would get injured in the crush. Unless they backed off, no one would get out of the room.

We call this an example of the fallacy of composition. What makes perfect sense for one person to do—rush to the door and pull it open—makes no sense when everyone tries to do it at the same time.

The paradox of thrift is a variant of the fallacy of composition. If everyone tries to save more, they will all end up saving less. Let's say that every week you save an extra $10 from your paycheck. At the end of a year, you will have saved an extra $520. Right? Right! Now, what if everyone tries saving an extra $10 a week? At the end of a year, we should have tens of billions in extra savings. Right? Wrong!

How come? Because what makes sense for one person to do does not make sense for everyone to do. If everyone tries to save more, everyone is cutting back on consumption. Business sales fall by hundreds of millions of dollars a week. If 130 million people each cut back by $10 a week, that comes to a weekly reduction of $1.3 billion. Over the course of a year, this will add up to $67.6 billion!

This $67.6 billion decline in consumption will have a multiplied effect on GDP. If the multiplier is 4, GDP will decline by $270.4 billion; if it is 6, GDP will decline by $405.6 billion. Surely such declines are typical of depressions.

But that's just for starters. When retailers get the idea that business will be off over the next few months, they do two things: lay off employees and cut back on their inventory. The workers who lose their jobs cut back on their consumption. Meanwhile, the retailers have begun canceling their orders for new inventory, prompting factories to lay off people and cut back on their orders for raw materials.

As the recession spreads, more and more people get laid off, and each will cut back on his or her consumption, further aggravating the decline in retail sales.

Now we come back to saving. Millions of people have been laid off and millions more are on reduced hours. Still others no longer get overtime. Each of these people, then, has suffered substantially reduced income. Each is not able to save as much as before the recession. Savings decline.

And so we're back where we started. We have the paradox of thrift: *If everyone tries to save more, they all will end up saving less.*

One of the biggest problems we have had since the early 1980s has been our low savings rate. So one may ask: If our savings rate is too low, don't we really need to save more, and will more saving really lead to a recession? One way that this dilemma can be resolved is to have a growing economy. Everyone's income goes up, everyone saves more and consumes more, and there's no recession.

---

[*]The paradox of thrift is not relevant today because we save less than 5 percent of our personal income. Then why talk about it? Because it does a great job of illustrating how the multiplier works.

centuries, we had small surpluses or deficits. Perhaps if the deficit or surplus were less than $10 billion, we'd call that a balanced budget. Remember, we're dealing with a budget that calls for a total of nearly $4 trillion in taxes and spending, so if tax revenue and expenditures were within $10 billion of each other, that would be close enough to call the budget balanced.

Deficits and Surpluses: The Record

Back in Chapter 7, we talked about federal government spending and federal government tax receipts. Let's put all that data together and focus on how well the government has covered its spending with tax revenue. Let's look at the record since the 1950s (see Figure 6).

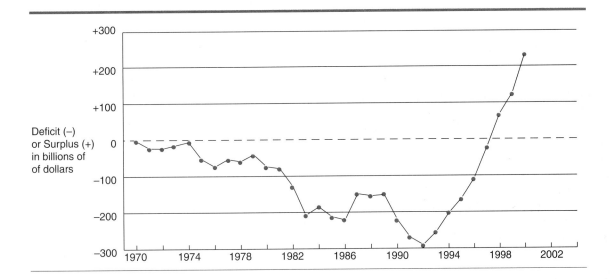

F*igure* 6

The Federal Budget Deficit, Fiscal Years 1970–2001

There were mounting deficits through most of the 1980s and early 1990s, followed by steadily declining deficits beginning in 1993. Finally in 1998 we had our first surplus since 1969.

Sources: Economic Report of the President, 2001; *Economic Indicators,* March 2001.

How do we interpret the data? On the surface, it's obvious that the deficit went throug the roof in the 1980s. Indeed, during the late 1940s the government ran three surpluses, in the 1950s it ran four, it ran just one in the 1960s, and it ran none between 1970 and 1997. Since 1998 we have run surpluses.

What has brought the deficit down since 1992? Congress passed two huge deficit reduction packages in 1990 and in 1993. To secure the spending cuts he wanted in 1990, George ("Read my lips: no tax increase") Bush agreed with the Democratic leaders of Congress to a tax increase, raising the top personal income tax bracket from 28 percent to 31 percent, which probably cost him reelection in 1992. The $492 billion five-year deficit reduction package had a major impact.

Then, three years later, President Clinton pushed a five-year $433 billion deficit reduction package through Congress. About half this package was tax increases and half was government spending reductions. Its main feature was raising the top personal income tax bracket from 31 percent to 39.6 percent. So, over a three-year period, the top income tax bracket went from 28 percent to 39.6 percent.

Is there a "real" surplus that is much smaller than the "official" surplus? In fiscal year 2000 the Social Security Trust Fund (which exists only as a computer entry in the federal government's accounts) took in about $148 billion more (in tax receipts and interest on the federal debt it holds) than it paid out. Without these revenues, the federal surplus for fiscal year 2000 would have been just $89 billion, rather than the official figure of $237 billion. Perhaps our real deficit worries will not begin until the second decade of the 21st century, when the baby boomers begin to retire and the Social Security Trust Fund surplus turns into a deficit.

How does our deficit compare with those of other nations? Until the late 1990s, we were among those running the highest deficits. But as you can see by glancing at Figure 7, we were running larger surpluses by 1998.

Why Are Large Deficits So Bad?

Let us count the ways. Number one: They raise interest rates, which, in turn, discourages investment. Our real interest rate (the nominal interest rate less the rate of infla-

Figure 7

The Surplus or Deficit as a
Percentage of GDP, Selected
Countries, 1999
While most of these countries have
been running deficits, the U.S. has
been running larger and larger
surpluses since 1998.

*In 2000 the U.S. surplus rose to
2.4 percent of GDP.

Sources: Business Week, April 2, 2001,
p.48; *New York Times Almanac,* 2001.

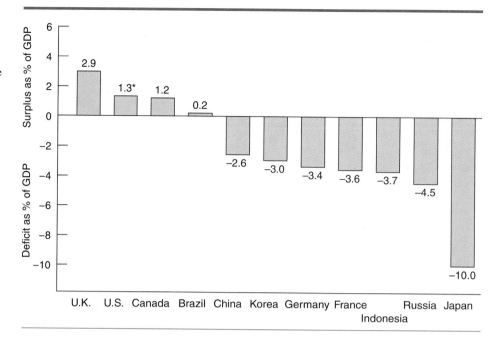

tion) during the latter half of the 1980s and all of the 1990s was three times as high as
the real interest rate in Japan, and it was much higher than those in most Western European countries as well. The Japanese, who had been investing in plant and equipment at
more than twice our rate (as a percentage of GDP)—and more than we had in absolute
numbers as well—have been able to tap a huge domestic pool of savings and *still* have
more than $100 billion a year left over to invest in the United States and other coun-
tries. The Japanese today have a savings pool of more than $10 trillion. In fact, had it
not been for this vast inflow of savings from Japan and Western Europe, our interest
rates would have been much higher.

Number two: The federal government had become increasingly dependent on foreign savers to finance the deficit—in the early- and mid-1990s foreigners financed more
than half the deficit.

Number three: Until the mid-1990s the deficit sopped up more than half the personal savings in this country, making that much less savings available to large corporate
borrowers seeking funds for new plant and equipment. We'll talk about this when we
discuss the crowding-out effect in the appendix to this chapter.

On the positive side, budget deficits stimulate the economy. The only problem is
that we should not have needed this stimulus during the "prosperous" mid- to late 1980s,
when we were running huge deficits. And, as Senator Lloyd Bentsen put it during his
televised vice presidential debate with Senator Dan Quayle in 1988, anyone could induce
prosperity by writing hundreds of billions of dollars of "hot checks." We would do well
to remember that John Maynard Keynes advocated writing those checks during recessions and paying them off during prosperity.

Will We Be Able to Balance Future Budgets?

We finally managed to run a federal budget surplus in 1998, and the Congressional
Budget Office forecasts a string of surpluses well into the new millenium. But no
sooner were these surpluses forecast than Congressional Republicans and Democrats
proposed dueling plans to dispose of those surpluses with various combinations of
tax cuts and spending increases. Interestingly, however, no elected official proposed
even slowing down the projected increases in Social Security spending (see box, "The
Special Interest Groups").

The Special Interest Groups

> Government is not a candy store in which every group can pick from any jar it wants.
>
> —Ross Perot[*]

During every election campaign people make allusions to special interest groups—wealthy contributors, lobbyists, labor unions, defense contractors, and the like—who exert undue political influence and receive special favors. For example, the government has been paying farmers billions of dollars a year in subsidies, ostensibly to save the family farm. But in the 6 decades that this program has been in operation, 7 out of every 10 family farms have disappeared; three-quarters of the payments go to large corporate farms.

But the group that has fed the most at the government trough is the elderly. Since 1960 the dollars of federal benefit outlays per elderly person has more than quadrupled, from a little over $3,000 to more than $15,000 (both in constant 2001 dollars). Military pensions, civil service pensions, veterans' benefits, Medicare payments, and, of course, Social Security retirement benefits have all skyrocketed over the last three decades. And the lion's share of this money has gone to the middle-class and wealthy elderly rather than to the elderly poor. Peter G. Peterson and Neil Howe have explained just how the system works:

> In the end, what we wound up with was a kind of "government by grievance." Each nonpoverty entitlement program acquired and nurtured a public constituency, which, with the aid of its corresponding bureaucratic and congressional constituency (not to mention the battalions of special interest lawyers), protected and assured its continual expansion. As time went on, the entire fiscal system acquired a strong bias favoring budget deficits and the current consumption of national resources.[†]

---

[*]Ross Perot, *United We Stand* (New York: Hyperion, 1992), p. 36.

[†]Peter G. Peterson and Neil Howe, *On Borrowed Time* (New York: Simon & Schuster, 1988), p. 16.

The centerpiece of George W. Bush's presidential campaign was a $1.6 trillion tax cut, which would be spread out between 2001 and 2011. Because a cumulative surplus of $5.6 trillion was forecast over this period, perhaps $2.9 trillion of which was earmarked for the Social Security and Medicare trust funds, a tax cut of this magnitude would apparently still permit us to continue running very sizeable surpluses. Most of his proposed tax cut would have gone toward lowering personal income tax rates, doubling the child care tax credit to $1,000, and eliminating the marriage penalty (under which married couples usually paid higher taxes than they would have had they filed separately). In addition, Bush proposed phasing out the estate tax, which was paid by fewer than 50,000 estates a year, and clearly was a burden that fell almost exclusively upon the rich.

In early 2001, the Republican majority in the House of Representatives passed the president's $1.6 trillion tax cut intact. However the Senate, without getting into specifics, passed a tax cut of just $1.2 trillion in April. This book had to go to press before Congress completed action on this tax bill, which would have gone to the White House for the president's signature.

A related issue which arose during congressional debate was possibly "front-loading" the tax cut to provide some economic stimulus to our slowing economy. As Congress debated, it was still unclear whether the economic slowdown that had begun in the fourth quarter of 2000 would develop into a full-fledged recession. Clearly a substantial tax cut would be the proper fiscal policy to pursue if, indeed, we were in a recession. But in April of 2001 (to paraphrase an old Clairol shampoo ad), even President Bush's economists did not know for sure.

But all good things *do* come to an end. A recession, a decline in stock prices, a tax cut, or an increase in government spending programs can easily push the deficit back up again. And keep in mind that after the year 2015, as the baby boom generation attains senior citizenship, the Social Security Trust Fund will quickly be depleted, and, unless the government has already raised Social Security taxes or cut benefits, the federal budget surplus will quickly become a large and growing deficit.

Balancing the Budget over the Business Cycle

Do you remember the Old Testament story of Joseph, the man who had a real talent for interpreting dreams? One day he was asked by the king to interpret this dream: Seven fat cows walked by, followed by seven emaciated cows. That was an easy one for Joseph. Seven fat years, or good harvests, would be followed by seven lean years, or bad harvests. Joseph's policy prescription: Store all the surplus grain grown during the seven years of plentiful harvests and use this bounty to feed everyone during the lean years.

What should we have learned from that story? We should have learned that during years of economic prosperity, we need to run budget surpluses. And that we could use those surpluses to finance the deficits we incur during recessionary years. So, over the entire business cycle, we have balanced the budget.

Part VI: The Proposed Balanced Budget Amendment and the Line Item Veto

To come back to the dictum that we must balance our budget each year—something the government really tried to do even into the early 1930s—the economic wisdom today tells us that we should have deficits in lean years and surpluses in fat years. But perhaps over the course of the business cycle, we should balance the budget (see the box, "Balancing the Budget over the Business Cycle").

Of course, it hasn't worked out that way. From 1961 through 1997 we managed only one surplus. Our national debt rose year after year as we ran budget deficits in fat years as well as in lean years. (See the box, "Micawber's Equation.")

The first step in passing a Constitutional amendment is a two-thirds vote in both houses of Congress. Then it would still need to be ratified by three-quarters of the states before it became part of our Constitution. Despite some very close votes in 1994, 1995, 1996, and 1997, the balanced budget amendment failed in one or the other house of Congress.

Those advocating a balanced budget amendment to the Constitution use our history of deficits and our mounting national debt to make their case. If our political leaders are unwilling or unable to exercise restraint, they will be required by law to do so.

Do we want to put ourselves in an economic straitjacket?

Most economists oppose such an amendment because it would put us in an economic straitjacket. No longer would we be able to fight recessions with deficits. Even our automatic stabilizers would be taken from us (as they are sure to cause deficits in recession years), leaving us vulnerable not just to recessions but to depressions as well.

The irony and even hypocrisy of this proposed amendment lay with its greatest advocate, President Ronald Reagan. It was remarkable that the man who presided over eight

Micawber's Equation

Do you remember Mr. Micawber from *David Copperfield*? This poor man was almost always just one step ahead of his creditors. Here is the advice he offered David, who was visiting him in debtors' prison:

> He solemnly conjured me, I remember, to take warning by his fate; and to observe that if a man had twenty pounds a-year for his income, and spent nineteen pounds nineteen shillings and sixpence, he would be happy, but that if he spent twenty pounds one he would be miserable.*

Should we apply Micawber's equation to the federal budget? Will future budget deficits and mounting public debt lead to national misery? There are plenty of people out there who would agree with Mr. Micawber that our government must not spend one penny more than it receives in taxes.

---

*Charles Dickens, *David Copperfield* (Harmondsworth, Middlesex, England: Penguin Books), p. 221.

of the largest deficits in our entire history was supporting a balanced budget amendment. "Stop me," he seemed to be pleading, "before I spend again!" His successor, George Bush, who went on to run even larger deficits than Reagan, pleaded again and again for the balanced budget amendment, as if that measure would magically wipe out all the red ink. Of course there's plenty of blame to go around considering that the president can't spend one penny without having Congress pass the necessary legislation.

In still another effort to lower the deficit, Congress passed a law in 1996 to permit the president to veto parts of tax and spending bills he opposes, without vetoing the entire legislation. This line item veto can be eventually overridden by a two-thirds vote in each house of Congress. In August 1997 President Clinton used the line item veto to strike down three relatively minor tax and spending items, while declaring, "From now on, presidents will be able to say no to wasteful spending or tax loopholes, even as they say yes to vital legislation." By December 1997 he had vetoed less than $2 billion of spending items, a minuscule fraction of the federal budget. Opponents of the line item veto claimed that it can be enacted only by constitutional amendment. In February 1998 a federal judge ruled the line item veto unconstitutional because it gave the president powers that Article I of the Constitution reserved for Congress.

Part VII: The Public Debt

The debt is like a crazy aunt we keep down in the basement. All the neighbors know she's there, but nobody wants to talk about her.

—Ross Perot

The public, or national, debt is the amount of currently outstanding federal securities that the Treasury has issued. Although nearly half is held by various federal agencies, most notably the Social Security Trust Fund and Federal Reserve, it is reasonable to say that the public debt is what the federal government owes to the holders of Treasury bills, notes, bonds, and certificates.

In 1981 the public debt went over the $1 trillion mark. Do you remember how much money $1 trillion is? Write it out with all the zeros right here:

Written out, it looks like this: $1,000,000,000,000.[5] In 1986 the national debt broke the $2 trillion mark. That means it took the federal government just five years to accumulate as much debt as it had accumulated between 1776 and 1981. The $3 trillion barrier was breached in 1989. We passed the $4 trillion mark in 1992 and the $5 trillion mark in 1996 (see Figure 8).

Exactly what is the national debt? It is *the cumulative total of all the federal budget deficits less any surpluses.* Much of it was run up during recessions and wars. It is owed to the holders of Treasury bills, notes, certificates, and bonds. For example, if you own any of these, you are holding part of the national debt. (For extra help in differentiating between the deficit and the debt, see the Extra Help box.)

Who holds the national debt? Private American citizens hold a little less than half. Foreigners hold almost one third. The rest is held by banks, other business firms, and U.S. government agencies. Those who say we owe it to ourselves are substantially correct. As a taxpayer, you owe part of that debt. And if you happen to own any U.S. government securities, you are also owed part of the debt, so you literally owe it to yourself.

Is the national debt a burden that will have to be borne by future generations? As long as we owe it to ourselves, the answer is no. If we did owe it mainly to foreigners,

The attractiveness of financing spending by debt issue to the elected politicians should be obvious. Borrowing allows spending to be made that will yield immediate payoffs without the incurring of any immediate political cost.

—James Buchanan, *The Deficit and American Democracy*

Exactly what is the national debt?

A nation is not in danger of financial disaster merely because it owes itself money.

—Andrew W. Mellon, Secretary of the Treasury in the 1920s

---

[5]If big numbers still make you nervous, you would do well to review the box "A Word about Numbers," near the beginning of Chapter 5.

Differentiating between the Deficit and the Debt

It's easy to confuse the federal budget deficit and the national debt. The *deficit* occurs when federal government spending is greater than tax revenue. The *debt* is the cumulative total of all the federal budget deficits less any surpluses.

Until 1998 the last time we had a budget surplus was in 1969. This means that our public debt had been rising steadily since that year.

Now suppose that our deficit declined one year, say, from $200 billion to $150 billion. What would happen to the national debt? Can you guess? It would still go up. By how much? By $150 billion. So every year that we have a deficit—even a declining one—the national debt will go up.

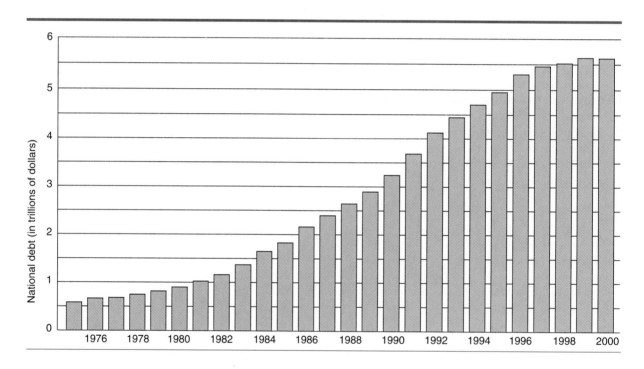

F*igure* 8

National Debt, 1975–2000*

The steady rise in the national debt through the 1970s, 1980s, and almost the entire 1990s was caused by the federal budget deficits that we ran each year. And when we finally began running surpluses in the late 1990s, we were able to start paying down the debt.

*Debt on January 1 of each year.

Source: Economic Report of the President, 2001.

and if they wanted to be paid off, it could be a great burden. But that is certainly not the case at this point.

In 1960 foreigners held about 3 percent of the national debt. They have increased their holdings so substantially in recent years almost entirely because Americans love to spend and hate to save, and because the U.S. federal government had run megadeficits from the early 1980s to the mid-1990s. Because our saving rate was so low, there wasn't enough domestic saving available to finance the federal budget deficits; but foreigners, particularly the Japanese, were awash with dollars, so they simply recycled them by lending them to the U.S. government. Today foreigners hold more than 30 percent of the public debt.

The national debt rose substantially during wars. We paid for these wars partly by taxation and partly by borrowing. It was considered one's patriotic duty during World War II to buy war bonds. Unfortunately, however, it was also a terrible investment because the buyers were locked into low interest rates—between 1 and 1½ percent for 7 to 10 years—while immediately after the war, prices jumped 35 percent in 3 years.

In wartime a nation will invest very little in plant and equipment; all available resources must go toward the war effort. As a result, during the first half of the 1940s, we built no new plant and equipment. Had there been no war, billions of dollars' worth of plant and equipment would have been built. The generation that came of age after the war inherited less capital than it would have had no war been fought. To that degree, a burden was placed on their shoulders.

Those who would point at the huge increase in the national debt during the war as the cause of our having less plant and equipment have misplaced the blame. It was the war, not the increase in the debt, that prevented wartime construction of capital goods.

When do we have to pay off the debt? We don't. All we have to do is roll it over, or refinance it, as it falls due. Each year several hundred billion dollars' worth of federal securities fall due. By selling new ones, the Treasury keeps us going. But there is no reason why the national debt ever has to be paid off.

When do we have to pay off the national debt?

Why not go ahead and just pay off the debt? Economists predict that following this course would have catastrophic consequences. If we tried to pay the debt off too quickly it might even send us into a deep depression. According to our earlier analysis, when the economy is experiencing high unemployment, we need to run budget deficits, not surpluses. But during prosperity, particularly when inflation becomes a problem, we need to run budget surpluses, paying off part of the debt. This is the part of a countercyclical policy we have ignored during most of the last three decades.

Let's return to two of the dicta stated at the beginning of this chapter: (1) The public debt is a burden on future generations. (2) We owe it to ourselves. To the degree that the debt is being held increasingly by foreigners, we can no longer say we owe it (only) to ourselves. In the future, even if we never pay back one penny of that debt, our children and our grandchildren will have to pay foreigners hundreds of billions of dollars a year in interest. At least to that degree, then, the public debt *will* be a burden to future generations.

Blessed are the young, for they shall inherit the national debt.
—Herbert Hoover

Believe or not, if we keep running large surpluses and pay down the national debt, this will cause a problem for both the Social Security Trust Fund and the Federal Reserve. Both have huge investments in U.S. government securities. But, as the national debt gets paid down, there won't be any of these securities for them to buy. Since the Social Security Trust Fund is required by law to invest in Treasury bonds, the law may have to be changed. Still, it is a whole lot better to have problems like these than those caused by running huge budget deficits year after year.

Questions for Further Thought and Discussion

1. Describe the differences between an inflationary gap and a deflationary gap.

2. Explain why large deficits are so bad.

3. It can be argued that there really is no fiscal policy. How would you make this argument?

4. To what degree is the public debt a burden to future generations?

5. Explain how, in general, the automatic stabilizers work. Then use one automatic stabilizer to illustrate this.

6. Suppose income taxes and unemployment compensation were cut by an equal amount. How would aggregate demand be affected?

7. Right now is there an inflationary gap or a deflationary gap?

8. Can you remember the last good or service you purchased? Explain how the money you spent will lead to a multiplied chain of increased income and spending.

9. As late as 1992 we were running budget deficits of nearly $300 billion. How do you explain the decline in the deficits through the rest of the decade?

Workbook for Chapter 12

Name _____ Date _____

Multiple-Choice Questions

Circle the letter that corresponds to the best answer.

1. In the late 1970s and early 1980s, the goals of fiscal policy were _____.
   a) completely attained
   c) largely unattained
   b) largely attained
   d) completely unattained

2. When equilibrium GDP is too small, we have _____.
   a) a deflationary gap
   c) an inflationary gap
   b) a depression
   d) none of these

3. There is an inflationary gap when _____.
   a) equilibrium GDP is equal to full-employment GDP
   b) equilibrium GDP is smaller than full-employment GDP
   c) equilibrium GDP is larger than full-employment GDP
   d) none of these occur

4. Fiscal policy and monetary policy are _____.
   a) different means used to attain different goals
   b) different means used to attain the same goals
   c) the same means to attain the same goals
   d) the same means to attain different goals

5. Budget surpluses are most appropriate during _____.
   a) depressions   b) recessions   c) inflations

6. Each of the following is an automatic stabilizer except
   a) unemployment compensation
   b) direct taxes
   c) welfare payments
   d) Social Security benefits

7. If you lost a $300-a-week job and were eligible for unemployment insurance, you would probably collect about _____.
   a) $240   b) $200   c) $160
   d) 120   e) $80

8. When there is a recession, the biggest decline is in _____.
   a) Social Security tax receipts
   b) personal income tax receipts
   c) consumer spending
   d) corporate aftertax profits

9. The automatic stabilizers _____.
   a) help smooth out the business cycle
   b) make the business cycle worse
   c) eliminate the business cycle

10. Each of the following is an example of discretionary fiscal policy except _____.
    a) public works spending
    b) making the automatic stabilizers more effective
    c) changes in tax rates
    d) the unemployment insurance program

11. The proposed balanced budget amendment to the Constitution would have required the federal budget to be balanced _____.
    a) over the business cycle
    b) every three years
    c) every year
    d) every nonrecession year

12. Fiscal policy is made by _____.
    a) the president only
    b) Congress only
    c) both the president and Congress
    d) neither the president nor Congress

13. The requirement to override a presidential veto is
    _____.

    a) a majority vote in each house of Congress

    b) a two-thirds vote in each house of Congress

    c) a three-quarters vote in each house of Congress

    d) a majority vote of both houses of Congress combined

14. If we passed a constitutional amendment requiring a balanced budget every year, this would probably
    _____.

    a) make our recessions into depressions

    b) prevent recessions

    c) create inflations

    d) raise interest rates

15. If equilibrium GDP is $5.5 trillion and full employment GDP is $5 trillion, there is _____.

    a) definitely an inflationary gap

    b) probably an inflationary gap

    c) definitely a deflationary gap

    d) probably a deflationary gap

16. Statement 1: A tax cut will have the same impact on the deflationary gap as an increase in G only if people spend the entire tax cut.
    Statement 2: The paradox of thrift is more relevant today, when savings are so low, than it was back in the 1950s and 1960s.

    a) Statement 1 is true and statement 2 is false.

    b) Statement 2 is true and statement 1 is false.

    c) Both statements are true.

    d) Both statements are false.

17. Statement 1: Although the federal budget deficit was higher in the 1980s than in the 1970s, it was a somewhat smaller percentage of GDP.
    Statement 2: The federal budget deficit reached $5.5 trillion in 1998.

    a) Statement 1 is true and statement 2 is false.

    b) Statement 2 is true and statement 1 is false.

    c) Both statements are true.

    d) Both statements are false.

18. Which statement is true?

    a) About one-third of the national debt is rolled over (or refinanced) every year.

    b) The national debt is doubling every 10 years.

    c) Unless we balance the budget within the next five years, the United States stands a good chance of going bankrupt.

    d) None of these statements is true.

19. Since 1945 the national debt has _____ as a percent of GDP.

    a) risen

    b) fallen

    c) remained about the same

20. Which statement is true?

    a) The national debt is larger than GDP.

    b) The national debt will have to be paid off eventually.

    c) Most of the national debt is held by foreigners.

    d) None of these statements is true.

21. If the federal government attempts to eliminate a budget deficit during a depression, this will
    _____.

    a) alleviate the depression

    b) contribute to inflation

    c) make the depression worse

    d) have no economic effect

22. During times of inflation, we want to _____.

    a) raise taxes and run budget deficits

    b) raise taxes and run budget surpluses

    c) lower taxes and run budget surpluses

    d) lower taxes and run budget deficits

23. Which statement is true?

    a) The public debt is larger than our GDP.

    b) The public debt is the sum of our deficits minus our surpluses over the years since the beginning of the country.

    c) We have had budget deficits only during recession years and wartime.

    d) None of these statements is true.

24. Through the 1970s, 1980s, and most of the 1990s, the public debt _____; each year since 1998 the public debt _____.
    a) fell, rose
    b) rose, fell
    c) fell, fell
    d) rose, rose

25. A major advantage of the automatic stabilizers is that they _____.
    a) simultaneously stabilize the economy and tend to reduce the size of the public debt
    b) guarantee that the federal budget will be balanced over the course of the business cycle
    c) automatically produce surpluses during recessions and deficits during inflations
    d) require no legislative action by Congress to be made effective

26. The most valid argument against the size of the national debt is that it _____.
    a) will ruin the nation when we have to pay it back
    b) is owed mainly to foreigners
    c) leaves future generations less plant and equipment than would be left had there been a smaller debt
    d) will bankrupt the nation because there is a limit as to how much we can borrow

27. The Budget Act of 1990 was designed to lower the deficit over the next five years by a total of nearly $ _____ billion.
    a) 100
    b) 200
    c) 300
    d) 400
    e) 500

28. Currently we have a _____.
    a) very small deflationary gap
    b) a very large deflationary gap
    c) a very small inflationary gap

29. Between 1998 and 2000 the federal budget surplus and the national debt held by the public _____.
    a) rose, rose
    b) fell, fell
    c) rose, fell
    d) fell, rose

Fill-In Questions

1. The means that fiscal policy uses to attain those goals are the manipulation of _____ and _____.

2. We could eliminate inflationary gaps and deflationary gaps by making _____ GDP equal to _____ GDP.

3. The two ways of eliminating an inflationary gap are
   (1) _____
   and (2) _____.

4. The two ways of eliminating a deflationary gap are
   (1) _____
   and (2) _____.

5. Welfare spending, unemployment compensation, and direct taxes are all examples of _____.

6. If you are earning $200 a week before taxes and then collect unemployment insurance benefits, you can expect to collect about $ _____ a week.

7. Perhaps the most countercyclical of all the automatic stabilizers is the _____.

8. In addition to the automatic stabilizer, we have _____ fiscal policy.

9. Fiscal policy was invented by _____.

10. When equilibrium GDP is equal to full-employment GDP, we have an inflationary gap equal to _____.

Problems

1. **a.** In Figure 1, is there an inflationary gap or a deflationary gap? **b.** How much is it? **c.** How much is the multiplier?

Figure 1

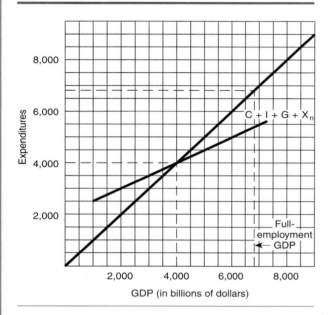

2. To remove the gap in Figure 1, what two fiscal policy measures would you recommend?

3. When the MPC is .8, how much is the multiplier?

4. If the MPC is .6, how much is the multiplier?

5. If C rises by $10 billion and the multiplier is 4, what happens to the level of GDP?

6. If I falls by $20 billion and the multiplier is 5, what happens to the level of GDP?

7. If GDP is 3,400, the multiplier is 5, and I rises by 15, what is the new level of GDP?

8. If GDP is 3,900, the multiplier is 8, and G falls by 10, what is the new level of GDP?

9. Suppose that Saddam and George each have MPCs of .5. If Saddam receives one dollar of income, how much of that dollar would he be expected to spend? If George receives all of the money that Saddam spent, how much would George be expected to spend?

10. If equilibrium GDP is $400 billion greater than full-employment GDP and there is an inflationary gap of $50 billion, how much is the multiplier?

11. If the full-employment GDP is $1 trillion greater than equilibrium GDP and the multiplier is 5, how much is the deflationary gap?

12. If George receives $1,000 from his newly created government job and gives $900 to Bill for writing him a speech, and then Bill gives $810 to Ralph for installing a computer system, assuming everyone else in the nation has the same spending pattern: **a.** How much is the multiplier? **b.** If $10 billion of new investment had been made, by how much would our GDP rise?

13. Suppose that in the year 2020 our national debt were $10 trillion and our budget deficit were $300 billion. If a plan to gradually reduce the deficit and to balance the budget in the year 2030 were successful, make an estimate of the national debt in 2030.

14. In Figure 2: **a.** Is there an inflationary gap or a deflationary gap? **b.** How much is it? **c.** How much is the multiplier?

Figure 2

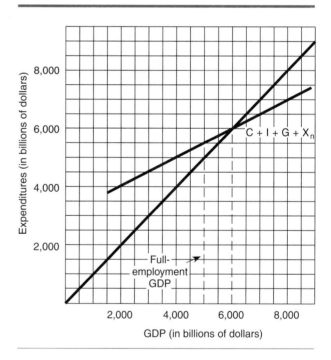

15. Krista Chavez was earning $600 a week after taxes and saved $50. If she lost her job, how much did she now spend each week on consumption? Show how you got your answer.

Appendix

The Full-Employment Budget and the Crowding-Out and Crowding-In Effects

There is fairly widespread agreement among economists that the government needs to run budget deficits during recessions and surpluses during periods of prosperity, full employment, and inflation. But how big should those deficits and surpluses be? That question is answered by setting up the full-employment budget. A second issue, raised by many conservative economists, is whether large budget deficits don't crowd private borrowers out of the financial markets. Or whether, as the Keynesians maintain, these large deficits actually lead to *more* private borrowing. In this appendix we will examine the issue of crowding out versus crowding in.

APPENDIX OBJECTIVES

In this appendix you will learn about:

* The full-employment budget.
* The crowding-out effect.
* The crowding-in effect.

The Full-Employment Budget

One question I have sidestepped is the size of deficits or surpluses. Besides saying that if the deficit or surplus is less than $10 billion the budget is virtually in balance and that our country's $200 billion-plus deficits in the early 1990s were huge indeed, I have not distinguished among the various sizes of deficits during the past few decades. To do that, I will use the concept of the full-employment budget.

To better understand this concept, let's start with an economy that is at full employment with a balanced budget. The unemployment rate is 5 percent, and federal expenditures are equal to tax revenues. What would happen if the unemployment rate rose just

How big should our deficits be during recessions?

1 percentage point to 6 percent? Economists have calculated that federal tax revenues would fall and government spending would rise by approximately $40 billion. The government would be taking in less in taxes because 1.45 million workers lost their jobs and corporate profits probably declined somewhat.[1] Also, government expenditures for transfer payments, particularly unemployment benefits, food stamps, welfare, and Medicaid, would rise. Together, then, the decline in tax revenue and the rise in government expenditures would total some $40 billion. In other words, we'd have a budget deficit of $40 billion.

Now we'll take it a step further by raising the unemployment rate to 7 percent, forcing up the deficit another $40 billion to a grand total of $80 billion.

Assuming no changes in the tax structure and no new government spending programs, let's figure out how much of a deficit the government would have been running had the economy been at full employment. Think about it. Tax revenue would have been higher because 2.9 million more people would have been working. Government expenditures would have been much lower because more than one million fewer people would have been collecting unemployment benefits; food stamp and welfare payments also would have been much lower.[2] In fact, the deficit would have been zero.

When the deficit is zero, the budget is balanced. Had our economy been at full employment then, we would have had a balanced budget. In other words, with a 7 percent unemployment rate and a $80 billion deficit, we would still say that we had a full-employment balanced budget.

A deficit of $80 billion when the unemployment rate is 7 percent would provide the same economic stimulus that a balanced budget would provide when there is full employment. (If this is not entirely clear to you, see the Extra Help box.)

All of this seems to fly in the face of our recent experience. After all, our unemployment rate has been below 5 percent since mid-1997. How can we still define full employment at a 5 percent unemployment level—let alone a level of 5½ or 6 percent? You've just asked a very good question. The answer is that extraordinary circumstances have pushed the unemployment rate below 5 percent, but those circumstances may prove temporary. If that's true, then we shall soon see the unemployment rate go back up again. If not, then maybe we'll need to reset the unemployment rate that defines full employment.

The Crowding-Out and Crowding-In Effects

The great debate: Monetarists: Deficits cause crowding-out. Keynesians: Deficits cause crowding-in.

Welcome to the first debate we are going to be sponsoring between the monetarists and the Keynesians over the next few chapters. In this debate the monetarists will argue in favor of the crowding-out effect, while the Keynesians will take the side of the crowding-in effect.

The monetarists maintain that Keynesian deficits designed to raise aggregate demand will have little, if any, positive effect. First, budget deficits drive up interest rates, thus discouraging investment. Second, the more money the government borrows to finance the deficit, the less that will be available to private borrowers.

If the proper fiscal policy during recessions is a large budget deficit, one would wonder where the Treasury will get all this money. Presumably it will go out and borrow it. But from whom?

If it borrows funds from individuals who would have otherwise made this money available for business investment, won't business borrowers be "crowded out" of the financial markets by the government? And won't interest rates be driven up in the process, further discouraging investment? Won't increased government spending financed by borrowing be replacing private investment spending?

---

[1] We are assuming a labor force of 145 million people.

[2] We are assuming that only 40 percent of the unemployed receive unemployment insurance benefits.

Read Only if the Full-Employment Balanced Budget Is Not Clear to You

The full-employment balanced budget means the federal government's spending equals its tax receipts when there is full employment. So if the unemployment rate is 5 percent, the deficit is zero. That's our starting point. For every 1 percent that the unemployment rate rises, the federal budget deficit rises by $40 billion (because such expenditures as unemployment benefits and welfare payments would automatically go up, while tax revenues would decline). OK, so if the unemployment rate were 6 percent, and if the deficit were 40 then we'd have a full-employment balanced budget.

A deficit of 40 would be exactly right for our economy if the unemployment rate were 6 percent. It would stimulate the economy (through more spending and lower tax receipts) and move the country back toward full employment.

What if the deficit were 50? It would be 10 too big. Instead of a full-employment balanced budget, we'd have a full-employment budget deficit of 10.

Now we'll see how much you've learned. If we have an unemployment rate of 8 percent, how large a deficit *should* we run? Work it out here:

The answer is 120. Because the unemployment rate is 3 percent over the full-employment rate of 5 percent, we need to run a deficit of 120 to have a full-employment balanced budget.

Next question: What if the deficit were only 80 and we had an unemployment rate of 8 percent? What would we have? Would it be a full-employment budget surplus or a full-employment budget deficit? It would be a full-employment budget surplus because it would be as if we were running a surplus when we were at full employment.

One more question: If we *did* run an actual deficit of 80 when the unemployment rate was 8 percent, how much of a full-employment budget surplus would we be running? The answer is 40. We *needed* a deficit of 120, but it was only 80; we were 40 short. By running a deficit of just 60, we were, in fact, running a full-employment budget surplus of 40.

The answer is yes to all three questions. Yes—but to what degree?

During recessions business firms cut back on their investing, so the government would be tapping a relatively idle source of funds, and during recessions interest rates tend to fall.

Even during relatively prosperous times, such as the mid-1980s, there is enough money to go around if the Federal Reserve allows the money supply to grow at a fairly rapid clip and if foreign investors are willing to make a few hundred billion dollars available each year to major corporations as well as to the U.S. Treasury.

Nevertheless, the crowding-out effect cannot be dismissed out of hand, particularly during times of tight money, such as the late 1970s and early 1980s. That any borrower as big as the U.S. government crowds other borrowers out of financial markets is a fact (see box, "Is the Federal Government Crowding Out Private Borrowers?"). And as the late Israeli defense minister Moshe Dayan once put it, "You can't argue with a fact."

Let's take a closer look at the Keynesian position. When there is substantial economic slack, one would not expect increased government borrowing to have much impact in financial markets. Not only would there be little effect on interest rates, but the Treasury would be sopping up funds that would otherwise go unclaimed. When orthodox Keynesian fiscal policy is followed, it is precisely during times of economic slack that large budget deficits are incurred.

One might also mention a possible "crowding-in" effect caused by deficit financing. This results from the stimulative effect that the deficit has on aggregate demand. If a massive personal income tax cut causes the deficit, consumption will rise, pulling up aggregate demand and inducing more investment. Similarly, increased government spending will raise aggregate demand, also inducing more investment. In other words, any rise in aggregate demand will induce a rise in investment.

This leaves us with one last question: which is larger, the crowding-in or the crowding-out effect? It doesn't really matter. The point is that as long as there is a sizable

Is the Federal Government Crowding Out Private Borrowers?

In the late 1980s and early 1990s the government was running massive budget deficits, although the unemployment rate was hovering around 5 percent. The Treasury was sopping up over half of all personal saving just to finance these deficits. But foreigners were also financing just over half of the deficit. Because virtually all our personal savings was indeed available to private borrowers, it could be argued that there was no crowding-out effect.

However, had the Treasury not been borrowing so heavily from foreigners, *that* money would have been available to American corporations seeking funds to replace and expand their plant and equipment. Furthermore, because of the huge deficits the Treasury was financing, real interest rates were much higher than they would have otherwise been. These high rates further discouraged private borrowing.

In sum, there definitely *was* a large crowding-out effect in the late 1980s. But it would have been a lot larger had it not been for the great inflow of foreign funds.

In the aftermath of the recession of 1990–91, not only did the government run the two largest budget deficits in U.S. history, but the Federal Reserve tried to accommodate private borrowers by pushing interest rates down to 15-year lows. And still President Bush was forced to term the recovery "anemic." One of the problems was that many banks were happy to pay only 2 or 3 percent interest for deposits and then buy U.S. government securities of varying maturities paying more than 5 percent interest. What we had here was a classic crowding-out effect at a time when it clearly hurt our economy.

So in the late 1980s and early 1990s, the conservative critics of an expansionary fiscal policy could point to a tangible crowding-out effect. What is ironic is that during the time under scrutiny, the White House was occupied by two self-proclaimed fiscal conservatives, Ronald Reagan and George Bush.

crowding-in effect, every dollar the government borrows will not crowd out a dollar of private borrowing. Thus, all we need to demonstrate is that there is a substantial crowding-in effect.

It appears that if we accept one fact—that the total amount of loanable funds is not fixed—there probably will be a substantial crowding-in effect. If there is indeed a fixed pool of saving, then it follows that every dollar the government borrows is one less dollar available to private savers. But *is* this total pool of saving fixed? If aggregate demand, stimulated by massive budget deficits, *does* rise, won't people save more money (as well as spend more)?

Therefore, as more saving becomes available, not every dollar borrowed by the government will actually be taken from private borrowers. Furthermore, as aggregate demand rises, more investment will be stimulated. If the crowding-in effect dominates the crowding-out effect, not only will government borrowing rise but so will private borrowing and investing. All we need to show is that total borrowing—government and private—rises.

What do *you* think? Are the monetarists right in saying that government borrowing crowds out private borrowing? Or are the orthodox Keynesians correct in saying that the crowding-in effect may dominate the crowding-out effect? The betting here is that the truth lies somewhere between these two extremes.

Questions for Further Thought and Discussion

1. Explain the crowding-in and crowding-out effects. How valid are these two concepts?

2. Why is the concept of the full-employment budget more meaningful than the budget that the federal government uses? Specifically, why are the full-employment budget's deficits and surpluses more meaningful than those reported by the government?

Workbook for appendix to Chapter 12

Name _____ Date _____

Multiple-Choice Questions

Circle the letter that corresponds to the best answer.

1. When there is a federal budget deficit, there could be a full-employment budget surplus if there happened to be _____.
   a) inflation
   b) full employment
   c) an unemployment rate of more than 5 percent
   d) a declining national debt

2. When the unemployment rate goes up one percentage point, this increases the federal budget deficit by about _____.
   a) $40 million   c) $40 billion
   b) $80 million   d) $80 billion

3. The crowding-out effect cancels out at least part of the impact of _____.
   a) expansionary fiscal policy
   b) expansionary monetary policy
   c) restrictive fiscal policy
   d) restrictive monetary policy

4. The crowding-out effect is _____.
   a) much stronger during a recession than during prosperity
   b) much stronger during prosperity than during a recession
   c) equally strong during a recession and prosperity

5. In 1991 and 1992 we were running _____.
   a) full-employment budget deficits
   b) full-employment budget surpluses
   c) full-employment balanced budgets

6. Which of the following is an example of crowding out?
   a) Federal government spending causes changes in state and local government spending.
   b) Government spending reduces private spending.
   c) Tax changes perceived as temporary are largely ignored.
   d) Government spending causes the price level to rise.

7. Between 1992 and 1997 the actual deficit _____.
   a) declined, and the full employment deficit rose
   b) declined, and the full employment deficit stayed about the same
   c) declined, and the full employment deficit declined
   d) rose, and the full employment deficit rose
   e) rose, and the full employment deficit stayed about the same
   f) rose, and the full employment deficit declined

Fill-In Questions

1. During a recession we need to run a budget deficit; the full-employment balanced budget tells us _____ _____ that deficit should be.

2. The crowding-out effect is associated with _____ economists, while the crowding-in effect is associated with _____ economists.

3. A full-employment balanced budget means the budget _____ _____.

4. The crowding-out effect states that when the Treasury borrows a lot of money to finance a budget deficit, _____.

Problems

1. If we had a budget deficit of $135 billion and an unemployment rate of 9 percent, would we have a full-employment surplus or deficit? Of how much?

2. If the unemployment rate were 7.5 percent, how large should our budget deficit be?

3. If we had a budget deficit of $60 billion and an unemployment rate of 8 percent, would we have a full-employment surplus or deficit? Of how much?

4. If the unemployment rate were 10 percent, how large should our budget deficit be?

5. We should run a balanced budget when our unemployment rate is about _____ percent.

6. Given: tax receipts, 1,500; government spending, 1,800; unemployment rate, 8.5 percent. **a.** How much is the actual deficit? **b.** How much is the full-employment budget deficit or surplus?

7. Given: tax receipts, 1,250; government spending, 1,500; unemployment rate, 9 percent. **a.** How much is the actual deficit? **b.** How much is the full-employment budget deficit or surplus?

Chapter 13

Money and Banking

W hy would it be a dumb idea to keep your money under your mattress, especially during times of inflation? What backs up our money supply? How much is a dollar worth today? What would happen if everyone tried to get their money out of the bank at the same time? By the time you've gotten to the end of the chapter, you'll know the answers to these questions.

Banks create money. The rate of monetary growth itself is controlled by the Federal Reserve, which serves as our nation's central bank. In this chapter we'll look at our country's money supply and banking system, and in the next, at the Federal Reserve System.

First we'll talk about the money supply in the United States and the jobs it does. Next we'll work in a little monetary theory; we'll look at the demand for money and how interest rates are set. Then we'll turn to banking, beginning with its origins in medieval times; moving right along, we'll look at modern banking. So fasten your seat belt; in the words of the late Jackie Gleason, "And away we go!"

CHAPTER OBJECTIVES

We will discuss the following interesting topics:

- The four jobs of money.
- What money is.
- M1, M2, and M3.
- The demand for money.
- The origins of banking.
- The creation and destruction of money.
- Branch banking and bank chartering.
- The FDIC.
- The savings and loan debacle.

Money

The Four Jobs of Money

How important *is* money? Imagine trying to get by without any. How well would you manage if you were dropped off in some strange town with no money, no credit cards, and no friends or family? What if there were no such thing as money? If you were hungry, maybe you could find a place where you'd be able to trade your wristwatch for a meal. But then, how would you pay for your *next* meal? And where would you sleep that night? And the next?

So wouldn't you agree that money is pretty important? Sometimes we don't know quite how important until we're caught without it. Money is important to us as individual consumers, and it is also essential to our economy. It performs four important jobs that enable our economy to function smoothly and productively.

Medium of Exchange

Money's most important job

Money is a terrible master but an excellent servant.
—P.T. Barnum,
Circus owner

By far the most important job of money is to serve as a medium of exchange: when any good or service is purchased, people use money.

Money makes it much easier to buy and to sell because money is universally acceptable. With money I can go out and buy whatever I want—provided, of course, I have enough of it. Similarly, a seller will sell to anyone who comes along with enough money; he won't have to wait for a buyer who's willing to trade something the seller needs.

Money, then, provides us with a shortcut in doing business. By acting as a medium of exchange, money performs its most important function.

Standard of Value

A currency, to be perfect, should be absolutely invariable in value.
—David Ricardo,
Works

Wanna buy a brand name DVD player? A new sports car? A Swiss watch?

"Sure," you say. "How much?"

Thus money performs well at its second job—as a standard of value. If I told you that I got gasoline at 50 cents a gallon, you'd want to know the exact location of that gas station. But if I said that I bought a cheeseburger at a fast-food place for $8.50, you might wonder whether I have both oars in the water. A job that pays $2 an hour would be nearly impossible to fill, while one paying $50 an hour would be swamped with applicants.

Does money work well as a standard of value? You tell *me*.

Is money a good standard of value?

Store of Value

I measure everything I do by the size of a silver dollar. If it don't [sic] come up to that standard, then I know it's no good.
—Thomas A. Edison

In economics we have a hard time doing scientific experiments because they won't allow us to use those Bunsen burners. We also have a hard time explaining why we need test tubes and litmus paper. So, I'll ask you to excuse my lack of equipment as I try to conduct a scientific experiment. I'll count on your help by asking you to use your imagination.

Imagine that in 1980 you put $100 under your mattress and took out that same hundred dollars in 2000. (I *do* hope you were changing the sheets regularly.) How much was that $100 worth?

In other words, if you could buy 100 units of goods and services with your $100 in 1982, how many units could you buy with $100 in 2000? Eighty? No, fewer. Seventy? No, but very close. OK, I'll put you out of your misery. You could have bought just 51 units.

Did someone sneak into your bedroom in the middle of the night and steal most of your money? No; but over the years, inflation took its toll. During this 20-year period, inflation robbed the dollar of almost half of its purchasing power.

advanced WORK

Money versus Barter

Imagine living in a country with no money. Every time you needed something, you would have to find someone who had what you wanted and was willing to trade for something that you had.

But if there were money, a widely accepted medium of exchange, you wouldn't need to barter. You could just go out and buy what you wanted without having to find someone willing to trade.

Money also provides a standard of value. Every good and service has a price that's expressed in terms of dollars and cents. If there were no money, then everything we traded would be valued in terms of what we traded for. For example, a haircut might trade for three movie tickets. Suppose there were just three goods and services in our economy, *a*, *b*, and *c*. The price of *a* would be expressed in terms of *b* and *c*, and the price of *b* would be expressed in terms of *c*. If there were four goods and services—*a*, *b*, *c*, and *d*—then the price of *a* would be expressed in terms of *b*, *c*, and *d*, the price of *b* would be expressed in terms of *c*

and *d*, and the price of *c* would be expressed in terms of *d*. So four goods would have six prices in a barter economy.

As the number of goods and services in a barter economy increases, the number of prices increases exponentially (see the table below). It sure is hard to do business when you have to keep track of so many prices.

Number of Goods and Services	Number of Prices in a Money Economy	Number of Prices in a Barter Economy
2	2	1
3	3	3
4	4	6
10	10	45
100	100	4,950
1,000	1,000	499,500

This brings us back to the third job of money. Is money a good store of value or wealth? Over the long run, and particularly since World War II, it has been a very poor store of value. However, over relatively short periods of time, say, a few weeks or months, money does not lose much of its value. More significantly, during periods of price stability, money is an excellent store of value. Of course, the best time to hold money is during deflation because the longer you hold it, the more it's worth. For example, if you held money under your mattress from late 1929 to early 1933, it would have doubled in value during those years.

Is money a good store of value?

Standard of Deferred Payment

Many contracts promise to pay fixed sums of money well into the future. A corporate bond may pay a specified amount of interest every quarter for 30 years and then, upon maturity, pay out the principal as well. A 20-year mortgage obligates the homeowner to send the bank a monthly payment covering interest and principal for the next 240 months. These contracts call for the payment of money years into the future, illustrating how money functions as a standard of deferred payment.

When Dave Winfield signed a 10-year, $23 million contract to play the outfield for the New York Yankees in 1980, he really got stuck, because over the next 10 years the consumer price index went up by almost 59 percent. Today when a professional ballplayer, entertainer, or virtually anyone else signs a long-term contract, she or he is generally protected by an escalator clause, which calls for increased payments to compensate for any future inflation.

How well does money do its job as a standard of deferred payment? About as well as it does its job as a store of value—usually quite well in the short run, but not well at all over the long run of, say, three years or more.

Try to imagine how hard it would be to do business without money. Whenever you shopped, you'd have to have something to trade that the shopkeeper wanted. Your employer would have to pay you with something that you could trade for at least some of the things you needed. You'd have to find a way to make your car payments and your rent or mortgage payments, and pay for electricity, gasoline, food, clothing, appliances, and anything else you needed. In short, to carry out every transaction, you would need to find someone with whom you had a double coincidence of wants.

Money versus Barter

Everything, then, must be assessed in money; for this enables men always to exchange their services, and so makes society possible.
—Aristotle
Nicomachean Ethics

Without money, the only way to do business is by bartering. "How many quarter sections of beef do you want for that car?" or "Will you accept four pounds of sugar for that 18-ounce steak?"

For barter to work, I must want what you have and you must want what I have. This makes it pretty difficult to do business. (See the Advanced Work box, "Money versus Barter.")

Our Money Supply

What does our money supply consist of?

What does our money supply consist of? Gold? No! U.S. government bonds? No! Diamonds? No! Money consists of just a few things: coins, paper money, demand (or checking) deposits, and checklike deposits (commonly called NOW—or negotiable order of withdrawal—accounts) held by the nonbank public. Coins (pennies, nickels, dimes, quarters, half-dollars, and silver dollars) and paper money (dollar bills, fives, tens, twenties, fifties, and hundreds) together are considered currency. (By the way, where did the *dollar* come from? See the box on this topic.)

Six out of every 10 dollars in our money supply are demand deposits and other checkable deposits. Virtually all the rest is currency (see Figure 1). We have to be careful, however, to distinguish between checks and demand (or checking) deposits. Jackie Gleason used to tell a story about two guys who get into an argument in a bar about who is more miserly (or cheaper). Suddenly one of them pulls out a dollar bill and a book of matches, lights the bill on fire, and lets it burn to a crisp. Not to be outdone, the other guy pulls out a five, lights it, and watches it burn to a crisp. So then the first guy does the same thing with a $10 bill. Well, the other guy doesn't want to look bad, so he reaches into his pocket, pulls out his checkbook, writes out a check for $1,000, lights it, and watches it burn to a crisp.

Checks are *not* money. Checking deposits *are*.

Where Did the Dollar Come From?

The U.S. dollar traces its roots back to the old Spanish-milled silver dollar. You didn't think it was based on the British system, did you? You'd really have to be crazy to try to copy a system that uses pence, shillings, guineas, and pounds.

Are you any good at trivia questions? In Robert Louis Stevenson's *Treasure Island,* there was a parrot who, as parrots will do, kept repeating the same phrase over and over. OK, what was the phrase? You have eight seconds to answer the question. What was the phrase that the parrot, who, by the way, was acquainted with Long John Silver, kept repeating? Did you guess? Sorry—time's up.

The answer is "Pieces of eight. Pieces of eight." See that? You learn something every day.

By the way, how much money is two bits? It's a quarter. And four bits? That's right—50 cents. Eight bits? A dollar.

What was that parrot getting at with his "Pieces of eight. Pieces of eight"? He was talking dollars, Spanish-milled silver dollars. Those dollars were milled in such a way, that eight pieces—or bits—could be torn from each dollar, like perforated slices in a metal pie. That way, if you had a dollar and wanted to spend just 25 cents, you tore off two pieces or bits. To this day, some South American countries have coins worth 12 ½ centavos.

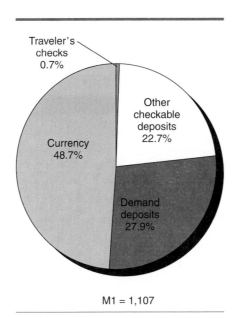

M1 = 1,107

Figure 1

The Components of M1, March, 2001

Almost half our money supply consists of currency, and the rest consists of demand deposits (or checking deposits) and other checkable deposits (negotiable order of withdrawal accounts, automatic transfer service accounts, and share drafts accounts). Demand deposits and other checkable deposits are all similar in that depositors can write checks on them whenever, and in whatever amount, they choose.

Source: Federal Reserve Statistical Release, April 5, 2001.

Incidentally, demand deposits are so named because they are payable "on demand." When you write a check, your bank must honor it, provided, of course, that you have enough money in your account to cover the check. Banks also insist that a certain number of business days go by before they will cash a specific check. It is usually 5 days for a local check and 7 to 10 days for an out-of-town check. Banks call this waiting period the time it takes for a check to clear. But any money in your checking account that has been cleared is available to depositors on demand.

Our currency is legal tender for all debts, public and private. But don't take *my* word for it. You'll find those words written just to the left of George Washington's portrait on the one dollar bill, or to the left of Abraham Lincoln's on the five. So the government says that your money must be accepted for payment of all debts. Does the government say that about checks and credit cards? No! Now what does it say on the back of each dollar just below "THE UNITED STATES OF AMERICA"? It says, "IN GOD WE TRUST." And as many people say: "In God we trust—all others pay cash."

M1, M2, and M3

Until a few years ago the money supply in the United States was defined as including just two things—currency and demand deposits. But the Federal Reserve was well aware of NOW accounts (accounts that allow negotiable orders of withdrawals) held at savings institutions other than commercial banks. After all, aren't these really checking accounts that just happen to pay interest? Then why not include them in the money supply?

Our money supply now includes not just currency and demand deposits but also traveler's checks and what the Federal Reserve terms "other checkable deposits," which include the NOW accounts and "share draft accounts," or checking accounts issued by credit unions. (Are credit cards money? See the box with that title.) The components of M1 are shown in Figure 1.

M1 is shown, along with M2 and M3, in Figure 2. As of March 2001, our money supply totaled $1,107 billion. Nearly everyone considers M1 our money supply, but we're going to consider two broader measures of money, M2 and M3.

By adding savings deposits, small-denomination time deposits, and money market mutual funds held by individuals to M1, we get M2. You know what savings deposits are. Time deposits hold funds that must be left in the bank for a specified period of time—a week, a month, three months, a year, five years, or even longer.

M1 = currency, demand deposits, traveler's checks, and other checkable deposits.

M1 + savings, small-denomination time deposits, and money market funds = M2.

Are Credit Cards Money?

The answer is no. Credit cards are ID cards that enable you to buy a whole range of goods and services without having to pay until the end of the month. Who pays? The bank that issued your credit card pays the merchant; then, a few weeks later, you repay the bank.

What the bank would really like you to do is run up a large balance and pay 18 or 20 percent interest on that balance for years and years. That's the main reason they will give you a credit line of $5,000 or $10,000.

Bank of America issued the first bank credit cards in 1958, but most people didn't begin using them regularly until the 1970s. Through the 1960s people used cash and checks to pay for all purchases. Today Americans hold 1.2 billion credit cards, about 10 for every cardholder. These include not just bank credit cards but gasoline, department store, restaurant, and telephone credit cards.

Bank credit cards like VISA, MasterCard, and American Express have become extremely important in our economy. Not only can you travel and make major purchases without having to carry hundreds or thousands of dollars in cash, but you won't be able to rent a car, stay in some hotels, or transact certain types of business without such a card. But remember, they're only pieces of plastic—not money.

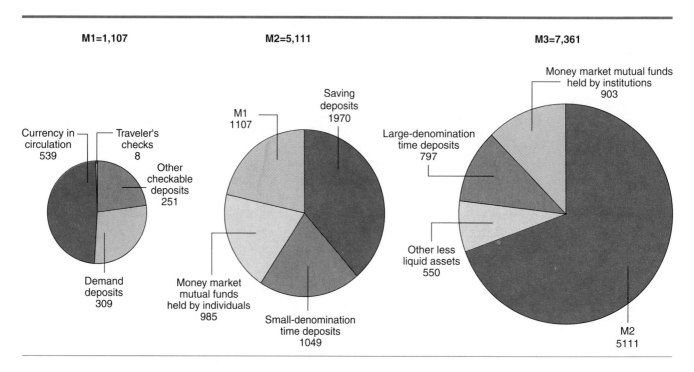

Figure 2

M1, M2, M3, March 2001

We showed M1 in Figure 1. By adding savings deposits, small-denomination time deposits, and money market mutual funds held by individuals to M1, we get M2. Adding large-denomination time deposits (of $100,000 or more) and money market mutual funds held by institutions, we get M3.

Source: Federal Reserve Bulletin, March 2001.

Remember the bank ads that warn, "There is a substantial penalty for early withdrawal"? These warnings are another way of saying that under the conditions of a time deposit, you are legally required to leave your money in the bank for a specified period of time. And so, unlike a demand deposit, time deposits are not payable until a certain date.

Technically, the money held in time and savings deposits does not have to be paid to the depositors "on demand." When you fill out a withdrawal slip to take money out of your savings account, you are completely confident that you will walk out of the bank

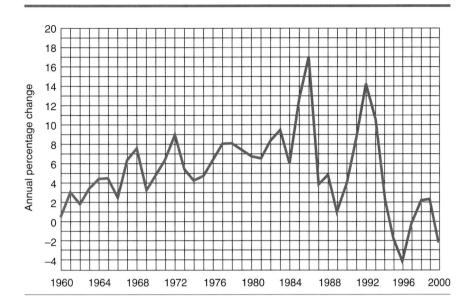

*F*igure 3

Annual Percentage Change in the Money Supply, M1, 1960–2000

Between 1960 and 1983, there was a fairly steady upward trend in the annual growth of M1 from less than 1 percent to just over 9 percent. But since then there have been extremely sharp fluctuations, ranging from an increase of 17 percent to a decrease of about 4 percent.

Sources: Economic Report of the President, 2000; Federal Reserve Statistical Release, April 5, 2001.

with your money. Legally, however, your bank can require up to 30 days' written notice before giving you these funds. In practice, of course, no bank ever does this. Although nearly every bank in the country is insured by the Federal Deposit Insurance Corporation, it is quite possible that, if a 30-day waiting period were enforced, many nervous depositors would rush into their banks to get their money while they could. Money market mutual funds are issued by stockbrokers and other institutions, usually pay slightly higher interest rates than banks, and offer check-writing privileges.

We get from M2 to M3 by adding large-denomination time deposits, money market mutual funds held by institutions, and other less liquid assets. How large is large? The dividing line between small-denomination and large-denomination time deposits is $100,000. Any deposit of less than $100,000 is small.

M2 + large-denomination time deposits = M3

A strong case can be made to designate M2 as our basic money supply rather than M1. First point, it is the monetary measure most closely watched by the Federal Reserve, the agency that controls the growth of our money supply. Second, with the enormous growth of money market deposit accounts, time deposits, and money market mutual funds, which people can quickly convert into cash, attention has shifted to M2. But I'm enough of a traditionalist to keep calling M1 our basic money supply—at least until the next edition of this text.

Our Growing Money Supply

Our money supply grows from year to year as the amount of currency in circulation goes up and as our checking deposits and checklike deposits go up as well. How fast does the money supply grow? Figure 3 shows monetary growth from the 1960s through the late 1990s.

Monetary growth has not been smooth. You'll notice a huge jump, for example, in 1985 and 1986. The Federal Reserve controls the rate of monetary growth. How? Read all about it in the next chapter. (To learn how much money is out there, see the box on this topic.)

The Demand for Money

How much of *your* assets do you hold in the form of money? A typical middle-class family might own a home, two cars, several thousand dollars' worth of corporate stock, and perhaps one or two U.S. Treasury bonds. Of course, none of that is money. But the

How Much Money Is Out There Anyway?

How much currency do we have circulating in the country? Is the answer $539 billion? The U.S. Treasury said it was in March 2001. There's something comforting about such a precise figure. It assures us that someone has gone to great trouble to calculate something to the nearest 10th. The only problem is that the Treasury and the Federal Reserve have absolutely no idea how much currency is actually circulating in the United States.

The reason they don't know is over $400 billion American dollars are circulating abroad. Most of this money is used as a second currency. For example, in Trinidad, Barbados, Jamaica, and other Caribbean nations, the British West Indian dollar—or BWI (pronounced beewee)—is the official currency. But U.S. dollars are gladly accepted.

Try this experiment. Pick a country—any country in the world. Buy a plane ticket and fly there. Get off the plane, go through customs, hop in a cab, and ask the driver to take you to the best restaurant he knows. When you pay the driver, ask whether he accepts U.S. dollars. Then go in the restaurant and order the most expensive thing on the menu, and, again, pay in U.S. dollars. Very often you'll find that your dollars are readily acceptable.

Now, back to our story. How do U.S. dollars end up circulating in other countries? Tourists spend them there, Americans send money to their relatives in other countries, and retired Americans often live abroad because of the relatively low cost of living in many countries. In addition, increasingly U.S. dollars are being shipped abroad to pay for cocaine and other illegal drugs.

You may recall the box entitled "Our Number One Export" near the beginning of Chapter 8, in which I argued that, in a sense, U.S. currency is our largest export, since we give dollars to foreigners in exchange for their goods and services. As long as we continue to run annual trade deficits of more than $300 billion a year, and as long as foreigners are willing to accept this form of payment, we will continue to ship more than $100 billion a year in U.S. currency to foreign countries. Actually they keep $15–$20 billion and invest most of the remaining dollars in U.S. government securities and corporate bonds and stock.

By the way, have you ever heard of "Eurodollars"? These are deposits denominated in U.S. dollars at banks and other financial institutions outside the United States. Why are they called Eurodollars? Because until about 20 years ago, nearly all this money was held in Western Europe. Now Eurodollar deposits are held all over the world. How much? Would you believe well over $1 trillion?

Is any of this money counted in our money supply? It does not show up in M1, but some Eurodollars held by U.S. residents are included in M2 and M3.

How much of our currency is circulating in foreign countries? In 1989 Federal Reserve chairman Alan Greenspan told Congress that "perhaps more than half of U.S. currency is outside the United States." Nice. Here's the guy who's supposed to be in charge of our money supply, and *he* doesn't even have a clue.

same family may also have a couple of bank accounts and $800 in cash. Let's consider the reasons why people hold some of their assets in the form of money.

Why do people hold money?

The classical economists of the 19th century believed money was merely a medium of exchange, something that burned a hole in your pocket. By that they did not mean that money was hot (in any sense of the word), but that people didn't hold it for very long. But economists today recognize that people hold money for a variety of purposes. John Maynard Keynes noted that people had three reasons for holding money: to make transactions, for precautionary reasons, and to speculate. Economists have since identified four factors that influence the three Keynesian motives for holding money: (1) the price level, (2) income, (3) the interest rate, and (4) credit availability.

The amount of money that people hold is called money balances. It consists of currency, checking deposits, checklike deposits held at financial institutions, and traveler's checks. After we discuss the Keynesian motives for holding money, we shall look at the influences that shape the demand for holding money.

The Keynesian Motives for Holding Money   John Maynard Keynes said people have three motives for holding money. Instead of holding their assets in other forms–stocks, bonds, real estate, commodities–everyone opts to hold at least some of their assets in the form of currency or demand deposits. First we'll look at the transactions motive.

Individuals have day-to-day purchases for which they pay in cash or by check. You take care of your rent or mortgage payment, car payment, monthly bills, and major purchases by check. Cash is needed for groceries, gasoline, most restaurant meals, the movies, and nearly every other small purchase. Businesses, too, need to keep substantial checking accounts to pay their bills and to meet their payrolls. Individuals and businesses, then, both need to hold a certain amount of money for regular expenses. Keynes called this the transactions motive for holding money. *Transactions motive*

Next we have the precautionary motive. People will keep money on hand just in case some unforeseen emergency arises. They do not actually expect to spend this money, but they want to be ready if the need arises. *Precautionary motive*

One good example dates to the 1950s and earlier, when women did not have to share the expenses when they went out on dates. In the 1950s many women carried a $10 bill on all their dates—just in case. They called it "mad money," which they would use for cab fare if their date went beyond the limits prescribed by the social mores of those times.

Finally, there is the speculative motive for holding money. When interest rates are very low—as they were during the Great Depression when Keynes was writing—you don't stand to lose much by holding your assets in the form of money. Alternatively, by tying up your assets in the form of bonds, you actually stand to lose money should interest rates rise, because you'd be locked into very low rates. In effect, the speculative demand for money is based on the belief that better opportunities for investment will come along and that, in particular, interest rates will rise. *Speculative motive*

Four Influences on the Demand for Money   The amount of money we hold is influenced by four factors: (1) the price level, (2) income, (3) interest rates, and (4) credit availability. Changes in these factors change how much money we hold.

(1) The Price Level   As prices rise you need more money to take care of your day-to-day transactions. As a young man during those prosperous years before World War I, I didn't need to carry much money around. After all, those were the days, my friend. The days of nickel beer and nickel hot dogs. And, believe it or not, two kids could see a movie for a nickel.

A popular mid-1950s Broadway musical, *The Most Happy Fella,* had a hit song, "Standin' on the Corner,"[1] which had this couplet:

> Saturday and I'm so broke
> Couldn't buy a girl a nickel Coke.

Today it costs a family of four at least $50 to take in a neighborhood movie and a meal at McDonald's. In Manhattan, where movie tickets are $10 and parking costs more than $15 for the first hour, this outing would cost more than $80. Thus, as the price level goes up, so does the demand for money balances. Nobody leaves home with just a nickel anymore.

Today we must pay a substantial penalty for holding our assets in the form of money. In fact, there are two closely related penalties. First, there's inflation. If the inflation rate is 5 percent, then $100 held for a year will be worth only about $95. That is, $100 will buy as much as $95 bought one year ago.

During times of inflation, then, we don't want to hold more than is necessary in currency or checking deposits. In other words, we want to get some kind of return on our money, or in some other way protect its purchasing power.

By holding our assets in the form of money, not only would we be forgoing interest, but our money would be losing its purchasing power from month to month. Therefore, in times of high interest rates and inflation (the two generally go together), people prefer to hold as little as possible of their assets in the form of money.

---

[1]This song actually made the charts on three different occasions, with versions by the Four Lads, the Four Freshman, and the Four Aces.

We should distinguish between two contradictory influences on money balances with respect to the price level. As the price level rises, people need to hold higher money balances to carry out their day-to-day transactions. But as the price level rises (that is, with inflation), the purchasing power of the dollar declines; so the longer you hold money, the less that money is worth.

A distinction between short run and long run would be helpful. Assume a constant inflation rate of 10 percent so that the price level rises by exactly 10 percent every year. The cost of living would double every seven years.[2] So you would need to carry double the money balance in 2007 that you did in 2000 to handle exactly the same transactions.

However, with a 10 percent rate of inflation, the longer you hold assets in the form of money, the less that money will buy. Even though there is an inflation penalty for holding money for relatively long periods of time, you will surely keep enough on hand to take care of your day-to-day transactions. And if you compared your money balance in 2000 with that of 2007, you'd find that in 2007 you would be holding about double what you held in 2000, all other things remaining the same.

We are left with this conclusion: Even though people tend to cut down on their money balances during periods of inflation, as the price level rises people will hold larger money balances.

Money is the poor people's credit card.
—Marshall McLuhan

(2) Income Poor people seldom carry around much money. Check it out. The more you make, the more you spend, and the more you spend, the more money you need to hold as cash or in your checking account. Even if you use a credit card, you still have to pay your bill at the end of the month. Therefore, as income rises, so does the demand for money balances.

(3) The Interest Rate So far we've had two positive relationships: the quantity of money demanded rises with the level of prices and income. Are you ready for a negative relationship? All right, then. The quantity of money demanded goes down as interest rates rise.

Until recently people did not receive interest for holding money. Cash that you keep in your wallet or under your mattress still pays no interest, and until the late 1970s neither did checking deposits. Even today nearly all checking deposits pay less than 2 percent interest, and some don't pay any interest whatsoever. The alternative to holding your assets in the form of money is to hold them in the form of bonds, money market funds, time deposits, and other interest-bearing securities. As interest rates rise, these assets become more attractive than money balances. Thus, there is a negative relationship between interest rates and money balances.

Do you remember the concept of opportunity cost, which was introduced in Chapter 2? What is the opportunity cost of holding money? It's the interest that you forgo.

(4) Credit Availability If you can get credit, you don't need to hold so much money. Thirty years ago most Americans paid cash for their smaller purchases and used checks for big-ticket items. The only form of consumer credit readily available was from retail merchants and manufacturers. The last three decades have seen a veritable explosion in consumer credit in the form of credit cards and bank loans. Over this period, then, increasing credit availability has been exerting a downward pressure on the demand for money.

We can now make four generalizations:

1. As interest rates rise, people tend to hold less money.

2. As the rate of inflation rises, people tend to hold more money.

3. As the level of income rises, people tend to hold more money.

4. People tend to hold less money as credit availability increases.

---

[2]Any number that increases by 10 percent a year will double in seven years. This is an application of the rule of 70: Any number that increases by 1 percent a year doubles in 70 years. You can check this out on your calculator or by consulting a book of compound interest tables.

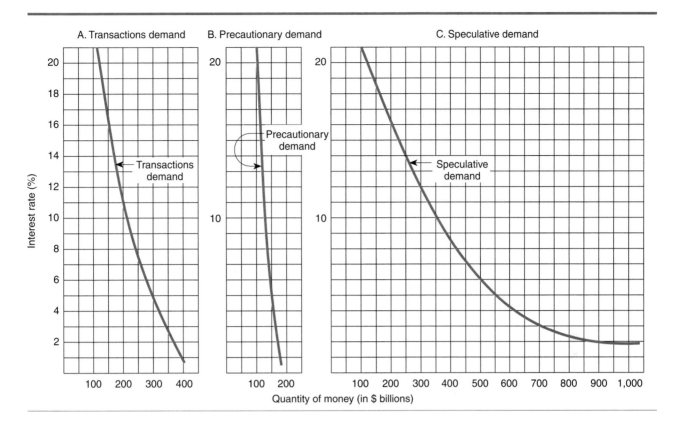

Figure 4

The Three Demands for Money

The amount of money that people hold for precautionary reasons has almost no responsiveness to interest rate changes, while the amount held for day-to-day transactions is somewhat responsive to interest rate changes. However, the speculative demand for money is very responsive, and, at relatively low interest rates, people wish to hold very large money balances.

The Demand Schedule for Money

For purposes of analysis, we shall use the Keynesian motives for holding money to derive the demand schedule for money. This schedule, when brought together with the money supply schedule in the next section, will enable us to derive the interest rate. Right now we'll be combining the transactions, precautionary, and speculative demands for money.

How much money individuals and business firms need to hold for their transactions really depends on the size of GDP, or total spending. The more we spend, the more we need to hold at any given time. The transactions demand for money is somewhat responsive to interest rate changes (see Figure 4A). Corporate comptrollers used to leave relatively large balances in their checking accounts in the 1950s when interest rates were very low and checking accounts paid zero interest. Today those funds might be held in the form of seven-day certificates of deposit or other very short-term, very liquid assets to take advantage of the relatively high interest rates. Individuals, too, because of today's higher interest rates as well as the widespread use of credit cards, carry much smaller money balances than they would have back in the 1950s.

The precautionary demand for money is least responsive to interest rate changes (see Figure 4B) because people have a specific purpose for holding these funds. However, even these funds would be at least partially converted into other assets at extremely high interest rates.

The speculative demand for money is, as we would expect, the most responsive to interest rate changes (see Figure 4C). The people who are holding these funds would obviously hold a lot more at low interest rates than they would at higher rates.

The transactions demand

The precautionary demand

The speculative demand

Figure 5

Total Demand for Money

This is the sum of the transactions demands, precautionary demands, and speculative demands for money shown in Figure 4.

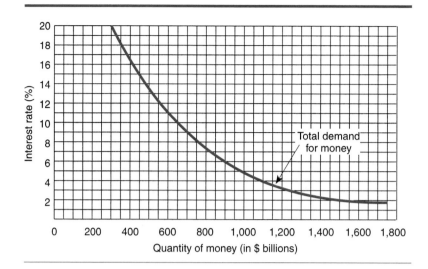

The Liquidity Trap

At very low interest rates, people don't lend out their money.

When John Maynard Keynes carried his speculative motive for holding money to its logical conclusion, he determined that at very low interest rates people would not lend out their money, would not put it in the bank, would not buy bonds with it, but would simply hold it. That's right—they'd sit on it, they'd hoard it, but they wouldn't spend it or make it available to anyone else.

Why should they? When the interest rate declines to, say, 2 percent, why would people risk their money for such a low rate of return? And why would they tie it up at such a low interest rate when within a few months the interest rate might rise? *Then* they would sink it into interest-bearing assets, not now. This reasoning is reflected by the horizontal section of the Keynesian money demand curve (which he called a liquidity preference curve) shown in Figure 5.

Using the data from Figure 4, we can derive the total demand schedule for money, shown in Figure 5. This demand curve is the sum of the three demand curves shown in Figure 4—the transactions demands, precautionary demands, and speculative demands for money. In the next section we combine this curve with the money supply curve to determine the interest rate.

Determination of the Interest Rate

The demand for and the supply of money determine the interest rate.

If you would know the value of money, go and borrow some.
—Benjamin Franklin

In banking it is axiomatic that the richest customers paid the least for borrowed money; highest interest rates were for the poor.

—Arthur Hailey,
The Moneychangers

In Figure 5 we assumed various interest rates and determined that as the interest rate declined, the amount of money that the public wished to hold went up. But what determines the interest rate? If we think of the interest rate as the price of money, then the interest rate, like the price of anything else, is set by the forces of supply and demand.[3]

The supply of money is controlled by the Federal Reserve.[4] At any given time supply is fixed, so we'll represent it as a vertical line at 800 in Figure 6. Taking the demand curve from Figure 5, we find that it crosses the money supply curve in Figure 6 at an interest rate of about 7.2 percent. It's as simple as that. Find the point at which the demand curve and supply curve cross, and you've got the interest rate.

Of course, both our demand and supply curves are hypothetical, so the interest rate we've found is hypothetical as well. OK, then, let's get real. How much is the interest

---

[3]The last section of Chapter 3 provides a cogent explanation of the workings of supply and demand.

[4]We'll go over how the Federal Reserve sets the money supply in the next chapter.

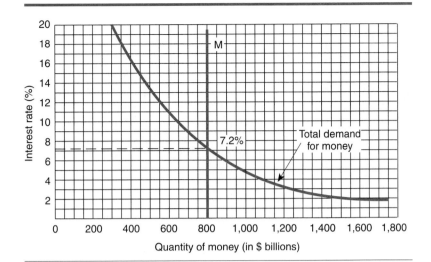

Figure 6

Total Demand for Money and Supply of Money

The interest rate of 7.2 percent is found at the intersection of the total demand for money and the supply of money (M). We used the total demand for money curve shown in Figure 5 and added a vertical M curve. Since at any given time the supply of money is fixed, it can be represented as a vertical line.

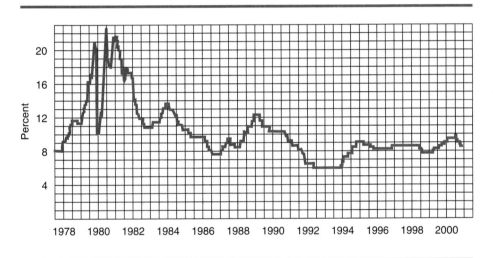

Figure 7

The Prime Rate of Interest Charged by Banks on Short-Term Business Loans, 1978–2001

Although the prime rate is set by the nation's largest banks, it is strongly influenced by the actions of the Federal Reserve Board of Governors.

Source: Federal Reserve Bulletin, 1978-2001.

rate right now? 5 percent? 8 percent? 10 percent? How much *is* it? How much is it on *what*? On passbook savings? On home mortgages? On Treasury bills? Are we talking about the interest rate that you *get* for your money or the interest rate that you *pay*? Guess which is always higher?

There are literally scores of interest rates (see box, "Keeping Track of Interest Rates"). People may receive between 2 and 5 percent on their savings, and a lot more during times of inflation, and may have to pay somewhere between 6 and 15 percent on a house mortgage. Large corporations with good credit ratings pay the prime rate, while smaller and less creditworthy firms might pay 1 or 2 percent above prime.

Interest rates may vary from day to day, and there may be considerable variation over the course of a year or two. Figure 7 shows the average rate of interest that banks charged on short-term business loans from 1978 through early 2001. Because all interest rates move up and down together, you can easily observe their cyclical nature. This particular rate (along with the prime rate, which is generally slightly lower) rose from 11 percent in 1980 to 21 percent in 1981 and then fell to 10 percent in early 1983.

Who controls interest rates?

Who controls interest rates? Is it the people who borrow money? Is it the banks? Is it the Federal Reserve? The answer is yes to all three questions. But most experts point to the Federal Reserve Board of Governors as playing the dominant role. However, board

Keeping Track of Interest Rates

The Wall Street Journal and other major newspapers track interest rates, often on a weekly basis, so readers can follow the ups and downs of these important series. The graphs below plot the short-term and long-term interest rates for the second half of 1989. The dividing line between the short-term and long-term is one year.

Treasury bills are very short-term borrowing, usually for just 91 days, at $10,000 denominations. *"Federal funds* are loans of reserves [which we'll be discussing in the next chapter] by one bank to another, and *commercial paper* is short-term debt sold on the open market by large corporations (kind of a private T bill)."*

Note how the rates all move up and down virtually in lockstep while maintaining the same distances from each other. These six are just a few of the interest rates we could have plotted. But no matter which ones you follow, all interest rates move up and down together.

Why are there so many different interest rates? The main reason is the possibility of default. When you buy a three-month U.S. Treasury bill, you know that you will be paid back in three months. But you're taking something of a risk when you purchase a corporate "junk bond." So the riskier the loan, the more interest the borrower must pay. Long-term interest rates are generally higher than short-term rates to protect lenders against the possibility of inflation. For example, in mid-1995 there was a spread of about four points between short-term and long-term rates.

---

*Michael B. Lehmann, *The Wall Street Journal Workbook,* Instructor's Manual (Burr Ridge, IL: Richard D. Irwin, 1990), p. 190.

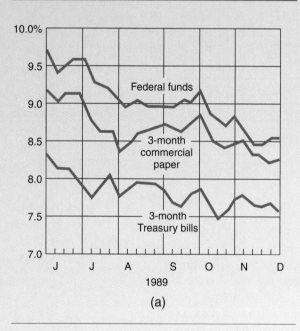

(a)

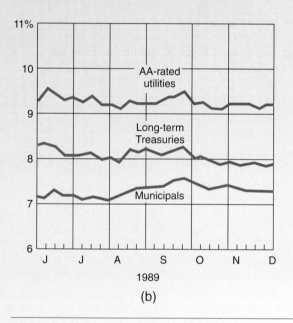

(b)

Source: Federal Reserve Bank of New York, as reported in *The Wall Street Journal,* December 7, 1989.

Source: Merrill Lynch Securities Research, as reported in *The Wall Street Journal,* December 11, 1989.

members would probably respond the way Casey Stengel did when he was congratulated (and then fired, incidentally) after managing the Yankees to 10 pennants and 7 World Series wins in 12 years. His exact words were "I couldn't have done it without my players." Neither can the Federal Reserve.

Banking

A Short History of Banking

There are slightly more than 8,000 commercial banks in the United States. These are defined as banks that hold demand deposits, but other banks—mutual savings banks, savings and loan associations, credit unions, and mutual money market funds—also issue checking accounts. The distinction between commercial banks and other savings institutions is blurring.

We'll talk about the origins of banking before we discuss how banking is conducted today in the United States. The first banks were run by goldsmiths back in the Middle Ages. We'll see that these fellows invented not only banking, but paper money as well.

In medieval times, about the only secure place for your money was in the safes of the goldsmiths, so anybody who was anybody kept his money with the local goldsmith. These gentlemen would give receipts that possibly looked a little like the hatcheck slips you get at some of the fancier restaurants. If you left 10 gold coins with the smith, he wrote 10 on your receipt. If you happened to be rich, it was very important to be able to count past 10.

The origins of banking

Although no one is quite sure who was the first to accept paper money—that is, goldsmiths' receipts—it might well have happened this way:

A knight was having his castle completely redone—new wallpaper, new bearskin rugs, new dungeon, new drawbridge—the works! When the job was finally completed, the contractor handed him a bill for 32 gold pieces.

The knight told the contractor, "Wait right here. I'll hitch up the team and take the oxcart into town. I'll get 32 gold coins from the goldsmith. I shouldn't be gone more than three days."

"Why bother to go all the way into town for the 32 gold coins?" asked the contractor. "When you give them to me, I'll have to ride all the way back into town and deposit the coins right back in the goldsmith's safe."

"You mean you're not going to charge me for the job?" The knight, while able to count past 10, came up short in certain other areas.

"Of course I want to get paid," replied the contractor. "Just give me your receipt for 32 gold coins."

It took the knight a little while to figure this out, but after the contractor went over it with him another six or eight times, he was finally able to summarize their transaction: "If I give you my receipt, we each save a trip to the goldsmith." And with that, paper money began to circulate.

The goldsmiths were not only able to count higher than anyone else in town, but they generally had a little more upstairs as well. Some of them began to figure out that they could really start to mint money, so to speak. First, they recognized that when people did come in to retrieve their gold coins, they did not insist on receiving the identical coins they had left. Second, they noticed that more and more people were not bothering to come in at all to get their money because they were paying their debts with the receipts. And so, the goldsmiths were struck with this evil thought: Why not lend out some of these gold coins just sitting here in the safe?

This was the moment modern banking was born. As long as the total number of receipts circulating was equal to the number of gold coins in the safe, there was no banking system, but when the number of receipts exceeded the number of coins in the safe, a banking system was created. For example, if a goldsmith had 1,000 coins in his safe and receipts for 1,000 coins circulating, he wasn't a banker. What if he knew that his depositors would never all come to him at the same time for their money and he decided to lend out just 10 gold coins? He would then still have receipts for 1,000 coins circulating, but he'd have only 990 coins in his safe.

Moment at which modern banking was born

The "paper money" issued by the goldsmith is no longer fully backed by gold, but there's really nothing to worry about because not everyone will show up at the same

Figure 8

Goldsmith's Receipts and
Reserves

Three questions: What is the
goldsmith's reserve ratio when there
are (a) 1,000 receipts in circulation
and 1,000 coins in his safe? (b)
1,000 receipts in circulation and
500 coins in his safe? (c) 1,000
receipts in circulation and 250 coins
in his safe? Answers: (a) 100
percent; (b) 50 percent; (c) 25
percent.

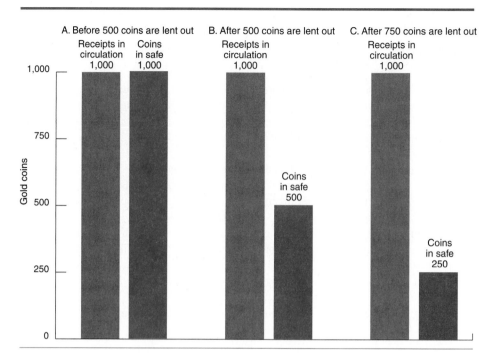

time for their gold. Meanwhile, the goldsmith is collecting interest on the 10 gold pieces
he lent out.

"But why stop there?" asks the goldsmith. "Why not lend out 100 gold coins, or
even 500?" And so he does. With 500 coins lent out, he still has 500 in his safe to cover
the 1,000 receipts in circulation. And what are the chances that half his depositors will
suddenly turn up demanding their coins?

Now we have 500 coins backing up 1,000 receipts, or a reserve ratio of 50 percent.
As long as no panics occur, 50 percent is certainly a prudent ratio. As the ratio declines
(from 100 to 50 percent), let's see what happened to the money supply, the gold coins,
and the goldsmith's receipts in the hands of the public (Figure 8).

Initially the goldsmith has 1,000 coins in the safe (or bank) and 1,000 receipts circulating. The reserve ratio is 100 percent (1,000 coins backing 1,000 receipts). Next he
has 500 coins in the safe and 500 circulating, along with the 1,000 receipts in the hands
of the public. His reserve ratio is 50 percent (500 coins backing 1,000 receipts). And the
money supply? It's grown to 1,500—1,000 receipts and 500 coins in circulation. Thus,
as the reserve ratio declines, the money supply rises.

Let's go a step further and have the goldsmith lend out an additional 250 gold coins.
See if you can figure out the reserve ratio and the size of the money supply.

Because there are now 250 coins backing 1,000 receipts, the reserve ratio is
25 percent. Meanwhile the money supply has grown from 1,500 to 1,750, because in
addition to the 1,000 receipts, 750 coins are in the hands of the public.

If the goldsmith were to continue lending out gold coins, he would end up with none
in his safe. His reserve ratio would sink to zero, and the money supply would be 2,000
(1,000 receipts and 1,000 coins).

Being a clever fellow, the goldsmith has noticed that his receipts circulate as easily
as gold coins. And so, long before he has lent out all his coins, which he really needs
as reserves (or backing for his receipts), he begins to make loans in the form of his
receipts. For example, suppose you need to borrow 10 gold coins. The goldsmith merely
writes up a receipt for 10 gold coins and off you go with your money.

What is to prevent the goldsmith from writing up receipts every time someone wants to borrow? We call this printing money. For example, with his original 1,000 gold coins tucked away in his safe, the goldsmith prints up 1,000 receipts (in addition to the 1,000 receipts he already gave to the owners of the 1,000 gold coins). How much would the reserve ratio be and what would be the size of the money supply?

With 1,000 coins backing up 2,000 receipts, the reserve ratio is 50 percent. The money supply consists of the 2,000 receipts in the hands of the public. Suppose the goldsmith lent out another 2,000 (units) in the form of receipts. The reserve ratio would be 25 percent (1,000 coins backing 4,000 receipts), and the money supply would be the 4,000 receipts.

If the goldsmith so chose, he could even print up 10,000 receipts, which would bring about a reserve ratio of 10 percent (1,000 coins backing 10,000 receipts) and a money supply of 10,000 receipts. Or he could lend out 100,000, bringing the reserve ratio down to 1 percent (1,000 coins backing up 100,000 receipts) and creating a money supply of 100,000 receipts.

The system worked as long as the goldsmiths did not get too greedy and as long as the depositors maintained their confidence in their goldsmith's ability to redeem his receipts in gold coins. From time to time, however, individual goldsmiths went too far in lending out money, whether in the form of gold coins or receipts. When depositors began to notice so many receipts in circulation, they asked themselves whether the goldsmith could possibly have enough coins in his safe to redeem them all. And when they thought he might not, they rushed into town to withdraw their gold coins before everyone else tried to.

> The system worked as long as the goldsmiths did not get too greedy.

If too many people reached the same conclusion, a panic ensued and the goldsmith could not possibly meet the demands of his depositors. In effect, then, he went bankrupt, and those left holding his receipts found them worthless. Of course, that was all before the days of the Federal Deposit Insurance Corporation (FDIC), so there was no one to whom depositors could turn.

Modern Banking

Like the early goldsmiths, today's bankers don't keep 100 percent reserve backing for their deposits. If a bank kept all its deposits in its vault, it would lose money from the day it opened. The whole idea of banking is to borrow money at low interest rates and then lend out that same money at high interest rates. The more you lend, the more profits you make.

Banks would like to keep about 2 percent of their deposits in the form of vault cash. As long as depositors maintain confidence in the banks—or at least in the FDIC—there is really no need to keep more than 2 percent on reserve.`

Unhappily for the banks, however, they are generally required to keep a lot more than 2 percent of their deposits on reserve. All the nation's commercial banks, credit unions, savings and loan associations, and mutual savings banks now have to keep up to 10 percent of their checking deposits on reserve. (See Table 1 of Chapter 14.)

Let's take a closer look at our banks. A bank as a financial institution accepts deposits, makes loans, and offers checking accounts.

Commercial Banks These banks account for the bulk of checkable deposits. Until the passage of the Depository Institutions Deregulation and Monetary Control Act of 1980, which is outlined near the end of the next chapter, only commercial banks were legally allowed to issue checking deposits, and they were the only institutions clearly recognized as "banks." Traditionally, banks lent money for very short-term commercial loans, but in the last few decades they have branched out into consumer loans, as well as commercial and residential mortgages. Today some even offer brokerage services. Usually they have the word "bank" in their names. There are slightly more than 8,000 commercial banks in the United States, and they hold nearly all demand deposits and almost half of total savings deposits.

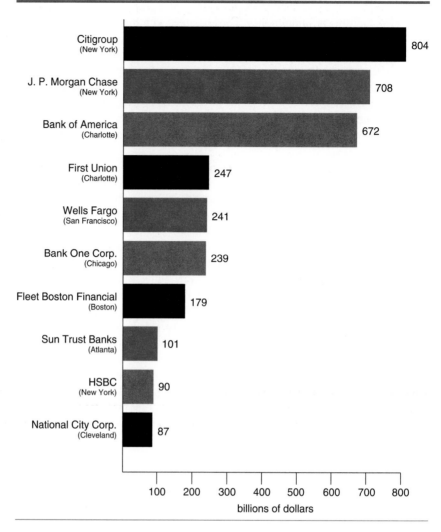

Figure 9

The Top Ten American Banks, Ranked by Assets, 2000

Total bank assets in 2000 were roughly $6 trillion. What percentage of those assets were held by (a) the top three banks? (b) the top ten banks?

Source: americanbanker.com.

Answers:

(a) 36%

(b) 56%

Savings and Loan Associations   Although originally established to finance home building, these associations also offer most of the services offered by commercial banks. The nearly 1,100 S&Ls invest more than three quarters of their savings deposits in home mortgages. Later in the chapter we'll cover the savings and loan debacle of the 1980s, which ultimately reduced the number of S&Ls by almost two-thirds.

Mutual Savings Banks   Mostly operated in the northeastern United States, these institutions were created in the 19th century to encourage saving by the "common people." They traditionally made small personal loans, but today, like savings and loan associations, they offer the same range of services as commercial banks. There are nearly 1,600 mutual savings banks.

Credit Unions   Although there are nearly 11,000 credit unions in the United States, they hold less than 5 percent of total savings deposits. While these banks, like the others we've mentioned, do offer a full range of financial services, they specialize in small consumer loans. They are cooperatives that generally serve specific employee, union, or community groups.

The Banking Act of 1980 blurred the distinctions between commercial banks and the three other depository institutions. The main distinction—that before 1980 only commercial banks were legally allowed to issue checking accounts—was swept away in 1980.

The Big Banks   Figure 9 lists our country's top 10 banks by size of assets in 2000. Nearly all are familiar names. You may notice that 3 of the top 25 are located in New York City, which was the financial capital of the world for a long time. Although it remains the financial capital of America, New York has been superseded by Tokyo as the preeminent financial center of the world.

Total U.S. bank assets at the end of the year 2000 were roughly $6 trillion. Do you think a substantial percentage of those assets was in the hands of the nation's ten largest banks listed in Figure 9? Calculate that percentage.

Would you say that 56 percent is substantial? That's certainly a lot of money in the hands of a relatively small number of institutions. There has been a trend toward consolidation of financial institutions for more than 20 years, and that consolidation means a lot less competition in the industry. Since competition is what drives firms to be efficient, we certainly have cause for concern.

This disturbing trend has been largely offset by the growing presence of foreign banks in the United States. For example, HSBC (Hong Kong and Shanghai Bank Corporation), a British bank, purchased two major New York banks, Marine Midland and Republic National, and is the third largest bank in New York state. In California, Japanese banks hold more than one-third of that state's banking assets. Clearly, banking has become a global industry.

Consolidation has also brought about huge economies of scale—most notably ongoing computerization and the spreading network of ATMs—efficiencies that are necessary for American banks to compete in global markets. Considering the trend toward financial supermarkets providing one-stop shopping, the efficiencies from consolidation may even outweigh the efficiency losses resulting from diminished competition.

How do the banks listed in Figure 9 rank internationally? Table 1 lists the world's top 25 commercial banks. There are 7 Japanese and 5 German banks in the top 25, but just 3 American banks—Citigroup (number 2), Bank of America (number 5), and Chase Manhattan (number 20). Since Chase Manhattan and JP Morgan (number 36 on the list) merged in 2000, their combined assets would have placed the bank in the number 5 position on the international list shown in Table 1.

Bank Lending   Banking is based on one simple principle: Borrow money at low interest rates and lend that money out at much higher interest rates. Even when interest rates are very low, as they were in the spring of 2001, banks charge their borrowers a lot more than they pay their depositors. Just look at the rates that banks post in their windows or in their lobbies. They come right out and admit that they pay either zero or up to maybe 3 percent interest on most deposits—and perhaps 1 or 2 points more if you leave your money on deposit for a few years—but they charge about 7 percent for fixed-rate mortgages, a bit more for most business loans, and about 18 percent on credit card loans. (See box, "Welfare Banks.")

Financial Intermediaries   Financial intermediaries channel funds from savers to borrowers. Basically they repackage the flow of deposits, insurance premiums, pension contributions, and other forms of savings into larger chunks—$10,000, $1 million, $50 million, or even more—for large business borrowers. And, of course, they pay relatively low rates of interest to their lenders and charge relatively high rates to their borrowers. We're all familiar with banks, but this function is performed by a variety of other financial intermediaries (see box, "Nonbank Financial Intermediaries").

Sometimes business borrowers dispense with financial middlemen altogether by borrowing directly from savers. The U.S. Treasury does this every month by issuing new bonds, certificates, notes, and bills. And increasingly, large business borrowers are doing the same thing by issuing relatively short-term commercial paper and long-term bonds.

One way that banks and other financial intermediaries differentiate between the relatively well off and the less fortunate is in the home mortgage market. Just over two-thirds of all American families own their home, nearly all of which have outstanding mortgages.

TABLE 1	The World's Top 25 Commercial Banks, Ranked by Assets		
Rank 12/31/99	Institution	Headquarters	Total Assets 12/31/99
1	Deutsche Bank AG	Frankfurt, Germany	$843,879,555
2	Citigroup	New York, USA	716,937,000
3	BNP Paribas	Paris, France	701,964,428
4	Bank of Tokyo-Mitsubishi Ltd.	Tokyo, Japan	697,263,000
5	Bank of America Corp.	Charlotte, NC	632,574,000
6	UBS AG (Group)	Zurich, Switzerland	614,558,603
7	HSBC Holdings PLC	London, United Kingdom	569,139,000
8	Fuji Bank, Ltd.	Tokyo, Japan	552,290,000
9	Sumitomo Bank Ltd.	Osaka, Japan	509,819,000
10	HypoVereinsbank AG	Munich, Germany	505,660,559
11	Dai-Ichi Kangyo Bank Ltd.	Tokyo, Japan	489,618,130
12	ABN Amro Bank NV	Amsterdam, Netherlands	460,100,000
13	Sakura Bank, Ltd.	Tokyo, Japan	456,634,645
14	Credit Suisse Group	Zurich, Switzerland	451,716,250
15	Credit Agricole (Group)	Paris, France	441,600,810
16	Sanwa Bank, Ltd.	Tokyo, Japan	425,462,600
17	Barclays Bank PLC	London, United Kingdom	410,956,452
18	Societe Generale	Paris, France	406,541,000
19	Fortis Bank	Brussels, Belgium	406,109,300
20	Chase Manhattan Corp.*	New York, USA	406,105,000
21	Industrial Bank of Japan, Ltd.	Tokyo, Japan	399,864,093
22	Dresdner Bank, AG	Frankfurt, Germany	396,846,000
23	Westdeutsche Landesbank	Dusseldorf, Germany	393,754,018
24	Bank of China	Hong Kong	373,687,000
25	Commerzbank, AG	Frankfurt, Germany	372,040,000

*Chase Manhattan merged with J.P. Morgan in 2000. Had these banks merged by 12/31/99, their combined assets of $667,003,000 thousand would have placed the bank fifth on this list. Separately Chase Manhattan was in 20th place and J.P. Morgan was in 36th place (not shown in this table).
Source: www.americanbanker.com.

There are two distinct mortgage markets. The conventional market, in which commercial banks, savings banks, savings and loan associations, and credit unions provide middle class and relativley well off homeowners conventional mortgages at interest rates which hovered around the seven-to-eight percent range in 2000 and 2001. The subprime market caters to poorer homeowners, and has interest rates that are double what they are in the conventional market. Banks generally do not lend directly to homeowners in the subprime market, but they either provide the funds to consumer lending companies like Countrywide Credit or Household International, that provide the actual mortgages, or else huge banks, such as Bank of America and Citicorp own these subprime lenders outright.

There have been moves on the local, state, and federal levels to more closely regulate these subprime lenders. Their defenders point out that without this market, millions of relatively poor families would be unable to own homes. However, the high interest rates and other financial charges have caused hundreds of thousands of families to lose their homes each year. The case of Veronica Harding, which was reported in *The New York Times*, illustrates the plight of relatively poor homeowners. Ms Harding "... bought a row house in North Philadelphia for $7,500 in 1980, but now owes about $35,000 after refinancing five times in four years. The last loan generated $5,600 in fees, or 16 percent of the loan value.[5]

---

[5]Richard A. Oppel, Jr. and Patrick McGeehan, "Lenders Try to Fend Off Laws on Subprime Loans," *The New York Times,* April 4, 2001, page C17.

"Welfare Banks"

Most of us take for granted the services provided by our neighborhood banks. They cash our paychecks; they operate 24-hour cash machines; and, if we need the money to buy a new car or even a house, they lend it to us.

But where do poor people do their banking? Chances are, they go to the "welfare bank," which is what the check-cashing stores are called. You'll find at least one in virtually every poor neighborhood. Where did the name come from? Well, on "check day," which almost always falls on the 1st and the 16th of every month, 7 million Americans receiving public assistance get their checks in the mail. Why don't they cash them at their neighborhood banks? First of all, many poor neighborhoods don't have banks. Second, you usually need to have a minimum balance of at least $1,500 or the bank will charge you some pretty stiff fees for its services. Third, people receiving public assistance are not allowed to have bank accounts; they have no choice but to find someplace else to cash their checks.

The check-cashing outlets not only cash checks but also sell money orders. Who pays their bills by money order? Poor people do. And, of course, a money order may cost $1, or $2, or even more. To cash a check, you usually pay a fee of 1 to 3 percent of the value of the check, but some check-cashing stores will charge you as much as 20 percent.

You may ask why banks almost always require a minimum balance on checking accounts in the first place. The reason is that every banking transaction—depositing money, withdrawing money, processing checks, even posting interest—costs the banks money. However, the poor, especially those on welfare, can least afford to pay the fees charged by check-cashing services. Congress, as well as state legislatures, has considered passing laws requiring banks to cash welfare and Social Security checks, and to provide other banking services to people who cannot afford to keep the stipulated minimum balances, but the American Bankers Association, one of the nation's most powerful special interest groups, has easily beaten back this legislation.

In the 1990s the number of check-cashing outfits tripled to 7,000; These outfits charged poor people between 4 and 10 times what they would have paid for the same services at a bank. And yet most poor people are unaware that several states (including Illinois, Massachusetts, New Jersey, New York, Rhode Island, Vermont, and Minnesota) have laws that require banks to offer accounts with minimum deposits of $100 or less and monthly fees of no more than $3. Although banks are often required to post information about low-cost checking accounts, few actually do, because these laws are rarely enforced.

Nonbank Financial Intermediaries

Banks offer their customers checking deposits that are included in M1. Some nonbank financial intermediaries may come close, but no cigar. Money market mutual funds, for instance, often allow their investors to write checks on their balances, but usually only a few a month, and for at least $500 or $1,000.

Pension funds, generally set up by large corporations are another major form of financial intermediary. TIAA-CREF, which nearly all college professors have joined, is the largest, with a stock and bond portfolio worth several hundred billion dollars. Where did it get all this money? From our paychecks, with matching contributions from our employers.

Insurance companies collect billions of dollars in premiums every year, which they invest in real estate, stocks and bonds, and mortgages. Consumer finance companies—such as Beneficial Finance and Household Finance—borrow at very low rates, because they have excellent credit ratings, and charge their customers 25, 30, or even 40 percent interest rates. Why are these people willing to pay so much? Because they don't have much choice—if their credit ratings had been better, they could have borrowed from a bank.

The Creation and Destruction of Money

The Creation of Money

Money consists of checking deposits, checklike deposits, and currency in the hands of the public. To create money, banks must increase either currency held by the public or checkable deposits. The way banks do this is by making loans.

Banks create money by making loans.

A businessperson walks into Bank of America and requests a loan of $10,000. Later that day she calls the bank and finds out that her loan is granted. Because she already has a checking account at Bank of America, the bank merely adds $10,000 to her balance. In return she signs a form promising to pay back the loan with interest on a specified date. That's it. Money has been created. Checking deposits have just increased by $10,000.

If, for some reason, the businessperson had asked to be paid in cash, the public would have held $10,000 more in currency. And the bank? The $10,000 it loaned out merely inventory; it was not counted as part of our money supply.

The point is that the bank just created $10,000. Whether checkable deposits or currency held by the public rose by that amount, our money supply rose by $10,000.

This may sound like a license to print money. It is, but it's a very restricted license. A bank may make loans only if it has some available reserves. And who determines whether banks have these reserves? You *guessed* it—the Federal Reserve. So we really have three parties involved in the creation of money: the person who wants to borrow the money, the bank that creates the money, and the Federal Reserve, which allows this creative act to take place.

The Destruction of Money

Whoever creates can usually destroy as well. That's what happens when the businessperson pays back her loan. She'll probably write a check on her account for $10,000 plus the interests she owes, and when the bank deducts that amount from her account, down goes the money supply. Or if she pays back the loan in cash, again—down goes the money supply. In this case the currency leaves the hands of the public (literally) and goes into the bank's inventory. The bank will stamp the loan agreement form "paid," and the transaction is completed.

Money is destroyed when a loan is repaid to the bank.

The creation and destruction of money is a major function of banking. The basic way this is done is through loans. The most important commercial bank loans are commercial and industrial loans, although consumer loans have grown considerably in importance since World War II.

Limits to Deposit Creation

Most bank loans involve giving the borrower an additional deposit in his or her checking account; therefore, it would appear that banks can create all the money they wanted by doing this. All you need is a simple bookkeeping operation. A $20,000 loan means you increase that customer's account by $20,000—on paper or by an entry into a computer.

Remember the goldsmith who kept writing receipts until there were 1,000 gold coins in his safe backing 100,000 receipts? Why can't bankers keep issuing loans by increasing the checking accounts of their customers?

The first limit would be prudence. Most banks would try to keep about 2 percent of their demand deposits on reserve in the form of vault cash; in case some of their depositors came in to cash checks, there would be enough money on hand to pay them. Thus, if left to their own devices, bankers would expand their loans only up to the point at which they had just 2 percent cash reserves, or a reserve ratio of 2 percent. Of course, most bankers would more prudently opt for reserve ratios of 3 or 4 percent.

But no banker has that choice. The Federal Reserve sets legal requirements to which the banks must adhere, and, as I've already mentioned, these limits are substantially higher than those that might be set by the most prudent of bankers.

Bank Regulation

Branch Banking and Bank Chartering

Branch Banking versus Unit Banking   Banking is legally defined as accepting deposits. Branch banking, therefore, would be the acceptance of deposits at more than one location. Branch banking rules are set by the state in which a bank is located. Bank of America, for example, is subject to California banking law, while Citibank and Chase Manhattan are regulated by New York banking law.

Three types of branch banking have evolved under various state laws. First is unrestricted branch banking, under which a bank may open branches throughout the state. Bank of America and Wells Fargo have branches all over California.

A second variation is restricted, or limited, branch banking. For example, a bank may be allowed to open branches only in contiguous communities. What is permissible varies from state to state.

Finally, there is unit banking, in which state law forbids any branching whatsoever. A bank that opens an office that receives deposits at a particular location cannot open any other branches. This obviously restricts the size of banks in those states. In fact, banks in unit banking states are, on the average, about one-fifth the size of banks in states that permit unrestricted branching.

Right now two out of five states, nearly all in the East and Far West, have unlimited branching. Another two out of five states, mainly in the Midwest and the South, allow limited branching. And finally, the remaining states, mostly in the Midwest, permit only unit banking.

There are about 75,000 bank branches throughout the nation—an increase of 10,000 since 1985—but some banks are closing branches and replacing them with automated teller machines. Why the shift to ATMs? Processing a teller transaction costs more than double what an ATM transaction costs. By the end of 2000 there were about 250,000 ATMs in the United States doing more than 13 billion transactions a year. As this trend continues, we may begin to see a decline in branch offices.

But now, you can withdraw money from your checking account at hundreds of thousands of retail outlets with a debit card. The vast majority of the 70 million debit cards in circulation were issued by MasterCard and VISA. But instead of getting a month to pay off your balance, as you would on your credit card, your money is automatically withdrawn almost instantly from your checking account to pay for your purchases. Like the advent of the ATM the debit card promises to make personal banking almost obsolete.

The ATM Wars   Should banks be allowed to charge fees—usually $1 to $2—to noncustomers? Virtually all bankers and most economists (including the author) would answer "yes!"

First, there's the issue of fairness. Six out of seven ATM users don't pay surcharges. The fees hit only users who go to "foreign" ATMs—machines not owned by their own bank. Why should a bank's customers underwrite the noncustomers who demand access to cash wherever they are? And why should a bank provide a free service to people who do not otherwise patronize it? Indeed, after Santa Monica and San Francisco banned the fees, Bank of America and Wells Fargo briefly stopped allowing noncustomers in those cities to use their machines.

Second, we need to think of an ATM as a convenience. We pay more to shop at a "convenience store" than at a supermarket. We pay more for soda from a vending

The three types of branch banking are
(1) unrestricted branching,
(2) limited branching,
(3) unit banking.

Questions for Further Thought and Discussion

1. When would you expect to find barter used instead of money?

2. What happens to the demand for money as (*a*) the price level rises; and (*b*) the availability of credit rises? Explain your answers.

3. Describe the conditions that were necessary for modern banking to be born.

4. What were the conditions that led to the savings and loan debacle?

5. How could rapid inflation undermine money's ability to perform each of its four basic jobs?

6. What distinguishes money from other assets, such as corporate stock, goverment bonds, and expensive jewelry?

7. Our money supply is defined as M1. But the Board of Governors of the Federal Reserve and many others believe M2 would better define our money supply. Can you think of one reason to support M1 and one reason to support M2?

8. Why do most interest rates go up and down together over time?

9. Financial intermediaries perform an important job. What is that job, and how do they perform it?

10. What percentage of your money balance do you hold for transactions purposes, precautionary purposes, and speculative purposes?

11. What percentage of your or your family's bills are paid by cash, by check, and by credit card?

W*orkbook* for Chapter 13

Name _____ Date _____

Multiple-Choice Questions

Circle the letter that corresponds to the best answer.

1. Each of the following except _____ is a job of the money supply.
   a) medium of exchange
   b) store of value
   c) standard of value
   d) receipt for gold
   e) standard of deferred payment

2. Which is the most important job of money?
   a) medium of exchange
   b) store of value
   c) standard of value
   d) receipt for gold
   e) standard of deferred payment

3. The basic alternative to money in the United States would be _____.
   a) gold   c) stealing
   b) barter   d) the underground economy

4. Barter involves _____.
   a) money
   b) specialization
   c) a double coincidence of wants
   d) demand deposits

5. Which one of the following is not part of our money supply?
   a) dollar bills   c) traveler's checks
   b) demand deposits   d) gold

6. Which statement is true?
   a) M1 is larger than M2.
   b) M1 + M2 = M3.
   c) M2 + large-denomination time deposits + money market mutual funds held by institutions = M3.
   d) M1 × M2 = M3.

7. Which statement is true?
   a) Checks are not money.
   b) A small part of our money supply is silver certificates.
   c) Most of our money supply is in the form of currency.
   d) None of these statements is true.

8. The U.S. dollar is based on _____ currency.
   a) British   c) Dutch
   b) French   d) Spanish

9. Which is not in M2?
   a) currency
   b) demand deposits
   c) small-denomination time deposits
   d) large-denomination time deposits

10. Which statement is true?
    a) Credit cards are a form of money.
    b) M1 is closer to the size of M2 than M2 is to the size of M3.
    c) M2 is almost five times the size of M1.
    d) M3 is about $2 trillion.

11. The Financial Institutions Reform, Recovery, and Enforcement Act of 1989 provided for each of the following, except _____.
    a) selling off the assets of failed S&Ls
    b) the closing down of failing S&Ls
    c) allowing the S&Ls to make commercial loans
    d) the borrowing of enough money to pay off all the shareholders of failed S&Ls

12. In early 2001 M1 was more than $_____ billion.
    a) 600   c) 1,000
    b) 800   d) 1,400

13. Over the last three decades our money supply _____.

    a) grew steadily at about the same rate

    b) fell steadily at about the same rate

    c) rose steadily through the 1970s and fell steadily through the 1980s and 1990s

    d) fell steadily through the 1970s and rose steadily through the 1980s and 1990s

    e) grew most years, but at widely varying rates

14. The interest rate on business loans _____ the interest rate that banks pay their depositors.

    a) is higher than

    b) is lower than

    c) has no relationship to

15. The too-big-to-fail doctrine _____.

    a) is the basis for the savings and loan bailout

    b) has had little relevance since the Great Depression

    c) was the basis for the bailouts of Franklin National, Continental Illinois, and other large banks

    d) was proclaimed by President Franklin Roosevelt and extended by nearly all of his successors

16. Which statement is true?

    a) The too-big-to-fail doctrine covers banks with assets of more than $1 billion.

    b) The largest bank bailout in our history was that of the Bank of New England.

    c) The FDIC has financed 15 bailouts costing more than $1 billion each.

    d) None of these statements is true.

17. John Maynard Keynes identified three motives for holding money. Which motive listed below did Keynes not identify?

    a) transactions   c) psychological

    b) precautionary   d) speculative

18. As the price level rises, amount of money demanded for transactions purposes _____.

    a) rises

    b) falls

    c) remains about the same

19. As the interest rate rises, the quantity of money demanded _____.

    a) rises

    b) falls

    c) remains about the same

20. People tend to hold more money as _____.

    a) incomes rise and credit availability rises

    b) incomes fall and credit availability falls

    c) incomes rise and credit availability falls

    d) incomes fall and credit availability rises

21. The distinction between commercial banks and other banks is _____.

    a) very clear   c) nonexistent

    b) becoming blurred   d) none of these

22. Banking began in _____.

    a) biblical times   c) the 19th century

    b) medieval times   d) the 20th century

23. What led to the bankruptcy of many goldsmiths was that they _____.

    a) had a reserve ratio that was too high

    b) had a reserve ratio that was too low

    c) lent out gold coins instead of receipts

    d) lent out receipts instead of gold coins

24. Bankers would like to hold a reserve ratio of about _____.

    a) 2 percent   c) 50 percent

    b) 10 percent   d) 100 percent

25. Which statement is true?

    a) Most financial institutions are commercial banks.

    b) There are currently fewer than 1,000 commercial banks in the United States.

    c) Nearly all banks today are regulated by both the Federal Reserve and the FDIC.

    d) About half the banks in the United States are members of the FDIC.

26. Which statement is false?

   a) About 99 percent of all banks are members of the FDIC.

   b) If the FDIC runs out of money, the federal government will supply it with more funds.

   c) The FDIC would rather have another bank take over an ailing institution than be forced to pay off its depositors.

   d) None of these statements is false.

27. Which statement is true?

   a) Most states allow only unit banking.

   b) Most states allow unlimited branching.

   c) Most banks have national charters.

   d) None of these statements is true.

28. To get a bank charter, you need to demonstrate each of the following, except _____.

   a) that your community needs a bank or an additional bank

   b) that you have sufficient banking experience

   c) that you have enough capital to start a bank

   d) that you are of good character

29. Money is created when someone _____.

   a) takes out a bank loan   c) spends money

   b) pays back a bank loan   d) saves money

30. Bank deposit creation is limited by _____.

   a) reserve requirements

   b) the interest rate

   c) whether a bank is nationally or state chartered

   d) whether a bank is in a large city or a rural area

31. Which statement is true?

   a) About half the savings and loan associations went bankrupt in the early 1980s.

   b) The savings and loan associations were helped by high interest rates in the late 1970s and early 1980s.

   c) Most savings and loan associations were locked into low-interest-rate mortgages in the 1950s and 1960s.

   d) None is true.

Fill-In Questions

1. The most important job of money is as _____ _____. The other three jobs of money are _____, _____, and _____. The job money performs the most poorly is as _____.

2. The alternative to money would be _____ _____. To do this, you would need a _____.

3. The three main components of our money supply are (1) _____ (2) _____; and (3) _____.

4. The U.S. dollar is based on the _____.

5. The basic function of credit cards is _____.

6. To get from M2 to M3, we add _____.

7. M2 is almost _____ times the size of M1.

8. Another name for checking deposits is _____. How did they get this name? _____.

9. About _____ percent of the states allow only unit banking.

10. About _____ percent of all banks have state charters.

11. The main way that banks create money is by _____; the main way that money is destroyed is when _____.

12. The interest rate is set by the _____ _____ and the _____.

13. The total demand for money is the sum of (1) the _____ demand; (2) the _____ _____ demand; and (3) the _____ _____ demand.

14. The four main influences on the amount of money that people tend to hold are (1) _____; (2) _____; (3) _____; and (4) _____.

15. John Maynard Keynes identified the following three motives to explain why people hold money: (1)_____;(2)_____; and (3)_____.

16. People tend to hold more money as_____ and_____rise; they tend to hold less money as _____ and _____ rise.

17. People hold more money for their _____ motive than for the other two motives.

18. According to Keynes's liquidity trap, at very low interest rates, people would _____ _____.

19. The world's first bankers were the _____ _____.

20. Modern banking was born when the first bankers noticed two things: (1) _____ _____ and (2) _____ _____.

21. The world's first paper money was in the form of ___ _____.

22. If a goldsmith had 100 gold coins sitting in his safe and lent out 50 of them, this would imply a reserve ratio of _____ percent.

23. The bankruptcy of the goldsmiths who lent out part of the gold they were safekeeping was caused by ___ _____.

24. Most bankers today would like to hold a reserve of about _____ percent.

25. Banks are very heavily regulated. The main reason for this is that _____ _____.

26. The FDIC insures all bank deposits of up to $____.

27. Rather than pay off depositors of a failed bank, the FDIC would prefer that _____ _____.

Problems

1. If M2 were 2,500, small-denomination time deposits were 250, large-denomination time deposits were 300, and money market mutual funds held by institutions were 200, how much would M3 be?

2. a) A goldsmith has 1,000 gold coins in his safe and 1,000 receipts circulating. How much are his outstanding loans and what is his reserve ratio?
   b) The goldsmith then lends out 100 of the coins. What is his reserve ratio?

3. A goldsmith has 100 gold coins in his safe. If there are 500 receipts in circulation, how much is his reserve ratio?

4. a) A banker lends a businessowner $100,000. How does this affect the money supply? (Hint: You need to have a dollar amount in your answer.)

b) The businessowner pays back the loan. How does this affect the money supply?

5. How much would M2 be if M1 were 500; small-denomination time deposits, savings deposits, and money market mutual funds held by individuals totaled 1,200; and large-denomination time deposits were 300? How much would M3 be?

Chapter 14

The Federal Reserve and Monetary Policy

In the first part of the chapter, we'll examine the organization and management of the Federal Reserve System (the Fed), especially how it uses open-market operations, changes in the discount rate, and changes in reserve requirements to control the rate of growth of the money supply.

The goals of monetary policy are price stability, relatively full employment, and a satisfactory rate of economic growth. If you go back to the first page of Chapter 12, you'll see that the goals of fiscal and monetary policy are identical. The melodies are the same, but the lyrics are quite different. Fiscal policy is the use of government spending and taxation to affect the overall economy, while monetary policy uses controls on the money supply's rate of growth to affect the overall economy.

CHAPTER OBJECTIVES

The main topics of this chapter are:

- The organization of the Federal Reserve System.
- Reserve requirements.
- The deposit expansion multiplier.

- The tools of monetary policy.
- The Fed's effectiveness in fighting inflation and recession.
- The Banking Act of 1980.

The Federal Reserve System

Unlike most other industrial nations, the United States was without a central bank until 1913.[1] While the Bank of England and the Bank of France acted as each country's central

---

[1]There had been a First United States Bank (1791–1811) and a Second United States Bank (1816–36), but the charters of both had been allowed to lapse, mainly for political reasons.

banking authority, Americans were left defenseless when financial panics set in. Every few years in the 1880s, 1890s, and early 1900s, financial crises developed and eventually receded until, finally, we had the Panic of 1907.

During this panic, people rushed to their banks to take out their money, and business was severely disrupted. The public demanded that the government take steps to prevent this from ever happening again. After six years of intermittent debate, Congress finally passed the Federal Reserve Act of 1913. One of the hopes of its framers was that the 12 Federal Reserve district banks would, at times of crisis, act as a "lender of last resort." In other words, if U.S. bankers were caught with their pants down, someone stood ready to give them a little time to get their affairs back in order.

In the very first paragraph of the Federal Reserve Act, Congress outlined its main objectives:

> An Act to provide for the establishment of Federal reserve banks, to furnish an elastic currency, to afford means of rediscounting commercial paper, to establish a more effective supervision of banking in the United States, and for other purposes.

What's an elastic currency? It's a money supply that expands when the economy is growing rapidly and businesses need more money. Rediscounting, which we'll talk about later in the chapter, is a way for the Federal Reserve to lend money to banks, which, in turn, would lend that money to businesses.

The Federal Reserve has five main jobs:

1. Conduct monetary policy, which is, by far, the most important job. Monetary policy is the control of the rate of growth of the money supply to foster relatively full employment, price stability, and a satisfactory rate of economic growth.

2. Serve as a lender of last resort to commercial banks, savings banks, savings and loan associations, and credit unions.

3. Issue currency (see box, "Who Issues Our Currency?").

4. Provide banking services to the U.S. government.

5. Supervise and regulate our financial institutions.

The Federal Reserve District Banks

The 12 Federal Reserve District Banks

There are 12 Federal Reserve District Banks, one in each of the nation's Federal Reserve districts. These are shown in the map in Figure 1. Each of these banks issues currency to accommodate the business needs of its district.[2] (To learn who actually issues our currency, see box.)

You'll notice in Figure 1 that the Federal Reserve District Banks are concentrated in the East and Midwest. This reflects the concentration of banks and business activity in 1913. Why haven't we moved some of the banks to the West, perhaps paralleling the movement of the old Brooklyn Dodgers, New York Giants, and Philadelphia Athletics? Evidently, it's a lot easier to move a baseball team than a Federal Reserve District Bank. To accommodate the needs of western banks, branch offices of the San Francisco, Kansas City, Dallas, and Minneapolis Federal Reserve District Banks have been set up in several cities (see Figure 1). For example, in the 12th district, in which the San Francisco bank is situated, there are branches in Los Angeles, Portland, and Salt Lake City.

Each Federal Reserve District Bank is owned by the several hundred member banks in that district. A commercial bank becomes a member by buying stock in the Federal Reserve District Bank, so the Fed is a quasi public–private enterprise, not controlled by the president or by Congress. However, effective control is really exercised by the Federal Reserve Board of Governors in Washington, D.C.

---

[2]The Bureau of Engraving in Washington does the actual printing, but why be picky?

Who Issues Our Currency?

The U.S. Treasury issues it, right? Wrong! Our currency is issued by the 12 Federal Reserve District Banks.* Check it out. Pull a dollar out of your wallet and look at it. What does it say right near the top, about a half inch above George Washington's picture? That's right—"Federal Reserve Note."

If you thought the Treasury issues our currency, it used to (and the secretary of the Treasury still signs every bill). The last thing it issued, until the mid-1960s, was $1 and $5 silver certificates. These certificates are now out of circulation, snapped up by collectors. The Treasury still issues our pennies, nickels, dimes, quarters,

half dollars, and metal (no longer silver) dollars, but, as you might have suspected, that's just the small change of our money supply.

And what about the backing for the dollar? Look on the back of the bill just above the big "ONE." What's the backing for our currency? That's right—"In God We Trust." Actually, there is backing for our currency—the government's word, as well as its general acceptability.

_____

*As noted in footnote 2, the actual printing is done by the Federal Bureau of Engraving.

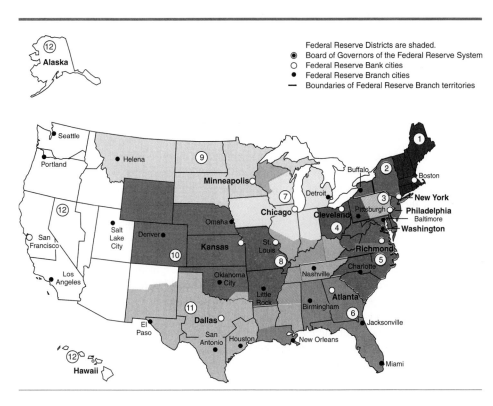

Figure 1
The Federal Reserve System

Federal Reserve Districts are shaded.
- ◉ Board of Governors of the Federal Reserve System
- ○ Federal Reserve Bank cities
- ● Federal Reserve Branch cities
- — Boundaries of Federal Reserve Branch territories

The Board of Governors

The seven members of the Board of Governors are nominated by the president, subject to confirmation by the Senate. Each is appointed for one 14-year term and is ineligible to serve a second term. The terms are staggered so that vacancies occur every two years. That way, in every four-year term, a president appoints two members of the Board of Governors.

Usually, however, a president gets to appoint three or even four members during a single executive term because many Governors do not serve their full 14-year terms. Why not? Mainly because they could make much more money "on the outside." Serving on the Board looks great on your résumé, and it's done in the spirit of serving one's country, but 14 years is a bit long to live on a government paycheck.

The seven members of the Federal Reserve Board

The chairman of the Board, who generally exercises considerable influence, serves a 4-year term, which is part of his or her 14-year tenure as a member of the Board. He or she is also appointed by the president and may serve more than one term as chairman.

Independence of the Board of Governors

Should the Board of Governors be controlled by or answerable to anyone else?

Does the president "control" the Board of Governors and its chairman? The answer is, generally, no. First, unless there is a vacancy caused by death or resignation, the president would have to serve two terms to appoint four members to the Board.[3] Second, once someone is appointed to the Board, there is no reason to expect that person to do the president's bidding.

The president does get to appoint a chairman sometime during his or her term. However, Jimmy Carter had to deal with Arthur Burns (Richard Nixon's appointee) for the first part of his term; Ronald Reagan did not always see eye-to-eye with Jimmy Carter's appointee, Paul Volcker. And Bill Clinton, who inherited Alan Greenspan from George Bush,[4] could not have been that pleased to see the Federal Reserve push up short-term interest rates seven times between early 1994 and early 1995. There have been proposals that the president be allowed to appoint his own chairman at the beginning of the executive term so that monetary and fiscal policy can be coordinated, but no action has been taken thus far.

Once a Board member or chairman is confirmed by the Senate, she or he is not answerable to the president or Congress. Although the chairman is legally required to make an annual report to Congress, he or she is free to stand before that body and tell them, "We have completely defied your wishes. You wanted us to increase the money supply and we lowered it. You wanted interest rates to drop and they've gone up. That is our report."

Of course, things are much more cordial than that between the Fed and Congress and between the Fed and the president, but the bottom line remains that the Federal Reserve is an independent agency. Some feel that for a group of unelected officials, the members of the Board have too much power. When interest rates soar or inflation rages out of control, these rascals cannot be turned out of office by an angry electorate. About all we can do is hope that better people will eventually be appointed to the Board.

Others feel that the difficult, unpopular decisions of monetary policy must be made by those who are insulated from the wrath of the voters. Tight money is hardly a popular policy, but when the Federal Reserve Board members think it will help control inflation, why should they be inhibited by fears of political reprisal?

Of course, the members of the Board of Governors are not immune to the reactions of their fellow citizens, but their independence permits them to follow unpopular policies if they feel that doing so is in the best economic interest of the nation. Attempts have been made in recent years to make the Federal Reserve Board more responsive to the wishes of Congress and the administration, but none has been successful.

How independent is our central bank in comparison to other leading central banks? The Bank of England and La Banca d'Italia (which you probably figured out is the central bank of Italy) have relatively little independence from political control. Consequently, these banks are often under pressure to increase the money supply and stimulate the economy, leading to relatively high inflation rates.

Germany's Deutsche Bundesbank (nicknamed "the Bubba") is quite independent. Indeed, according to German law, the Deutsche Bundesbank has the "assigned task of preserving monetary stability" and "shall be independent of instructions from the federal

---

[3]Because of a slew of resignations, President Ronald Reagan was able to appoint all seven members in his first seven years in office. Interestingly, two of those who resigned did so because the president would not promise them the chairmanship.

[4]George Bush, in turn, inherited Greenspan from Ronald Reagan, who appointed him chairman in 1987. Bill Clinton reappointed Greenspan to a third term.

government." Interestingly, Germany has experienced relatively little inflation during the last two and a half decades of the 20th century.

The Federal Reserve, the Bank of Canada, and the Bank of Japan are in the middle rank of central banks in terms of independence. Both enjoy considerable independence but still come under some political pressure.

You may recall the 11-member European Monetary Union from Chapter 8. Its common currency, the euro, gradually begins to replace each member nation's currency through 2002. It is issued by the European Central Bank, which will coexist with Deutsche Bundesbank, La Banca d'Italia, and each of the other nations' central banks. Its powers, as well as its independence, are very limited, but that may change when the euro eventually replaces the lira, the mark, the franc, and the other national currencies.

Legal Reserve Requirements

The Federal Reserve has various jobs, the most important of which is to control the money supply. When it was set up in 1913, the framers of the Federal Reserve Act envisaged the Fed as a "lender of last resort." Obviously, the record of widespread bank failures in the early 1930s is a sad commentary on how well the Fed was able to do that job.

The Federal Reserve's most important job

Before we consider how the Fed works today, we will look at the focal point of the Federal Reserve's control of our money supply: legal reserve requirements. Every financial institution in the country is legally required to hold a certain percentage of its deposits on reserve, either in the form of deposits at its Federal Reserve District Bank or in its own vaults. As neither Federal Reserve deposits nor vault cash pays interest, no one is very happy about holding 10 percent of most demand deposits on reserve (see Table 1).

We'll be using some technical terms, so let's be very clear on their meanings. *Required reserves* is the minimum amount of vault cash and deposits at the Federal Reserve District Bank that must be held by the financial institution. *Actual reserves* is what the bank is holding. If a bank is holding more than required, it has excess reserves. Therefore, *actual reserves − required reserves = excess reserves.*

If a bank had $100 million in checking deposits, how much reserves would it be required to hold? Work it out right here, using the information in Table 1:

TABLE 1	Legal Reserve Requirements, March 1997	
Checking accounts:		
$0–$42.8 million*	3%	
Over $42.8 million	10	
Time deposits	0%	

*Up to $5.5 million of deposits has a zero percent reserve requirement. This amount varies from bank to bank, so we shall ignore it.

Source: Federal Reserve Bulletin, March 2001.

Solution:

$$3 \text{ percent of } \$42.8 \text{ million} = \$1,284,000$$
$$10 \text{ percent of remaining } \$57.2 \text{ million} = \$5,720,000$$
$$\text{Required reserves} = \$1,284,000 + \$5,720,000$$
$$= \$7,004,000$$

If this bank happened to be holding reserves of, say, $9 million, then it would be holding excess reserves of $1,996,000. Because banks earn no interest on their reserves, they try to keep them down to a bare minimum. In fact, a bank ideally holds no excess reserves whatsoever; its goal is zero excess reserves.

Let's try another question. If a bank had demand deposits of $1 billion and held $120 million in actual reserves (in the form of deposits at the Federal Reserve District Bank and vault cash), calculate (1) its required reserves and (2) its excess reserves.

Solution:

$$(1) \ 3\% \text{ of } \$42.8 \text{ million} = \$1,284,000$$
$$10 \text{ percent of remaining } \$957.2 \text{ million} = \$95,720,000$$
$$\$1,284,000 + \$95,720,000 = \$97,004,000$$
$$\text{Required reserves} = \$97,004,000$$
$$(2) \ \text{Actual reserves} - \text{Required reserves} = \text{Excess reserves}$$
$$\$120,000,000 - \$97,004,000 = \$22,996,000$$

Can a bank ever end up with negative excess reserves? Think about it. Time's up: what do you think? If actual reserves are less than required reserves, then excess reserves are negative. Or, in simple English, the bank is short of required reserves. If a bank does find itself short, it will usually borrow reserves from another bank that has some excess reserves. The reserves it borrows are called *federal funds,* and the interest rate charged for them is called the *federal funds rate.* A bank short of reserves may also borrow at the discount window of its Federal Reserve District Bank, a process we'll discuss later in the chapter.

The Monetary Control Act of 1980 (which will be discussed in detail toward the end of this chapter) called for uniform reserve requirements for all financial institutions—commercial banks, savings banks, savings and loan associations, money market mutual funds, and credit unions. Until 1987, when the uniform reserve requirements were fully phased in, only Federal Reserve member banks, about 5,000 in number, were subject to relatively high reserve requirements. The other 28,000 or so of the nation's financial institutions were subject to much lower requirements.

You'll notice in Table 1 that the reserve requirement for time deposits is zero. Because time deposits, by definition, are held for relatively long periods of time, the Federal Reserve Board eliminated reserve requirements for all time deposits in 1992.

Primary and Secondary Reserves

A bank's *primary reserves are its vault cash and its deposits at the Federal Reserve District Bank.* These reserves pay no interest; therefore the banks try to hold no more than the Federal Reserve requires. Ideally, then, they hold zero excess reserves.

Bankers are, if nothing else, prudent. Their main aims, other than making high profits, are to protect their depositors and to maintain liquidity. Liquidity is the ability to convert assets quickly into cash without loss.

Even without legal reserve requirements, bankers would keep some cash on reserve to meet the day-to-day needs of their depositors as well as to meet any unforeseen large withdrawals. The cash that banks do keep on hand, together with their deposits at the Federal Reserve District Banks, is sometimes called primary reserves. In addition, every bank holds secondary reserves, mainly in the form of very short-term U.S. government securities.

What are the three main aims of bankers?

Treasury bills, notes, certificates, and bonds (that will mature in less than a year) are generally considered a bank's secondary reserves. These can quickly be converted to cash without loss if a bank suddenly needs money, whether because of increased withdrawals or perhaps a shortage of primary reserves. Generally, in the case of a shortage of primary reserves, a bank will borrow on a daily basis from other banks in the federal funds market. Another source of short-term funds is the Federal Reserve District Bank's discount window.

In the spring of 1993, when short-term interest rates had fallen to 15-year lows, banks were paying their depositors less than 3 percent interest on everything except long-term CDs. What did they *do* with these deposits? The banks held hundreds of billions of dollars' worth of short-term U.S. government securities that paid about 4 percent interest. These investments were not only profitable and risk free, but they incurred no administrative costs, as individual and commercial loans would have. And so, well into 1998, banks held a very high level of secondary reserves.

Deposit Expansion

How Deposit Expansion Works

To see how deposit expansion works, we'll assume a 10 percent reserve ratio because that's an easy number with which to work. Suppose someone comes into a bank and deposits $100,000.

We know that banks don't like to have idle reserves because they don't earn any interest on them. So what does the bank do with the $100,000? It lends out as much as it can.

With a 10 percent reserve requirement, the bank can lend $90,000. To keep matters simple, we'll assume the $90,000 was lent to a single company. The bank added $90,000 to the company's checking account by making an entry in its computer.

Normally, the bank would need an additional $9,000 in reserves to cover the new $90,000 demand deposit. But why did the company borrow $90,000? Obviously it was needed for certain business expenses; no one pays interest on borrowed money just to sit on it.

Again, keeping things simple, suppose this company wrote a check for $90,000 to pay for additional inventory. The company receiving the check deposits it in its bank, and the process is repeated. The bank keeps the required 10 percent ($9,000) on reserve and lends out the remaining $81,000. This money is spent and eventually deposited in a third bank, which keeps 10 percent ($8,100) on reserve and lends out $72,900.

We could go on and on. Indeed, we have in Table 2. Were we to continue the process with an infinite number of banks, we would eventually end up with $1 million in deposits and $100,000 in reserves.

The Deposit Expansion Multiplier

Remember the multiplier in Chapter 12? Now we'll look at the deposit expansion multiplier, which is based on the same principle and nearly the same formula.

Any new money injected into the banking system will have a multiplied effect on the money supply. How large this multiplied effect will be depends on the size of the multiplier. In general, when the reserve ratio is low, the multiplier will be high and vice versa.

TABLE 2	Hypothetical Deposit Expansion with 10 Percent Reserve Requirement
Deposits	**Reserves**
$100,000.00	$10,000.00
90,000.00	9,000.00
81,000.00	8,100.00
72,900.00	7,290.00
65,610.00	6,561.00
59,049.00	5,904.90
53,541.00	5,354.10
48,186.90	4,818.69
43,368.21	4,336.82
39,031.39	3,903.14
35,128.25	3,512.83
31,615.43	3,161.54
28,453.89	2,845.39
25,608.50	2,560.85
23,047.65	2,304.76
20,742.89	2,074.29
18,668.60	1,866.86
16,812.00	1,681.20
15,130.80	1,513.08
13,617.72	1,361.77
—*	—*
—	—
—	—
$1,000,000.00	$100,000.00

*To save space, the rest of the calculations are omitted.

The formula for the deposit expansion multiplier is:

$$\text{Deposit expansion multiplier} = \frac{1}{\text{Reserve ratio}}$$

$$\frac{1}{\text{Reserve ratio}}$$

If the reserve ratio is .10, we substitute and solve to find the multiplier:

$$\frac{1}{\text{Reserve ratio}} = \frac{1}{.10} = 10$$

Remember, how many dimes are in a dollar?

If the reserve ratio is .25, find the deposit expansion multiplier. Do it right here.

Using the formula, we get:

$$\frac{1}{\text{Reserve ratio}} = \frac{1}{.25} = 4$$

How many times does .25 go into 1? How many times does a quarter go into a dollar?

Three Modifications of the Deposit Expansion Multiplier

Not every dollar of deposit expansion will actually be redeposited and lent out repeatedly. Some people may choose to hold or spend some of their money as currency. For example, an individual receiving a $300 check may deposit $200 and receive $100 back as cash.

This cash leakage tends to cut down on the deposit expansion multiplier because not all the money lent out is redeposited. For example, if $90,000 is lent out but only $81,000 is redeposited, this would have the same effect on the multiplier as a 10 percent increase in the reserve ratio.

It is also possible, although unlikely in times of inflation, for banks to carry excess reserves. To the degree that they do, however, this cuts down on the deposit expansion multiplier. Why? Because it, in effect, raises the reserve ratio. For example, if the reserve ratio rose from .20 to .25 because banks were carrying a 5 percent excess reserve, the multiplier would fall from 5 ($1/.2 = 5$) to 4 ($1/.25 = 4$).

Currency leakages do take place, especially during times of recession and low interest rates. During such times, it is quite possible for banks to carry excess reserves. One might also keep in mind that during recessions, banks might carry excess reserves because of a scarcity of creditworthy borrowers.

Finally, there are leakages of dollars to foreign countries caused mainly by our foreign trade imbalance. Our imports far exceed our exports, so there is a large drain of dollars to foreigners. And then, too, there is all the currency that American tourists spend abroad plus the tens of billions sent covertly to international drug traffickers. Some of these dollars return to the United States in the form of various investments (particularly in U.S. government securities, corporate securities, and real estate), but there is a definite net outflow of dollars, which, in turn, depresses still further the deposit expansion multiplier.

Where does all this leave us? It leaves us with the conclusion that the deposit expansion multiplier is, in reality, quite a bit lower than it would be if we based it solely on the reserve ratio. In other words, if the reserve ratio tells us it's 10, perhaps it's only 6.

Now that I've made you do these calculations, a confession is in order. The deposit expansion multiplier is a bit less wonderful than I led you to believe. It's just too big. You can probably get on with your life just accepting this fact, but if you happen to be from Missouri (the Show Me State), then you can check out the Advanced Work box, "Three Modifications of the Deposit Expansion Multiplier."

Cash, Checks, and Electronic Money

One of the jobs of the Federal Reserve is called check clearing. Through this process, once the checks you write are deposited by the people you gave them to, they make their way through our financial system, facilitated by the Fed, and eventually wind up in your mailbox at the end of the month. How did they get there? Read the box, "Check Clearing."

Increasingly, money is changing hands electronically rather than in the form of checks. Today, more than $1.7 trillion a day is transferred electronically—80 percent of the total payments made worldwide in dollars. About $600 billion of these transfers are carried out by the Federal Reserve's electronic network, while the other $1.1 trillion are done by the Clearing House Interbank Payments System (CHIPS), which is owned by 11 big New York banks.

Does all this mean that we are well on our way to a checkless, cashless society? Yes and no. We still carry out nearly 85 percent of our monetary transactions in cash—everything from paying for our groceries to tipping the hairdresser. But when we consider the total dollars actually spent, cash covers less than 1 percent of the total value of transactions, while electronic transfers account for five out of every six dollars that move in the economy.

The Tools of Monetary Policy

The goals of monetary policy were outlined at the beginning of the chapter. To attain these goals, the Fed regulates the rate of growth of the nation's money supply. This effort focuses on the reserves held by financial institutions. The most important policy tool used by the Fed to control reserves and, indirectly, the money supply, is open-market operations. To reiterate, the most important job of the Fed is to control the money supply; its most important policy tool to do that job is open-market operations.

How Open-Market Operations Work

What are open-market operations?

Open-market operations are the buying and selling of U.S. government securities in the open market. What are U.S. government securities? They are Treasury bills, notes, certificates, and bonds. The Fed does not market new securities.[5] That's the Treasury's job. Rather, the Fed buys and sells securities that have already been marketed by the Treasury, some of which might be several years old.

The total value of all outstanding U.S. government securities is more than $4 trillion. If this number is familiar, it should be; it's our national debt. Many students are under the misconception that the Federal Reserve sells newly issued securities for the Treasury, but all it does is buy and sell chunks of the national debt.

What open-market operations consist of, then, is the buying and selling of chunks of the national debt. The Fed does this by dealing with government bond houses, which are private bond dealers. If the Fed wants to buy, say, $100 million of Treasury notes that will mature within the next three months, it places an order with a few of these bond houses, which then buy up the securities for the Fed. When the Fed wants to sell securities, it again goes to the government bond houses and has them do the actual selling.

How the Fed increases the money supply

When the Fed wants to increase the money supply, it goes into the open market and buys U.S. government securities. You might ask, "What if people don't want to sell?" Remember the line from *The Godfather,* "I'll make you an offer you can't refuse"? Well, that's exactly what the Fed does. It tells the government bond houses, "Buy us 30,000 Treasury bills no matter what the price."

Question: What do you get when you cross the Godfather with an economist? Answer: An offer you can't understand.

If the Fed goes on a buying spree in the open market, it will quickly drive up the prices of U.S. government securities. All this buying will push down interest rates. Let's see why.

Suppose a bond is issued by the Treasury with a face value of $1,000 and an interest rate of 8 percent. This means the bond costs the initial buyer $1,000 and pays $80 interest a year. The price of the bond will fluctuate considerably over its life; but when it matures, the Treasury must pay the owner $1,000, its face value. And every year the Treasury must pay the owner $80 interest.

Using the formula

$$\text{Interest rate} = \frac{\text{Interest paid}}{\text{Price of bond}}$$

$$\text{Interest rate} = \frac{\text{Interest paid}}{\text{Price of bond}}$$

we can observe that a $1,000 bond paying $80 interest pays an interest rate of 8 percent:

$$\frac{\$80}{\$1,000} = 8 \text{ percent}$$

We have been talking about the Fed going into the open market and buying government securities. Suppose the Fed bought enough securities to bid up their price to $1,200.

---

[5]The Fed is legally limited to buying no more than $5 billion in newly issued government securities a year, which is less than 1 percent of what the Treasury issues.

Check Clearing

If you have a checking account at your local bank, at the end of each month you receive a statement listing all your deposits and withdrawals. The withdrawals are more numerous than the deposits because every time you write a check, that money is withdrawn from your account. Together with your statement, your bank encloses a pile of checks you wrote that month.

Did you ever wonder how, if you wrote a check, it ended up with your statement at the end of the month? No? Well, I'm going to tell you anyway. The whole process is called check clearing, and it is a service provided by the Federal Reserve System.

In 1976 we had a series of birthday parties for the nation. The United States of America was 200 years old that year. I was visiting some friends out in San Francisco at the time, and one of them, Bob, sold me a beat-up old bugle, which actually *looked* like it might have dated from the American Revolution.

This bugle has come in quite handy at my 8:00 A.M. classes. At the time I bought it, though, the big question was how I would pay for it. I didn't have $50 in cash I could spare. But what was really good about Bob was that he took out-of-state checks.

I gave Bob my check for $50. It was written on Citibank back in Brooklyn. Bob deposited it in his account at Bank of America. From there it went to Bank of America's main office in San Francisco, which, in turn, sent it on to the San Francisco Federal Reserve District Bank. Bank of America's reserves were raised by $50 (the amount of the check). Doing this was a simple book-keeping operation.

The check was sent to the New York Federal Reserve District Bank, which deducted $50 from the reserves of Citibank. The check then went to Citibank's main office in Manhattan, and then to my branch out on Flatbush Avenue in Brooklyn. The $50 was then deducted from my account, and at the end of the month, the canceled check was mailed to me with my statement.

All of these transactions are shown pictorially in the diagram below. The check I gave Bob in San Francisco was sent back to me by my Brooklyn bank with my statement at the end of the month.

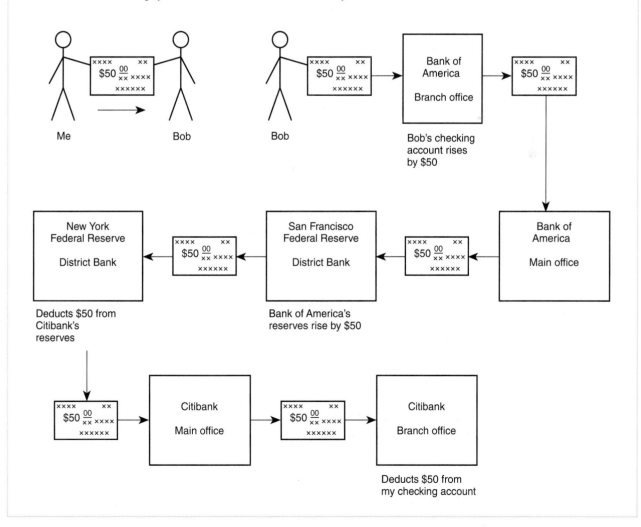

Remember, these securities still pay $80 interest a year. Let's calculate their new interest rate:

$$\text{Interest rate} = \frac{\text{Interest paid}}{\text{Price of bond}} = \frac{\$80}{\$1,200} = 6\tfrac{2}{3} \text{ percent}$$

You see that, as previously noted, when the Fed goes into the open market to buy securities, it bids up their price and lowers their interest rates. In the process, as we shall soon see, this also expands the money supply.

The $6\tfrac{2}{3}$ percent is the effective, or market, rate of interest. Although the U.S. Treasury is still paying 8 percent ($80) on the face value ($1,000) of the bond, the Federal Reserve has effectively lowered the market rate of interest to $6\tfrac{2}{3}$ percent. Incidentally, if the Treasury were to issue new bonds that day, it would need to pay an interest rate of just $6\tfrac{2}{3}$ percent (that is, $66.67 on a $1,000 bond).

How the Fed contracts the money supply

When the Fed wants to contract the money supply, or at least slow down its rate of expansion, it goes into the open market and sells securities. In the process, it lowers bond prices and raises interest rates.

When selling securities, the Fed also uses the "Godfather principle." Again, it makes an offer that can't be refused (in this case, an offer to sell securities at low enough prices to get rid of a certain amount).

If the Fed bids bond prices down to $800, we use the same formula to find that the interest rate has risen to 10 percent.

$$\text{Interest rate} = \frac{\text{Interest paid}}{\text{Price of bond}} = \frac{\$80}{\$800} = 10 \text{ percent}$$

When the Fed sells securities on the open market to contract the money supply, bond prices fall and interest rates rise. Falling bond prices and rising interest rates generally accompany a tightening of the money supply.

You should note that although the Fed deals only with U.S. government securities, interest rates and bond prices move together in a broad range. When the Fed depresses the prices of U.S. government securities, all government and corporate bond prices tend to fall. And when the Fed pushes up the interest on U.S. government securities, all interest rates tend to rise.

Let's try another interest rate problem. Find the interest rate on a bond that pays $100 a year in interest and is currently selling for $800. Work it out right here:

Solution:

$$\text{Interest rate} = \frac{\text{Interest paid}}{\text{Price of bond}} = \frac{\$100}{\$800} = 12.5 \text{ percent}$$

The Federal Open-Market Committee

How the open-market operations are conducted

Open-market operations are conducted by the Federal Open-Market Committee (FOMC), which consists of 12 people. Eight are permanent members—the seven members of the Board of Governors and the president of the New York Federal Reserve District Bank (he or she is a permanent member because nearly all open-market purchases are made in the New York federal securities market). The other four members of the FOMC are presidents of the other 11 Federal Reserve District Banks; they serve on a rotating basis.

Incidentally, when Paul Volcker, who had been serving as president of the New York Federal Reserve Bank, was appointed chairman of the Board of Governors by President Carter in 1979, he continued to serve on the FOMC, along with Anthony Solomon, the new president of the New York Federal Reserve Bank.

The FOMC meets about once every six weeks to decide what policy to follow. This is not to say that every three weeks the committee changes directions from buy to sell to buy again.

To fight recessions, the FOMC buys securities.

Assume the FOMC decides to ease credit a bit, perhaps because of the threat of a recession. It might decide to buy $100 million of securities on the open market. The New York Bank, as agent of the Federal Reserve, places an order with several government bond houses. The bonds are paid for by checks written on various Federal Reserve District Banks. Each government bond house deposits the checks in its own commercial bank. From there the checks are sent to the New York Federal Reserve District Bank, which adds the amount of the checks to the banks' reserves.

Say, for example, the Fed gives a $10 million check to bond house number one, which deposits it in its account at Bankers Trust. From there the check is sent a few blocks away to the New York Federal Reserve District Bank, which adds $10 million to the reserves of Bankers Trust.

What does Bankers Trust do with $10 million of reserves? Assuming it now has excess reserves of $10 million, it will lend most of it out. Up goes the money supply! As we have noted, banks seldom keep excess reserves because they don't earn interest. Thus we have a multiple expansion of deposits.

The process works the same way if the government bond houses are not the ultimate sellers of the securities. Usually those sellers are individuals, corporations, or banks. If an individual sells a $10,000 bond to the government bond house, which, in turn, sells it to the Fed, the government bond house is only the middleman. When the Fed pays the government bond house, this money will be turned over to the person who sold the bond. When she deposits her check at her local bank, say the National State Bank of New Jersey, the check will still be sent to the New York Federal Reserve District Bank. Ten thousand dollars will be added to the reserves of the National State Bank, which is now free to lend it out.

When banks lend out money, the money supply increases. When the Fed buys $100 million of securities, it is making $100 million of reserves available to the banking system. Most of this money will be lent out, and through the deposit expansion multiplier, it will create a multiplied deposit amount. For example, if the reserve ratio were 10 percent, the multiplier would be 10 (Multiplier = 1/Reserve ratio = $1/.10$ = 10). However, allowing for currency leakages and bank holdings of some excess reserves, we'll say that the multiplier is actually only 6. A $100 million open-market purchase will lead to about a $600 million expansion of deposits (and, therefore, a $600 million expansion of the money supply).

To fight inflation, the FOMC sells securities.

During periods of inflation, when the FOMC decides to sell securities, we have exactly the opposite set of events. If the FOMC were to give the government bond houses $100 million of securities with orders to sell them at whatever the market will bring, we can easily trace the steps.

Customers will be found, and they will pay by check. For example, a corporation with an account at Sun Trust Bank in Atlanta might buy $50,000 of securities. When its check reaches the Atlanta Federal Reserve District Bank, $50,000 is deducted from the reserves of Sun Trust Bank. Similar reserve deductions occur around the country. Soon reserves for the entire banking system are reduced by $100 million.

That's just the first step. The banks will probably be short of reserves as they carry little, if any, excess. Where do they get the money? They can borrow from their Federal Reserve District Bank's discount windows, but this will only tide them over temporarily, and they're reluctant to do this anyway. They can go into the federal funds market, which is an overnight market in which banks borrow from each other on a day-to-day basis if they are short of reserves. But because most banks are short because of FOMC sales, this source of funds has constricted.

Ultimately, the banks will have to curb their loans, which is what the FOMC wanted all along. Initially, then, we would expect that $100 million less reserves will mean $100 million less in loans. But *had* those loans been made, with a multiplier of six, there would have been some $600 million worth of loans, and the money supply would have been $600 million higher.

We're saying that if reserves are reduced by $100 million, this will, with a multiplier of six, ultimately reduce the money supply by $600 million. Or, put slightly differently, when reserves are reduced, the money supply will end up being lower than it would otherwise have been.

Are you ready to apply your knowledge of the monetary multiplier to determine the potential effect of the sale of some securities on the open market? Suppose the Fed buys $200 million of securities and the reserve ratio is 12 percent. By how much could our money supply increase?

Solution:

Excess reserves	×	Monetary multiplier	=	Potential expansion of the money supply
$200 million	×	$1/.12$	=	
$200 million	×	$100/12$	=	
$200 million	×	8.3	=	$1,660,000,000[6]

I mentioned a few pages back that the federal funds rate is what one bank charges another to borrow some of its reserves. When the Federal Reserve wants to tighten or ease credit, it will do so by manipulating the federal funds rate. To tighten credit, it sells U.S. government securities to commercial banks, pushing up the federal funds rate. To lower that rate, the Fed buys U.S. securities from the banks, driving down the federal funds rate.

Discount Rate Changes

The discount rate is the interest rate paid by member banks when they borrow at the Federal Reserve District Bank. The main reason today's banks borrow is that they are having trouble maintaining their required reserves. In general, however, by resorting to the discount window, member banks are calling attention to their difficulties, perhaps inviting closer audits when their Federal Reserve inspectors visit. Also, there is always the chance of being turned down for these loans.

The original intent of the Federal Reserve Act of 1913 was to have the District Banks lend money to member banks to take care of seasonal business needs. In the busy period before Christmas, firms would borrow money from their banks, which would, in turn, borrow from the Federal Reserve District Banks. Borrowing, then, was really note discounting. You technically borrowed $1,000, but if the interest rate was 8 percent, the interest—$80 for a one-year loan—was deducted in advance. All you got was $920; you paid back $1,000.

How discounting works

This was called discounting. When the commercial banks took these IOUs or commercial paper to the Federal Reserve District Bank, they would borrow money to cover these loans. This was called rediscounting.

---

[6]Because we rounded after one decimal, we got 8.3. If you rounded after four decimals, you would have gotten 8.3333, giving you a deposit expansion of $1,666,660,000.

Today banks no longer rediscount their commercial paper. Instead, they borrow directly from the Federal Reserve and call the interest they pay the discount rate. Although each of the 12 District Banks sets its own discount rate, they agree virtually all the time—perhaps with an occasional prod from the Board of Governors—to charge the same rate.

Rather than borrow from the Fed, banks usually borrow excess reserves from each other, usually for no more than a few days at a time. The interest rate they pay is called the federal funds rate. Concerned about inflationary pressures, the Federal Reserve Open-Market Committee sold enough securities from February 1994 to February 1995 to double the federal funds rate. Since all other short-term interest rates also move up sharply during this period, the economy began to slow in the first half of 1995.

Open-market operations are the Fed's day-to-day and most important policy weapon. After selling securities in the open market and still not getting the banks to cut back enough on their loans, the Fed will raise the discount rate. Because, however, member banks don't borrow heavily from the District Banks, raising the discount rate is more of a symbolic gesture. Although discount rate changes do occasionally have some impact on the financial markets,[7] more often than not these changes merely reflect the Fed's desire to keep the discount rate in line with other interest rates.

Kathleen Madigan of *BusinessWeek* describes what happens when the Fed changes the discount rate and the federal funds rate simultaneously:

> The Fed can also change the discount rate when it alters the federal funds rate, a one-two punch called "banging the gong" because it reverberates across global markets. The discount rate is charged when a member bank borrows from the Fed, a move done when the bank can't borrow anywhere else. The discount rate is usually set equal to or a half-point below the funds rate.[8]

Figure 2 provides a record of the movements of the prime rate, the federal funds rate, and the discount rate from 1989 through 2000. The prime rate, which banks charge mainly for loans to large corporations, is set by the banks themselves, but it almost always responds to changes in the federal funds target rate. Because the Fed can directly influence the federal funds rate, either by buying or by selling U.S. government securities on the open market, we may consider the federal funds target rate to be identical to the federal funds rate.

Changing Reserve Requirements

A changing of reserve requirements is really the ultimate weapon of the Federal Reserve System. Like nuclear weapons, which are rarely—if ever—used, it can be nice to know that the mechanism is there.

The Fed's ultimate weapon

The Federal Reserve Board has the power to change reserve requirements within legal limits, but in practice it does this perhaps once in a decade. The limits for checkable deposits are between 8 and 14 percent.[9] Before the Board takes this drastic step, it usually issues numerous warnings.

The discount rate will be raised by the District Banks, often in unison, as engineered by the Board of Governors. The FOMC will be actively selling securities; credit will be getting tighter; the chairman will be publicly warning the banks that they are advancing too many loans. This is called moral suasion, and like other appeals to morality, it rarely achieves the desired results (unless the Fed has been following President Teddy Roosevelt's advice: "Speak softly and carry a big stick"). If it doesn't do the job—if the banks are still

---

[7]An unexpected rise in the discount rate sometimes causes about a 50-point drop in the Dow Jones Index of stock prices and a similar decline in the prices of bonds. Unexpected declines in the discount rate sometimes cause these markets to rally.

[8]Kathleen Madigan, *BusinessWeek*, February 7, 2000, pp. 124 and 126.

[9]If five members of the Board deem it desirable, the maximum can be raised to 18 percent, and if conditions are extraordinary, any rate whatsoever may be set.

Figure 2

The Discount, Federal Funds, and Prime Rates, 1989–2000

You'll notice that these three rates move in lockstep, generally rising at the same time. In 1989–mid-1992 credit was eased to counter the 1990–91 recession. Credit was tightened in 1994 and again in 1999–2000 because the Fed feared the economy was overheating. Note that the discount rate is generally slightly below the federal funds rate and that the prime rate is about 2–2½ percent above the federal funds rate.

Sources: Federal Reserve; Associated Press

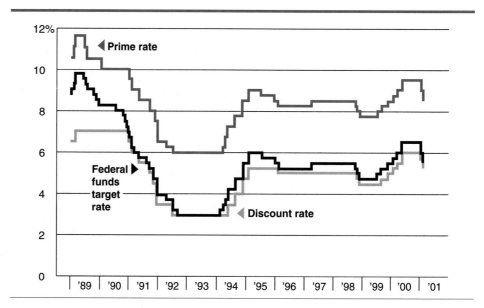

advancing too many loans and if the money supply is still growing too rapidly—the Fed reaches for its biggest stick and raises reserve requirements. The last time this happened, in October 1980, the resulting credit crunch sent the prime rate of interest soaring above 20 percent as the economy plunged into the worst recession since the Great Depression.

The basic reserve rate was set at 12 percent in 1980 for most checking deposits, but in April 1992 it was lowered to 10 percent. The Board of Governors took this strong measure to help the economy recover from the lingering effects of the 1990–91 recession. In banking circles this 10 percent rate is often referred to as the *reserve ratio,* ignoring the 3 percent ratio that must be held on the first $42.8 million of checking deposits.

This weapon is so rarely used because it is simply too powerful. For example, if the Federal Reserve Board raised the reserve requirement on demand deposits by just one half of 1 percent, the nation's banks and thrift institutions would have to come up with nearly $4 billion in reserves.

Reserve requirements, then, are raised reluctantly by the Board of Governors, and only after all else fails. However, when the economy is gripped by recession, the Fed becomes less reluctant to turn to its ultimate weapon; but even then, reserve requirement changes are a last resort.

The Fed has three ways of increasing our money supply: lowering reserve requirements, lowering the discount rate, and buying government securities on the open market. What about printing currency? Does *this* raise our money supply? If you think the answer is yes, then you definitely should read the box "Does Printing More Money Increase Our Money Supply?"

Why does the Fed rarely change reserve requirements?

Does Printing More Money Increase Our Money Supply?

When the Federal Reserve Banks issue currency, doesn't this increase our money supply? Surprisingly, the answer is no, Now I'm going to prove it.

What is the money supply? It's currency, demand deposits, and other checkable deposits held by the public. So the question is, When the Fed prints currency, how does it get into the hands of the public?

Suppose the Federal Reserve Bank of San Francisco issues 10 one-hundred-dollar bills and gives them to Security Pacific Corp., which pays by having its reserves lowered by $1,000. (Actually, its reserves stay the same, because this money goes into its vault.) Next, a local businesswoman writes a check for $1,000 on her account at Security Pacific and walks out of the bank with the 10 one-hundred-dollar bills.

Did that transaction increase the money supply? What do you think? On the one hand, when the teller gave the woman the cash, that increased the amount of money in the hands of the public by $1,000. But what the bank gave with that one hand, it took away with the other by decreasing her checking account by $1,000.

To recap: When the Federal Reserve Bank of San Francisco issued $1,000 in currency, did that lead to an increase in the money supply? No, it did not. When the Fed prints money, it does so to accommodate the needs of the public. If the public wishes to hold more of its money in the form of currency—and, parenthetically, less in the form of checking deposits—the Fed will accommodate these wishes.

While we're on the subject, I'd like you to take a look at the money you have in your wallet. You'll find the signature of the Secretary of the Treasury in the lower right of the face of each bill. Chances are Robert E. Rubin or Lawrence H. Summers signed most of your money. You might even have a bill signed by James Baker or Donald Regan, both of whom served under President Reagan. What happened to all the currency issued before 1980? Nearly all of it was withdrawn from circulation as it wore out; it was replaced by crisp new bills. Does *this* increase our money supply? Obviously not. So the next time someone walks up to you on the street and asks you whether the Fed increases the money supply by issuing currency, tell him no.

Summary: The Tools of Monetary Policy

What three things can the Fed do to fight a recession? List them right here:

1.

2.

3.

The answers are (1) lower the discount rate, (2) buy securities on the open market, and, ultimately, if these two don't do the job, (3) lower reserve requirements.

What three things can the Fed do to fight inflation? List them here:

1.

2.

3.

The answers are (1) raise the discount rate, (2) sell securities on the open market, and, ultimately, if these two don't do the job, (3) raise reserve requirements. (For further results of monetary policy, see the Advanced Work box, "The Effectiveness of Monetary Policy in an Open Economy.")

389

The Effectiveness of Monetary Policy in an Open Economy

Suppose the Fed tightens money and interest rates rise. Investors all over the world will be attracted to the higher interest rates they can earn by purchasing U.S. bonds; corporate bonds, and other assets. But in order to invest, they will need to exchange their money for U.S. dollars.

This will drive up the dollar relative to foreign currencies. In other words, you will now be able to get more marks, yen, and pounds for your dollars. Foreign goods will become cheaper to Americans and our imports will soar. Meanwhile, foreigners will be getting fewer dollars for their marks, yen, and pounds, so they will find American goods more expensive. And they will cut back on their purchases of those goods.

Let's recap: Tight money drives up interest rates, making American investments more attractive to foreigners. They will bid up the dollar, thus lowering our exports and raising our imports. So tight money works to lower our net exports (exports minus imports).

Did you get all that? We've really gotten a bit ahead of ourselves, because the effects to exchange rate changes on foreign trade are not analyzed until the last chapter of this book. But while we're at it, how would an expansionary monetary policy affect our net exports?

It would have just the opposite effect of a contractionary policy. Monetary expansion would lower our interest rates. Lower interest rates are not attractive to foreign investors, whose demand for U.S. dollars will drop. If the dollar falls relative to foreign currencies, that makes our exports cheaper and our imports more expensive. Thus, an expansionary monetary policy will raise our net exports and further stimulate our economy.

The Fed is more effective in fighting inflation than recession.

The government fighting inflation is like the Mafia fighting crime.
—Laurence J. Peter

The Fed's Effectiveness in Fighting Inflation and Recession

Federal Reserve policy in fighting inflation and recession has been likened to pulling and then pushing on a string. Like pulling on a string, when the Fed fights inflation, it gets results—provided, of course, it pulls hard enough.

Fighting a recession is another matter. Like pushing on a string, no matter how hard the Fed works, it might not get anywhere.

First we'll consider fighting inflation. Assume all three basic policy tools have been used: Securities have been sold on the open market, the discount rate has been raised, and, ultimately, reserve requirements have been raised. The results are that bond prices have plunged, interest rates have soared, and money supply growth has been stopped dead in its tracks. Banks find it impossible to increase their loan portfolios. There's a credit crunch and there's credit rationing. Old customers can still borrow, but their credit lines are slashed. (My own line of credit, for example, was cut by Citibank during the 1980 credit crunch from $3,500 to $500.) Nearly all new customers are turned away.

During times like these, the rate of inflation has got to decline. It's hard to raise prices when no one is buying anything. No one can buy because no one has any money. Of course, the Fed is somewhat reluctant to tighten up too much or too long because such a policy generally brings on recessions.

The Fed has a far harder time dealing with a recession. Again, assume the standard tools have been used: securities have been purchased on the open market, the discount rate has been lowered, and reserve requirements have been lowered. All this creates excess reserves for the banks. But now the $1,000,000 question: What do they *do* with these reserves?

Do they lend them out? Is that your final answer? Yes! To whom should they lend them? To a businessowner who needs a loan to keep going? To a firm that can't meet its next payroll without a loan? To an individual who has just lost her job and can't meet her car payments?

All these examples bring to mind the first law of banking: Never lend money to anyone who needs it. If you ever want a bank loan, you've got to convince the loan officer that you don't really need the money. I don't mean to make the banks sound bad, but from their point of view, they simply can't afford to take the risks inherent in these loans. A banker's first concern must be "Will the bank be paid back?"

During recessions, businesses that might have been good credit risks during prosperity have become poor risks. Individuals, too, lose creditworthiness during recessions, particularly if they've just been laid off. And so the very segment of the economic community most in need of help during recessions is least likely to be accommodated.

Meanwhile, many of the top credit-rated corporations are not coming in to borrow large sums of money. During recessions the companies to whom the banks will lend money are not borrowing. Why? Because business isn't so great for them either. Would you borrow to buy more equipment—even at low interest rates—if your equipment was one-third idle? Would you expand your factory if sales were down 20 percent—even if the interest rate fell to 4 percent?

In fact, in October 1982 the economy's capacity utilization rate had fallen to just 68.4 percent—an all-time low since this statistic was first compiled in 1948.[10] The Fed had by then loosened credit, but not until sales finally picked up in early 1983 did investments begin to rise appreciably.

All of this said, may we conclude that easy money has little or no effect in ending a recession? Not at all! It's like the adage "You can lead a horse to water, but you can't make him drink." But if that horse happens to be thirsty, just try to *stop* him from drinking.

The Fed was able to help end the recessions of 1980 and 1981–82 by relaxing credit and driving down interest rates. However, the excruciatingly slow and halting recovery of 1991–92 was not very responsive to the lowest interest rates in 15 years. Furthermore, even though the banks had plenty of money that they could have loaned out to individuals and business firms, many banks preferred to purchase short-term U.S. government securities.[11]

The American Economy According to Chairman Greenspan

When Chairman Alan Greenspan talks, the stock market listens. When he says that the market is exhibiting "irrational exuberance," the Dow Jones Average sometimes tumbles 300 or 400 points. The Federal Reserve, for which Dr. Greenspan speaks, can quickly push up interest rates, which makes bonds more attractive to investors, thereby depressing stock prices.[12]

But it isn't just stock market and bond market investors who are affected by Chairman Greenspan's announcements, which often foreshadow open market operations in the coming months. Rising interest rates will depress business investment, hurt car sales, and wreak havoc in the housing market.

Greenspan and his colleagues on the Federal Reserve Open Market Committee have long sought to maintain a Goldilocks economy—not too hot and not too cold. Too cold would be very slow or no economic growth—a stagnant economy that might slip into recession. But what's too hot? That would be an unsustainable rate of economic growth of much more than 4 percent a year. Why is that rate unsustainable? Because our labor force grows about 1 percent each year, and our productivity may be growing at as much as 3 percent. That would imply a sustainable growth rate of 4 percent. But if we were to exceed that speed limit by too much, we would generate pressures leading to a

Never lend money to anyone who needs it.

A bank is a place where they lend you an umbrella in fair weather and ask for it back again when it begins to rain.
—Robert Frost

---

[10]The capacity utilization rate is the percentage of the nation's plant and equipment that is being used. The full-employment and full-production section of Chapter 2 indicated that a capacity utilization rate of 85 to 90 percent would employ virtually all our usable plant and equipment.

[11]Do you recall the crowding-out effect discussed in the appendix of Chapter 12? It shows how private borrowers are crowded out of financial markets by the U.S. Treasury, thus offsetting some of the effects of an expansionary fiscal policy.

[12]An increase rate increase would push down bond prices, and investors might sell some of their stocks and buy bonds. This could involve a shift of hundreds of billions of dollars.

Margin Requirements

The Federal Reserve Board has the power to set margin requirements in the stock market. In Chapter 1 ("Our Financial House of Cards") we talked about how in the 1920s stock market speculators could borrow 90 percent of the price of a stock from a stockbroker and put up just 10 percent of their own money. If the stock went up, they made a lot of money. But when the market crashed in 1929, not only were these speculators wiped out but so were their stockbrokers, who were not repaid. They, in turn, could not repay the banks all they had borrowed.

Today the margin requirement is set by the Federal Reserve Board, which has pegged it at 50 percent since 1974. This means that, if you wanted to invest $10,000 in the stock market, you would need to put up $5,000 of your own money. When Alan Greenspan, who has repeatedly expressed concern about the "irrational

exhuberance" of the stock market, was asked why he didn't raise the margin requirement, he replied that an increase would be unfair to small investors. Perhaps, but margin debt has grown at an alarmingly rapid rate since 1990. In that year margin debt was just over 4 percent of all consumer debt. By the end of 2000 it was more than 16 percent.

If—or perhaps one should say when—the market turns down sharply, the stockbrokers will ask their margin customers to put up more money, or else they will sell their stocks. Most won't have the money, so their stocks will be sold, driving stock prices down still further. Although we are not nearly as vulnerable as we were in 1929, the huge and growing overhang of margin debt makes it increasingly likely that a sharp decline in stock prices could lead to a stock market crash.

demand-pull inflation. "Overall demand for goods cannot chronically exceed the underlying growth rate of supply," Greenspan said in March, 2000.

Too many dollars chasing too few goods might occur because aggregate supply would be unable to keep up with aggregate demand. That would be our demand-pull inflation. And then, to attract more employees—and to hold on to current ones—employers would be forced to pay higher salaries. There goes cost-push inflation.

Greenspan has long agonized over what economists call the "wealth effect," the idea that rising stock prices translate into higher spending levels by consumers. He has maintained that historical evidence suggests that 3 to 4 cents of every dollar in additional stock market wealth is reflected in increased purchases by consumers.

From the beginning of 1995 to the beginning of 2000, the total value of U.S. stocks tripled to more than $12 trillion. If just 3 cents of every dollar of this $8 trillion of additional wealth were spent on consumption, how much would that come to?

It would add $240 billion over five years, or about $50 billion a year, a sum that is none too shabby even in a $10 trillion economy. By the Fed's estimate, the booming stock market added about a percentage point a year to GDP growth over this five-year period (see box, "Margin Requirements").

In the early 1990s, as we began the longest economic expansion in our entire history, a consensus emerged between the Clinton administration and the Federal Reserve. There would be a steadily declining federal budget deficit—a fiscal policy that was aided by Republican congressional majorities after 1994. And there would be a pre-emptive monetary policy—small hikes in interest rates at the hint of inflation and a flood of liquidity when disaster strikes, such as the 1998 Asian debt crisis.[13]

---

[13]The Asian debt crisis is discussed in the last chapter.

A tacit deal had been struck between the Clinton administration and the Fed that, as long as the deficit was reduced, the Fed would allow the money supply to grow quickly enough to accommodate business needs and to keep interest rates low. But when the deficit turned into a surplus in 1998, congressional Republicans began making plans for a massive tax cut. Chairman Greenspan joined President Clinton in denouncing such a tax cut as irresponsible. But in early 2001, after George W. Bush took office as president, Chairman Greenspan joined him in calling for a substantial tax cut. The times had changed, and the Chairman's views changed with them. Bush had long advocated a $1.6 trillion tax cut over a 10-year period, and Greenspan, while not specifying any amount, agreed to a tax cut, as long as it did not lead back again to budget deficits. He also said that he would not be happy to see the national debt grow too small, because that would force the U.S. Treasury, Federal Reserve, and Social Security Trust fund, and other government agencies to invest in corporate bonds and stocks.

The Depository Institutions Deregulation and Monetary Control Act of 1980

I have waited until now to deal with the Depository Institutions Deregulation and Monetary Control Act of 1980. It is clearly the most important piece of banking legislation passed since the 1930s.

Economic historians will mark the 1970s and 1980s as decades of swift and significant change in American banking. During this period, the distinction between commercial banks and thrift institutions (savings banks, savings and loan associations, and credit unions) became blurred to the point where it's hard to tell what is a bank and what isn't.

What is a bank and what isn't?

Until 1980 there was a clear line of demarcation between commercial and thrift institutions. Banks (meaning commercial banks) could issue checking deposits; savings banks, savings and loan associations, and credit unions could not. The only problem was that more and more of the thrifts were doing just that. The way they got around the law was to call those checking deposits something else—namely, negotiable order of withdrawal accounts (or NOW accounts). Thus, technically, people who had deposits at these thrift institutions were not writing checks; they were writing negotiable orders of withdrawal.

While Federal Reserve regulation prohibited commercial banks from paying any interest on checking deposits, the thrifts were paying their depositors about 5 percent interest on their NOW accounts. Because these were technically savings accounts rather than checking accounts, it was OK to pay interest. Therefore, the thrifts had it both ways: They were able to give their depositors checking accounts and pay interest on them—which gave them a considerable competitive advantage over commercial banks.

The commercial banks complained to the Fed and to anyone else who would listen, but to little avail. Finally Congress took matters into its own hands and passed the Depository Institutions Deregulation and Monetary Control Act of 1980. It had three key provisions:

The three key provisions of the Banking Act of 1980

1. All depository institutions are now subject to the Fed's legal reserve requirements. Before this act, only those commercial banks that were members of the Federal Reserve—about one-third of all commercial banks were members—were subject to these requirements. The other commercial banks and thrift institutions were subject to state reserve requirements, which were substantially lower.

2. All depository institutions are now legally authorized to issue checking deposits. Furthermore, they may be interest bearing. Previously, commercial banks were forbidden to pay interest on checking accounts, while the thrift institutions claimed to be paying interest on savings accounts.

3. All depository institutions now enjoy all the advantages that only Federal Reserve member banks formerly enjoyed—including check clearing[14] and borrowing from the Fed (discounting).[15]

Remember that the main job of the Federal Reserve is to control the money supply. By bringing all depository institutions—especially the nonmember commercial banks and the savings banks that had NOW accounts—under the Fed's control, the Monetary Control Act made this job a lot easier.

The number of financial institutions is shrinking quickly.

Another important consequence of this law is that by the end of the 1990s, intense competition reduced the 40,000-plus financial institutions that existed at the beginning of the 1980s to a little more than half that number. The lifting of the prohibition against interstate banking, combined with further advances in electronic banking, will create greater consolidation, with perhaps just 30 or 40 giant financial institutions doing most of the business. "Virtually all observers agree that the ability of the new financial system to generate credit and meet credit demands will be enhanced because the system will consist of big, nationwide, all-purpose institutions."[16]

The Banking Act of 1999

In 1980 the jurisdiction of the Federal Reserve had been extended to all commercial banks and thrift institutions. In 1999 it was further extended to insurance companies, pension funds, investment companies, securities brokers, and finance companies.[17]

The new law repealed sections of the Glass-Steagall Act of 1933, which was based on the premise that America's financial house could best be restored if bankers and brokers stayed in separate rooms. It was thought that this could reduce the potential conflicts of interest between investment banking[18] and commercial banking, which had contributed to the speculative frenzy leading to the stock market crash of 1929. Under Glass-Steagall, commercial banks could receive no more than 10 percent of their income from the securities markets, a limit so restrictive that most simply abandoned business on Wall Street selling stocks and bonds to their customers. Over time, Federal judges and regulators chipped away at Glass-Steagall and other restrictions on cross-ownership of banks, insurance companies, and securities firms, enabling, for instance, Citibank to merge with Travelers in 1998 to form Citigroup, the world's largest financial services company. Indeed, this merger helped secure the scrapping of Glass-Steagall.

One purpose of the 1999 law was to give all financial firms, including banks, the chance to sell all sorts of investments. In this way they would be similar to banks in other countries that already provide such services. According to *The Economist,* "Banks in America and Japan—where laws based on Glass-Steagall were imposed by the

---

[14]Check clearing is the mysterious process by which all the checks you wrote during the month are mailed to you by your bank at the end of the month. If you're not clear on how this gets done, you'd better check back to the box titled "Check Clearing" earlier in this chapter. The Federal Reserve System processes, or clears, billions of checks each year.

[15]"Reserves of nonmember depository institutions may be held at a correspondent depository institution holding required reserves at a Federal Reserve Bank, a Federal Home Loan Bank, or the National Credit Union Administration Central Liquidity Facility, if such reserves are passed through to a Federal Reserve Bank. The Board may, by regulation or order that is applicable to all depository institutions, permit them to maintain all or a portion of their required reserves in the form of vault cash." See *The Federal Reserve Bulletin,* June 1980, p. 446.

[16]*BusinessWeek,* November 17, 1980, p. 139.

[17]The Federal Reserve and the Treasury Department will share jurisdiction over the new financial institutions, while the Securities and Exchange Commission will continue its jurisdiction over the nation's stock markets.

[18]Investment banks sell new stock and new bonds for existing companies and help arrange corporate mergers.

Americans during the post-war occupation—suffered from a lack of diversification compared with 'universal' banks in continental Europe."[19] The new law allows banks, securities firms, and insurance companies to merge and to sell each other's products. The measure will probably fuel a wave of mergers as companies compete to build financial supermarkets offering all the services customers need under one roof.

Robert Kuttner, writing in *BusinessWeek,* was less confident that consumers will benefit. "The Banking Act of 1933 was enacted after investigations showed that large financial houses had abused their fiduciary duties, peddling all manner of dubious securities, often with conflicts of interest and insider profiteering at the expenses of customers." He concludes that "it was repealed mainly to pave the way for more megamergers."[20]

Fiscal and Monetary Policies Should Mesh

It should be apparent that until the early 1990s there was little coordination in the making of fiscal and monetary policies. Indeed, there is little fiscal policy as such, but rather a series of compromises within Congress and between Congress and the president. Further, given the independence of the Federal Reserve Board, different groups of people are responsible for monetary and fiscal policy.

Because of the need for these policies to mesh rather than work at cross-purposes (as they sometimes have), we should consider ways to unify monetary and fiscal policy. One step in this direction would be to allow each newly elected president to appoint a new chairman of the Board.

Last Word

During the last few years it would be hard to find a news magazine, business magazine, or daily newspaper that did not at least mention Alan Greenspan and the job he was doing as the Chairman of the Federal Reserve. Much of the credit has gone to Greenspan and to the Federal Reserve Board of Governors for our rapid economic growth and our low rates of unemployment and inflation. Clearly, much of that credit is well deserved, especially when we look at the stop-and-go monetary policies under some of Greenspan's predecessors. But credit must also be given to President Clinton and to Congress for helping to turn huge federal budget deficits into mounting surpluses.

As the economy slowed in late 2000 and early 2001, some of the praise heaped upon Chairman Greenspan turned to blame. Perhaps he pushed up interest rates too quickly in 1999 and early 2000, helping to end the bull market in stocks and to bring about the precipitous fall in technology stock prices. And perhaps he moved too slowly in finally pushing down interest rates in early 2001, well after the booming economy had begun to cool, and after great fortunes had been lost in the stock market. If the economy rights itself before the end of 2001, Greenspan's reputation will probably be safe. But if the slowdown that began in late 2000 becomes a full-fledged recession in 2001, then Dr. Greenspan's reputation will sink along with the economy.

---

[19]*The Economist,* "The Wall Falls," October 30, 1999, p. 79.

[20]Robert Kuttner, "A Requiem for Glass-Steagall," *BusinessWeek,* November 15, 1999, p. 28.

Questions for Further Thought and Discussion

1. Should the Federal Reserve Board of Governors remain independent? What is the strongest argument on either side?

2. Is the Federal Reserve more effective in fighting recessions or inflations? Explain your answer, if possible, using a flow chart.

3. What is the most important job of the Federal Reserve? What makes it so important?

4. What are open-market operations? How are they conducted to fight inflation and recession?

5. Draw a diagram showing the impact on bond prices, interest rates, and the level of investment of (a) an expansionary monetary policy; (b) a contractionary monetary policy.

6. Distinguish between the prime interest rate and the federal funds rate.

7. Why has the power to set the discount rate become a less effective monetary policy tool over the last eight decades?

8. In 1980 and in 1999 two major banking laws were passed. Explain how each law affects bank consolidation.

9. What is the current macroeconomic situation in the United States? What should the Fed do about it?

10. What monetary policy tools should the Fed use to achieve the result you recommended in question 9?

11. Why would it be beneficial for you as a consumer to buy all your financial services from a bank? Do these benefits outweigh the problems raised by Robert Kuttner?

12. How is money created and destroyed? Explain the concept of the money multiplier, and discuss the factors that influence its size.

W*orkbook* for Chapter 14

Name _____ Date _____

Multiple-Choice Questions

Circle the letter that corresponds to the best answer.

1. Fiscal and monetary policy have
   a) the same means and ends.
   b) different means and ends.
   c) the same means and different ends.
   d) different means and the same ends.

2. Which statement is true?
   a) The United States has always had a central bank.
   b) The United States has never had a central bank.
   c) The United States had a central bank until 1913.
   d) The United States has had a central bank since 1913.

3. The most important Federal Reserve policy weapon is _____.
   a) changing reserve requirements
   b) changing the discount rate
   c) moral suasion
   d) open-market operations

4. To restrict monetary growth, the Federal Reserve will _____.
   a) raise the discount rate and sell securities
   b) raise the discount rate and buy securities
   c) lower the discount rate and sell securities
   d) lower the discount rate and buy securities

5. Monetary policy is conducted by _____.
   a) the president only
   b) Congress only
   c) the president and Congress
   d) the Federal Reserve

6. Which statement about the Federal Reserve Board of Governors is true?
   a) They serve seven-year terms.
   b) There are 14 members.
   c) Every president appoints his own board.
   d) The members serve at the pleasure of the president, who can force their resignations at any time.
   e) None of these statements is true.

7. Control of the Federal Reserve System is vested in _____.
   a) the president
   c) the Board of Governors
   b) Congressd
   d) the District Banks

8. Basically the Board of Governors is _____.
   a) independent
   b) dependent on the president and Congress
   c) powerless
   d) on a par with the District Banks

9. Legal reserve requirements are changed _____.
   a) very often
   c) never
   b) on rare occasions
   d) none of these

10. Which of these is a secondary reserve?
    a) Treasury bills
    b) gold
    c) vault cash
    d) deposits at the Federal Reserve District Bank

11. The larger the reserve requirement, the _____.
    a) smaller the deposit expansion multiplier
    b) larger the deposit expansion multiplier
    c) easier it is for banks to lend money

12. Each of the following is a leakage from the deposit expansion multiplier except _____.
    a) cash
    b) the foreign trade imbalance
    c) excess reserves
    d) all of these are leakages

13. Check clearing is done by _____.
    a) the bank where a check is deposited
    b) the bank on which a check is written
    c) the Federal Reserve System
    d) the comptroller of the currency

14. Open-market operations are _____.
    a) the buying and selling of U.S. government securities by the Fed
    b) borrowing by banks from the Fed
    c) the selling of U.S. government securities by the U.S. Treasury
    d) raising or lowering reserve requirements by the Fed

15. When the Fed wants to increase the money supply, it _____.
    a) raises the discount rate
    b) raises reserve requirements
    c) sells securities
    d) buys securities

16. To buy securities, the Fed offers _____.
    a) a low price and drives up interest rates
    b) a low price and drives down interest rates
    c) a high price and drives up interest rates
    d) a high price and drives down interest rates

17. Which statement is the most accurate?
    a) The federal funds rate and the discount rate generally rise and fall together.
    b) The prime rate of interest is usually about a half percentage point below the federal funds rate.
    c) The federal funds rate did not change at all during the late 1990s.
    d) The Federal Reserve has little influence on interest rates.

18. The original intent of the Federal Reserve Act was to have the District Banks lend money to _____.
    a) individual borrowers, particularly business firms
    b) member banks to take care of seasonal needs
    c) the U.S. Treasury
    d) none of the above

19. Which statement is true?
    a) The Fed is more effective at fighting inflation than fighting recession.
    b) The Fed is more effective at fighting recession than fighting inflation.
    c) The Fed is effective at fighting both recession and inflation.
    d) The Fed is effective at fighting neither inflation nor recession.

20. The Depository Institutions Deregulation and Monetary Control Act of 1980 had three key provisions, one of which was _____.
    a) uniform reserve requirements for all financial institutions
    b) zero reserve requirements for all time deposits
    c) that no interest may be paid on checking deposits
    d) that vault cash would no longer count toward reserves

21. The main job of the Fed is to _____.
    a) control the rate of growth of the money supply
    b) to manage the national debt
    c) provide low-interest loans to all financial institutions
    d) raise and lower tax rates

22. One of the main results of the Depository Institutions Deregulation and Monetary Control Act of 1980 may be to _____.
    a) lessen the number of financial institutions in the United States
    b) increase the number of financial institutions in the United States
    c) discourage the formation of big, nationwide, all-purpose financial institutions
    d) make it easier for the member banks to borrow money from the Federal Reserve District Banks

23. Reserve requirements are changed _____.
    a) once a week
    b) three or four times a year
    c) once every two or three years
    d) once every eight or ten years
    e) only if Congress passes a new law

24. Suppose that the deposit expansion multiplier were 7. After taking into account its three modifications, we might estimate the true deposit multiplier to be _____.

    a) 14   d) 4

    b) 9   e) 1

    c) 7

25. Statement 1: Currency leakages take place especially during times of recession and low interest rates. Statement 2: The process of check clearing is being partially replaced by the electronic transferring of money.

    a) Statement 1 is true and statement 2 is false.

    b) Statement 2 is true and statement 1 is false.

    c) Both statements are true.

    d) Both statements are false.

26. Which is the most accurate statement? The Federal Reserve _____.

    a) markets new treasury bills, notes, certificates, and bonds

    b) runs a check clearing operation for U.S. government checks, but does not handle checks written by private individuals or business firms

    c) Open-Market Committee is part of the U.S. Treasury

    d) buys and sells chunks of the national debt

27. The limits set by law for reserves on checking accounts are between _____.

    a) 0% and 9%   c) 8% and 14%

    b) 3% and 12%   d) 12% and 18%

28. Which statement best describes the role of Federal Reserve Chairman Alan Greenspan?

    a) He has been much too quick to curb the rate of growth of the money supply and has been responsible for sending our economy into three recessions.

    b) He has tried to steer an economic course that avoided unsustainable growth on one side and stagnation and recession on the other.

    c) He fought constantly with the Clinton administration over monetary and fiscal policy.

    d) He has long supported a massive tax cut, even if that would cause new federal budget deficits.

29. The repeal of Glass-Steagall in 1999 _____.

    a) had the objective of allowing banks, securities firms, and insurance companies to merge and to sell each others' products

    b) will result in a huge expansion in the number of financial institutions doing business in the United States

    c) will result in the same abuses that led to the passage of the original act in 1929

    d) will make it much harder for U.S. financial institutions to merge

30. Statement I: There was an implicit deal between Chairman Alan Greenspan to allow the money supply to grow quickly enough to accommodate business needs in exchange for President Clinton's ensuring that the federal budget deficit was steadily reduced. Statement II: Alan Greenspan's concern about the rising stock market in the latter 1990s was that about 3 or 4 percent of the resulting added wealth would be spent on consumption.

    a) Statement I is true and statement II is false.

    b) Statement II is true and statement I is false.

    c) Both statements are true.

    d) Both statements are false.

31. Which one of the following statements is true?

    a) The Federal Reserve Board of Governors has raised stock margin requirements three times during the year 2000.

    b) The current stock margin requirement is 50 percent.

    c) Stock market margin debt is nearly 40 percent of all consumer debt.

    d) A higher stock market margin debt makes a stock market crash much less likely.

32. Which would be the most accurate statement?

    a) The Federal Reserve Board of Governors has more power than the monetary authorities of any other country.

    b) The Deutsche Bundesbank has more power than the Federal Reserve.

    c) The Bank of England and La Banca d'Italia are two of the most powerful central banks.

    d) The European Central Bank is the most powerful central bank in the world.

Fill-In Questions

1. The Federal Reserve System was established in the year _____.

2. There are _____ Federal Reserve districts.

3. The members of the Board of Governors are appointed by _____, subject to confirmation by the _____.

4. Control of the Federal Reserve is held by _____

5. Currently, nearly all checking deposits are subject to a legal reserve requirement of _____ percent.

6. Time deposits are subject to no reserve requirement because _____ _____

7. All reserves pay an interest rate of _____ percent.

8. Primary reserves are held in the form of _____ _____ and _____ _____; secondary reserves are held in the form of _____.

9. The process by which a check you write is deposited in another bank, goes through the Federal Reserve System, and is sent back to your own bank is known as _____ _____.

10. The three goals of monetary policy are

    (1) _____;
    (2) _____;
    and (3) _____.

11. Open-market operations are the _____ _____.

12. If the Fed wants to increase the money supply, it will follow these two steps: (1) _____ _____; (2) _____ _____; and if these do not prove sufficient, it may _____.

13. If the Fed wanted to decrease the money supply, it would go into the open market and _____ _____; this would also _____ interest rates.

14. Open-market policy is conducted by the _____ _____, which is part of the Fed.

15. The main reason that banks borrow from the Fed is because they _____.

16. The Federal Reserve Board of Governors will _____ _____ only as a last resort.

17. It has been much easier for the Fed to fight _____ than _____.

18. Until 1980 there was a clear line of demarcation between commercial banks and the thrifts: commercial banks could _____ while the thrifts could not.

19. Our paper currency is issued by _____ _____.

20. Our currency is backed by _____.

Problems

1. If you ran a bank with demand deposits of $20 million, you would need to hold reserves of how much?

2. If you ran a bank with demand deposits of $400 million, you would need to hold reserves of a little less than how much (assuming you don't remember the cutoff point)?

3. If the reserve requirement were 15 percent, how much would the deposit multiplier be?

4. Using your answer from the previous problem, if the Federal Reserve increased bank reserves by $100 million, by how much would the money supply rise?

5. How much is the effective, or market interest rate on a bond that has a face value of $1,000 and a selling price of $1,200 and that pays $120 interest?

6. If a bank has reserves of $21 million and demand deposits of $200 million, how much are the bank's: a) required reserves? b) excess reserves?

7. Approximately how much in reserves does a bank with $5 billion in demand deposits have to hold?

8. If a bank has reserves of $100 million and demand deposits of $700 million, how much are the bank's: a) required reserves? b) excess reserves?

9. How much reserves would a bank have to hold on: a) $1 billion of time deposits that will mature in less than 18 months? b) $1 billion of time deposits that will mature in more than 18 months?

10. Use the information in Table 1 to find this bank's required reserves.

TABLE 1

Demand deposits: $1 billion
Time deposits: $300 million

Chapter 15

Twentieth-Century Economic Theory

Economists are not easy to follow when they talk about familiar, day-to-day events like unemployment rate changes and the rising consumer price index. When they talk theory, however, even their fellow economists have difficulty understanding, let alone agreeing with, what they are saying to each other. I'll repeat the words of George Bernard Shaw: "If all economists were laid end to end, they would not reach a conclusion."

John Maynard Keynes put all of this into perspective much more elegantly:

> The ideas of economists and political philosophers, both when they are right and when they are wrong, are more powerful than is commonly understood. Indeed, the world is ruled by little else. Practical men, who believe themselves to be quite exempt from any intellectual influences, are usually slaves of some defunct economist.

What conclusion will you reach at the end of this chapter? If you're like my fellow economists, you will choose one school of economic thought to defend while attacking each of the others. I hope you'll take each economic theory with a grain of salt, ferreting out what you can't accept while appreciating the cogency of the arguments that have been advanced. No attempt is being made to do more than outline some of the underlying ideas of each of the five main schools of this century. The appendix to this chapter presents "The Great Money Debate: The Keynesians versus the Monetarists."

An economist is someone good with numbers who didn't have the personality to become an accountant.

—Anonymous

CHAPTER OBJECTIVES

After you've read this chapter, you will have a better understanding of the basics of:

- The equation of exchange.
- The quantity theory of money.
- Classical economics.
- Keynesian economics.
- The monetarist school.
- Supply-side economics.
- The rational expectations theory.

The Equation of Exchange

Much of the Keynesian-Monetarist debate revolves around the quantity theory of money, which itself is based on the equation of exchange. So in the first two sections let's look at these two concepts before we deal specifically with the Classical School, the Keynesian School, or any of the other schools of twentieth-century economic theory. The equation of exchange and the quantity theory of money are easily confused, perhaps because the equation of exchange is used to explain the quantity theory. I warn my students every term about how easily the unwary test taker writes down the equation of exchange when asked for the quantity theory, or vice versa. Many of my students take these warnings to heart, remaining faithful to the tradition of confusing the two concepts on the next exam.

The equation of exchange is

$MV = PQ$

$$MV = PQ$$

What do these letters stand for? M represents the number of dollars in the nation's money supply—the currency, demand deposits, and checklike deposits.

The velocity of circulation, or the number of times per year that each dollar in our money supply is spent, is represented by V. If we were to multiple M times V, or MV, that would be our money supply multiplied by the number of times per year each dollar is spent—in other words, total spending. Total spending by a nation during a given year is GDP. Therefore,

$$MV = GDP$$

Now for the other side of the equation. P represents the price level, or the average price of all the goods and services sold during the year. Finally, there's Q, which stands for the quantity of goods and services sold during the year. Multiplying P times Q, we get the total amount of money received by the sellers of all the final goods and services produced by the nation that year. This is also GDP. Things equal to the same thing are equal to each other (MV = GDP; PQ = GDP); therefore MV = PQ.

We'll get a better idea of how this equation works by replacing the letters with numbers. For M we can substitute $900 billion, and we'll give V a value of 9,

$$MV = PQ$$
$$900 \times 9 = PQ$$
$$8,100 = PQ$$

This gives us a GDP of 8,100, or $8.1 trillion. As a form of shorthand, economists write billions of dollars without the dollar sign. The money supply of $900 billion becomes 900, and the GDP of $8,100 billion becomes 8,100.

So far we have MV = 8,100; therefore, PQ also = 8,100. How much are P and Q? We don't know. All we do know is that $P \times Q = 8,100$.

What we'll do, so we can fool around with this equation, is arbitrarily assign values to P and Q. That might not be very nice or proper, but let me assure you that people do this sort of thing every day. Let's take P. Who can guess what the average price of all the final goods and services sold actually is? In other words, could you guess the average price of all those cars, houses, hot dogs, pairs of shoes, toothbrushes, cans of beer, cavity fillings, and so on? As there's no way of even guessing, we'll make the number $81. Why $81? Because it will be easy to work with. But perhaps $61.17 or $123.98 is what P actually denotes. We'll never know.

Now we'll consider Q. How many final goods and services were sold during the year? 23 billion? 345 billion? Again, we can't possibly know, so we'll assign a number. If we've already picked $81 for P, and PQ = 8,100, then Q must equal 100 (meaning, in economists' shorthand, 100 billion). Therefore:

$$MV = PQ$$
$$900 \times 9 = 81 \times 100$$
$$8,100 = 8,100$$

That's the equation of exchange. It must always balance, as must all equations. If one side rises by a certain percentage, the other side must rise by the same percentage. For example, if MV rose to 9,000, PQ would also rise to 9,000.

The Quantity Theory of Money

The quantity theory of money has both a crude version and a more sophisticated version. The crude quantity theory of money holds that when the money supply changes by a certain percentage, the price level changes by that same percentage. For example, if the money supply were to rise by 10 percent, the price level would rise by 10 percent. Similarly, if M were to double, then P would double. Using the same figures we assigned to the equation of exchange, let's see what happens if M and P double.

The crude version of the quantity theory

$$MV = PQ$$
$$900 \times 9 = 81 \times 100$$
$$1,800 \times 9 = 162 \times 100$$
$$16,200 = 16,200$$

If we double M, then MV doubles, and if we double P, PQ doubles. Because both sides of the equation must be equal, it appears that the crude quantity theory of money works out.

There are only two problems here. We are assuming V and Q remain constant. Do they? If they do, the crude quantity theory is correct. But what if they don't? For example, what if M, P, and Q all double? For the equation to balance, V would have to double. Similarly, what if M doubles and V declines by 50 percent? In that case, the rise in M would be canceled by the decline in V. If M doubles and MV stays the same, can we expect an automatic doubling of P?

Let's take a closer look at V and then at Q. Since 1950 V has risen fairly steadily from about three to nearly seven. In other words, individuals and businesses are spending their dollars much more quickly. Alternatively, they are making more efficient use of their money balances.

During a period of very tight money in the late 1970s and early 1980s, V rose to nearly seven.

There are several explanations for the rise of V. First, there's inflation. Why hold large money balances when they lose their value over time? Second, why hold idle cash balances when they could be earning interest? Finally, the use of credit cards and automatic teller machines, especially during the last decade, has allowed people to carry less cash. As a result, V has more than doubled since the mid-1950s.

Now let's see about Q, the quantity of final goods and services produced. During recessions, production, and therefore Q will fall. For example, during the 1981–82 recession Q fell at an annual rate of about 4 percent during the fourth quarter of 1981 and the first quarter of 1982. During recoveries, production picks up, so we go from a declining Q to a rising Q.

Obviously, then, we cannot consider V or Q to be constants. Therefore, the crude version of the quantity theory is invalid.

The real problem with the early quantity theorists is that they overstated their case. Clearly, rapid monetary growth will invariably lead to inflation. But does a given rate of increase in the money supply lead to precisely the same rate of growth in the price level? Not in *my* book, which happens to be the one you are reading.

Today's modern monetarists, those who believe the key economic variable is changes in M, have come up with a more sophisticated quantity theory. They assume any short-

The sophisticated version of the quantity theory

Figure 1

Hypothetical Aggregate Supply Curve

Moving from the extreme left side of the aggregate supply curve, we can raise output without raising prices until we begin to approach full-employment GDP. After continuing to raise output, accompanied by a rising price level, we reach full-employment GDP, at which point any further movement along the aggregate supply curve will raise prices without increasing output.

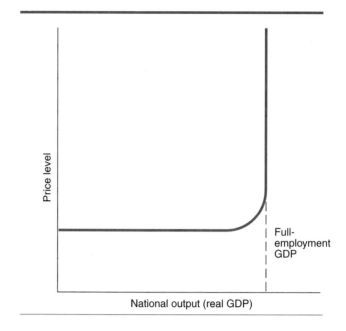

Full-employment GDP

National output (real GDP)

The value of money . . . varies inversely as its quantity; every increase of quantity lowering the value, and every diminution raising it, in a ratio exactly equivalent.

—John Stuart Mill, *Principles of Political Economy*

Sophisticated quantity theory in brief

term changes in V are either very small or predictable. The situation with Q, however, is another story.

Let's say M rises by 10 percent and V stays the same: MV will rise by 10 percent and PQ will rise by 10 percent. So far, so good. In fact, so far the crude and sophisticated quantity theories are identical. But what happens next is entirely up to the level of production, Q.

If there's considerable unemployment and we increase M, most, if not all, of this increase will be reflected in an increase in production, Q. Money flowing into the economy will lead to increased spending, output, and employment. Will it lead to higher prices as well? Probably not. Although our recent experience during recessions makes us a little more wary of large surges in the money supply, it is reasonable to expect most of the rise in M to be reflected in a rise in Q.

As we approach full employment, however, further increases in M will begin to lead, more and more, to increases in P, the price level (see Figure 1)[1]. And it is there that the sophisticated quantity theory becomes operative. We therefore can make two statements summarizing the sophisticated quantity theory:

1. If we are well below full employment, an increase in M will lead mainly to an increase in Q.

2. If we are close to full employment, an increase in M will lead mainly to an increase in P.

That's the sophisticated quantity theory of money. Please don't confuse it with the crude quantity theory, and don't confuse either quantity theory with the equation of exchange.

What is the sophisticated quantity theory supposed to do? Like most theories, it makes a prediction. In its least rigorous version, it says that changes in M's rate of growth lead to similar changes in PQ's rate of growth. If M is increasing slowly, PQ will increase slowly; rapid growth in M leads to rapid growth in PQ. Although no precise mathematical relationship is claimed (as under the crude quantity theory), the monetarists say changes in M lead to predictable changes in PQ.

We've deftly sidestepped the whole question of whether V is stable in the short run. The monetarists tell us it is, and the validity of the modern or sophisticated quantity the-

---

[1]Do you recognize our old friend, the aggregate supply curve, which appeared in Figures 6 and 9 of Chapter 11?

ory depends on the short-run stability of V. We'll deal with the question of the short-run stability of V in the appendix to this chapter.

Classical Economics

The United States suffered very bad recessions, even depressions, in the 1830s, 1870s, and 1890s, but always did eventually recover. If the government tried to get the country out of a recession, said the classicals, it only made things worse.

The classical school of economics was mainstream economics from roughly 1775 to 1930. Adam Smith's *The Wealth of Nations,* a plea for laissez-faire (no government interference), was virtually the economics bible through most of this period. The classicals believed our economy was self-regulating. Recessions would cure themselves, and a built-in mechanism was always pushing the economy toward full employment.

As we saw at the beginning of Chapter 11, the centerpiece of the classical system was Say's law: Supply creates its own demand. Everything produced gets sold. Why? Because people work so that they can spend.

What if people save some of their incomes? No problem, said the classicals, because that savings will be invested. With that, they pointed to Figure 2, which shows a graph of saving and investment. The two are equal at an interest rate of 10 percent.

What if the amount of money people wanted to save at 10 percent interest were greater than the amount businesspeople wanted to invest? Still no problem, said the classicals. The interest rate would fall automatically. People would be inclined to save less at lower interest rates, and businesspeople would be inclined to invest more. Eventually, the interest rate would fall far enough so that savings and investment would be equal.

The classicals also assumed downwardly flexible wage rates and prices. If there happened to be a temporary recession and business firms could not sell their entire inventories, they would simply lower their prices until their inventories were depleted. Similarly, if some workers were unemployed, they would offer to work for lower wages and would find new jobs.

Another basic classical tenet was the quantity theory of money, which we discussed earlier in this chapter. Stated in its crudest version, when the money supply changes by

Recessions cure themselves.

Say's law

Savings will be invested.

Interest rate mechanism

Flexible wages and prices

Quantity theory of money

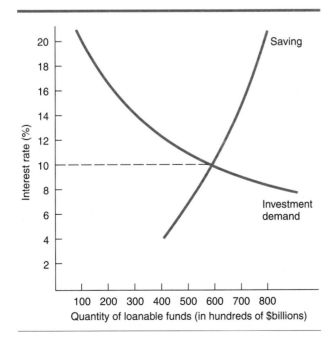

Figure 2

The Interest Rate Mechanism

An interest rate of 10 percent is found at the intersection of the saving curve and the investment demand curve.

a certain percentage, the price level changes by that same percentage. Thus, when the money supply is increased by 5 percent, the price level rises by 5 percent.

Resorting once again to the equation of exchange (whose components are defined in the first section of this chapter):

$$MV = PQ$$

If M rises by 5 percent and P rises by 5 percent, that means V and Q remain constant. We shall hold a full-scale debate between the Keynesians and the monetarists about the stability of V in the appendix to this chapter and shall conclude that V is stable during nonrecession and peacetime years. And Q? Well, Q, the output of goods and services, rises during nonrecession years and falls during recession years.

Where does all this leave us as regards the quantity theory? In its crude version, which the classicals espoused, we could hardly expect V *and* Q to stay constant from year to year. So much, then, for the crude quantity theory.

Finally, let's take a closer look at the classical contention that recessions are temporary phenomena, which, with the help of Say's law, the interest rate mechanism, and downwardly flexible wages and prices, cure themselves. This leads to the basic classical macroeconomic policy when there is a recession: Do nothing!

If the government attempted to cure a recession by spending more money or cutting taxes, these measures would not get the economy out of the recession. Why not? Because the recession would cure itself. Government intervention could not help, and it might even hurt.

What about monetary policy? If there were a recession, the standard monetary policy would be to increase the rate of growth of the money supply. What would this accomplish? Ask the classicals. Because the recession would be curing itself, output, Q, would go up automatically. Because V would be stable, a rise in M would simply be translated into a rise in P, so the attempt to cure the recession by means of monetary policy would only cause inflation.

The classical school dominated economic thought until the time of the Great Depression. If recessions cure themselves automatically, asked John Maynard Keynes in the 1930s, why is the entire world economy dragging along from year to year in unending depression? And if the economy isn't curing itself, said Keynes, government intervention is in order.

Keynesian Economics

John Maynard Keynes wrote his landmark work *The General Theory of Employment, Interest, and Money* during the depths of the Great Depression. While President Herbert Hoover (perhaps the last political leader to uphold the theories of classical economics) was telling everyone who would listen that recovery was just around the corner, things were going from bad to worse. As the unemployment rate mounted, production plummeted, and soup kitchens proliferated, more and more Americans demanded that the federal government do something. When Franklin Roosevelt defeated Hoover by a landslide in 1932, he had a mandate for the government to do whatever was necessary to bring about recovery.

Keynes provided a blueprint. The problem, he said, was inadequate aggregate demand. People were just not buying enough goods and services to employ the entire labor force. In fact, aggregate demand was so low that only the government could spend enough money to provide a sufficient boost.

Keynes defined aggregate demand as consumer spending, investment spending, and government spending (plus net exports, which at that time were negligible). Consumption is a function of disposable income. When disposable income is low, said Keynes, consumption is low. This was the problem Americans were having during the Great Depression.

Investment, which is largely a function of the marginal efficiency of investment, or the expected profit rate, was also very low during the Depression. So we could not hope that an upturn in investment would lead the way out of the Depression. The only hope was for the government to spend enough money to raise aggregate demand sufficiently to get people back to work.

What type of spending was necessary? Any kind, said Keynes. Quantity is much more relevant than quality. Even if the government employed some people to dig holes, said Keynes, and others to fill up those holes, it would still be able to spend the country out of these economic woes.

Where would the government get the money? There were two choices: print it or borrow it. If the government printed it, wouldn't that cause inflation? Keynes thought this unlikely; during the Depression, the country had been experiencing *de*flation, or falling prices. Who would even think of raising prices when he was having trouble finding customers?

What about budget deficits? Nothing improper about these, said Keynes. Although the common wisdom of the times was that the government must balance its budget, there was absolutely nothing wrong with deficits during recessions and depressions. It was necessary to prime the pump by sucking up the idle savings that businesses were not borrowing and using those funds to get the economy moving again.

Once government spending was under way, people would have some money in their pockets. And what would they do with that money? You guessed it—they'd spend it. This money would then end up in other people's pockets, and they, in turn, would spend it once again.

That money would continue to be spent again and again, putting more and more people back to work. In the process, the deficit would melt away. The government could cut back on its spending programs while tax receipts swelled, so we could view the budget deficits as a temporary expedient to get the economy off dead center.

But what of the classical automatic mechanism that ensured that the economy always moved toward full employment? In the long run, Keynes conceded, maybe it really did work. But in the long run, noted Keynes, "we are all dead."

Why didn't the classical mechanism work in the short run? Keynes observed that interest rates fell to about 2 percent during the Great Depression, but business firms still were not borrowing all that much to build new plant and equipment. After all, who in his right mind would invest in new plant and equipment when his factory was operating at only 30 or 40 percent of capacity? Besides, said Keynes, at an interest rate of 2 percent, many people would not be willing to lend out their savings. Why tie them up at such a low interest rate? Why not just sit on this money until interest rates rose again?

So much for the interest rate mechanism. With respect to downwardly flexible wages and prices, there were institutional barriers. Labor unions would oppose lowered wage rates, while highly concentrated industries would tend to prefer output decreases to price cuts during recessions.

Keynes also raised some objections to the quantity theory of money. Most significant, he asked what would happen to the money that would be printed if the government did increase the money supply. The classicals had assumed it would be spent, thus pushing up the price level. This could happen, conceded Keynes, but during a bad recession perhaps people would just hold their money, waiting for interest rates to rise before they lent it out.

Wouldn't they spend it, as the classicals suggested? Poor people would. But if they were poor, what would they be doing with money in the first place? If the money supply were increased during a bad recession, said Keynes, that money would simply be held as idle cash balances by relatively well-to-do people. Nothing would happen to the money until the economy was well on its way toward recovery, interest rates rose, and more investment opportunities became available.

By the mid-1930s the classical school of economics had lost most of its adherents. Not everyone became a Keynesian. Conservative economists in particular could never fully reconcile themselves to the vastly increased economic role that the Keynesians

The cure for recession is government spending.

In a campaign speech in Brooklyn in the fall of 1932, Roosevelt castigated Hoover for not balancing his budget.

Why invest in new plant and equipment when most of your capacity is idle?

If M rises, what if people don't spend additional money, but just hold it?

Is Keynesian economics valid
just during recessions?

awarded to the federal government. In fact, the remaining economic schools to be considered here—the monetarists, the supply-siders, and the rational expectationists—would
all rail against the evils of big government.

But big government was here to stay. Although the massive spending programs of
Franklin Roosevelt's New Deal did not get the country out of the Depression, the much
bigger defense spending during World War II certainly did. There was no question that
Keynes had been right, but since the war Americans had been plagued not just by periodic recessions but by almost unending inflation. There was growing feeling among the
populace as well as professional economists that perhaps Keynesian economics was just
recession and depression economics, that it could not satisfactorily deal with curbing
inflation.

Keynesian economics may have reached its high point in 1964, when personal
income tax rates were cut by about 20 percent. This tax cut, combined with accelerating military spending during the country's escalating involvement in the Vietnam War,
brought about a rapid rate of economic growth in the mid- to late 1960s; but this growth
was accompanied by increasing inflation, which reached double-digit proportions in the
early 1970s. By the time President Richard Nixon proclaimed, "We are all Keynesians
now," this school of economics had already been receiving a lot of bad press. In the
1970s being a Keynesian was out; to be in, you had to be a monetarist.

The Monetarist School

The Importance of the Rate of Monetary Growth

Monetarists are obsessed with
the growth rate of M.

Monetarism begins and ends with one obsession: the rate of growth of the money supply. According to monetarists, most of our major economic problems, especially inflation and recession, are due to the Federal Reserve's mismanagement of our rate of
monetary growth.

Milton Friedman, an economist who did exhaustive studies of the relationship
between the rate of growth of the money supply and the rate of increase in prices, reached
a couple of not surprising conclusions. First, the United States has never had a serious
inflation that was not accompanied by rapid monetary growth. Second, when the money
supply has grown slowly, the country has had no inflation.

In a study of the monetary history of the United States during the period of nearly
a century after the Civil War, Friedman and his longtime collaborator Anna Jacobson
Schwartz reached this conclusion: "Changes in the behavior of the money stock have
been closely associated with changes in economic activity, money income, and prices."[2]
Once again, the answer to all important economic questions is the rate of growth of the
money supply.

Monetarists modified crude
quantity theory.

Building on the quantity theory of money, the monetarists agreed with the classicals
that when the money supply grows, the price level rises, albeit not at exactly the same
rate. But they refuted Keynes's argument that if the money supply were raised during a
recession, people might just hold on to these added funds. Like the classicals, the monetarists assumed that to get it is to spend it—not necessarily on consumer goods, but on
stocks, bonds, real estate, and other noncash assets.

If people *did* spend this additional money, the prices of what they bought would be
bid up. In other words, the monetarists were saying that the quantity theory basically
holds true.

Monetarists' analysis has been
borne out by the facts.

So far, so good. Now for recessions. What causes them? When the Federal Reserve
increases the money supply at less than the rate needed by business—say, anything less

[2]Milton Friedman and Anna Jacobson Schwartz, *A Monetary History of the United States, 1867–1960*
(Princeton, NJ: Princeton University Press, 1971), p. 676.

than 3 percent a year—the economy is headed for trouble. Sometimes, in fact, the Fed does not let it grow at all and may even cause it to shrink slightly.

By and large the facts have borne out the monetarists' analysis. Without a steady increase in the money supply of at least 3 percent a year, there is a high likelihood of a recession.

The Basic Propositions of Monetarism

(1) The Key to Stable Economic Growth Is a Constant Rate of Increase in the Money Supply
Has our economic history been one of stable growth? No inflation? No recessions? Since World War II alone, we've had at least four waves of inflation and 10 recessions.

The monetarists place almost the entire blame on the Federal Reserve Board of Governors. If only they had been increasing the money supply by a steady 3 percent a year, we could have avoided most of this instability.

The Fed is blamed for our economic instability.

Let's trace the monetarist reasoning by analyzing the Fed's actions over the course of a business cycle. As a recession sets in, the Fed increases the rate of growth of the money supply. This stimulates output in the short run, helping to pull the economy out of the recession. In the long run, however, this expanded money supply causes inflation. So what does the Fed do? It slams on the monetary brakes, slowing the rate of growth in the money supply. This brings on a recession. And what does the Fed do in response? It increases the rate of monetary growth.

"Is this stop-go, stop-go monetary policy any way to run an economy?" ask the monetarists. This type of policy inspires about as much confidence as the student driver approaching a red light. First he hits the brakes about 100 yards from the corner. Then, overcompensating for his error, he hits the accelerator much too hard. When the car shoots forward, he hits the brakes again, bringing the car to a dead stop about 50 yards from the corner. Then he repeats the whole process.

Stop-go monetary policy

In the first half of the 1940s, the Fed helped finance the huge increase in the national debt (incurred by World War II) by pumping up the money supply by tens of billions of dollars. The 1950s, however, were a time of tight money, marked, incidentally, by three recessions.

In the late 1960s, an accelerating rate of monetary growth was accompanied by a rising rate of inflation, which, in the early 1970s, reached double-digit proportions. In 1973 the Federal Reserve Board put on the brakes, and we went into the worst recession we had suffered since World War II. In 1975 the Fed eased up and we recovered. Then, in late 1979, the brakes were applied. The prime rate of interest soared to more than 20 percent, and in January 1980 we went into a sharp six-month recession. What happened next? You guessed it. The Fed eased up again. Interest rates came down, and economic recovery set in. But in 1981 the Fed, alarmed at the rising inflation rate, stepped on the monetary brakes, and we entered still another recession in August 1981. The prime once again soared to more than 20 percent. This recession proved even deeper than that of 1973–75, In summer 1982 the Fed saw no course but to ease up on the brakes; sure enough, by November of that year the recession had ended.

(2) Expansionary Monetary Policy Will Only Temporarily Depress Interest Rates
In the short run, when the Fed increases the rate of monetary growth, interest rates decline. If the interest rate is the price of money, it follows that if the money supply is increased and there is no change in the demand for money, then its price (the interest rate) will decline.

The monetarists tell us that in the long run an increase in monetary growth will not lower interest rates; the increased money supply causes inflation. Lenders will demand higher interest rates to compensate them for being repaid in inflated dollars.

In the long run, a rise in M pushes up inflation and interest rates.

Let's say, for example, there's no inflation and the interest rate is 5 percent. This is the real rate of interest. The rate of inflation then rises to 8 percent; that means if it cost you $10,000 to live last year, your cost of living is now $10,800. If lenders can anticipate the rate of inflation, they will insist that they be paid not just for the real interest rate of 5 percent but also for the anticipated inflation of 8 percent. This raises the interest rate from 5 percent to a nominal rate of 13 percent.

When the Federal Reserve allows the money supply to grow quickly, interest rates are kept down for a while until lenders realize the rate of inflation (caused by faster monetary growth) is rising. They will then demand higher interest rates. Thus, a higher rate of monetary growth in the short run will keep interest rates low, but in the long run it will lead to higher interest rates.

(3) Expansionary Monetary Policy Will Only Temporarily Reduce the Unemployment Rate The first two basic propositions partially explain the third. First, when monetary growth speeds up, output is expanded, but in the long run only prices will rise. Because rising output would lower the unemployment rate, in the short run unemployment is reduced. But in the long run, an increase in the rate of monetary growth will raise prices, not output, so the unemployment rate will go back up. We'll come back to why this happens.

The second basic proposition states that expansionary monetary policy only temporarily depresses interest rates. In the short run, more money means lower interest rates. These lower interest rates encourage more investment and, consequently, less unemployment.

But in the long run the added money in circulation causes inflation, which, in turn, raises interest rates. As interest rates rise, investment declines and the unemployment rate goes back up.

The monetarists have explained the temporary reduction in the unemployment rate more directly. As labor union members begin to anticipate inflation, they will demand higher wage rates. New labor contract settlements will reflect the higher cost of living, but these higher wage settlements will price some workers out of the market, thus raising the unemployment rate.

(4) Expansionary Fiscal Policy Will Only Temporarily Raise Output and Employment Here we have another conflict—this time a basic one—between the monetarists and the Keynesians. The Keynesians believe fiscal policy, particularly heavy government spending, will pull us out of a recession. But how is this spending going to be financed? By borrowing. The Treasury goes into the market for loanable funds and borrows hundreds of billions of dollars to finance the deficit.

Crowding-out effect

The monetarists point out that such huge government borrowing comes directly into conflict with that of business firms and consumers. Not only will it be harder for these groups to borrow, but interest rates will be driven up. This crowding-out effect represents, according to the monetarists, a substitution of public for private spending. All we're really doing is spending more on government goods and services and less on consumer and investment goods and services. Aggregate demand is not increased.

How well would a budget surplus restrain inflation? Not very, say the monetarists. The Treasury would not be borrowing now, but rather repaying part of the national debt, which would tend to push down interest rates and make borrowing easier. Private borrowing would replace public borrowing. The hoped-for restraint would not materialize because private borrowers would now be spending these borrowed funds on goods and services. In effect, then, we would still have the same level of spending.

The Monetary Rule

Increase the money supply at a constant rate.

The policy prescription of the monetarists is simply to increase the money supply at a constant rate. When there is a recession, this steady infusion of money will pick up the economy. When there is inflation, a steady rate of monetary growth will slow it down.

You might ask why the money supply should be increased at all during inflation. There are two answers. First, the monetarists would tell you that if we didn't increase the money supply at all, we would be going back to the old, failed discretionary monetary policies of the past—the start-and-stop, start-and-stop policies that only made the business cycle worse. Second, over the long run the economy does need a steady infusion of money to enable economic growth.

The monetarists' steady monetary growth prescription is analogous to the feeding policy of the American Army. Every day, in every part of the world, at every meal, the soldiers walk along the chow line and receive, in addition to the main course and dessert, two pieces of white bread, two pats of butter, and one pint of whole milk. The main course is also dished out in equal portions. The food servers do not dole out portions whose sizes vary with that of the eater. They look from the serving pan to the eater's tray, slopping out serving spoonfuls of whatever it is that the Army decided to cook that day.

So, we have a 6-foot 6-inch 300-pound person getting the same size portion as does a 5-foot 6-inch 130-pound person. My theory is that the Army wants everyone to be the same size—a theory that seems to be borne out by the single uniform size that is issued. If everyone eats the same portion, presumably they will all end up this same size.

Perhaps the monetarists got the idea of increasing the money supply by a constant percentage by observing Army chow lines. They believe our economic health will be relatively good—if not always excellent—if we have a steady diet of money. No starts and stops, no extreme ups and downs, and, to complete the analogy, no very fat years and no very lean years.

The Decline of Monetarism

It's interesting that when the Fed really began to pay attention to what the monetarists were saying, this may have led to the ultimate decline of the monetarists. In October 1979 Federal Reserve chairman Paul Volcker announced a major policy shift. No longer would the Fed focus only on keeping interest rates on an even keel. From now on the Fed would set monetary growth targets and stick to them.

This new policy was followed for most of the next three years. The double-digit inflation that prevailed in 1979 and 1980 was finally brought under control by late 1982—but not until we had gone through a period of sky-high interest rates, very high unemployment, and two recessions.

Even though the Fed had finally followed the advice of the monetarists—at least to a large degree—and even though the nagging inflation of the last 15 years had finally been wrung out of the economy, people began to look elsewhere for their economic gurus. They looked to the White House, which had become a stronghold of the latest school of economics, the supply-side school.

Supply-Side Economics

Supply-side economics came into vogue in the early 1980s when Ronald Reagan assumed the presidency. Supply-siders felt that the economic role of the federal government had grown much too large and that high tax rates and onerous government rules and regulations were hurting the incentives of individuals and business firms to produce goods and services. President Reagan suggested a simple solution: get the government off the backs of the American people. How? By cutting taxes and reducing government spending and regulation.

Cut tax rates, government spending, and government regulation.

The objective of supply-side economics, then, is to raise aggregate supply, the total amount of goods and services the country produces. The problem, said the supply-siders, is that high tax rates are hurting the incentive to work and to invest. All the government needs to do is cut tax rates, and voila: up goes production.

Raise aggregate supply.

Many of the undesirable side effects of high marginal tax rates are explained by the work effect, the savings and investment effect, and the elimination of productive market exchanges, which we shall take up in turn.

The Work Effect

Work–leisure decisions

People are often confronted with work-leisure decisions. Should I put in that extra couple of hours of overtime? Should I take on a second job? Should I keep my store open longer hours? If you answer yes to any of these, you'll have to give the government a pretty big slice of that extra income. At some point you may well conclude, "I'd have to be nuts to take on any extra work; I'd only be working for the government."

At what point do you start working for the government? When it takes 20 cents out of each dollar of extra income (a marginal tax rate of 20 percent)? When it takes 30 cents? Or 40 cents? Each of us makes his or her own decision about the cutoff point. If you are a wage-earner, you will have to pay Medicare and Social Security tax, federal income tax, and, possibly, some state income tax. Back in 1980, before the passage of the Kemp-Roth tax cut and the tax cuts that came under the Tax Reform Act of 1986, people earning more than $50,000 a year often had marginal tax rates of more than 50 percent.[3] If you paid more than half of your overtime earnings in taxes, would you consider yourself to be working for the government? This is an especially important consideration for married couples (see box, "How High Taxes Discourage Married Women from Working").

Why work if the government gets most of your money?

Facing high marginal tax rates, many people refuse to work more than a certain number of hours of overtime or take on second jobs and other forms of extra work. Instead, they opt for more leisure time. In sum, high marginal tax rates rob people not only of some potential income but of the incentive to work longer hours. People working shorter hours obviously produce less, so total output is lower than it might have been with lower marginal tax rates. This and the saving-investment argument (considered next) are the two key points made by supply-siders for lower marginal tax rates.

The Saving and Investment Effect

The supply-side economists really make two arguments against high marginal tax rates. The first is the work effect. Next is the saving and investment effect. When people save

---

How High Taxes Discourage Married Women from Working*

Slightly more than half of all married women of child-bearing age are now working. But many more would work if our progressive income tax structure didn't push second earners into higher marginal tax brackets. In a *New York Times* article, Virginia Postrel presented this argument:

> Far more than men or single women, married women act like supply siders. Cut their marginal tax rates, and they get jobs. Raise their taxes and they stay home.
>
> By disproportionately punishing married women's work, the tax system distorts women's personal choices. And by discouraging valuable work, it lowers our overall standard of living.

Postrel cites a study by Nada Eissa, an economist at the University of California at Berkeley, and the National Bureau of Economic Research. In 1986, when marginal tax rates were slashed, the percentage of married women in the 99th percentile of family income (the top 1 percent) who worked jumped from 46 percent to 55 percent, while those who had jobs increased their hours 13 percent. But since the marginal tax rates have been raised, someone in the 39.6 percent bracket would possibly be paying more than half her income in federal and state income taxes as well as Social Security and Medicaid taxes.

---

*Virginia Postrel, "The U.S. Tax System Is Discouraging Married Women from Working," *The New York Times*, November 2, 2000, p. C2.

---

[3]Under Kemp-Roth, personal income taxes were slashed 23 percent between 1981 and 1984. The top marginal tax rate was cut from 70 percent to 50 percent. Personal income tax rates were cut further under the Tax Reform Act of 1986 to marginal rates of 28 and 15 percent.

money, they earn interest on their savings. But a high marginal tax rate on interest income will provide a disincentive to save, or at least to make savings available for investment purposes.

Similarly, people who borrow money for investment purposes—new plant and equipment and inventory—hope that this will lead to greater profits. But if those profits are subject to a high marginal tax rate, once again there is a disincentive to invest.[4]

If people are discouraged from working, total output will be reduced. And if they are discouraged from saving and investing, the economy will be stagnant. Supply-side economists point to the economic stagnation of the late 1970s and early 1980s as proof of the basic propositions of their theory. On the other hand, the economic record during the Reagan years, particularly with respect to saving, investment, and economic growth, was nothing to write home about either.

The Elimination of Productive Market Exchanges

Most people have jobs at which they are good; an accountant, a carpenter, an automobile mechanic, and a gourmet chef are all relatively good at their professions. That's probably why they chose those lines of work to begin with—and all that on-the-job training didn't hurt either.

When you need your taxes prepared—especially if you stand to save several thousand dollars—you go to an accountant. When you need your transmission fixed, unless you're a skilled mechanic, you'll certainly be better off going to someone who is. In fact, one of the main reasons our standard of living is so high in the United States is because a large proportion of our labor force is composed of individuals with specialized skills.

What happens when your roof must be reshingled? Do you hire a roofer, or do you do it yourself? Do you do it yourself because it's cheaper?

Well, maybe it's cheaper and maybe it isn't. Suppose you can reshingle your roof in 100 hours and a roofer can do the job in 60 hours. If the roofer charges you $12 an hour (in addition to materials), it will cost you $720. How many hours would you have to work to earn $720? Suppose your clerical job pays $9 an hour and you are in the 40 percent marginal tax bracket. You take home only $5.40 an hour (that is, 60 percent of $9).

Do you hire the roofer or do it yourself? If you do it yourself, it will take you 100 hours. If you hire the roofer, you must pay him $720. How many hours would you have to work to bring home $720? Figure it out: $720/$5.40 = 133⅓ hours. I think even *I* would rather spend 100 hours on my roof than 133⅓ hours in front of a class. And I'm afraid of heights!

There is a serious misallocation of labor when the productive market exchange—your clerical work for your roofer's labor—is eliminated; but because of the high marginal tax rate, it pays for you to work less at your regular job (at which you are presumably good) and more at household tasks (at which you are not so good). When you add up all the productive market exchanges short-circuited by high marginal tax rates, you may well be talking about hundreds of billions of dollars in misallocated resources.

The Laffer Curve

Supply-side economists have one basic policy prescription: Cut tax rates! This will raise output. However, there *is* one slight problem. Won't federal tax revenue fall precipitously? Some supply-side economists feel this would not be an altogether bad idea. After all, the more the federal government takes in, the more it spends. All the Democrats did,

---

[4]Under the Tax Reform Act of 1986, the basic corporate income tax rate was reduced from 46 percent to 34 percent.

The Laffer Curve

At a marginal tax rate of 0, tax
revenues are 0. Tax revenue can be
increased by raising the marginal
tax rate to point C, at which they
will be maximized. If marginal tax
rates are raised still higher, tax
revenue will decline. And, if the
marginal tax rate were 100 percent,
no one would work, and tax
revenue would be 0. The rationale
of the Laffer curve is that, when
the marginal tax rate is too high,
say, at 50 percent (see point A), we
can raise tax revenue by lowering it
to 40 percent (see point B).

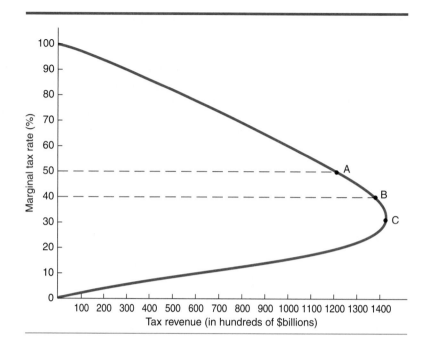

they argue, was "tax, tax, tax, spend, spend, spend." But Arthur Laffer, an orthodox supply-side economics professor, said it isn't necessarily true that a tax rate cut will lead to
a fall in tax revenue. *Au contraire.* (That's French for "just the opposite.")

Imagine that we're at point A on the Laffer curve drawn in Figure 3. We cut the
marginal tax rate from 50 percent to 40 percent, and lo and behold, tax revenue rises
from $1,200 billion to nearly $1,400 billion. Is this sophistry? (That's Greek for "pulling
a fast one.")

Let's see how this works by looking at the case of a specific individual. Suppose
this person pays $50,000 on an income of $100,000. If this person's tax rate were lowered to 40 percent, she would pay $40,000. Right? Wrong, say the supply-siders. She
would now have an incentive to work harder. How much harder? Hard enough, say, to
earn $130,000 by working every available hour of overtime or taking on a second job.

How much is 40 percent of $130,000? It comes out to exactly $52,000. How much
did the government collect from her before the tax cut? Only $50,000. So by cutting tax
rates, say the supply-siders, the government will end up collecting more revenue.

Is this true? If we look at the Laffer curve, it appears to be—at least at very high
tax rates. But when the government cut tax rates in 1981 and 1982, tax revenue actually
declined. Of course, there was a recession going on.

What if we were at, say, point C on the Laffer curve and we cut tax rates? What
would happen to federal tax revenue? Obviously, it would decline.

The problem, then, is to figure out where we are on the Laffer curve, or what the
parameters of the curve itself are, before we start cutting taxes. There really is a Laffer
curve out there. The trouble is we don't know exactly where, so when we try to use it
as a policy tool, it's kind of like playing an economic version of pin the tail on the donkey. When you play a game blindfolded, you run the risk of looking a lot like the six-
year-old kids who miss the donkey completely. And this game is for somewhat higher
stakes.

During the last two years of the Reagan administration, it had become apparent that
supply-side economics was an idea whose time had gone. Although inflation had been
brought under control and interest rates had declined as well (largely because of the
efforts of the Federal Reserve), the supply-side-policies had not yielded the rapid rate of
economic growth that the public had been led to expect. Perhaps the greatest legacies of
supply-side economics were huge budget deficits and a monumental national debt.

Arthur Laffer, American economist
(Collections of the Library of
Congress)

Before we bury supply-side economics, we might note that in 1995 the new Republican congressional majority, in its quest to cut taxes and the federal budget deficit simultaneously, embraced a new term, "dynamic scoring." And what, exactly, is dynamic scoring? Apparently, it is a new term for the Laffer curve. If it yields the same results in the late 1990s as it did through the 1980s, then we can look forward to a rising tide of budgetary red ink.

In any case, after the Reagan years, conservative economists, many of whom had never been entirely comfortable with supply-side economics, had yet another banner to rally round. This one was called rational expectations.

Waiting for supply-side economics to work is like leaving the landing lights on for Amelia Earhart.
—Walter Heller

Rational Expectations Theory

Whatever else you have learned about economic policy, you have certainly learned that economists don't all agree on what policies we should follow. Nevertheless, with certain notable exceptions, most economists today would more or less agree on two sets of policies. To fight inflation, you want to lower the rate of growth of the money supply and reduce federal government budget deficits. And to fight recessions, you want to do the opposite: increase the rate of growth of the money supply and increase the size of the deficits. Although some economists would only partially acquiesce to these policies, there has been a greater consensus for these stated policies than for any others.

Most economist agree on two sets of policies.

You probably never saw *Monty Python and the Holy Grail,* but in that movie there was a group of knights who distinguished themselves solely by saying "Neee." No matter what questions they were asked, they would always answer "Neee." Assuming "Neee" was Middle English for nay or no, those knights were the rational expectations theorists, or the new classical economists of their day.

Like the "old" classical economists, today's rational expectationists say no to any form of government economic intervention. Such intervention, no matter how well intentioned, would do a lot more harm than good. In fact, they maintain that anti-inflationary and antirecessionary policies, at best, would have no effect whatsoever. More likely, say the new classical economists, these policies would end up making things worse.

It would be best for the government to do nothing, even if there were a recession or a substantial amount of inflation. The economy will automatically and quickly right itself, ending up again with full employment and little or no inflation. The reason that fiscal and monetary policy would have little effect, according to the rational expectationists, is that they affect mainly aggregate demand but that the prime economic mover is aggregate supply.

They argued that at any given time there was a natural level of real GDP, toward which the economy gravitated. The deflationary and inflationary gaps that so perplexed policymakers during the 1974s weren't gaps at all. Instead they reflected changes in the economy's own natural level of output. When oil prices went through the roof in 1973 and again in 1979, said the rational expectationists, they created declines in aggregate supply, lowering the natural level of GDP. There was nothing the government could do about these new economic facts, except to keep out of the way and let our economy quickly adjust to them as it moved to its new natural level of output.

Robert Lucas of the University of Chicago, a 1995 Nobel Prize-winner, is clearly top gun among the new classical economists. Lucas believes that people can anticipate government policies to fight inflation and recession, given their knowledge of policy, past experience, and expectations about the future. Consequently, they act on this anticipation, effectively nullifying the intended effects of those policies. What, then, should the government do? It should follow strict guidelines rather than try to use discretionary policy to tinker with the economy.

The view of Robert Lucas

Rational expectations theory is based on three assumptions: (1) that individuals and business firms learn through experience to anticipate the consequences of changes in monetary and fiscal policy; (2) that they act instantaneously to protect their economic interests; and (3) that all resource and product markets are purely competitive.

The three assumptions of rational expectations theory

Now we'll translate. Imagine the Federal Reserve decides to increase the money supply's rate of growth sharply. Why would the Fed do this? To stimulate output and raise employment.

The scenario, according to the Fed, would be as follows: (1) the money supply rises; (2) business firms order more plant and equipment and more inventory; (3) more jobs are created and output rises; (4) wages do not rise right away, but prices do; (5) because prices rise and wages stay the same, profits rise; (6) eventually wages catch up to prices, profits go back down, and the expansion comes to an end.

This may have happened in the old days, say the rational expectations theorists, but surely people have learned something from all this experience. Everybody knows that when the Fed sharply increases the monetary growth rate, inflation will result. Business firms, of course, will raise prices. But what about labor? Anticipating the expected inflation, wage-earners will demand wage increases now. No more playing catch-up after the cost of living has already risen.

If wage rates are increased along with prices, do profits increase? No! If profits are not rising, there goes the main reason for increasing output and hiring more people—which, of course, was why the rate of monetary growth was raised in the first place.

Let's return to the rational expectations theorists' three assumptions. The first one is plausible enough—that through experience, we learn to anticipate the consequences of changes in monetary and fiscal policy. So, if a sharp increase in the rate of growth of the money supply always leads to inflation, eventually we will all learn to recognize this pattern. (See the box "Rational Expectations versus Adaptive Expectations.")

It would follow from the next two assumptions that the intended results of macroeconomic policy shifts will be completely frustrated. Why? If you knew that prices would be increasing, would you be willing to sit back and passively accept a decline in your standard of living? Wouldn't you demand a higher wage rate to keep pace with rising prices? The rational expectations theorists say people can always be expected to promote their personal economic interests, and furthermore, in a purely competitive market, they are free to do so.

In a purely competitive labor market, workers are free to leave one employer for another who offers higher wages. In a purely competitive products market, all firms are subject to the law of supply and demand, and will automatically pass along any wage increases in the form of higher prices.

Most macroeconomic policy changes, say the rational expectations theorists, are readily predictable. When there's inflation, there are extended debates in Congress, demands for cuts in government spending and tax increases, and a slowdown in the rate of monetary growth. Both Congress and the Federal Reserve generally telegraph policy moves, often months in advance. The point is that when these moves are made, no one is surprised. And because the public anticipates these policy changes, their intended effects are canceled out by the actions taken by individuals and business firms to protect their economic interests. In the case of policies aimed at raising output and employment, all the government gets for its efforts is more inflation.

What should the government do? It should do, say the rational expectations theorists, as little as possible. Like the classical economists and the monetarists, they believe the more the government tries to be an economic stabilizing force, the more it will destabilize the economy.

Basically, then, the federal government should figure out the right policies to follow and stick to them. What *are* the right policies? As you might expect, they've taken up the conservative economists' agenda: (1) steady monetary growth of 3 to 4 percent a year (the monetarists' monetary rule) and (2) a balanced budget (favored by the classical economists, among others).

Like every other school of economics, the rational expectations school has certainly received its share of criticism. In fact, only a small minority of economists today would consider themselves new classical economists, mainly because this group just goes too far in ascribing rationality to both the general population and themselves.

advanced WORK

Rational Expectations versus Adaptive Expectations

How do we predict the future? The simplest way is to assume that past trends will continue. The *adaptive expectations hypothesis* is based on the assumption that the best indicator of the future is what happened in the past.

Suppose the price level has been rising at an annual rate of 6 percent for the last three years. Under adaptive expectations, people will expect prices to rise about 6 percent in year 4. Now let's add a wrinkle. Suppose that in year 4 the rate of inflation rises to 9 percent. So what rate of inflation do people now predict for year 5? They predict 9 percent. Well, suppose that in year 5 it rises to 14 percent. What will everyone predict for year 6? Fourteen percent? Fine. Except that in year 6 it goes down to 10 percent. So for year 7 everyone predicts 10 percent. But in year 7 the inflation rate falls to just 5 percent.

Under adaptive expectations, forecasts of the future rate of inflation may be right on the money, but they may also exhibit systematic error. When inflation is accelerating, forecasts will tend to be too low. And when inflation is decelerating (that is, disinflation is taking place), then forecasts will tend to be too high.

The *rational expectations hypothesis* makes the assumption that people do not keep making the same mistakes over and over again when predicting future events. After getting burned once or twice, they do not systematically keep assuming that past trends will necessarily continue into the future.

The rational expectations hypothesis assumes that future expectations are based not just on past trends but on an understanding of how the economy works. For example, to form their expectation of the inflation rate, decision makers will use all available information, including past inflation rates, the impact of expected policy actions and their knowledge of macroeconomic relationships within our economy.

So which hypothesis is right—rational expectations or adaptive expectations? To the degree that people have sense of how our economy operates—and to the degree that they don't just blindly assume that past trends will continue into the future—the rational expectations hypothesis appears to have greater validity. But it falls far short of its adherents' claim that it is so powerful that it nullifies descretionary monetary and fiscal policy.

Is it reasonable to expect individuals and business firms to predict the consequences of macroeconomic policy changes correctly when economists themselves come up with widely varying predictions, most of which are wrong? Economists place little faith in each other's rationality; is it rational for them to ascribe a greater prescience to the general population than they give themselves?

In a world of constant change, is it possible for people to accurately predict the economic consequences of policy changes? Indeed, when a continually changing cast of policy makers, each with his or her own economic agenda, seems to be calling for entirely new economic approaches every few years, it's awfully hard to tell the players without a scorecard—it's even harder to predict the final score.

A second criticism of the rational expectations school is that our economic markets are not purely competitive; some are not competitive at all. Labor unions are not an economist's idea of purely competitive labor market institutions. Nor would industries such as those that produce automobiles, petroleum, cigarettes, and breakfast cereals, each of which has just a handful of firms doing most of the producing, be considered very competitive.

Finally, critics raise the question of the rigidities imposed by contracts. The labor union with the two- or three-year contract cannot reopen bargaining with employers when greater inflation is anticipated because of a suddenly expansionary monetary policy. Nor can business firms that have long-term contracts with customers decide to charge higher prices because they perceive more inflation in the future.

Should we summarily dismiss the rational expectations school because it is so vulnerable to criticism? Most economists would probably concede that this school is correct in calling their attention to how expectations may affect the outcome of macroeconomic policy changes. In recent years, then, economists have become more aware that to the

An economist is someone who cannot see something working in practice without asking whether it would work in theory.
—Walter Heller

419

degree policy changes are predictable, people will certainly act to protect their economic interests. Because they will succeed to some degree, they will partially counteract the effect of the government's macroeconomic policy.

In other words, rational expectations theory has a certain validity, as do each of the other theories we discussed. The question we're left with is: How valid is each theory relative to each of the others? Perhaps this question is answered by the first and second laws of economics:

The First Law of Economics: For every economist, there exists an equal and opposite economist.

The Second Law of Economics: They're both wrong.

Are Wages Downwardly Flexible?

When a recession hits and millions of workers are laid off, do many companies give their employees the choice of either accepting lower wages or being laid off? Wouldn't the workers be better off working for lower wages than not working at all? And wouldn't the employers be better off paying lower wages and thereby lowering their costs?

But very few workers are given the choice of accepting lower wages or being laid off. There are three reasons for this.

1. *Labor Contracts and the Minimum Wage*   As we've noted earlier many firms may not be able to cut wage rates because they are under contract, sometimes for two or three years, to pay their workers at specified wage rates. Usually these are union contracts, and while some workers might prefer pay cuts to layoffs, the vast majority (who do not face layoffs) would refuse to have *their* wages cut as well. In other words, if your employer asked everyone to take a pay cut to save some jobs, would *you* accept a pay cut to save someone *else's* job? Furthermore, in the case of workers earning the minimum federal or state wage rate, employers cannot legally lower their hourly earnings.

2. *Efficiency Wage Theory*   One thing every employer would like to do is pay an efficiency wage. *An efficiency wage is one that minimizes the firm's labor cost per unit of output.* Generally, the more you pay, the better quality labor you'll attract. For instance, people being paid $20/hour will usually produce more than people earning $10/hour. What if the people earning $20/hour, on average, produced more than double those earning $10/hour? Then the firm's cost per unit of output could be lowered by paying workers $20/hour. If, by trial and error, the firm found that $18/hour minimized its labor cost per unit of output, then $18/hour would be that firm's efficiency wage.

   In addition to attracting more productive workers, paying higher wages can result in a greater work effort, since workers would have a stronger incentive to retain their relatively high-paying jobs. Supervisory costs would be lower, since these highly paid workers would have less incentive to shirk, or slack off. And, finally, higher pay discourages workers from voluntarily leaving their jobs and, parenthetically, makes it harder for rival firms to lure them away with better job offers.

3. *The Insider-Outsider Theory*   Life is very much about being "in" or being "out." Think of the little poor girl, her nose pressed against the toy store window. The curtain separating the coach seats from the first class seats on nearly all commercial flights. The line of people behind the rope waiting to be recognized by the doorman at the club. As a friend once put it, "That place was so exclusive, I couldn't even get in with the 'out' crowd."

When millions of workers are laid off during a recession, they become the outsiders, while those who hang on to their jobs are now the insiders. We would expect many outsiders to offer to work for less than the current wage rate. And we would also expect many firms to accept such wage offers, since this would reduce their costs. Not according to the *insider-outsider theory*. The insiders, those still working for these firms, would greatly resent the new workers, who are not only undermining years of efforts to raise wages but who are replacing their co-workers who had been laid off. Many insiders would refuse to cooperate with these outsiders, whom, they may consider, as replacement workers, or, even worse, "scabs" (a term used to describe workers hired to replace those on strike). Employers may conclude that hiring outsiders at lower wages would end up being much more costly than not hiring them.

O.K., we've now established that wages are *not* downwardly flexible. Yet the belief that they are is a basic assumption of the classical economists and the rational expectationists. But most mainstream economists today believe that wages are inflexible downward for long periods, so that recovery from a recession might well take years.

This leaves us with a major economic policy disagreement: What should the government do when there's a recession? "Nothing," say the monetarists because policy makers are too incompetent to make the right decision. "Nothing," say the classical economists and the rational expectationists, since the economy will quickly and automatically move back to full employment. But this is definitely a minority view. Most economists today would agree that, since it might take years for our economy to work its way out of a recession, some monetary and fiscal policy actions would need to be taken.

In the event of inflation, this same policy dichotomy would be apparent. Although the monetarists might be somewhat amenable to a large degree of monetary restraint, the classical economists and rational expectationists would again suggest that the government do nothing. But the large majority of economists would again advocate some monetary and fiscal policy actions.

Twenty-First Century Economic Theory

In just the first two years of the new century we've already had a mild revival of the supply-side school, and the rise of a completely new school of economic thought— economic behaviorism. Here are some preliminary observations.

The Supply-Side Revival

In the early months of 2001 tax-cut fever swept through the nation's capital. With a projected federal budget surplus of $5.6 trillion over the next ten years, President George W. Bush asked Congress for a $1.6 trillion tax cut, most of which would be devoted to lowering federal personal income tax rates. Not to be outdone, Congressional Republicans, who held razor-thin majorities in both houses, opted for somewhat larger tax cuts, while Congressional Democrats called for cuts of a smaller magnitude than the president had proposed (see box, "Is Supply-Side Economics Enjoying a Revival?").

The basic premise of supply-side economics is that lower marginal tax rates would give people a greater incentive to work. Under President Bush's plan, for example, the top marginal tax rate of 39.6 percent would be cut to 33 percent, while taxpayers in each of the lower brackets—36 percent, 33 percent, 28 percent, and 15 percent—would also receive substantial tax cuts.

The question is: If your marginal tax rate is lowered (enabling you to keep more of your earnings), would you work more hours? The supply-siders say "Yes!"

As of spring, 2001, it seemed inevitable that a substantial tax cut would be enacted, but the details had not yet been worked out. And most important, the effects of this tax cut will not be apparent for at least another couple of years.

Is Supply-Side Economics Enjoying a Revival?

In the 1980s, when supply-side economics was in its ascendancy, personal income tax rates were slashed. Once again, at the beginning of the second Bush Administration, the president has proposed a large tax cut and Congress seems to be providing nearly all of the $1.6 trillion cut that he asked for. So it is reasonable to ask if supply-side economics is now enjoying a revival.

Back in 1980, when President George W. Bush's father, George Bush ran against Ronald Reagan for president in the Republican primaries, he dismissed Reagan's tax cut proposals as voodoo economics. Instead of being a coherent economic policy, supply-side economics, Bush implied, was more like sticking pins in a doll and then sitting back waiting for the magic to take effect. A few months later, having lost the Republican presidential nomination to Reagan, Bush agreed to run for vice president, even claiming to be a new convert to Reagan's faith in supply-side economics. He served as vice president under Reagan for eight years, watching as the president persuaded Congress to slash personal income tax rates (including a cut in the top marginal rate from 70 percent to just 28 percent).

When Bush finally got the Republican presidential nomination in 1988, he ran pretty much as a Ronald Reagan clone, even making his famous pledge, "Read my lips: no new taxes." Just two years later, as the federal budget deficit approached the $300 billion mark, President Bush very reluctantly agreed with the Democratic Congressional leaders to raise the top personal income tax rate to 31 percent in exchange for federal spending cuts. Not only was he violating his campaign pledge, but he was abandoning even the pretense of any belief in supply-side economics.

Ten years later, a son of the former president, George W. Bush, was elected president. His main campaign pledge? Cut taxes by $1.6 trillion over the next ten years. Question: Are we seeing a revival of supply-side economics?

Answer: Yes and no, but mainly no. Indeed, some observers have labeled Bush's tax proposals "supply-side lite." In 1981, Reagan secured an across-the-board income tax cut of 23 percent over three years. Bush is proposing a cut of about 10 percent over 10 years. While Reagan brought down the top marginal rate from 70 to 28, Bush hopes to bring it down from 39.6 to 33.

But a more fundamental difference is what each president hoped to accomplish. Ronald Reagan inherited an economy mired in an inflationary recession and a budget deficit that was large and growing. He expected that the tax cuts would not only restore our economic health, but increase the work incentive, raise tax revenue, and eliminate the budget deficit. The tax cuts did stimulate the economy, but were largely responsible for budget deficits that were threatening to spiral out of control.

The economy that George W. Bush inherited when he took office in January 2001 was one of great prosperity (unless you want to get picky by talking about the slowdown that had started during the last three months of the Clinton administration). In addition, we were running a budget surplus in fiscal year 2001 of some $237 billion. So Bush presented his tax cut simply as restoring to the American taxpayers what was rightfully theirs. And, almost as an afterthought, as the economic slowdown continued (only a few pessimists were calling it a recession), he talked more about how cutting taxes would stimulate the economy not just in the long run (over the next decade), but in the short run as well (preventing the slowdown from becoming a recession).

Although George W. Bush would never term it voodoo economics, he may be no more of a believer in supply-side economics than his father. Not only does he never utter the words "supply-side," but, unlike the administration of President Ronald Reagan, he has very few supply-side adherents working for him. At this early stage, in what school of economic thought would we place the president? I would say none. If nothing else, George W. Bush is an economic pragmatist.

The Economic Behaviorists

Believe it or not, in economics, like in popular music, we often ask ourselves, who's hot and who's not? Let's talk about a hot new group of young economists, many of whom are barely out of graduate school and are complete newcomers to the economic theory scene. Their work is just beginning to appear in some of the big economics journals, so it may be a while yet before they work their way up to the top of the charts. They call themselves economic behaviorists, and they're definitely going to hit it big.

Until the behavioral economists arrived upon the scene, a core belief among economists of all schools of thought was that people's actions were guided by rational, unemotional self-interest. So if you won the lottery, you would put most of this money aside for the rest of your life. The behavioral economists observed that most lottery winners quickly spent most or all of their winnings. Not very rational behavior, but very *human* behavior.

What would Americans do with President Bush's proposed tax cut? Mainstream economists believe a substantial portion would be saved. But the behavioral economists are probably right in predicting that nearly all of this tax cut will be spent. Instead of rationally balancing spending and saving over a lifetime, most people are indebted from youth to old age. How well does this behaviorist view describe your *own* finances?

The behaviorist view of the business cycle also departs from mainstream economic thinking. When the good times are rolling, most people seem to think that they will continue indefinitely. Remember the stock market boom in the 1990s? People kicked themselves for not putting more of their money in the market. Then, when the market tanked, those who were most heavily invested were the ones kicking themselves. During the economic boom during the late 1990s, many people thought the "new economy" had ushered in permanent prosperity. But should the economic slowdown of late 2000 and early 2001 develop into a full-fledged recession, the national psyche might quickly swing from overly optimistic to overly pessimistic.

In sum, the behavioral economists are not challenging the mainstream beliefs that rational behavior and economic self-interest are important motivators of economic behavior. But they *are* challenging the belief that these are the *only* motivating factors. Their goal is to apply a wider range of psychological concepts to economic theory.

Conclusion

What policies *should* we follow? Classical economists subscribed to Thomas Jefferson's dictum "The government that governs best, governs least." Because recessions will cure themselves, said the classicals, the government should adhere to a laissez-faire policy, allowing the private economic system to function without interference.

What policies should we follow?

The Keynesians stress fiscal policy. During recessions, run federal budget deficits; during inflations, run surpluses. Monetary policy? The latter-day Keynesians conceded that an expansionary monetary policy would be helpful, but Keynesian economics has always stressed the primacy of fiscal policy.

The supply-side school, sometimes considered the flip side of the Keynesian school, stresses the importance of tax rate cuts to give people greater work incentives. Although supply-siders basically believe in balanced budgets, temporary deficits are justified as unfortunate by-products of the tax rate cuts.

The monetarists want rules—a 3 to 4 percent rate of monetary growth and balanced budgets. Why? Because we simply don't know enough about the workings of our economy to successfully practice discretionary macroeconomic policy.

Despite the fact that he [Labor Secretary John Dunlop] is an economist, basically I have great confidence in him.
—George Meany

Finally, we have the new classical economists, who believe macroeconomic stabilization policy is self-defeating because people not only anticipate government actions, they also protect their own economic interests so that the intended effects of the government policy are immediately and fully canceled out.

Murray Weidenbaum, who served as chairman of President Reagan's Council of Economic Advisors, puts a lot of what we've been talking about in this chapter into perspective:

> Each of the major schools of economic thought can be useful on occasion. The insights of Keynesian economics proved appropriate for Western societies attempting to get out of deep depression in the 1930s. The tools of monetarism were powerfully effective in squeezing out the inflationary force of the 1970s. Supply-side economics played an important role in getting the public to understand the high costs of taxation

Economics is the only field in which two people can share a Nobel Prize for saying opposing things.

—Roberto Alazar

and thus to support tax reform in the 1980s. But sensible public policy cannot long focus on any one objective or be limited to one policy approach.[5]

Where does all of this leave us? It leaves us just about where we were at the beginning of this chapter: about the only thing economists can agree on is that they disagree.

Don't despair. After the great debate between the monetarists and the Keynesians in the appendix to this chapter, I'll try to tie things together in the next chapter on macroeconomic policy. I'll attempt to draw on the collective wisdom of the five schools of economics to attain the oft-stated goals of stable prices, high employment, and a satisfactory rate of economic growth.

Questions for Further Thought and Discussion

1. According to the classical economists, how did Say's law, the interest rate mechanism, and downwardly flexible wages and prices ensure that recessions would cure themselves?

2. According to John Maynard Keynes, what was the basic problem during recessions, and what was his solution?

3. What is the monetary rule and why is it favored by the monetarists?

4. What is the Laffer curve? How do supply-siders use it with respect to tax rates?

5. What are the three basic assumptions of the rational expectations theorists? Are they valid?

6. Are wages flexible downward? Explain your answer.

7. Is there any consensus among at least some of the different schools of economic thought with respect to the effectiveness of monetary and fiscal policy?

8. How does the crude quantity theory of money differ from the modern, sophisticated version?

9. When a recession begins, if the federal government spent tens of billions of dollars on a highway building program and consequently ran a large deficit, how would this fiscal policy measure be judged by each of the five main schools of 20th century economic thought?

---

[5]Murray Weidenbaum, *Rendezvous with Reality* (New York: Basic Books, 1988), p. 23.

Workbook for Chapter 15

Name _____ Date _____

Multiple-Choice Questions

Circle the letter that corresponds to the best answer.

1. Say's law states that _____.
   a) supply creates its own demand
   b) demand creates its own supply
   c) demand will always exceed supply
   d) supply will always exceed demand

2. The bible of classical economics was written by _____.
   a) John Maynard Keynes
   b) Milton Friedman
   c) Karl Marx
   d) Adam Smith

3. According to the classical economists, if the quantity of money that people wanted to save was greater than the amount that people wanted to invest, _____.
   a) there would be a recession
   b) there would be inflation
   c) the interest rate would fall
   d) the interest rate would rise

4. The classical economists believed _____.
   a) both wages and prices were downwardly flexible
   b) neither wages nor prices were downwardly flexible
   c) wages, but not prices, were downwardly flexible
   d) prices, but not wages, were downwardly flexible

5. The classicals believed recessions were _____.
   a) impossible
   b) potential depressions
   c) temporary
   d) hard to end without government intervention

6. The problem during recessions, said John Maynard Keynes, was _____.
   a) inadequate aggregate supply
   b) inadequate aggregate demand
   c) too much inflation
   d) too much government intervention

7. According to Keynes, _____ was necessary to get us out of a depression.
   a) investment spending
   b) consumer spending
   c) foreign spending
   d) any kind of spending.

8. Keynes believed budget deficits were _____.
   a) to be avoided at all costs
   b) bad during recessions
   c) good during recessions
   d) good all the time

9. The key to investment spending, said Keynes, was _____.
   a) the interest rate
   b) the expected profit rate
   c) foreign spending
   d) government spending

10. Classical economics lost most of its popularity in _____.
    a) the 1920s   c) the 1960s
    b) the 1930s   d) the 1980s

11. Big government was ushered in during the _____.
    a) 1920s   c) 1960s
    b) 1930s   d) 1980s

12. To the monetarists, the most important thing was _____.
    a) the rate of growth of the money supply
    b) balancing the federal budget
    c) raising the federal government's tax base
    d) giving the Federal Reserve free reign

13. During a recession, if the money supply were increased _____.

    a) the Keynesians and the monetarists agree that people would probably just hold on to these funds

    b) the Keynesians and the monetarists agree that people would spend this money on assets of one kind or another

    c) the Keynesians believe people would probably just hold on to these funds, while the monetarists believe people would spend this money on assets of one kind or another

14. Which of the following is a basic proposition of monetarism?

    a) The key to stable economic growth is a constant rate of increase in the money supply.

    b) Expansionary monetary policy will permanently depress the interest rates.

    c) Expansionary monetary policy will permanently reduce the unemployment rate.

    d) Expansionary fiscal policy will permanently raise output and employment.

15. The monetary rule states that _____.

    a) the federal budget must be balanced every year

    b) the money supply must increase at the same rate as the price level

    c) the money supply must remain a constant from year to year

    d) the money supply must be increased at a constant rate

16. The monetarists criticized _____.

    a) the stop-and-go policies of the Federal Reserve

    b) the ineffectiveness of monetary policy at fighting inflation

    c) the importance given to money by the Keynesians

    d) the Fed for keeping a heavy foot on the monetary brake and allowing the money supply to rise by only 3 percent a year

17. Supply-siders felt _____.

    a) the federal government played too large an economic role

    b) the federal government played too small an economic role

    c) tax rates were too low

    d) the federal government was not spending enough to meet the needs of the poor

18. According to the supply-siders, each of the following resulted from high marginal tax rates except _____.

    a) the work effect

    b) the savings-investment effect

    c) the elimination of productive market exchanges

    d) lagging demand for imported goods and services

19. Each of the following is associated with supply-side economics except _____.

    a) Ronald Reagan   c) Milton Friedman

    b) Arthur Laffer   d) Kemp-Roth

20. According to the Laffer curve, when very high marginal tax rates are lowered, tax revenue will _____.

    a) decline considerably   c) stay the same

    b) decline slightly   d) increase

21. The rational expectations theorists said anti-inflationary policy will _____.

    a) generally work

    b) definitely do more harm than good

    c) either do no good or do harm

22. According to the rational expectations theorists, everyone learns that when the Fed sharply increases monetary growth _____.

    a) inflation will result and people must move to protect themselves

    b) a recession will result and people must move to protect themselves

    c) people will continue to make the same mistakes over and over again

23. The effects of most macroeconomic policy changes, say the rational expectations theorists, are _____.
   a) very hard to predict
   b) very easy to predict
   c) slow—that is, they take place over a period of many years
   d) irrational

24. The advice the rational expectations theorists give the federal government is to _____.
   a) change macropolicy often
   b) figure out the right policies to follow and stick to them
   c) figure out what the public is expecting and then do the opposite

25. Which school would advocate government spending to end a recession?
   a) classical   d) supply-side
   b) Keynesian   e) rational expectations
   c) monetarist

26. Which school would consider cutting tax rates as the cure for all our economic ills?
   a) classical   d) supply-side
   b) Keynesian   e) rational expectations
   c) monetarist

27. MV = PQ _____.
   a) all the time   c) some of the time
   b) most of the time   d) never

28. The output of our economy is represented by the letter in the equation of exchange.
   a) M   c) P
   b) V   d) Q

29. If MV rises, PQ _____.
   a) must rise   c) must stay the same
   b) may rise   d) must fall

30. The crude quantity theory of money states that if MV rises by 20 percent, PQ will _____.
   a) fall by 20 percent   d) rise
   b) fall   e) rise by 20 percent
   c) stay the same

31. The modern monetarists believe _____.
   a) V is very unstable
   b) V never changes
   c) any changes in V are either very small or predictable
   d) if M rises, V will fall by the same percentage

32. As we approach full employment, what will probably happen?
   a) V will fall   d) P will rise
   b) Q will fall   e) P will fall
   c) Q will rise

33. Each of the following explains why wages are not downwardly flexible *except* _____.
   a) the efficiency wage theory
   b) the law of diminishing returns
   c) the insider-outsider theory
   d) labor contracts
   e) the minimum wage

34. The rational expectationists believe that fiscal and monetary policy are _____.
   a) most effective fighting recessions
   b) most effective fighting inflation
   c) more effective in influence aggregate supply than aggregate demand
   d) not effective

35. The tax cut proposed by President George W. Bush in 2001 was most in accord with the _____ school.
   a) classical
   b) Keynesian
   c) monetarist
   d) rational expectationist
   e) supply-side

36. Which of the following is the most accurate statement?
    a) A large cut in marginal tax rates will not result in an increase in the number of hours that people work.
    b) President Bush's proposed tax cut in 2001 was opposed by virtually all economists and nearly all members of Congress.
    c) The behaviorist economists predict Americans would spend nearly all of a substantial tax cut.
    d) The Keynesians oppose tax cuts because they are afraid that federal government budget deficits will result.

37. The behaviorial economists believe that economic behavior is guided _____.
    a) entirely by rational, unemotional self-interest.
    b) entirely by emotions.
    c) by both rational self-interest and emotions.
    d) by neither rational self-interest nor emotions.

Fill-In Questions

1. Say's law states that _____ _____.

2. According to the classical economists, if there is a recession, the government should _____ _____.

3. The classicals, applying Say's law, believed all our income would be _____; all our production would be _____, and all our savings would be _____.

4. The classicals said if the amount of money people wanted to save was greater than the amount business-people wanted to invest, _____ _____.

5. The classical school dominated economic thought until _____.

6. John Maynard Keynes defined aggregate demand as _____ plus _____ plus _____.

7. According to Keynes, the most important determinant of the level of investment was the _____.

8. According to Keynes, the main institutional barriers to downward wage and price flexibility were (1) _____ and (2) _____.

9. The main success of Keynesian economics in the 1960s was _____.

10. John Maynard Keynes said that during recessions and depressions, the main problem was _____ _____.

11. To solve that problem, Keynes suggested _____ _____.

12. Monetarism begins and ends with one obsession: _____.

13. Milton Friedman concluded that we have never had a serious inflation that was not accompanied by _____.

14. The monetarists believed that if the money supply were raised during a recession, people would _____.

15. According to the monetarists, recessions are caused by _____.

16. The key to stable economic growth, according to the monetarists, is _____.

17. The record of the Fed, say the monetarists, is analogous to _____.

18. The monetary rule states that _____ _____.

19. The monetarists say expansionary monetary policy will _____ depress interest rates and the unemployment rate. They further say expansionary monetary policy will _____ raise output and employment.

20. Supply-side economics came into vogue in_____ _____.

21. The objective of supply-side economics is to _____ _____. The problem, said the supply-siders, was that _____ were hurting the incentive to work and invest.

22. The way to get people to work more, say the supply-siders, is to _____.

23. According to the Laffer curve, reducing very high marginal tax rates will result in _____ federal tax revenue.

24. Most macroeconomic policy changes, say the rational expectations theorists, are _____ _____.

25. The main criticism leveled at the rational expectations theorists is that _____ _____.

Problems

1. If M were 600 and V were 10, how much would PQ be?

2. According to the crude quantity theory of money, if M were to increase by 10 percent, what would happen to V, P, and Q?

3. If M were 800, P were 20, and Q were 400, how much would V be?

4. Initially $M = 600$, $V = 8$, $P = 16$, and $Q = 300$. According to the crude quantity theory of money, if M rose to 720, how much would P be?

5. If P were 7 and Q were 800, how much would MV be?

Appendix A

The Great Money Debate:
The Keynesians versus the Monetarists

The Keynesian and monetarist schools of economic thought have been spoiling for a fight since way back in Chapter 10. After keeping them apart all this time, I've decided to let them fight it out once and for all. After a preliminary bout following the objectives, you'll see the main event, a scheduled four-rounder for the economic title of the world. (Actually, the title is split several ways, but why get into that now?)

APPENDIX OBJECTIVES

These four topics will be debated:

- The stability of V.
- The transmission mechanism.
- Monetary policy.
- A question of timing.

Preliminary Debate

As I've frequently noted, the only thing on which economists seem to agree is that they disagree on just about everything. The two groups of economists who disagree with each other the most are the monetarists and the Keynesians. We're going to take up three major areas of disagreement, each of which happens to be related to money.

First, there's the question of how stable V, the velocity of money, happens to be. Then, there's the transmission mechanism, which is the mechanism by which changes in the demand for and the supply of money affect aggregate demand. Finally, we'll look at the effectiveness of monetary and fiscal policy.

The time has finally arrived to let the Keynesians and the monetarists duke it out. This appendix has been given over to them for that purpose. I'll step back and let them go at it, only occasionally intervening to separate them in the clinches and ring the bell at the end of each round. You'll decide who won the bout.

Round 1: How Stable Is V?

Velocity and Changes in the Money Supply

The Keynesians believe changes in the level of the money supply affect the level of aggregate demand through the interest rate. An increase in the money supply lowers the interest rate, raising investment and, consequently, aggregate demand. Similarly, a decrease in the money supply raises the interest rate, thus lowering investment and aggregate demand.

The monetarists see a more direct link between the money supply and the level of GDP than the Keynesians see. When the money supply is increased, it creates excess money balances held by individuals. This money burns a hole—so to speak—in their pockets, so they spend it. Poof! Up goes aggregate demand, or GDP.

A decrease in the money supply, say the monetarists, has the opposite effect. Consumers and business firms find themselves short of funds. They would like to carry certain money balances but find themselves carrying less. What do they do? They cut back on spending, and down goes aggregate demand.

In this reasoning, there is an implicit assumption about V (velocity), which, you may or may not recall, is part of the equation of exchange we discussed at the beginning of the chapter: $MV = PQ$ (M is the money supply; V is the velocity of circulation, or the number of times each dollar in our money supply is spent during the year; P is the price level, or the average price of all final goods and services sold during the year; and Q is the quantity of transactions, or the number of things sold during the year, or simply output).

If a rise in M raises PQ (or GDP), V must be constant. This, the monetarists maintain, is true in the short run, which might be for a year or two.

If velocity were a perfect constant—that is, a number that stayed exactly the same—changes in M would lead to precisely predictable changes in PQ or GDP. The application of monetary policy would become an exact science, something even the most ardent supporters of the Federal Reserve Board would not dare to hope for. Imagine the power of monetary policy if we knew that a 3 percent rise in the money supply, M, would lead to exactly a 3 percent rise in GDP (PQ). Unfortunately, V will not hold still for us. But the monetarists say V is relatively stable in the short run. And that's the next best thing.

How Stable Is Velocity in the Short Run?

The Keynesians and the monetarists clash sharply with respect to the short-run stability of V. In a word, the monetarists say V is stable, and the Keynesians say it isn't. Perhaps more significant, the monetarists claim V is predictable in the short run, while the Keynesians say it isn't.

The Keynesians maintain that V is sensitive to interest rate changes. When interest rates rise, people will be more likely to hold more interest-bearing assets and less money. Conversely, when interest rates decline, people tend to increase their money holdings. This responsiveness of money balances to interest rate changes is Keynes's speculative demand for money.

Now, if interest rates rise and people hold less money, they will have to make more efficient use of their money balances to meet their day-to-day transactions needs—V will rise. And if interest rates fall, people will tend to hold more money, some of which will lie idly, thus pushing down V.

The Keynesian view of how changes in M affect V is diametrically opposed to the monetarist position. The latter, of course, holds that in the short run V will be constant, but the Keynesians say a change in M may lead to a change in V in the opposite direction.

The Keynesians maintain that a decline in the money supply pushes up interest rates. Consequently, people buy more bonds (whose prices have fallen). This churns the money supply, increasing velocity.

Similarly, if the money supply rises, interest rates fall, bond prices rise, and people sell some of the bonds they are holding.[1] They end up holding more cash, thereby decreasing velocity.

The Keynesians therefore conclude that velocity varies inversely with changes in the money supply. Consequently, an expansionary monetary policy may be partially or fully negated by a decline in velocity. And contractionary monetary policy may be similarly canceled by a rising velocity. Although changes in the money supply and velocity are inversely related, the Keynesians have no way to measure the magnitude of the changes in velocity caused by changes in the money supply.

It follows that there is no way, according to the Keynesians, of predicting how changes in the money supply will affect the price level.

The monetarists, however, dispute the Keynesians' claim that velocity is unstable in the short run. What determines velocity in the short run? The monetarists have identified three determinants: (1) the frequency with which people are paid; (2) people's inflationary expectations; and (3) the level of real interest rates.

The first determinant changes only very gradually. Employers, as a group, do not suddenly change from paying their employees once a week to once a month, or vice versa.

Expectations of inflation also do not suddenly arise, nor do they suddenly subside. It takes years for an inflation to gather momentum and for the public's perception of that inflation to take hold. Similarly, when inflation begins to subside, it will take a few years for inflationary expectations to subside as well.

Finally, we have real interest rates. These are the rates of return that bondholders receive after inflation. Suppose you receive 12 percent interest on a bond when there is currently a 5 percent inflation rate. We would say that the 12 percent interest rate is only the nominal rate, and that after the 5 percent rate of inflation is deducted, you are left with a real rate of interest of only 7 percent. Again, the monetarists believe that while nominal interest rates will rise and fall with the inflation rate, real interest rates remain relatively stable, at least in the short run.

Thus, the monetarists contend, because each of the three determinants of velocity is stable in the short run, then velocity must be stable in the short run as well.

Whether or not the monetarists have made a convincing case about the short-run stability of V, they have left themselves an escape hatch: V does not have to be stable in the short run for the sophisticated quantity theory to hold up. It just has to be predictable in the short run. Is it?

Again, the Keynesians just say no! They point to the experience of the 1930s and 1940s when V fluctuated widely, plunging from 4 in 1929 to 3 in 1932 and, after fluctuating widely through the rest of the decade, dropping to 2 during World War II. The monetarists prefer to look at the postwar period, particularly the 1960s and 1970s (see Figure 1). "Aha!" reply the Keynesians. "Then why not look at the 1980s as well?" During this decade V certainly had its ups and downs.

The stability of V is certainly in the eye of the beholder. But we can make a few generalizations. During wars and recessions, V is prone to decline as people tend to hold on to their money. We may account for V's decline in the mid-1980s by the change in how the Fed counted our money supply. Until then, only currency and demand deposits at commercial banks were counted. But suddenly the Fed was also including checklike deposits at thrift institutions. We can show the effect of this change algebraically: GDP is total spending. So is MV (the money supply multiplied by the number of times per year each dollar is spent). Therefore, MV = GDP.

Now divide both sides of this equation by M.

$$MV/M = GDP/M$$

$$V = GDP/M$$

The monetarists have identified three determinants of V in the short run.

The stability of V is in the eye of the beholder.

MV = GDP

$$V = \frac{GDP}{M}$$

---

[1] The section "How Open-Market Operations Work" in Chapter 14 showed that bond prices and interest are inversely related.

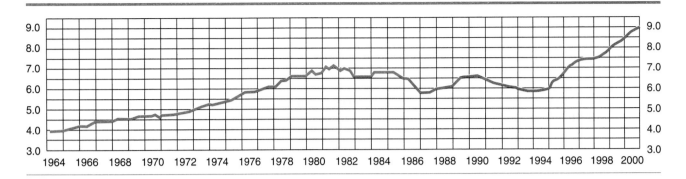

Figure 1

The Velocity of Money Circulation, 1964–2000

Velocity has risen from below 4 in 1964 to nearly 8 in 2000 mainly because individuals and businesses have grown increasingly reluctant to hold idle money balances.
Source: Economic Report of the President, 1994, 1995, and 2001.

What happens to the value or size of V if M gets larger? It goes down.

Quite possibly, then, the reason V declined in 1985 and 1986 was because of the change in the definition of M. We could conclude that except for times of war and recession, V has changed very little from one year to the next.

There has been a historical upward trend in V, which the monetarists readily acknowledge. This has been due to the expanded use of credit and credit cards, both of which, the monetarists would remind us, are fully predictable. Because people rely more on credit, they make better or more efficient use of their money balances, thereby pushing up V. In addition, there was a slow but steady decline in the money supply since 1994.

Is V stable?

Is V predictable? The monetarists make an excellent case for the "normal years" of the last three and a half decades. But during the "abnormal years" of the Depression and World War II, V has been neither stable nor predictable. So we may conclude that as long as our economy behaves normally, V is predictable (if not completely stable) in the short run and that the sophisticated quantity theory does hold up.

Round 2: The Transmission Mechanism

Introduction

Before championship bouts begin, we are usually treated to exhaustive analyses of the strategies and tactics of the two opponents. This section will do just that. The next three sections will bring you the Keynesian view, the monetarist view, and, finally, a comparison of the Keynesian and monetarist transmission mechanisms. The Keynesian position: an increase in the money supply depresses the interest rate. Given a certain MEI (marginal efficiency of investment) schedule, investment becomes more attractive and, therefore, increases. This, in turn, pushes up aggregate demand, and as we approach full employment, prices will rise as well. The monetarist position: a large increase in the money supply creates an imbalance in the money balances held by the public. People are holding more money than they wish to. What do they do? They spend this surplus on stocks and bonds, real estate, money market funds, and consumer durables. This, in turn, pushes up the prices of these assets. Finally, interest rates rise as lenders demand an inflation premium to compensate them for being repaid in inflated dollars.

Effects of a money supply increase: Keynesian and monetarist views

We can now sum up the effects of a money supply increase as seen by the Keynesians and the monetarists, respectively:

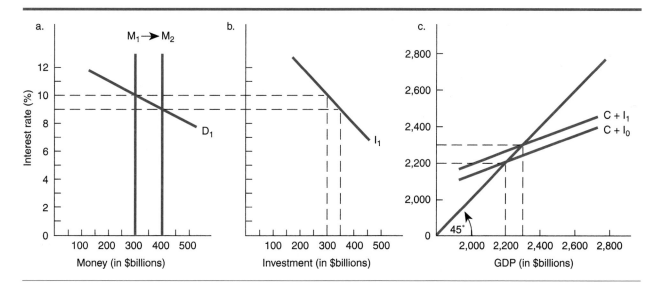

Figure 2

The Keynesian Transmission Mechanism

An increase in the money supply (from 300 to 400) in panel (a) leads to an interest rate decline of 1 percent (from 10 percent to 9 percent) and an increase in the level of investment from 300 to 350 in panel (b), which, in turn, leads to an increase in GDP from 2200 to 2300 in panel (c). Note that the $100 billion increase in the money supply lowered the interest rate by *just* 1 percent, that investment rose by *just* $50 billion, and that GDP rose by *just* $100 billion.

Keynesians: M $\uparrow$ → Interest rates $\downarrow$ → Prices$\uparrow$

Monetarists: M $\uparrow$ → Interest rates $\uparrow$ → Prices$\uparrow$

The monetarists and the Keynesians both believe large increases in the money supply will lead to rising prices. But they differ with respect to how interest rates and the level of investment are affected. The monetarists expect that rising prices will push up interest rates[2] and that, consequently, investment will fall. The Keynesians, on the other hand, look for a different sequence of events. A large increase in the money supply will push down interest rates and raise the level of investment.

When the Federal Reserve increases the money supply, what effect does this have on the level of interest rates, investment, and GDP? That depends on who answers this question.

The Keynesian View

A rise in the money supply will lead to a decline in the interest rate. At this lower interest rate, people will want to hold more money. Why? Number one: the opportunity cost of holding money (the interest rate) has gone down. Number two: at a lower interest rate, the price of bonds has gone up. Why buy bonds now? Why not wait until bond prices come back down?

We'll go over the entire process—what an increase in the money supply does to interest rates, the level of investment, and the level of GDP—step-by-step, using the graphs in Figure 2. *Step 1* is shown in Figure 2a. The demand for money, D1, is relatively flat. An increase of $100 billion in the money supply (from M1 to M2) leads to a decline of only 1 percent in the interest rate (from 10 percent to 9 percent).

Keynesians: A rise in M will lead to a decline in the interest rate.

---

[2]This is in the long run. They concede that in the short run interest rates may fall when the money supply goes up.

Step 2. In Figure 2b, what effect does this 1 percent decline in the interest rate have on the level of investment in the Keynesian system? It will raise investment, but not by much. Why? Because business firms are much more responsive to change in the expected profit rate (or the marginal efficiency of investment) than they are to interest rate changes.

Figure 2b shows a relatively steep investment demand curve, I_1, which means investment will not rise much in response to a decline in the interest rate. Here, a 1 percent interest rate decline leads to a rise in investment of just $50 billion.

Step 3. Before we began this whole process, equilibrium GDP stood at 2,200. Now we have a $50 billion increase in investment. By how much will this raise GDP? That depends entirely on the size of the multiplier. Here we'll assume a multiplier of 2, so a $50 billion increase in investment leads to a $100 billion increase in GDP. This last move is shown in Figure 2c.

Let's review the three steps of the Keynesian transmission mechanism. In this particular case, when the Fed raises the money supply by $100 billion, the interest rate falls by just 1 percent. This, in turn, leads to an increase in the level of investment of just $50 billion. Finally, with a multiplier of 2, the $50 billion rise in investment leads to a $100 billion rise in GDP. Perhaps $100 billion seems like a big increase, but it is relatively small when compared to the increase that takes place under the monetarist transmission mechanism.

The Monetarist View

Monetarists: A rise in M leads to a rise in spending.

Changes in the money supply, according to the monetarists, cause people to change their spending behavior. When the money supply rises sharply, people find themselves holding more money than they wish to. So what do they do? They spend it.

I don't mean they rush out to the shopping mall and buy up everything in sight. Rather, they add to their portfolios of assets. They might put the money into stocks and bonds, money market funds, real estate, or perhaps gold, a new car, or a video system.

People are constantly shifting their holdings among the various assets in their portfolios. If real estate becomes relatively attractive, they will shift into that from stocks and bonds and money market funds. If bond prices should fall (i.e., interest rates rise), people will put more money into bonds.

When the money supply is rising quickly, people will be pouring their excess cash balances into these various portfolio holdings, which, in turn, will drive up the prices of these holdings. This explains the heading for this section—the transmission mechanism. As the money supply grows, individual wealth holders transmit this increase into price increases. Put more succinctly by the monetarists, because money burns holes in people's pockets, they will spend it, thereby driving up prices.

Let's turn to Figure 3.

Step 1. In Figure 3a, when the Fed increases the money supply by $100 billion, from M1 to M2, this leads to a substantial decline in the interest rate—from 10 percent to 8 percent. Why? Because when people get their hands on this money, they buy things with it. Bonds are among the things they buy. When the demand for anything goes up, given a fixed supply, its price is driven up. Because bond prices and the interest rate are inversely related, as bond prices go up, interest rates fall.

Why does the interest rate come down so much? Because the demand for money, D_2, is relatively steep, according to the monetarists. Why? Because people have one basic reason to hold money: for transactions purposes. They will hold just enough money to handle their day-to-day personal and business needs, regardless of the interest rate. Thus, people would not alter their money balances much in response to even substantial interest rate changes.

Step 2. In Figure 3b, a 2 percent decline in the interest rate (from 10 percent to 8 percent) leads to a big increase in investment, from $300 billion to $500 billion. Why so big? Because the investment demand curve, I_2, is relatively flat. In other words, according to the monetarists, investment is very responsive to interest rate changes.

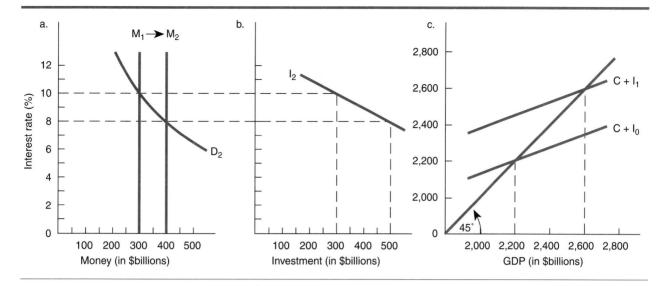

F*igure* 3

The Monetarist Transmission Mechanism

An increase in the money supply (from 300 to 400) in panel (a) leads to an interest rate decline of 2 percent (from 10 percent to 8 percent) and an increase in the level of investment from 300 to 500 in panel (b), which, in turn, leads to an increase in GDP from 2200 to 2600 in panel (c). Note that the $100 billion increase in the money supply lowered the interest rate by 2 percent, that investment rose by $200 billion, and that GDP rose by $400 billion. In Figure 2, under the Keynesian transmission mechanism, a $100 billion increase in the money supply led to a decline of just 1 percent in the interest rate, an increase of just $50 billion in investment, and an increase of just $100 billion in GDP.

Step 3. In Figure 3c, this $200 billion investment increase gives rise to a $400 billion increase in GDP, assuming, once again, a multiplier of 2.

Let's review the steps. An increase of $100 billion in the money supply leads to a 2 percent decline in the interest rate, which, in turn, leads to a $200 billion increase in the level of investment. Assuming a multiplier of 2, GDP will then rise by $400 billion.

Comparison of Keynesian and Monetarist Transmission Mechanisms

When the money supply rises by $100 billion, why does the monetarist analysis lead to a GDP increase four times larger than that of the Keynesian analysis ($400 billion compared to $100 billion)?

There are two reasons. First, look at the slopes of the money demand curves, D_1 (in Figure 2a) and D_2 (in Figure 3a). Notice that D_2 is much steeper than D_1. In other words, the demand for money is much less responsive to the interest rate under monetarist analysis. The Keynesians believe people will want to hold a lot more money as the interest rate declines.

The second basic difference has to do with how responsive the demand for investment funds is to interest rate changes. The monetarists believe investment demand is very responsive to interest rate changes, while the Keynesians feel it is not.

These two very basic differences lead to very different conclusions. The Keynesians feel an increase in the money supply will not lead to a substantial increase in investment; the monetarists think it will. As we shall see, the Keynesians do not believe monetary policy can have a substantial impact on our economy, while the monetarists believe changes in the rate of growth of the money supply have a powerful economic effect.

The monetarists believe an increase in M will lead to a much greater increase in GDP than the Keynesians do.

the brake too soon, we have another round of inflation. If it doesn't, we have a severe recession. Thus, once more we're faced with their only policy prescription: the monetary rule.

Round 4: A Question of Timing

The Lags

Timing, in economic policy as in most other areas, is of utmost importance. The effectiveness of both monetary and fiscal policy depends greatly on timing. Unfortunately, both of these policies are subject to three lags: the recognition, decision, and impact lags.

Suppose our economy enters a recession and the government provides a counteracting stimulus. What if this stimulus does not have full impact until recovery has set in? The end result of this well-intentioned government policy will be to destabilize the economy by making the recovery and subsequent prosperity far too exuberant. Similarly, if the government were to try to damp down an inflation, but the effects of its policy were not felt until the economy had already entered a recession, the policy would end up making the recession that much worse.

The recognition lag is the time it takes for policy makers to realize that a business cycle's turning point has been passed, or that either inflation or unemployment has become a particular problem. The decision lag is the time it takes for policy makers to decide what to do and to take action. And finally, the impact lag is the time it takes for the policy action to have a substantial effect. The whole process may take anywhere from about nine months to more than three years.

Fiscal Policy Lags

The lengths of the three lags under fiscal policy are not well defined. First, the recognition lag is the time it takes the president and a majority of both houses of Congress to recognize that something is broken and needs fixing—either an inflation or a recession. You would be amazed at how long this can take. In August 1981 we entered a recession, but in the spring of the following year President Reagan still could not bring himself to admit that we were actually in a recession (which, incidentally, proved to be the worst downturn since the Great Depression).

Congress, which at the time was divided between a Republican Senate and a Democratic House, also took some time to recognize the problem. This state of affairs was similar to that of 1967; inflation was beginning to get out of hand, but the president and Congress were reluctant to recognize the obvious.

Once the president *and* Congress recognize that something needs to be done about the economy, they must decide what action to take. After investigating the problem with his advisers, the president may make a fiscal policy recommendation to Congress. This recommendation, among others, is studied by appropriate subcommittees and committees, hearings are held, expert witnesses called, votes taken. Eventually bills may be passed by both houses, reconciled by a joint House-Senate committee, repassed by both houses, and sent to the president for his signature. This process usually takes several months. Finally, if the president likes the bill, he signs it. (If he doesn't, Congress may override his veto, but it usually doesn't.)

All this delay is part of the decision lag. We still have the impact lag. Once a spending bill, say a highway reconstruction measure, has been passed for the purpose of stimulating an economy that is mired in recession, a year may pass before the bulk of the appropriated funds is actually spent and has made a substantial economic impact. By then, of course, the country may already have begun to recover from the recession.

Monetary Policy Lags

One would expect monetary policy time lags to be somewhat shorter than fiscal policy time lags. The Board of Governors, which always has at least three or four professional economists among its membership, continually monitors the economy. Further, because the Board has only seven members, with the chair playing the dominant role, a consensus with respect to policy changes is reached far more easily than it is under our political method of conducting fiscal policy. While the legislative wrangling among the members of each house of Congress, between the two houses, and between the president and Congress may take several months, consensus among the seven members of the Fed is reached relatively quickly. The decision lag is thus fairly short.

How long is the impact lag—the time until monetary policy changes have a substantial effect? Economists estimate this time as anywhere from nine months to about three years. Further, there is some agreement that a tight money policy will slow down an inflation more quickly than an easy money policy will hasten a recovery. Still, there is no general agreement on whether monetary policy or fiscal policy is faster—or more effective.

While the goals of monetary policy and fiscal policy are identical—low unemployment and stable prices—the effects of each are felt in different economic sectors. Fiscal policy is generally directed toward the consumer sector (tax cuts) or the government sector (spending programs). Monetary policy, however, has its strongest impact on the investment sector. In brief, tight money discourages investment, and a rapidly growing money supply has the opposite effect. The only question, then, is how long it takes before the investment sector feels the impact of monetary policy changes.

Corporate investment does not fall off precipitously when the interest rate rises, nor does it shoot up when the interest rate falls. Although investment in plant and equipment becomes more attractive when the interest rate declines, as a rule large corporations take months, and sometimes years, to formulate investment plans. Therefore, transitory changes in the availability of investment funds or the rate of interest do not have a substantial impact on the level of investment in the short run. However, over a two- or three-year period, it's another story.

Thus, when we talk about the impact lag for monetary policy, we have to discuss that lag in terms of years rather than months. This is not to say that monetary policy changes have no impact for years, but rather that the substantial impact of these changes may not be felt for two or three years.

During a period of inflation, the proper monetary policy for the Fed to pursue is to slow down or even halt the growth of the money supply. But what if, by the time this is done and has had any impact, the economy has already entered a recession? Clearly it will make that recession even worse.

During a period of recession, what is the proper monetary policy? To speed up the rate of growth of the money supply. But suppose that by the time this policy has had any impact, recovery has begun? Oh no! Now this monetary expansion will fuel the next round of inflation.

To sum up, because of the recognition lag, the decision lag, and especially the impact lag, monetary policy is too slow to have its intended effect. By the time the monetary brakes are working to halt an inflation, the economy may have already entered a recession; and when an expansionary monetary policy is pursued to bring the economy out of a recession, recovery has already set in. Thus, because of the time lags, monetary policy may actually destabilize the economy. The Fed surely did not intend to have that effect, but the road to economic instability is often paved with good intentions.

The time lag in monetary policy invites a good-news/bad-news scenario. The good news is that there's a time lag. That's the *good* news? What's the *bad* news? It's a variable time lag. How variable? Monetarists believe it may be as short as six months or a long as two years.

Therefore, even if the Fed could take the time lag into account when it decides to slow the monetary growth rate to fight an inflation, how long a lag should it allow for? Six months? A year? A year and a half? Two years?

Recognition lag is usually shorter for monetary than for fiscal policy.

Fiscal versus Monetary Policy: A Summing Up

The Keynesians argue that fiscal policy is a much more powerful and reliable macro-policy tool than monetary policy. Why? Because fiscal policy, particularly increasing government spending during a recession, has a direct and substantial effect on GDP, where monetary policy is relatively weak and uncertain in effect.

When the government spends more money, G rises and has a multiplied effect on GDP. It happens one, two, three: (1) G rises; (2) it has a multiplied effect on GDP; and (3) GDP rises. That's fiscal policy—short and sweet.

But monetary policy, say the Keynesians, involves a longer and more variable sequence. Let's look at the effects of an expansion in the money supply. The Fed buys securities on the open market, creating more bank reserves. Will the banks lend out all these reserves? Only if they want to and are able to. Will there be a sufficient number of creditworthy borrowers who will want to borrow money during a recession to build new plant and equipment and expand their inventories?

If this money *is* lent out, the money supply will expand, but keep in mind the Keynesian assumptions of a relatively flat monetary demand curve and a relatively steep investment demand curve. A substantial increase in the money supply will lead to a relatively small decline in the interest rate. This, in turn, will lead to a small increase in investment and, eventually, a small increase in GDP.

Unlike the Keynesians, the monetarists believe a change in monetary policy has a short, direct, and powerful effect on GDP. An increase in M, assuming a stable or predictable V, will have a direct and predictable effect on PQ (which is GDP). The monetarists, like the classical economists before them, believe the private economy tends to operate near, or at full employment. Therefore, any large increase in M will be translated into increases in P.[4]

Where does all this leave us? Who won the fight? I think you would agree that both the monetarists and the Keynesians got in some good licks. But who won? That's a good question. I don't know. Who do *you* think won?

Questions for Further Thought and Discussion

1. How does the Keynesian view of the transmission mechanism differ from the monetarist view?

2. How do the Keynesians' and the monetarists' policy prescriptions differ with respect to fighting (a) inflations and (b) recessions?

3. Is velocity stable in the short run? Where does the evidence point?

4. Suppose the money supply rose by 5 percent during the year, while nominal GDP remained the same. What could we conclude about velocity?

5. How much money do you usually have (including cash and the balance in your checking account)? Divide this into your total income over the past year to obtain your own personal velocity.

---

[4]If the economy is near or at full employment, Q can't increase much; the only give would be in P. Because PQ must rise in proportion to the increase in M, the rise in PQ will be all, or nearly all, in P.

Workbook for Appendix A to Chapter 15

Name _____ Date _____

Multiple-Choice Questions

Circle the letter that corresponds to the best answer.

1. The two groups of economists who disagree with each other more than any others are the _____ .

   a) supply-siders and Keynesians

   b) supply-siders and monetarists

   c) monetarists and Keynesians

2. The Keynesians believe a change in the level of the money supply affects _____ through the interest rate.

   a) velocity

   b) the level of aggregate supply

   c) the level of aggregate demand

   d) the price level

3. One of the basic disagreements between the Keynesians and the monetarists is with regard to the _____ .

   a) stability of V

   b) rate of growth of M

   c) level of prices

   d) importance of real GDP versus nominal GDP

4. Which statement is true?

   a) Both the Keynesians and the monetarists believe V is sensitive to interest rate changes.

   b) Neither the Keynesians nor the monetarists believe V is sensitive to interest rate changes.

   c) The Keynesians believe V is sensitive to interest rate changes while the monetarists do not.

   d) The monetarists believe V is sensitive to interest rate changes while the Keynesians do not.

5. The Keynesians say a change in M will lead to _____ .

   a) no changes in V

   b) proportionate changes in V

   c) changes in V in the same direction

   d) changes in V in the opposite direction

6. The Keynesians say a decline in the money supply _____ .

   a) pushes down interest rates and causes people to buy more bonds

   b) pushes down interest rates and causes people to buy fewer bonds

   c) pushes up interest rates and causes people to buy more bonds

   d) pushes up interest rates and causes people to buy fewer bonds

7. Each of the following has been identified by the monetarists as a determinant of velocity in the short run except _____ .

   a) people's inflationary expectations

   b) the frequency with which people are paid

   c) changes in the level of output

   d) the level of real interest rates

8. Is V predictable in the short run?

   a) The monetarists say yes and the Keynesians say no.

   b) The Keynesians say yes and the monetarists say no.

   c) The Keynesians and the monetarists both say yes.

   d) The Keynesians and the monetarists both say no.

9. Which statement is true about the Keynesian and monetarist transmission mechanisms when the money supply is increased?

   a) Under both, aggregate demand will rise.

   b) Under both, aggregate demand will decline.

   c) Under the Keynesian mechanism, aggregate demand will rise; but under the monetarist mechanism, it will fall.

   d) Under the monetarist mechanism, aggregate demand will rise; but under the Keynesian mechanism, it will fall.

10. According to the Monetarists, when the money supply rises, _____.

    a) interest rates rise

    b) inflation declines

    c) people spend less on assets

    d) people spend more on assets

11. An increase in M of $100 billion will lead to _____.

    a) the same increase in GDP under the Keynesians as under the monetarists

    b) a larger increase in GDP under the Keynesians than under the monetarists

    c) a larger increase in GDP under the monetarists than under the Keynesians

    d) none of the above

12. The Keynesians and the monetarists have three basic disputes connected with the transmission mechanism. They include each of the following except _____.

    a) the effect of an increase in the money supply on GDP

    b) the stability of interest rates

    c) the stability of V

    d) the stability of the private sector

13. The Keynesians believe monetary policy is _____.

    a) more effective in fighting inflations than recessions

    b) more effective in fighting recessions than inflations

    c) effective in fighting both inflations and recessions

    d) effective in fighting neither inflations nor recessions

14. The monetarists say that if we are in a recession, the Fed should _____.

    a) increase the rate of growth of M

    b) decrease the rate of growth of M

    c) do nothing

15. Which statement is true?

    a) The monetarists agree with the Keynesians that easy money is a good way to fight inflation.

    b) The monetarists disagree with the Keynesians' contention that easy money is a good way to fight inflation.

    c) The monetarists agree with the Keynesians' contention that tight money is a good way to fight inflation.

    d) The monetarists disagree with the Keynesians' contention that tight money is a good way to fight inflation.

16. Each of the following is a policy lag except the _____ lag.

    a) psychological   c) recognition

    b) impact   d) decision

17. The lags under fiscal policy are _____ the lags under monetary policy.

    a) more clearly defined than

    b) as well defined as

    c) less defined than

18. Monetary policy lags may last _____.

    a) up to six months

    b) up to one year

    c) from six months to two years

    d) from nine months to three years

19. Which statement is true?

    a) The Keynesians and the monetarists agree that fiscal policy is more effective than monetary policy.

    b) The Keynesians and the monetarists agree that monetary policy is more effective than fiscal policy.

    c) The Keynesians believe more in fiscal policy and the monetarists in monetary policy.

    d) The Keynesians believe more in monetary policy and the monetarists in fiscal policy.

20. The Keynesians assume a _____ monetary demand curve and a _____ investment demand curve.

    a) relatively flat, relatively flat

    b) relatively steep, relatively steep

    c) relatively steep, relatively flat

    d) relatively flat, relatively steep

21. The monetarists believe monetary policy has a
    _____ effect on GDP.

    a) direct and powerful

    b) direct but not powerful

    c) indirect and powerful

    d) indirect and weak

Fill-In Questions

1. The monetarists see a _____
   between the money supply and the level of GDP.

2. If V were a perfect constant, a change in M would
   lead to a _____.

3. The Keynesians believe changes in the level of the
   money supply affect the level of aggregate demand
   through the _____.

4. The best course of action for the Fed, say the
   monetarists, would be to have the money supply
   grow at
   _____.

5. The monetarists say V is _____ and the
   Keynesians say V is
   _____.

6. If interest rates rise, according to the Keynesians,
   people hold less money and will have to _____.

7. Compared to the monetarist position, the Keynesian
   view of how changes in M affect V is _____.

8. The Keynesians maintain that an increase in M
   _____ interest rates.

9. The Keynesians say that V varies _____ with M.

10. The monetarists have identified three determinants of
    V in the short run: (1) _____;
    (2) _____; and
    (3) _____.

11. You can most easily predict V in _____
    _____ years; it is harder to predict
    in _____ years.

12. According to the monetarists, a large increase in the
    money supply creates an _____. In response,
    people _____.

13. Both the Keynesians and the monetarists believe a
    large increase in M will lead to _____
    _____.

14. The monetarists expect rising prices to push up
    _____.

15. The effect of a large increase in the money supply
    on the level of investment, say the Keynesians, will
    be _____
    _____.

16. The long-run consequences of a large-scale increase
    in the money supply when the economy is operating
    at less than full employment will lead to _____
    _____ according to the Keynesians;
    it will lead to _____
    according to the monetarists.

17. The three basic disputes between the Keynesians and
    the monetarists with respect to the transmission
    mechanism are (1) _____;
    (2) _____;
    and (3) _____.

18. The Keynesians say that if we are in a recession, the
    Fed should _____,
    while the monetarists say the Fed should _____
    _____.

19. The Keynesians place much greater faith in the Fed's
    ability to fight _____ than to fight _____.

20. The three policy lags are (1) the _____ _____ lag; (2) the _____ _____ lag; and (3) the _____ _____ lag.

21. The monetarists believe the monetary policy lags last between _____ and _____.

22. The Keynesians argue that _____ policy is a much more powerful and reliable macropolicy tool than _____ policy.

23. Unlike the Keynesians, the monetarists believe changes in the monetary policy have a _____, _____, _____, and _____ effect on GDP.

Appendix B

A Guide to Macropolicy

The three main goals of macropolicy are stable prices, high employment, and a satisfactory rate of economic growth. All economists agree to these goals; they disagree about the means of achieving them.

This will necessarily be a very short chapter because virtually nothing I can say about macropolicy will not offend at least one school of economists. What I will propose here, while not particularly daring or innovative, will give the reader some sense of overall macropolicy, its potential, and its limitations.

APPENDIX OBJECTIVES

After you have read this appendix, you will have a better understanding of:

- Conventional fiscal and monetary policy to fight recession.
- Conventional fiscal and monetary policies to fight inflations.

- How to fight inflationary recessions.
- The limits of macropolicy.

Fighting Recessions

We're going to talk about the conventional fiscal and monetary policies that are advocated by most economists. But as we saw in the last chapter, a significant minority opinion—especially among the monetarists and rational expectationists—runs counter to the majority opinion on macropolicy. So if you happen to disagree with conventional fiscal and monetary policy, just grit your teeth, work your way through the next few pages, and be thankful that this is a short chapter.

Conventional Fiscal Policy

Run deficits to fight recessions.

We'll begin with the simplest of fiscal policy measures drawn from Chapter 11; then we'll get a bit more fancy. The most conventional fiscal policy for fighting a recession is to run a budget deficit. Indeed, given the automatic stabilizers as well as our tax laws, deficits are virtually inevitable during recessions.

The question, then, is how big the deficits should be. Assuming the deficit rises about $40 billion for each point the unemployment rate rises and a 5 percent unemployment rate represents full employment, at a 6 percent unemployment rate, we should run a deficit of about $40 billion. How much should the deficit be when the unemployment rate is 7 percent? You got it—$80 billion. This is our famous full-employment balanced budget.

Conventional Monetary Policy

Speed up M growth to fight recessions.

Were we to enter a recession, the conventional monetary policy would be to speed up the rate of growth of the money supply. Here we need to be careful: if we were to speed it up too much, we would have to worry about an inflation and possibly rising interest rates, which, in time, would kill off any recovery. Surely there would be no justification for as much as a 10 percent rate of monetary growth over any extended period of time.

Two Policy Dilemmas

Suppose we are running a budget deficit of $90 billion and the annual rate of monetary growth is 8 percent. What would go wrong?

Huge budget deficits are financed by massive borrowings by the Treasury. As the economy begins to recover, business and consumer borrowing picks up as well. What does all this loan demand do to interest rates? It drives them up. And when interest rates, which were high even during the recession, rise still higher in the early stages of recovery, what happens next? The recovery collapses.

Thus, a budget deficit, designed to stimulate the economy, necessitates massive Treasury borrowing, driving up interest rates and ultimately choking off recovery.

Is there any way to resolve this dilemma? How about gradually reducing the deficit as the recovery progresses?

Let's consider rapid monetary growth. It stimulates recovery, making funds available to business firms and consumers. Interest rates may decline. So far, so good. But when we increase the money supply this rapidly, we also court inflation, and with inflation, people will demand more interest for their savings. With inflation and higher interest rates, it won't be long before the recovery sputters to a stop.

Can you think of a way out of this dilemma? We could try to reduce the rate of monetary growth as recovery begins to set in.

Fighting Inflation

Conventional Fiscal Policy

To fight inflation, reduce the deficit.

To fight inflation, we would immediately want to try to reduce the size of the federal budget deficit—if we happen to be running one. It would be too much of a shock to reduce it by more than $60 billion or $80 billion in one year, but in the face of persistent inflation, we would need to reduce the deficit year by year and ultimately run budget surpluses.

Conventional Monetary Policy

To fight inflation, slow the rate of M growth.

The obvious policy move here would be to slow down the rate of growth of the money supply, indeed; if inflation were beginning to rage out of control, not only would the

Fed have to stop the money supply from growing, but it would have to cause it to contract slightly.

Fighting Inflationary Recessions: Two More Policy Dilemmas

Some people think of inflations and recessions as separate problems. They once were. However, beginning with the recession in 1957–58, the price level has risen during every recession. To add insult to injury, during three of the four most recent recessions, 1973–75, 1980, and 1981–82, inflation was of double-digit proportions.

Let's review conventional fiscal policy to fight recession and inflation. To fight recession, we run budget deficits; to fight inflation, we run surpluses. Very well, then, what do we do to fight an inflationary recession? That's one dilemma.

We'll go on to the second dilemma. What is the conventional monetary policy to fight a recession? It's to speed up the rate of monetary growth. And to fight an inflation? Slow it down.

Here's the $64,000 question: How do we fight an inflation and a recession simultaneously using conventional fiscal and monetary policy? The answer: We can't.

Don't give up; there *is* hope.

One approach would be to try a combination of tight money to fight the inflation and a large budget deficit to provide the economic stimulus needed to fight the recession. The country kind of stumbled onto this combination during the recession of 1981–82, but not until the Fed eased up on the tight money part did the economy finally begin to recover. By then, much of the inflation had been wrung from the economy.

This suggests a second approach. First deal with the inflation, then cure the recession. In the early 1950s the United States suffered from a surge of inflation brought on by the Korean War. Three recessions occurred over the course of just eight years. By the end of the third recession, the consumer price index was virtually stable. Then, through almost the entire decade of the 1960s, the economy went through a recession-free expansion.

Conventional monetary and fiscal policy tools are sufficient to deal with simple recessions or inflations, but inflationary recessions pose additional problems. Conventional macropolicy cannot cure them without a great deal of suffering, especially by those who lose their jobs.

Conventional policies are not ideal for fighting inflationary recessions.

The Limits of Macropolicy

There is no question that the federal government can easily alter the course of our economy; but during the last decade, substantial changes took place that sharply limited its power. The internationalization of our economy has completely altered the rules of the macroeconomic policy game.

Marc Levinson noted these changes several years ago:

> International capital flows . . . have made it much more difficult for the central bank to plot the nation's monetary course.
>
> Suppose, for example, that the Fed wants to boost the economy's growth rate. When international capital flows were small, the central bank could stimulate borrowing by pumping up the money supply or cutting the discount rate. But now, lower real interest rates will spur investors to move their capital out of dollar-denominated vestments. Economists can't even begin to estimate the likely extent of those capital flows.[1]

---

[1]Mark Levinson, "Economic Policy: The Old Tools Won't Work," *Dun's Business Month,* January 1987, pp. 30–33.

Levinson's analysis is supported by that of Kenichi Ohmae, who reasons that if the Fed tightens the money supply and pushes up interest rates, money will flow in from abroad, attracted by our relatively high interest rates. This will frustrate the tight-money and high-interest-rate objectives of the Fed, and, in effect, render the traditional instruments of monetary policy obsolete.[2]

As our economy becomes even more closely integrated into the world economy—a topic we'll pursue in the last two chapters in this book—it is clear that macropolicy will become less important. And so, as we begin counting down the years until the turn of the century, macropolicy may no longer be the only economic game in town. But it is still, by far, the biggest game.

Conclusion

Where does this leave us? Clearly, the economics profession does not have all the answers. But we do occasionally come up with some interesting questions, and we're very good at providing cogent explanations about why our predictions almost always seem to go awry.

As we approach the millennium, the problem of our lagging rate of economic growth has become quite apparent. How low *has* our growth been? *Why* has it been so low? *What* can we do to speed it up? I'm glad you asked. You'll find the answers in the next chapter.

Question for Further Thought and Discussion

1. Outline the conventional monetary and fiscal policies for fighting an inflation. Then outline the conventional monetary and fiscal policies for fighting a recession. Why would an inflationary recession pose a dilemma for those who would attempt to apply conventional monetary and fiscal policies?

---

[2]Kenichi Ohmae, *The Borderless World* (New York: HarperCollins, 1990), p. xi.

Workbook for Appendix B to Chapter 15

Name _____ Date _____

Multiple-Choice Questions

Circle the letter that corresponds to the best answer.

1. The conventional fiscal policy to fight a recession would be to _____.
   a) increase the rate of monetary growth
   b) decrease the rate of monetary growth
   c) run budget deficits
   d) run budget surpluses

2. The conventional monetary policy to fight inflations would be to _____.
   a) increase the rate of monetary growth
   b) decrease the rate of monetary growth
   c) run budget deficits
   d) run budget surpluses

3. One problem or dilemma we might face in fighting a recession is that _____.
   a) we might end up with budget surpluses
   b) output might rise too quickly
   c) interest rates might fall
   d) interest rates might rise

4. During recessions, we want _____.
   a) budget deficits and faster monetary growth
   b) budget deficits and slower monetary growth
   c) budget surpluses and faster monetary growth
   d) budget surpluses and slower monetary growth

5. During inflations, we want _____.
   a) budget deficits and faster monetary growth
   b) budget deficits and slower monetary growth
   c) budget surpluses and faster monetary growth
   d) budget surpluses and slower monetary growth

6. Which statement is true?
   a) In recent years inflation and recession have become separate problems.
   b) In recent years inflation and recession have become related problems.
   c) Inflation and recession have never been related problems.
   d) Inflation and recession have always been related problems.

7. In recent years macropolicy has _____.
   a) become more powerful
   b) become less powerful
   c) remained about as powerful as it was 15 years ago

Fill-In Questions

1. The three main goals of macropolicy are
   (1) _____; (2) _____
   _____; and (3) _____.

2. The conventional fiscal policy to fight a recession is to _____ while the conventional monetary policy is to _____
   _____.

3. The conventional fiscal policy to fight an inflation is to _____, while the conventional monetary policy is to _____
   _____.

4. One problem with both expansionary monetary and fiscal policies used to fight recessions is that they could lead to _____
   _____.

5. The dilemma of fighting an inflationary recession with conventional fiscal policy would be _____

_____

_____.

6. The dilemma of fighting an inflationary recession with conventional monetary policy would be

_____

_____

_____.

Chapter 16

Economic Growth and Productivity

All the way back in Chapter 1, I outlined the history of the American economy. Now I shall return to our country's recent economic history, this time examining the factors most responsible for slowing our economic growth from the mid-1970s to the mid-1990s and its reinvigoration since the mid-1990s. What were the causes of this slowdown, and what reversed this trend? To answer these questions, we need to put economic growth in an historical and international context.

Our problems pale in comparison to those of the less developed countries of Asia, Africa, and Latin America. They are just beginning the journey to development that we undertook more than two centuries ago. But, unlike us, they are beginning from a base of such abject poverty that many of them may never get far.

CHAPTER OBJECTIVES

To understand:

- Economic growth in the United States: The record.
- The role of productivity.
- The reasons our productivity has varied.
- The roles of savings, capital, and technology.

- The declining quality of our labor force.
- Economic growth in the less developed countries.
- The Malthusian theory of population.

The Industrial Revolution and American Economic Development

Prior to the Industrial Revolution about two and a half centuries ago, one generation lived about as well as the next—or as badly. In fact, except for a few rich families,

453

Economic Growth During the Last Millennium

For most of the last millennium, growth in world output per head averaged little more than 0.1 percent a year. But that growth accelerated to 1.2 percent a year since around 1800. The accompanying chart shows that world GDP today is more than 30 times as great as it was 1,000 years ago.

The Industrial Revolution set off this great burst of sustained economic growth. We should note that, until the mid-20th century, nearly all this growth was confined to Europe, the United States, Canada, Australia, New Zealand, and Japan.

Source: The Economist, September 23, 2000, p. 7.

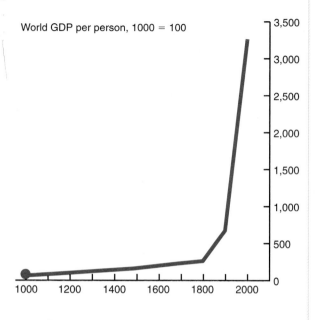

World GDP per person, 1000 = 100

almost everyone was poor. Throughout the world, you were lucky if you had the basics—three square meals a day, some homespun clothes on your back, and a thatched roof over your head.

If you were *really* lucky, you might live to see your old age, which began around your 40th birthday. You lived and died within a few miles of where you were born, you spent most of your time farming, and you were illiterate. About the only good thing in life before the Industrial Revolution was that you never had to worry about finding a parking space.

The Industrial Revolution made possible sustained economic growth and rising living standards for the first time in history (see accompanying box, "Economic Growth During the Last Millennium"). The steam engine, the factory system, mass production, the mechanized cotton spindle, the blast furnace (for smelting iron), railroads, and scores of other innovations ushered in a massive increase in productivity and output.

Although living standards in the industrializing nations of Western Europe and in the United States rose steadily, not until the 1920s did the age of mass consumption truly arrive. Homes were electrified; electric appliances, telephones, and cars became commonplace; and most working people were even beginning to enjoy increasing amounts of leisure time. After the Great Depression and World War II, the industrialized nations were able to pick up where they had left off in 1930, and by 1990 living standards in most of these countries had tripled. Chapter 1 of this book traced American economic development over the last two centuries.

Starting in 1780, England needed 58 years to double its per capita GDP. The American industrial revolution following the Civil War was a bit faster, with per capita output doubling in 47 years. Beginning in 1885, Japan doubled its per capita GDP in 34 years.

But borrowing heavily on earlier technology and making use of a great influx of Japanese capital, South Korea doubled its per capita output in just 11 years, starting in 1966. And now, China is roaring along with its own industrial revolution, doubling its per capita output every 10 years.

The Industrial Revolution, which began in England around the middle of the 18th century, entered its second phase in America in the early years of the 20th century. It was based on the mass production of cars, electrical machinery, steel, oil, and chemicals.

The Industrial Revolution made possible sustained economic growth and rising living standards for the first time in history.

But in the last two decades, the third phase of the Industrial Revolution has taken hold in Japan, Western Europe, and newly industrialized countries of Southeast Asia, as well as in the United States. This phase is based largely on consumer electronics, computer systems, communications systems, computer software, and advances in manufacturing processes. Since the 1980s we have been in the fourth phase of the Industrial Revolution—the information age. During this period nearly all business firms and most homes in the world's industrial countries have computerized.

The American economy is the largest in the world and will continue to be in the foreseeable future. We have one of the world's highest standards of living and a larger stock of capital than any other country. Japan, our nearest competitor, has a GDP slightly more than half the size of ours. Well, that's the *good* news.

The good news: We're still number one.

The *bad* news is that our standard of living, which was number one in the world 20 years ago, has barely increased over the last two decades. Our rate of capital formation is lower than Japan's, a country with only half our population and half our productive capacity. In the early 1970s our rate of productivity growth, or output per hour, slowed to one-third the rate at which it grew in the 1950s and early 1960s.

The bad news: We're losing our lead.

Since the early 1970s our economy has been plagued by all sorts of problems—inflation, recession, high interest rates, a low savings rate, a trade imbalance, huge federal budget deficits, lagging productivity, and a ballooning national debt. But by the mid-1990s, we seem to have had a change in economic fortune. Our federal budget deficits got smaller, interest rates came down, productivity growth began to pick up, and the economic expansion that began in the spring of 1991 would become the longest in our history in February, 2000. In the next section we'll look at the record of our economic and productivity growth, and in the following section we'll consider why our economy tanked in the mid-1970s and why it boomed again from the mid-1990s into the new millennium.

The hopeful news: Things are looking up.

The Record of Economic and Productivity Growth

Although our record of economic growth was relatively poor from the early 1970s through the mid-1990s, an economic boom beginning in 1995 has carried into the new century. That boom was made possible by higher productivity growth.

Productivity is output per unit of input. For example, a telephone switchboard operator handles 100 calls per hour. So the output is 100 calls handled, and input is one hour of labor. If, one year later, the switchboard operator handles 103 calls per hour, his productivity has grown 3 percent.

The faster our productivity grows, the faster our output, or real GDP will grow. New ways of doing things can sometimes drastically boost productivity. Before we began shipping freight in standard-sized containers in the 1960s, it would take 300 longshoremen 10 days to unload a large freighter. Today it takes 30 longshoremen just one and a half days to do the same job. Another example: I'm old enough to remember the photocopy machines that looked liked elongated toasters. You'd place the page to be copied in one slot and about 30 seconds later it would emerge from the other slot. And your copy would emerge from a third slot at the same time. Of course you'd have to wait another minute or so for that copy to dry. And if you weren't careful, you'd get chemicals all over your original. That happened to my friend when he tried to make a copy of a ten-dollar bill and it turned brown. Today, machines make hundreds of copies in a minute. So we could say that the productivity of photocopy machines—and longshoremen as well—has improved by several thousand percent since the 1950s.

Let's look at the record of our productivity growth since 1960 in Table 1. Clearly productivity growth slowed markedly in the 1970s and even more in the 1980s. But sometime in the 1990s productivity growth picked up again.

Figure 1 provides a year-to-year accounting of these four decades. You'll notice the dotted line drawn at 2.5%, which may be about as fast as we can expect our productivity

TABLE 1	Productivity Growth from the 1960s through the 1990s (Percentage change in worker productivity from the last quarter of the previous decade)
Decade	% Change
1960s	+31.8
1970s	+21.7
1980s	+15.6
1990s	+21.5

Source: Economic Report of the President, 2001.

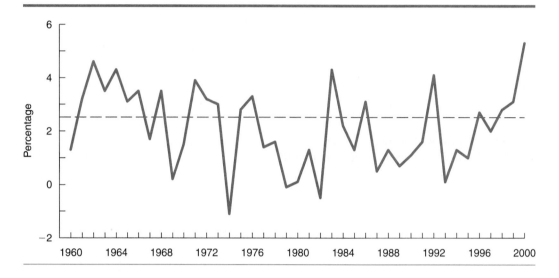

Figure 1

Annual Rate of Productivity Growth, 1960–2000
Source: Economic Report of the President, 2001.

to grow on a sustained basis. Our rate of productivity growth was more than 2.5% in 7 years during the 1960s. In the 1970s it exceeded 2.5% in 5 years. Our rate of productivity growth was more than 2.5% just twice in the 1980s. From 1977 through 1995 we had only three years of more than 2.5% growth. But in the five-year period between 1996 and 2000 our growth exceeded that benchmark four times.

All of this sets up two questions. First, why was our rate of productivity growth so low from the mid-1970s through the early 1990s? And second, why did it pick up again in the late 1990s?

Factors Affecting Productivity Growth

Basically we're looking for the factors that depressed our productivity growth from the mid-1970s through the mid-1990s, and, secondarily, we're looking for those factors that pushed up our productivity growth in the late 1990s.

Low savings rate means low productivity growth.

Our Low Savings Rate There is no one clear reason why our rate of productivity increase slowed in the 1970s and 1980s, but a reason singled out by many economists is our low savings rate. Americans have been poor savers for generations, but through

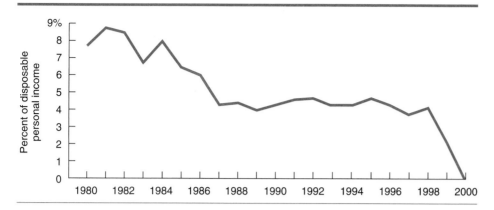

Figure 2
The Personal Savings Rate:
Saving as a Percentage of
Disposable Income, 1980–2000

Our savings rate, which averaged
about 8 percent in the early and
mid-1980s, has fallen to 0 in 2000
and −1 percent in the first quarter
of 2001 (not shown).
*Source: Economic Report of the
President, 2001.*

most years of the 1950s, 1960s, and 1970s, we still managed to put away around 7 to 8 percent of disposable income. This changed in the 1980s, however, when savings averaged just 5.4 percent of disposable income. In the second half of the 1990s it declined steadily, reaching 0 in 2000 and −1 percent in the first quarter of 2001.

Why do Americans save so little? Perhaps the explanation lies in the phenomenon called the "me generation" (see box). Perhaps Americans just want to have fun, and fun costs money. Whatever the reason—whether an inability to accept deferred gratification or the built-in savings disincentives of our tax laws—our savings rate is extremely low.

Although their savings rate is extremely low, Americans are putting away hundreds of billions for their retirement in the form of 401Ks, IRAs, and mutual funds, as well as

> The generations that came of age in the 1980s and 1990s have not done as well as their parents' generations.

The Me Generation and Generation X

"I want it *all* and I want it *now*!" That was the rallying cry of the "me generation," which came of age in the 1980s. These investment bankers, corporate lawyers, doctors, and computer whizzes gave new meaning to Thorstein Veblen's *conspicuous consumption.*

While most members of the so-called me generation may well have shared the material aspirations of their yuppie brethren, they just didn't have the dollars to make them happen. In fact, the generation of the 1980s has not done as well economically as their parents did when *they* were in their 20s.

In the 1960s most couples in their 20s could afford to buy a home; today less than one-third can. In terms of dollars of constant purchasing power, wages are virtually the same as they were 30 years ago. Family incomes have risen only because so many homemakers have gone back to work. Two may be able to live as cheaply as one, but only if they live on two salaries rather than one.

Harvard economist Benjamin Friedman wrote about an implicit compact between generations:

> The thesis of this book is that the radical course upon which the U.S. economic policy was launched in the 1980s violated the basic moral principle that

had bound each generation of Americans to the next since the founding of the republic; that men and women should work and eat, earn and spend, both privately and collectively, so that their children and their children's children would inherit a better world. Since 1980 we have broken with that tradition by pursuing a policy that amounts to living not just in, but for, the present. We are living well by running up our debt and selling off our assets. America has thrown itself a party and billed the tab to the future. The costs, which are only beginning to come due, will include a lower standard of living for individual Americans and reduced American influence and importance in world affairs.*

The so-called Generation X, which came of age in the 1990s, has clearly maintained the prolific spending habits of its generational precursors. Its members have also been "born to shop" and believe that you must "shop till you drop." And so far, it appears that Generation Y, which has been coming of age in the first decade of the 21st century, is maintaining the spending habits of the Me Generation and Generation X.

---

*Benjamin M. Friedman, *Day of Reckoning* (New York: Random House, 1988), p. 4.

the purchase of individual corporate stocks and bonds. Most of this does not count as personal savings, but a large chunk of these funds find their way into corporate investment.

Personal savings is just one part of the total amount saved by Americans, which we call *gross saving*. Businesses save as well as does the government (I'm lumping together the federal, state, and local governments). Businesses save money through retained earnings (that is, profits plowed back into the business), but most of their savings is in the form of depreciation (or capital consumption) allowances (which we talked about in Chapter 6). These funds are used to replace the plant and equipment that has worn out or become obsolete, and they are also used to purchase additional plant and equipment.

The federal government ran budget deficits from 1970 through 1997, while the state and local governments have generally run surpluses. Beginning in the late 1970s, the federal deficits far outweighed the state and local surpluses, so the government contribution to the gross savings rate became a big minus. Today, of course, the huge federal surplus, combined with the state and local surplus, make government saving a huge plus.

One of the bright spots in our savings picture is that the massive federal budget deficits of the early 1990s fell during the rest of the decade, and by 1998 we were running surpluses. As these surpluses mounted, they more than canceled the declining saving of individuals and boosted our gross savings rate (see Figure 3).

What does our gross savings rate look like? In Figure 3 you can see an unmistakable downward trend from the late 1940s to the early 1990s, and then an apparent reversal beginning in 1993.

Once we allow for using some of our savings to replace our worn out and/or obsolete plant and equipment, we are left with our net savings rate. How does our net savings rate compare with those of other leading industrial nations? Very badly. We're way over to the right in Figure 4. Our net savings rate was about half that of Japan from 1975 through 2000.

Because we save so little, we generate a very low flow of funds for investment. Over the last decade we've been running huge trade deficits, and foreigners have been recycling most of the dollars we sent them by making investments in the United States. Our investment is consequently much higher than it would otherwise have been due to this influx of dollars from abroad.

Foreign investors have been attracted by our high interest rates.

For foreigners, the key attraction of investing in the United States is the relatively high interest rates that we pay. Real interest rates (after subtracting the rate of inflation from nominal, or actual rates) were about three times as high in the United States as in Japan through most of the 1980s and 1990s. This meant Japanese firms were borrowing at about one-third the interest rate that their American competitors were paying. This factor—which can be traced back to our low savings rate—has put American firms at a great disadvantage and is a major reason why we have been losing our product markets to Japanese competitors.

Figure 3

U.S. Gross Savings Rate: Gross Saving as a Percentage of GDP, 1947–2000

For most of this period our gross savings has been in the 14–18 percent range, with a marked upward trend since 1992.
Source: Economic Report of the President, 2001.

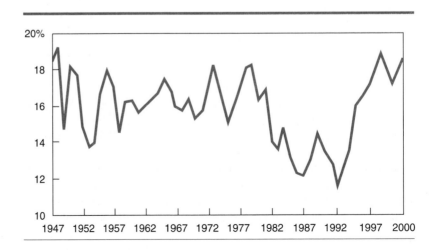

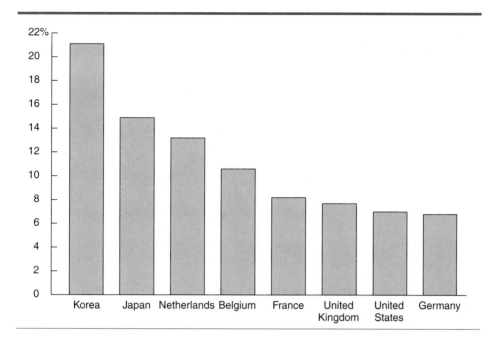

F*igure* 4

Net National Saving as a Percentage of GDP, Annual Average, Selected Countries, 1998

The net natinal savings of the United States as a percent of its GDP is among the lowest of all industrial countries—one-third the rate of Korea and one-half the rate of Japan.

Source: Organization for Economic Cooperation and Development.

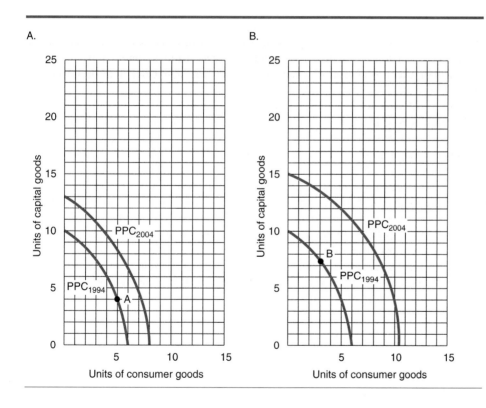

F*igure* 5

Capital Spending and Economic Growth

Panels A and B show identical production possibility curves in 1994. If a nation allocates its production of capital goods and consumer goods at point A of panel A, in 10 years it will be at PPC$_{2004}$. If it allocates its production of capital goods and consumer goods at point B of panel B, in ten years it will be at much higher PPC$_{2004}$.

Our Low Rate of Investment To increase our output at a satisfactory rate, we need to keep replacing worn-out and obsolete capital with the most up-to-date and technologically advanced plant and equipment. And we need not only to replace the capital that we've cast off, but also to keep increasing our capital stock.

Do you recall the production possibilities curves from Chapter 2? Figure 5 reproduces a few of them. The production possibilities curve provides a snapshot of our economy at full employment producing just two types of goods. Here they're capital goods and consumer goods. A country that devotes a higher proportion of its resources to capital goods than to consumer goods will grow faster than another country that initially has the same production possibilities curve but emphasizes consumer goods.

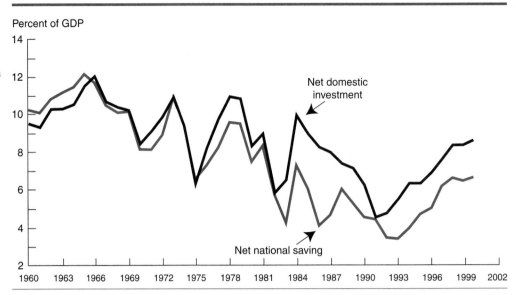

As you can see, the country shown in Figure 5B has a much higher rate of growth than the one in Figure 5A. And the reason why it has enjoyed this relatively high growth should be obvious. Perhaps the two countries in question are the United States and Japan (leaving aside the fact that Japan's economy is only half the size of ours). The lesson our nation must learn is that until we begin to devote more resources to capital goods production and less to consumer goods production, our growth rate will be lower than it would have otherwise been.

Let's make sure we're clear on the difference between gross investment and net investment. Gross investment − depreciation = net investment. Our nation's capital stock can grow only if gross investment exceeds depreciation. We've been hammering away that our relatively low savings rate has held down our rate of investment. Figure 6 shows this relationship.

In 1991 our net investment rate reached a minimum of 4.5 percent and then began to rise sharply. Our net national savings rate bottomed out in 1992 and 1993, and then rose just as sharply. So far, so good. But you'll also notice that, for most of the period from 1960 through 2000, our net investment rate exceeded our net savings rate. So how did we make up this difference?

We depended on foreign investors to provide us with some of *their* savings. And where did they get all those dollars? We supplied them ourselves by running massive trade deficits in recent years. As long as foreigners are willing to accept our dollars in payment for these trade deficits and to send most of them back to us in the form of investment, we can keep our financial heads above water. But, as Federal Reserve Chairman, Alan Greenspan, has repeatedly warned, foreigners will not be willing to accommodate us forever.[1]

The Labor Force: Rising Quantity and Declining Quality

In 1870, Americans, Germans, French, Japanese, and British workers averaged nearly 3,000 hours a year on the job. Now it is less than 2,000 hours, with much of the decline having come since World War II. How does our labor force stack up against those of the rest of the industrial world? Are we growing flabby and complacent? Some things are easier to measure than others, so we'll start with the easiest: the declining average workweek.

---

[1]We'll talk further about this problem in the last two chapters of the book.

(1) The Average Workweek

The average workweek has declined from 60 hours in 1900 to less than 35 hours by the mid-1970s. Today most people put in the standard nine-to-five (or eight-to-four) with an hour for lunch. Until the 1920s most Americans were putting in a six-day week. From there we went to a standard Monday-to-Friday plus half a day on Saturday, and finally, by the late 1940s, we got it down to the five-day week.

In the 1950s, if George Washington's birthday fell on a Saturday, you had to celebrate it on your own time. But today his birthday (as well as several other holidays) is celebrated on Monday, ensuring that everyone not only has the day off but also gets to enjoy a three-day weekend. In fact, most full-time workers are guaranteed 10 paid holidays. When you figure in vacation time, paid sick leave, and personal leave, it's a wonder anyone ever has to show up to work at all. And if you run out of sick leave, you can always call in dead.

But as much as the average workweek has fallen and vacation days have increased, Americans work slightly more hours than do their counterparts in Japan and considerably more than those in Germany. And, unlike Western European workers who get about five weeks vacation, most Americans get relatively short vacations—usually just two or three weeks.

The Labor Department measures the average workweek per job, not per worker. What about all those people who hold two jobs, not to mention those who hold three? If you work 35 hours on one job and 25 hours on a second job, the Labor Department would say that you have an average work week of 30 hours. But, of course, you're actually working 60 hours.

According to an Economic Policy Institute study, the typical married-couple family with children put in 256 more hours of work in 1999 than in 1989.

More people working more hours certainly raises output, but what does it do for productivity, which we measure as *output per unit of input*? Employers realize that, after their employees work more than a certain number of hours, they become less productive. And as the unemployment rate declined in the late 1990s, some of the workers most recently hired—many of whom had recently left the welfare rolls—were not as productive as the workers who had more work experience, education, and training.

(2) Our Declining Educational System

Business firms are having trouble finding secretaries who can spell and put together grammatically correct sentences. Law firms spend millions of dollars teaching their attorneys how to write. And fast-food restaurant chains have found it necessary to place pictures of burgers, fries, sodas, and other items on their cash registers because so many of their clerks were numerically challenged.

It is truly paradoxical that at a time when more people than ever are attending college and millions of them are graduating every year, our labor force is less well-educated than those of previous generations. So I'll resolve the paradox. Our educational leaders figured out that they could get more students through the educational system by lowering standards every 10 or 15 years—kind of like a reverse game of limbo. They kept lowering the limbo stick and letting people step *over* it instead of having to squeeze *under* it. Peer pressure ("Don't appear too smart, or we won't accept you"), television (watching sitcoms rather than reading books), and less parental supervision (one-parent families or two parents holding down jobs) have also taken a toll.

More people are going to college, but our labor force is less educated.

Given the product of our educational system, it is no great surprise that the quality of our labor force has been derided, especially in comparison with those of other leading industrial nations. In an age when literacy, numerical skills, and problem-solving ability are crucial in the workplace, our schools are failing us.

There is something very wrong with the way our children learn. By the time they reach high school, most of them still cannot do simple arithmetic without a calculator, and when they enter college, one out of three freshmen must enroll in at least one

Let no child be left behind.
—President George W. Bush

remedial course. If this is called higher education, one shudders to think of what is happening on the lower levels.[2]

A large and growing number of 18-year-olds are entering an increasingly high-tech labor market, unable to find jobs that pay much more than the minimum wage rate ($5.15 an hour until at least mid-2001). This is the other half—those who don't go to college. Several Western European nations, most notably Germany, have work-study programs for most teenagers who are not planning to enroll in college. They are awarded certificates of competence upon completing these programs, which often lead to relatively high-paying technical jobs.

Despite all our educational problems, the United States must be doing something right. Although the United States has less than 5 percent of the world's population, in the 1990s Americans won 59 percent of the Nobel prizes in economics, 59 percent in physics, and 60 percent in medicine. And the United States has captured sizable world leads in many knowledge industries—computers, telecommunications, and finance. Clearly, the upper strata of our work force is very smart and well educated. But what about the rest of us?

Over the last 10 years many states have abolished automatic promotion, and several have introduced competency exams at various grade levels. Many school systems have gone "back to basics," which stresses mastering reading, writing, and arithmetic in the early grades. The charter school movement (which provides autonomy from local school boards for individual schools) and the growing popularity of private schools (most notably the Edison project) are promising developments. There is also growing support for school vouchers—a very controversial initiative—which would give parents a range of choices of public and private schools, rather than having to send their children to the local public school. Whatever the results of these reforms, there is virtual agreement that an improving educational system holds the key to high productivity growth and, ultimately, to a high rate of economic growth.

> Basically the dominant competitive weapon of the 21st century will be the education and skills of the work force.
> —Lester Thurow, former dean, MIT Sloan School of Management

(3) The Permanent Underclass: Poverty, Drugs, and Crime

We have a permanent underclass constituting 10 percent of our population.

One of the major factors holding the United States back is a permanent underclass of nearly 10 percent of our population. These people are supported by our tax dollars, and many are members of third- and fourth-generation welfare families. No other industrialized nation in the world has such a large dependent population.

Closely associated with poverty are drugs and crime. Although poor people are much more likely than any other population group to be afflicted by both drugs and crime, these problems have affected the lives of virtually every American. No community today is free of either drugs or crime, and they have taken an enormous toll, both economically and socially. Although we cannot quantify how the related problems of poverty, drugs, and crime have affected our rate of economic growth, they have clearly played a major role in lowering productivity and output, as well as our quality of life.

Poverty amid plenty

Poverty amid plenty is an apt description of America today. Although we try to avoid making value judgments in economics, it amazes me that so many Americans do not feel an urgent need to alleviate the poverty that is all around us. The homeless, especially in the downtown areas of large cities, have become invisible to most of us as we pass them by.

Just to begin to wipe out poverty and eradicate the epidemics of drugs and crime would take a massive effort. Somehow these 25 million Americans must be rewoven into our social fabric and become fully integrated, self-supporting members of our labor force. We *did* make a partial effort in the mid-1960s (President Lyndon Johnson's abortive War on Poverty), with mixed results, but since then we've done absolutely nothing.

---

[2]I'll acknowledge that my views on our educational system may not be greeted with universal acclaim. But if anyone is interested, I have expressed those views in more detail in an article entitled, "Pretend Colleges," which was published in *Culturefront,* Fall, 1996.

There are signs, however, since the mid-1990s, that some of these disturbing trends have been reversed. The poverty rate is down sharply, the welfare rolls have been cut in half, and the crime rate has fallen substantially all across the country. Since this does tend to happen during economic booms, it is too soon to tell whether these are the beginning of a long-term trend.

(4) Restrictions on Immigration

To say this country was literally built by immigrants would be no exaggeration. Immigration has been a tremendous source of strength to our nation. Even though immigrant families were always willing to start out on the bottom rung of the economic ladder and work their way up, the rise of "native American" groups eventually led to severe restrictions on the number of people allowed into this country.

This country was built by immigrants.

The Daughters of the American Revolution, many of whom trace their ancestry back to the Mayflower, used to invite the president of the United States to address them every year. In 1933 Franklin Roosevelt, whose forebears arrived in New York while it was still a Dutch colony, was invited to speak. His first words were, "Fellow immigrants." Needless to say, the Daughters never asked him back.

Roosevelt's point, of course, was that we are indeed a nation of immigrants—regardless of when our families arrived. And each new wave of immigrants—whether from Europe, Africa, Latin America, or Asia—worked hard so that their children would have a better life. Hard work and deferred gratification were the hallmarks of each immigrant group.

Before the early 1920s, when a series of increasingly restrictive immigration laws were passed, virtually anyone who wanted to come here was welcome.[3] In the early years of the 20th century, close to a million people came here each year, mostly from eastern and southern Europe. The prime motivation in restricting their numbers was to prevent further dilution of our vaunted northern European stock.

Immigrants are usually in their 20s or 30s, and they tend to be more adventurous, ambitious, and upwardly mobile than those who stay behind. As an added bonus, their educations have already been completed, so we reap the benefits while their native countries bear the costs. This phenomenon has been termed the *brain drain.*

Immigrants are often willing to work 14 to 16 hours a day, seven days a week. Within a couple of years, an immigrant has typically saved enough to open a small business. They may never get rich, but their children will go to college.

Until the 1920s immigrants were a tremendous source of economic strength. Not only did they help build the railroads, settle the West, staff the factories, and set up businesses, but they provided the energy, the ambition, and the drive that were often lacking in native-born Americans.

Today, with immigration restricted to slightly over 300,000 people a year, we are deprived of much of what made our economy go. There is no way to quantify how much this has cost us in terms of economic growth, but a remark overheard in the giant Hunts Point produce market in the Bronx sums it up well. An older man pointed at a hardworking Korean vegetable store owner and said to his friend, "*He* works like our *grand*fathers used to work."

This energy, ambition, and drive, is also vividly illustrated each year when the 40 finalists of the Westinghouse Science Talent Search competition are announced. In recent years nearly half the winners were foreign born or the children of immigrants. These young people are our future. Imagine if our educational system turned out millions just like them.

A study by the National Academy of Sciences released in 1997 concluded that immigration added perhaps $10 billion a year to our GDP. But it did slightly reduce

---

[3]Everyone, that is, except people from China and Japan. Fewer than 100 a year were allowed in under law and by the so-called Gentlemen's Agreement as well as the Chinese Exclusion Act of 1882. Just to be fair (I'm saying this tongue-in-cheek), Congress enacted the Immigration Act of 1924, whose quotas tried to limit Italian and Jewish immigration. From 1924 until after World War II, no one from Japan or China was allowed to enter the United States.

the wages and job opportunities of low-skilled American workers and temporarily placed a fiscal burden on state and local governments. On the average, the panel said, immigrant households have more school-age children and lower incomes, pay lower state and local taxes, and receive more state-financed social services than households of native-born Americans. But within 15 or 20 years the children of these families produce fiscal benefits as they finish school, start working, and begin to pay income and payroll taxes.

With unemployment rates at record lows in 1999 and 2000, many jobs, especially in high-tech fields, became increasingly difficult to fill. Thousands of employers got Congress to raise the annual cap on H-1B visas—temporary work permits for foreign professionals—to 195,000 for the years 2001–2003. Today nearly one-third of the entrepreneurs and higher-level employees in Silicon Valley come from overseas. Indians started some of the Valley's most famous companies—Vinod Khosla of Sun Microsystems and Sabeer Bhatia of Hotmail, for example—and together with Chinese entrepreneurs were responsible in 2000 for nearly one-third of the Valley's new start-ups, creating 60,000 jobs.

On the lower end of the job ladder were the nation's six or seven million illegal immigrants. If these immigrants were expelled tomorrow, thousands of restaurants, hotels, farms, poultry plants, and garment factories would be forced to close for lack of workers. Some economists believe the nation's record economic boom may have already sputtered without immigrants to fill millions of jobs.

Even the Immigration and Naturalization Service (INS) has stopped trying to pick up illegal aliens, allowing them to help American employers fill jobs. This approach is in marked contrast to that in most European countries, where unemployment rates are much higher than in the United States, and governments have tightened immigration laws. Of course a downturn in the American economy could lead the INS to revive its pursuit of illegal immigrants at work.

The Role of Technological Change

Way back in Chapter 2, I said that there are two basic ways to attain economic growth: (1) more inputs of capital and labor and (2) technological change. So far we've been talking about capital and labor. Now we'll turn to technological change.

Technological change enables us to produce more output from the same package of resources or, alternatively, to produce the same output with fewer resources. Technological change could be the creation of new or better goods and services. It also includes greater efficiency in market processes, improvements in the qualities of resources, improved knowledge about how to combine resources, and the introduction of new production processes.

Economic growth rate is largely determined by the rate of technological change.

The rate of technological change may well be the single most important determinant of a nation's rate of economic growth. Although the United States has long been at the cutting edge of technological change, the Japanese have applied that change to the production of high-quality manufactured goods—whether consumer electronics, cars, semiconductors, or steel. We keep coming up with great ideas, but the Japanese have been more adept at taking those ideas and running with them. For example, the industrial robot may have been invented in America, but Japanese companies employ almost three-quarters of the world's robots. Toyota, which uses robots extensively, produces half as many vehicles as General Motors with only 5 percent of GM's number of workers.

A nation's educational system plays a basic role in promoting a high rate of technological change. How well trained are its scientists and engineers, and how many graduate each year? How well trained are its workforce, its industrial managers, and its marketing people? Perhaps the answers to these questions are all too obvious with respect to the United States, given the performance of the American economy over the last two decades.

However (economists always seem to argue with both hands), over the last 15 years computer literacy has increased exponentially. Today more than 60 percent of all American homes have at least one personal computer and most ten-year-olds can use computers for a multitude of activities. And so, as basic reading, writing, and math skills have declined, computer skills have increased dramatically.

How has computerization affected productivity? Two statements by Nobel Prize winner Robert Solow may lend some insight. In 1987 he said, "You can see the computer age everywhere but in the productivity statistics." In 2000 he said, "You can now see computers in the productivity statistics." Between 1973 and 1995 the annual rate of productivity growth was about 1.5 percent, and it has more than doubled. But how much of this increase was due to computerization? The most comprehensive study of this question was conducted by two economists at the Federal Reserve, Stephen Oliner and Daniel Sichel, who concluded that computers were responsible for as much as two-thirds of this increase.[4]

This view is disputed by Robert Gordon of Northwestern University, who believes that labor productivity gains have been confined almost entirely to computer manufacturing and, more generally, to durable goods manufacturing. He found only negligible improvement in labor productivity in the remaining 88 percent of the economy.[5]

Can these opposing views be reconciled? Perhaps the problem lies in productivity measurement itself, especially in the service industries, which are notoriously difficult to measure. How do we measure the output, for example, of McDonald's, Delta Airlines, or your family doctor?

What is the tangible impact of the computer and the Internet? Many industries are benefiting: airlines and theaters through ticket sales on the Web, retailers through e-commerce, Wall Street through online trading. Perhaps most significant is business-to-business (B2B) commerce on the Internet, which has cut purchasing costs of some firms by as much as one-third.

Additional Factors Affecting Our Rate of Growth

In the 1970s six other factors retarding our rate of economic growth came into play: (1) higher energy costs, (2) environmental protection requirements, (3) health and safety regulations, (4) rising health care costs, (5) crumbling infrastructure, and (6) high military spending. When the OPEC nations quadrupled the price of oil in 1973, this not only set off a severe inflationary recession, but it permanently raised the cost of doing business and somewhat retarded our rate of growth. Similarly, environmental protection legislation requiring the expenditure of tens of billions of dollars to reduce air and water pollution also slowed economic growth. And then, too, new health and safety regulations—some of which were relaxed in the 1980s—ate up billions of dollars that would have otherwise been invested in plant and equipment or research and development.

Three other factors retarding our growth rate are
(1) higher energy costs,
(2) environmental protection requirements,
(3) health and safety regulations.

None of this is to say that environmental protection and health and safety measures were not needed. Indeed, they probably reduced medical expenses and sick time significantly and substantially improved the quality of our lives. But they did divert resources from investment, consequently slowing our rate of growth by perhaps as much as 1 percent a year.

Still another factor that has slowed growth has been our rising health care costs, which now claim 14 percent of our GDP. These impose a tremendous burden on taxpayers, who foot the bill for Medicare and Medicaid, and on private employers who must shell out tens of billions of dollars in medical insurance premiums.

The effect of health care

---

[4]*The Economist,* "Economic Focus: Productivity on Stilts," June 10, 2000, p. 86.

[5]*The Economist,* "Economic Focus: Performing Miracles," June 17, 2000, p. 78.

The United States spends more on health care per capita than any other industrial nation, but the quality of that care has come under heavy criticism, and more than 45 million Americans have no medical insurance. One out of every seven dollars of our GDP goes toward health care, but we are clearly getting less per dollar than the citizens of any other industrial country. Again, while there is no way of quantifying how much the inefficiencies of our health care system have slowed our economic growth, they have clearly played a major role.

The effect of a deteriorating infrastructure

Also retarding economic growth is the neglect of our nation's crumbling infrastructure. When you drive along our once glorious interstate highway network, you will often be slowed by long stretches of construction work, much of which could have been carried out years ago at considerably less cost. About 60 percent of our highways need work, ranging from repaving to major structural repairs, and perhaps 40 percent of all highway bridges—some 240,000 of them—are either structurally deficient or functionally obsolete.

We have also allowed our railways to fall into disuse, or disappear altogether, while Japan and our trade rivals in Western Europe have been upgrading their own rail systems. Because of our relatively large geographic area, it is extremely important for us to upgrade our crumbling infrastructure to enhance economic growth and enable us to better compete in the international economic arena.

The effect of military spending

How has military spending affected our economic growth? To what degree has it drawn away resources that might otherwise have been used to build up our productive capacity? Between World War II and 1990, while we devoted about 6 percent of our GDP to defense, the Japanese held military spending to less than 1 percent. Until 1990 more than half of all the R&D spending by our government was on defense, and 40 percent of all our scientists and engineers worked on military projects. Today about 3 percent of our GDP is spent on defense.

Most developed nations have experienced an eventual slowing of their growth rate. Mancur Olson, in his study titled *The Rise and Decline of Nations,* concludes that special interest groups—particularly labor unions, farmers' cooperatives, and employers' associations—become stronger as the economy grows.[6] These groups then make it more difficult to introduce new technologies that could continue to increase growth. For example, the International Longshoremen's Union prevented the containerization of freight for years until the shippers offered them an extremely lucrative retirement plan. And the farmers continue persuading Congress to provide them with billions of dollars a year in price supports and subsidies. An egregious practitioner of these politics is North Carolina Senator Jesse Helms, who, as the second-ranking Republican on the Senate Agriculture Committee (and its former chair) has seen to it that the tobacco growers of his state continued to receive their subsidies.[7]

How do we counteract the influence of these special interest groups? Olson suggests that we bring down the barriers to international trade. Look at what foreign competition has done for the automobile industry. The United Auto Workers Union has been forced to grant concessions to the big three automakers, resulting in lower costs and increased efficiency. And now Americans have a wider range of better-quality cars to choose from at lower prices. Olson also attributes the high growth rate of the European Union nations to the effects of free trade on diluting the power of special interest groups.

In an extensive study of American economic growth over the 1929–82 period, Edward Denison attributed about half our growth to added inputs of labor and capital and the rest to increased productivity.[8] The main source of productivity growth was advances in knowledge obtained through research and development. A second major source was improvements in the quality of labor, primarily the consequence of improvements in education and training.

---

[6]Mancur Olson, *The Rise and Decline of Nations* (New Haven, CT: Yale University Press, 1982).

[7]In effect, then, the U.S. Department of Agriculture has subsidized the tobacco farmers, while the surgeon general was discouraging cigarette sales by forcing the companies to print a warning such as "Cigarette Smoke Contains Carbon Monoxide" on every pack of cigarettes and in every ad.

[8]Edward S. Denison, *Accounting for Slower Economic Growth* (Washington, DC: Brookings Institution, 1979).

Conclusion

We've talked about a multitude of factors affecting our productivity, but we need a more integrated explanation of why our productivity growth was so low from the mid-1970s to the mid-1990s and why it picked up again.

1. *Our low savings rate* This had a depressing effect, although there were two mitigating factors—the turnaround from large federal budget deficits to growing surpluses and the influx of investment dollars from abroad. Furthermore, our gross savings rate rose substantially after 1992.

2. *Our low rate of investment* Net domestic investment trended downward from the late 1960s until 1992, when it began to rise sharply. So the downward trends in both savings and investment tended to depress productivity growth in the 1970s, 1980s, and the early 1990s. But a rising pool of savings (including a large influx of money from abroad) tended to raise our productivity growth by the mid-1990s.

3. *The rising quantity of labor* The average work week, which had been declining in the 1950s and 1960s, stopped declining in the 1970s and has increased over the last two decades. This may have depressed productivity growth since the 1970s.

4. *The declining quality of labor* Although more people than ever before are going to college, our educational standards today—from the first grade through college—are well below the standards we maintained 40 or 50 years ago. I realize that this viewpoint is controversial (there are many people who disagree with me), but virtually everyone would agree that a good education is crucial to performing most jobs in today's high-tech economy. Although computer literacy is extremely high in this country, a disturbingly high proportion of those entering the labor force today are profoundly weak in reading, writing, and arithmetic—skills that are required in the workplace. Therefore, the declining quality of labor has had a long-term depressing effect on our productivity growth.

5. *The growth of the permanent underclass and its attendant problems of poverty, drugs, and crime* This factor has also tended to depress productivity growth in the 1970s and 1980s. However, sharp declines in poverty and crime since the early 1990s may have contributed to productivity growth over the last decade.

6. *Restrictions on immigration* Immigration restrictions dating back to the 1920s have lowered productivity growth. Since the late 1990s, however, the INS has virtually stopped its pursuit of illegal aliens, and there has been increasing pressure to allow more highly skilled immigrants into the country.

7. *Computerization* The United States was computerized in the 1990s, and the long-awaited accompanying rise in productivity growth has apparently begun to materialize. We may eventually conclude that computers have had an increasingly salutary effect on productivity since the mid- to late-1980s.

The 1999 *Economic Report of the President* noted that "although the electric dynamo was invented well before the turn of the century, it did not seem to fuel large gains in productivity until many years later."[9] Productivity growth actually slowed between 1890 and 1913, but it increased rapidly between 1919 and 1929. If history repeats itself, then we should experience rapid productivity growth well into the first decades of the 21st century.

Lester Thurow, an economic historian, believes that computerization will have far-reaching effects that may completely change the way we live and work. "What historians will come to call the third industrial revolution (the steam engine being the first and electrification the second) is based upon technical breakthroughs in computers, telecommunications, microelectonics, robots, new materials, and biotechnology."[10]

[9]Studies were conducted in 1992, 1993, 1996, and 1997. The company has published an executive summary of the 1996 and 1997 studies.

[10]Page 77.

The Productivity of Labor: An International Comparison

Are you ready for a big surprise? All right, then, here it comes. Which country in the world has the highest productivity per worker? Japan? Germany? Sweden? The answer is none of the above. That's right! The number one country in the world, the country with the highest productivity per worker, is—are you ready?—the United States.

How can that *be*? Our productivity growth had slowed these last two decades, from the mid-1970s to the mid-1990s while that of our industrial rivals grew much more rapidly. How could we possibly still be in the lead? The answer, of course, is that our lead was so big that even though a few other countries have been gaining, they haven't quite caught us yet. Indeed, since the early 1990s, as the economies of Western Europe and Japan slowed and unemployment mounted, we have increased our lead.

A series of studies by McKinsey, the giant consulting firm, has confirmed that American workers are the most productive in the world.[11] In 1990 the average full-time American worker produced $49,000 worth of goods and services, as apposed to $47,000 by the French worker, $44,200 by the German worker, and just $38,200 by the Japanese worker.

Through the 1980s and into the 1990s the productivity of the Japanese autoworker was held up as an example to emulate. During the last two decades of the 20th century, American carmakers closed the gap, so today the American autoworker is almost as productive as her Japanese counterpart. However, Japanese retailers are still in the Dark Ages in comparison to Wal-Mart, McDonalds, Starbucks, and hundreds of other American retail powerhouses.

Protected by an array of rules and regulations, tiny mom 'n pop stores have long dominated Japanese retailing. Until the early 1990s larger firms were barred from competing by a long list of licenses, permits, and other regulatory barriers. Under deregulation, retail competition has grown, but the traditional Japanese mom 'n pop stores still account for more than half the retail employment, operating at about one-third the efficiency of the American mom 'n pop store (see Figure 7).

Although international comparisons of productivity must be taken with at least a couple of grains of salt,[12] the McKinsey study is considered "the most authoritative to date," according to *New York Times* economics writer Sylvia Naser.[13] While we have been surpassed by the Japanese in several manufacturing industries, the U.S. economy shines in the service sector. For example, we are more than twice as efficient as the Japanese in general merchandise retailing "largely because Japan's zoning laws save mom-and-pop stores from annihilation by the Japanese equivalents of Wal-Mart."[14] Similarly, our deregulated telecommunications industry is at least twice as efficient as Germany's government monopoly.

The problem in Germany is "overengineering." Too much plant and equipment is allocated to each worker, leading to low levels of capacity utilization. In France, where the minimum wage is almost double that in the United States, and fringe benefits are also much higher, millions of lower-skilled workers are priced out of the labor market because employers simply cannot afford to hire them.[15]

---

[11]*Forbes ASAP,* February 21, 2000, p. 82.

[12]Two reasons why international comparisons of worker output are difficult are (1) no two national accounting systems are identical, and (2) there are daily fluctuations in the exchange rates among the world's currencies.

[13]Sylvia Naser, "U.S. Output per Worker Called Best," *New York Times,* October 1, 1992, p. D1.

[14]Ibid.

[15]The minimum wage is discussed at the end of the chapter entitled "Labor Markets and Wage Rates" in *Economics* and *Microeconomics.*

Discounters
93%

Convenience stores
88%

Specialty chains
84%

Department stores
70%

Supermarkets
60%

Retail average
50%

Small traditional shops
33%

F*igure* 7

Retail Productivity in Japan, Compared with the Same Type of Store in the U.S., 1999

Based on operating income for each hour worked, Japanese retailing operates, on average, at about half the efficiency of American retailing.
Source: McKinsey & Company; see *The New York Times,* August 8, 2000, p. C1.

Economic Growth in the Less Developed Countries

Well, enough about *our* problems. Now let's talk about other people's problems. Let's talk about people who *really* have problems—those who live in less developed countries (LDCs).

The world can be divided into three groups of countries: the industrialized nations, the newly industrializing countries (NICs), and the less developed countries (LDCs). The big question, then, is how to get from LDC to NIC and, ultimately, to industrialized. And, parenthetically, at what cost?

The only way to industrialize is to build up capital in the form of new plant and equipment. There are two main ways of doing this: working more and consuming less. As some of the poor nations of the world are barely at subsistence level, it's pretty hard for them to consume less. And because there is often a great deal of unemployment in preponderantly agricultural economies, those who want to work more have a hard time finding work.

The only way to industrialize

Each of the LDCs shown in Table 2 has a per capita GDP of less than $200. The NICs, which have lifted themselves out of abject poverty during the last three or four decades, are well on their way to high standards of living. Among the industrial nations

TABLE 2	The Poorest Countries in the World

Country	GDP Per Capita, 1998 ($)
Ethiopia	100
Dem. Rep. of Congo	110
Sierra Leone	140
Burundi	140
Guinea-Bissau	160
Niger	190
Eritrea	200
Malawi	200
Mozambique	210
Nepal	210
Tanzania	210

Source: World Bank, Word Development Indicators.

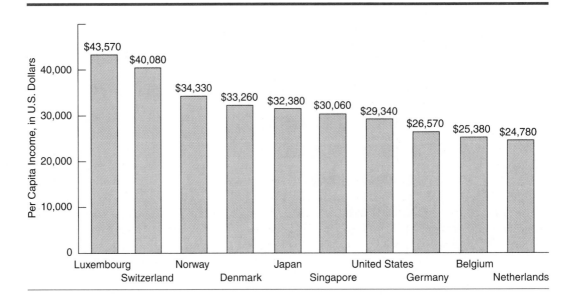

Figure 8

Per Capita GDP of the 10 Leading Nations, 1999

Although the United States is definitely not in the top five, international comparisons for per capita GDP are at least somewhat suspect because of varying national income accounting systems as well as fluctuations of foreign exchange rates.

Source: The World Bank, *World Development Indicators,* 2000.

(shown in Figure 8), it would appear that six have surpassed the United States. However, international comparisons should be made with a great deal of caution. Exchange rate fluctuations and varying systems of national income accounting make these comparisons somewhat problematical. Clearly the United States has one of the highest living standards in the world, but no one knows for sure who's number one—or who is number two, three, four, or five, for that matter.

Not all the LDCs have per capita incomes as low as $200, but two-thirds of the world's population live in countries with per capita incomes of less than $1,500. So what two out of every three people on this planet have in common is poverty.

Compounding the problems of the LDCs are rapidly growing populations. More than 200 years ago, an English economist named Thomas Robert Malthus predicted that the world's growth of food production would not be able to keep up with the growth of population (see box, "The Malthusian Theory of Population"). The Malthusian dilemma— a food supply growing at an arithmetic rate and a population growing at a geometric rate—is becoming a reality in some of the nations of sub-Saharan Africa, as well as in a few countries in Asia and in Latin America. Hundreds of millions face starvation, with virtually no chance to substantially raise their food output. The recurrent famines in Ethiopia and the Sudan may be mere dress rehearsals for a future crisis of much greater dimension.

Even more alarming in the long run, the birthrates of less developed nations show little indication of declining. And unless they decline, the emergency shipments of foodstuffs from the rest of the world are merely postponing the inevitable.

One way out of this dilemma may be the family planning programs that have been attempting to lower birthrates in the LDCs. Supported by government funding as well as grants from the Population Council, the International Planned Parenthood Federation, and the United Nations, the programs have had great success in lowering birthrates. In 1970 families in LDCs had an average of 6 children. Today that average is just 3. With fewer mouths to feed, these countries now have more savings available for development (see the box, "Family Planning and Economic Development").

Thomas Robert Malthus, English cleric and economist (The Granger Collection, New York)

The Malthusian Theory of Population

Economics is called the "dismal science" largely because of the Malthusian theory. As it was originally formulated, the theory predicted that famine and warfare would, within perhaps a few generations, beset the world. This was inevitable because of a tendency for the world's population to double every 25 years.

The Reverend Thomas Robert Malthus wrote the first edition of the *Essay on the Principle of Population* in 1798. His two main points were that population tended to grow in a geometric progression—1, 2, 4, 8, 16, 32—and that the only ways to stop population from growing this rapidly were the "positive checks" of pestilence, famine, and war. Not a very pleasant outlook.

In his second edition, Malthus held out slightly more hope for holding down the rate of the population increase. It could be contained by the "preventive check" of "moral restraint," which meant not getting married until one could support a family (and, it went without saying, no fooling around before you got married).

Malthus also noted that the food supply could not increase as rapidly as population tended to because the planet was limited in size and there was only a fixed amount of arable land. He felt the food supply would ultimately tend to grow in an arithmetic progression—1, 2, 3, 4, 5, 6—and it would not take a mathematical genius to conclude that we would be in trouble within a few generations. The relevant figures are shown in the table below.*

Year	Food Production	Population
1800	1	1
1825	2	2
1850	3	4
1875	4	8
1900	5	16
1925	6	32

The Malthusian theory is a variant of the law of diminishing returns. As increasing amounts of labor are applied to a fixed amount of land, eventually marginal output will decline.

Was Malthus right? Surely not in the industrialized countries, particularly the United States, Canada, and Australia, which are major exporters of wheat and other farm products. Two things happened in these countries to ward off Malthus's dire predictions. First, because of tremendous technological advances in agriculture—tractors, harvesters, better fertilizer, and high-yield seeds—farmers were able to feed many more people.† Second, as industrialization spread and more and more people left the countryside for the cities, the birthrate fell.

However, the less developed countries are caught in a double bind. The Malthusian positive check of a high death rate has been largely removed by public health measures, such as malaria control, smallpox vaccine, and more sanitary garbage disposal. But because these countries have not yet been able to industrialize and urbanize their populations, birthrates remain high. In most of Asia, Africa, and Latin America, populations are doubling every 30 to 35 years, putting hundreds of millions of people in peril of starvation. Famine is a reality in these countries, and it may well become even more wide-spread toward the end of this century.

---

*Malthus did not use actual years in his predictions; the years in the table are purely hypothetical to illustrate his theory. Also, Malthus did not predict that this would actually happen. Rather, he indicated that these were the tendencies, but that population increases could be checked by war, pestilence, famine, or moral restraint.

†Some observers have been encouraged by the so-called Green Revolution, which has enabled many large growers to double and triple yields by using better seeds and fertilizer. However, the prime beneficiaries have been the wealthy farmers and a few multinational agribusinesses, such as Dole, Del Monte, and Ralston Purina. They have profited by producing for export such crops as sugar, soybeans, bananas, and peanuts. But they have also forced millions of small farmers off the land and actually caused the production of indigenous food staples to decline, making these countries even more dependent on food imports.

Even *with* family planning programs, the populations of most LDCs continue to grow between 2 and 3 percent a year, and these countries must struggle to increase their food supplies at that rate just to keep pace. To industrialize, they would need to attain a high enough economic growth rate to be able to produce capital goods as well as the basic consumer necessities. Thus many LDCs clearly will never be able to begin industrializing without outside help.

There *is* one additional source of capital: grants and loans from the industrialized nations. Over the last four decades hundreds of billions of dollars have been provided by the United States, the Soviet Union, Western Europe, and Japan. But now that many LDCs are deeply in debt (some have defaulted on their loans), it is unlikely that more

Family Planning and Economic Development

Remember the riddle of the chicken and the egg? There's a similar one in family planning and economic development: Which comes first, economic development or a falling birthrate? Historically, as a nation urbanized and industrialized, its birthrate eventually fell. Once a nation reaches a certain threshold, or stage of development, families will begin to choose to have fewer and fewer children. The birthrate falls for three main reasons: (1) Children, who are economic assets on a farm, become just more mouths to feed in an urban setting. (2) Children used to be counted on for support in the parents' old age, but as development takes place, people are able to accumulate savings and will receive pensions when they retire. (3) As more children survive to adulthood, fathers don't need to have so many sons to ensure that at least one will survive to carry on the family name.

We know, then, that as development reaches a certain stage, the birthrate will fall. This enables a nation to save more, convert that savings into capital, and further increase its rate of economic growth. But why wait for birthrates to fall of their own accord? Why not induce them to fall by means of family planning programs *before* development has progressed very far?

Virtually every LDC has a policy of encouraging birth control to limit population growth. Some have had considerable success in lowering their birthrates, most notably China, Taiwan, Hong Kong, Singapore, South Korea, and several Caribbean nations.

Grants and loans from
industrialized nations

credit will be extended. In fact, the interest that must be paid out each year by the LDCs has become a tremendous burden.

During the 1980s some nations *did* attain the status of NIC. The "four tigers" of Asia—South Korea, Taiwan, Hong Kong, and Singapore—as well as Malaysia, Brazil, Indonesia, and Thailand have done this, largely through foreign investment. Unwise investments in South Korea, Indonesia, and Thailand, many of which are in default led to the 1997–1998 Asian financial crisis.[16]

Still another problem is that virtually all LDCs spend a major part of their budgets on armaments, which diverts desperately needed funds from development. Warfare in Southeast Asia, Afghanistan, Ethiopia, Sudan, Peru, Somalia, and the Persian Gulf has further exacerbated the situation. The United States, the former Soviet Union, China, and

Military spending and wars

several European nations have encouraged this unfortunate tendency by selling—or even giving—arms to developing nations.

China and India, the world's most populous nations, have made impressive strides toward development, although neither has yet attained NIC status (both, however, along with Pakistan, have managed to produce nuclear bombs). Today more than two-thirds of the people in the world live in LDCs, and in those countries about half live at or near the subsistence level. Most live out their lives in abject poverty, with no hope that they or their children will have better lives.

---

[16]This crisis will be fully discussed in the last chapter.

Questions for Further Thought and Discussion

1. How has our educational system affected the quality of our labor force?

2. Explain the Malthusian theory of population. Is it relevant today anywhere in the world? Explain where and why.

3. How does the American savings rate compare to that of other leading industrial nations? What accounts for the difference?

4. What changes took place during the Industrial Revolution that made possible sustained economic growth?

5. Why did our rate of productivity growth slow from the mid-1970s through the mid-1990s?

6. Why did our rate of productivity growth speed up in the late 1990s? Is this higher growth rate just temporary, or will it be sustained over the next 10 or 15 years?

7. Should we remove all barriers to immigration into the United States? What would be the consequences?

8. If we could let in an extra hundred thousand immigrants every year, should we favor certain immigrants over others? Why?

Workbook for Chapter 16

Name _____   Date _____

Multiple-Choice Questions

Circle the letter that corresponds to the best answer.

1. Our rate of productivity increase in the 1980s was
   _____ the rate of productivity increase in the
   1960s.
   a) faster than

   b) about

   c) slower than

2. Compared to Japan, our rate of savings is
   _____ and our rate of capital formation is
   _____.
   a) higher, higher   c) higher, lower

   b) lower, lower   d) lower, higher

3. Each of the following except _____ slowed
   our rate of economic growth in the 1970s.
   a) research and development spending

   b) pollution regulations and requiring pollution
      reduction

   c) health and safety regulations

   d) rising energy costs

4. The key to productivity growth is _____.
   a) an increasing labor force

   b) technological change

   c) expansion of land under cultivation

   d) the use of deteriorating and obsolete capital

5. Rising productivity could be each of these except
   _____.
   a) more units of output from more units of input

   b) More output per unit of input

   c) the same output from fewer units of input

6. Edward Denison attributes about _____ percent of our economic growth to increases in
   productivity.
   a) 10   d) 70

   b) 30   e) 90

   c) 50

7. Most of the people in the world live in
   _____.
   a) LDCs

   b) NICs

   c) industrialized countries

8. During the last 10 years, Americans were saving
   about _____ percent of their disposable
   incomes.
   a) 0 to 6   c) 9 to 12

   b) 6 to 9   d) 12 to 15

9. Which one of the following factors contributed
   most to our economic growth between 1995 and
   today?
   a) our high rate of savings

   b) our educational system

   c) technological change

   d) our high rate of investment

10. Sustained economic growth did not begin anywhere
    in the world until around _____.
    a) 1450   c) 1750

    b) 1600   d) 1900

11. Which statement is false?
    a) Net domestic investment has been much greater
       than net national savings since the early 1980s.

    b) As a percentage of GDP our net national savings
       rate is virtually the highest in the world.

    c) Our personal savings rate in 2000 was 0 percent.

    d) Americans worked more hours per year in 1999
       than they did in 1989.

12. Which statement is true?

a) Immigration has long been a tremendous drain on our economy and has slowed our rate of economic growth.

b) Congress raised the cap on immigration in high tech fields by 195,000 workers for each of the years from 2001 through 2003.

c) Our immigration policies in the 19th century favored Chinese immigrants.

d) Very few immigrants have found employment in California's Silicon Valley.

13. Which statement is true?

a) The generation that came of age in the 1980s has a much higher standard of living than their parents' generation did when they came of age.

b) Most people in their 20s and 30s could be considered "yuppies."

c) The "me generation" gave new meaning to Thorstein Veblen's term *conspicuous consumption*.

d) None of these statements is true.

14. Compared to the net savings rates of the other leading industrial nations, ours is _____.

a) among the lowest   c) higher than average

b) about average   d) the highest

15. All other things remaining equal, which country in the figure below would you expect to have a higher growth rate?

a) Country A

b) Country B

c) They would have the same growth rate.

d) There is no way of telling which would have the higher growth rate.

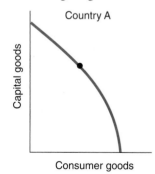

16. Our rate of productivity growth was highest in the decade of the _____.

a) 1960s   c) 1980s

b) 1970s   d) 1990s

17. Which statement best reflects the role of our educational system in preparing students for the workforce?

a) More people than ever are attending college, so our labor force is better educated than at any time in our history.

b) Business firms are having trouble finding secretaries who can spell and put together grammatically correct sentences.

c) Most people in our labor force are unable to perform their jobs because of their educational shortcomings.

d) Increased spending on teachers' salaries, science labs, and computer facilities will completely solve any educational problems this nation has.

18. Which statement is true?

a) The permanent underclass is basically an economic asset because it is a cheap source of labor.

b) The permanent underclass has slowed our rate of economic growth.

c) About 2 percent of all Americans are members of the permanent underclass.

d) Because the United States is a socially mobile society, there is no such thing as a permanent underclass.

19. Which is the most accurate statement?

a) The tremendous surge of immigrants into the United States has slowed our economic growth.

b) Most high-tech employers oppose increasing immigration quotas.

c) In 1999 and 2000 the flood of immigrants willing to take low-paying jobs has caused millions of Americans to be unemployed.

d) The Immigration and Naturalization Service has stopped trying to pick up illegal aliens.

20. Which statement is false with respect to the period 1945–1990?

a) More than half of all the research and development spending by our government was on defense.

b) Forty percent of all our scientists and engineers worked on military projects.

c) We spent about 6 percent of our GDP on defense.

d) None of these statements is false.

21. Mancur Olson suggests that the best remedy for overcoming the economic influence of special interest groups is _____.

a) bringing down the barriers to international trade

b) having the federal government curb the influence of special interest groups

c) raising tariffs on all imports that are putting American workers out of work

d) having the federal government nationalize all industries dominated by special interest groups

22. The only ways to build up capital are to _____.

a) consume more and save more

b) consume less and save less

c) consume more and save less

d) consume less and save more

23. Most people in the world live on incomes of less than _____ a year.

a) $200   c) $5,000

b) $1,500   d) $10,000

24. Rapid population growth _____ the economic development of LDCs.

a) severely hampers   c) slightly helps

b) slightly hampers   d) greatly helps

25. Malthus was correct in his predictions for _____.

a) at least some industrial countries and some LDCs

b) at least some industrial countries but no LDCs

c) at least some LDCs but no industrial countries

d) neither the LDCs nor the industrial countries

26. Which statement is false?

a) Children, who are economic assets on a farm, become just more mouths to feed in an urban setting.

b) Before economic development children are counted on for support in their parents' old age, but as development takes place, people become less dependent on this form of old-age support.

c) As economic development progresses, more children survive to adulthood, and the birthrate begins to fall.

d) None of these statements is false.

27. Since 1995 our productivity rose by more than 3 percent in _____ year(s).

a) 1   d) 11

b) 4   e) 15

c) 8

28. Which statement is true?

a) We have been spending a larger percentage of our GDP on our infrastructure than Japan and most of the nations of Western Europe.

b) Our health care costs are now nearly 10 percent of our GDP.

c) American productivity is the highest in the world.

d) None of these statements is true.

29. Which statement is true?

a) Americans work more hours and have a higher productivity than the workers of all other industrial nations.

b) The Japanese work more hours and have a higher productivity than the workers of any other industrial nation.

c) The Japanese work longer hours and Americans are more productive than the workers of any other industrial nation.

d) Americans work longer hours and the Japanese are more productive than the workers of any other industrial nation.

Fill-In Questions

1. An increase in the ratio of capital to workers is called _____.

2. Productivity is defined as _____
   _____.

3. Most Americans, French, Germans, Japanese, and British work a little under _____ hours a year.

4. In 2000 Americans were saving _____ percent of their disposable incomes.

5. The Industrial Revolution began over _____ centuries ago in _____.

6. Edward Denison attributes about _____ percent of our economic growth to increases in labor and capital and about _____ percent to increases in productivity.

7. Instead of waiting for economic development to lower birthrates, many LDCs are counting on _____ to do this.

8. The country with the highest productivity in the world is _____.

9. Sustained economic growth was made possible by the _____.

Problems

1. Given the information in Table 1, fill in Malthus's predictions for the years 2025, 2050, and 2075.

TABLE 1

Year	Food Production	Population
2000	1	1
2025	_____	_____
2050	_____	_____
2075	_____	_____

Chapter 17

Income Distribution and Poverty

The economic history of the United States has been one of tremendous growth, a rising standard of living, and a home in the suburbs for most American families. But income has not been distributed evenly, and tens of millions of Americans have been left far behind. Indeed, poverty amid plenty has been one of the basic failures of our society.

This chapter is divided into two parts: income distribution and poverty. If income were distributed evenly, every American would have an income of almost $30,000 a year—that's every man, woman, and child—and there would be no poverty. In fact, if income were distributed evenly, there would be virtually nothing to write about income distribution and poverty.

> The forces of a capitalist society, if left unchecked, tend to make the rich richer and the poor poorer.
>
> —Jawaharlal Nehru

CHAPTER OBJECTIVES

When you have finished this chapter, you will know the answers to these questions:

- How unequal is income distribution in the United States?
- What determines how income is distributed?
- How does the distribution of income differ from the distribution of wealth?
- How is poverty defined?
- Who are the poor?
- What are the main government transfer payments to help the poor?
- What are the causes of poverty?
- What are the solutions?

Income Distribution in the United States

The Poor, the Middle Class, and the Rich

I've been rich and I've been
poor; rich is better.
—Sophie Tucker

How unequal is income distribution in the United States? To answer this question, we must first answer three subsidiary questions: How unequal are the incomes of (1) the poor and the rich? (2) blacks and whites? and (3) males and females? There are no big surprises here. The rich make more money than the poor; whites make more than blacks; and men make more money than women. The question is, How much more?

Do you know what a quintile is? I'll bet no one ever asked you *that* before. A quinquennial is an event that occurs every five years; a quintuplet is one of five babies born at the same time. A *quintile* is one-fifth, just like a quarter is one-fourth. We'll use this term to measure income distribution.

Who is rich, who is middle class, and who is poor?

The poor are in the lowest quintile, the middle class in the next three quintiles, and the rich in the upper quintile. Is it accurate to say that 20 percent of our population is poor, 60 percent is middle class, and 20 percent is rich? Maybe not. But because social scientists can't agree about where to draw the dividing lines between the poor and the middle class and between the middle class and the rich, this arbitrary arrangement is as good as any other. And besides, we get to deal with nice round numbers—20, 60, and 20.

When all U.S. households are divided by income into quintiles, the middle 20 percent of households earns roughly between $30,000 and $50,000. Table 1 shows us how much the households in each quintile earned in 1999.

The Lorenz curve

Now we're going to analyze a Lorenz curve, named for M. O. Lorenz, who drew the first one in 1905. Let's begin by looking at the axes of Figure 1. On the horizontal axis we have the percentage of households, beginning with the poor (0 percent to 20 percent), running through the middle class (20 percent to 80 percent), and ending with the rich (80 percent to 100 percent). The vertical axis shows the cumulative share of income earned by these households.

Figure 1 has just two lines. The straight line that runs diagonally from the lower left to the upper right is the line of perfect equality. You'll notice that the poorest 20 percent of the households receive exactly 20 percent of the income, and that 40 percent of the households receive exactly 40 percent of the income. In other words, every household in the country makes exactly the same amount of money.

The curve to the right of the straight diagonal line is the Lorenz curve, which tells us how income is actually distributed. What percent of income does the poorest 20 percent of all households receive? And how much does the next poorest 20 percent receive? Put your answers here:

Lowest fifth:

Second fifth:

Third fifth:

TABLE 1	U.S. Household Income, by Quintile, 1999
Lowest quintile	$0–$16,799
Second quintile	16,800–30,828
Third quintile	30,829–49,015
Fourth quintile	49,016–76,009
Top quintile	76,010 and up

Source: The New York Times, October 25, 2000, Section E, p. E5.

Finding the Percentage of Income Share of the Quintiles in Figure 1

The lowest quintile receives 5 percent of all income. Right? How much does the second quintile get? It gets 7.5 percent. Where did we get that number? What is the percentage share of income earned by the lowest 40 percent of households? It looks like 12.5 percent—right? Now if the bottom quintile earns 5 percent, and the lowest two quintiles earns a total of 12.5 percent, how much do households in the second-lowest quintile earn? They earn 7.5 percent (12.5 percent − 5 percent).

Next question: How much is the cumulative percentage share of income of the lower 60 percent of households? It comes to 25 percent. So how much is the third quintile's income share? It's 12.5 percent (25 percent − 12.5 percent). In other words, we take the lower 60 percent of households' share (25 percent) and subtract from it the combined share of the lower two quintiles (12.5 percent).

The lower 80 percent receives 40 percent of income. From that, we subtract the income share of the lower 60 percent (25 percent), which leaves the fourth quintile with a 15 percent income share. One more quintile to go—the highest quintile. If 100 percent of all households receive 100 percent of all income and the lowest 80 percent of all households receive a total of 40 percent, what's left for the top quintile? You got it—60 percent.

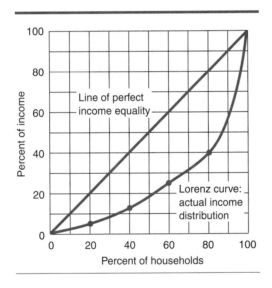

Figure 1

Hypothetical Lorenz Curve

The line of perfect income equality shows that any given percent of households receives that same percent of income. For example, the lowest 20 percent of all households would receive 20 percent of the income. Every household would receive the same income: There would be no rich or poor. The Lorenz curve shows the actual income distribution. In this particular example, the poorest 20 percent of all households receive about 5 percent of all income, while the richest fifth receives 60 percent.

Fourth fifth:

Highest fifth:

The lowest fifth receives just 5 percent of all income; the second fifth receives 7.5 percent; the third fifth receives 12.5 percent; the fourth fifth receives 15 percent; and the highest fifth receives 60 percent. (If you don't know how I got these numbers, please read the box, "Finding the Percentage of Income Share of the Quintiles in Figure 1.")

What do you think of *that* income distribution? Not very equal, is it? You'll notice the Lorenz curve is pretty far to the right of the diagonal line. That diagonal is the line of perfect equality, so the farther the Lorenz curve is from it, the less equal the distribution of income becomes.

Figure 2

Lorenz Curve of Income Distribution in the United States, 1999

Would you say that the United States has an equal distribution of income? No? I would agree. OK, what percentage of all income is received by those in the poorest 20 percent of all households, and what percentage of all income is received by those in the richest 20 percent of all households? The poorest 20 percent received 3.7 percent of all income; the richest 20 percent received 49.0 percent of all income.

Source: U.S. Bureau of the Census, *Current Population Reports, Series P–60.*

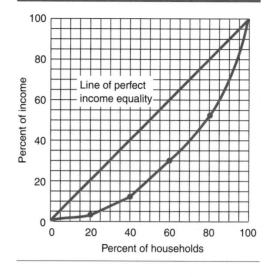

Definition of the Lorenz curve

Do you know what I forgot to do? I forgot to define the Lorenz curve. Do *you* want to take a stab at a definition? Here's mine: *A Lorenz curve shows the cumulative share of income earned by each quintile of households.*

How does our own income distribution look? It's plotted for you in Figure 2. Once again, figure out the distribution of income, and write your answers here:

Lowest fifth:

Second fifth:

Third fifth:

Fourth fifth:

Highest fifth:

Check your answers against those in the right-hand column of Table 2. Your figures don't have to match mine exactly because we're both making our own observations from the graph.

It doesn't take a rocket scientist to figure out that income distribution was more uneven at the end of the 1990s than it was in the 1960s and 1970s. We know that changes in our tax laws have been a major factor. Income tax rates and taxes on capital gains were cut, especially for the rich, while payroll tax rates were raised, taking a large bite out of the incomes of the working poor, the working class, and the lower-middle-class.

TABLE 2	Percentages of Total Income before Taxes Received by Each Fifth of American Families, 1960 and 1999	
Income Rank	1960	1999
Lowest fifth	4.8%	3.7%
Second fifth	12.2	9.0
Third fifth	17.8	15.1
Fourth fifth	24.0	23.3
Highest fifth	41.3	49.0

Source: U.S. Bureau of the Census, *Current Population Reports, Series P–60.*

Indeed, about 75 percent of all Americans pay more today in payroll taxes than they do in personal income tax.

The rich also reaped huge capital gains in the 1980s and 1990s, largely from increases in stock prices, real estate, and investments in their own businesses. During this same period the average hourly wage rate fell by more than 10 percent. Meanwhile the relatively high-paying manufacturing sector has been shedding hundreds of thousands of jobs almost every year, while employment in the relatively low-paying service sector has been rising rapidly.

Now, let's compare the distribution of income in 1999 with that in 1960. Has income become *more* evenly distributed or *less* evenly distributed? A society in which the poorest fifth of the population gets less than 4 percent of the income and the richest fifth gets nearly half has a very uneven distribution of income. Since 1960, the top fifth's share of income rose from 41.3% to 49.0%, whereas the share of each of the lower four-fifths declined. In short, then, the rich are getting richer and the poor are getting poorer.

When it is said that our income is unevenly distributed, we need to ask: relative to what standard? Obviously it is unevenly distributed relative to the line of perfect income equality in Figure 2. It is less evenly distributed relative to its distribution 40 years ago.

The global divide between the rich and the poor is much more apparent in the area of consumption spending. The richest 20 percent of humanity consume 86 percent of all goods and services, while the poorest fifth consume just 1.3 percent. In other words, when we look at the consumption rate of all the people on this planet, someone in the richest fifth consumes about 66 times as much as someone in the poorest fifth.

Has income become more equally distributed since 1960?

Distribution of Wealth in the United States

What did we learn from all those income figures in the last section? That rich people have higher incomes than poor people? But we already knew that. That rich people can enjoy a higher standard of living? We knew that, too. But we can surmise something else from these income distribution figures. The same guys who were pulling down $300,000 last year were doing it the year before and the year before that. So, over time, they were able to buy nice first homes, second homes, fancy cars, and expensive clothes; to go skiing on weekends; and maybe even to put a little bit aside for a rainy day.

And what about the working class and the poor? What have they got to show for all their years of work? Maybe a modest little home with a second mortgage, a beat-up car, and a lot of bills. Which brings us to an important conclusion: if we're going to compare living standards, we need to look not just at income distribution but at accumulated wealth. We do this in the box titled "Millionaires and Billionaires."

Has the distribution of wealth become less equal since 1980? Is it fair to call the decade of the 1980s the age of greed? Researchers at the Federal Reserve and Internal Revenue Service reported that in 1976 the richest 1 percent of our population held about 20 percent of the nation's household wealth. By 2000 the richest 1 percent held 40 percent.

Although more than 100 million Americans directly or indirectly (mainly through pension plans) own some corporate stock, the top 5 percent of all households own 77 percent of equity holdings. The bottom 80 percent own only 1.8 percent.

Let's make sure we're clear on the difference between wealth and income. Your income this year includes your annual wages or salary, as well as any interest, dividends, profits, rent and government transfer payments you received (for example, Social Security benefits, unemployment insurance benefits). Wealth includes housing and other real estate, checking and savings accounts, certificates of deposit, stocks and bonds, and other valuable assets. One reason for the greater concentration of wealth in the hands of the rich is the slashing of federal income tax rates paid by the very rich. In 1981 the top tax bracket was 70 percent; today it is 39.6 percent. But the main reason why the distribution of wealth in America is becoming less equal is because the distribution of income is becoming less equal. In summary, the rich are getting richer and the poor are getting poorer.

The rich are different from you and me.
—F. Scott Fitzgerald

Yes, they are different. They have more money.
—Ernest Hemingway

Millionaires and Billionaires

Whenever there is excessive wealth, there is also in the train of it excessive poverty; as where the sun is brightest the shade is deepest.

—Walter Savage Landor, "Aristoteles and Callisthenes," *Imaginary Conversations*

If you can count your money, you don't have a billion dollars.

—J. Paul Getty, founder, Getty Oil

Remember our discussion of millions, billions, and trillions way back in Chapter 5 of *Economics* and *Macroeconomics*? One million is written in digits with a one followed by two sets of three zeros: 1,000,000. And one billion? A one is followed by three sets of three zeros: 1,000,000,000.

So, what's a millionaire? Someone who earns a million dollars a year? No! No? That's right! To be a millionaire, all you need is a net worth of 1 million dollars. Take a minute to figure out your own net worth. Add up all your assets—your stocks and bonds, your bank deposits, and all your property. Don't forget your car, your summer cottage, or even your clothes, jewelry, and valuable stamp collection. After you've added up all your assets, do the same thing with your liabilities—that's everything you owe. Be sure to include your mortgage debt, bank loans, credit card balances, car loan, and any outstanding student loans.

Once you've added up all your assets and all your liabilities, subtract your liabilities from your assets:

$$\text{Assets} - \text{Liabilities} = \text{Net worth}$$

How much is your net worth? More than 1 million dollars? Then you're a millionaire. What happens if your liabilities are greater than your assets? Then you have a negative net worth. And what if your liabilities are 1 million dollars more than your assets? Then congratulations are in order because you are a negative millionaire.

Being a millionaire is not such a big deal in this country because there are 7 million of them. Think about it. If you owned a house that was situated in Palm Beach, Provincetown, Grosse Point, Westport, Palm Springs, Newport, or Manhattan's Park Avenue or Sutton Place, you'd be a millionaire simply because of where you lived. So, if you want to become an instant millionaire, all you need to do is move to a more affluent neighborhood.

The really rich are our billionaires—the folks with net worth in 10 figures. Yet even these people are becoming rather common. A total of 298 individuals or families have a net worth of at least $1 billion. In 1994 there were just 69.

The Forbes 2000 Top Ten List of American Billionaires*		
Name and Rank	Main Source of Income	Net Worth (in $billions)
1. William H. Gates III	Microsoft (cofounder)	63
2. Larry Ellison	Oracle (founder)	45
3. Paul Allen	Microsoft (cofounder)	36
4. Warren Buffett	Stock market	28
5. Gordon Moore	Intel (cofounder)	26
6. Philip Anschutz	Qwest Communications	18
7. Steven Balmer	Microsoft	17
8. The heirs of Sam Walton: Helen, John, Alice, S. Robson, and Jim	WalMart	17 each

*Because of a five-way tie for 8th place among the five Waltons, there are actually 12 people listed.

Source: Forbes, November 20, 2000.

Distribution of Income: Equity and Efficiency

Philosophers and economists have wrestled with these questions for centuries, but they still have not reached a conclusion. First we'll consider what a fair and just distribution of income would be, and then we'll talk about how income distribution affects the efficient operation of our economy.

We'll begin with the utilitarian view based on the law of diminishing marginal utility, which was discussed with great eloquence in the chapter on the theory of consumer behavior in *Economics* and *Microeconomics*. On the off chance that you don't fully recall this important law, I'll restate it: *As we consume increasing amounts of a good or service, we derive diminishing utility or satisfaction from each additional unit consumed.*

Let's seat a rich person and a poor person side by side in a booth at McDonald's and place a Big Mac in front of each of them. The rich person and the poor person wolf down the burgers with equal delight. So we place a second Big Mac in front of each of them and, if their appetites are big enough, a third and a fourth. When will they stop chowing down? When they've had enough. Who will stop first—the poor person or the rich person? We don't know. Would it be reasonable to guess that they would stop at about the same time? I think so.

What does all of this prove? It proves that Big Macs are enjoyed by people from all income groups. It also indicates that poor people and rich people get about the same satisfaction from Big Macs, Whoppers, Bruce Springsteen concerts, and all the other available goods and services.

The only problem is that the poor person can't afford to buy nearly as much as the rich person can. The rich person can buy all the Big Macs he wants, but the poor person can afford just one—without enough money remaining for a side of fries. What if the rich person gave one dollar to the poor person? The rich person would have more than enough money left. He can afford to buy all the Big Macs *and* french fries he'll ever want and *still* have plenty of money left over.

OK, so would it be such a bad thing for the rich guy to fork over a buck or two to the poor guy? After all, that money would mean a whole lot more to the poor guy. But now we'll carry this redistribution scheme to its logical conclusion. Let's have everyone who's earning more than the average income give his surplus to everyone who is earning less. When we've finished, we'll all have exactly the same income. I have just stated the utilitarian case for equality.

What do *you* think? Is this fair? What about the people who worked hard for their money, putting in hours of overtime, holding down two jobs, and never seeing their families or friends? And what about the lazy bums who don't even bother looking for a job because they know they'll have exactly the same income as the working stiffs?

So much for a fair and just distribution of income. How does income distribution affect our economic efficiency? Well, for starters, what would an equal distribution of income do to work incentives? Would *you* work hard if you'd end up with exactly the same income as a lot of people who just sat at home and waited for their checks? Two of the things that make our economy go are the carrot and the stick. The carrot is all the money you can make by working hard. And the stick is that if you don't work, you don't eat.

Another incentive that would suffer is the incentive to save. Considering that the interest you'd get from your savings would be divided among everyone, why bother to save at all? Why invest, for that matter? Why bother to engage in any productive activities whatsoever, when we'll all end up with the same income no matter what we do?

Of course, if we were to pursue this reasoning to its logical conclusion, we would end up with very little output (because only a few workaholics would still be producing) and therefore very little real income.

So what should we do? Neither extreme seems desirable. Complete income equality would rob us of our productive incentives. And great income inequality would mean a great deal of human suffering, because many of the poor would not be able to afford even the basic necessities of life.

The utilitarian view

Poverty is an anomaly to rich people; it is very difficult to make out why people who want dinner do not ring the bell.
—Walter Bagehot

Short of genius, a rich man cannot imagine poverty.
—Charles Péguy

How does income distribution affect our economic efficiency?

Whatever the means of income redistribution, the ends are always the same—to take from the rich and give to the poor. Robin Hood may not have won favor with the Sheriff of Nottingham or with the rich people he robbed, but most folks agree that the rich—*and* the middle class—should give some of their money to the poor. The only question is, How much?

What Determines Income Distribution?

What *does* determine income distribution? Remember the adage "It's not *what* you know; it's *who* you know"? (Actually, it's *whom* you know.) So is *that* all there is? Connections?

Did David Rockefeller rise quickly through the ranks to attain the presidency of Chase Manhattan Bank back in the 1960s solely because he had a Ph.D. in economics, while I couldn't even get an interview? (I really couldn't.) Not that his family's huge holding of Chase Manhattan stock had anything to do with it. In general, it is fair to say that connections don't hurt, but once you have your foot in the door you've got to have *something*. I might be able to get you a tryout with the Atlanta Braves, but if you can't pitch—or hit—don't hold out for *too* big a signing bonus.

Some people make a lot more money than most others do. Why? Is it training, education, intelligence, inborn skills, physical attributes, or just plain luck? Yes. Yes? Yes, it's all of the above. And don't forget about job discrimination. Few WASP males have encountered it, but just ask most women, blacks, Hispanics, and members of other racial, religious, and ethnic minorities about it.

About three-fifths of all personal income is earned in wages and salaries, so we'll concentrate on the factors causing these incomes to vary so widely. And then we'll take a look at property income, which accounts for a little less than one-quarter of all personal income. Finally, we'll look at government transfer payments, which account for the rest.

Differences in Wages and Salaries   Why do doctors make more than word processors? Why do professional athletes make more than cashiers? The questions may change from chapter to chapter, but the answer remains the same: supply and demand. Basically, the people in certain occupations are in relatively short supply. Relative to what? Relative to the demand for their services.

A doctor must go through not just four years of college and four years of medical school but also a year's internship and at least three years of residency. Consider all those years of little or no income, all that money going toward tuition and living expenses, all those student loans to pay back. And, incidentally, consider all that malpractice insurance that still has to be paid out in the years to come.

Doctors are in short supply relative to the demand for medical services. And they're kept in short supply by the American Medical Association, as noted in the chapter on labor unions in *Economics* and *Macroeconomics*. But I've overlooked the intelligence and ability of the person who becomes a doctor. These factors also greatly influence how much doctors earn. One might ask why, then, Ph.D.s in history, philosophy, or even economics don't earn what doctors do. Once again, we're back to supply and demand. I'm still waiting for that long-predicted Ph.D. shortage to materialize so college teaching salaries will finally start going up.

How important is education? We *do* know college graduates earn a lot more than high school graduates; M.B.A.s, particularly those who have taken the trouble to attend Harvard, Columbia, Wharton, or the University of Chicago, are getting starting salaries of $100,000 or more, and graduates of our more illustrious law schools are pulling down similar salaries.

How many times have you heard that in today's high-tech economy, you not only need to know reading, writing, and arithmetic, but you must be computer literate as well? As the blue-collar workforce shrinks, more and more people are getting office jobs, and there's a computer terminal on virtually every desk. Are training and education important? You tell *me*.

[margin note:] Why do some people earn more than others?

[margin note:] How important is education?

Everyone tells us that the longer we stay in school, the more money we'll make for the rest of our lives. Is this true? Yes, it is. The average college graduate will earn almost three times the income earned by someone who has not completed the eighth grade. Why? Because of everything the college graduate learned in school? Not necessarily. Because of the college diploma, which is the minimum entrance requirement for many jobs? Possibly.

The main reasons the college graduate earns so much more than the grade school dropout are that the college graduate is probably smarter, richer, and more motivated; has better connections; and comes from a home with a more supportive learning environment. In other words, the personal characteristics of the two people, rather than their respective educations, determine their earning power. This is not to say that education does not affect earning power at all or that many poor people, given the opportunity, could not do well in school and go on to brilliant careers selling junk bonds or even writing economics textbooks.

Why does a college graduate earn more than a grade school dropout?

But before we get too excited about the importance of education and training as determinants of income, we might want to take a look at the role credentials play in the hiring process. Employers use years of schooling mainly as a screening device. *Does more schooling make you more productive?* My nephew Jonah tells me that what he learned in law school has virtually nothing to do with what he's been doing these last 15 years in mergers, acquisitions, and trusts and estates. The title of Robert Fulghum's best-seller sums it up: *All I Really Need to Know I Learned in Kindergarten.*

How important is talent? Sometimes it's very important. Michael Jackson has brought home about $60 million a year since 1989. In the mid-1990s Oprah Winfrey (her mother loved Harpo Marx and named her after him by spelling his name backward) earned an average of $150 million a year. Another field where talent usually rises to the top is sales. Those with the best communication skills and the most extroverted personalities generally do the best, whether they're selling real estate, used cars, insurance, or aluminum siding.

How important is talent?

And yet talent is usually not a decisive factor in determining how much people earn. In most organizations, both public and private, new employees are hired at the same starting salaries, and they advance in lockstep from one pay level to the next. More than talent and ability, and education or training, the most important factor in determining pay level seems to be seniority.

Those who have really made it big have been able to climb the corporate ladder. Table 3 lists the 10 best-paid chief executive officers in corporate America. The average corporate chieftain now makes more in a single day than the typical American worker makes in a year.

How many women did you see listed in Table 3? Not one. Well, that's not fair. So we've listed the highest paid female corporate executives in Table 4. What do you notice about their compensation? First, they're very well paid. And second, they earn about one-tenth of the pay that their top ten male counterparts recieve.

The 1960s and 1970s were decades of great social upheaval. The women's liberation movement and the civil rights movement sought to place women, blacks, and other minorities squarely in the socioeconomic mainstream. Although these movements and the public- and private-sector hiring programs they engendered have had a major impact in promoting equal economic opportunity, employment discrimination persists.

Through the 1960s women working full time were stuck earning around 60 percent of what men earned. In 1973 the median wage for women was just 63 percent of that for men. By 2000 it had risen to almost 80 percent. The average college-educated woman, however, still earns less than the average high school-educated man.

Employment discrimination can be measured in two basic ways: by relative income and by occupation. Traditionally, blacks have earned about 60 percent of what whites have earned, while women working full time have also earned about 60 percent of what was earned by their male counterparts. Moreover, women have traditionally entered very specific occupations, most notably the three Ss (schoolteacher, secretary, and social

Blacks have traditionally earned 60 percent of what whites earned.

TABLE 3   The 10 Best-Paid CEOs in 2000

Rank	Name	Company	Total Compensation (in $millions)
1	John Reed*	Citigroup	$293.0
2	Sanford Weill	Citigroup	224.9
3	Gerald Levin	AOL Time Warner	163.8
4	John Chambers	Cisco Systems	157.3
5	Henry Silverman	Cendant	136.7
6	L. Dennis Kozlowski	Tyco International	125.3
7	Jack Welch	General Electric	122.6
8	David Peterschmidt	Inktomi	107.6
9	Kevin Kalkhoven	JDS Uniphase	106.9
10	David Wetherell	CMGI	103.7

*Retired April 2000
Source: BusinessWeek, April 16, 2001.

TABLE 4   The Highest-Paid Women in America

Rank	Name	Company	Total Compensation (in $millions)
1	Heather Killen	Senior Vice President, Yahoo!	$32.7
2	Dawn G. Lepore	Vice Chmn., Exec VP & CIO, Charles Schwab	22.3
3	M. Zita Cobb	Executive Vice President, JDS Uniphase	18.7
4	Susan D. Desmond-Hellmann	Executive Vice President, Genentech	16.1
5	Terri A. Dial	Group Executive Vice President Wells Fargo	12.8
6	Janice M. Roberts	Senior Vice President, 3Com	12.2
7	Lois D. Juliber	COO, Colgate-Palmolive	12.2
8	Donna S. Birks	Executive Vice President & CFO, Adaptive Broadband	10.4
9	Deborah C. Hopkins	Executive VP & CFO, Lucent Technologies	9.5
10	Leslie C. Tortora	CIO, Goldman Sachs Group	9.4

Source: BusinessWeek, April 23, 2001.

Women have traditionally earned 60 percent of what men have earned.

Unemployment is an important determinant of income level.

worker) as well as nurse, cashier, waitress, maid, telephone operator, and dressmaker. In fact, these occupations were long considered "women's work." Blacks and Hispanics also were confined largely to low-paid factory work, janitorial duties, and, until the late 1940s, farm labor.

Unemployment—or, more broadly, the lack of employment—is an important determinant of the income level of millions of Americans. We'll start with the fact that over the last four decades the unemployment rate for blacks has been consistently double that of whites. As noted previously, when it's a recession for whites, it's a depression for blacks.[1]

---

[1]See the box with this title in the chapter on economic fluctuations, unemployment, and inflation in *Economics* and *Macroeconomics.*

Property Income   Wages and salaries accounted for 62 percent of personal income in 1997, property income accounted for 26 percent, and government transfer payments for 12 percent. As you might have suspected, most property income goes to the rich. These payments are in the form of rent, interest, dividends, and profits (which include capital gains).

The two largest sources of wealth, exclusive of inheritance, have been the fortunes made in the stock market and the starting up of new companies. In the computer field alone, great fortunes were made by Lawrence Ellison (Oracle), Gordon Earle Moore (Intel), Steve Jobs (Apple), Kenneth Olsen (Digital), William Gates, Paul Gardner Allen, and Steven Anthony Ballmer (Microsoft), An Wang (Wang Laboratories), and David Packard (Hewlett-Packard), and, of course, Ross Perot (Electronic Data Systems). Stock market investors who hit it big include Warren Buffet, Edward Crosby Johnson III, and Ronald Owen Perelman.[2]

A *Fortune* magazine cover story, "America's Forty Richest Under 40," revealed the sources of wealth of these young billionaires (number 40 on the list was actually worth only $431 million). Virtually all, from Michael Dell ($17 billion) on down, made their fortunes in some aspect of computer technology, usually founding their own companies. Seventeen of the 40 are based in California's Silicon Valley.

Property income may also be derived from ownership of stocks, bonds, bank deposits, and other assets. Because the poor and the working class hold little property, little (if any) of their income comes from this source. Those in the middle class derive somewhat more of their income from property, but rarely more than 10 percent. And the rich? Well, the superrich, those whose annual incomes surpass $100 million, get most or all of their income from rent, interest, and profits. The people who live exclusively on their property income are sometimes called rentiers, which simply means they don't have to work for a living.

Income from Government Transfer Payments   In addition to wages, salaries, and property income, some people receive government transfer payments. For retirees, Social Security benefits may be their main means of support. For most people collecting unemployment benefits, these checks are usually their sole means of support. And public assistance recipients all depend on these benefits plus food stamps for nearly all of their income.

Social Security benefits, which constitute more than two-thirds of all federal government transfer payments, are not aimed specifically at the poor, but they do help millions of older people rise above the poverty line. Similarly, Medicare helps the elderly regardless of income level. Unemployment benefits, which go to less than half of the unemployed, happen to go disproportionately to those in lower income groups.

The public assistance and food stamp programs are targeted solely at poor people. The basic philosophy is to provide subsistence to those who are down on their luck and in dire need of help. However, as we shall see in the second part of this chapter, in recent decades a permanent underclass has become completely dependent on government aid.

Virtually all of us agree that a certain amount of income redistribution is needed, but where we part company is in specifying just how much should be redistributed. We all want to see a more equitable and yet more efficient society, but we are far from reaching a consensus as to how that can be attained.

This brings us to the question of poverty in America. We're painfully aware that it's out there, but we're not sure what should be done about it. Like other subjects in economics, poverty and income distribution raise a lot of interesting questions. Unfortunately, there is little consensus on the correct answers.

Some people's money is merited. And other people's money is inherited.

—Ogden Nash

The largest sources of wealth

Social Security benefits constitute more than two-thirds of all federal government transfer payments.

---

[2]*Fortune,* "America's Forty Richest Under 40," September 18, 2000.

Mobility

How income is distributed would be less important if our society were upwardly mobile. If millions of Americans went from rags to riches every year, whether by hitting the lottery, being handed $1 million by Regis Phibin, cashing in on stock options, or climbing the corporate ladder, then it wouldn't matter as much if the rich were getting richer and the poor were getting poorer. That's because so many of the rich used to be poor, and so many of the poor used to be rich. So the million-dollar question is this: Is America an upwardly mobile society? The answer will immediately become apparent when you glance at Figure 3.

Compared to several European countries, the United States is certainly not a very upwardly mobile society. Only 17 percent of all poor American whites rose out of poverty within one year, while just 8 percent of all poor blacks managed to do so. And yet, 44 percent of the poor Dutch and 37 percent of the poor Swedes were about to leave poverty within a year.

Figure 3

Upward Mobility: Europe vs. the United States**

Percentage share of poor who left poverty with a year in the 1980s
Source: BusinessWeek, February 26, 1996, p. 90. Data: Greg I. Duncan, Northwestern University.

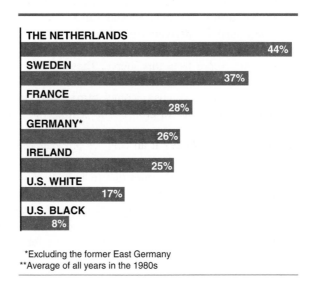

THE NETHERLANDS — 44%
SWEDEN — 37%
FRANCE — 28%
GERMANY* — 26%
IRELAND — 25%
U.S. WHITE — 17%
U.S. BLACK — 8%

*Excluding the former East Germany
**Average of all years in the 1980s

Poverty in America

In this part of the chapter we'll examine the dimensions of the poverty problem in the United States, some of its causes, how we're dealing with it, and some possible remedies. But first we need to define poverty.

Poverty Defined

The relative concept of poverty

There are two basic ways to define poverty: as a relative concept and as an absolute concept. So far, by defining the poor as the lowest income quintile (that is, the lowest 20 percent) in the nation, we set up poverty as a relative concept. In other words, this group of people is poor relative to the rest of the population.

But there are a couple of problems with this definition. First, suppose everyone's standard of living quadrupled from one year to the next. We'd *still* be calling those in the lowest quintile poor, even though most of the "poor" would be living better this year than the entire middle class lived last year. Although Jesus *did* say, "Ye have the poor always with you" (Matthew 26:11), *these* poor people would be driving late-model cars, living in nice houses, and eating in fancy restaurants three or four nights a week.

A second difficulty with the concept of relative poverty is that the lowest income quintile in the United States and other relatively rich countries is infinitely better off than the average citizens of the world's poorest nations. In Bangladesh, Ethiopia, and Somalia, most people struggle to survive on maybe $200 or $300 a year. Even our homeless population fares considerably better than that.

What about the absolute concept of poverty? Well, there's one basic problem here, too. Who gets to determine the dividing line between poor and not poor, and how is that determination reached? The best approach is to set up a minimum basic standard of living and figure out how much it costs to maintain that standard from year to year. So far, so good. OK, so who gets to set up this basic living standard, and what goods and services should go into it?

The absolute concept of poverty

The World Bank defines poverty as living on less than the equivalent of one U.S. dollar a day. Today 1.5 billion people (about one-quarter of the world's population)— mainly in Asia, Africa, and Latin America—live on less than a dollar a day. And half the world's population, some 3 billion people, struggle to survive on less than $2 a day. One quarter of the people in the world lack access to clean drinking water, and half the world's people have yet to make or receive a telephone call. By contrast, one of the biggest political questions is whether drivers should be allowed to talk on their cell phones.

The most widely used poverty standard in the United States is the official poverty line calculated each year by the U.S. Department of Agriculture. The department bases its estimate on the assumption that poor families spend about one-third of their incomes on food. Each year it calculates the minimum food budget for a family of four for one week, multiplies that figure by 52 for the family's annual food budget, and then triples that figure to get the official poverty line. In 1999 that line was set at $17,029 for a family of four.

The official poverty line

Can a family of four live on $17,029? It all depends on what you mean by living. Is it enough to put food on the table, clothes on your back, and a roof over your head? In some parts of the country, the answer is yes. In the more expensive cities such as New York, Boston, and San Francisco, as well as in many suburban communities, especially in the Northeast, $17,029 won't provide even the bare necessities, largely because of relatively high rents. Of course, all we're talking about here is a definition. When we get to the topic of public assistance in a few pages, we'll see that virtually none of the nation's thousands of locally administered welfare programs brings any of the poor up to the poverty line. Indeed, few even come close.

Once the poverty line has been established, we can find the poverty rate by dividing the number of poor people by the total population of the country. In other words, the poverty rate is the percentage of Americans who are poor.

The Census Bureau has been tracking the poverty rate since 1960. As you can observe in Figure 4, there was a sharp decline throughout the 1960s and early 1970s. In 1973 the rate bottomed out at 11.1 percent, about half the 1960 rate. The main causes of the decline were the prosperity of the 1960s and the War on Poverty conducted by the administration of President Lyndon Johnson. The federal government spent tens of billions of dollars on education, job training, and the creation of government jobs for millions of poor people.

But recessions in 1973–75, 1980, and 1981–82 pushed the poverty rate back up to 15.2 percent in 1983. Furthermore, President Ronald Reagan, who believed antipoverty programs were just "throwing money at problems," persuaded Congress to dismantle some of these programs. Reagan argued that his economic program—basically, massive tax cuts—would create enough jobs in the private sector to put millions of poor people to work in productive (rather than make-work) jobs. Indeed, from 1983 to 1989 1 million poor people or so were added to the employment rolls. Although the majority of these jobs were relatively low-paying positions in the service sector, the poverty rate *did* decline from 15.2 percent in 1983 to 12.8 percent in 1989. It rose again during the recession of 1990–91, peaking in 1993. The poverty rate has fallen steadily since then to 11.8 percent in 1999, a period of rapid economic growth and falling unemployment. But in 1999 there were still 32 million Americans living below the poverty line.

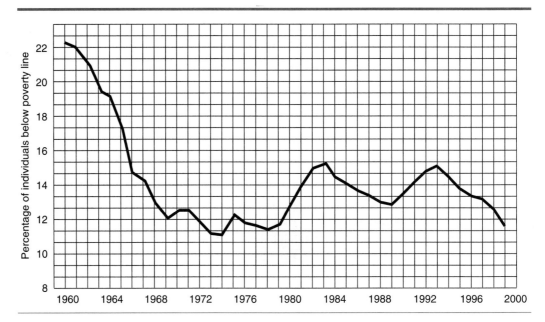

Figure 4

U.S. Poverty Rate: Percentage of Individuals Below the Poverty Line, 1960–99*

The poverty rate was cut in half between 1960 and 1973, largely because of President Lyndon Johnson's war on poverty, much of which was continued and even expanded under President Richard Nixon. However, the poverty rate rose again in the 1980s and began to decline once more in the mid- and late 1990s. However, it remains well above the low of 11.1 percent attained in 1973.

*In 1993 the Census Bureau adopted a different system of statistical weighting from the one used in previous years.

Source: U.S. Bureau of the Census.

> The poverty rate would be substantially lower if we counted the value of in-kind benefits.

Some conservative critics point out that the poverty rate would be substantially lower if we counted the value of noncash, or in-kind, benefits given to the poor by the government. These include Medicaid, housing subsidies, low-rent public housing, food stamps, and school lunches. If these in-kind benefits were counted, the poverty rate would have been 8.8 percent in 1999 rather than the reported 11.8 percent.

Who Are the Poor?

Who *are* the poor? Old people? Traditionally, people older than 65 have had a much higher poverty rate than the general population, but the advent of Medicare, higher Social Security benefits, and supplementary Social Security benefits over the last three decades has reduced the poverty rate for older Americans to well below the overall rate. In 1999 it was 9.7 percent.

> Most poor people are white.

Are most poor people black? No, most poor people are white. It *is* true that almost one out of four blacks is poor, but only 13 percent of our population is black. Figure 5 shows the relative poverty rates for white, black, and Hispanic Americans. Although one out of every three blacks lives below the poverty line, the poorest population group is Native American. The National Indian Policy Center says that 47 percent of the people living on Indian reservations and trust lands are poor.

OK, so our first two stereotypes of the poor as elderly and black or Hispanic were wrong. Ready for another shocker? Where do the majority of the poor live? In the cities? Wrong again! Most poor people actually live outside the cities. They live in the suburbs, in small towns, and in rural areas. While it *is* true that the majority of the poor are white residents of the suburbs, small towns, or the countryside, a disproportionate number of the poor are urban blacks and Hispanics. So if you want to be poor, you can increase your chances substantially by being black or Hispanic and living in a large city.

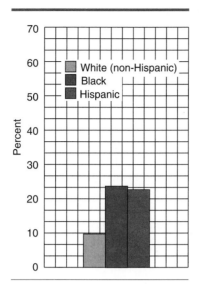

Figure 5
Poverty Rates by Race, 1999
The poverty rates of blacks and hispanics is nearly three times that of whites.
Source: U.S. Bureau of the Census.

Speaking of improving your chances of being poor, if you happen to be a member of a female-headed household with children, your chances improve to about one out of two. And if that household happens to be black or Hispanic, then you stand an even better chance. To a large degree, then, your chances of being rich or poor in the United States have a lot to do with how skillfully you have chosen your ancestors.

So who *are* the poor? About three-quarters are single mothers and their children. People living in the rural South and in the Appalachian region have relatively high poverty rates. In 1999 the state with the highest poverty rate was New Mexico with 20.5 percent, and Maryland, with 7.2 percent, had the lowest. Migrant farm workers, native Americans, and recent immigrants are also much more likely than the general population to be poor.

And then there are the people who once held jobs in declining industries like steel, automobiles, rubber, oil, textiles, and apparel, as well as in mining and farming. Many have been forced to take minimum-wage jobs in service industries, and others have found no jobs at all.

Americans work at or close to the minimum wage in fast-food restaurants, laundries, and hospitals, on farms, and even in illegal sweatshops around the country. A person earning $5.15 an hour for 35 hours a week earns an annual income of just $9,373 (before taxes), which would clearly leave a family of four—or three, for that matter—well below the poverty line.

All the people employed at or just above the minimum wage could be considered the working poor. Most of them receive little or no government benefits yet somehow manage to make ends meet from paycheck to paycheck. But even if they don't get one cent from the government, they are still part of our poverty problem. (And what about the homeless? See box.)

Finally, there are the chronically (long-term) unemployed and the discouraged workers. Although the U.S. unemployment rate has been very low during the last few years, this measure does not take into account the millions of Americans who have been out of work for years. The official unemployment statistics count only those who have actively sought employment; people who have given up looking for jobs are not included. The Bureau of Labor Statistics calls the latter group "discouraged workers." If the long-term unemployed—both officially unemployed and officially discouraged—were fully accounted for, we would be talking about another 3 or 4 million people.

God must love the poor—he made so many of them.
—Abraham Lincoln

The working poor

The long-term unemployed

The Homeless

The law, in its majestic equality, forbids the rich as well as the poor to sleep under bridges, to beg in the streets, and to steal bread.

—Anatole France

We've created a lot of $6-an-hour jobs and not much $6-an-hour housing.

—John Donahue
Chicago Coalition for the Homeless

There have always been homeless people in America—the hobo jungles of the Depression era, the skid rows (or skid roads, as they are known in the West), and, of course, the isolated shopping-bag ladies and other folks who lived out on the street, in doorways, or in train stations. But now there are literally millions of them. In a nation of some 281 million people, between 2 and 3 million are homeless.* During the winter of 2000–2001 New York City provided temporary shelter to more than 25,000 homeless people every night. And advocates of the homeless have estimated that another 60,000 to 90,000 sleep in privately run shelters, in bus and railroad terminals, or out on the street.

A convergence of four trends has multiplied the number of homeless people who congregate in all our large cities. Since World War II the number of entry-level factory jobs has steadily declined in every large city. Meanwhile, the availability of cheap housing (basically furnished rooms) has also declined as the cities' more dilapidated neighborhoods were demolished to make way for urban renewal projects.

A third trend has been gentrification, which has pushed rents through the roof, so to speak, in New York, San Francisco, Boston, Chicago, and most other major cities. Finally, the deinstitutionalization of the mentally ill over the last two decades (without the promised halfway houses to treat and shelter them) has further added to the homeless population.

The U.S. Department of Health and Human Services estimates that one-third of the homeless are mentally ill. That agency also estimates that half of the homeless are alcoholics or drug addicts, and few are receiving treatment. Interestingly, about one-quarter of the homeless work full time, according to the U.S. Conference of Mayors. The problem for them is being trapped between jobs that pay too little and housing that costs too much.

Not all of the homeless are poor. Most of the 20,000 homeless people have jobs in California's Santa Clara County, which covers most of the Silicon Valley. Since 1992 more than 250,000 new jobs have been created, but only 40,000 new housing units have been built. There are people earning more than $50,000 who live in shelters or in their cars.†

---

*There are widely varying estimates of the number of homeless people in the United States. Christopher Jencks (*The Homeless,* Cambridge, MA: Harvard University Press, 1994, chapter 1) makes an estimate of 400,000 to 500,000 for 1987 and presumably would make a much higher estimate today. While a reliable census of the homeless isn't possible, if we include individuals and families who are temporarily staying with relatives and friends, an estimate of 2 to 3 million is reasonable.

†*The Sunday Times,* Central Contra Costa, February 20, 2000, p. A. 16; Aaron Bernstein, "Down and Out in Silicon Valley," *BusinessWeek,* March 27, 2000, pp. 76–92.

Child Poverty

Perhaps the most striking thing about poverty in America is how it affects children. Particularly hard hit by poverty are black children and Hispanic children (see Figure 6). "Children are our future" may be a cliché, but they are nevertheless a future that we neglect at our peril.

The United Nations Children's Fund (Unicef) uses a relative measure of poverty. Children are defined as poor if they live in households with incomes below 50 percent of the national median. You can see from Figure 7 that the relative poverty rate of American children is extremely high. We cannot conclude that poor American children are worse off than poor Italian or British children or Canadian children. But we certainly *can* say that the standard of living of poor American children is extremely low compared to those of middle-class and rich American children.

Figure 7 provides a snapshot of the *relative* child poverty rates of many countries. In terms of *absolute* child poverty in the United States, in 1999 one of every six children lived in a household with an income below the official poverty line.

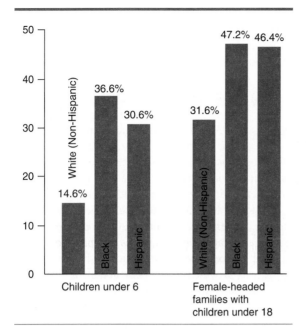

Figure 6
Poverty Rates of Selected
Population Groups, by Race,
1999

Of these population groups shown
here, the one most likely to be poor
is the black female-headed family
with children under 18.
Source: U.S. Bureau of the Census.

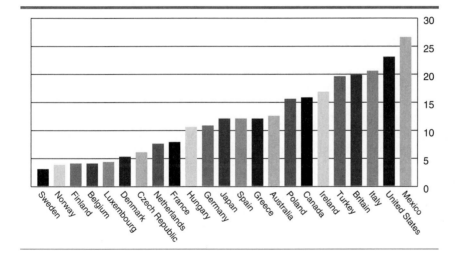

Figure 7
Children Living in Relative
Poverty, Selected Countries,
1999

Percentage living in households
with income below 50 percent of
the national median.
Source: Unicef

Large-scale, high-rise, low-income public housing projects have been especially good breeding grounds for this culture of poverty. In these neighborhoods at least three-quarters of the families are on welfare, most of the girls get pregnant before they are 18, and there is a great degree of drug dependency and an extremely high rate of violent crime. The gangs are the real authority in the ghetto, according to Nicholas Lemann. The gang "forces kids through physical terror, to give up school and work and become professional criminals."[3] To some degree this phenomenon has evolved in poor Hispanic and non-Hispanic white neighborhoods as well.

The civil rights revolution led by the Reverend Martin Luther King, Jr., in the early 1960s and the federal civil rights legislation passed in its wake gave rise to a tremendous black exodus from the ghettos as central city housing barriers came tumbling down. Everyone who could get out got out. These middle-class and working-class families fled the squalor, crime, and inferior schools of the ghettos for the apartments and private homes formerly owned by the white middle- and working-class families who had already made their own exodus—to the suburbs.

[3]Nicholas Lemann, "The Origins of the Underclass," *Atlantic Monthly,* June 1986, p. 39.

A decent provision for the poor
is a true test of civilization.
—Samuel Johnson

Later in the chapter we'll be discussing William Julius Wilson's view of how these events brought about the formation of a permanent black underclass in the ghettos of the nation's large cities. Right now let's see how the federal government has dealt with this great upsurge in urban poverty.

The Main Government Transfer Programs

The Social Security Act of 1935

The Social Security Act of 1935 set up three major programs: Social Security, unemployment insurance, and public assistance. Taxes paid by workers and their employers financed the first two programs. Public assistance, which was intended to help families experiencing temporary economic distress, was the only means-tested program. To obtain public assistance (or relief, as it was then called), you needed to demonstrate that your income or means of support was insufficient to cover your basic needs.

Medicare and Medicaid

Two major programs, Medicare and Medicaid, were added in the mid-1960s under President Johnson's Great Society program. Medicare, which was really a supplement to Social Security, provided retirees and their families with free or very low-cost medical care. Free medical care was provided to the poor under Medicaid.

Forty-five million Americans
have no health insurance.

There are about 45 million Americans who have no health insurance. Nearly all are among the working poor—too young to receive Medicare and too well-off to receive Medicaid. Their low-paying jobs do not provide health insurance, so they often must go without any medical care whatsoever.

Today one out of every ten Americans receives food stamps, which represents just 40 percent of those who are eligible. The food stamp program, which also began in the 1960s, enabled the very poor as well as the working poor to buy enough food. Like Medicare and Medicaid, it has expanded tremendously since the late 1960s.

Have these programs worked? Yes, they have. Each has accomplished what it was set up to do. But there are three major problems: (1) their costs have gone through the roof; (2) they have fostered a permanent dependency on government support among millions of poor families; and (3) they have not ended poverty.

Public assistance has been the greatest disappointment. About half the money spent goes to female-headed families that stay on the program for eight years or more. Intended to provide "temporary relief," public assistance has instead engendered a permanent dependence in millions of families.

The number of people receiving public assistance remained remarkably steady—at about 11 million—from 1975 through 1989. Although we were hit with back-to-back recessions from 1980 to 1982, which ordinarily would have produced an increase in the rolls, the Reagan administration managed to institute sharp eligibility cutbacks, which prevented such an increase. But the welfare rolls shot up from 11 million in mid-1993 to a peak of 14.4 million in March 1994. The main reason for this increase was the recession of 1990–91. By early 1994, the benefits of the subsequent economic expansion finally began to reach people at the bottom of the economic ladder, and the welfare rolls began to decline. Another important factor has been that many states have restricted eligibility for welfare.

One misconception about welfare mothers is that they keep having more and more children so that they can collect bigger checks. Indeed, many states no longer increase the size of a welfare grant if more children are born into a family. But 72 percent of all welfare families have only one or two children.

The welfare culture

A welfare culture has evolved over the last four decades, giving rise to second-, third-, and fourth-generation welfare families. Typically, teenage girls become pregnant, keep their babies, go on welfare, do not marry, and have no hope of becoming self-supporting. In a sense, the young mothers are provided with surrogate husbands in the form of public assistance checks. Eventually their children grow up, become teenage parents themselves, and continue the welfare pattern through another generation. The challenge we face is how to break this pattern and help these families become self-supporting.

What we keep coming back to is the overwhelmingly high poverty rate of children. Some 22 percent of Americans now aged 18 to 20 spent at least one year on welfare before they were 18; for 18- to 20-year-old blacks, that figure is 72 percent.

The words of one welfare mother are especially poignant: "I'm sorry I got myself into this and my children into this. And I don't know how to get them out of it. If I don't get them away from here, they're going to end up dead, in jail, or like me."[4]

Theories of the Causes of Poverty

Any theory of poverty must take into account our entire socioeconomic system, how it is set up, how it is run, and who gets what. Poor people live on the margin or even beyond the system. They are basically superfluous and rarely have much impact on the system. They are an unfortunate presence, by-products that have been discarded but are grudgingly tolerated by society's "productive" members.

At least a dozen theories of poverty have attracted support, and each has at least *some* apparent validity. But because there are so many different poverty groups, no single theory can have universal applicability. We'll begin by briefly outlining a few theories, and then we'll look at the two with the largest number of adherents: the conservative and liberal theories.

The Poor Are Lazy　This theory was popular through most of the 19th century and right up to the time of the Great Depression. God's chosen people, who were destined to go to heaven, worked hard all their lives and were rewarded by attaining great earthly riches. And the poor? Well, you can figure out for yourself where they were headed. This theory went down the tubes when the Great Depression hit and millions of relatively affluent Americans were thrown out of work, lost their life savings, and had to ask the government for handouts.

The Heritage of Slavery　Because blacks were brought here in chains and held back for three centuries by slavery and a feudal sharecropping system in the South, the current poverty of many blacks can be explained by centuries of oppression. Not only were blacks systematically excluded from all but the most menial jobs, but they were denied the educational opportunities open to almost all other Americans. Mortgage loans, restaurant meals, hotel and motel lodging, union membership, and apartment rentals were routinely denied. In effect, then, blacks were systematically excluded from the nation's economic mainstream until the 1960s. Is it any wonder, ask adherents of this theory, that after so many years of oppression both during and after slavery, many blacks still find themselves mired in poverty?

Employment Discrimination　All the way back in Chapter 2 we talked about how employment discrimination causes our economy to operate at less than its full potential. Employment discrimination has been especially strong in holding down the incomes of women, blacks, Hispanics, and other minorities. The fact that women working full-time have generally earned about four-fifths of what their male counterparts have earned clearly points toward discrimination. Similar figures for blacks and Hispanics arouse the same suspicion.

Full-time working women have earned 60 percent of what full-time working men earned.

But other factors have also contributed to these wage differentials—education, training, and experience, and, in the case of many women, the years taken off work to raise children. Social scientists generally believe that about half of these wage differentials result from employment discrimination and the other half from other factors. As more employment opportunities become available to women and to minorities, we may see a narrowing of wage differentials. Meanwhile, employment discrimination has obviously been playing a major role in the poverty of women, blacks, Hispanics, and other minorities.

---

[4]See Celia W. Dugger, "On the Edge of Survival: Single Mothers on Welfare," *New York Times*, July 6, 1992, p. B6.

Black Male Joblessness   Back in 1970, about 33 percent of all black families were headed by women. By the mid-1990s, the number had jumped to over 60 percent. The growing perception of a permanent welfare population of single black mothers and their children has raised the question of where the young black males are who got them pregnant. In college? Playing major-league ball? Hardly.

While more than four-fifths of all white males aged 20 to 44 are employed, only about half of their black counterparts have jobs. What are the rest of them doing? Some are officially unemployed, and some are "discouraged workers" who have stopped looking for work. And where are the rest of these guys? Some may be working in the underground economy—in either the legal or illegal sector. And others have just slipped through the cracks. (See the box, "The Darity–Myers Thesis.")

The decline in manufacturing has been especially brutal to young black men. According to William Julius Wilson, "48 percent of all employed black males, ages 20 to 24, were in well-paid, blue-collar, semiskilled crafts positions in 1974. By 1986, that figure had declined to 25 percent."[5]

The absence of eligible males does explain why there are so many single young black women, but it doesn't explain why these women are having so many children. Some conservatives, most notably Charles Murray,[6] believe that they allow themselves to get pregnant because they want to get on welfare. However, substantial research indicates that although public assistance is the main source of support once these girls give birth, peer pressure, the wish to go through the rite of passage into womanhood, and the desire for something to love are the real motivating factors.[7]

Only half of all black males aged 16 to 64 are employed.

The Darity–Myers Thesis: The Economic Marginality of Young Black Men

William A. Darity, Jr., and Samuel L. Myers, Jr., argue that "black men have become less useful in the emerging economic order; they are socially unwanted, superfluous, and marginal."* Consequently there is a shrinking pool of marriageable black men. This growing marginality has led to drug abuse, violent crime, incarceration, and a high death rate, further depleting the ranks of marriageable young black men. Cutting welfare benefits, Darity and Myers observe, will do nothing to lower the number of black female-headed households, because the underlying problem is finding meaningful employment for millions of black men.

Their conclusion is bleak:

The decline in the supply of marriageable mates has dire consequences for the future of black families. If the effects of violent crime, homicide, incarceration, and other aspects of the marginalization of black men rob the next generation of fathers and husbands and the next generation's mothers form families at earlier and earlier ages, then our best estimates suggest that the vast majority of all black families will be female headed by the year 2000.** These families will be poor and increasingly isolated from the mainstream of American society. Curbing welfare will have no effect in halting this trend. And, unfortunately, not much hope seems to exist for slowing the withdrawal of young black men from productive spheres of the economy.

---

*William A. Darity, Jr., and Samuel L. Myers, Jr., "Family Structure and the Marginalization of Black Men: Policy Implications," presented at the American Economic Association Meetings, Washington, D.C., January 1995.

**About 60 percent of all black families are headed by females.

---

[5]See Bob Herbert, "Who Will Help the Black Man?" *New York Times Magazine,* December 4, 1994, p. 74.

[6]Charles Murray, *Losing Ground: American Social Policy, 1950–1980* (New York: Basic Books, 1984).

[7]P. Cutright, "Illegitimacy and Income Supplements," *Studies in Public Welfare,* paper no. 12, prepared for the use of the Subcommittee on Fiscal Policy of the Joint Economic Committee, Congress of the United States (Washington, DC: Government Printing Office, 1973); C. R. Winegarden, "The Fertility of AFDC Women: An Economic Analysis," *Journal of Economics and Business* 26 (1974), pp. 159–66; William Julius Wilson, *When Work Disappears* (New York: Knopf, 1996), pp. 107–9.

Let's pause here for a minute to catch our breath. We've been talking for a while about the causes of what is mainly black poverty. Keep in mind that most poor people are white. But when we distinguish between short-term poverty and a permanent underclass, we are talking mainly about a problem that has affected blacks, who constitute about 60 percent of the long-term poor.

Poverty Breeds Poverty   Poverty itself generally breeds poverty. Before birth an infant may suffer from poor prenatal care or even acquire an addiction to drugs, particularly crack. During childhood inadequate nutrition and a lack of medical and dental care also take their tolls. An unsafe—or even violent—environment, emotional deprivation, and a broken home also militate against a good childhood. This situation makes it extremely difficult to do well in school, so the easiest course is to give up.

Inadequate Human Capital   Human capital is defined as the acquired skills of an individual—education, training, and work habits. People who grew up poor usually had poor home learning environments, attended poor schools, dropped out before graduation, acquired little useful work experience, did not develop good work habits, and have poorly developed communication skills. In sum, they are virtually unemployable in today's economy.

The Conservative View versus the Liberal View

Now we're ready for the Super Bowl of poverty theory debate—the conservatives versus the liberals. Representing the conservative view will be Charles Murray, whose book *Losing Ground* depicts overly generous public assistance programs as perpetuating a dependent underclass. William Julius Wilson is perhaps the most prominent of Murray's liberal critics, so he'll represent their view.[8]

The conservatives and the liberals agree completely on ends—getting the long-term poor off welfare and into self-supporting employment—but they disagree completely on the appropriate means. Basically, the liberals favor the carrot approach, while the conservatives advocate the stick.

The conservatives and liberals agree on ends but disagree on means.

During the Great Depression, President Franklin Roosevelt's New Deal program attempted to lift one-third of all Americans out of poverty. Poverty wasn't rediscovered until the 1960s,[9] and the response was President Lyndon Johnson's Great Society program. Did this program and its extension through the 1970s actually help alleviate poverty? Here's Murray's response:

Did the Great Society program help alleviate poverty?

> In 1968, as Lyndon Johnson left office, 13 percent of Americans were poor, using the official definition. Over the next 12 years, our expenditures on social welfare quadrupled. And, in 1980, the percentage of poor Americans was—13 percent.[10]

Murray draws this conclusion: By showering so much money on the poor, the government robbed them of their incentive to work. Using the archetypal couple, Harold and Phyllis, he shows how in 1960 Harold would have gone out and gotten a minimum-wage job to support Phyllis and their newborn baby. But 10 years later the couple would be better off receiving public assistance and food stamps, living together without getting married, and having Harold work periodically. Why work steadily at an unpleasant, dead-end job, asks Murray, when you can fall back on welfare, food stamps, unemployment insurance, and other government benefit programs?

All of this sounds perfectly logical. But Murray's logic has been shot full of holes by his critics. We'll start with welfare spending. Although payments did increase from

---

[8]Wilson would probably reject any label, but his views are supported by nearly all liberals.

[9]Interest was sparked by Michael Harrington's book *The Other America* (New York: MacMillan, 1962).

[10]Murray, *Losing Ground*, p. 8.

Charles Murray, American economist
(© 1993 Susan Muniak)

1968 to 1980, when we adjust them for inflation these payments actually decreased between 1972 and 1980. Wilson really lowers the boom:

> The evidence does not sustain Murray's contentions. First, countries with far more generous social welfare programs than the United States—Germany, Denmark, France, Sweden, and Great Britain—all have sharply lower rates of teenage births and teenage crime.
>
> Second, if welfare benefits figured in the decision to have a baby, more babies would be born in states with relatively high levels of welfare payments. But careful state-by-state comparisons show no evidence that [public assistance] influences childbearing decisions; sex and childbearing among teenagers do not seem to be a product of careful economic analysis.[11]

Another problem with Murray's analysis is that the unemployment rate doubled between 1968 and 1980, yet the poverty rate remained constant. Why? Because of all the social programs that were in place—unemployment insurance, public assistance, food stamps, and Medicaid, among others. Although there was substantial economic growth throughout most of the 1970s, this growth was insufficient to absorb all of the housewives and baby boomers who had entered the labor market. And so the odd man out was the black male.

Murray's use of statistics and the conclusions he derives from them raise even more questions. If, instead of comparing the poverty levels in 1968 (when the Great Society program had pretty much run its course) and 1980 (when the poverty level had been rising due to long-term economic stagnation), he had looked at the period of 1965 to 1974 (when social spending was rising), he would have concluded that the percentage of Americans below the poverty line had been cut by more than 40 percent.

Still more to the point, social scientists warn of the difficulty of measuring the effects of a nonevent. The nonevent in question is the absence of antipoverty programs in the 1960s and 1970s. Had there been no such programs, would more people have been poor—as the liberals (and numerous other observers) maintain—or would there have been even less poverty, as Murray insists?

The offer of alms increases the supply of beggars.
—Simon Newcomb

Murray believes that not only did the social programs of the 1960s and 1970s not work, but they actually caused more poverty by destroying the incentive to work. Murray's view is seconded by Mickey Kaus:

> Although welfare might not cause the underclass, it sustains it. With [welfare] in place, young girls look around them and recognize, perhaps unconsciously, that girls in their neighborhood who have had babies on their own are surviving, however uncomfortably (but who lives comfortably in the ghetto?). Welfare, as the umbilical cord through which the mainstream society sustains the isolated ghetto society, permits the expansion of this single-parent culture.[12]

One conservative approach to welfare dependence is noted in the box "Dealing with Teenage Pregnancies."

Murray blamed the antipoverty programs for increasing poverty. Liberals would say he really had it backward: These programs prevented a bad situation from getting worse. During a time of rising unemployment, particularly among black males, it was actually a triumph of social policy to keep the poverty rate from rising.

All of this said, Murray's thesis should not be dismissed out of hand. There *are* plenty of people out there who choose welfare as the easy way out. Even more to the point, a culture of poverty *has* developed during the last four decades. Had he said that the largesse of the federal government had induced a sizable minority of the poor to succumb to the joys of living on the dole, he would have had a valid point. Murray simply overstated his case.

[11]William Julius Wilson, Introduction to Lisbeth B. Schorr and Daniel Schorr, *Within Our Reach* (New York: Doubleday, 1989), p. xxv.

[12]Mickey Kaus, "The Work Ethic State," *New Republic,* July 7, 1986, p. 24.

Dealing with Teenage Pregnancies

The birthrate among teenage girls in the United States is higher than that of any other industrial country— twice as high as the British and Canadian rates, more than three times the French rate, and more than four times the rates of the Swedes and Dutch. Among girls under 15, the contrasts are even sharper. For white teenagers alone, our birthrates are higher than those of teenagers in any other Western country.*

Think of a girl growing up in a slum who has had two or three children before she is out of her teens. By the time she's in her 40s she will have 8 or 10 grandchildren, virtually all of whom will be on welfare. Think of what a burden she and her offspring will be to our society.

Poverty is not only perpetuated but also expanded by the more than 200,000 babies born each year to poor, unwed teenage mothers. If the number of these births could be substantially reduced, we would go a long way toward reducing poverty. So the big question is, How do we get these girls to stop having babies?

Every proposal—unrestricted and free abortions, free contraceptives, sex education, and tubal ligations and vasectomies (that is, sterilization)—is highly controversial. Nevertheless, hundreds of thousands of children are having children every year, and our society has been unable to take any meaningful steps to deal with this growing problem.

In 1992 New Jersey became the first state to deny extra welfare benefits to women who had additional children. Formerly, these families would have received $64 per month upon the birth of each child. Many other states have imposed identical restrictions. It remains to be seen whether these measures will have any appreciable effect. It should be noted that almost three-fourths of the families receiving public assistance have only one or two children.

---

*Frances Fox Piven, a liberal, notes that these other rich countries provide far more generous assistance to single mothers. See "From Workhouse to Workfare," *New York Times,* August 1, 1996, p. A27.

Decades ago, when I was a case worker for the New York City Welfare Department, I saw hundreds of thick case folders documenting the lives of second-, third-, and fourth-generation welfare families, consisting of scores of people, virtually all of whom had spent most or all of their lives dependent on public assistance. Had Murray confined his theory to this group, he would have had the support of the large majority of those working directly with the welfare population. Again, there *is* no valid general theory of the causes of welfare dependency.

In his landmark work *The Truly Disadvantaged,* Wilson begins by describing the black ghettos as they were more than 40 years ago. Sure there was crime, but it was still safe to walk the streets at night. And sure there was joblessness, but nothing like what there has been these last 25 years. Then he goes on to describe other social problems:

Forty years ago the ghettos were a lot kinder and gentler places to live.

> There were single-parent families, but they were a small minority of all black families and tended to be incorporated within extended family networks and to be headed not by unwed teenagers and young adult women but by middle-aged women who usually were widowed, separated, or divorced. There were welfare recipients, but only a very small percentage of the families could be said to be welfare-dependent. In short, unlike the present period, inner-city communities prior to 1960 exhibited the features of social organization—including a sense of community, positive neighborhood identification, and explicit norms and sanctions against aberrant behavior.[13]

So what happened? What happened was the civil rights revolution led by Martin Luther King, Jr., in the early 1960s and the subsequent legislation that lowered racial housing and employment barriers. Until then the big-city ghettos had been socioeconomically integrated. But this quickly changed by the late 60s as millions of blacks, who had been penned up in the ghettos, were finally able to move out. They moved into the houses and apartments that had been vacated by the whites who had fled to the suburbs.

William Julius Wilson, American sociologist (Harvard).

---

[13]William Julius Wilson, *The Truly Disadvantaged* (Chicago: University of Chicago Press, 1987), p. 3.

The outward migration of middle- and working-class blacks had a significant impact on those left behind.

How did this outward migration affect those who were left behind?

> The exodus of middle- and working-class families from many ghetto neighborhoods removes an important "social buffer" that could deflect the full impact of the kind of prolonged and increasing joblessness that plagued inner-city neighborhoods in the 1970s and early 1980s. . . . Even if the truly disadvantaged segments of an inner-city area experience a significant increase in long-term joblessness, the basic institutions in that area (churches, schools, stores, recreational facilities, etc.) would remain viable if much of the base of their support comes from the more economically stable and secure families. Moreover, the very presence of these families during such periods provides mainstream role models that help keep alive the perception that education is meaningful, that steady employment is a viable alternative to welfare, and that family stability is the norm, not the exception.[14]

What's left behind is a neighborhood of impoverished people. Wilson notes that in 1980 only 7 percent of all poor whites lived in areas of extreme poverty, but 32 percent of all poor Hispanics and 39 percent of all poor blacks lived in such areas.[15] These areas became increasingly unsafe and were eventually shunned by those who didn't live in them, further isolating those who remained.

This isolation makes it harder to find a job; few ghetto dwellers are tied into the job network. And because few relatives or neighbors have steady work, tardiness and absenteeism are not considered aberrant behavior. Consequently, those who do find jobs seldom hold them very long.

Lack of jobs is the key.

So the key is jobs—or rather the lack of them:

> The black delay in marriage and the lower rate of remarriage, each associated with high percentages of out-of-wedlock births in female-headed households, can be directly tied to the employment status of black males. Indeed, black women, especially young black women, are confronting a shrinking pool of "marriageable" (that is, economically stable) men.[16]

Wilson also notes that the cities have lost far more than 2 million jobs in manufacturing and the wholesale and retail trades since the end of World War II. The loss of these jobs, as well as technological changes creating the need for a more highly trained and educated labor force, has made the job prospects of inner-city blacks and Hispanics bleak indeed.

Still another consequence of widespread joblessness is that most poor children fail to perceive any connection between schooling and future employment. When it comes to school, they think, Why bother? "In such neighborhoods, therefore, teachers become frustrated and do not teach and children do not learn."[17]

The migration of black middle- and working-class families from the ghettos removed the key social constraint against crime. And the erection of huge, high-rise, low-income public housing projects further destroyed the remaining sense of community. Place together a large number of female-headed families with a large number of teenage children (who commit more crime than any other population group) and you've got the recipe for not only high crime rates but almost complete social breakdown.

Wilson's thesis is a direct repudiation of Murray's, which blames public assistance and other social programs for the emergence of the permanent black underclass. Wilson finds no evidence to support that contention. Instead, he blames a whole range of social and economic forces, including past employment discrimination.

Has the government done too much for the poor?

The arguments that Wilson has advanced would not persuade many Americans, who would remain convinced that Murray and his conservative allies are right—that the government has done entirely too much for the poor, especially poor blacks and Hispanics.

---

[14]*Ibid.*, p. 56.

[15]*Ibid.*, p. 58.

[16]*Ibid.*, p. 145.

[17]*Ibid.*, p. 57.

As Wilson himself has acknowledged, no government program that is perceived as helping only the poor is likely to gain the support of a majority of Americans. At a time when more and more people—white as well as black (see box, "The Permanent White Underclass")—are faced with bleak economic prospects, the government will have to come up with programs that are geared toward helping tens of millions of working-class Americans, not just the poor.

Solutions

All poor people have one thing in common: They don't have nearly enough money. Or, in the words of the great wit Finley Peter Dunne, "One of the strangest things about life is that the poor, who need the money the most, are the very ones that never have it." So why not simply *give* it to them? In the box titled "The Negative Income Tax," a program that would do just that is described.

> The best way to help poor people is to not be one of them.
> —Reverend Ike, New York City preacher

The basic liberal solution—in addition to combating employment discrimination—is to provide the poor with better education and training, and with millions of government jobs. The conservatives have placed their faith in providing the poor with jobs mainly in the private sector. But the basic strain running through conservative thought about welfare recipients may be summed up in just three little words: Cut 'em off. A solution with widespread support, workfare, combines the liberal carrot of training and jobs with the conservative stick of cutting off the benefits of those who refuse to seek training or work.

The Conservative Solutions   To end the poor's dependency on government largesse, Charles Murray would simply pull the plug on the life-support system:

> [Scrap] the entire welfare and income-support structure for working-aged persons, including [public assistance], medicaid, food stamps, unemployment insurance, workers' compensation, subsidized housing, disability insurance, and the rest. It would leave the working-aged person with no recourse whatsoever except the job market, family members, friends, and public or private locally funded services.[18]

A somewhat more humane approach is advocated by Mickey Kaus: Replace all government aid with an offer of employment for every American citizen over 18 who wants it, in a useful public job at a wage slightly below the minimum wage. . . . If you showed up, and worked, you would be paid for your work. If you don't show up, you don't get paid. Simple.[19]

The Permanent White Underclass

There *is* no permanent white underclass. No? Tell that to the folks unkindly referred to as white trash. Tell that to the unemployed 50-year-old ex-autoworker whose wife works at the 7-Eleven and who makes ends meet with food stamps. Tell it to the high school dropout who hangs around drinking beer with his buddies all day. Or maybe talk to the crack-addicted unwed teenage mother whose alcoholic father used to beat her.

The permanent poverty problem among whites is not nearly as bad as it is among blacks and Hispanics, but it's growing quickly. You may have noticed that most of the street beggars and the homeless all across the United States are white. And there are millions of them. Look at them. They may be our future.

---

[18]Murray, *Losing Ground,* pp. 227–28.
[19]Kaus, "The Work Ethic State," p. 30.

The Negative Income Tax

The negative income tax is the logical extension of the federal personal income tax. People earning relatively high incomes pay nearly 40 percent of their incomes to the IRS. Those earning somewhat less are taxed at 28 percent, while those earning more moderate amounts are taxed at a 15 percent rate. And millions of low-income families pay nothing, so we can say their tax rate is 0 percent. Now, what about *really* poor families—those below the poverty line? Most of them are on welfare and Medicaid and receive food stamps. The negative income tax would largely or entirely replace these programs by simply sending the poor enough money to live on.

Isn't this just calling welfare by another name? Yes and no. Yes, it's still giving money to the needy, but it has five clear advantages over public assistance, food stamps, and Medicaid.

First, if money is mailed out by the IRS rather than by the hodgepodge of local departments of welfare, perhaps two or three billion dollars a year could be saved in administrative costs. More than 100,000 people are employed by county and municipal welfare departments, not to mention tens of thousands more employed by various state and federal bureaus and agencies whose sole purpose is to oversee the work done by the local departments. If all these people suddenly vanished, no one would miss them, least of all the poor.

A second advantage of the negative income tax over the current public assistance programs is that the poor would be freer to choose how to spend their money. Economists have long recognized that consumers spend their money most efficiently when they are free to buy what they want. Food stamps and Medicaid both place rigid restrictions on the types of food and medical services consumed by the poor. Add to that the administrative cost of these programs, and we may be talking about another two or three billion dollars of waste.

Of course, one may ask how many of the negative income tax dollars sent to the poor would be spent on crack or liquor or gambling—or whether even more children would turn up at school each morning without having had breakfast. On the other hand, how did you spend your last income tax refund? Oops—sorry—I should never have asked.

Third, this system would provide everyone in the United States with a guaranteed annual income. Instead of thousands of widely varying welfare programs, with payments in some states four or five times those in others, every poor person would get the same amount of money.

Finally, the negative income tax would afford the poor a certain measure of dignity, because the assistance would take the form of an income tax refund. This would be no small thing to people who endure the stigma of being on the dole, living in public housing projects, going to public health clinics, and having to pay for their grocery purchases with food stamps. Although some welfare critics have painted pictures of welfare queens and welfare chiselers living in great opulence, most people dependent on public assistance lead miserable lives, have very low self-esteem, and are barely able to keep the wolf from the door. Anything that provides a modicum of self-respect to welfare recipients would greatly improve the "welfare mess" that has become a permanent part of American life.

To illustrate how the negative income tax would work, the table below illustrates the negative income tax for a family of four. In the first column we have earned income. This could be from wages and salaries, unemployment benefits, child support payments, or any other cash income. The subsidy, or negative income tax, is shown in the second column. When earned income is zero, the family receives $5,000 from the government. In other words, every family would have a guaranteed annual income of $5,000.

Earned Income	+	Subsidy	=	Total Income
–0–		$5,000		$5,000
$2,000		4,000		6,000
4,000		3,000		7,000
6,000		2,000		8,000
8,000		1,000		9,000
10,000		–0–		10,000

As earned income rises, the subsidy declines. For every $2 earned income rises, by how much does the subsidy decline? That's right—it goes down by $1. In effect, every $2 of additional earnings is taxed by $1, which gives us a marginal tax rate of 50 percent.*

If we add the first two columns across, we get total income. A family with an earned income of $6,000 would receive a subsidy of $2,000, giving it a total income of $8,000. As earned income rose, the subsidy would decline until, at an earned income of $10,000, the subsidy would be zero.

Thus, at income levels of less than $10,000, the family receives the negative income tax. At an income of exactly $10,000, there is no negative income tax. And at incomes above $10,000, the family will be paying income tax, albeit not at a 50 percent marginal tax rate.   *(continued)*

The negative income tax has several drawbacks. First, despite administrative cost savings, it will cost the Treasury a good deal more than all the federal, state, and local aid to the poor combined. Second, it will still leave most of the nonworking poor well below the poverty line. Alternatively, if a guaranteed minimum income level of, say, $15,000 were set, the program would become prohibitively expensive.

A third problem has to do with work incentives. A 50 percent marginal tax rate may be too great a disincentive to work. But a much lower rate would mean raising the total income ceiling well above $10,000. In that case, families considerably above the poverty line would not be paying personal income taxes and yet they would be receiving negative income tax.

A few halfhearted attempts to enact a negative income tax were made in the 1970s, but Congress never passed the necessary legislation. Today the concept of the negative income tax lives only in economics texts.

Nevertheless, the earned income tax credit, which is written into our Internal Revenue Code, does provide a kind of backdoor negative income tax to low-wage workers. In 2000 a family with two children could receive as much as $3,800 a year from the credit. Families earning more than $30,000 are ineligible.

The earned income tax credit (EITC) is popular with liberals because it provides a substantial amount of income to the poor, and it is also popular with conservatives because only families with a working member are eligible. Today the EITC is, by far, the biggest single federal policy targeted at the poor. In addition, at least ten states have also introduced their own EITC programs that supplement the feederal credit.

---

*The marginal tax rate is found by dividing additional taxes paid by additional taxable income.

The Liberal Solutions   While the conservatives claim the government has done too much for the poor, the liberals believe much too little has been done. Barbara Ehrenreich and Frances Fox Piven, for example, point out that an increasing number of jobs do not pay enough to subsist on.[20] The solution? Government jobs.

Government jobs doing what? Jobs rebuilding the nation's crumbling highways and bridges, and staffing hospitals, schools, libraries, and day care centers. Jobs rebuilding dilapidated inner-city housing and cleaning up toxic waste dumps. In the 1930s, the Works Progress Administration (WPA) of the New Deal employed millions of Americans building highways, airports, bridges, parks, and school buildings. Much of this infrastructure is badly in need of repair. In addition we need millions of people to staff day care centers, libraries, and after-school programs. Why not create a labor-intensive, minimum-wage public service jobs program of last resort for today's low-skilled and jobless workers?[21]

Jobs, jobs, jobs

But some liberals acknowledge that even a massive jobs program won't get *all* of the poor off the dole. Remember that nearly all these people are women with young children.

Our country will need to go beyond providing jobs if we are to succeed in greatly reducing poverty. The lives of those in the permanent underclass are filled with hopelessness and despair. The lack of jobs put most of these families into this predicament, but it will take more than jobs, three or four generations later, to get them out of it.

More is needed than providing jobs.

Dr. David Rogers, president of the Robert Wood Johnson Foundation, remarked that "human misery is generally the result of, or accompanied by, a great untidy basketful of intertwined and interconnected circumstances and happenings"[22] that all need attention if a problem is to be solved. This point was amplified by Lisbeth and Daniel Schorr in their landmark work *Within Our Reach:*

> The mother who cannot respond appropriately to a child's evolving needs while simultaneously coping with unemployment, an abusive husband or boyfriend, an apartment without hot water, insufficient money for food, and her own memories of

---

[20]Barbara Ehrenreich and Frances Fox Piven, "The Alarm Clock Syndrome," *New Republic,* October 6, 1986, p. 18.

[21]See William Julius Wilson, *When Work Disappears* (New York: Knopf, 1996), pp. 225–38; and Sheldon Danziger and Peter Gottschalk, *America Unequal* (Cambridge, MA: Harvard University Press, 1995), p. 174.

[22]Robert Wood Johnson Foundation, *Annual Report,* 1984.

4. The two biggest benefit programs aimed solely at the poor are _____ and _____ .

5. About one out of every _____ black Americans is poor.

6. About _____ percent of all poor people are black.

7. The basic problem with the absolute concept of poverty is finding the _____ .

8. The negative income tax has five clear advantages over welfare, Medicaid, food stamps, and other programs to aid the poor. List at least three:

   (1) _____ ;

   (2) _____ ;

   and (3) _____ .

9. The superrich get most of their incomes from _____ .

10. The poverty line is set by the _____ .

Problems

Use Figure 1 to answer questions 1 through 4.

Figure 1

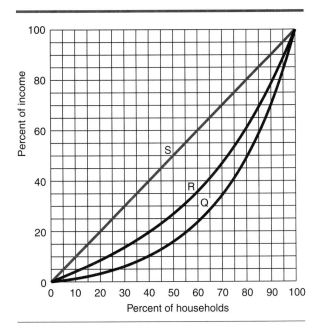

1. How much is the percentage of income received by the lowest quintile on line R?

2. How much is the percentage of income earned by the highest quintile on Lorenz curve Q?

3. How much is the percentage of income received by the highest quintile on line R?

4. How much is the percentage of income received by the middle three quintiles on line S?

   Use this information on a hypothetical negative income tax program to answer questions 5 through 7. Every family has a guaranteed annual income of $8,000. For every $2 earned income rises, the subsidy goes down by $1.

5. If the family earned $2,000: a) How much of a subsidy would it receive? b) Calculate the family's total income.

6. If the family earned $5,000: a) How much of a subsidy would it receive? b) Calculate the family's total income.

7. At what level of earned income would the subsidy be zero?

Chapter 18

International Trade

More and more of our imports come from overseas.
—President George W. Bush

Trillions of dollars' worth of business in international trade is conducted every year. Certain trading nations—Japan, the United Kingdom, Hong Kong, Korea, and Taiwan among them—draw their economic lifeblood from foreign trade, while others, such as the United States, France, Germany, Russia, and China, are relatively self-sufficient. Yet even the United States has become increasingly dependent on imported TVs, VCRs, compact cars, oil, and other consumer goods. Our growing dependency on imported goods was discussed in Chapter 8 of *Economics* and *Macroeconomics*.

How this trade is conducted is the subject of this chapter; how it is financed is the subject of the next. The thread that runs through international trade and finance is specialization and exchange. If all the nations of the world were self-sufficient, there would be no international trade and little need for international finance. But if that were to happen, the world would have a much lower standard of living.

CHAPTER OBJECTIVES

These are the topics you'll learn about:

- Specialization and trade.
- Domestic exchange equations.
- Absolute advantage and comparative advantage.
- Tariffs or quotas?
- The arguments for protection.

- The causes of our trade imbalance.
- What we can do to restore our balance of trade.
- Our trade deficits with Japan and China.
- U.S. trade policy: A historical view.

America is being flooded with imports, and millions of workers are being thrown out of work. Americans are buying not just foreign-made cameras and VCRs, but also foreign-made steel, textiles, apparel, personal computers, typewriters, and toys. But why worry? After all, the world is now a global village, and we all buy from and sell to each other. Why should we buy something from an American firm when we can get a better deal from a foreign firm?

International trade is really good for everyone. As consumers, we are able to purchase a whole array of goods and services that would not have otherwise been available—at least, not at such low prices. Hence, we can thank international trade for much of our high standard of living. As producers, we are able to sell a great deal of our output abroad, thereby increasing our employment and profits. So far, so good. The only trouble is that during the last two decades we were buying a lot more from foreigners than they were buying from us.

So what do we *do*? Do we throw up protective tariff barriers to keep out lower-priced foreign imports? Or, like the old Avis rent-a-car commercials, do we just try harder? After a brief history of U.S. trade, in Part II we'll consider the theory of international trade, why such trade is so wonderful, and why we should not do anything to impede its flow. In Part III we'll take a closer look at the practice of international trade and try to zero in on the causes of our trade imbalance and what we can do to redress it. And then, in Part IV, we'll look at why we've been running huge trade deficits with Japan and China.

Part I: A Brief History of U.S. Trade

The United States did not always run huge trade deficits. Indeed, we ran surpluses for virtually the first three quarters of the 20th century. Let's look at that record, and at U.S. government trade policy over the years.

U.S. Trade Before 1975

We ran trade surpluses before 1975 and deficits after 1975.

Why 1975? Because that's the last year we ran a trade surplus. Until 1971 the United States had run a surplus virtually every year of the 20th century.

Until the early 1900s we were primarily an agricultural nation, exporting cotton and grain to Europe in exchange for manufactured goods. These included not just consumer goods—shoes, clothing, books, and furniture—but also a great deal of machinery and equipment for our growing industrial sector. We ran relatively small trade deficits through most of the 19th century.

But once we had become a powerful industrial nation, by the turn of the 20th century, we had not only less need of European manufactures but we were now exporting our own manufactured goods. With the outbreak of World War I in 1914, we added armaments to our growing list of exports, as our trade surpluses mounted. In the 1920s we inundated the world with Model T Fords, as well as a host of other American vehicles, along with radios, phonographs, toasters, waffle irons, and other consumer appliances.

The Great Depression of the 1930s depressed not only worldwide production of goods and services but their export as well. Our trade surpluses rose again in the 1940s, with the advent of World War II, when, once again, we exported tens of billions of dollars worth of food and armaments to England, the Soviet Union, China, and our other allies. It took 15 years for the world's other leading industrial powers to recover from the devastation of the war, during which time we supplied the world from our cornucopia of manufacturing and agricultural products. During this period, and well into the 1960s, we continued running substantial trade surpluses.

U.S. Trade Since 1975

We faced increasing trade competition in the 1960s.

By the early 1960s Japan and the industrial nations of Western Europe had rebuilt their factories and stemmed the flood of American imports. Later in that decade these nations, especially Japan, were exporting cars, TVs, cameras, and other consumer goods to the United States and going head-to-head with American manufacturers throughout the world. By the late 1970s our trade deficits were mounting (see Figure 1). Although these deficits rose and fell over the years, by 1984 they crossed the $100 billion mark.

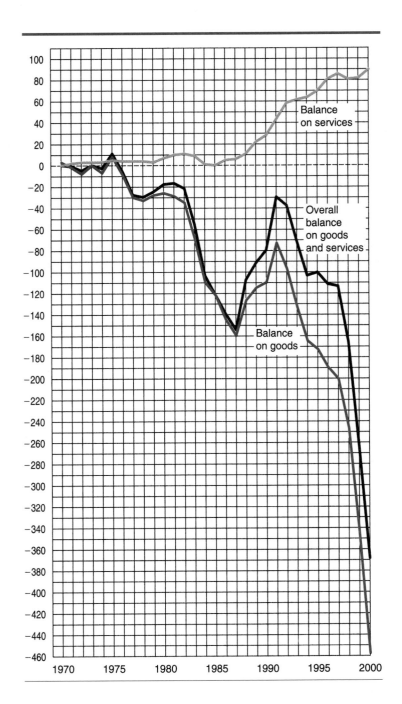

Figure 1

U.S. Balance of Trade in Goods and Services, and Overall Balance, 1970–2000 (in billions of dollars)[*]

Since the late 1980s we have been running a large and growing balance on services. Our balance on goods, which has been negative since the mid-1970s, has grown steadily worse since 1991 and totaled −$459 in 2000.

Sources: Economic Report of the President, 1985; *Survey of Current Business,* February 2001.

Figure 1 shows that we've been running large and growing trade surpluses on services, larger and growing trade deficits on goods. Since our deficits on goods are much greater than our surpluses on services, our overall trade deficits have gotten very large. In the second section of Chapter 8 of *Economics* and *Macroeconomics,* we discuss in detail U.S. imports and exports of goods and services. Very briefly, examples of goods (merchandise) include cars, toys, clothing, textiles, and steel. Examples of services would include insurance, airline travel, education (foreigners going to American schools or Americans attending foreign schools), and TV programming.

Until Part IV, we won't really distinguish between goods and services. We'll keep referring to our trade deficits. But since it is our huge and growing merchandise deficits that are driving up our overall trade deficits, most of the discussion is implicitly about our imports and exports of merchandise.

Why did our surpluses turn into deficits after 1975? To a large degree, we were no longer alone in the world as the only major industrial power. But there were several other reasons as well, which we'll be looking at in Part III.

U.S. Government Trade Policy

We can get a snapshot view of this policy over the last two centuries by glancing at Figure 2. The relatively high tariffs through most of the 19th century and during the Great Depression reflected the political climate of those times. In the 19th century we protected our growing manufacturing base from foreign competition, which, it was felt, would smother these infant industries before they could mature. We'll consider that argument in Part II.

Back in Chapter 1 we talked about the high protective tariff being a cause of the Civil War. How did that come to be?

Initially the tariff was purely a revenue-raising device, but after the War of 1812 war-born industries found it impossible to meet British competition, and the tariff took on a protective tinge. In 1816 the first protective tariff was adopted, followed in 1828 by the "Tariff of Abominations." But to whom was this tariff so abominable? To the South, which was primarily an agrarian economy, exporting cotton and importing manufactured goods. Of course the industrial Northern manufacturers wanted the South to buy their own goods rather than import them from Europe. However the South, allied with the Western states joining the union, was able to induce Congress to progressively lower tariffs until the Civil War. Note that, in 1861, when the 11 states of the Confederacy withdrew from the union, tariffs went right back up once more. Business-oriented Republican administrations kept them high until the Underwood Tariff of 1913, which, incidentally, was passed by a Southern-dominated Democratic Congress.

A century of high protective tariffs

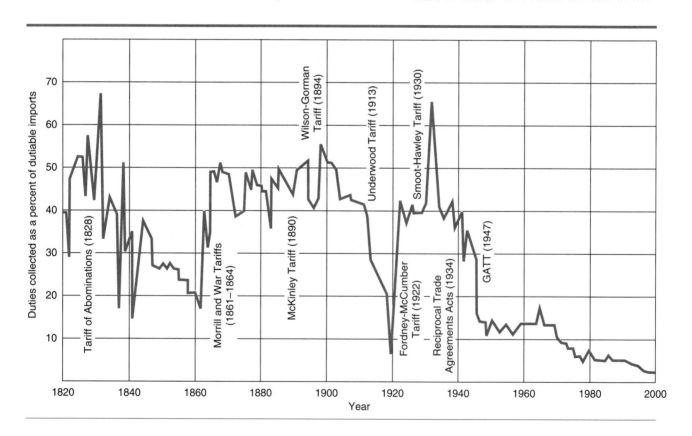

Figure 2
U.S. Tariffs, 1820–2000

Although tariffs fluctuated widely from the 1820s through the early 1930s, there has been a strong downward trend. Today tariffs are less than 5 percent of the price of our imported durable goods.
Source: U.S. Department of Commerce.

Again, during the Great Depression, virtually every industrial power, beset with massive unemployment, raised its tariffs to keep out foreign goods. Of course, since everyone was doing this, world trade dwindled to a fraction of what it had been in the 1920s. While certain jobs were protected, others, mainly in the export sector, were lost. Economists believe that these high tariffs, especially the Smoot-Hawley Tariff of 1930, made the depression a lot worse than it might have otherwise been.

The GATT (General Agreement on Trade and Tariffs) treaty of 1947 began a downward trend in tariffs all around the world, leading to the formation of the World Trade Organization, which was set up to further facilitate world trade. GATT and the World Trade Organization were discussed in Chapter 8 of *Economics and Macroeconomics.*

A downward trend in tariffs since 1947

Economists are virtually unanimous in their support of free trade, and increasingly, so are our politicians. Our last three presidents, Ronald Reagan (1981–89), George Bush (1989–93), and Bill Clinton (1993–2001) were all ardent supporters of free trade. However, many Americans, especially labor union members and environmentalists, prefer what they call "fair trade."[1]

Almost everyone seems to support free trade.

Let us consider now the theory of international trade, and, after that, the practice of international trade.

Part II: The Theory of International Trade

Recent years have seen a growing consensus in the United States that we need more protection against the import of foreign goods. As Japanese cars, Korean VCRs, Brazilian steel, Canadian lumber, and Hong Kong textiles have flooded American markets, we have seen an alarming trend in our balance of trade. Indeed, we went from a positive balance of $12 billion in 1975 to a negative balance of $370 billion in 2000.

The trend in our balance of trade is alarming.

What caused this dramatic turnaround? What can we do to reverse this trend? Should we restrict this profusion of imports, or should we listen to the reasoning of the economics profession, which is nearly unanimous in arguing for free trade?

Specialization and Trade

The basis for international trade is specialization. Different nations specialize in the production of those goods and services for which their resources are best suited. Such an allocation of the world's resources lends itself to the efficient production of goods and services. If you check back with our definition of economics in Chapter 2—the efficient allocation of the scarce means of production toward the satisfaction of human wants—you'll see that international specialization and trade conform to that definition.

Specialization is the basis for international trade.

If we go from individual specialization and trade to national and international specialization and trade, we'll see that each induces an efficient allocation of resources.

An individual who attempts to be entirely self-sufficient would have to make his or her own nails, grow his or her own food, spin his or her own cloth, sew his or her own clothes, make his or her own tools, ad infinitum. It is much easier and a lot cheaper to work at one particular job or specialty and use one's earnings to buy those nails, food, clothes, and so on.

What makes sense individually also makes sense internationally. Thus, just as it pays for individuals to specialize and trade, it pays for nations to do so. And that's exactly what we do: On a national basis we specialize and trade. But it would be impossible to do this unless there were a big enough market in which to buy and sell the goods and services we produce. Of course, the United States has long been the world's largest national market.

It pays for nations to specialize, just as it pays for individuals.

Adam Smith recognized the advantages of foreign trade more than two centuries ago when he wrote:

> If a foreign country can supply us with a commodity cheaper than we ourselves can
> make it, better buy it of them with some part of the produce of our own industry,

---

[1]This topic as well as NAFTA, WTO, and the European Union are discussed in Chapter 8 of *Economics* and *Macroeconomics.*

employed in a way in which we have some advantage. The general industry of the country . . . will not thereby be diminished . . . but only left to find out the way in which it can be employed with the greatest advantage.[2]

Smith's argument provides the basis for international trade. Country A specializes in making the products that it can make most cheaply. Country B does the same. When they trade, each country will be better off than they would have been if they didn't specialize and trade.

Suppose there are just two products in the world: photocopy machines and VCRs. The United States as well as every other industrialized country has the necessary resources and technology to produce both. The production possibilities curve in Figure 1A shows a hypothetical range of various combinations of outputs of photocopiers and VCRs.

You may recall from the discussion of the production possibilities curve in Chapter 2 that a couple of assumptions are made: (1) a nation is using all its resources to produce just two products, and (2) it is using the best available technology. You may further recall that if a nation is operating on its production possibilities curve, it is operating at full capacity and full employment.[3]

You may also have noticed that the production possibilities curves in Figure 3 are straight lines rather than the rounded (concave to the origin) curves of Chapter 2. This reflects constant opportunity costs; in Chapter 2 we showed increasing opportunity costs.[4]

Just by glancing at Figure 3 you will see that the United States is better at making photocopiers and South Korea is better at making VCRs. Before we conclude that the United States should specialize in photocopy machines and South Korea in VCRs, let's consider what would happen if each nation produced both products and they didn't trade.

Domestic Exchange Equations

If we examine a few points along the U.S. production possibilities curve (Figure 3A), we will find various combinations of photocopiers and VCRs that we could produce. At point A, with all of the country's resources devoted to photocopier production, the U.S. output is 80 copiers. At point B we make 60 copiers and 10 VCRs. At C it's 40 copiers and 20 VCRs; at D it's 20 copiers and 30 VCRs; and at E we make 40 VCRs.

From this information we can derive this equation:

Domestic exchange equation for the United States

$$2 \text{ photocopiers} = 1 \text{ VCR}$$

In other words, the opportunity cost of producing one more VCR is two photocopiers. Alternatively, the cost of producing two more copiers would be one VCR.

Let's turn now to Figure 3B, which depicts the production possibility curve of South Korea. At point F this country would make 40 photocopy machines. At G production would total 30 photocopiers and 20 VCRs. Thus the opportunity cost of 20 additional VCRs would be 10 copiers. Obviously, then, the South Korean domestic exchange equation is:

Domestic exchange equation for South Korea

$$1 \text{ photocopier} = 2 \text{ VCRs}$$

A comparison of the American and South Korean domestic exchange equations tells us that the South Koreans are twice as efficient at VCR production as they are at

---

[2]Adam Smith, *The Wealth of Nations,* vol. 1, ed. Edwin Cannan (London: University Paperbacks by Methuen, 1961), pp. 478–79.

[3]What I am hinting at in a not very subtle way is that if you don't recall these things, it would be a very good idea to reread the production possibility curve section of Chapter 2.

[4]In the real world every industry eventually faces increasing opportunity costs. But here we use constant opportunity costs because straight lines lend themselves much better to our analysis than do curved lines.

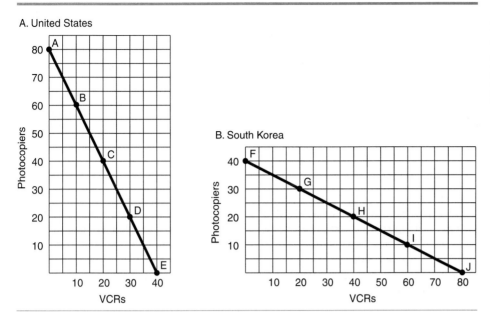

Figure 3

Production Possibilities Curves

The United States, operating at full capacity, can produce 80 photocopiers or 40 VCRs. South Korea, operating at full capacity, can produce 40 photocopiers or 80 VCRs.

making photocopy machines; Americans have precisely the opposite situation. Again, instinct tells us that it would make economic sense for South Korea to devote all its resources to VCR production and to trade its VCRs for American photocopiers, in whose production we would specialize.

The Terms of Trade

We're finally ready to set up trading between South Korea and the United States. We know that South Korea will trade its VCRs for our photocopiers. What we don't know are the terms of trade. Specifically, how many VCRs will South Korea be willing to trade for each copier? Alternatively, how many copiers will the United States be willing to trade for each VCR?

South Korea will trade its VCRs for our photocopiers, and we will trade our copiers for their VCRs.

To help answer these questions, we will make a couple of simple observations. Let's look at the American domestic exchange equation again:

$$2 \text{ photocopiers} = 1 \text{ VCR}$$

Surely the United States would be unwilling to trade more than two photocopiers for one VCR. But what if South Korea offered *more* than one VCR for two copiers? This would be a better deal for the United States than trying to produce VCRs by itself. Let's see why.

By devoting a fixed amount of resources, the United States could produce either two copiers or one VCR. If it devoted those resources to producing two copiers and trading them for more than one VCR, the United States would be better off than it would have been using those resources to produce just one VCR.

The same logic applies to South Korea, whose domestic exchange equation is

$$2 \text{ VCRs} = 1 \text{ photocopier}$$

Obviously, South Korea would be unwilling to trade two VCRs for anything less than one photocopier. If South Korea could trade two VCRs and get more than one photocopier in exchange, it would be better off concentrating on VCR production and trading some of them for copiers.

Two general observations

We can now make two general observations:

1. No nation will engage in trade with another nation unless it will gain by that trade.

2. The terms of trade will fall somewhere between the domestic exchange equations of the two trading nations.

The first observation is virtually a truism, but the second may require further elaboration. We'll state the two domestic exchange equations sequentially and then derive the terms of trade.

$$\text{United States:} \quad 2 \text{ photocopiers} = 1 \text{ VCR}$$

$$\text{South Korea:} \quad 1 \text{ photocopier} = 2 \text{ VCRs}$$

Looking at these two equations, we ask ourselves whether the United States and South Korea can do business. The United States is willing to trade two photocopiers for more than one VCR; the South Koreans are willing to trade two VCRs for more than one copier. Can a trade be worked out to the satisfaction of both parties? Go ahead and try to work out such an exchange. How many copiers for how many VCRs?

Use trial and error. Would the United States accept 1½ VCRs for 2 copiers? Yes! Would South Korea give up 1½ VCRs for 2 copiers? Yes! That's one possibility for what we call their terms of trade.

Here's another. Would the United States accept 2½ VCRs for 2 copiers? Obviously. Would the South Koreans give up 2½ VCRs for 2 copiers? Yes. There's another possibility. In fact, we could easily demonstrate a large number of possible terms of trade.

What are the terms of trade between the United States and South Korea?

At this point you may well ask, What *are* the terms of trade? The best we can do is say they will definitely be between the two domestic exchange equations. But where? That depends on the forces of supply and demand in the world market. Let's suppose VCRs are selling for $200 and copiers are also selling for $200. What do you think the terms of trade for these two products will be?

I hope you said one copier for one VCR. Would these terms of trade satisfy both the United States and South Korea? The answer is definitely yes.

Over the last two centuries economists have insisted that when two countries trade, both gain from the trade. Now we'll prove it. Figure 4 includes the production possibilities curves of the United States and South Korea from Figure 1 and shows their trade possibilities curves. The last tell us that these countries are trading copiers for VCRs on a one-for-one basis.

Both countries end up with more copiers and more VCRs.

In effect, through international trade both countries end up with more copiers *and* more VCRs. Suppose the United States had been operating at point C of its production possibilities curve (before discovering the benefits of international trade). At C we produced 40 copiers and 20 VCRs. But if we concentrate our resources on copier production (i.e., produce 80 copiers) and trade some copiers for VCRs, we go to point K of our trade possibilities curve. At K we have 50 copiers and 30 VCRs. What we've done, then, is produced 80 copiers and traded 30 of them for 30 VCRs.

You can easily demonstrate that South Korea experiences similar gains from trade. Start at point H on its production possibilities curve and figure out how much better off South Korea is at point L of its trade possibilities curve. Do your calculations in this space.

South Korea produces 80 VCRs and sells 30 of them to the United States in exchange for 30 copiers. It now has 50 VCRs and 30 copiers. At point H it had only 40 VCRs and 20 copiers. Its gain is 10 VCRs and 10 copiers.

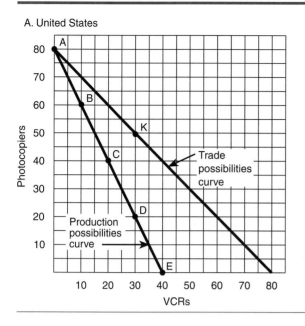

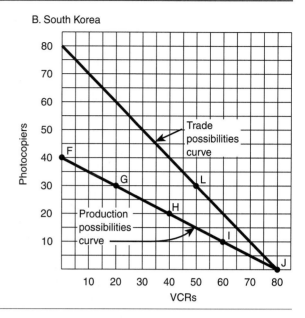

Figure 4

Trade Possibilities Curves: The United States and South Korea

The trade possibilities curves of the United States and South Korea tell us that each is willing to trade photocopiers for VCRs on a one-for-one basis.

Absolute Advantage and Comparative Advantage

In the trade example we just used, you may have inferred that South Korea makes VCRs more efficiently (that is, at a lower cost per unit) than the United States does and that the United States is more efficient than South Korea in photocopier production.

This may well be the case, but we don't have cost figures. If it *does* cost the United States the same amount to make a copier as it costs South Korea to make a VCR, clearly we're better at making copiers and they're better at making VCRs.

Absolute Advantage   *Absolute advantage is the ability of a country to produce a good or service at a lower cost than its trading partners.* For example, Saudi Arabia, which can produce crude oil at a much lower cost than can either the United States or Japan, exports hundreds of billions of barrels a year to each of these nations.

Let's assume that the United States *does* make copiers for exactly the same production costs as does South Korea for its VCRs. Expressed somewhat differently, it takes the United States an expenditure of the same resources to produce a copier as it does Korea to make a VCR. Suppose it costs South Korea $200 to make a VCR; it follows that it costs the United States $200 to make a copier.

Try this one on for size. If the United States attempts to produce its own VCRs, how much will it cost to make them? If you're not sure, look at Figure 2A. With the same amount of resources, we produce 80 copiers (point A) or 40 VCRs (point E), so it costs us twice as much to make a VCR as a copier (that is, it costs $400 per VCR).

The bottom line is that Americans can buy South Korean VCRs at half the price that American manufacturers would charge. Thus the South Koreans have an *absolute advantage* in making VCRs. They're better than we are at making VCRs, so we would do well to take advantage of their low prices while we concentrate on making things we're good at making.

South Koreans have an absolute advantage at making VCRs.

In this problem we are particularly good at making copiers. In fact, we are so good that we enjoy an absolute advantage over South Korea. And so, just as we find it advantageous to buy their VCRs, they buy American copiers rather than produce their own.

With absolute advantage it should be obvious that each country sells what it produces most efficiently and buys what it produces least efficiently. What about countries that do not enjoy an absolute advantage in producing anything? If your country can't make anything for less than other countries, what can it sell? In the next section, we'll find out.

Comparative Advantage   In the previous problem South Korea was better at making VCRs than it was at making copiers. How much better? A glance back at Figure 2 shows us that South Korea could turn out twice as many VCRs as copiers, using the same resources.

How about the United States? Using the same resources, the United States could turn out twice as many copiers as VCRs.

We found that there was a basis for trade because both countries stood to gain. Now let's go a step further and ask whether there would be any basis for trade if South Korea were more efficient than the United States at making both VCRs *and* copiers. What do you think? No? Guess again.

Imagine there are only two countries in the world (the United States and South Korea) and they produce only two goods (VCRs and copiers). To keep things simple, we'll assume the only resource used to make these goods is labor. We know it takes South Korea twice as much labor to produce a copier as a VCR.

Suppose it takes 10 hours to make a VCR in South Korea and 20 hours to make a copier. Using the same analysis for the United States, suppose it takes 30 hours to make a copier and 60 to make a VCR. This information is summarized in Table 1.

TABLE 1	Hours of Labor Required to Produce Copiers and VCRs in the United States and South Korea	
Country	Copiers	VCRs
United States	30 hours	60 hours
South Korea	20	10

Table 2 shows how many VCRs and copiers the United States and South Korea can make in 600 hours of labor. Because the United States can make one copier in 30 hours, in 600 hours it can make 20 copiers. Similarly, the United States can make 10 VCRs in 600 hours because it takes 60 hours to make one.

TABLE 2	Copiers and VCRs Produced by the United States and South Korea Using 600 Hours of Labor
United States	20 copiers or 10 VCRs
South Korea	30 copiers or 60 VCRs

What if the United States used 300 hours of labor to build copiers and 300 to build VCRs? In that case, we would have 10 copiers and 5 VCRs. Similarly, South Korea would produce 15 copiers and 30 VCRs. Therefore the United States and Korea could turn out a total of 25 copiers and 35 VCRs without trading. This is shown in Table 3.

Are you wondering what all this is leading up to? It's all leading up to Table 4, which will demonstrate how a shift in VCR and copier production will lead to an increased output of both VCRs and copiers. That's right! You're going to try to figure out which country should raise VCR production and which should increase its production of copiers. Use Table 3 as your starting point.

TABLE 3	Copiers and VCRs Produced by the United States and South Korea Using 600 Hours of Labor*
United States	10 copiers or 5 VCRs
South Korea	15 copiers or 30 VCRs
Total	25 copiers and 35 VCRs

*Each country devotes 300 hours to VCR and 300 hours to copier production.

You may have reasoned that because South Korea is relatively efficient at making VCRs, it will raise its VCR output while reducing its output of copiers. The United States will do the opposite. If that's what you figured, you figured right.

In Table 4 the United States shifts all 600 hours of labor into copier production and consequently produces 20 copiers. South Korea, on the other hand, shifts 120 hours of its labor from copiers to VCRs. Thus in 420 hours it turns out 42 VCRs; in 180 hours it makes 9 copiers.

TABLE 4	Copiers and VCRs Produced by the United States and South Korea Using 600 Hours of Labor*
United States	20 copiers and 0 VCRs
South Korea	9 copiers and 42 VCRs
Total	29 copiers and 42 VCRs

*The United States devotes 600 hours to copier production; South Korea devotes 180 hours to copier production and 420 to VCR production.

When we add up the total output of copiers and VCRs in Table 4, we find that we have exceeded the outputs in Table 3. There is a gain of 4 copiers (from 25 to 29) and 7 VCRs (from 35 to 42).

If South Korea and the United States are the only two countries in the world and copiers and VCRs are their only products, then we are ready to trade. The trade will be American copiers for South Korean VCRs. As we did in the previous problem, let's have a one-for-one exchange.

A one-for-one trade leaves both countries better off than they were before they specialized. Let's say South Korea trades 8 VCRs for 8 copiers. South Korea now has 34 VCRs and 17 copiers, while the United States ends up with 8 VCRs and 12 copiers (see Table 5).

How does this compare with what each country had before specialization? For this comparison, look back at Table 3. South Korea has a net gain of 2 copiers and 4 VCRs, while the United States has 3 more VCRs and 2 more copiers. These gains are summarized in Table 6.

TABLE 5	Copiers and VCRs Owned by the United States and South Korea after United States Trades 8 Copiers for 8 VCRs
United States	12 (20 − 8) copiers and 8 (0 + 8) VCRs
South Korea	17 (9 + 8) copiers and 34 (42 − 8)VCRs

TABLE 6	U.S. and South Korean Gains from Trade
United States	2(12 − 10) copiers and 3 (8 − 5) VCRs
South Korea	2(17 − 15) copiers and 4 (34 − 30) VCRs

This is what is meant by a trade that helps both parties. We see that even though one nation is better at producing both products, it still pays for each nation to specialize in the production of the product it is relatively good at making and to trade for the product the other is relatively good at making.

Let's go back once again to the concept of opportunity cost. What is the opportunity cost of producing one VCR for the United States? In other words, to raise VCR output by one unit, what do you give up? You give up two copiers. What is the opportunity cost of producing one VCR in South Korea? You guessed it: one-half of one copier.

Now we'll consider the opportunity cost of producing copiers. In the United States it's one-half of one VCR; in South Korea it's two VCRs. In other words, the opportunity cost of producing VCRs is lower in South Korea. How about the opportunity cost of producing copiers? It's lower in the United States.

The law of comparative
advantage: Total output is
greatest when each product is
made by the country that has the
lowest opportunity cost.

We're finally ready for the law of comparative advantage, which is what this section is all about. Are you ready? OK, here it comes. *The law of comparative advantage states that total output is greatest when each product is made by the country that has the lowest opportunity cost.* If the relative opportunity costs of producing goods (what must be given up in one good in order to get another good) differ between two countries, there are potential gains from trade. In our example, copiers should be made in the United States and VCRs in South Korea. This is so because the United States has a comparative

Absolute Advantage versus Comparative Advantage

One of the things economists are fond of saying is that you can't compare apples and oranges. Here's a corollary: you can't compare absolute advantage and comparative advantage. The words may not exactly trip off your tongue, but still they ring true. Let's see why.

First, what *is* absolute advantage? It means that one country is better than another at producing some good or service (that is, it can produce it more cheaply). For example, the United States enjoys an absolute advantage over Japan in building commercial aircraft. But the Japanese enjoy an absolute advantage over the United States in making cameras. They can turn out cameras at a lower cost than we can, while we can build planes at

a lower cost than the Japanese can.

So absolute advantage is a comparison of the cost of production in two different countries. What about comparative advantage? Let me quote myself: "The law of comparative advantage states that total output is greatest when each product is made by the country that has the lowest opportunity cost."

So we can say that as long as the relative opportunity costs of producing goods differ among nations, there are potential gains from trade even if one country has an absolute advantage in producing everything. Therefore *absolute* advantage is not necessary for trade to take place, but *comparative* advantage is.

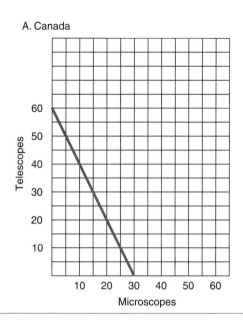

A. Canada

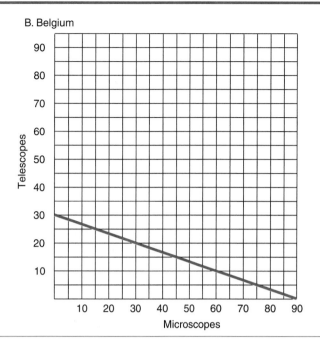

B. Belgium

Figure 5

Production Possibilities Curves

Operating at full capacity, Canada can produce 60 telescopes and 30 microscopes. Operating at full capacity, Belgium can produce 30 telescopes and 90 microscopes.

advantage in copiers while South Korea has one in VCRs. This is true even though South Korea can make both copiers and VCRs at a lower cost than the United States can. (See the box, "Absolute Advantage versus Comparative Advantage.")

Just for a change of pace, let's look at a couple of graphs instead of at tables. In Figure 5 we show the production possibilities curves of Canada and Belgium. See if you can answer these four questions: (1) Which country has a comparative advantage in producing telescopes? (2) Which country has a comparative advantage in producing microscopes? (3) Which country has an absolute advantage in producing telescopes? (4) Which country has an absolute advantage in producing microscopes?

Canada has a comparative and an absolute advantage in producing telescopes, while Belgium has a comparative and absolute advantage in producing microscopes.

Obviously Canada should be trading some of its telescopes for some of Belgium's microscopes. Canada would be willing to trade two telescopes for more than one microscope. And Belgium would be willing to trade three microscopes for more than one telescope. So clearly, they will be able to do business. The big question is: What are their terms of trade?

If Belgium and Canada were the only countries in the world, then their terms of trade would be determined by their relative bargaining power. But in today's world of international trade, their terms of trade are determined by the relative prices of microscopes and telescopes in the international market. So let's make it very easy. If telescopes sold for $1,000 and microscopes also sold for $1,000, then what are our terms of trade?

Our terms of trade would be 1:1, or one telescope for one microscope. We're ready, now, to add trade possibilities curves to our production possibilities curves. We've done that in Figure 6.

Now we can prove graphically how much better off a nation is when it trades. The production possibilities curve shows various combinations of two goods that a nation can produce. If it doesn't trade, then it will produce and consume one of these combinations. Suppose that Canada does this at point A—20 microscopes and 20 telescopes. But if Canada specialized in making just telescopes, it could make 60 telescopes (and

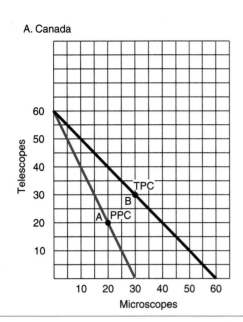

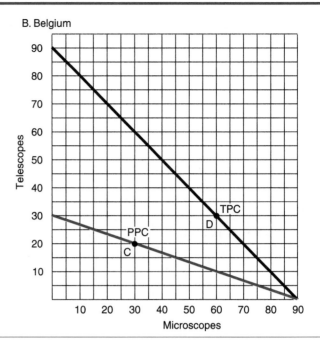

Figure 6

Production Possibilities Curves and Trade Possibilities Curves
What are our terms of trade? Our terms of trade would be 1:1.

no microscope) and trade away 30 of them to Belgium in exchange for 30 microscopes. This would place Canada at point B of its trade possibilities curve.

Talk about having your cake and eating it too! Specialization and trade enables Canada to go from point A (20 telescopes and 20 microscopes) to point B (30 telescopes and 30 microscopes). So by trading Canada gains 10 telescopes *and* 10 microscopes.

Now let's see how Belgium does by trading 30 of its microscopes for 30 of Canada's telescopes. We'll start at point C on Belgium's production possibilities curve. At that point Belgium is producing and consuming 20 telescopes and 30 microscopes. By specializing in making microscopes, Belgium produces 90, sends 30 of them to Canada in exchange for 30 microscopes, and ends up at point D of its trade possibilities curve. At that point it has 30 telescopes *and* 60 microscopes. Compared to point C, Belgium has 30 more microscopes and 10 more telescopes.

You may still have your doubts about these transactions. How can *both* countries gain by trading? Their gain really comes from specialization. Canada is especially good at making telescopes, while Belgium is better at making microscopes. It's as simple as that.

The Arguments for Protection

As America continues to hemorrhage manufacturing jobs, there is a growing outcry for protection against the flood of foreign imports. But American consumers are virtually addicted to Japanese cars; South Korean VCRs, TVs, and other consumer electronics; and hundreds of other manufactured goods from all over the world. How do we justify taxing or excluding so many things that so many Americans want to buy?

Four main arguments for protection

Four main arguments have been made for protection. Each seems plausible and strikes a responsive chord in the minds of the American public. But under closer examination, all four are essentially pleas by special interest groups for protection against more efficient competitors.

We'll first consider the argument that certain industries, while not as efficient as their foreign competitors, are essential to the defense of the country. The next three arguments, especially the last two, are related. Each uses the premise that industries based in foreign countries are not competing fairly with their American counterparts.

The infant industry argument is addressed to American consumers who would be seduced into buying foreign goods by their temporarily lower prices. The low-wage and the employment arguments are addressed to the workers who would be hurt by foreign competition. Interestingly, the owners of American companies who would stand to gain the most from protection are conspicuously silent about the benefits they would receive from protection.

(1) The National Security Argument   Originally this argument may have been advanced by American watchmakers, who warned the country not to become dependent on Swiss watchmakers because in the event of war Americans would not be able to make the timing devices for explosives without Swiss expertise. Yet during one long, drawn-out war, World War II, the United States was able to develop synthetics, notably rubber, to replace the supplies of raw materials that were cut off. And the Germans were able to convert coal into oil. It would appear, then, that the Swiss watch argument may have been somewhat overstated.

If our country were involved in a limited war, it is conceivable that our oil supplies from the Mideast might be cut off (although no American president would stand by passively while this happened), but we could probably replace these imports by producing more oil ourselves. When Iraqi forces invaded Kuwait in 1990 President George Bush was able to put together an international coalition that quickly defeated Iraq. And if there were a third world war we would certainly not have to worry about a cutoff of needed war material because the war would last only a few minutes.

If the national security argument is applied only to limited or local wars rather than to worldwide wars, it is possible that we do need to maintain certain defense-related industries. A justification that the United States should make its own aircraft, ordnance (bombs and artillery shells), and nuclear submarines might well be valid on a national security basis. But these industries have done extremely well in international markets and are hardly in need of protection.

Nevertheless, as our dependence upon Japanese technology grows, particularly in the area of semiconductor components, the national security argument has gained some validity. The time may come when major defense contractors become dependent on Japanese suppliers for critical components of entire weapons systems. Although that day might not arrive for decades, we had better start worrying right now.

Does our dependence on foreign suppliers make us vulnerable in time of war?

Of course, with the disintegration of the Soviet bloc and the end of the 45-year-old cold war, the world seems considerably safer. On the other hand, the continued spread of nuclear arms technology may soon make the national security argument much more relevant.

The national security argument can be extended to many other industrial nations, including smaller ones such as Israel, Iraq, and South Africa. These nations have not only thriving armament industries, but they strive to remain independent of foreign suppliers of crucial components.

(2) The Infant Industry Argument   In the late 18th century American manufacturers clamored for protection against "unfair" British competition. British manufacturers were "dumping" their products on our shores. By pricing their goods below cost, the British would drive infant American manufacturers out of business. Once their American competition was out of the way, the British companies would jack up their prices.

Whatever validity this reasoning once had has long since vanished. American manufactured products are no longer produced by infant industries being swamped by foreign giants. About the best that can be said is that some of our infant industries never matured, while others went well beyond the point of maturity and actually attained senility. Perhaps a senile industry argument might be more applicable to such stalwarts as steel, textiles, clothing, and automobiles.

Are American industries still infant industries?

An argument *can* be made that in a world of rapid technological change, a perfectly grown-up industry may become a helpless infant at any time. And hence some temporary protection is needed to allow American producers to catch up with the competition. The auto and steel industries provide excellent cases in point. After receiving some protection from foreign competition during the 1980s, both have made impressive comebacks.

How can the United States compete against countries that pay sweatshop wages?

(3) The Low-Wage Argument   The reasoning here is best summed up by this question: How can American workers compete with foreigners who are paid sweatshop wages (see box)? Certain goods and services are very labor intensive (that is, labor constitutes most or nearly all of the resource costs). Clothing manufacturing, domestic work, rice cultivation, most kinds of assembly-line work, and repetitive clerical work are examples. There is no reason for American firms to compete with foreign firms to provide these goods and services. If we look at our national experience over the last 150 years, Americans have always left the least desirable, most labor-intensive, low-paying work to immigrants. The Irish did the domestic work, built the railroads and canals, and did much of the rest of the backbreaking work of the mid-19th century. Then, in sequence, the Germans, Chinese, Italians, Poles, other Eastern Europeans, Jews, Mexicans, and, more recently, Vietnamese, Koreans, Indians, and Pakistanis have been accorded the lowest place on the economic totem pole. And, of course, a special place near the bottom has long been reserved for blacks and Hispanics—not because they were recent immigrants, but simply because they were systematically excluded from the economic mainstream by discrimination.

Those were the rules of the game, and by and large they served us well. Gradually they started to change in the early 1970s as a growing number of relatively cheap foreign imports began to dominate the American market.

What happened? What brought about these changes? First, Japan and West Germany, which had been rebuilding their industrial plants from scratch since World War II, had finally attained parity with the American industrial plant. At the same time their workers were being paid, on the average, less than half the wages of American workers. But in the 1970s the wages of both German and Japanese workers rose very sharply relative to those of American workers (the average German worker earned more than the average American worker by 1980). Throughout the 1970s, however, our trade balances with both these countries continued to deteriorate.

Why are some countries high-wage countries, while others are low-wage countries?

Why *are* certain workers paid higher wage rates than others? Why *are* some countries high-wage countries, while others are low-wage countries? In general, high-wage

Sweatshop Labor

Sweatshop employees put in very long hours under very poor working conditions for very low pay. Most of the clothing and footwear we import is produced by sweatshops. Reebok, Nike, Liz Claiborne, the Gap, J.C. Penney, Kmart, Wal-Mart, and Target are some of the leading producers and sellers of goods made in sweatshops in Asia and Latin America.

In El Salvador alone, 200 factories make clothing for the American market. In 1995, conditions were so bad in her factory, a contractor for the Gap, Abigail Martinez, helped lead a strike that got the Gap's attention. This is a *New York Times* then-and-now account:

> Six years ago, Abigail Martinez earned 55 cents an hour sewing cotton tops and khaki pants. Back then, she says, workers were made to spend 18-hour days in an unventilated factory with undrinkable water. Employees who displeased the bosses were denied bathroom breaks or occasionally made to sweep outside all morning in the broiling sun.

> Today, she and other workers have coffee breaks and lunch on an outdoor terrace cafeteria. Bathrooms are unlocked, the factory is breezy and clean, and employees can complain to a board of independent monitors if they feel abused.

> The changes are a result of efforts by Gap, the big clothing chain, to improve working conditions at this independent factory, one of many that supply its clothes.

> Yet Ms. Martinez today earns 60 cents an hour, only 5 cents more than six years ago.

But consider the alternative. If Abigail quits, will she get a better job? And if wages in El Salvador were to rise, the Gap and other foreign clothing firms would move to another low-wage country.

Source: Leslie Kaufman and David Gonzalez, "Labor Standards Clash With Global Reality," *The New York Times*, April 24, 2001, p. A1.

Having the Best of Both Worlds

The low-wage countries of Asia, Africa, and Latin America have a competitive advantage. So do the high-capital countries of Japan, the United States, Canada, and the European union. Why not combine the best of both worlds—low wages and high capital?

That's just what American multinational corporations have done around the world. Just across the Rio Grande in northern Mexico, thousands of factories churn out everything from cars and refrigerators to water beds and garage-door openers; they then ship most of these goods back into the United States. The factories are called *maquiladoras,* from the Mexican word for handwork. The workers are seldom paid much more than $1 an hour, or maybe a quarter of the U.S. minimum wage of $5.15.* There is great concern that the free trade agreement that President George Bush negotiated with Mexico in 1992 and the 1993 NAFTA pact will eventually lead to a flood of low-priced Mexican goods, but that flood began *years* ago.

Japanese multinational corporations have invested heavily in Mexico, Brazil, and the nations of the Pacific Rim. They are farming out the less profitable tasks, such as assembly work, while keeping the most advanced high-value work, such as product design and engineering, in Japan. In Thailand, for instance, Japan has established more than 50 electronics companies since 1985. While Japan's consumer electronics exports to America have been falling, exports of microwave ovens, VCRs, and TVs from Japanese companies in Thailand have soared.

---

*General Motors pays its American assembly-line workers about $18 an hour plus about another $18 an hour in fringe benefits; it pays its Mexican assembly-line workers $1.50 an hour and almost no fringe benefits.

---

workers produce more than low-wage workers. The main reason workers in high-wage countries produce more is that they have more capital with which to work than do workers in low-wage countries.

And so labor was paid more in the United States than anywhere else in the world during the three decades following World War II because we had more capital (plant and equipment) per worker than any other country. But as other countries succeeded in rebuilding and adding to their capital, our advantage began to disappear.

A new group of industrializing nations, among them South Korea, Taiwan, Thailand, Malaysia, Indonesia, Singapore, and Brazil, is challenging the older industrial powers. By combining capital with low wage rates, they are able to undersell even Japan (see box, "Having the Best of Both Worlds"). Although the wage rates in these emerging industrial nations will rise over time to reflect the growing productivity of their workers, they *do* have a clear competitive edge over higher-wage nations.

The question, then, is how to deal with low-wage competition. The answer is to deal with it the way we always have. We have always imported labor-intensive goods—sugar, handmade rugs, wood carvings, even Chinese back scratchers—because they were cheap. And we always let immigrants do the most backbreaking, low-paying, thankless labor. By specializing in the production of goods and services in which we excel, we can use the proceeds to buy the goods and services produced by people who are forced to work for low wages.

(4) The Employment Argument   Hasn't the flood of imports thrown millions of Americans out of work? The answer is, yes—but.

First we'll deal with the yes. There is no denying that hundreds of thousands of workers in each of the industries with stiff foreign competition—autos, steel, textiles, clothing, consumer electronics, and petroleum—have lost their jobs due to this competition. If we had restricted our imports of these goods by means of tariffs or quotas, most of these workers would not have lost their jobs.

Unfortunately, the governments of our foreign competitors would reciprocate by restricting our exports. Furthermore, a nation pays for its imports by selling its exports.[5]

If we restrict our imports, our exports will decline.

---

[5]The United States, Argentina, Brazil, Mexico, Poland, and several other countries have discovered another way of paying for imports. Together they have borrowed hundreds of billions of dollars a year to finance their spending binge. In the next chapter we'll take a closer look at this borrowing.

By curbing our imports, we will be depriving other nations of the earnings they need to buy our exports. In sum, if we restrict our imports, our exports will go down as well.

Even such unabashed free traders as President Reagan's Council of Economic Advisors conceded that 25,000 to 30,000 jobs may be lost for each additional billion dollars of imports. They go on to say, "Protection may save jobs in import-competing industries, but this is likely to be matched by the less visible loss of jobs elsewhere in the economy."[6]

The jobs we save in steel, autos, textiles, clothing, consumer electronics, and petroleum will be lost in our traditional export industries—machinery, office equipment, aircraft, chemicals, and agricultural products. From an economic standpoint, this would involve a considerable loss because we would be shifting production from our relatively efficient export industries to our relatively inefficient import industries. Is that any way to run an economy?

What about the workers who lose their jobs because of imports?

Nevertheless, you may ask about the human cost. What happens to the workers who are thrown out of work by foreign competition? Should their employers help them or should the government? And what can be done to help them?

Ideally, these displaced workers should be retrained and possibly relocated to work in our relatively efficient industries. Those who cannot be retrained or cannot move should be given some form of work, if only to keep them off the welfare rolls.

Who should help these displaced workers adjust? In a sense, their employers are responsible because these people were loyal and productive employees for perhaps 20 or 30 years. Unfortunately, the companies that should bear most of the responsibility for helping their employees are hardly in a position to do so. After all, they wouldn't be laying off workers if business were good to begin with.

That leaves the party of last resort: the federal government. What does the federal government do for workers who are displaced by foreign competition? Not very much. These workers receive extended unemployment benefits, are eligible for job retraining, and may receive some moving expenses. But the bottom line is that a middle-aged worker who loses her $15-an-hour job will probably not find another one that pays close to that, and government programs will not begin to compensate for this loss.

Does this mean we should keep out foreign goods that displace so many workers? No, not at all. We need better government retraining programs to get these people into well-paid, productive jobs.

Tariffs or Quotas

Politically, it is very hard to resist the pleas of millions of Americans who have been losing their jobs because of imports. Furthermore, some powerful industries have been hurt by imports, most notably the auto industry. Surely General Motors, Ford, and Chrysler are not without influence in the halls of Congress.

Although economists are loathe to be in such a situation, suppose it came down to choosing between the two main forms of protection: tariffs and import quotas. Which would be better? Or, more accurately, which is the lesser of two evils? Perhaps an apt analogy for this choice is picking the good guy of the 20th century with Hitler and Stalin as the only nominees.

A tariff is a tax on imports.

A tariff is a tax on imports. Throughout most of U.S. history until World War I, the tariff was our main source of federal revenue. The United States, which has lower tariffs than most other countries, charges less than 5 percent of the value of most imports.

A quota is a limit on the import of certain goods.

A quota is a limit on the import of certain goods. Sometimes this is a legal limit (as in the case of steel, apparel, textiles and sugar), and sometimes it is a "voluntary" limit (as was the case with cars from Japan). In the early and mid-1980s the Japanese limited their export of cars to the United States to fewer than 2.5 million a year, but only because of the threat of more stringent legal limits in the form of higher tariffs.

---

[6]*Economic Report of the President,* February 1986, pp. 107–8.

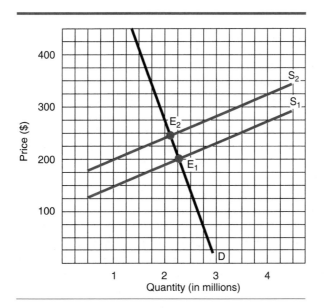

Figure 7
A Tariff Lowers Supply

This $50 tariff lowers supply from S_1 to S_2. Price rises from $200 to about $245, and quantity purchased falls from 2.25 million to 2.1 million. We move from equilibrium point E_1 to E_2. The tariff of $50 is the vertical distance between S_1 and S_2.

A third interference with free trade is export subsidies. Although several countries, most notably Japan and South Korea, do subsidize their export industries, this is a relatively minor expedient in the United States. The effect of export subsidies, of course, is to make the products cheaper, an effect that many Americans complain gives foreign competitors an "unfair advantage."

Both tariffs and quotas raise the price that consumers in the importing country must pay. However, there are three important differences in the effects of tariffs and quotas.

First, the federal government receives the proceeds of a tariff. Under import quotas there *are* no tax revenues.

Second, a tariff affects all foreign sellers equally, but import quotas are directed against particular sellers on an arbitrary basis. For example, in 1986 various Japanese car manufacturers had widely varying quotas, but the import of South Korean Hyundais was unrestricted.

A third difference involves relative efficiency. Efficient foreign producers will be able to pay a uniform tariff that less efficient producers will not be able to meet. But arbitrary import quotas may allow relatively inefficient foreign producers to send us their goods while keeping out those of their more efficient competitors. This comes down to somewhat higher prices for the American consumer because less efficient producers will charge higher prices than more efficient producers.

Figure 7 illustrates the effects of a tariff. A $50 tariff on cameras raises the price of a camera from $200 to about $245. And it causes the quantity purchased to fall from 2.25 million to 2.1 million.

Incidentally, a tariff, like any other excise tax, causes a decrease in supply—that is, a smaller quantity is supplied at every possible price. The effect of taxes on supply was discussed at length in the chapter on supply in *Economics* and *Microeconomics*.

To summarize, tariffs are better than quotas, but free trade is best. In the long run, the American consumer must pay for trade restrictions in the form of higher prices. (See the box, "What Does It Cost to Save Jobs?")

Tariffs are better than quotas, but free trade is best.

Conclusion

The case for free trade is one of the cornerstones of economics. (See box, "Petition of the Candlemakers to Shut out the Sun.") Economics is all about the efficient allocation of scarce resources, so there is no reason why this efficient allocation should not be applied beyond national boundaries. A baseball team that has more pitchers than it knows

No nation was ever ruined by trade.

—Benjamin Franklin

What Does It Cost to Save Jobs?

Almost everything costs something. How much does it cost to save an American job from foreign competition? Sometimes it costs hundreds of thousands of dollars a year.

Various estimates have been made for jobs in different industries. In specialty steel it costs consumers about $1 million a year in the form of higher prices to save one American job. To save a job making television sets in the United States costs more than $400,000 a year. Saving other jobs in steel production, shipping, and chemicals also costs the American consumer hundreds of thousands of dollars.

We need to ask ourselves: Is it worth all this money to save certain jobs? Would American consumers support high tariffs or import quotas if they knew how much it cost to save each job?

Former Secretary of Labor Robert Reich has noted that much of what we produce is purchased by other industries:

For one thing, every time one industry gained protection, another industry, dependent on the first for material or components, found itself squeezed. Once the steel industry successfully warded off cheaper foreign steel, the Big Three American automakers discovered that they had to pay 40 percent more for it than did their global competitors, thus putting the American automakers at a greater competitive disadvantage and, paradoxically, making them all the more needful of protection. The same proved true for American apparel manufacturers when textiles were first protected, and American computer manufacturers when foreign semiconductors were blocked from the American market.[*]

_____

[*]Robert Reich, _The Work of Nations_ (New York: Knopf, 1991), p. 78.

what to do with but needs a good-hitting shortstop will trade that extra pitcher or two for the shortstop. It will trade with a team that has an extra shortstop but needs more pitching. This trade will help both teams.

International trade helps every country; we all have higher living standards because of it. To the degree that we can remove the tariffs, import quotas, and other impediments to free trade, we will all be better off.

It has been estimated that lower-priced imports kept the rate of inflation one or two points below what it would otherwise have been since the mid-1980s. This is still another important reason for not restricting imports.

Imports pressure American companies to become more efficient. It is obvious, for example, that Toyota, Nissan, Honda, and the other Japanese automakers drove Detroit to make far better cars with far fewer workers than it used to. Indeed, our annual productivity gains of 10 percent would have been inconceivable without the spur of Japanese competition. Our chemical, steel, pharmaceutical, computer, textile, apparel, commercial aircraft, machine tool, paper copier, and semiconductor industries have all been spurred to much higher levels of efficiency by their foreign competitors.

None of this is to deny that there are problems. The millions of workers who are losing their jobs due to foreign competition cannot be expected to cheerfully make personal sacrifices in the interest of the greater national economic well-being. Nor will the American people stand by patiently awaiting the readjustment or deindustrialization of our economy to conform to the new world economic order. In the long run we may all be better off if there is worldwide free trade, but, as John Maynard Keynes once noted, "In the long run we are all dead."

The economics profession nearly unanimously backs free trade.

While the economics profession is nearly unanimous in advocating free trade, there is nearly complete disagreement over what to do about our huge trade deficit. If we do nothing, as fervent free traders advocate, can we count on our trade imbalance to eventually correct itself? Or will foreigners—especially the Japanese—continue to outsell us? These are just two of the questions I'll try to answer in the third part of this chapter.

Petition of the Candlemakers to Shut out the Sun

The case of protection against "unfair" competition was extended to its absurd conclusion by Frédéric Bastiat, a mid-19th-century French economist who wrote an imagined petition to the Chamber of Deputies. Parts of that petition follow.

> We are suffering from the intolerable competition of a foreign rival, placed, it would seem, in a condition so far superior to ours for the production of light, that he absolutely inundates our national market with it at a price fabulously reduced. The moment he shows himself, our trade leaves us—all consumers apply to him, and a branch of native industry, having countless ramifications, is all at once rendered completely stagnant. This rival . . . is no other than the Sun. What we pray for is, that it may please you to pass a law ordering the shutting up of all windows, skylights, dormerwindows, outside and inside shutters, curtains, blinds, bull's eyes; in a word, of all openings, holes, chinks, clefts, and fissures, by or through which the light of the sun has been in use to enter houses . . .*

Frédéric Bastiat, 19th-century French economist. Courtesy Roger-Viollet.

*Frédéric Bastiat, *Economic Sophisms* (Edinburgh: Oliver and Boyd, Tweeddale Court, 1873), pp. 49–53.

Part III: The Practice of International Trade

Let's distinguish between our balance of payments and our balance of trade. Our balance of trade, which we'll be discussing in this section, *compares the dollar value of merchandise and services we buy from foreigners with the dollar value of the merchandise and services they buy from us.* Our balance of trade is the main component of our overall balance of payments, which is *our country's record of all transactions between its residents and the residents of all foreign nations.* We'll get to our balance of payments in the next chapter.

Our balance of trade versus our balance of payments

What Are the Causes of Our Trade Imbalance?

Not only have we been losing our national markets to foreign imports, but we have been losing our share of *foreign* markets as well. In 1969 we made 90 percent of our nation's machine tools, 88 percent of our cars, and 82 percent of our TVs. And today? We make half our machine tools; we make just over 60 percent of our cars (not counting the output of the Japanese transplants); and our only remaining TV maker, Zenith, moved its only remaining production facilities to Mexico in 1992.

We have been losing market share both at home and abroad.

In the 1970s, 8 of the top 10 makers of semiconductors were American. By the end of the 1980s, 8 of the top 10 were Japanese, 1 was Korean, and 1 American. In the 1970s the world's top 10 banks were all American; today none is. And now there are signs that we may even be losing our lead in commercial aircraft manufacturing and in computer software engineering.[7]

---

[7]Given our high rate of economic growth since the mid-1990s, perhaps I am coming down too hard on corporate America. Howerver, most of the impetus for our recent growth spurt has come from tiny start-up enterprises, nearly all of which have relatively long time horizons.

Our Oil Import Bill

In 1990, for the first time in our history, we imported half of the oil we consumed. To lend some perspective, in 1973, when the Arab oil embargo produced our first oil-price shock, we imported just 39 percent of our oil. And in 1979, when Iran cut production after the fall of the Shah, we imported 45 percent. Yet both times the price of oil went through the roof and we had gas lines six blocks long.

So are we vulnerable to future shocks? Yes, we are. And over time we'll become even more vulnerable. American domestic production has been declining, as the output from fields in Alaska's North Slope declines and many other fields mature. In 2000 our bill for oil imports was almost $80 billion.

Most Americans believe gasoline taxes are too high and only grudgingly went along with the 12-cent-a-gallon increase that was part of the deficit reduction package passed by Congress in October 1990. But American gasoline taxes (federal plus state and local), at 41 cents a gallon, on average, are the lowest in any major industrial country. The French and the Italians pay more than $3 a gallon in tax, the Germans, $2.75.

Would Americans be willing to pay an extra two or three bucks a gallon? Never! Even if it meant we'd be able to cut our foreign energy dependence in half and maybe even cut our trade deficit in half as well? Still no! Hey, there are priorities around here, buddy. And nobody messes with American priorities. Americans like to drive, and they like their gasoline to be cheap—no matter who has to pay for it in the long run.

In 2000 our motor vehicle trade gap set a new record. We imported $116 billion more in cars, light trucks, and parts than we exported. Added to our oil import bill of almost $80 billion, our driving habit is responsible for over half of our $370 billion trade deficit.

The three biggest culprits are our oil bill and our deficits with Japan and China.

Why have we been losing our markets to foreign competitors, and why have we been running such large trade deficits? Before we turn to the underlying reasons, I want to mention three of the most obvious culprits: our huge bill for imported oil and our very large trade deficits with Japan and China. Together, these three account for nine-tenths of our overall deficit. I've summarized the U.S. problem with oil imports in the box titled "Our Oil Import Bill," but our trade problems with Japan and China will be dealt with separately in Part IV of this chapter.[8]

Why did the United States, which has run positive trade balances practically every year since the turn of the century, begin running small negative trade balances in the 1970s and huge ones in the 1980s? There is no single answer to this question, but each of the following seven factors provides part of the answer. The second, third, fourth, and fifth factors were more fully discussed in Chapter 16 of *Macroeconomics* and *Economics*. Each bears directly on our productivity rate of growth, which had been lagging until the mid-1990s.

A rising dollar makes our exports more expensive and our imports cheaper.

(1) The Rise of the Dollar Between 1980 and 1985 the dollar rose by 74 percent against the world's major currencies. How much of this increase was due to our huge budget deficits is still being debated, but the effect of this spectacular increase in the dollar's value on our balance of trade is clear. A rising dollar depresses our exports because it makes our goods more expensive relative to foreign goods. Similarly, it makes imported goods cheaper relative to American products, thus encouraging the consumer to switch.

In 1980 our balance of trade stood at −$19 billion. By 1985 it stood at −$122 billion (see Figure 1). There is no way to determine how much of this decline was caused by the rising dollar, but it seems likely that the rising dollar played a large role. The dollar rose again from 1995 to 1998, and again our trade deficit rose sharply.

(2) Our Low Saving Rate Americans have become notoriously poor savers, averaging less than 5 percent of their disposable personal income since the mid-1980s. The

---

[8]Our deficits with Japan averaged over $50 billion from 1986 through 1997. Sony now makes TVs in Westmoreland County, PA.

Japanese have been putting away more than 20 percent a year. The Germans, the South Koreans, the Taiwanese, and other people experiencing a rapid rate of economic growth—and, not coincidentally, a positive balance of trade—have all had very high savings rates.

If you don't save, you can't invest, and if you don't invest, you don't grow. It's as simple as that, which leaves business firms with just one choice: borrow from foreigners. This strategy has worked up to a point. While tens of billions of dollars in investment funds have been flowing in from abroad each year, they have come here only because of our relatively high interest rates.

> A penny saved is a penny earned.
> —Benjamin Franklin

(3) The High Cost of Capital

Because the Japanese, with a population half the size of ours, generate the largest pool of savings in the world, Japan's cost of capital measured by real interest rates (that is, nominal interest rates less the rate of inflation) has been just one-third that in the United States over the last two decades. One of the few things on which all economists agree is the central role of interest rates in determining the level of investment.

Mainly because of our low saving rate and partially because of the huge federal budget deficits we had been running, high real interest rates have discouraged investment in plant and equipment as well as in technological innovation. Indeed, these high real interest rates have attracted investment funds from the Japanese and other foreign sources. This inflow has only partially offset the lack of investment funds generated by American savers.

> We are consuming more than we are producing, borrowing more than we are saving, and spending more than we are earning.
> —Murray Weidenbaum

(4) High Defense Spending

The defense expenditures of the United States have dwarfed those of every other industrial power, except, incidentally, those of the former Soviet Union. One-third of our research-and-development (R&D) spending goes toward defense, and until 1990 about half of our engineers and scientists were involved in military projects.

Can we afford to devote such a large proportion of our resources to defense, especially when the countries we are presumably defending spend so little? While 3 percent of our GDP goes toward defense, the Japanese spend barely 1 percent of theirs. Nearly all of their R&D dollars and engineering and scientific talent go into the production of goods and services, which have been displacing those made in America. One can only ask whether we have our priorities straight, and whether, in a time of diminishing military tension, we should be diverting our dollars to defense from areas where they could be used more productively.

(5) Our Failing Educational System

The American educational system, once second to none, is now second to practically everyone's. The illiterate high school graduate is no longer the rare exception, and about one-third of all college freshmen need remedial work in the three Rs—reading, writing, and arithmetic. Nearly every college—even in the Ivy League schools—has special classes for students unprepared to do college work. In test after test, Americans rank at or near the bottom of the industrial countries.

> Our schools are turning out students who cannot read or write.

Half our high school math and science teachers are unqualified to teach those subjects. In Florida and in Massachusetts, thousands of teachers failed exams testing them on the very subject matter they had been hired to teach. No wonder that our educational system turns out one million functional illiterates every year—not exactly job candidates for today's high-tech economy.

(6) The Role of Multinationals

Before the 1960s the vast low-wage workforces of the world's poorer nations were no threat to the workers in the high-wage economies like the United States. Our workers were many times more productive than those in the poorer nations because they had so much more capital to work with.

All of this began to change in the 1960s as multinational corporations began to move their manufacturing operations offshore to take advantage of this low-wage labor pool. By providing these workers with sufficient plant and equipment, the multinationals were able to increase their productivity to the level of American assembly-line workers.

> More capital, higher productivity, and higher wages.

Much of the manufacturing of apparel, shoes, toys, and consumer electronics, which had been done largely by the "four tigers," has been shifting to China, India, Indonesia, the Philippines, Thailand, and other low-wage countries. Capital has long been much more mobile than labor, and that capital has been flowing very rapidly to the low-wage nations.

The hollow corporation

The term *hollow corporation* has gained currency in the last decade as more and more companies put their names on imported goods. These companies' sole function is to sell such goods as the Dodge Colt or the Panasonic typewriter, both of which are made in Japan. Yet our import business is not dominated by firms that market goods for the Japanese and other foreign producers, but rather by our own multinational corporations that have shifted most of their production overseas. Joel Kurtzman describes their operations:

> These multinationals have transformed themselves from producers of goods to importers and marketers of goods made overseas by their foreign divisions and affiliates. Because so many of our imports come to us in the form of trade between the different divisions of American multinationals, the balance-of-payments deficit has become structurally integrated into our economy.[9]

(7) Relative Growth Rate   So far we've talked about all our deficiencies contributing to our balance of trade deficit. But even our virtues seem to contribute to that deficit. Since 1995 we have had one of the highest rates of economic growth of any industrial nation. Most of Western Europe and Japan went through a period of recession, while the new industrial countries of Southeast Asia went through severe financial crises and accompanying recessions. Countries with high economic growth rates import more goods and services than they would if they had low growth rates. The bad news, then, is that while we have been importing record amounts of goods and services, foreign demand for U.S. exports has been lagging. But the good news is that as the economies of Western Europe, Japan, and Southeast Asia pick up again, they will be importing more from us.

What Can We Do?

Devalue the dollar.

One thing that should have helped reduce our negative trade balance was a fall in the value of the dollar relative to other currencies. Let's consider the decade of the 1980s. From 1980 to 1985 the dollar rose by 74 percent relative to the world's other major currencies. But then, in 1985, the dollar began to fall, reaching its 1980 level by 1989.

What do you think happened to our negative trade balance between 1985 and 1989? It got smaller, right? Glance back at Figure 1. You'll see that our trade deficit actually got *larger* from 1985 to 1987 before it finally began to shrink in 1988. Question: If the rising value of the dollar drove up our trade deficit from 1980 through 1985, why didn't it go back down when the dollar began to fall in 1985?

One explanation is that Japan, the "four tigers" (Taiwan, Korea, Singapore, and Hong Kong), and some of our other trading partners whose sales to us expanded between 1980 and 1985 refused to give up those gains. As the dollar declined, so did their prices. What they did, then, was defend their markets by cutting their profit margins, even taking occasional losses.

The J-curve effect

Another explanation is provided by the J-curve effect (sorry, no pictures). When the dollar is devalued, the trade deficit actually continues to rise for another year or year and a half—which is exactly what happened from 1985 through 1987.

At the onset of devaluation, why do things get worse before they begin to get better? The first thing to happen is that our exports become cheaper to foreigners (that is, our exports' prices decline), while imports to the United States become more expensive

---

[9]Joel Kurtzman, *The Decline and Crash of the American Economy* (New York: W. W. Norton, 1988), p. 131.

(their prices rise). Hence foreigners are getting higher prices for the goods they send us, but we're getting lower prices for our exports. Do you follow so far?

But if the prices of our exports decline, won't foreigners buy more? Yes—only not right away. It takes time for advertisements to wean them away from domestic products. And don't forget that our foreign competitors are reluctant to give up market share, especially on their home turf.

The same goes for imports. It takes a year or two to get Americans to switch from foreign imports to American goods, and again, our foreign rivals will cut prices to hold their market share.

Clearly the 1980–85 dollar rise does not fully explain the huge jump in our trade deficit; if it did, then the 1985–94 devaluation should have returned the deficit to its 1980 level. All the other causes outlined in the previous section have also played roles. So, as we cast about for remedies, let's see what else we can fix.

The core of our trade problem is that the so-called "me generation" of the 1980s went on a spending spree that has continued through the 1990s and that it still hasn't paid for. We need to put a lid on consumption; then, we hope, all the other pieces will fall into place.

> We need to put a lid on consumption.

Various measures could be taken to curb consumption and, concurrently, raise saving. A national sales tax or, alternatively, a value-added tax (like those in several European countries) would not only hold down consumption but would also raise tens of billions of dollars in federal revenue. A value-added tax, unlike a sales tax, is collected at each stage of the production process.

Economists have always believed in providing incentives to get people to "do the right thing" (which was even made into a film by Spike Lee). One thing we want people to do is save more, and the way to get them to do that is to make at least some of their savings tax free.

> We need to save more.

Individual retirement accounts (IRAs) were tax free from 1982 to 1986, when the personal savings rate averaged 7.2 percent. But from 1987, when the tax exemption was removed, the savings rate sank below 5 percent (in 2000 it fell to 0 percent). It would appear that making the first $1,000 of interest earned on bank accounts and other forms of savings, we could push up our savings rate well above 5 percent. One might note that the Japanese have built powerful savings incentives into their tax code.

> Bring back the tax-free IRA.

One of the few bright spots in recent years has been our declining defense spending. What we must guard against, however, are the blandishments of the defense establishment to "not let down our guard" (that is, keep spending money on new weaponry).

> Defense spending should fall.

Turning around our failing education system may be the key to turning around our economy. One part of the problem, which may be a little too sensitive to discuss (but I'll discuss it anyway), is that our best and our brightest do not become teachers. In fact, those majoring in education have consistently scored among the lowest of all students taking the Scholastic Aptitude Test (SAT). Who scored the lowest? Those with the lowest scores were physical education majors. (But then, how do you *teach* gym?)

> Educating our future labor force is the key.

My own plan is to pay teachers enough to attract bright and highly motivated people, allow the schools to expel "students" who are consistently disruptive, and abolish all college departments of education. The latter not only offer courses of almost no intellectual substance, but they perpetuate standards that rarely soar to even a level of mediocrity. I would also get rid of any teacher who could not read at an eighth-grade level. I might extend the school day and the school year, make two hours of homework a night mandatory, and abolish automatic promotion. If this program were followed—and I have no illusions that it ever will be—our schools would no longer graduate illiterates and semiliterates, who are completely unqualified for today's workforce.

Protectionist legislation is a real possibility if our foreign competitors are indeed dumping goods below cost on our shores. Although the economics profession and many people in government remain firmly opposed to any interference with free trade, the pressure for such measures will continue to grow if our trade deficit does not shrink to an acceptable level.

> Protectionist legislation is a real possibility.

Part IV: Our Trade Deficit with Japan and China

For most of the 1980s and 1990s, Japan was not only our fiercest trade competitor, but was running huge trade surpluses with us. In the long run, however, our largest trade deficits may be with China, who finally overtook Japan in 2000. (See Figure 8.)

Please note that the data in Figure 8 are virtually the same as *merchandise* trade deficits with Japan and China. Although we do maintain small service surpluses with both Japan and China, our big problem is with our huge and growing merchandise deficits. Our merchandise deficits with Japan are substantially underestimated because Japanese multinational corporations have shifted much of their production offshore to Thailand, Indonesia, Malaysia, Singapore, China, Korea, and Mexico. For instance, that Sony TV that you just bought may well be one of the 14 million sets turned out just across the Rio Grande in Tijuana. (See again box "Having the Best of Both Worlds" earlier in this chapter.)

There are two factors that compromise our official trade deficits with China. Until July 1, 1997, when China repossessed Hong Kong, a substantial part of the goods shipped

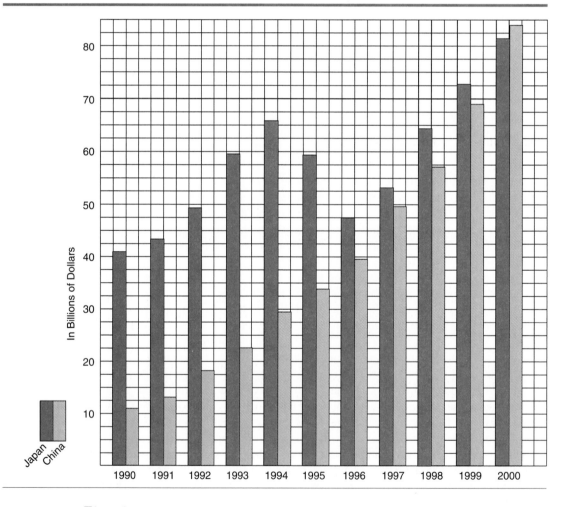

Figure 8

U.S. Trade Deficit with Japan and China

Our trade deficit with Japan, which topped $50 billion in 1992, has apparently leveled off, while our deficit with China grew steadily through the 1990s and is now equal to that with Japan.

Sources: Economic Report of the President, 1998; *Survey of Current Business,* July 1997; February, 1998; *U.S. Statistical Abstract,* 1999 & 2000.

here were made in China. If these goods were counted as imports from China—and not from Hong Kong—our trade deficits with China would have been a great deal higher.

On the other hand, our exports to China are also underestimated. Chinese officials themselves admit that high tariffs have led to rampant smuggling of cigarettes and other consumer goods. In 1997 out of about 100 billion American and other foreign-brand cigarettes that were sold in China, not a single one was legally imported.

Many goods once made elsewhere in Asia—in Japan, Taiwan, Singapore, South Korea—are now produced in foreign-owned factories that have been moved to China. Our growing deficit with China is largely offset by declining deficits with other Asian nations.

Japanese Trading Practices

Are the Japanese dumping, or selling their products below cost, to drive American producers out of business? Because they are selling many of their products below cost, it is reasonable to ask whether they are unfairly—and, according to our laws, illegally—competing by dumping their products on our shores. Clearly, the *effect* of selling below cost is to drive out American competitors. But what is their *motivation*? Perhaps Japanese firms' motivation in charging so little is to minimize their losses in the short run by producing and selling a large volume of output, and spreading their fixed costs to take advantages of economies of scale. This, of course, is exactly what every economist would tell a firm to do.

Are the Japanese dumping?

But when we look at the other side of the coin, at how Japanese society pulls together to keep foreign manufacturers out of the Japanese market, at how the Japanese consumer is willing to pay double what the American consumer pays for the same Japanese products, it is fair to say that driving American competitors out of business provides a great deal of the motivation for Japanese manufacturers to sell us their goods below cost—at least in the short run. (The question of whether Japanese markets are closed to imports is discussed in the accompanying box.)

Other theories attempting to explain the success of Japanese manufacturers attribute much of it to the just-in-time manufacturing system, to the lifetime employment practices of large corporations, to a strong work ethic, to weak labor unions, and to worker involvement in decision making. All of these certainly describe important differences between the Japanese workplace and ours, and they also likely account for much of the Japanese success. Many observers believe the fundamental difference between ourselves and the Japanese is product quality.

The fundamental difference between ourselves and the Japanese is product quality.

The same conclusion was reached by the MIT Commission on Industrial Productivity: "Mass production was the driving force behind American postwar prosperity, but it is often no longer an appropriate model for managers and workers in the changed circumstances of today."[10] The commission uses the Japanese automobile industry as an example of how product quality can be raised:

> The Japanese have succeeded by providing different products for each segment of the market. To do so efficiently and profitably, they have developed technologies, product development methods, and patterns of workplace organization that allow them to reduce the volume of production and increase the speed with which new products are brought to market.[11]

What it all comes down to is that the Japanese compete not just on the basis of price but on the basis of product quality. They have taken our system of mass production one step further, turning out a wide range of customized variations, while we continue to concentrate on single standardized products.

The Japanese compete on the basis of price and quality.

[10]Michael L. Dertouzos, Richard K. Lester, and Robert M. Solow, *Made in America: Regaining the Productive Edge* (Cambridge, MA: MIT Press, 1989), p. 46.

[11]Ibid., p. 48.

Are Japanese Markets Closed to Imports?

The Japanese have always considered themselves different, and the rest of us are forced to agree with them. An insular society shut off from the rest of the world until the mid-19th century, the Japanese are an ethnically and culturally homogeneous nation. They have no immigrant population to speak of, and more than almost any other people, the Japanese are just plain clannish. Is it any wonder, then, that they prefer doing business among themselves rather than with outsiders?

American exporters have long complained that Japanese markets were largely closed to them. The record shows that our exports to Japan have been inordinately low, even in fields where we are selling a superior product at prices well below those charged by Japanese producers. And yet Japan's tariff barriers are by and large no higher than our own.

One trade barrier is the *keiretsu* (economic group), which is described by Clyde Prestowitz as an alliance "linked by cross-shareholdings, common banking affiliations, and the use of the same trading company to procure raw materials and to distribute products."[*] This makes for quite a tidy arrangement. Although group members don't always deal with each other, they usually do. After all, what is a *keiretsu* for?

Less formal but very powerful obstacles are placed in the way of imports. These are described by Murray Sayle, an Australian journalist who lived in Japan for several years:

> The Japanese exporter to the United States needs only to offer a better or cheaper product, and he's honorably in. But the would-be exporter to Japan finds the marketplace already seized up solid with a dense network of "friendships," of layer upon layer of middlemen who have been doing business together for years, and who are, of course, all Japanese.[†]

The relationship between the large manufacturer and the supplier is an especially close one. In fact, the vaunted just-in-time inventory control system is based on it. As Prestowitz notes, "When the whole production system depends on precisely timed delivery of zero-defect products, it is absolutely critical to have a high degree of confidence in the supplier. Such confidence requires working closely with him and even assisting him in parts design and the manufacturing process."[‡] The bond between these firms is not easily severed by outsiders, especially foreign outsiders.

---

[*]Clyde V. Prestowitz, Jr., *Trading Places* (New York: Basic Books, 1988), p. 157.

[†]Murray Sayle, "The Japanese Exporter: Japan Victorious," *New York Review of Books,* March 28, 1985.

[‡]Prestowitz, *Trading Places,* p. 165.

What do we sell the Japanese? Agricultural products. And what do we buy from them? Manufactured products. When a nation supplies another nation with raw materials and gets back, in return, manufactured goods, it is a colonial relationship.

In the years before the American Revolution, the British strongly encouraged their American colonies to send them raw materials in exchange for manufactured goods. Which, incidentally, was one of the grievances over which we rebelled.

Japan picks winners and then makes sure they win.

The Japanese game plan is to pick industries that look like long-run winners for Japan—cars, consumer electronics, computer chips, cameras—and to give them backing not just from the government but from fellow industrialists, from employees, consumers, and basically from the entire society. The government provides R&D funding, helps keep out imports, and holds down the interest rate, so the new industry has virtually unlimited low-interest funding. Competitors cooperate rather than compete. The Japanese consumer automatically prefers indigenous products—no matter how costly or qualitatively inferior—to foreign imports. And as a whole the Japanese people prefer doing business among themselves rather than with foreigners. In the box titled "How the Japanese Drove American TV Manufacturers Out of Business," I discuss in more detail the Japanese game of international trade and how it is played.

Well, you might ask, why can't we just put up high tariffs to keep out imports? Good question! Aside from the fact that our competitors would reciprocate with tariffs of their own to keep out American goods, there's an even more important reason. Americans would simply not stand for it. It would mean no VCRs, no TVs, and no cameras. Most of all, it would mean a sharp decline in our standard of living, which most Americans

How the Japanese Drove American TV Manufacturers Out of Business*

You'd have to be at least in your mid-50s to remember those old Dumonts, RCAs, GEs, and Sylvanias, with their nine-inch screens, back in the late 1940s. Howdy Doody, Gene Autry, Hopalong Cassidy, and Farmer Gray cartoons were all the rage. Well, TV programming has come a long way, but it's still by and large produced by American companies. However, TV manufacturing, like so much else in consumer electronics, has come to be dominated by the Japanese. Today there are no American companies still making television sets in this country.

It all started back in 1956 when a cartel of Japanese television makers was formed. The Home Electric Appliance Market Stabilization Council had two objectives: first, to gain complete control of the Japanese TV market, and then, to gain control of the far larger American market.

At the time GE, Westinghouse, and RCA produced the state-of-the-art TVs. Because the cartel effectively excluded the sale of American TV sets in Japan, these companies "each licensed and then transferred its monochrome technology to members of the cartel. In 1962, RCA went one step further and licensed its color technology to the Japanese."[†]

Next came the plan's second phase. The American market would be inundated with television sets that would be sold well below cost. To subsidize this venture, the Japanese consumer was charged double what Americans paid. Indeed, while Americans were paying an average of just $350 a set, Japanese consumers were forking out $700 for identical TVs.

*Much of this information may be found in Chapter 6 of Pat Choate's book *Agents of Influence* (New York Touchstone, 1990). Choate ran for vice president in 1996 on the Reform Party ticket with Ross Perot.

†Ibid p. 80.

would find intolerable. High tariffs might well have been feasible 20 or 30 years ago, but not today when the American consumer has become so dependent on foreign imports.[12]

The Japanese consumer has long accepted a lower standard of living because it was necessary for the greater economic good. But how many Americans would be willing to make that sacrifice? Certainly not those whose lifestyle is best described as "born to shop" and "shop till you drop." The concept of subordinating our personal interests to those of our society is as foreign to us as our concept of the ascendancy of the individual is to the Japanese.

Some fundamental societal differences help explain why we have run such large trade deficits with Japan. Stephen Cohen describes these differences:

The United States and Japan are very different societies.

> The United States as a whole maximizes consumption and recreation, pursues instant gratification, extols the spirit of the individual, and adheres to a belief in the glory of the free market. Japan as a whole opts to work, to save, to sublimate the self to the interests of a larger group, to plan and to sacrifice for the long run, and to adhere to an economic system based primarily on enhancing the size and power of entrenched domestic interests.[13]

We need to be asking the Japanese some hard questions: Why do we manage to export our manufactured goods to other industrial countries without much ado, while it's such a struggle to export them to Japan? Why do so many other countries also complain about how Japan's markets are closed? And why have the Japanese been running huge bilateral trade surpluses in manufactured goods with nearly *all* their trading partners—even the newly industrialized economies of Southeast Asia?

[12]American manufacturers—indeed, manufacturers around the world—have become extremely dependent on imported components and raw materials. We depend heavily on foreigners for such manufacturing inputs as oil, machine tools, computer chips, and steel.

[13]Stephen Cohen, *Cowboys and Samurai* (New York: HarperBusiness, 1991), p. 3.

Our Trade Deficit with China

When we began trading with China in the mid-1970s, after President Richard Nixon's historic trip to open relations with that nation, American exporters had great hopes that the world's most populous nation would eventually become the world's largest consumer market. Twenty-five years later, toys, athletic shoes, clothing, and other relatively low-price manufactured goods are flooding into the United States, along with an increasing stream of higher-priced goods such as tools, auto parts, electronic gear, microwave ovens, and personal computers. Although U.S. exports to China are growing rapidly, our exports are only about one-quarter of our imports.

Why are we importing so much from China? Mainly because U.S. retailers are seeking the cheapest goods available and finding them in China. Wal-Mart Stores imported nearly $3 billion worth of goods in 2000, and Kmart and Toys 'R' Us also found that the price was right in China.

One of the big trade issues between China and the United States is that thousands of Chinese factories, many controlled by top officers of the Chinese army, have been making unauthorized, or knock-off, copies of American movies, CDs, and most important, computer software. According to a *New York Times* article, an American official said that Chinese officials disputed the United States estimates that 95 percent of computer software used in China was pirated and asserted that it was closer to 25 to 30 percent—and that they would take steps to lower that amount.[14]

Trading with China and Japan: More Differences than Similarities

Our trading position with Japan is very much like a colony and a colonial power. Our trading relationship with the Chinese is very different. We send airplanes, computers, movies, compact disks, cars, cigarettes, power-generating equipment, and computer software in exchanges for toys, clothing, shoes, and low-end consumer electronics.

Still another difference between China and Japan is that the latter was never open to foreign direct investment. Japanese factories are Japanese-owned. But China, since the mid-1980s, has been open to foreign direct investment, which has been attracted mainly by extremely low wages, about $50 a month, except in the southern provinces surrounding Hong Kong. American, Japanese, British, Korean, and Taiwanese corporations have invested some $200 billion to set up assembly lines that use semiskilled labor to turn out cheap manufactured goods. Foreign-owned companies are then required to export a certain percentage of what they produce.

The percentage of its exports made by enterprises with foreign investment grew from 1 percent in 1985 to nearly 50 percent in 1998. So we have American multinational corporations using cheap Chinese labor to produce toys, clothing, watches, shoes, and other low-end consumer products for the American market. Much of what they're sending to us used to come from Japan back in the 1950s. "Made in Japan" has been replaced by "Made in China."

Japanese gains in the production of semiconductors, machine tools, steel, autos, TVs, and VCRs have led directly to the loss of millions of well-paying American jobs. Although Chinese products may compete on a broader scale with American goods in the future, Chinese exports so far have generally not translated into job losses in the United States. China's leading exports are products that have not been produced in large quantity by American factories for more than a decade.

The Chinese, like the Japanese before them, have insisted on licensing agreements and large-scale transfer of technology as the price for agreeing to imports. These agreements, of course, lead to the eventual elimination of imports from the United States.

---

[14]Seth Faison, "U.S. and China Sign Accord to End Piracy of Software, Music Recordings and Film," *New York Times,* February 27, 1995, p. D6.

However, the Chinese have taken this process one step further. Sometimes, instead of entering into licensing agreements, Chinese factories simply manufacture pirated versions, or knock-offs, of American videos, CDs, computer software, and designer apparel.

Final Word

To reduce our overall trade deficit further we need to make a combination of four things happen. First, we need to maintain our high rate of productivity growth and keep improving the quality of American goods and services. Second, we need to lower our dependence on oil imports, perhaps by raising the tax on gasoline. Third, we must reduce our trade deficit with Japan—a problem we share with many other nations. And finally, we need to do something about our rapidly rising deficit with China.

But perhaps our best hope to reduce our trade deficit lies with the rapidly expanding Internet, which makes it much easier to provide services of all types—banking, education, consulting, retailing, and even gambling—through a Web site that is globally accessible. Since the United States has long had a large and growing positive trade balance in services, there is good reason to expect the Internet to continue pushing up our export of services.

> No man is an island, entire of itself.
>
> —John Donne

Questions for Further Thought and Discussion

1. Explain what comparative advantage is. Make up an example to illustrate this concept.
2. What is wrong with having tariffs and quotas? Which is the lesser of two evils, and why?
3. To what degree are we at fault for our huge trade deficit with Japan? To what degree are the Japanese at fault?
4. What would you suggest we do to reduce our trade deficit?
5. We run huge trade imbalances with two countries. Explain the cause of the imbalances.
6. Should we be worried about our trade deficit? Explain why or why not.
7. What is the economist's case for free trade?
8. Can you think of any valid reason for tariff protection? Try to make a case for it.

Workbook for Chapter 18

Name _____ Date _____

Multiple-Choice Questions

Circle the letter that corresponds to the best answer.

1. Our balance of trade _____.
   a) has always been positive
   b) turned negative in the mid-1970s
   c) turned negative in the mid-1980s
   d) has always been negative

2. Which makes the most sense economically?
   a) individual self-sufficiency
   b) national self-sufficiency
   c) national specialization
   d) none of these

3. If the United States were to devote all its resources to producing washing machines, it could turn out 50 billion a year; if it devoted all its resources to producing cars, it could turn out 10 billion a year. Our domestic exchange equation is _____.
   a) 5 cars = 1 washing machine
   b) 5 washing machines = 1 car
   c) $\frac{1}{5}$ of a washing machine = 1 car
   d) $\frac{1}{2}$ of a car = 1 washing machine

4. If the United States were to trade its cars for another country's washing machines, it would not trade one car unless it received at least _____ washing machines. (Use data in question 3.)
   a) at least one   c) at least five
   b) more than one   d) more than five

5. Which statement is false?
   a) No nation will engage in trade with another nation unless it will gain by that trade.
   b) The terms of trade will fall somewhere between the domestic exchange equations of the two trading nations
   c) Most economists advocate free trade.
   d) None of these statements is false.

6. If Hong Kong can make TVs more efficiently than France can, it enjoys _____.
   a) a comparative advantage
   b) an absolute advantage
   c) no advantage

7. Under the law of comparative advantage, total output is greatest when each product is made by the country that _____.
   a) enjoys an absolute advantage
   b) has the lowest opportunity cost
   c) has the lowest wage rates
   d) has the lowest degree of specialization

8. The least applicable argument for protecting American industry from foreign competition would be the _____ argument.
   a) national security   c) low-wage
   b) infant industry   d) employment

9. Imports would be lowered by _____.
   a) tariffs only
   b) import quotas only
   c) both tariffs and import quotas
   d) neither tariffs nor import quotas

10. Of these three choices—tariffs, quotas, and free trade—economists like _____ the most and _____ the least.
    a) tariffs, quotas   d) free trade, quotas
    b) tariffs, free trade   e) quotas, free trade
    c) free trade, tariffs   f) quotas, tariffs

11. Our biggest trade deficit was a little more than _____ billion.
    a) $150   d) $300
    b) $200   e) $350
    c) $250

12. In the 1980s Japanese real interest rates were about _____.

    a) triple ours

    b) one-and-a-half times ours

    c) about the same as ours

    d) somewhat lower than ours

    e) one-third ours

13. Each of the following has contributed to our trade deficit except _____.

    a) high military spending

    b) the high cost of capital

    c) the cost of our educational system

    d) our short time horizon

    e) none of the above

14. Since the 1950s the percentage share of the world's manufacturing of _____.

    a) multinationals and of U.S. firms has declined

    b) multinationals and U.S. firms has risen

    c) multinationals has declined and of U.S. firms has risen

    d) multinationals has risen and of U.S. firms has declined

15. Which statement is false?

    a) The J-curve theory explains why devaluation does not lead to an immediate reduction in the trade deficit.

    b) The 1980–85 rise in the dollar does not fully explain the rise in the trade deficit.

    c) A declining dollar will eventually reduce the trade deficit.

    d) None of these statements is false.

16. Each of the following would reduce our trade deficit except _____.

    a) increasing saving

    b) cutting defense spending

    c) increasing investment

    d) improving our educational system

17. The best example of unfair Japanese trade practices may be found in the _____ industry.

    a) computer software   d) textile

    b) photocopier   e) TV manufacturing

    c) camera

18. Statement 1: If we eliminated our trade deficit with Japan and our oil import bill, we would be running trade surpluses.
    Statement 2: Americans pay lower taxes on gasoline than do the citizens of most of the nations in Western Europe.

    a) Statement 1 is true, and statement 2 is false.

    b) Statement 2 is true, and statement 1 is false.

    c) Both statements are true.

    d) Both statements are false.

19. Statement 1: Japanese industrialists pay much lower interest rates than do American industrialists.
    Statement 2: Like Americans, Japanese consumers are born shoppers who look for high quality and low prices, regardless of which country produces the goods.

    a) Statement 1 is true, and statement 2 is false.

    b) Statement 2 is true, and statement 1 is false.

    c) Both statements are true.

    d) Both statements are false.

20. Statement 1: It costs more to save an American job making specialty steel from foreign competition than it does to save a job making television sets.
    Statement 2: Although saving American jobs from foreign competition may raise prices, the cost is well worth it.

    a) Statement 1 is true, and statement 2 is false.

    b) Statement 2 is true, and statement 1 is false.

    c) Both statements are true.

    d) Both statements are false.

21. To save a job making television sets in the United States from foreign competition would cost consumers about _____ a year in the form of higher prices.

    a) $400   d) $400,000

    b) $4,000   e) $4 million

    c) $40,000

Questions 22–24 refer to Table 1.

TABLE 1

	One Nigerian Worker	One Romanian Worker
Basketballs	5	12
Barbie Dolls	10	18

22. Nigeria has an absolute advantage in the production of _____.
   a) basketballs
   b) Barbie Dolls
   c) both basketballs and Barbie Dolls
   d) neither basketballs nor Barbie Dolls
   e) none of the above

23. The opportunity cost of producing one basketball in Romania is _____.
   a) $^2/_3$s of a Barbie Doll
   b) 1 Barbie Doll
   c) $1^1/_2$ Barbie Dolls
   d) 4 Barbie Dolls
   e) 6 Barbie Dolls

24. Romania has a comparative advantage in the production of _____.
   a) basketballs
   b) Barbie Dolls
   c) both basketballs and Barbie Dolls
   d) neither basketballs nor Barbie Dolls
   e) none of the above

Fill-In Questions

1. The basis for international trade is _____ _____.

Use Figure 1 to answer questions 2 through 6.

Figure 1

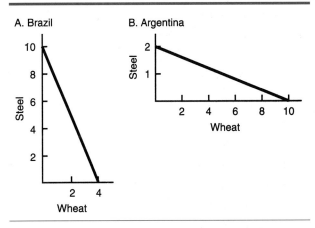

2. Brazil is better at producing _____ than at producing _____. Argentina is better at producing _____ than at producing _____.

3. The domestic equation of exchange for Brazil is _____. The domestic equation of exchange for Argentina is _____.

4. If Argentina and Brazil traded, Argentina would trade _____ for _____, while Brazil would trade _____ for _____.

5. Brazil would be willing to trade one ton of steel for more than _____ ton(s) of wheat. Argentina would be willing to trade five tons of wheat for more than _____ ton(s) of steel.

547

6. State the terms of trade in steel and wheat.

   a) One ton of steel will be exchanged for more than _____ and less than _____ tons of wheat.

   b) One ton of wheat will be exchanged for more than _____ and less than _____ tons of steel.

7. If one country is better at growing wheat than another country, it enjoys a(n) _____ advantage in wheat production.

8. The law of comparative advantage states that total output is greatest when each product is made by the country that has the _____ _____.

9. Four main arguments have been made for trade protection: (1) the _____ argument, (2) the _____ argument; (3) the _____ argument; and (4) the _____ argument.

10. Although economists dislike both, they would prefer tariffs to _____.

11. A tariff is a tax on _____; a quota is a limit on _____.

12. If it costs three times as much to make a car in Nigeria as it does in Mexico and it costs twice as much to grow wheat in Mexico as it does in Nigeria, we say Mexico enjoys an absolute advantage in the production of _____, and Nigeria enjoys an absolute advantage in the production of _____.

13. A company that puts its name on imported goods is called a _____ corporation.

14. One thing we could do to reduce our trade imbalance is to _____ the dollar.

15. Our trade deficit set a record in the year _____, when it was $ _____ billion.

16. _____ was the last year in which we ran a trade surplus.

Problems

Assume Bolivia and Chile use the same amount of resources to produce tin and copper. Figure 2 represents their production possibilities curves. Use it to answer questions 1 through 8.

Figure 2

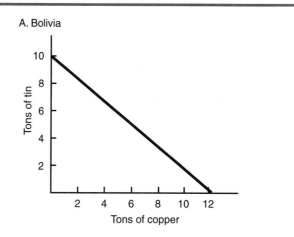

A. Bolivia

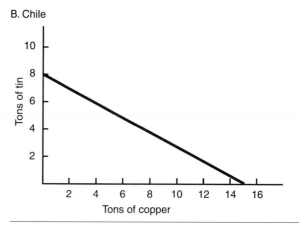

B. Chile

1. What is the domestic exchange equation of Bolivia?

2. What is the domestic exchange equation of Chile?

3. Bolivia would be willing to trade 5 tons of tin for how much copper?

4. Chile would be willing to trade 15 tons of copper for how much tin?

5. Bolivia has a comparative advantage in the production of which metal?

6. Chile has a comparative advantage in the production of which metal?

7. Bolivia has an absolute advantage in the production of which metal?

8. Chile has an absolute advantage in the production of which metal

Chapter 19

International Finance

The United States is the world's largest economy, and we are the world's largest trading nation. We import more and export more than any other nation. We also run the world's largest negative trade balance—now $370 billion.

How do we finance all this trading, and how do we finance our negative balance in trade? International trade is just one part of international finance. The other part encompasses foreign investment, exchange rates, and other international transactions, as well as the finance of international trade.

One consequence of our mounting trade deficits is that foreigners are buying up American assets. How much of America is foreign owned today, and will most of this country one day be owned by foreigners? Stay tuned, and by the end of the chapter you will learn the answers to these important questions.

CHAPTER OBJECTIVES

These are the topics you'll learn about:

- Financing international trade.
- The balance of payments.
- Exchange rate systems.
- Globalization of the U.S. dollar.
- Growing foreign ownership of American assets.

The Mechanics of International Finance

Think of international trade and finance as an extension of our nation's economic activities beyond our borders. Instead of buying microchips from a firm in California, we buy them from a firm in Japan. Instead of selling Cadillacs in Miami, we sell them in Rio de Janeiro. And rather than building a factory in Chicago, we build one in Hong Kong.

The balance of trade is part of the balance of payments.

We discussed the whys and wherefores of international trade in the last chapter; now we'll see how that trade is financed. Ideally, our exports should pay for our imports; but since the mid-1970s the United States has had a very large negative balance of trade. That is, our imports have grown much faster than our exports.

The balance of trade is only part of the big picture of international finance. That picture includes imports and exports of services as well as goods. Also included are investment income, transfers of funds abroad, and capital inflows and outflows. The whole shooting match is called the balance of payments, which we'll take up after we look at the mechanics of financing trade. Toward the end of this part of the chapter we'll talk about international exchange rate systems, including the gold standard.

Financing International Trade

When an American importer buys $2 million of wine from a French merchant, how does she pay? In dollars? In francs? In gold? Gold is used only by governments, and then only on very rare occasions, to settle international transactions. Dollars, although sometimes acceptable as an international currency, are not as useful as francs to the French wine merchant. After all, the merchant will have to pay his employees and suppliers in francs.

There's no problem exchanging dollars for francs in either the United States or France. Many banks in New York have plenty of francs on hand, and virtually every bank in the country can get francs (as well as yen, marks, pounds, and other foreign currencies) within a day or two. In Paris and every other French city dollars are readily available from banks. On any given day—actually, at any given minute—there is a market exchange rate of francs for dollars; all you need to do is find the right teller and you can exchange your dollars for francs or francs for dollars within minutes.

Financing international trade is part of the economic flow of money and credit that crosses international boundaries every day. For the rest of this chapter we'll see where these funds are going and, in particular, how the United States is involved. We'll begin with the U.S. balance of payments, which provides an accounting of our country's international financial transactions.

The Balance of Payments

Often people confuse our balance of payments with our balance of trade. Actually, the balance of trade is a major part of the balance of payments. *The entire flow of U.S. dollars and foreign currencies into and out of the country constitutes the balance of payments,* while the trade balance is just the difference between our imports and our exports.

Until the mid-1970s we generally had a positive balance of trade; that is, the value of our exports was greater than that of our imports. All this changed drastically due to the quadrupling of oil prices in late 1973, as well as several other factors I'll be enumerating toward the end of this chapter. But an unmistakable trend, which had been going on for decades, foreshadowed the negative trade balances we have been experiencing every year since 1976.

The balance of payments has two parts: the current account and the capital account.

The balance of payments consists of two parts. First is the current account, which summarizes all the goods and services produced during the current year that we buy from or sell to foreigners. The second part is the capital account, which records the long-term transactions that we conduct with foreigners. The total of the current and capital accounts will always be zero; that is, our balance of payments never has a deficit or a surplus. When we look at these accounts in more detail, the picture should become clearer.

Table 1 shows the U.S. balance of payments in 2000. The great villain of the piece is our huge merchandise trade deficit of $459 billion. The next item, services, comprises mainly income from insurance, tourist spending, and legal financial services. Now we have income from investments. From the turn of the century to the early 1980s the United States had a substantial net investment income because Americans invested much more abroad than foreigners invested in the United States. Because of our huge trade deficits

TABLE 1 U.S. Balance of Payments, 2001* (in $billions)

1. **Current account**	
2. Merchandise	
3. Exports	+790
4. Imports	−1,249
5. Balance of trade	−459
6. Services	
7. Exports	+308
8. Imports	−220
9. Balance of services	+128
10. Income from investments	
11. Income receipts	+343
12. Income payments	−361
13. Net investment income	−18
14. Net unilateral transfers abroad	−50
15. **Balance on current account**	−399
16. **Capital account**	
17. Capital inflows	+898
18. Capital outflows	−430
19. **Balance on capital account**	+468
20. Statistical Discrepancy	−69
21. **Totals**	0

*Figures may not add up due to rounding.
Source: Survey of Current Business, April 2001.

in recent years, however, foreigners have been left holding hundreds of billions of dollars, most of which they have invested in the United States. The return on this investment has been growing rapidly. In fact, in 1997, for the first time since the early years of this century, the flow of income from investments—interest, profits, dividends, and rent—turned negative. Why? Because foreigners have invested a lot more in the United States than Americans have invested abroad.

Finally, we have net transfers, which include foreign aid, military spending abroad, remittances to relatives living abroad, and pensions paid to Americans living abroad. Because the United States does not receive foreign aid, no foreign troops are stationed here, and few personal remittances or pensions are paid to U.S. residents from abroad, net transfers will continue to be a negative figure into the foreseeable future.

Our balance on the current account is a clear indicator of how we're doing. To arrive at that balance in Table 1, just add items 5 (balance of trade), 9 (balance of services), 13 (net investment income), and 14 (net unilateral transfers abroad). Adding −459 +128 −18 and −50, we get −399. A negative balance on the current account of $399 billion means that we went $399 billion deeper into debt with foreigners.

When we add up the numbers that go into our current account, it is easy to see why this figure is negative and why our current account deficit has been growing in recent years. (See Figure 1.) But what international finance takes away with one hand, it pays back with the other. Thus, by definition, our current account deficit is balanced by our capital account surplus.

Our current account deficit is balanced by our capital account surplus.

What have foreigners done with the dollars they have earned from trading with us as well as from their other current account dealings with us? Nearly all of this money has been reinvested in the United States in the form of corporate stocks and bonds; U.S. Treasury bills, notes, and bonds; and real estate and direct investment in plant and equipment.

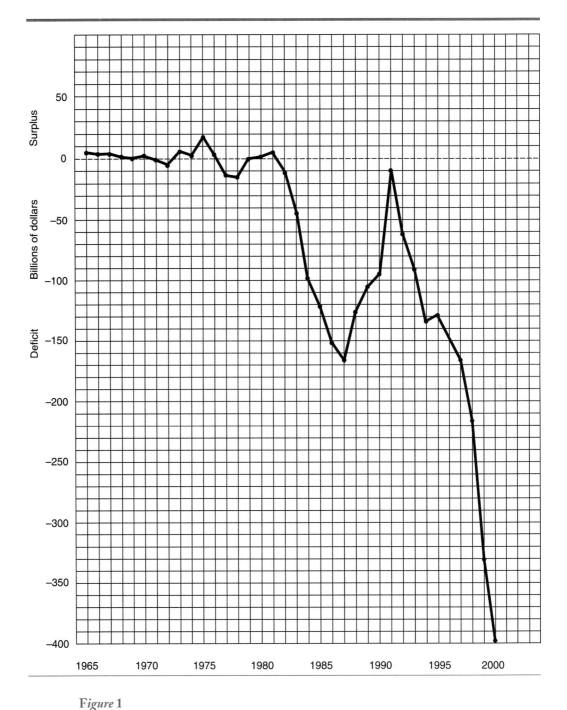

Figure 1

Current Account Surpluses and Deficits, 1965–2000

Before the early 1980s, we ran very small current account deficits and surpluses, but we went from a small surplus in 1981 to a deficit of more than $160 billion in 1986. Although this deficit was almost wiped out by 1991, we suffered another reversal of fortune for the rest of the 1990s, until, by 2000 our deficit reached $399 billion.

Source: Survey of Current Business, April 1998; March 2001.

    Before the early 1980s Americans were investing much more in foreign countries than foreigners were investing in the United States. But as our balance of trade worsened it was inevitable that the flow of capital would be reversed. Some relatively minor items are included in the capital account, most notably the statistical discrepancy. Now,

$69 billion is a pretty big discrepancy. This money flowed into the United States but was never recorded.[1]

Technically there are no balance-of-payment deficits or surpluses because the current account deficit, by definition, will be balanced by a capital account surplus. In 2000 we ran a $399 billion current deficit, which was matched by a $468 billion capital account surplus plus the $69 billion statistical discrepancy.

Technically, the balance of payments has no deficits or surpluses.

Was this a coincidence? Not at all! As you can see in Figure 1, we've been running substantial current account deficits since 1982, but they have been matched dollar-for-dollar by capital account surpluses plus or minus statistical discrepancies.

The way it works is that we buy much more from foreigners than they buy from us. In effect, they lend or give us the money to make up the difference between our imports and our exports. It would not be an exaggeration to say that we borrow so much from foreigners to finance our current account deficits that we sell them pieces of the American rock, so to speak. Those pieces consist mainly of corporate stock and real estate, but they also lend us tens of billions of dollars each year in the form of purchases of corporate and government bonds and other debt instruments.

Now that foreigners own more investment assets in the United States than Americans own abroad, they are receiving more interest, rent, dividends, and profits than we are. In the early 1980s, when we held more assets abroad than foreigners held in the United States, Americans earned a net investment income of over $30 billion a year. This net inflow fell sharply over the next decade as foreigners bought up more and more American stocks, bonds, and real estate, and purchased American corporations or built their own factories, office buildings, and retail outlets. In 2000 there was a net outflow of $18 billion in investment income.

In future years, we can expect this net outflow of investment income to continue to grow. Unless we can reduce our deficit in the trade of goods and services, our current account deficit will keep growing, and foreigners will have little choice but to keep sending most of those dollars back here to buy up more and more of our assets.

While technically we don't run balance-of-payments deficits, we *do* go deeper and deeper into hock each year. Should this last another three or four decades, foreign investors will own most of the country, so it is hard to refrain from calling the huge shortfalls in our balance-of-payments account "deficits."

We go deeper and deeper into debt each year.

Exchange Rate Systems

The basis for international finance is the exchange of well over 100 national currencies. Until the 1930s the world's currencies were based on gold. Since then a relatively free-floating exchange rate system has evolved. Under this system exchange rates are determined largely by the forces of supply and demand. In other words, how many yen, marks, francs, or pounds you can get for your dollars is determined largely by the impersonal forces of the market.

An exchange rate is the price of a country's currency in terms of another currency. If you received 100 Japanese yen for $1, then you could say that a yen is worth about one cent. And if a British pound were exchanged for $2, then you could say that a dollar is worth about half a pound. In August 2000, you needed about 110 euros (the euro is becoming the official currency of Germany, Finance, Italy, and eight other European countries) to get $1. So a euro was worth about 90 cents.

We'll consider three fairly distinct periods in the recent history of exchange rates. First, we'll examine the period before 1934, when most of the world was on the gold

Three distinct periods

---

[1] Statistical discrepancy is another way of saying, "Something's just not adding up." This very issue came up once in a course taught by the late Oskar Morgenstern, the mathematical economist.

Sometime during the 1930s Austria exported 10,000 horses to Czechoslovakia, but the Czechs had no record of having imported 10,000 horses. "Did the horses disappear into thin air when they crossed the border?" asked Morgenstern. No, he concluded. The 10,000 horses were swallowed by a statistical discrepancy.

standard. Second, we'll look at the period from 1934 to 1973, when international finance was based on fixed exchange rates. Finally, we shall review the period from 1973 to the present, when we have had relatively freely floating exchange rates.

The Gold Standard

Exactly what is the gold standard?

There has been a lot of talk in recent years about a return to the gold standard, but it's not going to happen. Exactly what *is* the gold standard, what are its advantages, and what are its disadvantages? Funny you should ask.

A nation is on the gold standard when it defines its currency in terms of gold. Until 1933 the U.S. dollar was worth 1/23 of an ounce of gold. In other words, you could buy an ounce of gold from the Treasury for $23 or sell this department an ounce for $23. Paper money was fully convertible into gold. If you gave the Treasury $23, you would get one ounce of gold—no ifs, ands, or buts. In 1933, just before we went off the gold standard (along with the rest of the world), we raised the price of gold to $35 an ounce, which meant a dollar was worth 1/35 of an ounce of gold.

To be on the gold standard, a nation must maintain a fixed ratio between its gold stock and its money supply. That way, when the gold stock rises, so does the money supply. Should gold leave the country, the money supply declines.

That brings us to the third and last requirement of the gold standard: there must be no barriers to the free flow of gold into and out of the country.

When we put all these things together, we have the gold standard. The nation's money supply, which is based on gold, is tied to the money supply of every other nation on the gold standard. It is the closest the world has ever come to an international currency. This system worked quite well until World War I, when most of the belligerents temporarily went off the gold standard because many of their citizens were hoarding gold and trying to ship it off to neutral nations.

How the gold standard works

Ideally, here is how the gold standard works. When Country A exports as much as it imports from Country B, no gold is transferred. But when Country A imports more than it exports, it has to ship the difference, in gold, to the trading partners with whom it has trade deficits.

Suppose the United States had to ship 1 million ounces of gold to other countries. This would lower our gold stock and, consequently, our money supply. When our money supply declined, so would our price level. This would make our goods cheaper relative to foreign goods. Our imports would decline and our exports would rise because foreigners would find American imports cheaper than their own goods.

A self-correcting mechanism

What we had, then, was a self-correcting mechanism. A negative balance of trade caused an outflow of gold, a lower money supply, lower prices, and ultimately, fewer imports and more exports. Thus, under the gold standard, negative trade balances eliminated themselves.

After World War I the nations that had left the gold standard returned to the fold, but some nations' currencies were overvalued (relative to their price in gold) while others' currencies were undervalued. Adjustments were difficult because the nations whose currency was overvalued would have faced a gold drain and, consequently, lower prices and lower wages. But wages and prices are rarely downwardly flexible.

An alternative was to devalue—that is, lower the price of money in relation to gold. For example, a 10 percent devaluation would mean that instead of getting 10 British pounds for an ounce of gold, you now get 11. As the Great Depression spread, one nation after another devalued, and within a few years virtually everyone was off the gold standard.

Evaluation of the gold standard

Let's step back for a moment and evaluate the gold standard. It *did* work for a long time, automatically eliminating trade surpluses and deficits. And it *did* stimulate international trade by removing the uncertainty of fluctuating exchange rates.

But the gold standard has a downside. First, it will work only when the gold supply increases as quickly as the world's need for money. By the early 20th century this was no longer the case. Second, it will work only if participating nations are willing to accept the periodic inflation and unemployment that accompany the elimination of trade imbalances. In today's world political leaders must pay far more attention to their domestic constituencies than to their trading partners. Finally, strict adherence to the gold standard would render monetary policy utterly ineffective. If gold were flowing into the United States, the Federal Reserve would be powerless to slow the rate of monetary growth and the ensuing inflation. And if there were an outflow of gold, the Federal Reserve would be unable to slow the decline in the money supply and thereby prevent the advent of a recession.

With the breakdown of the gold standard in the 1930s, protectionism returned as one nation after another raised tariff barriers higher and higher. Devaluation followed devaluation until the entire structure of international trade and finance was near complete collapse. Then came World War II—and with it, a great revival of economic activity. While the war was still raging, the Bretton Woods conference was called to set up a system of international finance that would lend some stability to how exchange rates were set.

The Gold Exchange Standard, 1934–73

The Bretton Woods (New Hampshire) conference set up the International Monetary Fund (IMF) to supervise a system of fixed exchange rates, all of which were based on the U.S. dollar, which was based on gold. The dollar was defined, as it had been for the previous 10 years, as being worth 1/35 of an ounce of gold, so gold was $35 an ounce, and dollars were convertible into gold at that price.

Fixed exchange rates

Other currencies were convertible into dollars at fixed prices, so these currencies were indirectly convertible into gold. But this was short of a gold standard because the money supplies of these nations were not tied to gold and no longer would trade deficits or surpluses automatically eliminate themselves. If a nation ran consistent trade deficits, it could devalue its currency relative to the dollar. A devaluation of 10 percent or less could be done without the IMF's permission (larger cuts required permission).

The new system functioned well for 25 years after World War II. The United States ran almost continual balance-of-payment deficits during the 1950s and 1960s, which eventually led to an international financial crisis in 1971. But until that year these deficits contributed to international liquidity. This is because U.S. dollars as well as gold were held as reserves for international payments by virtually every country in the world but the United States.

During this period millions of American tourists went abroad (while fewer foreign tourists could afford to come here) and spent billions of dollars a year. More than 1 million American troops were stationed in Western Europe, Korea, Japan, and scores of other countries, and they spent most of their pay locally. Meanwhile, it took billions of dollars a year to supply these troops with food and other daily necessities, most of which were purchased locally. Finally, we dispensed billions of dollars a year in foreign economic and military aid.

So you may think of the United States during the 1950s and 1960s as a kind of financial Johnny Appleseed, walking the earth throwing U.S. dollars to the wind. Had any other nation spread its currency around the way we did, that currency would have quickly found its way back to its treasury to be redeemed in gold. But not the almighty U.S. dollar, which for years was literally as good as gold.

Why were U.S. dollars acceptable to other nations? First, the United States held the largest stock of gold in the world and stood ready to sell that gold at $35 an ounce to the central banks of every nation. Second, the American economy was by far the largest and strongest in the world.

Why were U.S. dollars so acceptable?

By the late 1960s, as our gold stock dwindled and as foreign governments found themselves with increasing stocks of dollars, these nations began to ask some embarrassing questions. If the United States continued to run balance-of-payments deficits, would we be able to redeem the dollars they were holding for gold at $35 an ounce? Would the United States be forced to devalue the dollar, thus making other countries' dollar holdings less valuable?

Sure enough, in 1971 President Richard Nixon announced that the United States would no longer redeem dollars for gold. In one fell swoop the Bretton Woods agreement to maintain fixed exchange rates went out the window. The dollar would now float, and with it, every other currency. Now the forces of demand and supply would determine exchange rates.

Why did the U.S. balance of payments deteriorate in the 50s and 60s?

Let's step back for a minute and ask why the U.S. balance of payments deteriorated so badly during the 50s and 60s. There were several reasons, but one that is easily overlooked is really the most important. You see, our positive balance of payments and, in particular, our huge trade surpluses in the late 1940s were only a temporary situation brought about by World War II. Of all the major belligerents, only the United States escaped unscathed from the vast war damage. The industrial machines of Germany and Japan, not to mention those of England, France, Italy, and the rest of Europe, were reduced to rubble.

Renewed foreign competition

Thus our industrial goods had virtually no competition in the world's markets until well into the 1950s, when the postwar recovery finally took hold. At that time the best our competitors could do was narrow our leads in some areas and provide products we didn't bother to manufacture, most notably small cars. But by the early 1950s our huge trade surpluses began to narrow.

Military and foreign aid spending

A second reason for our growing payments deficits was our huge military and foreign aid spending. American soldiers stationed abroad required the expenditure of billions of dollars a year, as did the military and economic aid we provided to our foreign friends and allies. The cost of the Vietnam War must be added to the bill too.

Increasing private investment abroad

A third factor was rapidly increasing U.S. private investment abroad, which went from an annual rate of just $2 billion in the early 1950s to $8 billion in the late 1960s.

Inflation

Then there was inflation, particularly in the late 1960s and through the 1970s and early 1980s. Because our inflation rate was higher than those of most of our trading partners, some American goods were priced out of both foreign and domestic markets.

Oil price shocks

Just two more to go. First is the oil price shock of 1973, when oil prices quadrupled, and the subsequent shock of 1979, when oil prices again rose sharply (not to mention the oil shock of 1990). This put our balance of trade into the negative column and has helped keep it there.

The productivity factor

Finally, we have the productivity factor. Believe it or not, the United States still produces more goods and services than any other country in the world (Japan, number two, produces a little more than half as much), and American workers are still the world's most productive. The problem is that we have been losing our productivity lead. That, combined with Americans' prodigious appetite for consumer goods—both American and foreign—and our refusal to save, has added considerably to our mounting trade deficits.

The Freely Floating Exchange Rate System, 1973 to the Present

To return to 1971, when our payments deficits finally forced us to abandon the gold exchange standard—and forced the rest of the world off as well—the IMF needed to set up a new system fast, and that system was, in computer terminology, a default system.

We were back to the law of supply and demand.

We were back to the old system that economists fondly refer to as the law of supply and demand. How does it apply to foreign exchange? The same way it applies to everything else.

Figure 2 shows hypothetical supply and demand curves for German marks. Inferring from these curves, you can get 1.5 marks for a dollar, or one mark for 67 cents—and vice versa.

Who sets this exchange rate? Basically, the forces of supply and demand do. The question then is, Where does the supply and demand for marks come from?

The demand curve for marks represents the desire of Americans to exchange their dollars for marks. Why do they want marks? To buy German goods and services, stocks, bonds, real estate, and other assets.

Likewise, the supply curve of marks represents the desire of German citizens to purchase American goods, services, and financial assets.

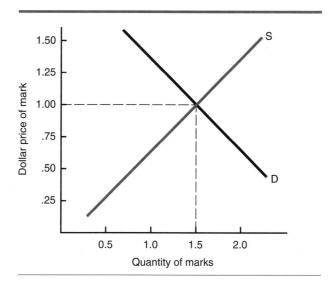

Figure 2
Hypothetical Demand for and
Supply of German Marks

How is the exchange rate set
between dollars and marks? It is set
by the forces of demand and
supply.

Now we get to the beauty of the law of supply and demand. The point at which the two curves cross tells us the exchange rate of marks and dollars. In Figure 2 we have a rate of five marks for one dollar.

With freely floating exchange rates, currencies will sometimes *depreciate* in value relative to other currencies. If the pound, for instance, depreciates with respect to the lira, it may fall from one pound equals 300 lira to one pound equals 280 lira. Similarly, a currency can *appreciate* in value relative to another currency. Before appreciation 20 francs equaled one mark, but after the franc appreciated 19 francs equaled one mark.

If we had completely free-floating exchange rates (that is, no government interference), the market forces of supply and demand would set the exchange rates. To a large degree, this is what happens; but governments do intervene, although usually for a limited time. In other words, government intervention may temporarily influence exchange rates, but exchange rates are set by the forces of supply and demand in the long run.

We don't have completely free-floating exchange rates.

Three factors influence the exchange rates between countries. (Let's continue to use the United States and Germany as an example.) The most important factor is the relative price levels of the two countries. If American goods are relatively cheap compared to German goods, there will be a relatively low demand for marks and a relatively high supply of marks. In other words, everyone—Germans and Americans—wants dollars to buy American goods.

A second factor is the relative growth rates of the American and German economies. Whichever is growing faster generates a greater demand for imports. If the American economy is growing faster, it will raise the demand for marks (to be used to buy imported goods from Germany) while decreasing the supply of marks (the Germans will hold more marks and fewer dollars because they are not buying many American goods).

The third and final factor is the relative level of interest rates in the two countries. If the interest rates are higher in Germany than they are in the United States, American investors will want to take advantage of the higher rates by buying German securities. They will sell their dollars for marks, driving up the price of marks. In effect, then, the demand for marks will rise and their supply will decline.

In 1980 and 1981 U.S. interest rates went through the roof. Banks, the U.S. Treasury, and major corporations were paying more than 15 percent—and sometimes more than 20 percent—to borrow money. These high rates, which were double or triple what could be earned abroad, made the American dollar exceedingly attractive to foreigners, because they generally needed to convert their currencies into dollars to invest here. So it was our relatively high interest rates that provided most of the impetus for the rising dollar during the first half of the 1980s (see Figure 3).

Remember that the exchange rate reflects the demand of foreigners for U.S. dollars and the demand of Americans for foreign currencies. By the late 1980s American interest

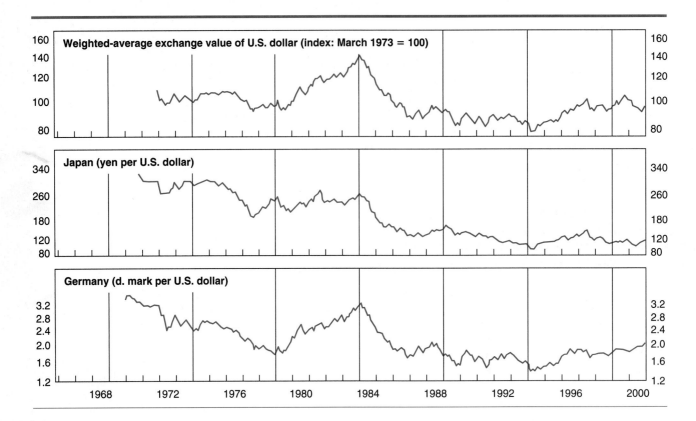

Figure 3

International Exchange Rates, 1970–2000

The value of the U.S. dollar in relation to the yen, mark, and other currencies has fluctuated rather widely over the last three decades. To a large degree the dollar has appreciated and depreciated relative to all other major currencies, moving up in value in the early 1980s, down in the later 1980s, and up in the 1990s.

Source: Business Cycle Indicators, March 2001.

rates had fallen to the levels of foreign interest rates. This cut sharply into the foreign demand for U.S. dollars, pushing the dollar all the way back down (see Figure 3). The cheaper dollar, incidentally, helped reduce our huge imbalance of trade by the early 1990s. If Figure 3 confuses you, then help is on the way. You'll find it in the box, "Interpreting the Top Line in Figure 3."

Two of our major trading partners are Germany and Japan. Figure 3 shows how the dollar has fluctuated against the mark and the yen since 1971.

When we had fixed exchange rates in the 1950s and 1960s, there were no fluctuations in the exchange rate between dollars and yen or between dollars and marks. Since then, of course, there has been nothing *but* fluctuation. In addition, the dollar has been on a long-term downward trend against both the mark and the yen. In the 1950s you could get 350 yen for your dollar, but in early 2001 you could get only about 130 yen. Similarly, in the 1950s you could get more than four marks for one dollar, but in early 1998 you could get about 1.8 marks for a dollar.

Let's see how the dollar stacks up against the currencies of our leading trading partners as of January, 2001. Figure 4 tells us how many marks, pounds, yen, and other foreign currencies we can get for a dollar.

Suppose you bought a Volkswagen Beetle for 11,500 euros. How much would that come to in dollars and cents?

Interpreting the Top Line in Figure 3

The graph line at the top of Figure 3 shows how the U.S. dollar has fluctuated against other major currencies since 1970. When the line rises, that means the dollar has risen in value against a weighted average of 10 major foreign currencies. What does this mean in plain English?

First, a weighted average of currencies is similar to your grade point average. If you're really curious about how weighted averages are constructed, look at the box "Construction of the Consumer Price Index" in the chapter on economic fluctuations in *Economics* and *Macroeconomics*.

Figure 3 charts an index of the dollar's relationship to other major currencies, with a base of March 1973. Let's say that in March 1973 a dollar traded for 50 francs. We set that base year at 100. Suppose the index rises to 200 a few years later. Then you might be able to get 100 francs for your dollar.[*]

The index did rise from the low 80s in 1980 to just over 145 in 1985; so the dollar rose by about 75 percent. What did this mean to American consumers? It meant that on the average they could get about 75 percent more foreign currency for their dollars than they could have just five years before.

Suppose a Honda Accord cost 1,000,000 yen in 1985. If 250 yen exchanged for one dollar, the car cost an American $4,000 (1,000,000/250). By 1988 you could get only 125 yen for your dollar. If that new Accord still cost 1,000,000 yen, how many dollars did you need to buy it? Don't wait for me to tell you. I'd like you to work out the answer here:

Here's the solution: 1,000,000/125 = $8,000.

When the dollar rises in value, foreign goods become cheaper; at the same time American goods become more expensive to foreigners. What do you think this does to our trade balance? That's right—it makes it worse. Since the late 1980s the index has generally fluctuated within a range of 80 to 100. Most economists believe that the dollar has fallen low enough to reduce our trade deficit.

[*]This is, of course, an oversimplification, because the dollar will not have risen by 100 percent against every currency during this period. It will have risen by more than 100 percent against some and by less than 100 percent against others.

$1 Will Buy

- 1.83 German marks
- .61 British pounds
- 1.43 Canadian dollars
- 8.19 Mexican pesos
- 1.50 Swiss francs
- 6.14 French francs
- 129 Japanese yen
- 1618 South Korean won
- 1804 Italian lira
- 1.11 Euros

Figure 4

Exchange Rates: Foreign Currency per American Dollar, January 31, 2000.

How many German marks would you get for a dollar? Can you figure out how many dollars (actually how many cents) would you get for a mark? You would get 54.6 cents, or about 55 cents. Exchange rates fluctuate from minute to minute, and they are usually calibrated to hundredths, or even thousandths of a cent.

Solution: First, note that, since the exchange rate in Figure 4 is 1.11 euros for a dollar, the number of dollars you need to pay is less than the number of euros. To find the answer, divide the 11,500 euros by the exchange rate of 1.11:

$$\frac{11,500}{1.11} = \$10,360.36$$

How Well Do Freely Floating (Flexible) Exchange Rates Work?

So far, so good.

Until 1973 most countries had fixed exchange rates because they feared flexible rates would fluctuate wildly. Has that happened since 1973? While there certainly have been some ups and downs, most notably with the dollar, we can still say so far, so good.

The dollar declined by well over 20 percent relative to other major currencies during the late 1970s, but this trend was completely reversed in the early 1980s. Between 1980 and early 1985 its value rose by 74 percent. But then another major decline set in (see Figure 3). International trade and finance have adjusted extremely well to these ups and downs, while government intervention has not been a major factor. Barring a major international financial crisis—such as a chain of loan defaults by Third World countries or the refusal of foreign investors to extend further credit to the U.S. government and to American corporations—we will continue to have freely floating exchange rates. While far from perfect, it may be the best system we have known.

The Euro

On January 1, 1999, most of Western Europe introduced a single currency, the euro. The European Monetary Union has eleven members—Austria, Belgium, Finland, France, Germany, Ireland, Italy, Luxembourg, Netherlands, Portugal, and Spain. To qualify, each nation needed to meet three criteria—an annual budget deficit of less than 3 percent, an inflation rate of less than 3 percent, and a public debt of less than 60 percent of GDP. Having a common currency not only facilitates trade among the members, but it may also spur economic growth.

Imagine if the United States were divided into 50 states, each with its own currency. Think how hard it would be to do business. Not only would exchange rates change, literally from minute to minute, but, since business payments are often made 30 or 60 days after delivery, you might end up paying 5 or 10 percent more—or less—than the contractual price. This added element of uncertainty would make it much harder to do business. So, what the members of the euro area are doing, then, is attempting to move toward a unified market with a single currency, just like the one we've long enjoyed in the United States.

The euro was worth $1.17 at the beginning of 1999, but it fell in value over the course of the year, slipping below $1 in January, 2000. For most of 2000 and the first four months of 2001 the euro traded within the 85 cents to 95 cents range. Has this hurt the economies of the 11 member nations? Apparently it hasn't. Their rates of economic growth picked up in 1999 and 2000, while their unemployment rates declined. The euro has fostered the continued unification of the European market and may have given added impetus to the growing prosperity of its members.

When a nation's currency declines relative to other currencies, the main effect is to make that nation's imports more expensive and its exports cheaper. All other things being equal, the effect of the currency decline will be to raise that nation's exports and lower its imports. In 1985 the dollar fell sharply, but real GDP grew by 3.9 percent. The dollar also fell substantially in 1999, when real GDP grew by 4 percent. Similarly, the decline of the euro in 1999 had no perceivable effect on the economies of the 11 member nations. Indeed, the only casualty may have been the wounded pride of the officers of the European Central Bank.

The main reason for the euro's decline has been the remarkable strength of the American economy, which grew about twice as fast as the euro zone nations in 1999 and 2000. Consequently, the United States has attracted vast amounts of foreign capital, which, of course, has tended to raise the value of the dollar.

All this poses a dilemma for the European Central Bank, which also came into existence on January 1, 1999. It can stem the decline of the euro by raising interest rates, thereby making the euro more attractive. But raising interest rates might undermine economic growth.

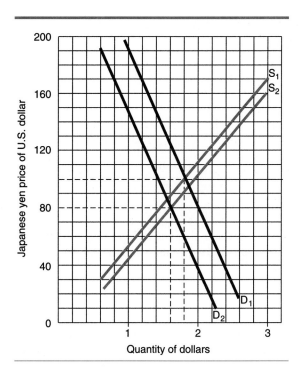

Figure 5

Hypothetical Supply of and Demand for Dollars Relative to Yen

If the supply of dollars outside the United States were to go up, while the demand for dollars went down, what would happen to the price of the dollar relative to yen? It would go down, in this case from 100 yen to 80 yen.

The Decline of the Dollar and the East Asian Financial Crisis

The years between 1994 and 1998 were marked by turmoil in the world's currency markets. First came the Mexico peso crisis, which was quickly resolved by a $53 billion American bailout. In 1994 and 1995, the U.S dollar fell relative to other major currencies. And then, in late 1997, a major financial crisis hit Southeast Asia and threatened to spread throughout the world.

The 1994–95 Decline of the Dollar

Because the value of the dollar vis-à-vis other currencies is set by the market forces of supply and demand, and because over $1 trillion a day passes through the hands of currency traders, if these people think that the dollar is overvalued relative to other currencies, they will sell dollars. In 1994, when we ran a huge current account deficit, currency traders began selling dollars, mainly for Japanese yen and German marks.

The dollar, which had been holding its own against most other major currencies in the early 1990s (see Figure 3), fell substantially throughout 1994 and then more sharply in early 1995.

What happened to the supply of dollars outside the United States in 1994 and what happened to the demand for U.S. dollars? Clearly the supply went up and the demand went down. Now if the supply of anything goes up while the demand for it goes down, what happens to its price?

Its price must go down. This is illustrated in Figure 5, which shows a change in the supply of dollars and the demand for dollars relative to yen. Although this graph is hypothetical, it does show how the dollar's value is determined by the forces of supply and demand.

The East Asian Financial Crisis

In late 1997 a financial crisis hit South Korea, Indonesia, and Thailand and threatened to spread through the rest of Asia and even beyond. Indeed, it was so reminiscent of the Mexican peso crisis that it appeared to be, in the words of baseball philosopher Yogi Berra, "déjà vu all over again."

Here's what happened. Japanese, Western European, and American banks lent nearly $400 billion to South Korean, Thai, and other East Asian banks. Nearly all these loans were very short term, having maturities of less than one year, and had to be repaid in yen, pounds, francs, marks, or dollars.

A Korean bank, for example, relent this money to local businesses, many of whom, it turned out, were poor credit risks. When they defaulted, the bank could not repay its creditors. To make matters worse, the Korean currency, the won, fell precipitously against the yen, pound, franc, mark, and dollar. This placed Korean (as well as Thai and Indonesian) banks in danger of default. The problem was compounded because so many of these short-term loans were falling due. Normally, of course, the Japanese, Western European, and American banks would have automatically renewed the loans, but now they refused to do so without credible guarantees that they would eventually be repaid. The International Monetary Fund, with strong backing from the governments of the world's leading industrial powers, agreed to provide over $100 billion—twice the cost of the Mexican bailout—to South Korea, Indonesia, and Thailand.

The bailout worked. The financial crisis was over by February 1998. But one may ask whether by making the lenders whole, this did not encourage more careless lending and future crises. If lenders were confident that they would be bailed out whenever they got into trouble, they would continue to make loans that should not have been made.

Running up a Tab in the Global Economy

What should be pretty clear by now is that, as a nation, we have been living well beyond our means for more than 20 years—and that the party can't last forever. The United States quickly shifted from being the world's largest creditor nation to the largest debtor. What happened?

From Largest Creditor to Largest Debtor

During the second half of the 19th century the United States borrowed heavily from Great Britain and other European nations to finance the building of railroads and the construction of much plant and equipment. Our country was a classic debtor nation, importing manufactured goods, exporting agricultural products, and borrowing capital in order to industrialize.

During World War I the United States became the world's leading creditor nation.

On the eve of World War I with the process of industrialization largely completed, we finally became a creditor nation. In 1914 foreigners owed us more than we owed them. The assets Americans held in foreign countries—factories, real estate, office buildings, corporate stock and bonds, and government bonds—was greater than the assets foreigners held in the United States. Our creditor status rose substantially during the war as we loaned the Allies billions of dollars. We became the world's leading creditor nation, a position we held until 1982.

How did we lose this position and fall into debt, quickly becoming the world's largest debtor? How could the largest, most productive economy in the world—a nation with low unemployment and stable prices—manage to run up such a huge tab?

The main reason for this turnaround was our mounting trade deficits, which we discussed in the last chapter. As a nation we are living for today and not worrying about what will happen tomorrow. To say that, as a people, Americans are world class consumers would not be that much of an exaggeration. "Born to shop" and "shop till you drop" are apt descriptions of millions of American consumers.

Along with being the world's only economic superpower, we are also the world's number-one military power. Although the cold war with the Soviet Union ended in 1989, we continue to station hundreds of thousands of troops abroad, extend billions of dollars in military aid each year, all of which adds to our Current Account deficit.

As our foreign debt mounts, the interest, rent, dividends, and profits we pay to foreigners continue to grow. In 1987 the net inflow of factor payments (that is, what we received less what foreigners got as a return on their American assets) was $22 billion.

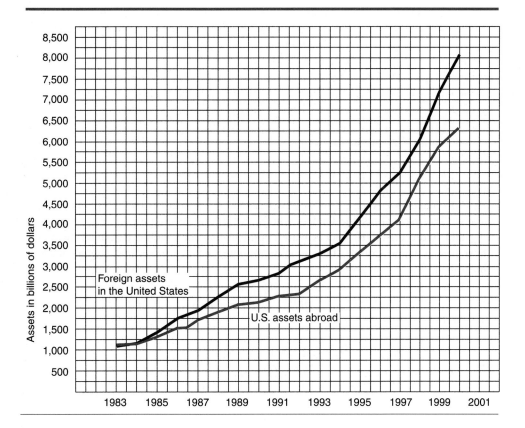

Figure 6

U.S. Assets Abroad and Foreign Assets in the United States, 1983–2000

Until the mid-1985s we went from being a creditor nation to a debtor nation. Each year since 1985 the gap between foreign assets in the United States and U.S. assets abroad keeps growing. Today that gap is more than $1.6 trillion.

Sources: Economic Report of the President, 1992 and 1995; *Survey of Current Business,* March, 2001.

In 2000 there was a net outflow of $18 billion, since foreign investors hold so many more American assets than Americans hold abroad. As our net debt keeps climbing, this net outflow will continue to rise rapidly, pushing up our Current Account deficit.

Let's do the math. In the year 2000 we ran a Current Account deficit of almost $400 billion. If foreigners invested $300 billion of that money in American assets and received a 6 percent return on their investment, it would add $18 billion to next year's Current Account deficit.

You can see the trend in foreign assets in the United States and U.S. assets abroad by looking at Figure 6. In 1985 we became a net debtor nation, and since that year, foreign investment in the United States has far outstripped our investment abroad. These trends will continue into the foreseeable future as foreigners continue accumulating dollars and using them to buy up our assets.

If we add up all the assets that foreigners own in the United States and subtract the assets that Americans own abroad we would get the U.S. stock of net foreign assets. In 1980 the U.S. stock to net foreign assets was about 12 percent of our GDP. By the year 2000, the U.S. stock of net foreign assets was minus 17 percent of our GDP.

Something's gotta give. Most likely the dollar will decline. This will make our exports cheaper, so foreigners will buy more from us. Similarly, the lower-valued dollar will make imported goods and services more expensive, so we'll import less. When the dollar falls—note that I said "when" and not "if"—our exports will rise, our imports will fall, and so our trade deficit will shrink.

But a declining dollar, as Paul Krugman notes, makes foreign investment in dollar-denominated assets much less attractive, thereby slowing the inflow of foreign investment:

> Right now foreign investors are willing to hold 10-year U.S. government bonds, even though they pay only a slightly higher interest rate than their European counterparts. Those investors seem to believe, in other words, that today's strong dollar will persist for another 10 years. But the size of our trade deficit makes that unlikely. So foreign investors, and therefore the value of the dollar, are arguably doing a Wile E. Coyote—one of these days they will look down, realize that they have already walked over the edge of the cliff, and plunge.[2]

Well more than $1 trillion of our currency remain abroad where they circulate as a medium of exchange. The Federal Reserve estimates that 60 percent of all the U.S. currency being printed is eventually used as unofficial legal tender in China, Russia, Mexico, Romania, Bolivia, the Philippines, Tajikistan, Vietnam, and dozens of other countries. Lithuania, Argentina, and Brazil have formally pegged their currencies to the dollar, while many others have done so informally. In effect, then, much of the world is unofficially on the dollar standard.

The U.S. dollar is actually the official currency of more than two dozen countries, the largest of which are Ecuador and Panama. On January 1, 2002, the dollar will become El Salvador's primary legal tender. And several others, including Mexico and Argentina, have been considering dollarization.

As long as we can maintain a low inflation rate and currency stability, the world may continue to accept our dollars in exchange for a multitude of goods and services. We're certainly getting a great deal. We get to buy tens of billions of dollars' worth of stuff each year and pay for it just by printing money. So it would not be unreasonable to say that dollars are our largest export.

The U.S. Treasury depends on the foreign saver to finance the deficit.

The foreign saver has a strong voice in setting the interest rates—not just for U.S. government securities but indirectly for other interest rates as well. As our dependence on funds from abroad grows, we are abdicating not just our role as the world's leading economic power but our economic sovereignty. As time goes by, decisions affecting the American economy will be made not in New York and Washington but in Tokyo, London, Frankfurt, and other financial capitals outside the United States.

We are living for today and not worrying about tomorrow.

As a nation we are living for today and not worrying about what will happen tomorrow. "America has thrown itself a party and billed the tab to the future," says Harvard economist Benjamin Friedman.[3] But all parties must end sometime, and someone is going to be left with a mess to clean up. (See the box, "The Role of Drug Money," for a discussion of another aspect of our living for today.)

Living beyond Our Means

The root cause of our problems has been that we as a nation have been consuming more than we have been producing, spending more than we have been earning, or, in short, living for today without providing for tomorrow. In the 19th century, when this country also ran up a large international debt, we were financing capital expansion. This investment in the future enabled us to vastly expand our production and quickly pay off our debt.

Today we are following a radically different course. We are not borrowing from abroad to finance capital expansion but rather to pay for a massive spending spree. What are we buying? We're buying consumer electronics, cars, designer clothes, and oil.

We are a nation of consumption junkies.

America has become a nation of consumption junkies. This is not, in itself, such a terrible thing if we support our habit. But we can't. So we ask foreigners to indulge us. And so far they have—at a price. We've been giving them IOUs in the form of U.S. dollars, and more and more, foreigners have been cashing them in for pieces of America.

---

[2]Paul Krugman, "Deficit Attention Disorder," *The New York Times,* March 26, 2000, Section 4, p. 17.

[3]Benjamin M. Friedman, *Day of Reckoning* (New York: Random House, 1988), p. 4.

The Role of Drug Money

There are no hard figures or even reliable estimates on the amount of money sent abroad to pay for cocaine and heroin imports. But considering that the United States is clearly the world's leading drug importer, it is reasonable to say that more than $20 billion is sent abroad to drug growers and traffickers. The transfer of funds is done by cash or electronically through the worldwide banking network and is not easy to trace.

How does this affect our balance-of-payments deficit? It doesn't, except that we often run "statistical discrepancies" of some $50 billion to $100 billion. Now

where could all that money be coming from? And where could it be going?

Some of it is coming back into the United States to purchase legitimate businesses, some to buy luxury condominiums along South Florida's "Gold Coast," and some may even be going to help lower the national debt. The point is, however reprehensible the drug dealers are, the economic effect of their transactions is similar to the effects of any other imports. The bottom line is that Americans are buying today's pleasures with tomorrow's income.

It seems as though everyone—the British, the Japanese, the Dutch, the Canadians, the Germans—owns a piece of the rock.

Since the early 1980s we've seen a massive recycling of dollars. As our trade deficits rose, the dollars we sent abroad were lent back to us as foreigners took advantage of our relatively high interest rates to purchase Treasury securities and corporate bonds. But they have increasingly been using their dollar stash to buy up pieces of America in the form of real estate and corporate stock. One might say foreigners are now not just America's creditors but its owners as well.

We are selling off the rock— piece by piece.

Closing Word: Will Foreigners Soon Own America?

Over the last three decades foreigners have accumulated well over 1 trillion U.S. dollars (a sum exceeding our current money supply). Most of this money is being held abroad. But in recent years as our trade deficit soared, and especially following the depreciation of the dollar, foreigners have been using their holdings of U.S. dollars to buy up large chunks of America.

Is it true that foreigners will soon own most of our country? Well, there's some good news and some bad news. The good news is that of the roughly $40 trillion of real assets in this country, foreigners own no more than 15 percent. And the bad news? At the rate they're going, within another 15 years they'll own more than one-third.

The American automobile industry is an interesting case. The Japanese transplants have reached over 20 percent of the U.S. capacity, but they have been built from the ground up rather than simply acquired. Honda, now America's number four automaker, may soon overtake Daimler-Chrysler. In fact, the transplants are actually exporting cars, some of them to Japan.

The Japanese have three good reasons for building plants in the United States. They save a couple of hundred dollars right off the top in shipping costs for every car built here. Second, they have billions of dollars that they need to invest, so why not build plants in a politically stable country with a fairly well-educated labor force? And perhaps most important in the long run, by substituting cars put together here for cars made in Japan, they are placing themselves within any tariff wall that may be erected in coming years.

Martin Feldstein, who once served as the chair of President Reagan's Council of Economic Advisors, cited these and other factors:

Will foreigners soon own most of this country?

Japanese automobile transplants

Why do the Japanese want to make cars here?

America has been selling off the family jewels to pay for a night on the town.
—Representative John Bryant, D-Texas

The United States is, of course, fundamentally attractive to foreign investors because of its massive $5 million marketplace, its political stability, its continuing flow of technological and product innovations, and its relatively flexible labor and product markets.[4]

Foreign bank ownership

Another sector with a strong foreign presence is banking. Foreign banks hold about 20 percent of all the banking assets in the United States and provide perhaps 30 percent of all business loans. The heaviest concentration of foreign banking interests is in California, where the Japanese alone hold more than one-third of that state's banking assets and control 5 of the 10 largest banks. The main reason for this imposing presence is the number of other Japanese firms that these banks service.

Before we get too upset with the Japanese, we need to consider two factors. First, which foreign country owns a larger chunk of America than any other? Disregard your first guess—it's not Japan. Great Britain owns more of us than any other foreign country. And one more word about the Japanese. Largely because of financial problems at home—their recent stock market crash and their plunging real estate prices—they have greatly scaled back on their American investments.

For at least another decade, we will continue running huge Current Account deficits, and foreigners will be buying a lot more American assets. But these foreigners will not take these assets home with them. Furthermore, within the context of the global economy, does it matter whether real estate, corporate stock and bonds, and U.S. Treasury bills are owned by Americans or foreigners?

Right now it doesn't seem to matter. However, we are financing our spending spree by printing money.[5] Much of this money circulates in dozens of countries around the world, and a lot more is held as reserve currencies by virtually every foreign government. In addition, foreigners recycle perhaps $300 billion a year as investments in the American economy. This process of running huge Currrent Account deficits and financing them by printing and exporting U.S. dollars cannot continue indefinitely.

Ours is the largest economy in the world, our currency is universally accepted, and we have been enjoying the longest economic expansion in our nation's history. Right now our current account deficit is our only major economic problem. One hopes that, before too long, we will at least bring it under control.

Questions for Further Thought and Discussion

1. What is meant by our balance of payments? Explain what current account and capital account are.

2. What is the gold standard? How does it work?

3. Why does the dollar fluctuate with other currencies?

4. How did the United States go from being the world's largest creditor nation to the world's largest debtor?

5. Foreigners are buying up hundreds of billions of dollars in American assets. In what ways should this be a matter of concern to Americans?

6. Can there be a deficit on Current Account and a deficit on Capital Account at the same time? Explain.

---

[4]"The United States in the World Economy: Introduction," in *The United States in the World Economy,* ed. Martin Feldstein (Chicago: University of Chicago Press, 1988), p. 7.

[5]When the Federal Reserve Banks issue currency each year, a large part of it—perhaps 30 or 40 percent—ends up abroad. Foreigners choose to hold those dollars rather than to use them to buy American goods and services, or to use them to invest in American assets. Each year the stash of U.S. currency held abroad grows much larger. This is a great deal for the United States. In effect, we're printing some of the money they use. Americans give foreigners that money in exchange for goods and services.

7. For several months before your vacation trip to Germany you find that the exchange rate for the dollar has increased relative to the euro. Are you pleased or saddened? Explain.

8. If the dollar depreciates relative to the Japanese yen, will the Sony VCR you have wanted became more or less expensive? What effect will this have on the number of Sony VCRs that Americans buy?

9. Explain why a currency depreciation leads to an improvement in a nation's balance of trade.

10. What is a foreign exchange rate? Provide a few examples.

11. How is the exchange rate determined in a freely floating rate system?

12. Who demands Japanese yen? Who supplies yen?

Workbook for Chapter 19

Name _____ Date _____

Multiple-Choice Questions

Circle the letter that corresponds to the best answer.

1. Which statement is true?
   a) The dollar rose from 1980 to 1985 and then declined.
   b) The dollar declined from 1980 to 1985 and then rose.
   c) The dollar has been rising since 1980.
   d) The dollar has been falling since 1980.

2. We became a debtor nation in _____.
   a) 1975   c) 1985
   b) 1980   d) 1990

3. In 2000 our net foreign debt was over _____ billion.
   a) $500   c) $1,500
   b) $1,000   d) $2,000

4. Which statement is true?
   a) In the 1980s we did not receive many dollars in investment funds from foreigners.
   b) In the 1980s foreign investment funds were attracted by our high interest rates.
   c) Our military spending has helped reduce our current account deficit.
   d) None of these statements is true.

5. During the 1980s, _____.
   a) both American investment abroad and foreign investment in the United States increased
   b) both American investment abroad and foreign investment in the United States decreased
   c) American investment abroad increased and foreign investment in the United States decreased
   d) American investment abroad decreased and foreign investment in the United States increased

6. The world's leading debtor nation is _____.
   a) Argentina   c) Mexico
   b) Brazil   d) the United States

7. Which statement is true?
   a) Foreigners own most of the assets in the United States.
   b) We own more assets in foreign countries than foreigners own in the United States.
   c) Foreigners own half of our cement industry and one-third of our chemical industry.
   d) None of these statements is true.

8. Which statement is false?
   a) The Japanese produce more than half of all cars built in the United States.
   b) The number four automobile producer in the United States is Honda.
   c) The Japanese will soon own about 20 percent of the capacity for producing cars in the United States.
   d) None of these statements is false.

9. An American importer of Italian shoes would pay in _____.
   a) dollars   b) gold   c) lira

10. The total of our current and capital accounts _____.
    a) will always be zero
    b) will always be negative
    c) will always be positive
    d) may be positive or negative

11. In recent years we bought _____ from foreigners than they bought from us, and we invested _____ in foreign countries than foreigners invested in the United States.
    a) more, more   c) less, more
    b) less, less   d) more, less

12. Today international finance is based on _____.
    a) the gold standard
    b) a relatively free-floating exchange rate system
    c) fixed rates of exchange

571

13. The international gold standard worked well until
_____.

   a) World War I   c) 1968

   b) 1940   d) 1975

14. If we were on an international gold standard,
_____.

   a) inflations would be eliminated

   b) recessions would be eliminated

   c) trade deficits and surpluses would be eliminated

   d) no nation would ever have to devaluate its
   currency

15. Which of the following is false?

   a) The gold standard will work only when the gold
   supply increases as quickly as the world's need
   for money.

   b) The gold standard will work only if all nations
   agree to devaluate their currencies
   simultaneously.

   c) The gold standard will work only if participating
   nations are willing to accept periodic inflation.

   d) The gold standard will work only if participating
   nations are willing to accept periodic unemployment.

16. The gold exchange standard was in effect from
_____.

   a) 1900 to 1934   c) 1955 to 1980

   b) 1934 to 1973   d) 1973 to the present

17. The United States first began running balance-of-
payments deficits in the _____.

   a) 1940s   d) 1970s

   b) 1950s   e) 1980s

   c) 1960s

18. Today currency exchange rates are set by
_____.

   a) the International Monetary Fund

   b) the U.S. Treasury

   c) bilateral agreements between trading nations

   d) supply and demand

19. The most important influence on the exchange rate
between two countries is _____.

   a) the relative price levels of the two countries

   b) the relative growth rates of the two countries

   c) the relative level of interest rates in both countries

   d) the relative wage rates of both countries

20. Devaluation would tend to _____.

   a) make the devaluating country's goods cheaper

   b) make the devaluating country's goods more
   expensive

   c) have no effect on the value of the devaluating
   country's goods

21. Which is the most accurate statement?

   a) Since the euro was introduced it has lost almost
   half its value.

   b) The euro has facilitated trade among the 11
   members of the euro zone.

   c) The euro is now the world's most important
   reserve currency.

   d) The euro circulates as currency in most of the
   countries of the world.

22. The main reason why we are the world's largest
debtor nation is _____.

   a) our military spending

   b) our trade deficit

   c) inflation

   d. high taxes

23. Which is the most accurate statement?

   a) There is a net outflow from the United States to
   foreigners of interest, rent, dividends, and profits.

   b) Foreigners invest all the dollars they receive from
   our Capital Account deficit to buy American
   assets.

   c) Our Current Account deficits are declining and
   should disappear before the year 2005.

   d) A declining dollar makes foreign investment in
   dollar-denominated assets much more attractive
   to foreigners.

24. Which of these is the most accurate statement?

   a) There is no basis for the claim that the United
   States is living beyond its means.

   b) There is virtually no foreign presence in American banking.

   c) Our current account deficit is our only major
   economic problem.

   d) Through most of 1999 and 2000 the dollar fell
   in value against the euro.

Fill-In Questions

1. The entire flow of U.S. dollars and foreign currencies into and out of the country constitutes our _____.

2. Most all the dollars that foreigners have earned from trading with the United States have been _____ in the form of _____ _____.

3. The basis for international finance is the exchange of _____.

4. A nation is on the gold standard when it _____ _____.

5. To be on the gold standard, a nation must maintain a fixed ratio between its gold stock and _____ _____.

6. Under the gold standard, if country J imports more than it exports, it has to ship _____ _____ to the trading partners with whom it has trade deficits. This will depress country J's _____, and its price level will _____.

7. Under the gold standard, if country K's price level declines, its imports will _____ and its exports will _____.

8. Today exchange rates are set by _____ and _____.

9. In the year 2004, if you wanted to buy wine from a French merchant, you would pay her with _____.

10. The main difference between our being a debtor nation in the 19th century and our being a debtor nation since the early 1980s was that in the 19th century we ran up a debt by _____ goods; since the early 1980s we have run up a debt buying _____ goods.

Problems

Use the exchange rates listed in Figure 4 to find how much it would cost in U.S. dollars and cents to make the purchases listed in problems 1–5.

1. A Toyota Corolla priced at 1.4 million yen

2. An bottle of Italian wine priced at 37,000 lire

3. A carton of Canadian paper priced at $9.00 Canadian

4. A British book priced at 12 pounds

5. A German camera priced at 250 euros

573

a

Ability-to-Pay Principle   The amount of taxes that people pay should be based on their ability to pay (that is, their incomes).

Absolute Advantage   The ability of a country to produce a good at a lower cost than its trading partners.

Accelerator Principle   If sales or consumption is rising at a constant rate, gross investment will stay the same; if sales rise at a decreasing rate, both gross investment and GDP will fall.

Accounting Profit   Sales minus explicit cost. Implicit costs are not considered.

Aggregate Demand   The sum of all expenditures for goods and services.

Aggregate Demand Curve   Curve showing planned purchase rates for all goods and services in the economy at various price levels.

Aggregate Supply   The nation's total output of goods and services.

Allocative Efficiency   Occurs when no resources are wasted; it is not possible to make any person better off without making someone else worse off.

Anticipated Inflation   The rate of inflation that we believe will occur; when it does, we are in a situation of fully anticipated inflation.

Antitrust Laws   These laws, including the Sherman and Clayton acts, attempted to enforce competition and to control the corporate merger movement.

Appreciation   An increase in the value of a currency in terms of other currencies.

Arbitration   An arbitrator imposes a settlement on labor and management if they cannot reach a collective bargaining agreement.

Asset Demand   Holding money as a store of value instead of other assets such as stocks, bonds, savings accounts, certificates of deposit, or gold.

Automatic Stabilizers   Programs such as unemployment insurance benefits and taxes that are already on the books to help alleviate recessions and hold down the rate of inflation.

Autonomous Consumption   The minimum amount that people will spend on the necessities of life.

Average Fixed Cost   Fixed cost divided by output.

Average Propensity to Consume   The percentage of disposable income that is spent; consumption divided by disposable income.

Average Propensity to Save   The percentage of disposable income that is saved; saving divided by disposable income.

Average Tax Rate   The percentage of taxable income that is paid in taxes; taxes paid divided by taxable income.

Average Total Cost (ATC)   Total cost divided by output.

Average Variable Cost (AVC)   Variable cost divided by output.

b

Backward-Bending Labor Supply Curve   As the wage rate rises, more and more people are willing to work longer and longer hours up to a point. They will then substitute more leisure time for higher earnings.

Balance of Payments   The entire flow of U.S. dollars and foreign currencies into and out of the country.

Balance of Trade   The difference between the value of our imports and our exports.

Balance on Capital Account   A category that itemizes changes in foreign asset holdings in one nation and that nation's asset holdings abroad.

Balance on Current Account   A category that itemizes a nation's imports and exports of goods and services, income receipts and payments on investment, and unilateral transfers.

Balanced Budget   When federal tax receipts equal federal government spending.

Bank   A commercial bank or thrift institution that offers checkable deposits.

Bank Run   Attempts by many depositors to withdraw their money out of fear that that bank was failing, or that all banks were failing.

Barrier to Entry   Anything that prevents the entry of new firms into an industry.

Barter   The exchange of one good or service for another good or service; a trade.

Base Year   The year with which other years are compared when an index is constructed: for example, a price index.

Benefits-Received Principle   The amount of taxes people pay should be based on the benefits they receive from the government.

Bonds   (See Government Bonds or Corporate Bonds.)

Break-Even Point   The low point on the firm's average total cost curve. If the price is below this point, the firm will go out of business in the long run.

Budget Deficit   When federal tax receipts are less than federal government spending.

Budget Surplus   When federal tax receipts are greater than federal government spending.

Business Cycle   Increases and decreases in the level of business activity that occur at irregular intervals and last for varying lengths of time.

C

CPI   (See Consumer Price Index.)

Capital   All means of production (mainly plant and equipment) created by people.

Capital Account   The section of a nation's international balance of payments statement in which the foreign purchases of that nation's assets and that nation's purchases of assets abroad are recorded.

Capitalism   An economic system in which most economic decisions are made by private owners and most of the means of production are privately owned.

Capital/Output Ratio   The ratio of capital stock to GDP.

Cartel   A group of firms behaving like a monopoly.

Certificate of Deposit (CD)   A time deposit (almost always of $500 or more) with a fixed maturity date offered by banks and other financial institutions.

Change in Demand   A change in the quantity demanded of a good or service at at least one price that is caused by factors other than a change in the price of that good or service.

Change in Supply   A change in the quantity supplied of a good or service at at least one price that is caused by factors other than a change in the price of that good or service.

Circular Flow Model   Goods and services flow from business firms to households in exchange for consumer expenditures, while resources flow from households to business firms in exchange for resource payments.

Classical Economics   Laissez-faire economics. Our economy, if left free from government interference, tends toward full employment. The prevalent school of economics from about 1800 to 1930.

Closed Shop   An employer may hire only union members; outlawed under the Taft-Hartley Act.

Collective Bargaining   Negotiations between union and management to obtain agreements on wages, working conditions, and other issues.

Collusion   The practice of firms to negotiate price and/or market share decisions that limit competition in a market.

Commercial Bank   A firm that engages in the business of banking, accepting deposits, offering checking accounts, and making loans.

Communism   An economic system characterized by collective ownership of most resources and central planning.

Comparative Advantage   Total output is greatest when each product is made by the country that has the lowest opportunity cost.

Competition   Rivalry among business firms for resources and customers.

Complementary Goods   Goods and services that are used together; when the price of one falls, the demand for the other rises (and conversely).

Concentration Ratio   The percentage share of industry sales by the four leading firms.

Conglomerate Merger   Merger between two companies in unrelated industries.

Constant-Cost Industry   An industry whose total output can be increased without an increase in long-run-per-unit costs; an industry whose long-run supply curve is flat.

Constant Dollars   Dollars expressed in terms of real purchasing power, using a particular year as the base of comparison, in contrast to current dollars.

Constant Returns to Scale   Cost per unit of production are the same for any output.

Consumer Price Index   The most important measure of inflation. This tells us the percentage rise in the price level since the base year, which is set at 100; represented by CPI.

Consumer Surplus   The difference between what you pay for some good or service and what you would have been willing to pay.

Consumption   The expenditure by individuals on durable goods, nondurable goods, and services; represented by C.

Consumption Function   As income rises, consumption rises, but not as quickly.

Contraction   The downturn of the business cycle, when real GDP is declining.

Corporate Bonds   This is a debt of the corporation. Bondholders have loaned money to the company and are its creditors.

Corporate Stock   Share in a corporation. The stockholders own the corporation.

Corporation   A business firm that is a legal person. Its chief advantage is that each owner's liability is limited to the amount of money he or she invested in the company.

Cost-of-Living Adjustments (COLAs)   Clauses in contracts that allow for increases in wages, Social Security benefits, and other payments to take account of changes in the cost of living.

Cost-Push Inflation   Rising costs of doing business push up prices.

Craft Unions   Labor unions composed of workers who engage in a particular trade or have a particular skill.

Creeping Inflation   A relatively low rate of inflation, such as the rate of less than 4 percent in the United States in recent years.

Crowding-Out Effect   Large federal budget deficits are financed by Treasury borrowing, which then crowds private borrowers out of financial markets and drives up interest rates.

Crude Quantity Theory of Money   The belief that changes in the money supply are directly proportional to changes in the price level.

Currency   Coins and paper money that serve as a medium of exchange.

Current Account   The section of a nation's international balance of payments that records its exports and imports of goods and services, its net investment income, and its net transfers.

Cyclical Unemployment   When people are out of work because the economy is operating below the full-employment level. It rises sharply during recessions.

d

Decreasing Cost Industry   An industry in which an increase in output leads to a reduction in the long-run average cost, such that the long-run industry supply curve slopes downward.

Deflation   A decline in the price level for at least two years.

Deflationary Gap   Occurs when equilibrium GDP is less than full-employment GDP.

Demand   A schedule of quantities of a good or service that people will buy at different prices; represented by D.

Demand Curve   A graphical representation of the demand schedule showing the inverse relationship between price and quantity demanded.

Demand Deposit   A deposit in a commercial bank or other financial intermediary against which checks may be written.

Demand, Law of   When the price of a good is lowered, more of it is demanded; when the price is raised, less is demanded.

Demand Schedule   A schedule of quantities of a good or service that people are willing to buy at different prices.

Demand-Pull Inflation   Inflation caused primarily by an increase in aggregate demand: too many dollars chasing too few goods.

Depository Institutions Deregulation and Monetary Control Act of 1980   This made all depository institutions subject to the Federal Reserve's legal reserve requirements and allowed all depository institutions to issue checking deposits.

Depreciation   A fall in the price of a nation's currency relative to foreign currencies.

Depression   A deep and prolonged business downturn; the last one occurred in the 1930s.

Deregulation   The process of converting a regulated firm or industry into an unregulated firm or industry.

Derived Demand   Demand for resources derived from demand for the final product.

Devaluation   Government policy that lowers the nation's exchange rate so that its currency is worth less than it had been relative to foreign currencies.

Diminishing Marginal Utility   Declining utility, or satisfaction, derived from each additional unit consumed of a particular good or service.

Diminishing Returns, Law of   If units of a resource are added to a fixed proportion of other resources, marginal output will eventually decline.

Direct Tax   Tax on a particular person. Most important are federal personal income tax and payroll (Social Security) tax.

Discount Rate   The interest rate charged by the Federal Reserve to depository institutions.

Discounting   The method by which the present value of a future sum or a future stream of sums is obtained.

Discouraged Workers   People without jobs who have given up looking for work.

Diseconomies of Scale   An increase in average total cost as output rises.

Disequilibrium   When aggregate demand does not equal aggregate supply.

Disinflation   Occurs when the rate of inflation declines.

Disposable Income   Aftertax income. Term applies to individuals and to the nation.

Dissaving   When consumption is greater than disposable income; negative saving.

Dividends   The part of corporate profits paid to its shareholders.

Division of Labor   The provision of specialized jobs.

Durable Goods   Things that last at least a year or two.

e

E-commerce   Buying and selling on the Internet.

Economic Goods   Goods that are scarce, for which the quantity demanded exceeds the quantity supplied at a zero price.

Economic Growth   An outward shift of the production possibilities frontier brought about by an increase in available resources and/or a technological improvement.

Economic Problem   When we have limited resources available to fulfill society's relatively limitless wants.

Economic Profit   Sales minus explicit costs and implicit costs.

Economic Rent   The excess payment to a resource above what it is necessary to pay to secure its use.

Economics   The efficient allocation of the scarce means of production toward the satisfaction of human wants.

Economies of Scale   Reductions in average total cost as output rises.

Efficiency   Conditions under which maximum output is produced with a given level of inputs.

Elasticity of Demand   Measures the change in quantity demanded in response to a change in price.

Entrepreneurial Ability   Ability to recognize a business opportunity and successfully set up a business firm to take advantage of it.

Equation of Exchange   Shows the relationship among four variables: M (the money supply), V (velocity of circulation), P (the price level), and Q (the quantity of goods and services produced). $MV = PQ$.

Equilibrium   When aggregate demand equals aggregate supply.

Equilibrium Point   Point at which quantity demanded equals quantity supplied; where demand and supply curves cross.

Equilibrium Price   The price at which quantity demand is equal to quantity supplied.

Excess Reserves   The difference between actual reserves and required reserves.

Exchange Rates   The price of foreign currency; for example, how many dollars we must give up in exchange for marks, yen, and pounds.

Excise Tax   A sales tax levied on a particular good or service; for example, gasoline and cigarette taxes.

Expected Rate of Profit   Expected profits divided by money invested.

Expenditures Approach   A way of computing GDP by adding up the dollar value at current market prices of all final goods and services.

Explicit Costs   Dollar costs incurred by business firms, such as wages, rent, and interest.

Exports   Goods and services produced in a nation and sold to customers in other nations.

Externality   A consequence of an economic activity, such as pollution, that affects third parties.

f

FDIC   (See Federal Deposit Insurance Corporation.)

Factors of Production   The resources of land, labor, capital, and entrepreneurial ability.

Featherbedding   Any labor practice that forces employers to use more workers than they would otherwise employ; a make-work program.

Federal Deposit Insurance Corporation   Insures bank deposits up to $100,000.

Federal Funds Rate   The interest rate banks and other depository institutions charge one another on overnight loans made out of their excess reserves.

Federal Open Market Committee (FOMC)   The principal decision-making body of the Federal Reserve, conducting open market operations.

Federal Reserve System   Central bank of the United States, whose main job is to control our rate of monetary growth.

Fiat Money   Paper money that is not backed by or convertible into any good; it is money because the government says it is money.

Financial Intermediaries   Firms that accept deposits from savers and use those deposits to make loans to borrowers.

Firm   A business that employs resources to produce a good or service for profit and owns and operate one or more plants.

Fiscal Policy   Manipulation of the federal budget to attain price stability, relatively full employment, and a satisfactory rate of economic growth.

Fiscal Year   Budget year. U.S. federal budget fiscal year begins on October 1.

Fixed Costs   These stay the same no matter how much output changes.

Fixed Exchange Rate   A rate determined by government and then maintained by buying and selling quantities of its own currency on the foreign exchange market.

Floating Exchange Rate   An exchange rate determined by the demand for and the supply of a nation's currency.

Foreign Exchange Market   A market in which currencies of different nations are bought and sold.

Foreign Exchange Rate   The price of one currency in terms of another.

Fractional Reserve Banking   A system in which depository institutions held reserves that are less than the amount of total deposits.

Free Trade   The absence of artificial (government) barriers to trade among individuals and firms in different nations.

Frictional Unemployment   Refers to people who are between jobs or just entering or reentering the labor market.

Fringe Benefits   Nonwage compensation, mainly medical insurance, that workers receive from employers.

Full Employment   When a society's resources are all being used with maximum efficiency.

Full-Employment GDP   That level of spending (or aggregate demand) that will result in full employment.

g

GATT (General Agreement on Tariffs and Trade)   An agreement to negotiate reductions in tariffs and other trade barriers.

GDP   (See Gross Domestic Product.)

GDP deflator   A price index used to measure price changes in the items that go into GDP.

GDP gap   The amount of production by which potential GDP exceed actual GDP.

Gold Standard   A historical system of fixed exchange rates in which nations defined their currency in terms of gold, maintained a fixed relationship between their stock of gold and their money supplies, and allowed gold to be freely exported and imported.

Government Bonds   Long-term debt of the federal government.

Government Purchases   All goods and services bought by the federal, state, and local governments.

Gross Domestic Product (GDP)   The nation's expenditure on all the goods and services produced in the country during the year at market prices; represented by GDP.

Gross Investment   A company's total investment in plant, equipment, and inventory. Also, a nation's plant, equipment, inventory, and residential housing investment.

h

Herfindahl-Hirschman Index   A measure of concentration calculated as the sum of the squares of the market share of each firm in an industry.

Horizontal Merger   Conventional merger between two firms in the same industry.

Household   An economic unit of one or more persons living under one roof.

Hyperinflation   Runaway inflation; in the United States, double-digit inflation.

i

Imperfect Competition   All market structures except perfect competition; includes monopoly, oligopoly, and monopolistic competition.

Implicit Costs   The firm's opportunity costs of using resources owned or provided by the owner.

Imports   Goods and services bought by people in one country that are produced in other countries.

Income Approach   Method of finding GDP by adding all the incomes earned in the production of final goods and services.

Income Effect   A person's willingness to give up some income in exchange for more leisure time.

Incomes Policy   Wage controls, price controls, and tax incentives used to try to control inflation.

Increasing Costs, Law of   As the output of a good expands, the opportunity cost of producing additional units of this good increases.

Increasing Returns to Scale   A situation in which a firm's minimum long-run average total cost decrease as the level of output rises.

Indirect Tax   Tax on a thing rather than on a particular person; for example, sales tax.

Induced Consumption   Spending induced by changes in the level of income.

Industrial Union   A union representing all the workers in a single industry, regardless of each worker's skill or craft.

Inelastic Demand   A demand relationship in which a given percentage change in price results in a smaller percentage change in quantity sold.

Inferior Goods   Goods for which demands decrease when people's incomes rise.

Inflation   A general rise in the price level.

Inflationary Gap   Occurs when equilibrium GDP is greater than full-employment GDP.

Innovation   An idea that eventually takes the form of new, applied technology or a new production process.

Interest Rate   Interest paid divided by amount borrowed.

Interlocking Directorates   When one person serves on the boards of at least two competing firms.

Intermediate Goods   Goods used to produce other goods.

Inventory Investment   Changes in the stocks of finished goods and raw materials that firms keep in reserve to meet orders.

Investment   The purchase or construction of any new plant, equipment, or residential housing, or the accumulation of inventory; represented by I.

j

Jurisdictional Dispute   A dispute involving two or more unions over which should represent the workers in a particular shop or plant.

k

Keynesian Economics   As formulated by John Maynard Keynes, this school believed the private economy was inherently unstable and that government intervention was necessary to prevent recessions from becoming depressions.

Kinked Demand Curve   The demand curve for a non-collusive oligopolist, which is based on the assumption that rivals will follow a price decrease and will ignore a price increase.

l

Labor   The work and time for which employees are paid.

Labor Force   The total number of employed and unemployed people.

Labor Union   Worker organization that seeks to secure economic benefits for its members.

Laffer Curve   Shows that at very high tax rates, very few people will work and pay taxes; therefore government revenue will rise as tax rates are lowered.

Laissez-Faire   The philosophy that the private economy should function without any government interference.

Land   Natural resources used to produce goods and services.

Law of Demand   An increase in a product's price will reduce the quantity of it demanded, and conversely for a decrease in price.

Law of Diminishing (Marginal) Returns   The observation that, after some point, successive equal-sized increases of a resource, added to fixed factors of other resources, will result in smaller increases in output.

Law of Increasing Costs   As the output of one good expands, the opportunity cost of producing additional units of this good increases.

Law of Supply   An increase in the price of a product will increase the quantity of it supplied; and conversely for a decrease in price.

Legal Reserves   Reserves that depository institutions are allowed by law to claim as reserves; vault cash and deposits held at Federal Reserve district banks.

Less Developed Countries (LDCs)   Economies in Asia, Africa, and Latin America with relatively low per capita incomes.

Leveraged Buyouts   A primarily debt-financed purchase of a controlling interest of a corporation's stock.

Limited Liability   The liability of the owners of a corporation is limited to the value of the shares in the firm that they own.

Liquidity   Money or things that can be quickly and easily converted into money with little or no loss of value.

Liquidity Preference   The demand for money.

Liquidity Trap   At very low interest rates, said John Maynard Keynes, people will neither lend out their money nor put it in the bank, but will simply hold it.

Loanable Funds   The supply of money that savers have made available to borrowers.

Long Run   When all costs become variable costs and firms can enter or leave the industry.

Lorenz Curve   Data plotted to show the percentage of income enjoyed by each percentage of households, ranked according to their income.

m

M   The money supply—currency, checking deposits, and checklike deposits (identical to M1).

M1   Currency, checking deposits, and checklike deposits.

M2   M1 plus savings deposits, small-denomination time deposits, and money market mutual funds.

M3   M2 plus large-denomination time deposits.

Macroeconomics   The part of economics concerned with the economy as a whole, dealing with huge aggregates like national output, employment, the money supply, bank deposits, and government spending.

Malthusian Theory of Population   Population tends to grow in a geometric progression (1, 2, 4, 8, 16), while food production tends to grow in an arithmetic progression (1, 2, 3, 4, 5).

Margin Requirement   The maximum percentage of the cost of a stock purchase that can be borrowed from a bank, stockbroker, or any other financial institution, with stock offered as collateral; this percentage is set by the Federal Reserve.

Marginal Cost (MC)   The cost of producing one additional unit of output.

Marginal Propensity to Consume (MPC)   Change in consumption divided by change in income.

Marginal Propensity to Save (MPS)   Change in saving divided by change in income.

Marginal Revenue (MR)   The revenue derived from selling one additional unit of output.

Marginal Revenue Product (MRP)   The demand for a resource, based on that resource's marginal output and the price at which it is sold.

Marginal Tax Rate   Additional taxes paid divided by taxable income.

Marginal Utility   The additional utility derived from consuming one more unit of some good or service.

Market   Any place where buyers and sellers exchange goods and services.

Market Failure   A less than efficient allocation of resources.

Maximum Profit Point   A firm will always produce at this point; marginal cost equals marginal revenue.

MC = MR Rule   For a firm to maximize its profits, marginal cost must equal marginal revenue.

Measure of Economic Welfare   A measure developed by James Tobin and William Nordhaus that modifies GDP by excluding "economic bads" and "regrettable necessities" and adding household, unreported, and illegal production.

Mediation   A third party acts as a go-between for labor and management during collective bargaining.

Medium of Exchange   Items sellers generally accept and buyers generally use to pay for a good or service; the primary job of money.

Microeconomics   The part of economics concerned with individual units such as firms and households and with individual markets, particular prices, and specific goods and services.

Minimum Wage   An hourly wage floor set by government that firms must pay their workers.

Mixed Economy   An economy in which production and distribution is done partly by the private sector and partly by the government.

Monetarism   A school of economics that places paramount importance on money as the key determinant of the level of prices, income, and employment.

Monetary Policy   Control of the rate of monetary growth by the Board of Governors of the Federal Reserve.

Monetary Rule   The money supply may grow at a specified annual percentage rate, generally about 3–4 percent.

Money   Main job is to be a medium of exchange; also serves as a standard of value and a store of value.

Money Supply   Currency, checking deposits, and checklike deposits (M or M1).

Monopolistic Competition   An industry that has many firms producing a differentiated product.

Monopoly   An industry in which one firm produces all the output. The good or service produced has no close substitutes.

Monopsony   A market in which a single buyer has no rivals.

Multinational Corporation   A corporation doing business in more than one country; often it owns production facilities in at least one country and sells in many countries.

Multiplier   Any change in spending (C, I, or G) will set off a chain reaction leading to a multiplied change in GDP. Equation is $1/(1 - MPC)$.

n

NNP   (See Net National Product.)

National Debt   (See Public Debt.)

National Income   Net domestic product minus indirect business taxes.

Natural Monopoly   An industry in which a single firm can provide cheaper service than could several competing firms.

Negative Income Tax   Cash payments by the government to the poor—an income tax in reverse. The cash payments decrease as income levels increase.

Net Exports   One country's exports to other countries minus its imports from other countries.

Net Investment   Gross investment minus depreciation.

Net National Product   Gross domestic product minus depreciation.

Net Productivity of Capital   The expected annual profit rate.

Nominal Interest Rate   The real interest rate plus the inflation rate.

Noncompeting Groups   Various strata of labor that do not compete for jobs; for example, doctors and secretaries, skilled and unskilled workers.

Nondurable Goods   Goods that are expected to last or be used for less than one year.

Normal Good   A good whose demand varies directly with income; nearly all goods are normal goods.

Normal Profits   The return to the businessowners for the opportunity cost of their implicit inputs.

North American Free Trade Agreement (NAFTA)   A free trade area consisting of the United states, Canada, and Mexico.

O

Oligopoly   An industry with just a few firms.

Oligopsony   A market in which there are only a few buyers.

Open Economy   An economy linked to the rest of the world through international trade.

Open-Market Operations   The purchase or sale of Treasury securities by the Federal Reserve; main monetary policy weapon.

Open Shop   When no one is forced to join a union even though the union represents all the workers in contract negotiations.

Opportunity Cost   The forgone value of what you give up when you make a choice.

Output Effect   When the price of any resource rises, the cost of production rises, which, in turn, lowers the supply of the final product. When supply falls, price rises, consequently reducing output.

P

P   The price level, or the average price of all goods and services produced during the current year.

Paradox of Thrift   If everyone tries to save more, they will all end up saving less.

Partnership   A business firm owned by two or more people.

Payroll Tax   (See Social Security tax.)

Per Capita Real GDP   Real GDP divided by population.

Perfect Competition   An industry with so many firms that no one firm has any influence over price, and firms produce an identical product.

Perfectly Elastic Demand Curve   A perfectly horizontal demand curve; the firm can sell as much as it wishes at that price.

Perfectly Elastic Supply Curve   A perfectly horizontal supply curve; the slightest decrease in price causes the quantity supplied to fall to zero.

Perfectly Inelastic Demand Curve   A perfectly vertical demand curve; no matter what the price is, the quantity demanded remains the same.

Perfectly Inelastic Supply Curve   A perfectly vertical supply curve; quantity supplied remains constant no matter what happens to price.

Permanent Income Hypothesis   Formulated by Milton Friedman, it states that the strongest influence on consumption is one's estimated lifetime income.

Personal Income   Income received by household, including both earned income and transfer payments.

Phillips Curve   Curve showing inverse relationship between the unemployment rate and the rate of inflation.

Plant   A store, factory, office, or other physical establishment that performs one or more functions in the production, fabrication, and sales of goods and services.

Poverty   A situation in which the basic needs of an individual or family exceed the means to satisfy them.

Poverty Rate   The percentage of the population with incomes below the official poverty line established by the federal government.

Present Value   The value today of the stream of expected future annual income that a property generates.

Price   The amount of money needed to buy a particular good, service, or resource.

Price Ceiling   Government-imposed maximum legal price.

Price Discrimination   Occurs when a seller charges two or more prices for the same good or service.

Price Floor   Government-imposed minimum price (used almost exclusively to keep agricultural commodity prices up).

Price Index   An index number that shows how the weighted average price of a market basket of goods changes through time.

Price Leadership   One firm, often the dominant firm in an oligopolistic industry, raises or lowers price, and the other firms quickly match the new price.

Price Level   A measure of prices in a given month or year in relation to prices in a base year.

Price System   Mechanism that allocates resources, goods, and services based on supply and demand.

Prime Rate   Rate of interest that banks charge their most creditworthy customers.

Product Differentiation   The distinction between or among goods and services made in the minds of buyers.

Production   Any good or service for which people are willing to pay.

Production Possibilities Frontier   A curve representing a hypothetical model of a two-product economy operating at full employment.

Productivity   Output per unit of input; efficiency with which resources are used.

Profit   The difference between total revenue and total cost.

Progressive Tax   Places greater burden on those with best ability to pay and little or no burden on the poor (for example, federal personal income tax).

Proprietorship   A business firm owned by just one person.

Proportional Tax   A tax whose burden falls equally among the rich, the middle class, and the poor.

Protective Tariff   A tariff designed to shield domestic producers of a good or service from the competition of foreign producers.

Public Debt   The amount of federal securities outstanding, which represents what the federal government owes (the accumulation of federal deficits minus surpluses over the last two centuries).

Public Goods   Goods or services produced by the government; they can be jointly consumed by many individuals simultaneously at no additional cost and with no reduction in quality or quantity.

q

Q   Output, or number of goods and services produced during the current year.

Quantity Theory of Money   Crude version: Changes in the money supply cause proportional changes in the price level. Sophisticated version: If we are well below full employment, an increase in M will lead to an increase in output. If we are close to full employment, an increase in M will lead mainly to an increase in P.

Quotas   Numerical limits imposed on the quantity of a specific good that may be imported.

r

Rational Expectations Theory   This is based on three assumptions: (1) that individuals and business firms learn through experience to anticipate the consequences of changes in monetary and fiscal policy; (2) that they act immediately to protect their economic interests; and (3) that all resource and product markets are purely competitive.

Real Balance Effect   The influence a change in household purchasing power has on the quantity of real GDP that consumers are willing to buy.

Real GDP   GDP corrected for inflation; actual production.

Real Interest Rate   Nominal interest rate minus inflation rate.

Real Wages   Nominal wages corrected for inflation.

Recession   A decline in real GDP for two consecutive quarters.

Recovery   Phase of business cycle during which real GDP increases from trough level to level of previous peak.

Regressive Tax   Falls more heavily on the poor than on the rich; for example, Social Security tax.

Rent   (See Economic Rent)

Rent Control   Government-set price ceiling on rent.

Required Reserve Ratio   Percentage of deposits that must be held as vault cash and reserve deposits by all depository institutions.

Required Reserves   Minimum vault cash or reserves; held at the Federal Reserve District Bank.

Reserves   Vault cash and deposits of banks held by Federal Reserve district banks.

Resources   Land, labor, capital, and entrepreneurial ability used to produce goods and services.

Retained Earnings   Earnings that a corporation keeps for investment in plant and equipment or for other purposes, rather than distributed to shareholders.

Right-to-Work Laws   Under the Taft-Hartley Act, states are permitted to pass these laws, which prohibit the union shop. (Union membership cannot be made a condition of securing employment.)

Rule of Reason   Mere size is no offense. Market conduct rather than market share should determine whether antitrust laws have been violated.

s

Saving   Disposable income not spent for consumer goods; equal to disposable income minus personal consumption expenditures.

Saving Function   As income rises, saving rises, but not as quickly.

Say's Law   Supply creates its own demand.

Scarcity   The inability of an economy to generate enough goods and services to satisfy all human wants.

Seasonal Unemployment   Unemployment resulting from the seasonal pattern of work in certain industries, with workers regularly laid off during the slow season and rehired during the busy season.

Secondary Boycott   A boycott of products or a company that sells the products of a company that is being struck.

Short Run   The length of time it takes all fixed costs to become variable costs.

Shortage   The amount by which the quantity demanded of a product exceeds the quantity supplied at a particular (below-equilibrium) price.

Shut Down   Cessation of a firm's operations as output falls to zero.

Shut-Down Point   The low point on the firm's average variable cost curve. If price is below the shut-down point, the firm will shut down in the short run.

Social Security Tax   A tax paid equally by employee and employer, based on employee's wages. Most proceeds are used to pay Social Security retirement and Medicare benefits.

Socialism   An economic system in which the government owns most of the productive resources except labor; it usually involves the redistribution of income.

Specialization   Division of productive activities so that no one is self-sufficient.

Stagflation   A period of either recession or stagnation accompanied by inflation.

Stock   (See Corporate Stock.)

Strike   When a collective bargaining agreement cannot be reached, a union calls for a work stoppage to last until an agreement is reached.

Structural Unemployment   When people are out of work for a couple of years or longer.

Substitute Goods   Products or services that can be used in place of each other. When the price of one falls, the demand for the other falls, and conversely with an increase of price.

Substitution Effect   If the price of a resource, say labor, goes up, business firms tend to substitute capital or land for some of their now-expensive workers. Also, the substitution of more hours of work for leisure time as the wage rate rises.

Supply (s)   A schedule of quantities that people will sell at different prices.

Supply, Law of   When the price of a good is lowered, less of it is supplied; when the price is raised, more is supplied.

Supply-Side Economics   Main tenets: economic role of federal government is too large; high tax rates and government regulations hurt the incentives of individuals and business firms to produce goods and services.

Surplus   The amount by which the quantity supplied of a product exceeds the quantity demanded at a specific (above-equilibrium) price.

Surplus Value   A Marxian term: the amount by which the value of a worker's daily output exceeds the worker's daily wage.

t

Tariff   A tax on imported goods.

Terms of Trade   The ratio of exchange between an imported good and an exported good.

Time Deposit   A deposit in a financial institution that requires notice of withdrawal or must be left for some fixed period of time.

Total Cost   The sum of fixed and variable costs.

Total Revenue   The price of a good or service multiplied by the number of units sold.

Transactions Demand for Money   The demand for money by individuals and business firms to pay for day-to-day expenses.

Transfer Payment   Payment by one branch of government to another or to an individual. Largest transfer payment is Social Security.

Transmission Mechanism   The series of changes brought about by a change in monetary policy that ultimately changes the level of GDP.

u

Unanticipated Inflation   A rate of inflation that is either higher or lower than expected.

Underground Economy   Unreported or illegal production of goods and services that is not counted in GDP.

Underemployment   Failure to use our resources efficiently. A situation in which workers are employed in positions requiring less skill and education than they have or other resources are employed in their most productive use.

Unemployment   The total number of people over 16 who are ready, willing, and able to work, who have been unsuccessfully seeking employment.

Unemployment Rate   Number of unemployed divided by the labor force.

Union Shop   All employees must join the union, usually within 30 days after they are hired.

Utility   The satisfaction you derive from a good or service that you purchase. How much utility you derive is measured by how much you would be willing to pay.

v

Variable Costs   These vary with output. When output rises, variable costs rise; when output declines, variable costs fall.

Velocity (V)   The number of times per year each dollar in the money supply is spent.

Vertical Merger   The joining of two firms engaged in different parts of an industrial process, or the joining of a manufacturer and a retailer.

w

Wage   The price paid for the use or services of labor per unit of time.

Wage and Price Controls   Rules established by the government that either place a ceiling on wages and prices or limit their rate of increase.

Workfare   A plan that requires welfare recipients to accept jobs or to enter training programs.

World Trade Organization (WTO)   The successor organization to GATT, which handles all trade disputes among member nations.

Index